marketing principles

2nd Asia-Pacific Edition

marketing principles

William M Pride

OC Ferrell

Bryan A Lukas

Sharon Schembri

Outi Niininen

Marketing Principles
2nd Edition
William M. Pride
O. C. Ferrell
Bryan A. Lukas
Sharon Schembri
Outi Niininen

Publishing manager: Dorothy Chiu
Publishing editor: Michelle Aarons
Senior developmental editor: Jessica Brennan
Senior project editor: Nathan Katz
Cover designer: Alicia Freile
Text designer: Leigh Ashforth (Watershed Design)
Editor: Sylvia Marson
Proofreader: Judith Bamber
Indexer: Russell Brooks
Permissions/Photo researcher: Jan Calderwood
Art direction: Danielle Maccarone
Typeset by MPS Limited

Any URLs contained in this publication were checked for currency during the production process. Note, however, that the publisher cannot vouch for the ongoing currency of URLs.

First Asia Pacific edition published in 2012.
Second Asia Pacific edition published in 2015.

For product information and technology assistance,
in Australia call **1300 790 853**;
in New Zealand call **0800 449 725**

For permission to use material from this text or product, please email
aust.permissions@cengage.com

National Library of Australia Cataloguing-in-Publication Data
Author: Pride, William M., author.
Title: Marketing principles / William M Pride, O. C. Ferrell, Bryan A Lukas, Sharon Schembri, Outi Niininen.
Edition: 2nd edition.
ISBN: 9780170254793 (paperback)
Notes: Includes index.
Subjects: Marketing--Asia--Textbooks. Marketing--Pacific Area--Textbooks.
Other Authors/Contributors: Ferrell, O. C., author. Lukas, Bryan A., author. Schembri, Sharon, author. Niininen, Outi, author.
Dewey Number: 658.8

Cengage Learning Australia
Level 7, 80 Dorcas Street
South Melbourne, Victoria Australia 3205

Cengage Learning New Zealand
Unit 4B Rosedale Office Park
331 Rosedale Road, Albany, North Shore 0632, NZ

For learning solutions, visit **cengage.com.au**

Printed in China by China Translation & Printing Services.
1 2 3 4 5 6 7 18 17 16 15 14

Brief contents

PART 1: MARKETING GROUNDWORK — 1

1   KEY CONCEPTS IN MARKETING — 3

2   MARKETING PLANNING AND STRATEGY IN A COMPETITIVE ENVIRONMENT — 39

3   MARKETING RESEARCH AND INFORMATION SYSTEMS — 85

PART 2: UNDERSTANDING MARKETS — 117

4   CONSUMER BEHAVIOUR — 119

5   SEGMENTATION, TARGET MARKETS AND POSITIONING — 155

6   BUSINESS MARKETS AND BUYING BEHAVIOUR — 191

PART 3 THE EXPANDED MARKETING MIX — 217

7   THE POWER OF BRANDING — 219

8   PRODUCT DECISIONS — 251

9   DEVELOPING AND MANAGING GOODS AND SERVICES — 289

10   PRICING DECISIONS — 331

11   DISTRIBUTION DECISIONS — 363

12   INTEGRATING MARKETING COMMUNICATIONS: DESIGNING PROMOTIONAL CAMPAIGNS — 411

13   MARKETING COMMUNICATIONS MIX VARIABLES: APPLICATION — 451

14   EXPANDING THE MARKETING MIX — 501

15   DIGITAL MARKETING AND SOCIAL NETWORKING — 539

Contents

Resources guide   xvii

Features matrix   xxii

Preface   xxiv

Acknowledgements   xxviii

About the authors   xxx

PART 1   MARKETING GROUNDWORK   1

CHAPTER 1   KEY CONCEPTS IN MARKETING   3

✹ Introduction   4

✹ Marketing defined   5

People are the focus   6

The strategic variables of marketing – the marketing mix and the expanded marketing mix   7

     Marketing in transition: Efficiency and size make tiny cars a winning segment   12

Marketing builds relationships with customers and stakeholders   14

Marketing occurs in a dynamic environment   15

     Ethical marketing: Facing ethical issues in marketing   17

✹ Understanding the marketing concept and market orientation   18

The evolution of how marketing has been interpreted   19

Modern marketing: being market-oriented   20

     Marketing in action: Surviving the outdoors with Bear Grylls: Marketing appeals to survivalists and more   21

✹ Managing customer relationships   22

Value-driven marketing   23

     Marketing in action: Does marketing increase the value of products?   25

✹ The marketing management process   25

✹ The role and importance of marketing in a global economy   26

Marketing costs consume a sizable portion of buyers' dollars   27

Marketing is used in non-profit organisations   27

Marketing is important to businesses   28

Marketing fuels our global economy   28

Marketing knowledge enhances consumer awareness   28

     Sustainable Marketing: Pedal power: Putting eco-responsibility into your customers' hands   29

Marketing connects people through technology   29

Socially responsible marketing can promote the welfare of customers and stakeholders   30

Marketing offers many exciting career prospects   30

STUDY TOOLS   31

     Case study: Kraft creates unhappy little Vegemites   35

CHAPTER 2   MARKETING PLANNING AND STRATEGY IN A COMPETITIVE ENVIRONMENT   39

✹ Introduction   40

✹ The marketing environment   41

Shaping and responding to the marketing environment   42

Competitive forces   43

Economic forces   45

Political forces   47

Legal and regulatory forces   47

Technological forces   49

Marketing in transition: New technology provides opportunities for social network marketing   51

Sociocultural forces   51

✳ Understanding the strategic planning process   52

Assessing organisational resources and opportunities   54

Establishing an organisational mission and marketing goals   57

Developing corporate, business-unit and marketing strategies   59

Sustainable marketing: Packaging … that does not cost the earth   64

✳ Creating the marketing plan   64

✳ Implementing marketing strategies   65

Customer relationship management   66

Marketing in action: Marketing new products   67

Marketing implementation through internal marketing   67

Ethical Marketing: The payoffs for being ethical   68

Organising marketing activities   68

Controlling marketing activities   71

✳ Incorporating social responsibility and ethics into strategic planning   73

Ethics and codes of conduct   73

Corporate social responsibility   74

STUDY TOOLS   **75**

Case study: Stormy ride for Queensland's tourism industry   79

CHAPTER 3   MARKETING RESEARCH AND INFORMATION SYSTEMS   85

✳ Introduction   86

✳ The importance of marketing research   86

Marketing in action: The billboard of the future   87

✳ The marketing research process   88

Determine the scope for marketing research   88

Select the research method   89

Collect and prepare the data   91

Marketing in transition: Nielsen company offers valuable insights for marketers   98

Analyse the data   101

Sustainable marketing: Message in a bottle: Secondary data provide recycling lessons   101

Transform the analysis results into insights   102

✳ Using technology to improve data analysis   102

Marketing information systems   103

Databases   104

Marketing decision support systems   105

✳ Issues in marketing research   105

The importance of ethical marketing research 105
International issues in marketing research 106
Ethical marketing: Privacy: Where do you draw the line online? 107
STUDY TOOLS **108**
Case study: Bom bom bom! Re-igniting Kmart's brand 112

PART 2   UNDERSTANDING MARKETS   117

CHAPTER 4   CONSUMER BEHAVIOUR   119

✳ Introduction 120
✳ The importance of understanding consumer behaviour 121
  Ethical marketing: Ethics and fast food marketing to children 122
✳ Consumer buying decision process 122
  Problem recognition 123
  Information search 124
  Evaluation of alternatives 124
  Purchase 125
  Marketing in action: Technology is changing consumption habits 125
  Post-purchase evaluation 126
✳ Level of involvement and consumer problem-solving processes 126
✳ Situational influences on the buying decision process 128
✳ Psychological influences on the buying decision process 130
  Perception 130
  Marketing in transition: QR code haircuts – clear in Thailand 131
  Motives 132
  Learning 132
  Attitudes 133
  Self-concept 134
  Lifestyles 135
✳ Social influences on the buying decision process 137
  Roles 130
  Reference groups 139
  Opinion leaders 139
  Sustainable marketing: Green car sales up and Aqua tops Prius 140
  Digital networks 141
  Culture and subcultures 141
  Marketing in action: The ritual of facebook 142
  Marketing in transition: Are all consumer reviews trustworthy? 145
  STUDY TOOLS **145**
  Case study: The importance of behavioural change in social marketing 150

CHAPTER 5   SEGMENTATION, TARGET MARKETS AND POSITIONING   155

✳ Introduction 156
✳ What is a market? 156
✳ Market segmentation 157

Variables for segmenting consumer markets | 159
Marketing in transition: Brave girl power or feeble female? | 160
Ethical marketing: Taking geek-chic a little too far? | 161
Sustainable marketing: It's not easy being green? | 167
Variables for segmenting business markets | 169

✳ Target-market selection process | 170
Step 1: Identify the appropriate targeting strategy | 170
Marketing in transition: Facebook geo-targeting delivers goats and 500 000 fans | 173
Step 2: Determine which segmentation variables to use | 174
Marketing in action: The Australian DIY lifestyle segmentation | 175
Step 3: Develop market segment profiles | 176
Step 4: Evaluate relevant market segments | 177
Step 5: Select specific target markets | 179

✳ Product positioning and repositioning | 179
Perceptual mapping | 180
Bases for positioning | 180
Repositioning | 181
STUDY TOOLS | **183**
Case study: Is there a Trek bicycle for everybody? | 186

CHAPTER 6   BUSINESS MARKETS AND BUYING BEHAVIOUR   191

✳ Introduction | 192

✳ Business markets | 192
Ethical marketing: When outsourcing goes bad | 193
Producer markets | 194
Reseller markets | 194
Government markets | 195
Institutional markets | 195

✳ Dimensions of marketing to business customers | 196
Characteristics of transactions with business customers | 197
Attributes of business customers | 197
Primary concerns of business customers | 197
Methods of business buying | 199
Sustainable marketing: Go green – pass it along | 200
Types of business purchases | 200

✳ Demand for business products | 201
Derived demand | 201
Inelastic demand | 201
Joint demand | 202
Marketing in action: Steelcase wants to keep business customers healthy | 202
Fluctuating demand | 203

✳ Business buying decisions | 203
The buying centre | 203
Marketing in transition: Partnering for profit | 204

✳ Stages of the business buying decision process | 205
Influences on the business buying decision process | 207

STUDY TOOLS   208
    Case study: The evolution of business banking – the impact
    of technology   212

PART 3	THE EXPANDED MARKETING MIX	217

CHAPTER 7	THE POWER OF BRANDING	219

✳ Introduction   221

✳ The strategic power of branding   221

✳ Value of branding   222

✳ Brand equity   223
    Marketing in action: Weet-bix brand culture   225
    Ethical marketing: The popularity of house brands and the
    effect on competition   228

✳ How brand names are selected and protected   229
  Selecting a brand name   229
  Protecting a brand   230

✳ Branding policies, brand extensions, co-branding
  and brand licensing   231
  Branding policies   231
  Brand extensions   232
  Co-branding   233
  Brand licensing   234
    Marketing in transition: R.M. Williams brand identity   235

✳ Building and sustaining brands   235
  Brand vision   237
  Organisational culture   237
  Brand objectives   238
  Auditing the brandsphere   238
  Brand essence   238
  Internal implementation   239
  Brand resourcing   239
  Brand evaluation   239

✳ Connecting the marketing mix and brands   239
  Brands and pricing   240
  Branding and physical distribution   240
    Sustainable marketing: Branding and corporate social
    responsibility   241
  Branding and promotion   241
  Branding and products   242
    Marketing in transition: Nike brand innovation   243
    Marketing in transition: Power shift from organisations
    to consumers   243
STUDY TOOLS   244
    Case study: Branding strategy within an unbranded market:
    A case of the Australian tobacco industry   247

CHAPTER 8	PRODUCT DECISIONS	251

✳ Introduction	252
✳ What is a product?	252
Classifying products	255
Consumer products	256
Marketing in action: Summer the surfer girl!	*256*
Business products	258
Sustainable marketing: Digging deeper into green claims	*260*
✳ Product line and product mix	262
✳ Product life cycles and marketing strategies	263
Introduction stage	264
Growth stage	265
Maturity stage	266
Ethical marketing: Reinventing tobacco products as electronic	*268*
✳ Product adoption process	269
Consumer adoption categories	270
✳ Packaging functions, design consideration and strategy	271
Sustainable marketing: Sustainable packaging at Gucci	*271*
Packaging functions	272
Major packaging considerations	272
Packaging and marketing strategy	273
Marketing in transition: How green is that product? Check the label	*276*
✳ Labelling and legal issues	276
STUDY TOOLS	**279**
Case study: Product strategy and innovation at Glacéau Vitaminwater	*283*

CHAPTER 9	DEVELOPING AND MANAGING GOODS AND SERVICES	289

✳ Introduction	290
✳ Developing new products	291
Idea generation	291
Ethical marketing: Building blocks and innovative communities	*293*
Screening	294
Concept testing	294
Marketing in action: 'Crazy' former comic laughs all the way to the bank – thanks to spanx!	*295*
Business analysis	295
Product development	396
Test marketing	396
Commercialisation	398
✳ Managing existing products	299
Line extensions	300
Product modifications	300
Marketing in transition: Samsung S4: Is the iPhone old school?	*303*
Product deletions	303

✷ Nature and importance of services 305
   Traditional characteristics of services 306

✷ Managing intangible (service) product components 310
   Creating marketing mixes for services 311
      Marketing in transition: @SBYudhoyono – Indonesian president twitter success! 313
      Marketing in action: Delivery by drones…! 316

✷ Product differentiation through quality, design and service components 317
      Marketing in action: This is not your grandmother's circus! 318
   Product quality 318
   Product design and features 319
      Sustainable marketing: Quality green beer 320
   Product support services 320
   STUDY TOOLS 321
      Case study: Pilates Studio 325

CHAPTER 10   PRICING DECISIONS 331

✷ Introduction 332

✷ The role of price 332

✷ Price and non-price competition 333
   Price competition 333
   Non-price competition 333

✷ Factors affecting pricing decisions and objectives 334
   Organisational and marketing objectives 335
   Types of pricing objectives 335
   Costs 335
   Marketing mix variables other than price 336
   Customer interpretations of, and responses to, a price 336
      Ethical marketing: Travel prices and fine print 337
   Customer perceptions of the product 338
   Demand 339

✷ Setting prices 340
   Development of pricing objectives 341
      Marketing in transition: Making 'freemium' pay off 341
      Sustainable marketing: Home-made energy 342
   Assessment of the target market's evaluation of price 342
   Evaluation of competitors' prices 343
   Selection of a basis for pricing 343
      Marketing in action: Reinventing the wheelie bin 344

✷ Selection of a pricing strategy 346
   Differential pricing 346
   New-product pricing 347
   Product-line pricing 347
   Psychological pricing 349
   Professional pricing 352
   Determination of a specific price 352

STUDY TOOLS 355
Case study: Spa Ceylon 359

CHAPTER 11   DISTRIBUTION DECISIONS   363

✳ Introduction 364

✳ The role of marketing channels 365
The significance of marketing channels 366
Types of marketing channels 367
Sustainable marketing: IKEA's sustainable geothermal energy initiative 368

✳ Physical distribution in supply-chain management and marketing strategies 369
Marketing in transition: Streamlining physical distribution to profit from your grocery shop 370
Order processing 371
Inventory management 372
Materials handling 373
Warehousing 374
Transportation 374

✳ Types of retailers and strategic issues in retailing 377
Major types of retail stores 378
Strategic issues in retailing 382
Marketing in action: Etsy creates a crafty channel 383
Ethical marketing: Which are more earth-friendly: online or traditional channels? 386

✳ Direct marketing 387
Catalogue marketing 387
Direct response marketing 387
Telemarketing 387
Television home shopping 388
Online retailing 388
Direct selling 388

✳ Wholesaling 389
Services provided by wholesalers 390
Types of wholesalers 391

✳ Strategic issues in marketing channels 395
Selecting marketing channels 396
Channel leadership, cooperation and conflict 398
STUDY TOOLS 401
Case study: Why own when you can share? New models of ownership and distribution in the automotive industry. 407

CHAPTER 12   INTEGRATING MARKETING COMMUNICATIONS: DESIGNING PROMOTIONAL CAMPAIGNS   411

✳ Introduction 412

✳ What is integrated marketing communications? 412
Marketing in action: Rum-road to recovery after floods 413

✱ The communication process — 415

   Sustainable marketing: Fight against green washing — *417*

✱ Message appeal styles — 419

   How target market characteristics and media channels guide message themes — *419*

✱ The role and objectives of promotion — 420

   Create awareness — *422*

   Marketing in transition: Near field communication (NFC) turns advertisements into interactive games — *423*

   Stimulate demand — *424*

   Encourage product trial — *425*

   Identify prospects — *425*

   Retain loyal customers — *425*

   Facilitate reseller support — *426*

   Reduce sales fluctuations/seasonality of demand — *426*

   Combat competitive promotional efforts — *426*

✱ Selecting elements for the marketing communications mix — 427

   Promotional resources, objectives and policies — *429*

   Target market characteristics — *429*

   Marketing in transition: Technology is changing billboards — *431*

   Product characteristics — *432*

   Costs and availability of promotional methods — *432*

   Push and pull channel policies — *433*

   The growing importance of word-of-mouth communications — *434*

✱ Criticisms and defences of promotion — 435

   Offensive advertisements — *436*

   Is promotion deceptive? — *438*

   Ethical marketing: Images in advertising are routinely photoshopped — *438*

   Does promotion increase prices? — *439*

   Does promotion create needs? — *439*

   Does promotion help customers without costing too much? — *440*

   Should potentially harmful products be promoted? — *440*

   STUDY TOOLS — **441**

   Case study: Promoting an alternative to the smartphone — *445*

CHAPTER 13   MARKETING COMMUNICATIONS MIX VARIABLES: APPLICATION — 451

✱ Introduction — 452

✱ Advertising — 453

   Developing an advertising campaign — *454*

   Marketing in transition: Will TV advertising be revitalised through targeted advertisements? — *460*

   Executing the campaign and evaluating advertising effectiveness — *463*

   Advertising you should be aware of — *465*

✱ Product placement — 465

✱ Public relations — 466

   Public relations tools — *466*

   Marketing in action: The six best jobs in the world? — *467*

✴ Sponsorship   471
Common types of sponsorship   472
Evaluating the effectiveness of sponsorship   473
Dealing with unfavourable sponsorship contracts   474
Ethical marketing: Professional athlete refuses to don sponsor's logo for religious reasons   475

✴ Personal selling   476
The personal selling process   477
Managing the sales force   480

✴ Sales promotion   480
Consumer sales promotion methods   482
Sustainable marketing: E-coupons benefit a variety of stakeholders, including the environment   483
Trade sales promotion methods   487
STUDY TOOLS   **489**
Case study: Bloggers and social media influence: New opportunities for brand marketers   494

CHAPTER 14   EXPANDING THE MARKETING MIX   501

✴ Introduction   502

✴ Strategic use of the expanded marketing mix variables   503
A marketing mix for the 'experience economy'   505
Mapping the customer experience   507
Marketing in action: Expanded marketing mix used to transform a UK haulage company into a superbrand   508

✴ The people variable   509
Personnel   509
Aesthetic labour   510
Ethical marketing: 'The community has a right to expect a professional image from its police officers'   511
Emotional labour   512
'Me as the customer' and other customers as participants   512
Passersby (or accidental participants)   514
Can marketing help solve these problems?   515

✴ The physical evidence/physical assets variable   515
Buildings, grounds and other physical assets   516
Atmospherics   517

✴ Processes   520
Flow and progress of customers   521
Marketing in action: was it really a queue?   521
Sensitivity, privacy and confidentiality of customer–company interactions   522
Digital technology and the service process   523
Marketing in transition: Body scanning helps you find perfectly fitting clothes   524
Curated convenience   524

✴ The partnerships variable   525
Ethical marketing: Does your tuna have the WWF stamp of approval?   525

| STUDY TOOLS | 528 |
| *Case study: The experience of learning in a museum* | *532* |

| CHAPTER 15 | DIGITAL MARKETING AND SOCIAL NETWORKING | 539 |

❋ Introduction · 540

❋ Growth and benefits of digital marketing · 540
  The interactivity of social media · *543*

❋ Consumer-generated marketing and digital media · 544
  Social networks · *544*
    Ethical marketing: Don't leave sacked employee in charge of your social media account! · *545*
  Media-sharing websites · *549*
  Virtual websites · *551*
  Mobile devices · *551*
  Applications and widgets · *553*
    Marketing in transition: Ethical apps · *554*
  Wearable technology · *555*

❋ Trends in digital marketing consumer behaviour · 556
  Online consumer behaviour · *556*
  E-marketing strategy · *557*
  Product considerations · *557*
  Distribution considerations · *558*
    Sustainable marketing: Are electronic textbooks really better for the environment? · *560*
  Promotion considerations · *560*
  Pricing considerations · *561*

❋ Digital media and the expanded marketing mix · 562
  People considerations · *562*
  Physical evidence considerations · *563*
  Process considerations · *564*
    Marketing in action: Mercedes-Benz has developed a QR code based app that could save lives · *565*
    Ethical marketing: Is it OK to offer minor medical procedures to customers as a convenience? · *566*
  Partnership considerations · *566*

❋ Ethical and legal issues · 567
  Privacy · *567*
    Marketing in transition: You as the target audience: Social media profiles are catching up with our real life purchases · *567*
  Online fraud · *569*
  Intellectual property · *569*
  STUDY TOOLS · 570
    Case study: How a plush toy manufacturer plans its marketing through crowdsourcing · *576*

Glossary 583
Index 594

For the student

As you read this text you will find a wealth of Part and Chapter features designed to enhance your study of marketing and help you understand how it is applied in the real world.

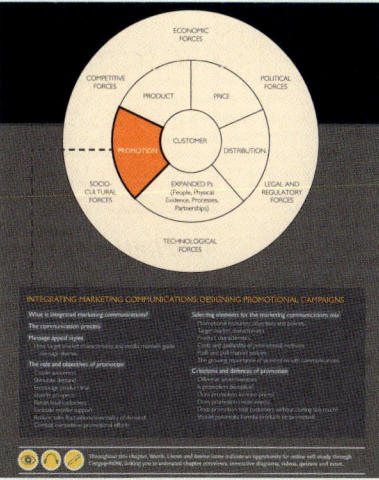

The **organisational diagram** at the beginning of each Part provides a 'road map' of the text and a visual tool for understanding the connection between various components of marketing. This diagram is revisited at the start of each chapter in a visual guide to the key chapter concepts.

1 *Learning objectives*, listed at the start of each chapter, give you a clear sense of the key outcomes that are covered. A learning objective icon appears in the margin to help identify where the text explores each objective in depth.

2 Each chapter opens with a real world vignette, the *Marketing Challenge*, which introduces you to the chapter concepts through an engaging real-world example relating to the topic covered in the chapter.

3 The *Marketing Challenge* question at the end of the vignette asks you to think more about the concepts and strategies explored. By thinking of different ways to resolve the question, you can relate learning objectives and key chapter concepts to their various applications in real-life scenarios.

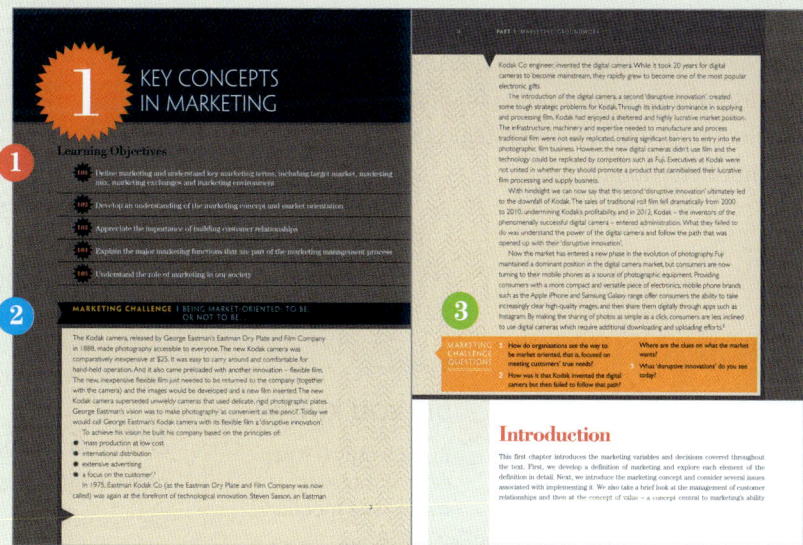

When **Key Terms** are used in the text for the first time, they are bolded for easy identification, and a definition is provided in the margin, as well as in the glossary, which can be found at the back of the text.

Marketing in Action explores marketing in the real world by profiling businesses, people and projects.

Ethical Marketing boxes discuss a controversial marketing issue related to ethics and social responsibility.

Marketing in Transition boxes explore how the dynamic changes in the world of marketing and technology are influencing marketing strategies and customer behaviour.

The **Sustainable Marketing** boxes focus on green initiatives that help organisations achieve both environmental and economic sustainability.

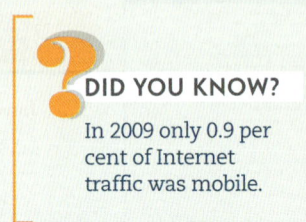

DID YOU KNOW?

In 2009 only 0.9 per cent of Internet traffic was mobile.

Did you know? boxes explore interesting facts about marketing.

At the end of each chapter you will find several learning tools to help you review the chapter and key concepts, and extend your learning.

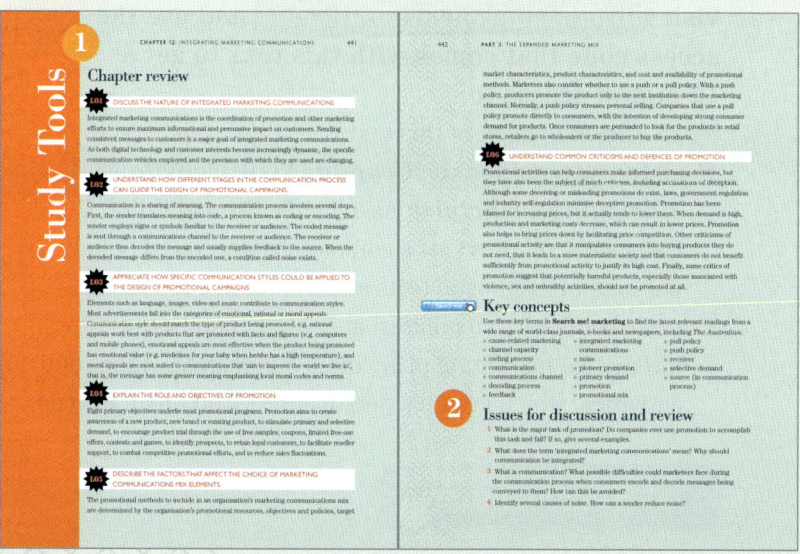

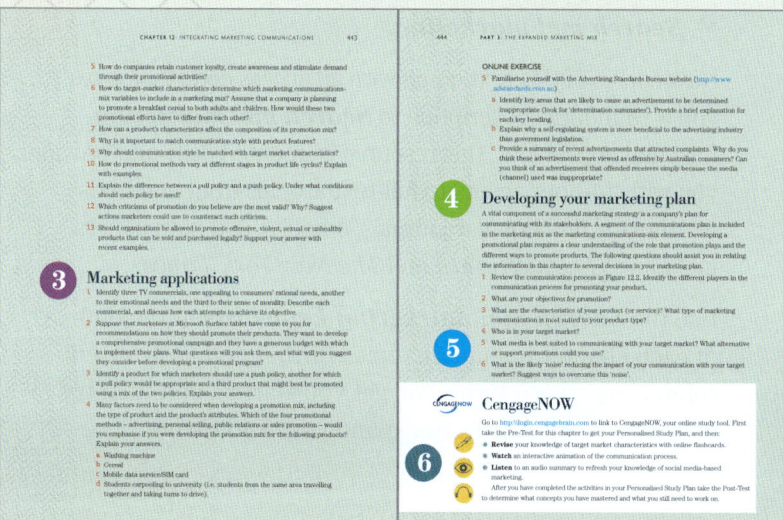

1 The **Chapter Review** outlines all the key points and provides a snapshot of the chapters' content. A list of **important key concepts** is also included to expand your marketing vocabulary.

2 **Issues for discussion and review** at the end of each chapter encourage further study and exploration of chapter content.

3 **Marketing Application** questions challenge and enhance your comprehension of important topics. An **online exercise** at the end of each chapter directs you to examine a website and assess more strategic issues associated with topics identified with that site.

4 **Developing your marketing plan** ties the chapter concepts into an overall marketing plan that can be created by completing the Interactive Marketing Plan activity found on the CengageNOW website. The *Developing your marketing plan* feature allows you to build on chapter topics as you develop and implement a marketing campaign.

5 At the end of each chapter the **CengageNOW** section profiles key online resources available through the CengageNow platform that will help to bring your study of the chapter concepts to life. A 12-month access to CengageNOW comes with each new copy of this text. An intelligent online study system, CengageNOW provides a completely integrated package of diagnostic tests and interactive resources that create a personalised study plan for you.

6 Watch, Listen and Revise icons throughout the text indicate an opportunity for online self-study, linking you to interactive quizzes, audio summaries and additional resources based on your level of understanding.

* A written *Case Study* at the end of each chapter illustrates concrete applications of marketing strategies and concepts.

Student online resources

Visit **http://login.cengagebrain.com** and use the access code that comes with this text to get a 12-month access to:

* an *eBook* version of this text
* all the materials on the *CengageNOW website* for *Marketing Principles* Asia Pacific Second Edition. CengageNOW provides a completely integrated online package of diagnostic tests and interactive resources, such as interactive quizzes, animated chapter overviews, interactive marketing plan, audio summaries, videos and activities, which create a personalised study plan for you.

* *Search me! marketing.*

New copies of this text come with an access code that gives you a 12-month subscription to *Search me! marketing*. Fast and convenient, this resource is updated daily and provides you with 24-hour access to full-text articles from hundreds of scholarly and popular journals, e-books, and newspapers, including *The Australian* and *The New York Times*.

Use the *Search me! marketing keywords* at the end of each chapter to explore topics further and find current references. These terms will get you started, and then try your own search terms to expand your knowledge.

For the instructor

Cengage Learning is pleased to provide you with an extensive selection of electronic and online resources to help you lecture in Marketing Principles. These teaching tools are available on the Instructor website accessible via **www.cengage.com/sso**

CengageNOW: Ensure that your students have the understanding they need with CengageNOW. This integrated, online course management and learning system combines the best of current technology to save time in planning and managing your course and assignments. You can reinforce comprehension with customised student learning paths and efficiently test and automatically grade assignments. Resources on CengageNOW include an *eBook, Interactive marketing plan*, interactive quizzes, audio summaries, animations and more.

Instructor's Manual. The Instructor's Manual provides you with a wealth of content to help set up and administer your marketing subject. It includes an outline of the chapter purpose and perspective, discussion starters, class exercises, a chapter quiz, as well as answers to problems within the text.

PowerPoint slides. PowerPoint presentations are available to accompany each chapter of *Marketing Principles.* Use these slides as they are to reinforce key marketing principles, or edit them to suit your particular needs.

ExamView

ExamView testbank. **ExamView** helps you create, customise and deliver tests in minutes for both print and online. The Quick Test Wizard and Online Test Wizard guide you step-by-step through the test-creation process. The program also allows you to see the test you are creating on the screen exactly as it will print or display online. With ExamView's complete word-processing capabilities, you can edit the questions provided, add an unlimited number of new questions to the bank and build tests of up to 250 questions using up to 12 question types. You can also export the files into Blackboard or WebCT.

Marketing Principles video package

Local Marketing videos. This video package, featuring large and small local companies, provides a relevant and engaging visual teaching tool for the classroom. Scenarios will link the application of marketing concepts to key graduate outcomes.

Marketing Video Case Series. This series contains videos specifically tied to cases relevant to each chapter. The videos, cases and suggested answers are available for Instructors on the Instructor companion website. Students can access the videos and cases on the CengageNOW website. Video cases cover a variety of interesting companies such as New Belgium Brewing, Raleigh, Campbell's, UNICEF, Ford and Pepsi.

Interactive Marketing Plan worksheets have been developed alongside a video program, allowing students to follow a company through the trials and tribulations of launching a new product. This video helps place the conceptual marketing plan into an applicable light and is supported by a summary of the specific stages in the marketing plan, as well as a sample plan based on the events of the video. The plan is broken up into three functional sections that can be completed in one simple project, or carried over throughout the semester.

Features matrix

Chapters	Part 1			Part 2			
	1	2	3	4	5	6	7
Marketing Challenge	Being market-oriented: to be, or not to be… p. 3	The supermarket wars p. 39	Social media's role in information systems p. 85	High flying consumers p. 119	The great Generation Y challenge p. 155	Business marketers and customers rely on virtual marketing p. 191	Pristine rainforest experience p. 219
Marketing in Transition	Efficiency and size make tiny cars a winning segment p. 12	New technology provides opportunities for social network marketing p. 51	Nielsen company offers valuable insights for marketers p. 98	QR code haircuts – Clear in Thailand p. 131 Are all consumer reviews trustworthy? p. 145	BRAVE girl power or feeble female? p. 160 Facebook geo-targeting delivers goats and 500 000 fans p. 173	Partnering for profit p. 204	R.M. Williams brand identity p. 235 Nike brand innovation p. 243 Power shift from organisations to consumers p. 243
Ethical Marketing	Facing ethical issues in marketing p. 17	The payoffs for being ethical p. 68	Privacy: Where do you draw the line online? p. 107	Ethics and fast food marketing to children p. 122	Taking geek-chic a little too far? p. 161	When outsourcing goes bad p. 193	The popularity of house brands and the effect on competition p. 228
Marketing in Action	Surviving the outdoors with Bear Grylls: Marketing appeals to survivalists and more p. 21 Does marketing increase the value of products? p. 25	Marketing new products p. 67	The billboard of the future p. 87	Technology is changing consumption habits p. 125 The ritual of Facebook p. 142	The Australian DIY lifestyle segmentation p. 175	Steelcase wants to keep business customers healthy p. 202	Weet-bix brand culture p. 225
Sustainable Marketing	Pedal power: Putting eco-responsibility into your customers hands p. 29	Packaging that does not cost the earth p. 64	Message in a bottle: secondary data provide recycling lessons p. 101	Green car sales up and Aqua tops Prius p. 140	It's not easy being green? p. 167	Go green – pass it along p. 200	Branding and corporate social responsibility p. 241
Written Case Study	Kraft creates unhappy little Vegemites p. 35	Stormy ride for Queensland's tourism industry p. 79	Bom Bom Bom! Re-igniting Kmart's brand p. 112	The importance of behavioural change in social marketing p. 150	Is there a Trek bicycle for everybody? p. 186	The evolution of business banking – the impact of technology p. 212	Branding strategy within an unbranded market: A case of the Australian tobacco industry p. 247

Part 3							
8	**9**	**10**	**11**	**12**	**13**	**14**	**15**
Welcome to the wonderful world of LEGO® p. 251	Wet 'n' Wild in the west p. 291	Amazon.com's best-selling pricing ideas p. 333	Target reinvigorates its brand p. 363	'No one sees it like you' by Canon p. 411	L'Oréal slogan celebrates 40 years of empowering women p. 451	5-star after sales service from Kubota Australia p. 503	Facebook befriends small businesses p. 539
How green is that product? Check the label p. 276	Samsung S4: is the iPhone old school? p. 303 @SBYudhoyono – Indonesian President Twitter success! p. 313	Making 'freemium' pay off p. 341	Streamlining physical distribution to profit from your grocery shop p. 370	Near Field Communication (NFC) turns advertisements into interactive games p. 423 Technology is changing billboards p. 431	Will TV advertising be revitalised through targeted advertisements? p. 460	Body scanning helps you find perfectly fitting clothes p. 524	Ethical apps p. 554 You as the target audience: Social media profiles are catching up with our real life purchases p. 567
Reinventing tobacco products as electronic p. 268	Building blocks and innovative communities p. 293	Travel prices and fine print p. 337	Which are more earth-friendly: online or traditional channels? p. 386	Images in advertising are routinely photoshopped p. 438	Professional athlete refuses to don sponsor's logo for religious reasons p. 445	'The community has a right to expect a professional image from its police officers' p. 511 Does your tuna have the WWF stamp of approval? p. 525	Don't leave sacked employee in charge of your social media account! p. 545 Is it OK to offer minor medical procedures to customers as a convenience? p. 566
Summer the Surfer Girl! p. 256	'Crazy' former comic laughs all the way to the bank - thanks to Spanx p. 295 Delivery by drones…! p. 316 This is not your grandmother's circus! p. 318	Reinventing the wheelie bin p. 344	Etsy creates a crafty channel p. 383	Rum-road to recovery after floods p. 413	The six best jobs in the world? p. 467	Expanded marketing mix used to transform a UK haulage company into a Superbrand p. 508 Was it really a queue? p. 521	Mercedes Benz has developed a QR code-based app that could save lives p. 565
Digging deeper into green claims p. 260 Sustainable packaging at Gucci p. 271	Quality green beer p. 320	Home-made energy p. 342	IKEA's sustainable geothermal energy initiative p. 368	Fight against green washing p. 417	E-coupons benefit a variety of stakeholders, including the environment p. 483		Are electronic textbooks really better for the environment? p. 560
Product strategy and innovation at Glaceau Vitaminwater p. 283	Pilates Studio p. 325	Spa Ceylon p. 359	Why own when you can share? New models of ownership and distribution in the automotive industry p. 407	Promoting an alternative to the smartphone p. 445	Bloggers and social media influence: New opportunities for brand marketers p. 494	The experience of learning in a museum p. 532	How a plush toy manufacturer plans its marketing through crowdsourcing p. 576

Marketing in the Asia-Pacific region

Marketing is a popular choice among business students because the subject matter is highly engaging and evident in everyday life. Marketing is a business function concerned with managing markets – managing the customers, competitors and collaborators of an organisation. *Marketing Principles*, now in its second edition, is a textbook that conveys the most relevant, contemporary marketing concepts and best practices in relation to managing markets. And, importantly, the book has been developed specifically with the Asia–Pacific region in mind.

This book's strong focus on the Asia–Pacific region is demonstrated with cases drawn from Australia and New Zealand, as well as other cases coming from individual countries across the Asia–Pacific. Case examples and discussions strewn throughout the book include high-profile brands such as Sony and Toyota, along with other less noticeable inclusions such as the discussion in Chapter 14 on aromatic seats offered in Japanese cinemas.

One of the reasons for producing a book with an Asia–Pacific focus is to specifically address the issues relevant to this region. Prescribing students a US-based text, for example, assumes that culture is the same throughout the world – and this is simply not the case. Culture matters! Another reason for producing an Asia–Pacific edition is to profile and highlight the success and innovation of local businesses and entrepreneurial ventures. Many businesses and operations throughout Australia, New Zealand and Asia are highly deserving of the intangible reward of recognition. The authors have therefore strived to deliberately highlight successful operations throughout the region.

Overall, the book's Asia–Pacific focus means the text will be as relevant in Singapore as it will be in Melbourne, Perth, Auckland and Hong Kong. The benefit for lecturers is less preparation around aligning marketing theory with an Asia–Pacific context, and the benefit for students with an Asia–Pacific background is that the interest level in the content will be high and, therefore, retention of the text content is more likely. Contextualisation of marketing theory and practice as presented in this Asia–Pacific text is, therefore, beneficial for both instructors and students alike.

Distinctive themes

In this second edition we continue with a distinct practical marketing focus, with many cases and examples presented throughout the book. This is essential for the learning of our target audience – undergraduate marketing students who are promising employees, entrepreneurs and business owners. As such, students need to be equipped with the understanding of marketing knowledge in action. Such actionable knowledge also helps organisations to benefit from anticipated changes in the business environment. To this end, the practical application of marketing theory as presented in this text is also an example of how the book is oriented towards market needs.

We have also focused on the need for marketing to change and adapt to existing and future developments of the business environment. Updated *Marketing in Transition* and *Marketing in Action* boxes, and a more detailed discussion of the *Expanded Marketing Mix*, reflect how marketing is changing and adapting to new technology, competitive forces and a now truly global economy. We have introduced a new feature, *Did you know?*, that includes unusual or unconventional examples of marketing practice to intrigue the experienced marketers, to challenge conventional thinking and, hopefully, whet the appetite for learning more marketing.

Presenting the standard 4Ps is no longer a sufficient introduction for our students. Hence, our inclusion of the *Expanded Marketing Mix* in this book – an important point of differentiation from other marketing texts with a similar target audience. The expanded marketing mix emphasises the importance of People, Physical Evidence, Process and Partnerships for making good marketing decisions and achieving competitive advantages in any industry. Students with a thorough understanding of the expanded marketing mix will obtain a significant head start in their marketing thinking early in their career.

Throughout the book, we emphasise a strong 'market-orientation' theme. To be market-oriented you must be in touch with the competitive environment, be alert to trends in the mark place and then to be able to adapt how you practise and apply marketing. Research shows that market-oriented firms usually out-perform firms that are not market-oriented, all else being equal. Rather than just outlining and explaining product-related decisions, we have designed most chapters from a market-oriented decision-making perspective.

The text is presented in three parts, with Part 1 giving a broad introduction, Part 2 focusing on markets and Part 3 presenting the Expanded Marketing Mix. We consider branding to be a powerful marketing tool and have, therefore, included a chapter dedicated to branding at the beginning of Part 3. In terms of prominence in the marketing landscape, branding is highly visible from the clothes we wear, to the companies we work for, the places we live and travel and the cars we choose to drive. As consumers, even deciding *not* to consume a particular brand is a statement that defines the brand, as well as ourselves. While brands and branding originally emerged at the product level in the area of Fast Moving Consumer Goods (FMCGs), branding is no longer restricted to this area and, therefore, a comprehensive and effective introductory marketing textbook needs to reflect that.

Another emphasis of this book is on the contribution the services sector makes to developed economies. For example, in Australia the services sector accounts for approximately 75 per cent of GDP and 85 per cent of employment. In line with contemporary issues, this edition has a distinct focus on emergent technology and sustainability issues. Technology is changing the way customers consume and, similarly, technology is changing the way we as marketers execute marketing. The emergence of social media and the uptake of these platforms, especially in developing countries, have enabled a level of communication throughout the world not achievable in previous eras. Importantly, being able to Skype or Tweet a business associate or a customer and not having to travel extensively saves carbon emissions and contributes towards a greener earth. We show our readers how innovative organisations can achieve greater customer value by adopting new technology for all/any of the Expanded Marketing Mix variables. Here in the Asia–Pacific region, and more than a decade into the 21st Century, marketers' roles are changing as the global economic climate changes. The process of meeting and exceeding customer needs in a commercially viable, socially just and sustainable manner becomes the new front, and a priority for effective and successful marketing efforts.

As businesses across the Asia–Pacific region increasingly recognise the importance of sustainability initiatives, we have further emphasised our sustainability, or green, theme throughout the book. We view sustainability as a strategic process to create meaningful long-term relationships with customers while maintaining, supporting and enhancing the natural environment. Sustainable strategies have become important to business because of the many challenges associated with maintaining a habitable world for generations to come. With carbon emissions becoming a focal point of most reports on how to minimise global warming, the need to reduce, reuse and recycle has become a source of green initiatives for most businesses and their communications with customers and stakeholders. Each chapter has a *Sustainable Marketing* box that relates marketing activities to sustainability and the natural environment.

Textbook organisation

We have organised this book into three parts. Part 1 provides an overview of marketing; Part 2 discusses the complexities involved with understanding markets, while Part 3 presents our expanded version of the marketing mix.

In **Part 1: Marketing groundwork,** we introduce the discipline of marketing and offer a broad perspective from which to explore and analyse the discipline's various components. Chapter 1 defines marketing and explores some key concepts, including customers and target markets, the marketing mix, relationship marketing, the marketing concept and market orientation. Leading from this introduction of marketing, Chapter 2 provides an overview of strategic marketing issues, such as the effect of organisational resources and opportunities on the planning process, the role of the mission statement, corporate, business-unit, and marketing strategies, and the creation of the marketing plan. These issues are profoundly affected by competitive, economic, political, legal and regulatory, technological and sociocultural forces in the marketing environment. Part 1 concludes with Chapter 3, providing a foundation for analysing buyers through a discussion of marketing information systems and the basic steps in the marketing research process.

Part 2: Understanding markets examines how marketers use information and technology to better understand and reach customers. Chapter 4 deals with how customers behave. Understanding elements that affect buying decisions enables marketers to better analyse customers' needs and to evaluate how specific marketing strategies can satisfy those needs. Chapter 5 addresses selecting and analysing target markets, which is one of the major steps in marketing strategy development. Chapter 6 stresses business markets, organisational buyers, the buying centre and the organisational buying decision process.

Part 3: The expanded marketing mix continues the focus on the customer, but in relation to elements of the marketing mix. Chapter 7 discusses the power and nature of developing and maintaining a successful brand for a company's products. Chapter 8 focuses on basic product concepts where products are considered to comprise both tangible and intangible components. This chapter therefore introduces both goods and services marketing. Chapter 9 analyses various dimensions of product management, including line extensions and the management of services. Chapter 10 discusses the importance of price and looks at some characteristics of price and non-price competition. Then an examination of the major factors that affect marketers' pricing decisions is presented. Chapter 11 discusses supply-chain management, marketing channels and the decisions and activities associated with the physical distribution of products. Retailing and wholesaling, including types of retailers and wholesalers, direct marketing and selling, and strategic retailing issues are also explored. Chapter 12 introduces the major components of integrated marketing communications including a discussion of matching the communication style to product characteristics and target segment features. Chapter 13 describes the major promotional methods that can be included in promotion mixes. The general characteristics of advertising, product placement, public relations (PR), sponsorship and sales promotion techniques are also explored. This chapter also deals with personal selling and the role it can play in a company's promotional efforts. Chapter 14 discusses how the marketing mix can be expanded to include additional variables that have become important for contemporary marketing. Finally, to further understand the contemporary marketplace, Chapter 15 covers digital marketing and social networking.

Your comments and suggestions are valued

As authors, our major focus has been on teaching and preparing learning material for introductory marketing students. We have worked extensively with students and understand the needs of professors and instructors of introductory marketing courses. Each of the authors teach, and have taught in previous years, introductory marketing courses, incorporating and testing the materials included in the book and other ancillary materials to make sure they are effective in the classroom.

We invite your comments, questions and criticisms. We want to do our best to provide materials that enhance the teaching and learning of marketing concepts and strategies. Your suggestions will be sincerely appreciated. Please write to us at anz.customerservice@cengage.com.

William M. Pride
O.C. Ferrell
Bryan A. Lukas
Sharon Schembri
Outi Niininen

Acknowledgements

The achievement of this new text has not happened without the extensive help and support of a number of individuals. Particular thanks must go to Lorien Latimer and Sharon-Lee Lukas for contributing to various aspects of the text, artwork, images and case studies of this book. A big thank you goes to Michelle Aarons, Jessica Brennan, Nathan Katz, Sylvia Marson and the publishing team at Cengage for developing and managing this book project. We would also like to thank all of the local businesses that have allowed us to profile them here as case examples. We sincerely hope inclusion in this text is a profitable experience for you and your business.

Sharon: I would also like to add that I am very grateful for the support provided by both my boys, Jac and Jorge. As my guiding light, Jac you have helped me get through the most difficult days and Jorge, your brilliance with graphic design continues to amaze me. Thank you for being my boys.

Outi: I would also like to say that my greatest thanks go to my family, Vuokko and Erik for their love and support through yet another big project!

Finally, the authors and publisher would like to thank the following reviewers and contributors, whose feedback shaped this second edition:

Case authors
- Wayne Binney, Deakin University
- Petra Bouvain, University of Canberra
- Nicolas Grigoriou, Monash University
- Mark Kilgour and Quentin Somerville, University of Waikato
- Raechel Johns, University of Canberra
- Sebastian Krook, Australian Catholic University
- Lorien Latimer, Freelance Consultant, Queensland Australia
- Anita Love, Griffith University
- Sharon-Lee Lukas, Marketing Consultant, Lukas & Company Pty Ltd
- Sandra Osorio, La Trobe University
- Owen Seamons, University of Queensland
- Sarah Sloan, Griffith University
- Ekant Veer, University of Canterbury
- Tania von der Heidt, Southern Cross University

Reviewers
- Delane Osborne, Curtin University
- Anita Love, Griffith University
- Fredy-Roberto Valenzuela, University of New England
- Philip Trebilcock, Latrobe University, Bendigo
- Frances M Woodside, University of Southern Queensland
- Tendai Chikweche, University of Western Sydney
- Sebastian Krook, Australian Catholic University
- Jennifer Banks, Central Queensland University

- Scott Weaven, Griffith University
- Maureen Griffiths, Monash University
- Dewi Tojib, Monash University
- Ahmed Shahriar Ferdous, Deakin University
- Delane Osborne, Curtin University / University of Western Australia

William M. Pride is Professor of Marketing, Mays Business School, at Texas A&M University. In addition to this text, he is also co-author of a market-leading *Principles of Marketing* text. William's research interests are in advertising, promotion and distribution channels. His research articles have appeared in major journals in the field of marketing, such as the *Journal of Marketing*, the *Journal of Marketing Research*, the *Journal of the Academy of Marketing Science* and the *Journal of Advertising*. William is a member of the American Marketing Association, Academy of Marketing Science, the Society for Marketing Advances and the Marketing Management Association. He has received the Marketing Fellow Award from the Society of Marketing Advances and the Marketing Innovation Award from the Marketing Management Association. Both of these are lifetime achievement awards.

O.C. Ferrell is Professor of Marketing and Bill Daniels Professor of Business Ethics at the Anderson School of Management at the University of New Mexico. O.C. has a distinguished teaching career with previous appointments at the University of Wyoming, Colorado State University, University of Memphis, University of Tampa, Texas A&M University, Illinois State University and Southern Illinois University. His teaching career is broad and includes courses such as Business & Society, Marketing & Society, Business Ethics and Marketing Ethics – both domestically and internationally. O.C. is also an accomplished author with contributions in more than 20 books. He has served as an expert witness in many high-profile civil litigation cases related to business ethics. More recently, O.C. has assisted international corporations and worked with state regulatory agencies in modifying marketing programs to maintain compliance with both ethical and legal requirements.

Brian A. Lukas is Professor of Marketing and Head of the Marketing discipline in the Faculty of Business and Economics at the University of Melbourne. Bryan is well known for promoting the importance of organisations being market-oriented and the marketing function being financially accountable to chief executives. He holds several academic awards, including Best Paper awards from the American Marketing Association and the Australian and New Zealand Marketing Association. Bryan has published many peer-reviewed research papers in leading international journals and conference proceedings and is a member of the American Marketing Association, Academy of Management, Academy of Marketing Science and Society for Marketing Advances. He is also an Associate Fellow (AFAMI) of the Australian Marketing Institute and is accredited as a Certified Practicing Marketer (CPM) by the same institute. In addition to his academic activities, Bryan has carried out consulting and executive teaching assignments in Asia, Australia, Europe and the US. Bryan's expertise is especially sought after in litigation proceedings.

Sharon Schembri was previously tenured at Griffith University and is now Assistant Professor at University of Texas – Pan American. With a focus on innovative teaching and learning approaches, Sharon's students receive personalised attention even in the larger classes, and this personalisation takes their learning and development to another level. As an animated, engaging and professional presenter who regularly speaks at academic conferences throughout the world, teaching is a passion. On the research front, her work has been published in the *Journal of Business Research, Psychology & Marketing, Marketing Theory, Journal of Product and Brand Management*, the *Journal of Management and Organization* and the *Journal of Customer Behavior*. As an experienced ethnographic researcher, Sharon has research themes that investigate health care, branding and visual-research methods. As a consultant, Sharon focuses on research-driven strategies.

Outi Niininen is a Senior Lecturer in Marketing in the La Trobe Business School, La Trobe University, Australia, enticing undergraduate students to the art and business of marketing through enthusiastic and innovative delivery of the key concepts of marketing. Before joining the Marketing team at La Trobe, Outi was in charge of several Masters courses for the Tourism Department of the University of Surrey, UK. She has also taught executive groups at Masters level in Zimbabwe and Jordan and advised managers from the Ministry of Tourism in Saudi Arabia regarding destination branding. Outi's research interests fall broadly under the heading of consumer psychology and to what extent perception influences consumer behaviour. Outi has recently been published in the *Journal of Business Research, Tourism Management, Tourism Analysis, Journal of Travel and Tourism Marketing, Journal of Services Marketing* and *Advances in Culture, Tourism and Hospitality Research*. Her research projects have focused on human-computer interaction, crisis management, utilising social media for research, destination loyalty, destination branding, as well as the Australian short break holiday market. Her current research focuses on Education- and Enquiry-Based Learning approaches.

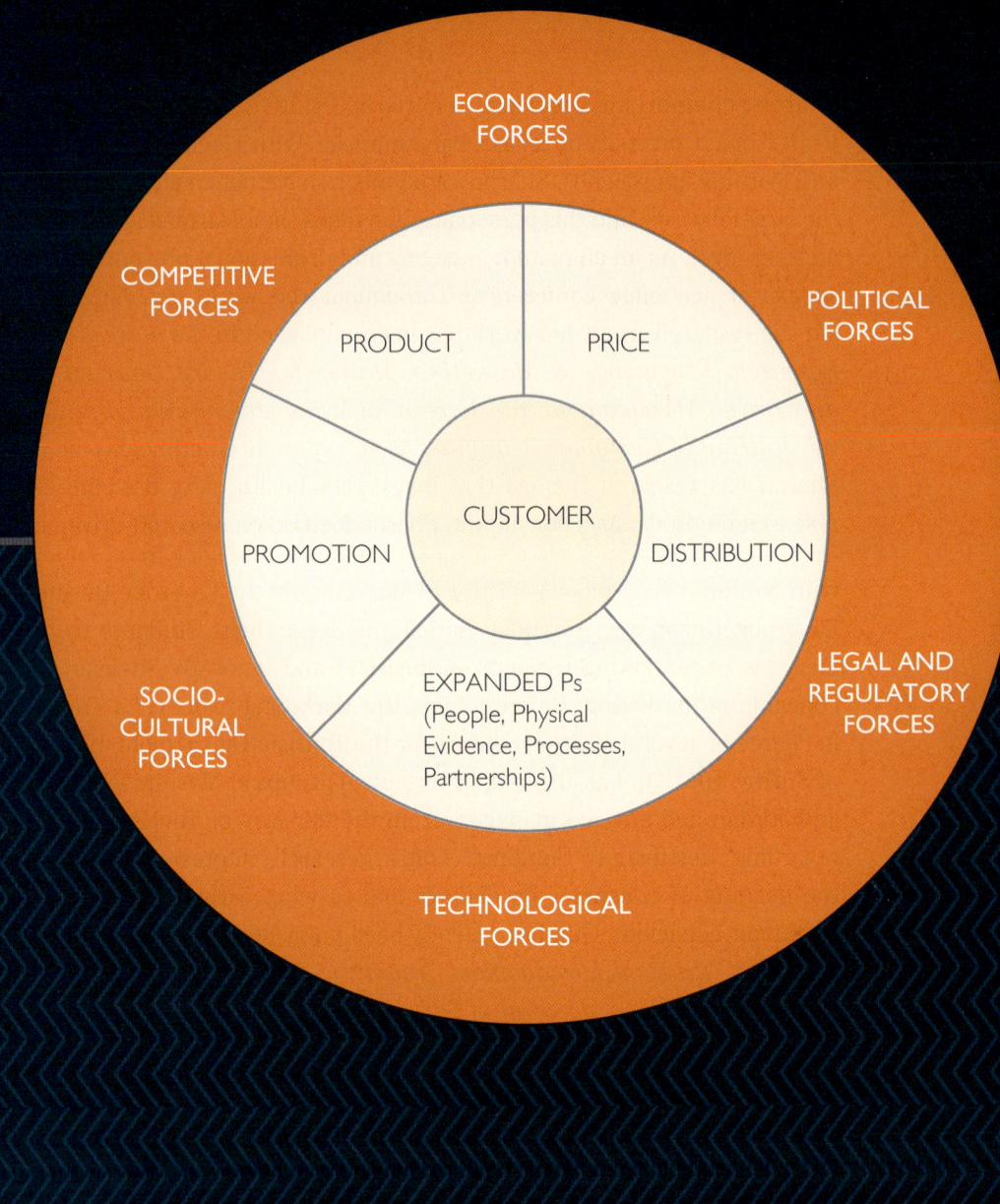

PART 1
MARKETING GROUNDWORK

CHAPTER 1   KEY CONCEPTS IN MARKETING

CHAPTER 2   MARKETING PLANNING AND STRATEGY IN A
COMPETITIVE ENVIRONMENT

CHAPTER 3   MARKETING RESEARCH AND INFORMATION SYSTEMS

WELCOME TO the world of marketing!

This text is presented as three parts. Part 1 introduces the marketing discipline and offers a broad perspective from which to explore and analyse the various concepts and components of marketing. Chapter 1 defines marketing and explores some key concepts, including customers and target markets, the marketing mix, relationship marketing, the marketing concept and market orientation. Chapter 2 provides an overview of strategic marketing issues, such as the effect of organisational resources and opportunities on the planning process, the role of the mission statement, corporate, business-unit and marketing strategies, and the creation of the marketing plan. These issues are profoundly affected by competitive, economic, political, legal and regulatory, technological and sociocultural forces in the macro environment. Chapter 3 provides a foundation for analysing buyers through a discussion of marketing information systems and the basic steps in the marketing research process.

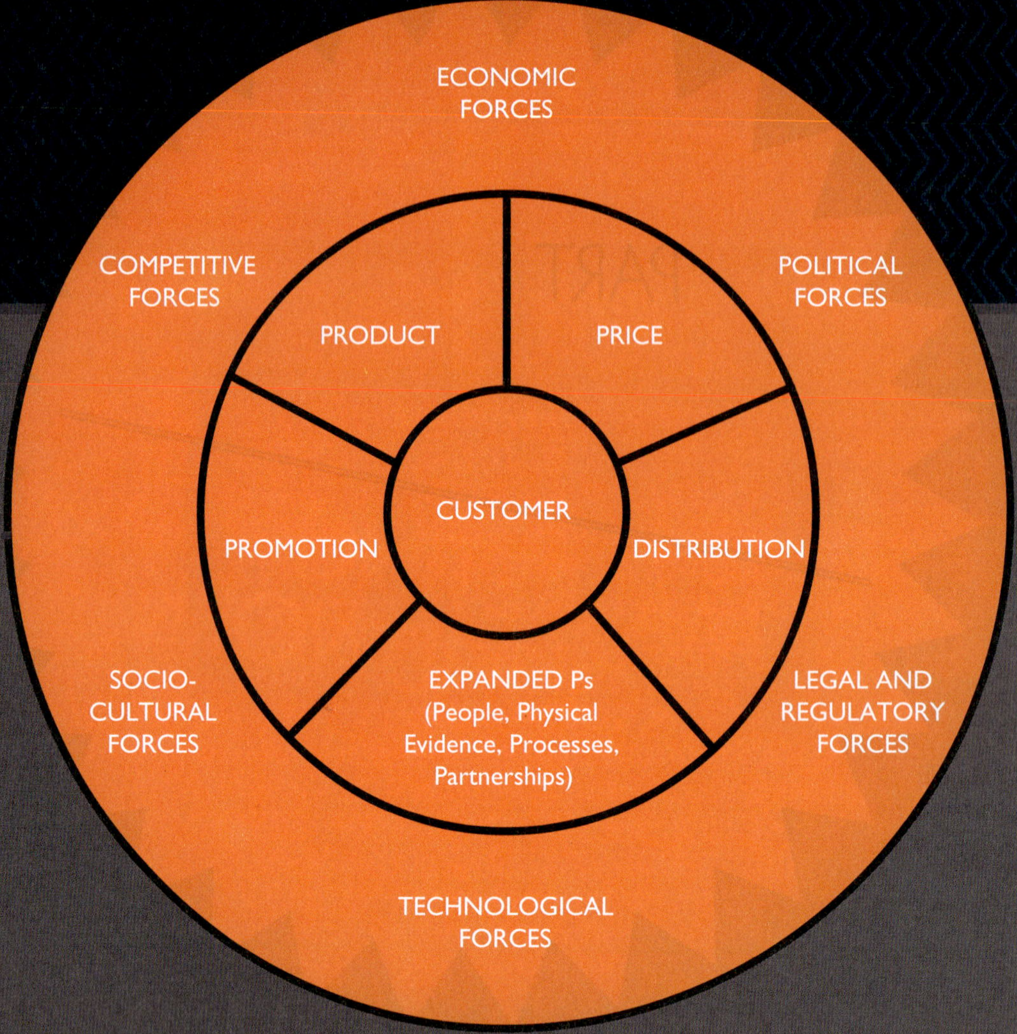

The diagram shows concentric circles with a central "CUSTOMER" surrounded by the marketing mix, surrounded by environmental forces.

Outer ring (environmental forces):
ECONOMIC FORCES

COMPETITIVE FORCES

POLITICAL FORCES

SOCIO-CULTURAL FORCES

LEGAL AND REGULATORY FORCES

TECHNOLOGICAL FORCES

Inner ring (marketing mix):
PRODUCT

PRICE

PROMOTION

DISTRIBUTION

EXPANDED Ps
(People, Physical Evidence, Processes, Partnerships)

Centre:
CUSTOMER

KEY CONCEPTS IN MARKETING

Marketing defined
People are the focus
Strategic variables – the marketing mix
Builds customer and stakeholder relationships
Occurs in a dynamic environment

Marketing concept and orientation
Evolution
Being market-oriented

Managing customer relationships
Value driven marketing

Marketing management

The role of marketing
Cost to consumers
Non-profit organisations
Important to business
Fuels global economy
Enhances consumer awareness
Connects people through technology
Promotes welfare of customers and stakeholders
Exciting career prospects

Throughout this chapter, Watch, Listen and Revise icons indicate an opportunity for online self-study through CengageNOW, linking you to animated chapter overviews, interactive diagrams, videos, quizzes and more.

1

KEY CONCEPTS IN MARKETING

Learning Objectives

LO1 Define marketing and understand key marketing terms, including target market, marketing mix, marketing exchanges and marketing environment

LO2 Develop an understanding of the marketing concept and market orientation

LO3 Appreciate the importance of building customer relationships

LO4 Explain the major marketing functions that are part of the marketing management process

LO5 Understand the role of marketing in our society

MARKETING CHALLENGE | BEING MARKET-ORIENTED: TO BE, OR NOT TO BE…

The Kodak camera, released by George Eastman's Eastman Dry Plate and Film Company in 1888, made photography accessible to everyone. The new Kodak camera was comparatively inexpensive at $25. It was easy to carry around and comfortable for hand-held operation. And it also came preloaded with another innovation – flexible film. The new, inexpensive flexible film just needed to be returned to the company (together with the camera) and the images would be developed and a new film inserted. The new Kodak camera superseded unwieldy cameras that used delicate, rigid photographic plates. George Eastman's vision was to make photography 'as convenient as the pencil'. Today we would call George Eastman's Kodak camera with its flexible film a 'disruptive innovation'.

To achieve his vision he built his company based on the principles of:

* 'mass production at low cost
* international distribution
* extensive advertising
* a focus on the customer'.[1]

In 1975, Eastman Kodak Co (as the Eastman Dry Plate and Film Company was now called) was again at the forefront of technological innovation. Steven Sasson, an Eastman

Kodak Co engineer, invented the digital camera. While it took 20 years for digital cameras to become mainstream, they rapidly grew to become one of the most popular electronic gifts.

The introduction of the digital camera, a second 'disruptive innovation', created some tough strategic problems for Kodak. Through its industry dominance in supplying and processing film, Kodak had enjoyed a sheltered and highly lucrative market position. The infrastructure, machinery and expertise needed to manufacture and process traditional film were not easily replicated, creating significant barriers to entry into the photographic film business. However, the new digital cameras didn't use film and the technology could be replicated by competitors such as Fuji. Executives at Kodak were not united in whether they should promote a product that cannibalised their lucrative film processing and supply business.

With hindsight we can now say that this second 'disruptive innovation' ultimately led to the downfall of Kodak. The sales of traditional roll film fell dramatically from 2000 to 2010, undermining Kodak's profitability, and in 2012, Kodak – the inventors of the phenomenally successful digital camera – entered administration. What they failed to do was understand the power of the digital camera and follow the path that was opened up with their 'disruptive innovation'.

Now the market has entered a new phase in the evolution of photography. Fuji maintained a dominant position in the digital camera market, but consumers are now turning to their mobile phones as a source of photographic equipment. Providing consumers with a more compact and versatile piece of electronics, mobile phone brands such as the Apple iPhone and Samsung Galaxy range offer consumers the ability to take increasingly clear high-quality images, and then share them digitally through apps such as Instagram. By making the sharing of photos as simple as a click, consumers are less inclined to use digital cameras which require additional downloading and uploading efforts.[2]

MARKETING CHALLENGE QUESTIONS

1 How do organisations see the way to be market oriented, that is, focused on meeting customers' true needs?

2 How was it that Kodak invented the digital camera but then failed to follow that path?

Where are the clues on what the market wants?

3 What 'disruptive innovations' do you see today?

Introduction

This first chapter introduces the marketing variables and decisions covered throughout the text. First, we develop a definition of marketing and explore each element of the definition in detail. Next, we introduce the marketing concept and consider several issues associated with implementing it. We also take a brief look at the management of customer relationships and then at the concept of value – a concept central to marketing's ability to contribute to an organisation's cash flow and overall performance. We then explore the process of marketing management, which includes planning, organising, implementing and controlling marketing activities to encourage marketing exchanges. Finally, we examine the importance of marketing in our global society.

Marketing defined

If you ask several people what marketing is, you are likely to hear a variety of descriptions. One of the most common descriptions is that marketing is all about advertising and selling, and nothing else. Such descriptions are disappointing because marketing actually encompasses many more activities. Indeed, marketing is about managing key aspects of an organisation's environment and includes a wide variety of strategic and managerial activities.

Source: Shutterstock.com

DID YOU KNOW?

Think of advertising and sales as the visible tip of an iceberg supported by the bulk of the marketing expertise [the majority of the iceberg is not visible as it is under water].

marketing
The process of maximising returns to stakeholders by developing exchanges with valued customers and creating an advantage for them

In this book, we define **marketing** as the process of maximising returns to stakeholders by developing exchanges with valued customers and creating an advantage for them. The central theme in this definition is that the customers receive an advantage through exchanges. Therefore, whether a marketing activity has been successful or not depends on whether the purchaser has acquired a meaningful advantage from the seller as a result of the seller's market activity. For example, such an advantage may be to feel more confident after choosing to go to a different hairdresser who offers more than just a style cut, but also a full makeover service. In this example, the chosen hairdresser offers the benefit of style and confidence, rather than just hairdressing.

Fundamentally, the customer expects to gain an advantage, or benefit, in excess of the costs incurred in a marketing exchange. But the marketer also expects to gain a benefit in return, generally a financial gain. Over time, these exchanges can result in relationships between the two parties. The contemporary goal of marketing is to develop relationships. Gourmet pizza chain Pizza Capers depend on relationships with satisfied customers, and customers' relationship willingness depends on being satisfied with the food, value and service during each exchange with Pizza Capers.

Customer satisfaction can come from anything received when buying and using a product. For instance, the Kindle e-reader provides users with access to thousands of printed texts from the one portable lightweight device. A Kindle has the capacity to store hundreds of books within an electronic memory, without the bulk or measurable mass that the physical books would hold. This product therefore provides the consumer a benefit of storage and mobility, without the bulk and weight of many books.

Overall, our definition of marketing is consistent with the world's most influential international marketing association, the American Marketing Association (AMA), which defines marketing as 'the activity, set of institutions, and processes for creating, communicating, delivering, and exchanging offerings that have value for customers, clients, partners, and society at large.'[3]

People are the focus

Products include goods, services and ideas or experiences, and people are purchasers and users of these products. Even if organisations buy from each other, it is the people in those organisations who make the purchase for their organisations. Hence, organisations develop, price, distribute and promote their products such that people are always the focal point of all marketing activities, as illustrated in Figure 1.1).

people
The actors involved with the process/experience, including personnel as well as other customers (and even passers-by) present when the product/service/experience took place, also referred to as participants

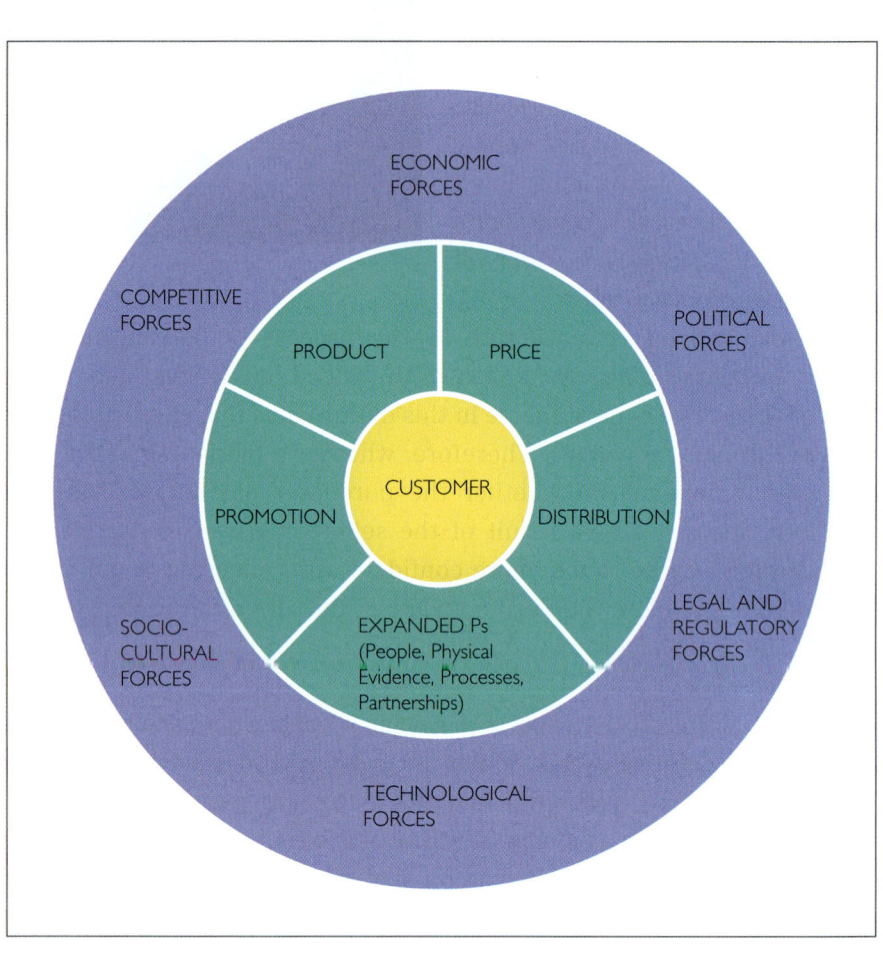

FIGURE 1.1
COMPONENTS OF
STRATEGIC MARKETING

 **WATCH** an interactive animation on the components of strategic marketing

Modern organisations define their products not as what the companies make or produce but as what they do to satisfy people. For example, the Australia Zoo in Queensland, Australia, associated with the late Steve Irwin, is not in the business of establishing zoos. Rather, Australia Zoo is in the business of making people happy, giving them memorable experiences and promoting ideas such as conservation and awareness of the environment. At Australia Zoo, people are guests, the crowd is an audience, and employees and animals can be thought of as cast members. In this way, Australia Zoo is an experience that includes the tangible structure of the zoo as well as the intangible atmosphere of a wildlife safari.

Individuals who purchase things for non-commercial reasons are consumers. Consumers who purchase products from a seller are customers (or clients depending on a particular industry's terminology). In the business-to-business environment, entire organisations can also be referred to as customers or clients. However, individuals will hold the responsibility of purchasing with the support of relevant decision makers.

When organisations focus their marketing efforts on a specific group of customers, they focus on what is called a target market. Marketing managers may define a target market as a vast number of people or a relatively small group. The Australian airline Jetstar Airways, for example, targets its domestic flights in Australia to people who want to fly to a destination without having to pay for things that are not essential to arriving at the destination safely and in good spirit. Other companies target multiple markets with different products, promotions, prices and distribution systems for each one. Nike also uses this strategy, marketing different types of shoes and apparel to meet specific needs of cross-trainers, joggers, aerobics enthusiasts and other athletic-shoe buyers.

Source: Reprinted with permission from Kellogg's and Salamagica

customers
Customers are the purchasers of products, such as goods, services, ideas and experiences. Customers are the focal point of all marketing activities

<< Appealing to target markets
Special K targets a mostly female health conscious consumer

target market
Customers on whom an organisation focuses its marketing efforts

The strategic variables of marketing – the marketing mix and the expanded marketing mix

Marketing is more than simply advertising or selling a product because marketing involves developing and managing a product that will satisfy customer needs. Marketing as a whole focuses on making the right product available in the right place and at the right price acceptable to buyers. Marketing also requires communicating information that helps customers determine if the product will satisfy their needs. These marketing activities are strategic activities and they are planned, organised, implemented and controlled to meet the needs of customers within the target market. Marketers refer to these activity variables – product, price, distribution and promotion – as the marketing mix. Another term often used instead of the marketing mix is the 4Ps, where distribution is traditionally referred to as place.

As our understanding of the marketing function in organisations has improved, marketing professionals and academics have suggested that the marketing mix should be expanded to include additional important variables such as people, physical evidence, process and partnership. This variation of the marketing mix is usually referred to as the expanded marketing mix, or 8Ps, and is outlined in this introductory chapter, as well as discussed in detail in Chapter 14. An important point to note, however, is that regardless of how many variables are ultimately

marketing mix
Four marketing activities (or variables) – product, pricing, distribution and promotion – that an organisation controls to meet the needs of customers within its target market

expanded marketing mix
Also known as the extended marketing mix, the concept includes the eight key variables a company can use to manage its markets under changing market conditions: product, place, promotion, price, people, physical evidence, process and partnership

considered within the marketing mix, the four original variables – product, pricing, distribution (i.e., place) and promotion – will always remain central to any marketing mix and represent the core strategic focus. This expanded marketing mix of the 8Ps is summarised in Figure 1.2.

A marketer's goal is to create and maintain the right mix of these marketing mix elements in order to satisfy customers' needs for a general product type. The marketing mix for a new model of Fords, such as the Ford Focus, for example, combines an economical vehicle with coordinated distribution, promotion and price appropriate for the target market of primarily younger drivers who value technology, driving dynamics and styling. The marketing mix for the Ford Focus therefore includes an economical engine, stylish compact design, a competitive price, dealership distribution and primetime TV commercial advertising. Within this marketing mix, while the style and design of the new model can be considered as the physical evidence of the product, so too can the network of dealerships that present the car to the public. More than that, there are many people, both on the frontline and within support roles, and many supply and retail partnerships involved in getting the new Ford Focus to market. There are, as well, many processes completed along the way. All of this complexity is marketing and referred to here as the expanded marketing mix.

Before marketers can develop an effective marketing mix, they must collect in-depth, up-to-date information about what benefits customers need. Such information might include data about people's preferences for product features, their attitudes toward competitors' products and the frequency with which they use the product. Descriptive data is also collected such as age, income, ethnicity, gender and educational level of people in the target market. Research by Wrigleys, for example, revealed that consumers want a gum that has a whitening function for use after drinking beverages such as coffee. This resulted in the introduction of Wrigley's Extra White chewing gum which not only freshens the breath, but also serves as a teeth whitening product.

The marketing mix

Let's look more closely at the decisions and activities related to the variables of the marketing mix.

THE PRODUCT VARIABLE

Successful marketing efforts result in products that become part of everyday life. Consider the satisfaction customers have had over the years from Sony MP3 players, Apple smart phones, Visa credit cards and 3M Post-it Notes. The product variable of the marketing mix deals with researching customers' needs and wants and designing a product that satisfies them. A **product** can be a good, a service, an idea, an experience or a combination thereof. *A good* is a physical entity you can touch. The Apple iPad, Ray-Ban sunglasses or a bottle of Grey Goose Vodka are all examples of goods. A *service* is the application of human and/or mechanical efforts to people or objects to provide intangible benefits to customers. Air travel, online banking, beauty salons and Google search engines are examples of services. *Ideas* include concepts, philosophies, images and issues. For instance, career guidance counsellors provide students with ideas and advice on career direction and effective career development. Other marketers of ideas include political parties, churches and schools. Experiences typically engage the customers on an emotional level too. For example, crying at a sad storyline in a movie or feeling nervous and excited before a bungee jump.

The product variable also involves creating or modifying brand names and packaging and may include decisions regarding warranty and repair services. Australian snowboarder Torah Bright is a global brand. She is endorsed by US-based companies such as Boost Mobile and also the international brands Roxy and Quicksilver.

product
A good, a service, an idea, an experience or a combination thereof

YOU'LL KNOW YOU'RE WEARING IT WHEN A ROCK FALLS ON YOUR HEAD. OTHER THAN THAT, PROBABLY NOT.

Source: Courtesy Petzl

<< Product
Petzl's ad focuses on the quality, comfort and reliability of its climbing helmet

Product variable decisions and related activities are important because they are directly involved with creating products that address customers' needs and wants. To maintain an assortment of products that helps an organisation achieve its goals, marketers must develop new products, modify existing ones and eliminate those that no longer satisfy enough buyers or that yield unacceptable profits. In the funeral home industry, for example, some companies have developed new products such as DVD memoirs, grave markers that display photos along with a soundtrack and caskets with drawers to hold mementos from the bereaved. To appeal to the growing number of people who prefer to be cremated, other companies are offering more cremation and memorial services. In the eco-friendly market, there are cardboard coffins being designed, delivered and very well received. In the pet-friendly market, there are pet crematoriums emerging. Of course, these products come at a price, with some deliberately priced at a premium to demonstrate status and others deliberately priced low, to achieve market penetration.

THE PRICE VARIABLE

The price variable relates to decisions and actions associated with establishing pricing objectives and policies and determining product prices. Price is a critical component of the marketing mix because customers are concerned about the value obtained in an exchange. Price is often used as a competitive tool, and intense price competition sometimes leads to price wars. High prices can be used competitively to establish a product's premium image. Louis Vuitton, Prada and Mont Blanc brands, for example, have an image of high quality and high price that has given them significant status. On the other hand, some luxury goods marketers are now offering lower-priced versions of their products to appeal to middle-class consumers who want to 'trade up' to prestigious brand names. For example, Volkswagen are renowned for their iconic Kombi and Beetle models and in more recent years have developed a range of smaller hatchback, fuel-efficient cars including the Golf. While this range of smaller Volkswagen cars contrasts with the large passenger and commercial ranges, the Golf range is deliberately designed and priced to compete with small cars made by Ford and Mazda.

Pricing is an important marketing mix variable because it is an adjustable variable that can directly improve the bottom line. By carefully pricing products, marketers can provide customers with an indicator of product quality while maximising profitability. In this way, price is an indicator of value.

In monetary terms, 'price' and 'profit' are relatively easy to understand. But how would a not-for-profit organisation utilise these concepts? For example, a charity like St Vincent de Paul Society (Vinnies) could count increased community awareness of homelessness as their profit and the effort of organising the CEO Winter Sleepout as the price for such an achievement. In this instance, the exchange is not monetary but rather informational. Price is therefore the cost of St Vincent de Paul's investment to achieve the goal of raising awareness on homelessness.

Price is also the cost of the product for the customer. For many products the price is simply a financial cost. However, customers could view the price variable as anything precious to them exchanged for a product; in other words, a personal trainer could cost us money, and that extra hour of sleep in the morning, as well as sweat or physical effort. Hence, price beyond the dollars also includes time and effort.

THE DISTRIBUTION (PLACE) VARIABLE

To satisfy customers, products must be available at the right time and in convenient locations. McDonald's, for example, locates not only in shopping centres, but also inside hospitals (such as the Royal Children's Hospital in Melbourne) and petrol stations. In dealing with the distribution variable, a marketing manager makes products available in the quantities desired by as many target-market customers as possible, keeping total inventory, transportation and storage costs as low as possible. A marketing manager may also select and motivate intermediaries (wholesalers and retailers), establish and maintain inventory control procedures and develop and manage transportation and storage systems. The Internet and e-commerce have dramatically influenced the distribution variable. Companies can now make their products available throughout the world without maintaining facilities in each country. Apple has benefitted from technological advances in distributing songs over the Internet via its iTunes store, rather than establishing brick and mortar venues to sell music.

Downloading iTunes to an iPhone provides consumers with the benefit of music on the move. Since the introduction of iTunes in 2003, billions of downloads have occurred.[4] This evolution of technology and accessibility is a support industry born out of the global success of the Apple iPhone, iPod and iPad. Hence the Apple brand has strategically developed their product beyond just the desktop computer market.

Source: Getty Images; Getty Images

^ **Price strategy**
Competitive pricing in the small car market. Pricing significantly lower than competitors is a pricing strategy designed to capture market share. You can see examples of competitive pricing with, for example, a Hyundai car, where the emphasis is on the price

REVISE your knowledge of promotion in the marketing mix with the online Media Quiz

THE PROMOTION VARIABLE

The promotion variable relates to activities used to inform individuals or groups about the organisation and its products. Promotion can aim to increase public awareness of the organisation and of new or existing products. Red Bull, for example, uses a Formula 1 racing team, air races flugtag and VW Beetles with oversize Red Bull cans strapped to the roofs to advertise and promote its products. Promotional activities also can educate customers about product features or urge people to take a particular stance on a political or social issue, such as smoking or drug abuse. For example, the rising number of incidents of drink driving in Australia has prompted the Australian government to launch advertising campaigns showcasing what can happen when driving under the influence of alcohol. Promotion can also help to sustain interest in established products that have been available for decades, such as Johnson & Johnson Baby Shampoo. Many companies are using the Internet to communicate information about themselves and their products. Social media is also changing how promotion is implemented and is, at times, outside of organisational control. Consumers communicating with other consumers can instigate viral marketing instances where a particular product is advocated by many or maybe announced or reviewed as unfavourable. However, a key element in devising promotional messages is the message itself. As the Marketing in Transition box discusses on the next page, Mini-Coopers and Smart cars are selling strong. As well as fuel efficiency, Mini-Coopers and Smart cars offer consumers a way to take action in being environmentally friendly in their transport choices.

With environmental concerns increasing, the automobile market has seen a global decline in sales and people are looking for smarter solutions to transportation. One answer appears to be: go tiny. While global car sales have been declining precipitously,

Source: Getty Images

the Mini Cooper (made by BMW) and Smart cars (Smart is a member of Mercedes-Benz Cars) are two bright spots on the car industry horizon. The Smart car is like no other car; despite its small size, test drivers have found the interior to be roomier than expected. Over 770 000 of the original Smart Fortwo coupes have been sold in 36 countries since 2001 and the current Smart model is doing well. It is the first car that can be factory ordered over the Internet. Toyota's answer to the tiny car is called the iQ, which was first launched in small-car-friendly Japan and Europe.

Part of the success of smaller vehicles is that they appeal to the practical and emotional sides of consumers. Fuel efficiencies are higher. For example, Toyota's iQ records an impressive 27.4 kpl and emissions of just 99 g/km. Increased parking options is another perk of the small car, especially in Australia's increasingly crowded cities where parking is a challenge. The cars also aim to be more affordable than their large counterparts.[5]

The marketing mix variables are often viewed as controllable because they can be modified. However, there are limits to how much and how often marketing managers can alter elements in the marketing mix. Economic conditions, competitive structure and government regulations may prevent a manager from adjusting prices frequently or significantly. Making changes in the size, shape and design of most tangible goods is expensive; therefore, such product features cannot be altered very often. In addition, promotional campaigns and methods used to distribute products ordinarily cannot be rewritten or revamped overnight.

The expanded marketing mix

Beyond these traditional 4Ps of the marketing mix discussed above are the other marketing mix variables that expand the marketer's toolbox. Now we discuss in detail the additional marketing mix variables of people, physical evidence, processes and partnerships.

THE PEOPLE VARIABLE

In the expanded marketing mix, the people variable refers to the human element of the product. This human element includes those people involved with preparing, producing and presenting the product, who are typically employees of an organisation and are paid to do a quality job.

Marketers can also utilise the people factor to add to the appeal or charm of a product experience. The formality of a fine dining restaurant is evident in the black and white pressed linen staff uniforms combined with posture of personnel on the front line. Similarly, the casual nature of a street café is also evident in the T-shirt and jeans worn by those working in the café combined with the fast and less formal communications of the front-line personnel.

Customers must also not be forgotten. Just like the employees of a fine dining restaurant demonstrate the product offering, so too do the actions and attire of the customers. There might be a dress code to instil a sense of customer exclusivity, for example, and anyone not adhering to these requirements might be refused entry. Potential customers will interpret the clues offered by the 8Ps and decide if they wish to have a meal in this restaurant (i.e. self-select).

THE PHYSICAL EVIDENCE VARIABLE

Just like the people and the attire of those people demonstrate the product and what it is about, so too does the location, décor, lighting and other physical elements associated with the product. The inner city bar, with industrial chic interiors, lounge areas, cocktail menus and soft background music is demonstrating that the bar is upmarket and you can therefore expect to pay higher prices. In contrast, your local pub, televising the cricket with bar stool seating is demonstrating a relaxed and casual atmosphere. Outside of the hospitality industry, physical evidence under the control of marketers can take the form of packaging. For example, bags of green tea presented in a plastic box demonstrates an inferior product quality compared with green tea presented as fresh leaves packaged in a wooden box or embossed tin.

THE PROCESS VARIABLE

Process is another variable used to enhance customer satisfaction. Process involves things such as automation or use of self-service technology. For example, passengers on international flights can reduce their queuing times at the airport by pre-booking their seat online and using self-service terminals for check-in or for arrivals processes like customs and immigration. Another example of how process is used as a marketing variable is provided by Woolworths, the 'Fresh Food People', who demonstrate the freshness and quality of their product by featuring the primary producers who participate in their supply chain in Woolworths TV advertising. The primary producers supplying Woolworths are shown to be farmers who care about the land and the fruit/vegetables they grow. In this way, Woolworths shows the farmers as being part of the process of creating a fresh-food experience.

THE PARTNERSHIP VARIABLE

Establishing, maintaining and nurturing partnerships throughout the supply chain is another recognised manageable marketing variable. Primary producers supplying Woolworths with fresh fruit and vegetables are important partners in marketing of the Woolworths product because they play a key role in the product quality and packaging. By working as partners in the supply chain, Woolworths gains efficiency and encourages reliability. Beyond supply, partnerships relevant to the marketing task include partnerships with the media, partnerships with unions and other lobby groups, partnerships with government and of course partnerships with customers and the broader community. Local sports teams and/or community service groups, for example, being sponsored by big name brands demonstrate these community partnerships. Notably, partnerships can be established, maintained and nurtured with the assistance of technology.

Electronic data shared across the supply chain can facilitate real-time information exchange and just-in-time delivery processes, which effectively reduce the cost of holding inventory and enable customers to get the right product at the right time. Through these exchanges, the company can also collect valuable data on customer satisfaction or for new product development processes. Social media and shared networks also enhance the potential of partnerships that can be established across borders and oceans that enhance an organisation's image. A two-way dialogue can be facilitated by an organisation engaging with customers via social media, as evidenced by the many organisations using Twitter and Facebook as marketing tools.

Marketing builds relationships with customers and stakeholders

Individuals and organisations engage in marketing to facilitate exchanges, the provision or transfer of goods, services and ideas in return for something of value. Any product (good, service or idea) may be involved in a marketing exchange. We assume only that individuals and organisations expect to gain a reward in excess of the costs incurred.

For an exchange to take place, four conditions must exist. First, two or more individuals, groups or organisations must participate, and each must possess something of value that the other party desires. Second, the exchange should provide a benefit or satisfaction to both parties involved in the transaction. Third, each party must have confidence in the promise of the 'something of value' held by the other. If you go to a Lady Gaga concert for example, you go with the expectation of a great theatrical performance. Finally, to build trust, the parties to the exchange must meet expectations.

Figure 1.3 depicts the exchange process. The arrows indicate that the parties communicate that each has something of value available to exchange. However, an exchange will not necessarily take place just because these conditions exist. When an exchange does occur, products are traded for other products or for financial resources.

Marketing activities should attempt to create and maintain satisfying exchange relationships.

exchanges
The provision or transfer of goods, services and ideas in return for something of value

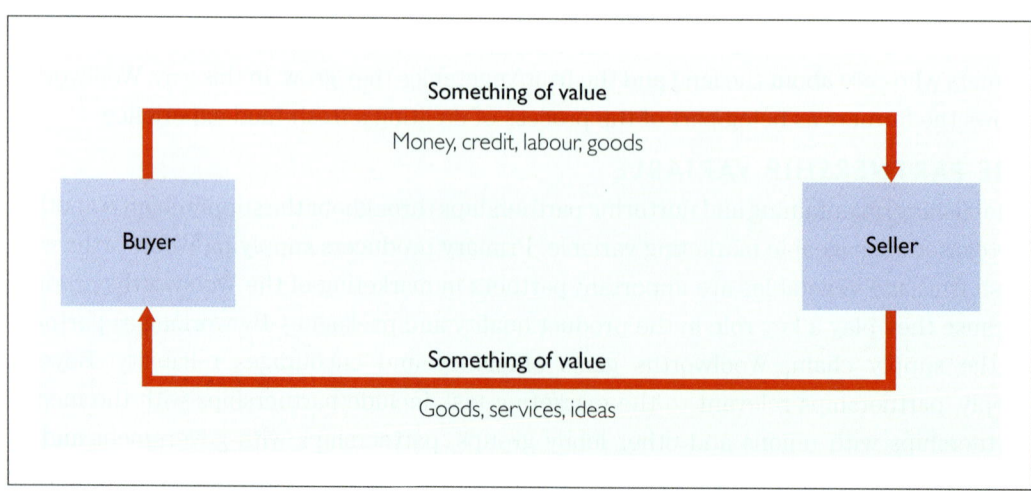

FIGURE 1.3
EXCHANGE BETWEEN
BUYER AND SELLER

To maintain an exchange relationship, buyers must be satisfied with the goods, service or idea obtained, and sellers must be satisfied with the financial reward or something else of value received. A dissatisfied customer who lacks trust in the relationship often searches for alternative organisations or products.

Marketers are concerned with building and maintaining relationships not only with customers but also with relevant stakeholders. Stakeholders include those constituents who have a 'stake', or claim, in some aspect of a company's products, operations, markets, industry and outcomes; these include customers, employees, investors and shareholders, suppliers, governments, communities and many others. Developing and maintaining favourable relations with stakeholders is crucial to the long-term growth of an organisation and its products.

Marketing occurs in a dynamic environment

Marketing activities do not take place in a vacuum. The marketing environment is the macro environment which includes various macro factors such as: competitive, economic, political, legal and regulatory, technological, ethical, ecological and sociocultural. Each of these macro factors, or forces, surrounds the customer and affects the marketing mix (see Figure 1.1). A simplistic framework often referred to in a macro-environmental analysis is the PEST framework. PEST is an acronym for four major macro environments: politics, economics, social and technology. However, macro marketing is far more complex than just these four factors, as depicted in Figure 1.1. The effects of these forces on buyers and sellers can be dramatic and difficult to predict. They can create threats to marketers but can also generate opportunities for new products and new methods of reaching customers.

The forces of the marketing environment affect a marketer's ability to facilitate exchanges in three general ways. First, they influence customers by affecting their lifestyles, standards of living and preferences and needs for products. Because a marketing manager tries to develop and adjust the marketing mix to satisfy customers, effects of environmental forces on customers also have an indirect impact on marketing-mix components. Responding to health concerns from consumers, McDonald's, for example, revamped their menu to include healthier children's menu options, such as fruit bags and chicken wraps instead of fries and hamburgers. Second, marketing-environment forces help to determine whether and how a marketing manager can perform certain marketing activities. Third, environmental forces may affect a marketing manager's decisions and actions by influencing buyers' reactions to the company's marketing mix.

Marketing environment forces can fluctuate quickly and dramatically, which is one reason why marketing is so interesting and challenging. Because these forces are closely interrelated, changes in one may cause changes in others. For example, evidence linking children's consumption of soft drinks and fast foods to health issues such as obesity, diabetes and osteoporosis has exposed marketers of such products to negative publicity and generated calls for legislation regulating the sale of soft drinks in public schools. These legal environmental factors have seen some companies respond to these concerns by voluntarily reformulating products to make them healthier or even introducing new products. Campbell's in Australia responded to consumer concerns

stakeholders
Constituents who have a 'stake', or claim, in some aspect of a company's products, operations, markets, industry and outcomes

marketing environment
The competitive, economic, political, legal and regulatory, technological and sociocultural forces that surround the customer and affect the marketing mix

about their health by introducing a line of reduced sodium soups made with natural sea salt. Campbell's also responded to consumer concerns about wasteful packaging by advertising that its condensed soup cans are smaller, and therefore more eco-friendly, than soups that have the water already added.[6] In another effort to respond to consumer needs, Campbell's sought the Heart Foundation tick of approval. A company's concern for sociocultural and environmental factors is one such ethical issue addressed in the Ethical Marketing box on the next page. Although changes in the marketing environment produce uncertainty for marketers, and at times negatively impact marketing efforts, changes in the broader operating environment also create opportunities. In reference to the economic forces and the recent global recession, customers wanted more attention, better quality and greater value for their money. In fact, during the recession, 90 per cent of large companies trimmed costs in other areas of their business in order to avoid cuts in their marketing budget.[7] Marketers who are alert to changes in environmental forces not only can adjust to and influence these changes but can also capitalise on the opportunities such changes provide.

Apart from legislative forces and economic forces, fast-advancing technological forces are widely impacting both consumption and marketing practice. The rising trend of online shopping, for example, is causing retailers to rethink their product offering and how it is promoted. Currently, Australian consumers purchasing from a retail store are charged GST; however, there is no GST charged on online purchases made from foreign websites provided they are valued at less than $AUD1000. An emerging trend is for consumers to visit retail outlets in their search for products and information prior to purchase, then going home to buy online at the best price. This consumer behaviour is a consequence of globalisation which is positive for consumers but negative for retailers. The dynamics of the marketing environment, therefore, mean that retailers need to improve their product offer put forward to the marketplace while also rethinking how it is promoted. In this way, the dynamics of the marketing environment drive innovation and change in what and how marketing occurs.

This identified change in consumer behaviour towards online shopping and/or searching for information can be described as a sociocultural force operating in the dynamic marketing environment. Given this emerging trend and the negative impact on retailers, innovative marketing efforts for retailers might include, for example, rethinking the level of service provided on the shop floor. Improving the customer's retail experience might include training staff to be proactive rather than reactive and using Internet technology together with visual technology to enable customers to find and buy what they are looking for. The goal is to enhance the customer's retail experience so as to bring consumers back to the shops and away from online shopping. Watch this space!

Astute marketers operating in this dynamic environment have to shift and shape their marketing efforts according to the demands of that broader environment. Marketing mix variables traditionally under control of marketers include product, price, distribution and promotion; the forces of the environment, however, are subject to far less control. Even though marketers know that they cannot predict changes in the marketing environment with certainty, they must nevertheless plan for them. Part of this planning process means monitoring the dynamics and changes within the broader operating environment.

A comprehensive and accurate system of information gathering to alert marketers to the changing dynamics within the broader environment needs to be established and continuously checked to ensure it is capturing the necessary information in an accurate and timely manner. More than that, this environmental scanning system needs to feed relevant information through to the marketers in a user-friendly form.

ETHICAL MARKETING | FACING ETHICAL ISSUES IN MARKETING

issue

Issue: What are the ethical responsibilities of marketers?

Below are actions that marketers can take in order to address typical ethical issues.

Issue category	Examples
Product	Disclose risks associated with a product
	Disclose information about a product's function, value or use
	Disclose information about changes in the nature, quality or size of a product
Price	Practice anti-price fixing behaviours so consumers are offered a fair price.
	Avoid undercutting your prices to drive out competitors (predatory pricing)
	Always clearly disclose the full price of a purchase
Place (Distribution)	Honour the rights and responsibilities associated with specific intermediary roles
	Refrain from manipulating product availability
	Never use coercion to force other intermediaries to behave in a certain way
Promotion	Practice true and clear advertising (avoid false or misleading information)
	Using honest and transparent sales promotions, tactics and publicity
	Never offer or accept bribes in personal selling situations
People	Never discriminate against recruits who are qualified for the job but do not have the desired appearance or are older that other applicants, e.g. a middle-aged mother might not look as glamorous as other job applicants
	Put adequate support systems in place for staff members who work in an emotionally demanding role requiring customer empathy, e.g. working in a funeral home can be emotionally draining. Managers might wish to consider regular counselling for staff members
Physical evidence	Take a long-term view towards facilities and buildings, taking into consideration the environment and local stakeholders, e.g. using sustainably-sourced and safe building materials
	Take measures to cater for your resource use, e.g. installing self-sufficient water supply rather than relying on sprinklers to maintain a green golf course when local residents have limited supply of water for domestic use
Process	Maintain confidentiality and anonymity requirements, even if sacrificing confidentiality would save the company money or time in essential processes. Ensure staff training emphasises the importance of these aspects. Align your expectations of staff members' problem-solving ability with the training, management support and facilities available to them
Partnership	Never enter into a business alliance with a plan to exploit the other business partners, e.g. planning to copy their technological innovation without sharing any of your expertise
	Never use the company size or volume of business to set extremely low prices for services provided for your customers by small independent operators, e.g. a large cruise liner company visiting a port regularly can haggle down taxi fares

Understanding the marketing concept and market orientation

Some companies have sought success by buying land, building a factory, equipping it with people and machines, and then making a product they believe buyers need. However, these companies frequently fail to attract customers with what they have to offer because they defined their business as 'making and then selling a product' rather than as 'helping potential customers satisfy their needs and wants'. For example, companies such as Apple developed the iTunes music store as well as new products like the iPod, iPhone and iPad to satisfy consumers' desire for portable, customised music libraries. Other companies, such as Pandora and Spotify, offered on-demand music streaming to computers and mobile devices. Companies that did not pursue such opportunities struggled to compete as digital music sales rose while physical album sales declined. Consider, also, turntable manufacturers. When CDs became more popular than vinyl records, turntable manufacturers had an opportunity to develop new products to satisfy customers' needs for home entertainment. Companies that did not pursue this opportunity, such as Dual and Empire, are no longer in business. Indeed, such organisations have failed to implement what is called the marketing concept.

According to the marketing concept, an organisation provides products that satisfy customers' needs through a coordinated set of activities that also allows the organisation to achieve its goals. Customer satisfaction is the major focus of the marketing concept. To implement the marketing concept, an organisation strives to determine what buyers

marketing concept
A marketing philosophy suggesting that an organisation should try to satisfy customers' needs through a coordinated set of activities that also allows the organisation to achieve its goals

Source: Reprinted with permission from CUB Pty Ltd

want and uses this information to develop satisfying products. It focuses on customer analysis, competitor analysis and integration of the company's resources to provide customer value, as well as make the organisation more valuable for its owners and other stakeholders.[8] The company must continue to alter, adapt and develop products to keep pace with customers' changing desires and preferences.

The marketing concept is not a second definition of marketing. It is a marketing philosophy guiding an organisation's overall activities. This philosophy affects all organisational activities, not just marketing activities. Production, finance, accounting, human resources and marketing departments must work together.

The marketing concept is also not a philanthropic philosophy aimed at helping customers at the expense of the organisation. A company that adopts the marketing concept must satisfy not only its customers' objectives but also its own, or it will not stay in business long. The overall objectives of a business might relate to increasing profits, market share, sales or a combination of all three.

The marketing concept >>
Carlton United Breweries (CUB) understand the importance of a customer orientation. Marketers for CUB have listened to their customers' requests for a more health-conscious beer and responded with a range of Pure Blonde low-carb options

The evolution of how marketing has been interpreted

Today, the marketing concept may seem like an obvious approach to running a business. However, business people have not always believed that the best way to make sales and profits is to satisfy customers (see Figure 1.4). A better understanding of how marketing has evolved over time will help us identify persistent problems in many of today's businesses.

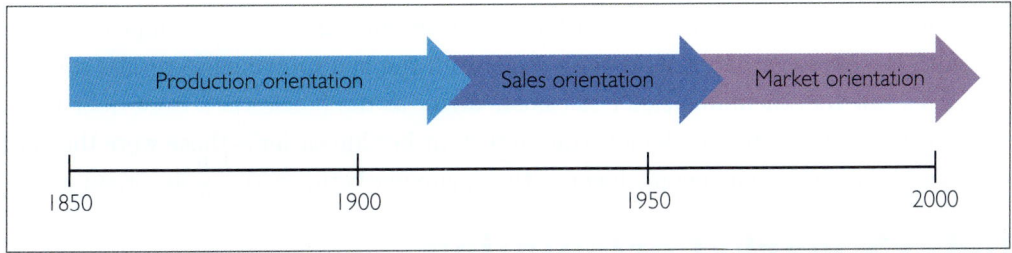

FIGURE 1.4 THE EVOLUTION OF THE MARKETING CONCEPT

Basic trading

The first stage in the evolution of marketing was simple trading of produce. During this era, those with excess wheat were able to trade this for other commodities such as meat; equally, families would have used some of their produce to obtain livestock or other basic possessions. Once townships were formed along key routes, more specialist trades (e.g. blacksmith) flourished. During this era the supply and demand for items was localised as the means of transporting or informing potential customers of produce available for trade had not yet developed. Another notable feature was that the producer (farmer) was also the trader (seller) and middle men were not used for distribution. Relationships between the customers and the producers were essential as many would only trade with people they trusted.[9]

The production orientation

During the second half of the nineteenth century, the Industrial Revolution was in full swing in most Western economies. Electricity, rail transportation, division of labour, assembly lines and mass production made it possible to produce goods more efficiently. With new technology and new ways of using labour, products poured into the marketplace, where demand for manufactured goods was strong. As a consequence, marketing was essentially interpreted as a production orientation. Henry Ford's T-model Ford released in 1910 embodied a production orientation. Known as the father of the assembly line, Henry Ford took his custom car shop to the extreme of efficiency by announcing, 'You can have any colour you want as long as it's black!'. Each worker was trained for a specific work station and a specific task. Specialisation meant standardisation which meant fewer errors and reduced cost, and black paint was cheap.

Branding gained importance, together with an increase in distribution middle men to help with sales expertise, as well as share some of the risks and costs involved with inventory. In the early stages, the demand for many industrial products was plentiful. Once the initial rush of demand was satisfied, the focus shifted to more aggressive sales tactics.[10]

The sales orientation

In the 1920s, strong demand for products subsided, and businesses realised that they would have to 'sell' products to buyers to maintain their mass manufacturing facilities. The production orientation shifted to a sales, or selling, orientation.

From the mid-1920s to the early 1950s, businesses viewed sales as the major means of increasing profits. Business people believed that the most important marketing activities were personal selling, advertising and distribution. This era gave birth to the term 'sales force' as some of the sales practices used would be labelled as aggressive. Deceptive advertising or making false claims were not unheard of, as successful marketing was supposed to lead to a sale. This strategy had a short-term focus with the aim to maximise profits sooner.[11] The 1950s saw the 'vacuum cleaner salesman' arrive at the housewife's front door with a charming smile and a product demonstration that 'makes life easier' – those were the hard-sell days. Today, still, some people incorrectly equate marketing with a sales orientation.

Today's market orientation

By the early 1950s, some business people began to recognise that efficient production and extensive promotion did not guarantee that customers would buy products. These businesses, and many others since, found that they must first determine what customers want and then produce those products rather than making the products first and then try to persuade customers that they need them. As more organisations realised the importance of satisfying customers' needs, the marketing concept we discussed earlier was born. Today's orientation is nothing less than the operationalisation of the marketing concept.

Modern marketing: being market-oriented

The marketing concept is the conceptual core of modern marketing, and since the early 1990s, being market-oriented is seen as the managerial operationalisation, or the implementation, of the marketing concept. A market orientation requires the organisation-wide generation of market intelligence. This intelligence is in relation to current and future customer needs, to the competition and to collaborators (such as suppliers and alliance partners). In addition, a market orientation requires the dissemination and inter-functional coordination of the intelligence across business functions. Further, a market orientation requires an organisation-wide responsiveness to the intelligence.[12]

Unless marketing managers implement a market orientation as an organisational culture, an organisation cannot operationalise the marketing concept. To implement a market orientation culturally, an organisation must establish some general conditions.

Management must first establish an information system to discover customers' real needs and then use the information to create satisfying products. For example, research has shown that women want products that are customisable and relevant to their lives. As food prices increase, food manufacturers such as Kraft have been engaged in large-scale tests to determine ways to cut costs on their food products. The company is feeling the pressure to keep prices low, while simultaneously satisfying customers. An information system is usually expensive; management

market orientation
An organisational culture expressed through the organisation-wide
(1) generation of market intelligence in relation to current and future customer needs, to the competition and to collaborators;
(2) dissemination and inter-functional coordination of the market intelligence across business functions; and
(3) responsiveness to the market intelligence

must commit money and time for its development and maintenance. Without an adequate information system, however, an organisation cannot hope to become market-oriented.

A company must also establish a way to coordinate all its activities. This may require restructuring the internal operations and overall objectives of one or more departments. If the head of the marketing unit is not a member of the organisation's top-level management, he or she should be. Some departments may have to be abolished and new ones created. Implementing the marketing concept demands the support not only of top management but also of managers and staff at all levels. For instance, non-marketing managers must communicate with marketing managers to share information important to understanding the customer. In the end, executives, marketing managers and non-marketing managers (those in production, finance, human resources and so on) are all important for establishing and carrying out a market orientation.

MARKETING IN ACTION | SURVIVING THE OUTDOORS WITH BEAR GRYLLS: MARKETING APPEALS TO SURVIVALISTS AND MORE

Source: Getty Images/NBC

Bear Grylls is ex-British Special Forces and a survivalist expert. He is one of the most recognisable faces of outdoor survival worldwide. After becoming one of the youngest climbers to reach the summit of Mount Everest, he went on to become the star of Discovery Channel's *Man Vs Wild* and *Born Survivor* TV series, which have reached over 1.2 billion viewers worldwide. In branding himself as a survivalist expert, Bear Grylls shares his survival skills, techniques and tools with the everyday outdoor adventurer through his range of books, DVDs and survival tools. His audience aspires to have adventures and be just as survival-savvy and well-equipped as their survival icon.

In reaching the outdoor enthusiast market, the Bear Grylls product line takes key extreme survival elements, such as warmth, water and safety, and brings them to the market in the form of easy to use, compact and stylish products. The Bear Grylls Survival Bracelet is both a critical emergency tool and a fashion statement, created from 3.65 metres of cobra woven high-strength Paracord with an inbuilt safety whistle, perfect for cliff descents and climbing trees to hide from wild animals. Similarly, the Bear Grylls Fire Starter features a fire starter and metal striker, SOS instructions, a waterproof tinder compartment and a whistle which all clip neatly

together to form the perfect survival tool. Backed by the Bear Grylls name and associated adventuring acclaim, the brand reaches consumers by providing a sense of trust in the quality of the tools. Consumers feel more prepared and equipped for the worst-case scenario with a Bear Grylls knife and Bear Grylls survival torch tucked away in their Bear Grylls technical day pack. Bear Grylls has essentially brought extreme survival to the mainstream market. ◼

Finally, a number of cultural values are required for implementing a market orientation. Trust, openness, honouring promises, respect, collaboration and recognising the market as the reason for existence are six values required by organisations striving to become more market-oriented.[13] (Refer to the Sustainable Marketing box on p. 31 for an example of a brand that has recognised the market as the reason for its existence, and in response developed a range of related products to meet their customers' needs and wants.)

Managing customer relationships

Each and every organisation must recognise relevant stakeholders and consider each stakeholder perspective. Stakeholders include, for example, shareholders, employees and suppliers as well as customers and the broader community. Achieving full stakeholder-value (e.g. cash-flow for the owners of an organisation and satisfaction for the customers of the organisation) should be the fundamental goal of an astutely market-oriented company. At the most basic level, stakeholder value can be obtained in the following ways: (1) by acquiring new customers, (2) by providing more value to customers and (3) by retaining customers.

Underpinning the creation of stakeholder value is the building of relationships with stakeholders, and the subsequent maintenance of these relationships. These relationships are critical because they bond stakeholders to the organisation and help them to feel involved in the organisation's success.

Maintaining relationships with customers is clearly an important goal for marketers. The term relationship marketing refers to 'long-term, mutually beneficial arrangements in which both the buyer and seller focus on value enhancement through the creation of more satisfying exchanges'.[14]

Relationship marketing continually deepens the buyer's trust in the company, and as the customer's confidence grows, this, in turn, increases the company's understanding of the customer's needs. Successful marketers respond to customer needs and strive to increase value to buyers over time. Eventually this interaction becomes a solid relationship that allows for cooperation and mutual dependency.

To build these long-term customer relationships, marketers are increasingly turning to marketing research and information technology. Customer relationship management (CRM) focuses on using information about customers to create marketing strategies that develop and sustain desirable customer relationships. By increasing customer value over time, organisations try to retain and increase long-term profitability through customer loyalty.[15] For example, many companies have a rewards program, wherein members collect reward points for every $1 spent, which can be redeemed for future purchases or gift certificates. Rewards programs are popular with large companies, such as Coles, Woolworths and Myer, as well as smaller operations such as Hudson's Coffee and chemist chain Priceline.

Managing customer relationships requires identifying patterns of buying behaviour and using that information to focus on the most promising and profitable customers.[16] Companies must be sensitive to customers' requirements and desires and establish communication

relationship marketing
Establishing long-term, mutually satisfying buyer–seller relationships

customer relationship management (CRM)
Using information about customers to create marketing strategies that develop and sustain desirable customer relationships

to build their trust and loyalty. Consider that the lifetime value of a Lexus customer will be usually much higher than that of a Red Rooster customer; but remember, there are many more Red Rooster customers. For either organisation, a customer is important. A customer's lifetime value results from his or her frequency of purchases, average value of purchases and brand-switching patterns.[17] In general, when marketers focus on customers chosen for their lifetime value, they earn higher profits in future periods than when they focus on customers selected for other reasons.[18] Because the loss of a loyal potential lifetime customer could result in lower profits, managing customer relationships has become a major focus of strategic marketing today. Companies need to understand the value of paying customers, but also the value of customers subsidised by other customers. Employment agencies, dating services and even IT providers provide the word-of-mouth advertising and social networking value for so-called free customers. Customers attracting other customers can grow your business.[19]

Through the use of Internet-based marketing strategies (e-marketing), companies can personalise customer relationships on a nearly one-on-one basis. A wide range of products, such as computers, jeans, golf clubs, cosmetics and greeting cards, can be tailored for specific customers. Customer relationship management provides a strategic bridge between information technology and marketing strategies aimed at long-term relationships. This process involves finding and retaining customers using information to improve customer value and satisfaction.

Value-driven marketing

Value is an important element of managing long-term customer relationships and implementing the marketing concept. We view value as a customer's subjective assessment of benefits relative to costs in determining the worth of a product.

Customer benefits include anything a buyer receives in an exchange. Hotels and motels, for example, basically provide a room with a bed and bathroom, but each provides a different level of service, amenities and atmosphere to satisfy its guests. YHA Backpacker Hostels provide basic share-room bunk-style accommodation, perfect for those travelling on a backpacker budget and favouring the social experience over comfort and luxury. In contrast, the Hilton provides every imaginable service a guest might desire and strives to ensure that all service is of the highest quality. Customers judge which type of accommodation offers the best value according to the benefits they desire and their willingness and ability to pay for the costs associated with the benefits.

Customer costs include anything a buyer must give up to obtain the benefits the product provides. The most obvious cost is the monetary price of the product, but non-monetary costs can be equally important in a customer's determination of value. Two non-monetary costs are the time and effort customers expend to find and purchase desired products. To reduce time and effort, a company can increase product availability, thereby making it more convenient for buyers to purchase their products. Another non-monetary cost is risk, which can be reduced by offering good basic warranties or extended warranties for an additional charge.[20] Another risk-reduction strategy is the offer of a 100 per cent satisfaction guarantee. This strategy is increasingly popular in today's catalogue/telephone/Internet

LISTEN to this chapter's Audio Summary for a recap of relationship marketing and CRM

value
A customer's subjective assessment of benefits relative to costs in determining the worth of a product

shopping environment. Many eBay-based businesses, for example, use such a guarantee to reduce the risk involved in ordering merchandise sight unseen.

The process people use to determine the value of a product is not highly scientific. All of us tend to get a feel for the worth of products based on our own expectations and previous experience. We can, for example, compare the value of tyres, batteries and computers directly with the value of competing products. We evaluate movies, sporting events and performances by entertainers on the more subjective basis of personal preferences and emotions. For most purchases, we do not consciously try to calculate the associated benefits and costs. It becomes an instinctive feeling that Kellogg's Corn Flakes are good value or that Pancake Parlour is a good place for a quick breakfast. The purchase of a car or a mountain bike may have emotional components, but more conscious decision making may also figure in the process of determining value.

In developing marketing activities, it is important to recognise that customers receive benefits based on their experiences. For example, many computer buyers consider services such as fast delivery, ease of installation, technical advice and training assistance to be important elements of the product. Customers also derive benefits from the act of shopping and selecting products. These benefits can be affected by the atmosphere or environment of a store. Even the ease of navigating a website can have a tremendous impact on perceived value. Therefore, companies such as Amazon.com, that tailor their website to individual customers, have been found to be far more successful at maintaining customer loyalty and generating customer interest in their products.

The marketing mix can be used to enhance perceptions of value. A product that demonstrates value usually has a feature or an enhancement that provides benefits. Promotional activities can also help to create an image and prestige characteristics that customers consider in their assessment of a product's value. In some cases, value may be perceived simply as the lowest price. Many customers may not care about the quality of the paper towels they buy; they simply want the cheapest ones for use in cleaning up spills because they plan to throw them in the rubbish anyway.

On the other hand, more people are looking for the fastest, most convenient way to achieve a goal and, therefore, become insensitive to pricing. For example, many busy customers are buying more prepared meals in supermarkets to take home and serve quickly, even though these meals cost considerably more than meals prepared from scratch. In such cases, the products with the greatest convenience may be perceived as having the greatest value. The availability or distribution of

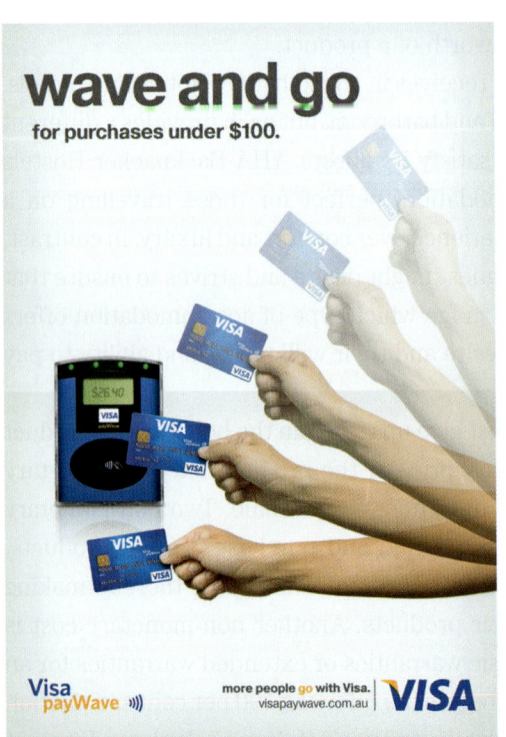

Source: Used with permission from Visa AP Australia) Pty Ltd

wave and go
for purchases under $100.

Visa payWave)))   more people go with Visa. visapaywave.com.au   **VISA**

Value-driven marketing >>
To drive customer value Visa have introduced a contactless payment method branded Paywave to their credit cards, increasing the ease and efficiency of using their products over competing credit card brands

products can also enhance their value. In Australia, Nandos wants to have its Portuguese-style fast-food products available at any time and at any place people are thinking about consuming food. It has, therefore, introduced Nando's products into supermarkets. Thus, the development of an effective marketing strategy requires understanding the needs and desires of customers and designing a marketing mix to satisfy them and provide the value that consumers want. Marketing, therefore, is more than just price or any other one element of the marketing mix. Marketing is about packaging up an idea to demonstrate the value to a particular consumer segment. When marketing demonstrates value, consumers recognise the benefit for them. Hence, why consumers might be willing to pay a premium for convenience, for example. The Marketing in Action box below looks at the arguments for and against in this debate.

MARKETING IN ACTION | DOES MARKETING INCREASE THE VALUE OF PRODUCTS?

Value is a subjective assessment of benefits relative to costs. Marketing has the ability to increase consumers' perceptions of a product's quality and social approval. For instance, retailers like Neiman Marcus use marketing to create awareness and promote the quality of their products. Consumers may be willing to pay more for products when the image of the product is enhanced through advertising, personal selling and publicity.

On the other hand, critics are concerned that consumers may pay more for products when benefits such as quality and functionality are not enhanced. For example, some name-brand pharmaceuticals have the exact same ingredients as generic brands. Additionally, certain products are advertised as natural and sustainable to justify higher prices. There is no evidence that consumers actually obtain more tangible benefits from these purchases.[21]

The marketing management process

In this chapter, we have provided an overview of modern marketing and how it has evolved. With what we have learned so far in mind, we must recognise that the function of marketing also has to be managed. Marketing management is the process of planning, organising, implementing and controlling marketing activities to facilitate exchanges effectively and efficiently. Effectiveness and efficiency are important dimensions of this definition. Effectiveness is the degree to which an exchange helps to achieve an organisation's objectives. Efficiency refers to minimising the resources an organisation must spend to achieve a specific level of desired exchanges. Therefore, the overall goal of marketing management is to facilitate highly desirable exchanges and to minimise the costs of doing so.

Planning is a systematic process of assessing opportunities and resources, determining marketing objectives and developing a marketing strategy and plans for implementation

marketing management
The process of planning, organising, implementing and controlling marketing activities to facilitate exchanges effectively and efficiently

and control. Planning determines when and how marketing activities are performed and who performs them. It forces marketing managers to think ahead, establish objectives and consider future marketing activities and their impact on society. Effective planning also reduces or eliminates daily crises.

Organising marketing activities involves developing the internal structure of the marketing unit. The structure is the key to directing marketing activities. The marketing unit can be organised by functions, products, regions, types of customers or a combination of all four.

Proper *implementation* of marketing plans hinges on coordination of marketing activities, motivation of marketing personnel and effective communication. Marketing managers must motivate marketing personnel, coordinate their activities and integrate their activities both with those in other areas of the company and with the marketing efforts of personnel in external organisations, such as advertising agencies and research companies. An organisation's communication system must allow the marketing manager to stay in contact with high-level management, with managers of other functional areas within the company and with personnel involved in marketing activities both inside and outside the organisation.

The marketing *control process* consists of establishing performance standards, comparing actual performance with established standards and reducing the difference between desired and actual performance. An effective control process has four requirements. It should ensure a rate of information flow that allows the marketing manager to detect quickly any differences between actual and planned levels of performance. It must accurately monitor various activities and be flexible enough to accommodate changes. The costs of the control process must be low, relative to costs that would arise without controls. Finally, the control process should be designed so that both managers and subordinates can understand it.

The role and importance of marketing in a global economy

As we conclude this chapter, we must further recognise that many companies view their marketing as an international activity. Local brands, such as Billabong and Sass & Bide, are competing on the global stage and in the global marketplace. Even individual businesses operating from home can join global competition by launching and operating on eBay or Etsy, for example. Choosing to limit operations to a national and domestic marketplace may be a deliberate strategic decision. However, in doing so, you may not escape global competition because some competitors may choose to market and operate in your domestic space. In effect, therefore, rather than considering international marketing and the global economy as something distinct, we have incorporated international examples throughout this book.

Marketing costs consume a sizable portion of buyers' dollars

Studying marketing will make you aware that many marketing activities are necessary to provide satisfying goods and services. Obviously, these activities cost money. About one-half of a buyer's dollar goes for marketing costs. If you spend $100 on a new pair of Nike running shoes, 40 to 50 per cent goes toward marketing expenses, including promotion and distribution.

Marketing is used in non-profit organisations

Although the term *marketing* may bring to mind advertising, marketing is also important in organisations working to achieve goals other than ordinary business objectives, such as profit. Government agencies at the federal, state and local levels engage in marketing activities to fulfil their mission and goals. The Australian Defence Force, for example, uses promotion, including TV ads and event sponsorships, to communicate the benefits of signing up to potential recruits. Universities engage in marketing activities to recruit new students, as well as to obtain donations from alumni and businesses.

In the private sector, non-profit organisations also use marketing activities to create, price, distribute and promote programs that benefit particular segments of society. The Red Cross, for example, must promote its slogan of 'one in three will need blood' to the public to increase awareness of their cause, encourage people to donate and raise funds.

Source: Alamy/imagebroker

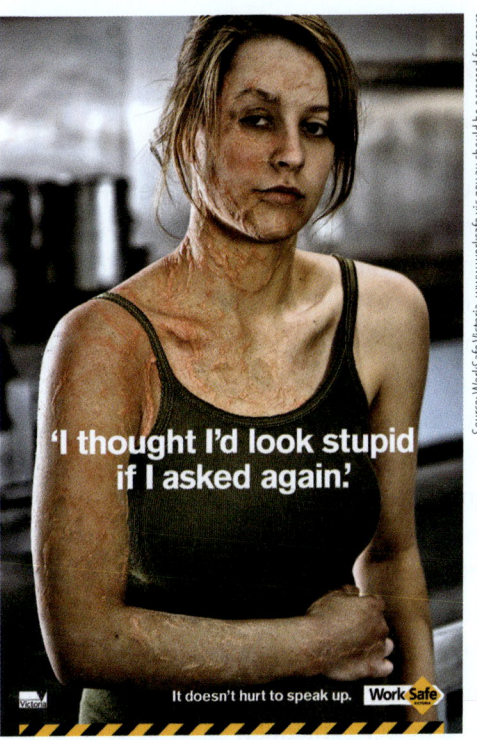

Source: WorkSafe Victoria, www.worksafe.vic.gov.au should be accessed for more information and future updates on the references used. Ad by Grey Group Australia.

<< Non-profit organisations
WorkSafe Victoria (http://www .worksafe.vic.gov .au/) and the World Wildlife Fund (WWF; http://www.wwf .org/) use marketing to promote their causes

Marketing is important to businesses

Businesses must sell products to survive and grow, and marketing activities help to sell their products. Financial resources generated from sales can be used to develop innovative products. New products allow a company to satisfy customers' changing needs, which, in turn, enables them to generate more profits. Even non-profit businesses need to 'sell' to survive.

Marketing fuels our global economy

Profits from marketing products contribute to the development of new products and technologies. Advances in technology, along with falling political and economic barriers and the universal desire for a higher standard of living, have made marketing across national borders commonplace while stimulating global economic growth. As a result of worldwide communications and increased international travel, many Australian and New Zealand brands have achieved widespread acceptance around the world. At the same time, customers in Australia and New Zealand have greater choices among the products they buy because foreign brands such as Toyota (Japan) sell alongside Australian brand Holden, and Christian Dior (France) sells alongside Australian fashion designer Collette Dinnigan. People around the world watch CNN and MTV on Toshiba and Sony televisions they purchased at The Good Guys. Electronic commerce via the Internet now enables businesses of all sizes to reach buyers around the world.

Marketing knowledge enhances consumer awareness

Besides contributing to the wellbeing of a country's economy, marketing activities help to improve the quality of people's lives. Studying marketing allows us to assess a product's value and flaws more effectively. Consider that research suggests that low-fat nutrition claims for a food product can actually increase the intake of that product, thereby countering the desired effects of consuming low-fat snacks to lose weight.[22] Similarly, gym members may be more inclined to spend longer on the exercise bikes knowing they are creating green energy at the same time (see the Sustainable Marketing box on the next page). We can determine which marketing efforts need improvement and how to attain that goal. For example, an unsatisfactory experience with a warranty may make you wish for stricter law enforcement so that sellers would fulfil their promises. You may also wish that you had more accurate information about a product before you purchased it. Understanding marketing enables us to evaluate corrective measures (such as laws, regulations and industry guidelines) that could stop unfair, damaging or unethical marketing practices. Thus, understanding how marketing activities work can help you to be a better consumer.

SUSTAINABLE MARKETING | PEDAL POWER: PUTTING ECO-RESPONSIBILITY INTO YOUR CUSTOMERS' HANDS

In order for businesses to run in a more environmentally friendly way, business owners are becoming innovative in how they source their electricity. One such trend is the advent of the people-powered gym, whereby gym members effectively convert their workout into clean energy to run the electrical components of the gym space, such as lighting and music. One such source of power is your humble exercise bike, which is specially configured to operate as a pedal-powered generator. The pedalling motion creates kinetic energy which is carried via a cable at the back of the machine into a storage unit and distributed to electrical equipment throughout the premises. Your spin class not only burns calories, but has a new purpose in keeping coal-burning electricity to a minimum.

This notion of pedal power is now available for the home gym, through products such as the Pedal-A-Watt bike. Other businesses are harnessing the interactive and eco-friendly pedal power concept, such as bars, whereby customers pedal power their blended margaritas. Similarly, major music festivals, such as Glastonbury, are going green, setting up pedal-powered generators to run visual displays and charge festival goers mobile phones. Even dance floors are being converted to energy producing machines. What will come next?[23]

Marketing connects people through technology

New technology, particularly technology related to computers and telecommunications, helps marketers to understand and satisfy more customers than ever before. Today, marketers must recognise the impact not only of websites but also of instant messaging, blogs, online forums, online games, mailing lists and wikis, as well as text messaging via mobile phones and podcasts. Increasingly, these tools are facilitating marketing exchanges. A consumer shopping for a new car, for example, can access car makers' websites, configure an ideal vehicle and get instant feedback on its cost. Consumers can visit websites to find professional reviews and obtain comparative pricing information on both new and used cars to help them find the best value. They can then purchase a vehicle online or at a dealership. Technology lets Carsales.com serve customers promptly and maybe without ever talking to an employee. With a minimal sales staff, they act as a link between buyers and sellers.

Source: iStockphoto.com

<< Marketing and the growth of technology
Apple manage the development of technology to produce customer satisfaction and loyalty

The Internet provides an opportunity for marketers of everything from computers to travel reservations to encourage exchanges. The Internet has also become a vital tool for marketing to other businesses. Successful companies are using technology in their marketing strategies to develop profitable relationships with these customers.[24] As more consumers adopt smartphones, mobile marketing is also becoming a major trend. We will discuss mobile marketing in more detail in Chapter 15, along with other low cost, no cost marketing strategies such as social media strategies.

Socially responsible marketing can promote the welfare of customers and stakeholders

The success of our economic system depends on marketers whose values promote trust and cooperative relationships in which customers and other stakeholders are treated with respect. The public is increasingly insisting that social responsibility and ethical concerns be considered in planning and implementing marketing activities. Although some irresponsible or unethical marketing activities end up on the front pages of *The Australian* or the *Australian Financial Review*, more companies are working to develop a responsible approach to developing long-term relationships with customers and society. In the area of the natural environment, companies are increasingly embracing the notion of green marketing, which is a strategic process involving stakeholder assessment to create meaningful long-term relationships with customers, while maintaining, supporting and enhancing the natural environment. The multinational enterprise Unilever, for example, not only produces and markets a variety of food and personal-care products around the world, but also operates a free community laundry in São Paulo, funds a hospital that provides free medical care in Bangladesh, provides financing and educational materials to help suppliers around the world convert to more environmentally friendly practices, and reports on its carbon dioxide and hazardous waste releases to interested stakeholders. Unilever's former chief executive officer, Patrick Cescau, believes that such activities are necessary to remain competitive in future decades, declaring, 'You can't ignore the impact your company has on the community and environment'. Even Hollywood is 'going green' with TV shows and movies incorporating more green themes. By being concerned about the impact of marketing on society, an organisation can protect the interests of the general public and the natural environment.

green marketing
A strategic process involving stakeholder assessment to create meaningful long-term relationships with customers while maintaining, supporting and enhancing the natural environment

Marketing offers many exciting career prospects

The marketing field offers a variety of interesting and challenging career opportunities throughout the world, such as advertising, brand management, customer relationship management, product management (including product development), business consulting, key account management, personal selling, packaging, retailing, sales management, transportation, marketing research and wholesaling. In addition, many individuals working for non-business organisations engage in marketing activities to promote political, educational, cultural, church, civic and charitable activities. Whether a person earns a living through marketing activities or performs them voluntarily for a non-profit group, marketing knowledge and skills are valuable personal and professional assets.

Study Tools

Chapter review

LO1 DEFINE MARKETING AND UNDERSTAND KEY MARKETING TERMS, INCLUDING TARGET MARKET, MARKETING MIX, MARKETING EXCHANGES AND MARKETING ENVIRONMENT.

Marketing is the process of maximising returns to stakeholders by developing exchanges with valued customers and creating an advantage for them.

A target market is the group of customers towards which a company directs a set of marketing efforts.

The variables – product, price, distribution and promotion – are known as the marketing mix because marketing managers decide what type of each element to use and in what amounts. Marketing managers strive to develop a marketing mix that matches the needs of customers in the target market. Before marketers can develop a marketing mix, they must collect in-depth, up-to-date information about customer needs.

Individuals and organisations engage in marketing to facilitate exchanges – the provision or transfer of goods, services and ideas in return for something of value. Four conditions must exist for an exchange to occur: (1) Two or more individuals, groups or organisations must participate, and each must possess something of value that the other party desires; (2) the exchange should provide an advantage, or benefit, to both parties involved in the transaction; (3) each party must have confidence in the promise of the 'something of value' held by the other; and (4) to build trust, the parties to the exchange must meet expectations. Marketing activities should attempt to create and maintain satisfying exchange relationships with all stakeholders – those constituents who have a 'stake', or claim, in some aspect of a company's products, operations, markets, industry and outcomes.

The marketing environment, which includes competitive, economic, political, legal and regulatory, technological and sociocultural forces, surrounds the customer and the marketing mix. These forces can create threats to marketers, but they also generate opportunities for new products and new methods of reaching customers.

LO2 DEVELOP AN UNDERSTANDING OF THE MARKETING CONCEPT AND MARKET ORIENTATION.

According to the marketing concept, an organisation should try to provide products that satisfy customers' needs through a coordinated set of activities that also allows the organisation to achieve its goals. The philosophy of the marketing concept emerged in literature during the 1950s after the production and sales eras. Organisations that develop a culture and activities consistent with the marketing concept become market-oriented organisations.

LO3 APPRECIATE THE IMPORTANCE OF BUILDING CUSTOMER RELATIONSHIPS.

Relationship marketing involves establishing long-term, mutually satisfying buyer–seller relationships. Customer relationship management (CRM) focuses on using information about customers to create marketing strategies that develop and sustain desirable customer relationships. Managing customer relationships requires identifying patterns of buying behaviour and using that information to focus on the most promising and profitable customers.

Value is a customer's subjective assessment of benefits relative to costs in determining the worth of a product. Benefits include anything a buyer receives in an exchange, whereas costs include anything a buyer must give up to obtain the benefits the product provides.

 **LO4** EXPLAIN THE MAJOR MARKETING FUNCTIONS THAT ARE PART OF THE MARKETING MANAGEMENT PROCESS.

Marketing management is the process of planning, organising, implementing and controlling marketing activities to facilitate effective and efficient exchanges. Planning is a systematic process of assessing opportunities and resources, determining marketing objectives, developing a marketing strategy and preparing for implementation and control. Organising marketing activities involves developing the marketing unit's internal structure. Proper implementation of marketing plans depends on coordinating marketing activities, motivating marketing personnel and communicating effectively within the unit. The marketing control process consists of establishing performance standards, comparing actual performance with established standards and reducing the difference between desired and actual performance.

 LO5 UNDERSTAND THE ROLE OF MARKETING IN OUR SOCIETY.

Marketing costs absorb about half of each buyer's dollar. Marketing activities are performed in both business and non-profit organisations. Marketing activities help business organisations to generate profits, and they help fuel the increasingly global economy. Knowledge of marketing enhances consumer awareness. New technology improves marketers' abilities to connect with customers. Socially responsible marketing can promote the welfare of customers and society. Finally, marketing offers many exciting career opportunities.

 # Key concepts

Use these key terms in **Search me! marketing** to find the latest relevant readings from a wide range of world-class journals, e-books and newspapers, including *The Australian*.

- customers
- customer relationship management (CRM)
- exchanges
- expanded marketing mix
- green marketing
- marketing
- market orientation
- marketing concept
- marketing environment
- marketing management
- marketing mix
- product
- relationship marketing
- stakeholders
- target market
- value

Issues for discussion and review

1 Define marketing. How has your definition changed after reading this chapter?
2 What is the focus of all marketing activities? How is this reflected in an organisation's market orientation?

3   What are the traditional 4Ps of marketing? What eight variables make up the expanded marketing mix?

4   What conditions must exist before a marketing exchange can occur? Describe these conditions in relation to a recent exchange in which you participated.

5   What forces shape the marketing environment? How can these forces affect a marketer's ability to facilitate exchanges?

6   Discuss the basic elements of the marketing concept.

7   What is the objective of customer relationship management? What elements influence a customer's lifetime value to an organisation?

8   What is value? How can marketers use the marketing mix to enhance the perception of value?

9   What types of activities are involved in the marketing management process?

10   Why is marketing important to businesses and to the global economy?

11   What is green marketing? Identify and discuss an Australian company that is engaged in socially responsible marketing.

Marketing applications

1   Identify a business that does not display a market-orientation. What characteristics of this organisation indicate that it doesn't have a market-orientation? How could the business implement the marketing concept?

2   Identify the probable target markets for the following products:

   a   Uncle Tobys Traditional Oats
   b   Jalna Biodynamic Yoghurt
   c   Australian Rules Football (AFL)

   What clues do the company websites give regarding the company's view of their product's target market?

3   Discuss the variables of the marketing mix (product, price, promotion, distribution, people/participants, physical evidence, processes, partnerships) as they might relate to each of the following companies:

   a   Visy, an innovative package provider and recycler (http://www.visy.com.au)
   b   Rod Laver Arena, a stadium at Melbourne Park that hosts major events and the Australian Open tennis (http://www.rodlaverarena.com.au)
   c   The Iconic, an online store (http://www.theiconic.com.au)
   d   Bailey's Sydney, a tour company (http://baileys-sydney.com)

ONLINE EXERCISE

4   ADMA (Association for Data-Driven Marketing & Advertising) is Australia's largest marketing and advertising association. Visit their website at http://www.adma.com.au and find the answers to the questions below.

   a   What is the association's overarching goal?
   b   Who does the association serve, and in what way?
   c   What services does the organisation provide?

Developing your marketing plan

Successful companies develop strategies for marketing their products. The strategic plan guides the marketer in making many of the detailed decisions about the attributes of the product, its distribution, promotional activities and pricing. A clear understanding of the foundations of marketing is essential in formulating a strategy and in the development of a specific marketing plan. To guide you in relating the information in this chapter to the development of your marketing plan, consider the following:

✳ Discuss how the marketing concept contributes to a company's long-term success.

✳ Describe the level of market orientation that currently exists in your company. How will a market orientation contribute to the success of your new product?

✳ What benefits will your product provide to the customer? How will these benefits play a role in determining the customer value of your product?

CengageNOW

Go to http:\\login.cengagebrain.com to link to CengageNOW, your online study tool. First take the Pre-Test for this chapter to get your Personalised Study Plan, and then:

✳ **Revise** your understanding of the key concepts of marketing with the online glossary

✳ **Watch** an interactive animation of strategic marketing to broaden your subject comprehension

✳ **Listen** to an audio summary of the learning objectives covered in this chapter.

After you have completed the activities in your Personalised Study Plan take the Post-Test to determine what concepts you have mastered and what you still need to work on.

KRAFT CREATES UNHAPPY LITTLE VEGEMITES

Case study

It's our very own piece of Australia. Aussies love it, and overseas visitors love to try it. But the classic Australian icon of Vegemite has not been without its share of controversy.

In 2009, Kraft, the makers of Vegemite, responded to consumer feedback which showed that consumers wanted a product that was creamier, easier to spread and that did not have to be mixed with butter. Following the development of a new product, a mix of original Vegemite and cream cheese, Kraft launched a competition among the Australian public to name the new product. This was in keeping with tradition, as the original name of Vegemite was chosen from a pool of consumer suggestions following its launch in 1923.

Source: Fairfax Ltd

Following a nationwide three-month naming competition which generated almost 50 000 suggestions, Kraft announced the new name to public outcry. West Australian Dean Robbins was pronounced the successful entrant of the competition with his winning suggestion iSnack 2.0, beating other suggestions such as Wow Chow and 2ritemite. Kraft said the name encapsulates the new brand, and that the choice was based on its reference to snacking, a personal call to action and the differentiation the product has from the original Vegemite. However, while the name may have come from a suggestion by a member of the public, the new product name iSnack 2.0 was met with criticism from the Australian public.

Responses to the new name included the hashtag #vegefail trending at number seven on Twitter on the day the name was announced. The name choice gained worldwide attention, including criticism from consumers who declared the name 'cheesy' and 'stupid' and marketing experts who declared the name will have a short

shelf life. So is all publicity good publicity? Despite the criticism for the name, more than three million jars of the product were shipped in the three months after the launch, indicating that Aussies still wanted a taste of this new variation to an old favourite.

However, a short time later Kraft seemingly caved to public pressure and announced it would change the name. It seemed Australians liked the taste, they just didn't like the name. Following an online and telephone public vote of more than 30 000 people, Cheesybite came out as the new name, attracting 36 per cent of the vote. This choice beat out other possibilities including Vegemite Smooth and Vegemite Vegemate. Following this announcement, which was met positively by the Australian public, the remaining iSnack 2.0 jars continued to be sold in supermarkets until the new labels could be distributed. Since then, Kraft's Vegemite Cheesybite has joined its predecessor to be among Australia's favourite breakfast spreads. Who knows, could we have another Australian icon in the making?

With the new-found success of Cheesybite, Kraft Foods chose to launch My First Vegemite, aimed at parents of young children in February 2011. This took the total number of products in the Vegemite product line to three, which is a huge growth considering Vegemite was the only product in the yeast category by Kraft since 1923. This growth in product lines is mirrored in market share growth. Despite the initial dilemmas surrounding the launch of Cheesybite in 2009, Kraft foods has seen a 35 per cent increase in its retail market to 2012, more than 24 per cent in front of their closest competitor, Ferrero. Can Kraft keep up this growth with new products? Only time will tell.[25]

Sarah Sloan, Griffith University

QUESTIONS FOR DISCUSSION

1 If the name was originally suggested by the Australian public, should Kraft be ultimately responsible for the iSnack 2.0 name?

2 What factors influenced Kraft to change the name of the new product from iSnack 2.0 to Cheesybite?

3 More than three million jars of iSnack 2.0 were sold in the three months after its launch, despite the public criticism of the product name. Why do you think this is?

Chapter endnotes

1. 'Building the Foundation,' Kodak, accessed September 27, 2013. http://www.kodak.com/ek/US/en/Our_Company /History_of_Kodak/Building_the_Foundation.htm.

2. 'Kodak moment,' Urban Dictionary, accessed September 27, 2013. http://www.urbandictionary.com /define.php?term=kodak%20moment.

3. 'Definition of Marketing,' American Marketing Association, accessed December 10, 2013. www. marketingpower.com > About AMA > Definition of marketing.

4. Ethan Smith and Yukari Iwatani Kane, 'Apple Changes Tune on Music Pricing,' *The Wall Street Journal*, (January 1, 2009): B1.

5. Kellen Schetter, 'Smart Car Offers Drivers New High MPG Option,' Greencar.com, 2008, http://www.greencar .com/features/smart-car.

6. 'Campbell's V8 Soups,' Campbell's Soup, http://www .campbellsv8soup.com.

7. Jena McGregor, 'When Service Means Survival,' *BusinessWeek* (March 2, 2009): 26–31.

8. Ajay K. Kohli and Bernard J. Jaworski, 'Market Orientation: The Construct, Research Propositions, and Managerial Implications,' *Journal of Marketing* (April 1990): 1–18; O. C. Ferrell, 'Business Ethics and Customer Stakeholders,' *Academy of Management Executive* 18 (May 2004): 126–129.

9. Jagdish N. Sheth and Atul Parvatiyar, 'The Evolution of Relationship Marketing', *International Business Review* 4 (4) (1995): 397–418, viewed July 23, 2011. http:// www.iei.liu. se/program/civilek/kurser/ar-3/722g60/

gruppernas_artiklar_och_presentationer/1.149402/ Artikel.GruppC3.pdf.

10. Ibid.

11. Ibid.

12. Kohli and Jaworski, 'Market Orientation: The Construct, Research Propositions, and Managerial Implications,' 1-18.

13. Gary F. Gebhardt, Gregory S. Carpenter, and John F. Sherry, Jr., 'Creating a Marketing Orientation,' *Journal of Marketing* 70 (October 2006), http://www .marketingpower.com.

14. Jagdish N. Sheth and Rajendras Sisodia, 'More Than Ever Before, Marketing Is under Fire to Account for What It Spends,' *Marketing Management* (Fall 1995): 13–14.

15. Lynette Ryals and Adrian Payne, 'Customer Relationship Management in Financial Services: Towards Information-Enabled Relationship Marketing,' *Journal of Strategic Marketing* (March 2001): 3.

16. Werner J. Reinartz and V. Kumar, 'On the Profitability of Long-Life Customers in a Noncontractual Setting: An Empirical Investigation and Implications for Marketing,' *Journal of Marketing* (October 2000): 17–35.

17. Roland T. Rust, Katherine N. Lemon, and Valarie A. Zeithaml, 'Return on Marketing: Using Customer Equity to Focus Marketing Strategy,' *Journal of Marketing* (January 2004): 109–127.

18. Rajkumar Venkatesan and V. Kumar, 'A Customer Lifetime Value Framework for Customer Selection and Resource Allocation Strategy,' *Journal of Marketing* (October 2004): 106–125.

19. Sunil Gupta and Carl F. Mela, 'What Is a Free Customer Worth?' *Harvard Business Review* (November 2008): 104.

20. O. C. Ferrell and Michael Hartline, *Marketing Strategy* (Mason, OH: South-Western, 2008), 108.

21. Original material from O. C. Ferrell and Michael Hartline, *Marketing Strategy* (Mason, OH: South-Western, 2008).

22. Kelly Geyskens, Mario Pandlelaere, Siegfried DeWitte, and Luk Warlop, 'The Backdoor to Overconsumption: The Effect of Associating 'Low-Fat' Food with Health References,' *Journal of Public Policy & Marketing* 26 (Spring 2007): 118–125.

23. 'The Pedal Power Revolution in Glastonbury Festival,' Daily Motion, accessed September 27, 2013. http://www.dailymotion.com/video/xrslmv_the-pedal-power-revolution-in-glastonbury-festival_tech; 'The Power Behind Festivals,' Green Festival Alliance, accessed September 27, 2013. http://www.agreenerfestival.com /wp-content/uploads/pdfs/Power_Behind_Festivals_Guide_2013_V1.2.pdf; 'Energy Floors,' Energy Floors, accessed 15 January 2014. http://www .sustainabledanceclub.com/.

24. Enid Burns, 'Online Retail Sales Grew in 2005,' ClickZ, (January 5, 2006), http://www.clickz.com/showPage. html?page=3575456.

25. 'And the winner is…a happy little vegemite,' *The Age* (September 27, 2009), accessed September 9, 2013. http://www.theage.com.au/executive-style/and-the-winner-is--a-happy-little-vegemite-20090926-g73s. html#ixzz2eMCL76av; Collerton, S. (September 28, 2009), 'iSuck 2.0: Unhappy little Vegemites,' *ABC News*, accessed September 9, 2013. http://www.abc. net.au/news/2009-09-28/isuck-20-unhappy-little-vegemites/1445034; Hildebrand, J. (October 7, 2009), 'Kraft's Vegemite iSnack 2.0 renamed Cheesybite,' accessed September 9, 2013. http://www.dailytelegraph. com.au/krafts-vegemite-isnack-20-renamed-cheesybite/ story-e6freuy9-1225783689707; Lanperd, R. (September 27, 2009). 'Name's a mite 2 cheesy,' *Herald Sun*, accessed September 9, 2013. http://www.heraldsun. com.au/archive/news/names-a-mite-2-cheesy/story-e6frf7l6-1225780224851; Lee, J. (September 29, 2009), 'Unhappy little Vegemites vent their fury over iSnack 2.0,' The Age, accessed September 9, 2013. http:// www.theage.com.au/business/media-and-marketing/ unhappy-little-vegemites-vent-their-fury-over-isnack-20-20090928-g997.html#ixzz2eMGbaurM; mUmBRELLA, (September 30, 2009), 'Kraft: We admit the new Vegemite name sucked and we're changing it,' accessed September 9, 2013. http://mumbrella.com.au/kraft-we-admit-the-new-vegemite-name-sucked-and-were-changing-it-9997; 'Spreads in Australia,' Euromonitor International, accessed December 13, 2012. http://www.euromonitor .com/spreads-in-australia/report.

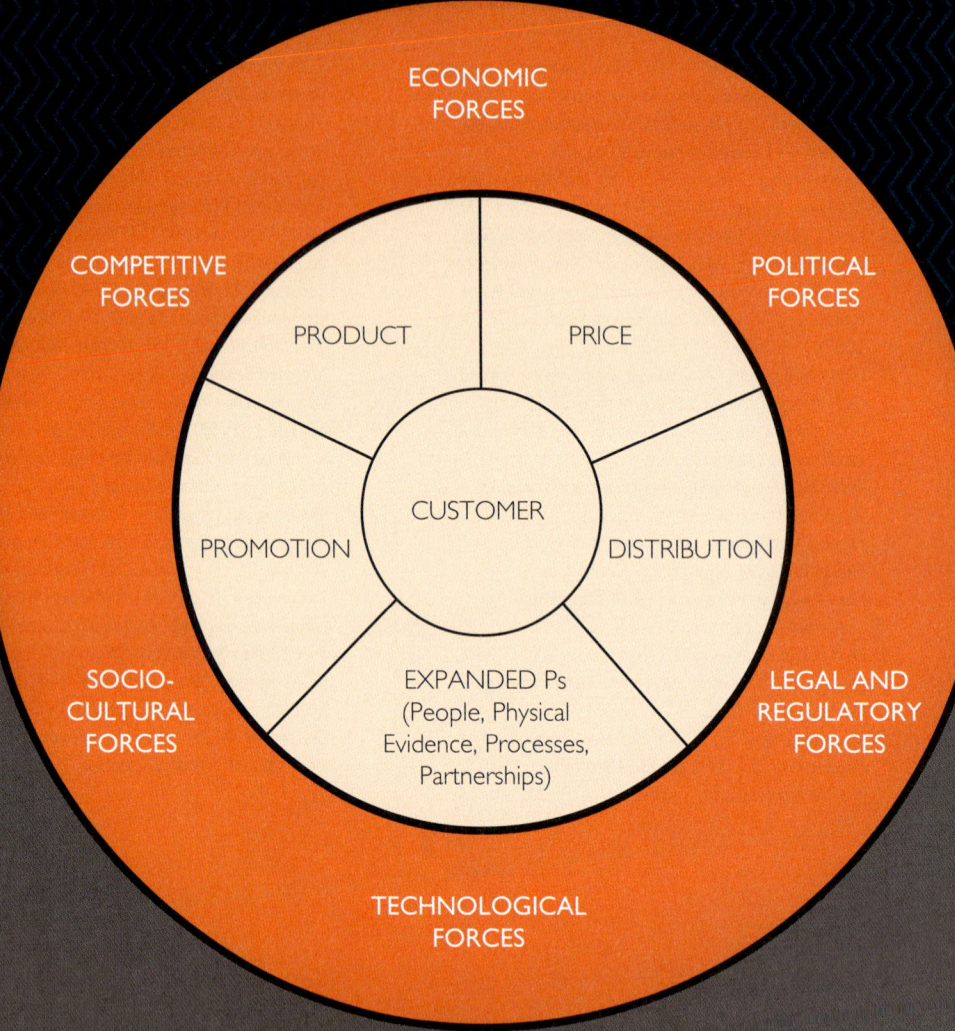

ECONOMIC
FORGES

COMPETITIVE
FORCES

POLITICAL
FORCES

PRODUCT

PRICE

CUSTOMER

PROMOTION

DISTRIBUTION

SOCIO-
CULTURAL
FORCES

EXPANDED Ps
(People, Physical
Evidence, Processes,
Partnerships)

LEGAL AND
REGULATORY
FORCES

TECHNOLOGICAL
FORCES

MARKETING PLANNING AND STRATEGY IN A COMPETITIVE ENVIRONMENT

The marketing environment
Competitive forces
Economic forces
Political forces
Legal and regulatory forces
Technological forces
Sociocultural forces

Strategic planning process
Assessing organisational resources and opportunities
Establishing an organisational mission and marketing goals
Developing corporate, business-unit and marketing strategies

Creating the marketing plan

Implementing marketing strategies
Customer relationship management
Internal marketing
Organising marketing activities
Controlling marketing activities

Social responsibility and ethics
Ethics and codes of conduct
Corporate social responsibility

   Throughout this chapter, Watch, Listen and Revise icons indicate an opportunity for online self-study through CengageNOW, linking you to animated chapter overviews, interactive diagrams, videos, quizzes and more.

2

MARKETING PLANNING AND STRATEGY IN A COMPETITIVE ENVIRONMENT

Learning Objectives

 LO1 Understand the importance of environmental scanning and the effects of competitive, economic, political, legal and regulatory, technological and sociocultural (PEST) factors on marketing strategies

 LO2 Describe the strategic planning process and how it is affected by organisational resources and opportunities

 LO3 Understand the process of creating a marketing plan

 LO4 Describe the marketing implementation process and the major approaches to marketing implementation

 LO5 Explain how to incorporate ethics and social responsibility into marketing strategy.

MARKETING CHALLENGE | THE SUPERMARKET WARS

It is very likely that you have recently been into a major supermarket. Was it a Woolworths, Coles, Aldi or Costco? Low-cost international supermarket giants Costco and Aldi are established fixtures of the Australian supermarket industry. Aldi opened its first Australian store in 2002 and now has over 305 sites. In 2013 Aldi outperformed both Coles' (4.8%) and Woolworths' (3.8%) half-yearly revenue growth by increasing revenue 6.9%. The entry of Aldi and Costco has dramatically changed Coles' and Woolworths' competitive environment.

Both the German-based Aldi and US-based Costco compete aggressively for customers with lower-priced products and spot bargains. Two reasons why they can compete effectively against traditional supermarket retailers are their lower operating costs and excellent understanding of the deep-discount environment. Experience and understanding, gained and tested primarily in their home markets, was brought with them to Australia.

The value proposition and marketing strategy that Costco and Aldi have adopted is different to Australia's traditional supermarkets and retail chains, such as Woolworths and Coles. Aldi was one of the world's first so-called 'box', or 'no-frills' stores; grocers that featured rock-bottom pricing by offering a limited inventory and eliminating all unnecessary costs, from vouchers to butcher shops to fancy displays. Similarly, at Costco, consumers are not surrounded by service staff, but rather large package-sized goods that come straight off the pallet. Many supermarkets have a labour factor of 12.5 to 16.5 per cent, but discounters' labour factor is between 5.5 and 7.5 per cent. Additionally, over 95 per cent of goods sold at Aldi are higher-margin private label products compared to 6 per cent at Woolworths and 25 per cent at Coles. They also rely heavily on word-of-mouth rather than advertising to promote their brand, which contributes to their low operating costs and low prices.

In the face of Aldi's fierce competition, Woolworths has adapted their strategy to maintain their competitiveness. As you walk the aisles of your local Woolworths you are likely to notice expanded categories, such as newsagents, pharmacies and other daily conveniences within the store. You'll see significantly more private-label product offerings on the shelves – and lower prices. These changes all aim to improve Woolworths' overall value proposition to customers. Each retailer is trying to improve upon the other, which, one would think, can only lead to more choice and better shopping experiences for consumers.[1]

Source: Getty Images; Getty Images

MARKETING CHALLENGE QUESTION

1   Consider Coles' and Woolworths' core value propositions. How are they seeking to differentiate themselves in the face of Aldi's and Costco's competition?

Introduction

Effectively satisfying customers and achieving organisational goals requires all organisations to engage in strategic planning. Indeed, we believe that good marketing starts with a good marketing strategy.

First, we define the marketing environment and consider why it is critical to scan and analyse it. Then we proceed with an overview of the strategic planning process, which necessarily begins with an assessment of the broader marketing environment and a continuous monitoring of relevant macro-environmental factors. Next, we examine how organisational resources and opportunities affect strategic planning and the role played by the organisation's mission statement. After discussing the development of both corporate and business-unit strategy, we explore the nature of marketing strategy and creation of the marketing plan. These elements provide a framework for the development and implementation of marketing strategies, as we will see throughout the remainder of this book.

The marketing environment

The marketing environment consists of external forces that directly or indirectly influence an organisation's acquisition of inputs (human, financial, natural resources and raw materials, and information) and creation of outputs (goods, services or ideas). Whether fluctuating rapidly or slowly, environmental forces are always dynamic. Changes in the marketing environment create uncertainty, threats and opportunities for marketers. Consider that companies providing digital products, such as software, music and movies, face many environmental threats as well as opportunities. Advancing technology provides digital delivery of these products, which is an efficient and effective way to reach global markets. On the other hand, websites such as Pirate Bay allow peer-to-peer transfers and are referred to as file-sharing websites or cyberlockers. These websites can operate in countries such as Russia, where intellectual property rights are weak. The movie and music industries want more effective legislation in place to crack down on the theft of their products. Most of these developments involve trying to influence controls to stop this threat.[2] Marketing managers who fail to recognise changes in environmental forces leave their organisations unprepared to capitalise on marketing opportunities or to cope with threats created by changes in the environment. Monitoring the environment, therefore, is crucial to an organisation's survival and to the long-term achievement of its goals.

To monitor changes in the marketing environment effectively, marketers engage in environmental scanning and analysis. Environmental scanning is the process of collecting information about forces in the marketing environment. Scanning involves observation of secondary sources such as business, trade, government and Internet sources, and marketing research. The Internet has become a popular scanning tool because it makes data more accessible and allows companies to gather needed information quickly. However, simply gathering information about competitors and customers is not enough; companies must know how to use that information in the strategic planning process. Managers must be careful not to gather so much information that sheer volume makes analysis impossible.

Environmental analysis is the process of assessing and interpreting the information gathered through environmental scanning. A manager evaluates the information for accuracy, tries to resolve inconsistencies in the data and, if warranted, assigns significance to the findings. By evaluating this information, the manager should be able to identify potential threats and opportunities linked to environmental changes.

Understanding the current state of the marketing environment and recognising threats and opportunities arising from changes within it help companies with strategic marketing planning. In particular, they can help marketing managers assess the performance of current marketing efforts and develop future marketing strategies.

environmental scanning
The process of collecting information about forces in the marketing environment

environmental analysis
The process of assessing and interpreting the information gathered through environmental scanning

Shaping and responding to the marketing environment

Marketing managers take two general approaches to environmental forces: accepting them as uncontrollable or shaping them.[3] An organisation that views environmental forces as uncontrollable remains passive and reactive toward the environment. Instead of trying to influence forces in the environment, its marketing managers adjust current marketing strategies to environmental changes. They approach with caution market opportunities discovered through environmental scanning and analysis. On the other hand, marketing managers who believe that environmental forces can be shaped adopt a more proactive approach. For example, if a market is blocked by traditional environmental constraints, proactive marketing managers may apply economic, psychological, political and promotional skills to gain access to and operate within it. Once they identify what is blocking a market opportunity, they assess the power of the various parties involved and develop strategies to overcome the obstructing environmental forces. Microsoft, Intel and Google, for example, have responded to political, legal and regulatory concerns about their power in the computer industry by communicating the value of their competitive approaches to various publics. The computer giants contend that their competitive success results in superior products for their customers.

A proactive approach can be constructive and bring desired results. To exert influence on environmental forces, marketing managers seek to identify market opportunities or to extract greater benefits relative to costs from existing market opportunities. Political action is another way to affect environmental forces. For example, globally, the pharmaceutical industry has lobbied very effectively for fewer restrictions on prescription drug marketing. However, managers must recognise that there are limits on how much environmental forces can be shaped, especially by smaller players. As one of the larger global organisations that does have some power in the shaping of legislation and regulation, Microsoft, for example, can take a proactive approach because of its financial resources and the highly visible image and philanthropic orientation of its founder, Bill Gates. Although an organisation may be able to influence legislation through lobbying, it is unlikely that a single organisation can significantly increase the national birth rate or move the economy from recession to prosperity.

Source: Image courtesy of the Advertising Archives

Responding to environmental forces >>
Ribena juice company demonstrates its commitment to environmental responsibility through its 100% recycled bottles

Competitive forces

Few organisations, if any, operate free of competition. In fact, for most products, customers have many alternatives from which to choose and therefore indirect competition is sometimes more relevant than direct competition. For example, while some of the best-selling soft drinks are Coke Classic, Coke Zero, Diet Coke, PepsiCola and Diet Pepsi, soft-drink sales in general have flattened as consumers have turned to alternatives such as bottled water, flavoured water, fruit juice and iced-tea products.[4] Thus, when marketing managers select the target market(s) their company will serve, they simultaneously select a set of competitors.[5] The number of companies that supply a product may affect the strength of competitors. When just one or a few firms control supply, competitive factors exert a different sort of influence on marketing activities than when many competitors exist.

Source: Getty Images; Getty Images

<< Brand and product competition
HTC and Samsung compete in the mobile phone handset market

Broadly speaking, all firms compete with one another for customers' dollars. More practically, however, a marketer generally defines **competition** as other firms that market products that are similar to, or can be substituted for, its products in the same target market segment. These competitors are called direct competitors because they are available in the target market segment and are considered to be viable alternatives by consumers. Direct competitors can be classified into one of four types. **Brand competitors** market products with similar features and benefits to the same customers at similar prices. For example, a thirsty, calorie-conscious customer may choose a diet cola such as Diet Coke or Diet Pepsi from the vending machine. However, these colas face competition from other types of beverages. **Product competitors** compete in the same product class but market products with different features, benefits and prices. The thirsty dieter, for instance, might purchase iced tea, juice, mineral water or bottled water instead of a cola. **Generic competitors** provide very different products that solve the same problem or satisfy the same basic customer need. Our dieter, for

competition
Other firms that market products that are similar to or can be substituted for a firm's products in the same target market segment

brand competitors
Firms that market branded products with similar brand features and brand benefits to the same customers at similar prices

product competitors
Firms that compete in the same target market segment but market products with different features, benefits and prices

generic competitors
Firms that provide very different products that solve the same problem or satisfy the same basic customer need

total budget competitors
Firms that compete for the financial resources of the same customers

example, might simply have a glass of water from the kitchen tap to satisfy his or her thirst. Total budget competitors compete for the limited financial resources of the same customers.[6] Total budget competitors for Diet Coke, for example, might include chewing gum, a newspaper and bananas. Although all four types of competition can affect a firm's marketing performance, brand competitors are the most significant because buyers typically see the different products of these firms as direct substitutes for one another. Consequently, marketers tend to concentrate environmental analyses on brand competitors.

When just one or a few firms control supply, competitive factors exert a different form of influence on marketing activities than when many competitors exist. Table 2.1 presents four general types of competitive structures: monopoly, oligopoly, monopolistic competition and pure competition. A monopoly exists when an organisation offers a product that has no close substitutes, making that organisation the sole source of supply. Because the organisation has no competitors, it controls supply of the product completely and, as a single seller, can erect barriers to potential competitors. In reality, most monopolies surviving today are local utilities, which are heavily regulated by local, state or federal agencies. An oligopoly exists when a few sellers control the supply of a large proportion of a product. In this case each seller considers the reactions of other sellers to changes in marketing activities. Products facing oligopolistic competition may be homogeneous, such as aluminum, or differentiated, such as cars. Monopolistic competition exists when a firm with many potential competitors attempts to develop a marketing strategy to differentiate its product. For example, Levi's Jeans conducted a Road Worthy competition inviting consumers to upload their favourite road trip photo to the Levi's Australia and New Zealand Facebook page. This consumer-generated photo portfolio depicted Levi's consumers as strong, adventurous and fun loving. This positioned Levi's from other jeans labels such as Lee and Wrangler. Although many competing brands of blue jeans are available, these firms have carved out market niches by emphasising differences in their products, especially style and image. Pure competition, if it existed at all, would entail a large number of sellers, none of which could significantly influence price or supply. One of the closest things to an example of pure competition is an unregulated farmers' market, where local growers gather to sell their produce. Pure competition is an ideal at one end of the continuum; monopoly is at the other end. Most marketers function in a competitive environment somewhere between these two extremes.

monopoly
A competitive structure in which an organisation offers a product that has no close substitutes, making that organisation the sole source of supply

oligopoly
A competitive structure in which a few sellers control the supply of a large proportion of a product

monopolistic competition
A competitive structure in which a firm has many potential competitors and tries to develop a marketing strategy to differentiate its product

pure competition
A market structure characterised by an extremely large number of sellers, none strong enough to significantly influence price or supply

TABLE 2.1   SELECTED CHARACTERISTICS OF COMPETITIVE STRUCTURES

Type of structure	Number of competitors	Ease of entry into market	Product	Example
Monopoly	One	Many barriers	Almost no substitutes	Water utilities
Oligopoly	Few	Some barriers	Homogeneous or differentiated (with real or perceived differences)	Toyota Motors (cars)
Monopolistic competition	Many	Few barriers	Product differentiation, with many substitutes	Wrangler, Levi Strauss (jeans)
Pure competition	Unlimited	No barriers	Homogeneous products	Vegetable/fruit farm (cauliflower/bananas)

Marketers need to monitor the actions of major competitors to determine what specific strategies competitors are using and how those strategies affect their own. Price is one of the marketing strategy variables that most competitors monitor. When Qantas or Emirates lowers the farc on a route, most other major international airlines catering to the same route will attempt to match the new price rather than lose market share. Environmental scanning and monitoring therefore guides marketers in developing competitive advantages and aids them in adjusting current marketing strategies and planning new ones.

In monitoring competition, it is not enough to analyse available information; the firm must develop a system for gathering ongoing information about competitors. Understanding the market and what customers want, as well as what the competition is providing, will assist in maintaining a market orientation.[7] Information about competitors allows marketing managers to assess the performance of their own marketing efforts and to recognise the strengths and weaknesses in their own marketing strategies. Data about market shares, product movement, sales volume and expenditure levels can be useful. However, accurate information on these matters is often difficult to obtain.

Economic forces

Economic forces in the marketing environment influence both marketers' and customers' decisions and activities. In this section we examine the effects of buying power and willingness to spend, as well as general economic conditions.

Buying power and willingness to spend

The strength of a person's buying power depends on economic conditions and the size of the resources – money, goods and services that can be traded in an exchange – that enable the individual to make purchases. The major financial sources of buying power are income, credit and wealth.

For an individual, *income* is the amount of money received through wages, rents, investments, pensions and subsidy payments for a given period, such as a month or a year. Normally, this money is allocated among taxes, spending for goods and services, and savings. Marketers are most interested in the amount of money left after payment of taxes because this disposable income is used for spending or saving. Because disposable income is a ready source of buying power, the total amount available in a nation is important to marketers. Several factors determine the size of total disposable income, including the total amount of income – which is affected by wage levels, the rate of unemployment, interest rates and dividend rates – and the number and amount of taxes. Disposable income that is available for spending and saving after an individual has purchased the basic necessities of food, clothing and shelter is called discretionary income. People use discretionary income to purchase entertainment, holidays, cars, education, pets, furniture, appliances and so on. Changes in total discretionary income affect sales of these products, especially cars, furniture, large appliances and other costly durable goods.

People's willingness to spend – their inclination to buy because of expected satisfaction from a product – is related, to some degree, to their ability to buy. That is, people are sometimes more willing to buy if they have the buying power. However, several other

buying power
Resources, such as money, goods and services, that can be traded in an exchange

disposable income
After-tax income

discretionary income
Disposable income available for spending and saving after an individual has purchased the basic necessities of food, clothing and shelter

willingness to spend
An inclination to buy because of expected satisfaction from a product, influenced by the ability to buy and numerous psychological and social forces

Source: Image courtesy of the Advertising Archives

Source: Image courtesy of the Advertising Archives

Economic forces >>
Tag Heuer and Omega rely on consumers with significant discretionary income to purchase their watches

elements also influence willingness to spend. Some elements affect specific products, others influence spending in general. A product's price and value influence almost all of us. Rolex watches, for example, appeal to customers who are willing to spend more for fine timepieces even when lower-priced watches are readily available. In recessions, consumers usually are not willing to spend as much on luxury products because of economic uncertainty. Credit is not as available given revised expectations about future employment, income levels, prices, family size and general economic conditions.

Economic conditions

The overall state of the economy fluctuates in all countries. Changes in general economic conditions affect (and are affected by) supply and demand, buying power, willingness to spend, consumer expenditure levels and the intensity of competitive behaviour. Therefore, current economic conditions and changes in the economy have a broad impact on the success of organisations' marketing strategies.

Fluctuations in the economy follow a general pattern, often referred to as the business cycle. In the traditional view, the business cycle consists of four stages: prosperity, recession, depression and recovery. During *prosperity*, unemployment is low and total income is relatively high. Assuming a low inflation rate, this combination ensures high buying power. During a *recession*, however, unemployment rises, while total buying power declines. Pessimism accompanying a recession often stifles both consumer and business spending. A prolonged recession may become a *depression*, a period in which unemployment is extremely high, wages are very low, total disposable income is at a minimum and consumers lack confidence in the economy. During *recovery*, the economy moves from depression or recession to prosperity. It is possible to have a recession without a full-blown depression. During this period, high unemployment begins to decline, total disposable income increases and the economic gloom that reduced consumers' willingness to buy subsides. Both the ability and willingness to buy increase.

business cycle
A pattern of economic fluctuations that usually has four stages: prosperity, recession, depression and recovery

The business cycle can enhance the success of marketing strategies. In the prosperity stage, for example, marketers may expand their product offerings to take advantage of increased buying power. They may be able to capture a larger market share by intensifying distribution and promotion efforts. In times of recession or depression, when buying power decreases, many customers may become more price-conscious and seek more basic, functional products. During economic downturns, a company should focus its efforts on determining precisely what functions buyers want and ensure that these functions are available in its product offerings. Promotional efforts should emphasise value and utility. Some firms make the mistake of drastically reducing their marketing efforts during a recession, harming their ability to compete.

Political forces

Political, legal and regulatory forces of the marketing environment are closely interrelated. Legislation is enacted, legal decisions are interpreted by courts, and regulatory agencies are created and operated, for the most part, by elected or appointed officials. Legislation and regulations (or their lack) reflect the current political outlook. Consequently, the political forces of the marketing environment have the potential to influence marketing decisions and strategies.

Reactive marketers view political forces as beyond their control and simply adjust to conditions arising from those forces. Some firms are more proactive, however, and seek to

Source: Fairfax Ltd

<< Political forces
More recently, in 2013 Woolworths lobbied the Australian Federal Government against increasing regulation that would include an industry code of conduct

influence the political process. In some cases, organisations publicly protest the actions of legislative bodies and this might be done as an industry collective.

In 2010, tax increases affecting the Australian mining industry, estimated at $10.5 billion of government revenue, saw the Minerals Council take out full-page newspaper advertisements in protest. Bankrolled by BHP Billiton, Rio Tinto and Xstrata, the ads received a large amount of publicity exposure across TV news reports, which consequently compounded the initial investment and sparked a controversial debate at dinner tables across the country.[8] In this way, the mining industry actively participated in the political process through lobbying to persuade public and government officials to favour a particular position in their decision-making related to tax legislation. Many companies concerned about the threat of legislation or regulation that may negatively affect their operations employ lobbyists to communicate their concerns to elected officials.

Legal and regulatory forces

There are a number of federal laws that influence marketing decisions and activities, including the 2011 *Australian Consumer Law*, which is the new name for the *Trade Practices Act 1974* (TPA). Regulatory agencies and self-regulatory forces also affect marketing efforts.

Regulatory agencies

Federal regulatory agencies influence many marketing activities, including product development, pricing, packaging, advertising, personal selling and distribution. Usually these bodies have the power to enforce specific laws, as well as some discretion in establishing operating rules and regulations to guide certain types of industry practices.

The Australian Competition and Consumer Commission (ACCC) is an independent Australian Government statutory authority. It was formed in 1995 to administer the *Trade Practices Act 1974* and the *Prices Surveillance Act 1983*. The ACCC promotes competition and fair trade in the market place to benefit consumers, business and the community. It also regulates national infrastructure services. Its primary responsibility is to ensure that individuals and businesses comply with the Commonwealth competition, fair trading and consumer protection laws. In fair trading and consumer protection its role complements that of the state and territory consumer affairs agencies, which administer the mirror legislation of their jurisdictions, and the Competition and Consumer Policy Division of the Commonwealth Treasury. In addition, all states, as well as many cities and towns, have regulatory agencies that enforce laws and regulations regarding marketing practices within their states or regions. State and local regulatory agencies try not to establish regulations that conflict with those of federal regulatory agencies. They generally enforce laws dealing with the production and sale of particular goods and services. Utility, insurance, financial and liquor industries are commonly regulated by state agencies. Among these agencies' targets are misleading advertising and pricing.

In an attempt to be good corporate citizens and to prevent government intervention, some businesses try to regulate themselves. Kraft Foods, for example, stopped advertising sugary snacks and cereals to children under the age of 12 in response to growing concerns about childhood obesity and its effects on children's long-term health. While some competitors were astonished by the decision, Kraft executives recognised that if food product marketers did not begin to police themselves, the government could impose restrictions on advertising to children, and the industry could face potential lawsuits [9]

Several trade associations have developed self-regulatory programs. You may not be aware that alcohol advertising in Australia is currently self-regulated under the Alcohol Beverages Advertising Code (ABAC). This voluntary code of practice is managed jointly by advertising and alcohol industries. However, there is no provision for penalising advertisers who breach the code, and its scope is limited to advertising content rather than the placement of advertisements. It also does not cover sponsorship and the full range of social media. [10]

Although these programs are not a direct outgrowth of laws, many were established to stop or stall the development of laws and governmental regulatory groups that would regulate the associations' marketing practices.

The Advertising Standards Bureau administers a national system of advertising self-regulation through a review process conducted by the Advertising Standards Board and the Advertising Claims Board. Based in Canberra, the Bureau operates as an advertising complaints resolution service that addresses both public and competitor complaints to ensure compliance with relevant advertising codes. Usually, complained-about ads relate to people's beliefs, values and personal choices. For example, a social health campaign produced by the Queensland Association of Health communities about safe sex for gay men portrayed two men hugging and kissing with the headline 'Rip & Roll' and was evaluated with 220 complaints received; however, the case was dismissed by the Board as compliant. Another ad, produced by the General Pants Group, featuring a topless woman with black tape on her nipples and male hands unzipping her pants received just 35 complaints and the Board determination was upheld as non-compliant. Notably, in the background the word 'sex' appeared in giant print while the word 'fashion' appeared in tiny print.[11]

Self-regulatory programs have several advantages over governmental laws and regulatory agencies. Establishment and implementation are usually less expensive, and guidelines are generally more realistic and operational. In addition, effective self-regulatory programs reduce the need to expand government bureaucracy. However, these programs have several limitations. When a trade association creates a set of industry guidelines for its members, non-member firms do not have to abide by them. Furthermore, many self-regulatory programs lack the tools or authority to enforce guidelines. Finally, guidelines in self-regulatory programs are often less strict than those established by government agencies.

Source: AAP Images/Queensland association for Healthy Communities

<< Regulatory agencies
Advertisers are required to comply with the Advertising Standards Bureau. Advertising regulation recognised community resistance to this billboard; however, the case was dismissed and the billboard appeared prominently on freeways throughout Queensland

Technological forces

The word *technology* brings to mind scientific advances such as information technology and biotechnology, which have resulted in the Internet, mobile phones, cloning, stem-cell research, electric cars, iPads and more. Such developments make it possible for marketers to operate ever more efficiently and to provide an exciting array of products for consumers. Technology has revolutionised the products created and offered by marketers and the channels by which they communicate about those products. However, even though these innovations are outgrowths of technology, none of them are technology.

Technology determines how we, as members of society, satisfy our physiological needs. In various ways and to varying degrees, eating and drinking habits, sleeping patterns, sexual activities, health care and work performance are all influenced by both existing technology and advances in technology. Because of the technological revolution in communications, for example, marketers can now reach vast numbers of people more efficiently through a variety of media. Email, voicemail, mobile phones, smart phones, iPods, iPads and other portable technology help marketers to interact with customers, make appointments and handle last-minute orders or cancellations. Consider that a growing number of households are giving up their landlines in favour of using mobile phones as their primary phones.

The proliferation of mobile devices has led marketers to employ text and multimedia messaging on mobile phones to reach their target markets. Many businesses send monthly

technology
The application of knowledge and tools to solve problems and perform tasks more efficiently

or weekly special offers to customers' mobile phones. Examples of businesses doing this include beauty salons and restaurants who can send their specials to subscribers' mobile phones.[12]

The Internet is a major tool in most households for communicating, researching, shopping and entertaining. The Marketing in Transition box on the next page illustrates how consumers' use of social media has created opportunities for social network marketing. The use of online videos through websites such as YouTube, is an essential part of the digital consumer experience in the Asia-Pacific region. Time spent on social networks also makes up a significant portion of a consumer's online activities. One study estimates that users worldwide spend 19 per cent of their time online on social networking websites.[13] As the lines between TV and online technology continue to blur, it is increasingly important for marketers to understand these audiences and how to reach and engage them effectively.

The effects of technology relate to such characteristics as dynamics and reach, and the self-sustaining nature of technological progress. The *dynamics* of technology involve the constant change that often challenges the structures of social institutions, including social relationships, the legal system, religion, education, business and leisure. *Reach* refers to the broad nature of technology as it moves through society.

Although technology has had many positive impacts on our lives, there are also many negative impacts to consider. We enjoy the benefits of communicating through the Internet; however, we are increasingly concerned about protecting our privacy and intellectual property. Hackers and those who steal digital property are also using advanced technology to harm others. Likewise, technological advances in the areas of health and medicine have led to the creation of new drugs that save lives; however, such advances have also led to cloning and genetically modified foods that have become controversial issues in many segments of society. Consider the impact of mobile phones. The ability to call from almost any location has many benefits, but it also has negative side effects, including increases in traffic accidents, increased noise pollution and fears about potential health risks.[14]

The *self-sustaining* nature of technology relates to the fact that technology acts as a catalyst to spur even faster development. As new innovations are introduced, they stimulate the need for more advancements to facilitate further development. For example, the Internet has created the need for ever-faster transmission of signals through broadband connections such as high-speed phone lines (ADSL), satellite and cable. Technology initiates a change process that creates new opportunities for new technologies in every industry segment or personal life experience that it touches. At some point there is even a multiplier effect that causes still greater demand for more change to improve performance.[15]

It is important for organisations to determine when a technology is changing an industry and to define the strategic influence of the new technology. To remain competitive, companies must keep up with and adapt to these technological advances. Through a procedure known as *technology assessment*, managers try to foresee the effects of new products and processes on their organisation's operation, on other business organisations and on society in general. With information obtained through a technology assessment, management aims to estimate whether benefits of adopting a specific technology outweigh costs to the company and to society at large. The degree to which a business is technologically based also influences its managers' response to technology.

MARKETING IN TRANSITION | NEW TECHNOLOGY PROVIDES OPPORTUNITIES FOR SOCIAL NETWORK MARKETING

In today's digital era, marketers are finding that many traditional marketing campaigns are losing effectiveness. People spend a lot of their time online, where they are constantly inundated with ads. With so many distractions and competing advertisements on the Internet, marketers must adapt their traditional marketing methods to attract consumers.

An important way that marketers are reaching consumers online is through social networks like Facebook, Google+, Twitter and Pinterest. These networks provide new ways to advertise products. Facebook websites, in particular, allow consumers to track ordinary aspects of their lives, such as their favourite venues and brand choices, and share them with online communities. They are hoping to use these Internet data collections to improve their own lives, but some companies are using this information to improve sales. Amazon.com, for example, uses personal information to profile customers and recommend new products for them.

Online communities are powerful tools for promoting products and gathering information. Many companies, like Johnson & Johnson, have created their own social networks for customers. One new tool marketers are using is rewards for consumers who pass company advertising messages on to other consumers in their online communities.

Of course, the amount of personal information consumers are providing online could have negative ethical consequences. For example, everything that you do online leaves a digital trail that can be traced, and some fear this may come back to haunt people. Yet for marketers, these traces create new opportunities to target customers and sell products.[16]

Source: Getty Images

Sociocultural forces

Sociocultural forces are the influences in a society and its culture(s) that bring about changes in attitudes, beliefs, norms, customs and lifestyles. Profoundly affecting how people live, these forces help to determine what, where, how and when people buy products. Like the other environmental forces, sociocultural forces present marketers with both challenges and opportunities.

Changes in a population's demographic characteristics – age, gender, race, ethnicity, marital and parental status, income and education – have a significant bearing on relationships and individual behaviour. These shifts lead to changes in how people live and ultimately in their consumption of products such as food, clothing, housing, transportation, communication, recreation, education and health services. We look at a few of the changes in demographics and diversity that are affecting marketing activities.

One demographic change affecting the Australian marketplace is the increasing proportion of older consumers, despite an increasing number of births: 309 000 in 2012 versus 251 000 in 2002.[17] According to the Australian Bureau of Statistics, Australia's population, like that of

sociocultural forces
The influences in a society and its culture(s) that change people's attitudes, beliefs, norms, customs and lifestyles

Source: Shutterstock.com

Sociocultural >> forces
The Australian population is an ageing population therefore enabling myriad opportunities for a burgeoning funeral industry

most developed countries, is ageing as a result of increasing life expectancy, which results in proportionately more elderly people. Over the next several decades, population ageing is projected to have significant implications for Australia, including for health, labour force participation, housing and demand for skilled labour. In countries such as Japan, Italy, Greece, Sweden and Hong Kong, the number of people aged 65 years and over already exceeds the number of children aged 0–14 years. In Australia, the number of people aged 65 years and over is projected to exceed the number of children aged 0–14 years around the year 2025.[18] Consequently, marketers can expect significant increases in the demand for healthcare services, recreation, tourism, retirement housing and selected skin-care products.

People today are also increasingly concerned about the foods they eat and, thus, are choosing more low-fat, organic, natural and healthy products. Marketers have responded with a proliferation of foods, beverages and exercise products that fit this new lifestyle. In addition to the proliferation of new Australian brands focused on organic products, such as Be Natural, Sukin Organics and Australia's Own Organic, many conventional marketers have introduced organic versions of their products, including Heinz, Sanitarium and Cadbury.

LISTEN to this chapter's Audio Summary for a recap of sociocultural forces

L02

Understanding the strategic planning process

strategic planning
The process of establishing an organisational mission and formulating goals, corporate strategy, marketing objectives, marketing strategy and a marketing plan

marketing objective
A statement of what is to be accomplished through marketing activities

Through strategic planning, a company responds to its environment. The process of strategic planning establishes an organisational mission and formulates goals, corporate strategy, marketing objectives, marketing strategy and, finally, a marketing plan.[19] A market orientation should guide the process of strategic planning to ensure that a concern for customer satisfaction is an integral part of the process. A market orientation is also important for the successful implementation of marketing strategies.[20] Figure 2.1 shows the components of strategic planning.

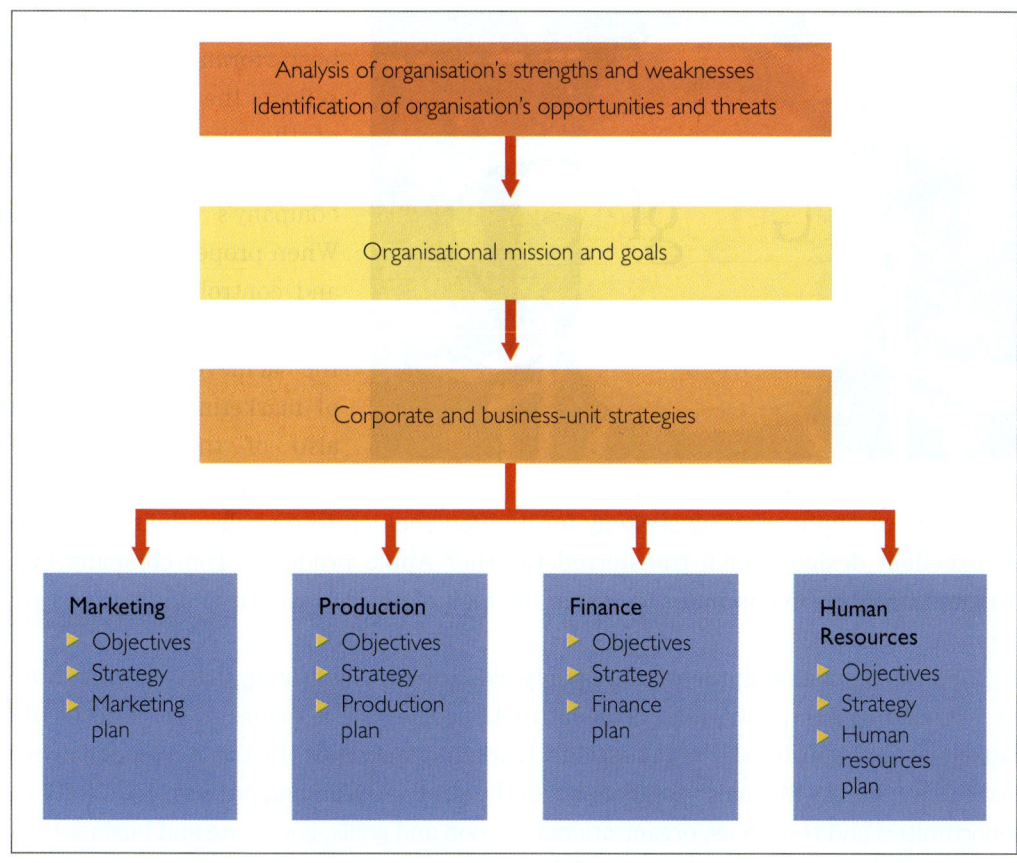

Source: From O. C. Ferrell and Michael Hartline, *Marketing Strategy* (Mason, OH: South-Western, 2008). Reprinted with permission of South-Western, a division of Thomson Learning: www.thomsonrights.com.

FIGURE 2.1
COMPONENTS OF STRATEGIC PLANNING

Beyond an analysis of the macro-environment, the strategic planning process includes a detailed analysis of an organisation's strengths and weaknesses and identification of opportunities and threats within the marketing environment. Based on this analysis, the company can establish or revise its mission and goals and then develop corporate strategies to achieve those goals. Next, each functional area of the organisation (marketing, production, finance, human resources and so on) establishes its own objectives and develops strategies to achieve them.[21] The objectives and strategies of each functional area must support the organisation's overall goals and mission. The strategies of each functional area should also be coordinated with a focus on marketing orientation.

Because our focus is marketing, we are most interested, of course, in the development of marketing objectives and strategies. Marketing objectives should be designed so that their achievement will contribute to the corporate strategy and can be accomplished through efficient use of the company's resources. To achieve its marketing objectives, an organisation must develop a marketing strategy, which includes identifying and analysing a target market segment and developing a marketing mix to satisfy individuals in that market segment. Thus a marketing strategy includes a plan of action for developing, distributing, promoting and pricing products that meet the needs of target consumers.

marketing strategy
A plan of action for identifying and analysing a target market segment and developing a marketing mix to meet the needs of that market segment

Source: Getty Images

Marketing strategy is best formulated when it reflects the overall direction of the organisation and is coordinated with all the company's functional areas. When properly implemented and controlled, a marketing strategy will contribute to the achievement not only of marketing objectives but also of the organisation's overall goals. Consider that Apple's successful marketing strategy for its iPods helped to revitalise their reputation for excellent design, which transferred to other Apple products. The company even designed its iMac G5 computer to mimic the look of an iPod with rounded corners and a translucent shell.[22]

The strategic planning process ultimately yields a marketing strategy that is the framework for a marketing plan, a written document that specifies the activities to be performed to implement and control the organisation's marketing activities. In the remainder of this chapter, we discuss the major components of the strategic planning process: organisational opportunities and resources, organisational mission and goals, corporate and business-unit strategy, marketing strategy, the role of the marketing plan and how to incorporate ethics and social responsibility into marketing strategies.

Assessing organisational resources and opportunities

Any strategic planning effort must assess an organisation's resources and competencies, as well as how the level of these factors is likely to change in the future. Aldi's core competency, efficiency in supply-chain management and product sourcing, has enabled the discount chain to build a strong reputation for low prices in the supermarket business and to become a major competitor of Coles and Woolworths.

An analysis of the marketing environment involves not only an assessment of resources and competencies, but also the identification of opportunities in the marketplace. When the right combination of circumstances and timing permits an organisation to take action to reach a particular target market and its segments, a market opportunity exists. For example, after Australian consumers began to perceive the prices of many national food brands as being rather expensive in comparison to food prices abroad, especially in Europe and the USA, Coles and Woolworths recognised a market opportunity for introducing their own private label brands priced significantly below the national brands. Such opportunities are often called strategic windows, temporary periods of optimal fit between the key requirements of a market and the particular capabilities of a company competing in that market.[23]

When a company matches a core competency to opportunities it has discovered in the marketplace, it is said to have a competitive advantage. In some cases a company may possess manufacturing, technical or marketing skills that it can match to market opportunities to create a competitive advantage. For example, communications provider Telstra is Australia's largest provider of fixed-line services, and as the owner of the majority of Australia's copper network, maintains dominance over this service sector. Telstra's dominance has now expanded into the mobile communications industry, through the establishment of their Next G network. By owning a network that provides more coverage and faster speeds than any other network available, Telstra have a clear competitive advantage over rival providers, such as Optus and Vodafone. More recently, heavy investment into their 4G network will see Telstra as one of the only networks that will be capable of supporting new 4G smartphone models as they enter the market. Reflected through their slogan 'the network without equal', Telstra hold both a technological and network competitive advantage.

Source: dl.library.com.au

competitive advantage
The result of a company's matching a core competency to opportunities in the marketplace

<< Market opportunity
In Australia, Kettle Chips is trying to reposition the brand as 'prestigious but laconic Australian' by targeting beer drinkers rather than consumers concerned about artificial ingredients and preservatives

Source: Advertising Archives; Advertising Archives

<< Competitive advantage
Environmentally friendly appeals have been used by many different products, all over the world to create a competitive advantage

SWOT analysis

SWOT analysis
A tool that marketers use
to assess an organisation's
strengths, weaknesses,
opportunities and threats

One tool that marketers use to assess an organisation's strengths, weaknesses, opportunities and threats is SWOT analysis. Strengths and weaknesses are internal factors that can influence an organisation's ability to satisfy its target markets. *Strengths* refer to competitive advantages and core competencies that give the company an edge in meeting the needs of its target market segments. Ella Baché salons, for example, promote their personalised service and global reputation in the beauty industry to emphasise the quality of their range of products and treatments. *Weaknesses* refer to any limitations that a company faces in developing or implementing a marketing strategy.

Both strengths and weaknesses should be examined from a customer perspective because they are meaningful only when they help or hinder the company in meeting customer needs. Only strengths that relate to satisfying customers should be considered true competitive advantages. Likewise, weaknesses that directly affect customer satisfaction should be considered competitive disadvantages.

Opportunities and threats exist independently of a company and therefore represent issues to be considered by all organisations, even those that do not compete with a company. *Opportunities* refer to favourable conditions in the environment that could produce rewards for an organisation if acted on properly. That is, opportunities are situations that exist but must be acted on if a company is to benefit from them. *Threats*, on the other hand, refer to conditions or barriers that may prevent a company from reaching its objectives. For example, Apple's top-selling iPod family of digital music players faced competition from mobile phone makers and services that incorporated MP3 technology into new mobile phones. Apple launched the iPhone, a mobile phone with easy-to-use iTunes software, and iTunes' prices remain highly competitive.[24] Threats must be acted on to prevent them from limiting the organisation's capabilities. Opportunities and threats can stem from many sources within the environment. When a competitor's introduction of a new product threatens a company, a defensive strategy may be required. If the company can develop and launch a new product that meets or exceeds the competition's offering, it can transform the threat into an opportunity.[25]

Figure 2.2 depicts a four-cell SWOT matrix that can help managers in the planning process. When an organisation matches internal strengths to external opportunities, it creates competitive advantages in meeting the needs of its customers. In addition, an organisation should act to convert internal weaknesses into strengths and external threats into opportunities. Procter & Gamble, for instance, converted the weaknesses of not having competitive advantages in five areas that are essential to succeeding in consumer

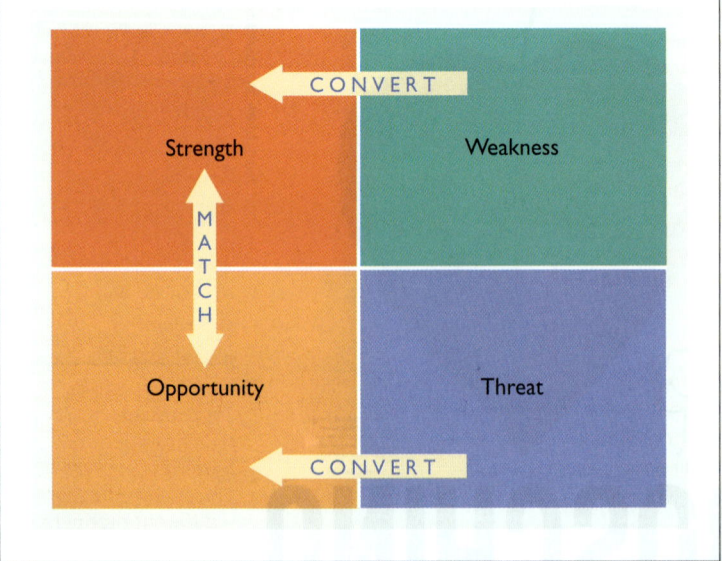

FIGURE 2.2
THE FOUR-CELL SWOT
MATRIX

Source: Reprinted from *Market-Led Strategic Change*, by Nigel F. Piercy, p. 371, copyright 1992 with permission from Elsevier Science.

products – consumer understanding, brand building, innovation, go-to-market capability and scale – into strengths by investing billions of dollars into areas such as marketing research and supply-chain management. Indeed, the company's research and development program has become a core competency that fosters significant innovation in areas such as enzymes, perfumes, flavours, polymers, substrates and surfactants.[26] A company that lacks adequate marketing skills can hire outside consultants to help convert a weakness into a strength.

Establishing an organisational mission and marketing goals

Once an organisation has assessed its resources and opportunities, it can begin to establish goals and strategies to take advantage of those opportunities. The goals of any organisation should derive from its mission statement, a long-term view, or vision, of what the organisation wants to become.

mission statement
A long-term view of what the organisation wants to become

When an organisation decides on its mission, it really answers two questions: Who are our customers? What is our core competency? Although these questions seem very simple, they are two of the most important questions any company must answer. Defining customers' needs and wants gives direction to what the company must do to satisfy them. Figure 2.3 displays the Google mission that addresses customer requirements.

Companies try to develop and manage their *corporate identity* – their unique symbols, personalities and philosophies – to support all corporate activities, including marketing. Managing identity requires broadcasting mission goals and values, sending a consistent message and implementing visual identity with stakeholders. Mission statements, goals and objectives must be implemented properly to achieve the desired corporate identity.[27]

An organisation's goals and objectives, derived from its mission statement, guide the remainder of its planning efforts. Goals focus on the end results that the organisation seeks. Ben & Jerry's ice cream is a brand well known for its commitment to social responsibility. It has a three-component mission statement to underscore this commitment. The social mission component focuses on improving the quality of life. The product mission, the second component, deals with maintaining high product quality through the use of natural ingredients. The third component is its economic mission. This component emphasises growth, which includes expanding development and career opportunities for employees.[28]

A marketing goal states what is to be accomplished through marketing activities. A marketing goal of Ritz-Carlton hotels, for example, is to have more than 90 per cent of its customers indicate that they had a memorable experience at the hotel. Marketing goals should be based on a careful study of the SWOT analysis and should relate to matching strengths to opportunities and/or the conversion of weaknesses or threats. These goals can be stated in terms of strategic objectives such as growth objectives and strategic focuses such as a sales volume focus.

marketing goal
A statement of what is to be accomplished through marketing activities

Marketing goals should possess certain characteristics. First, a marketing goal should be expressed in clear, simple terms so that all marketing personnel understand exactly what they are trying to achieve. Second, a goal should be written so that it can be measured accurately. This allows an organisation to determine if and when the goal has been achieved. If a goal is to increase market share by 10 per cent, the company should be able to measure

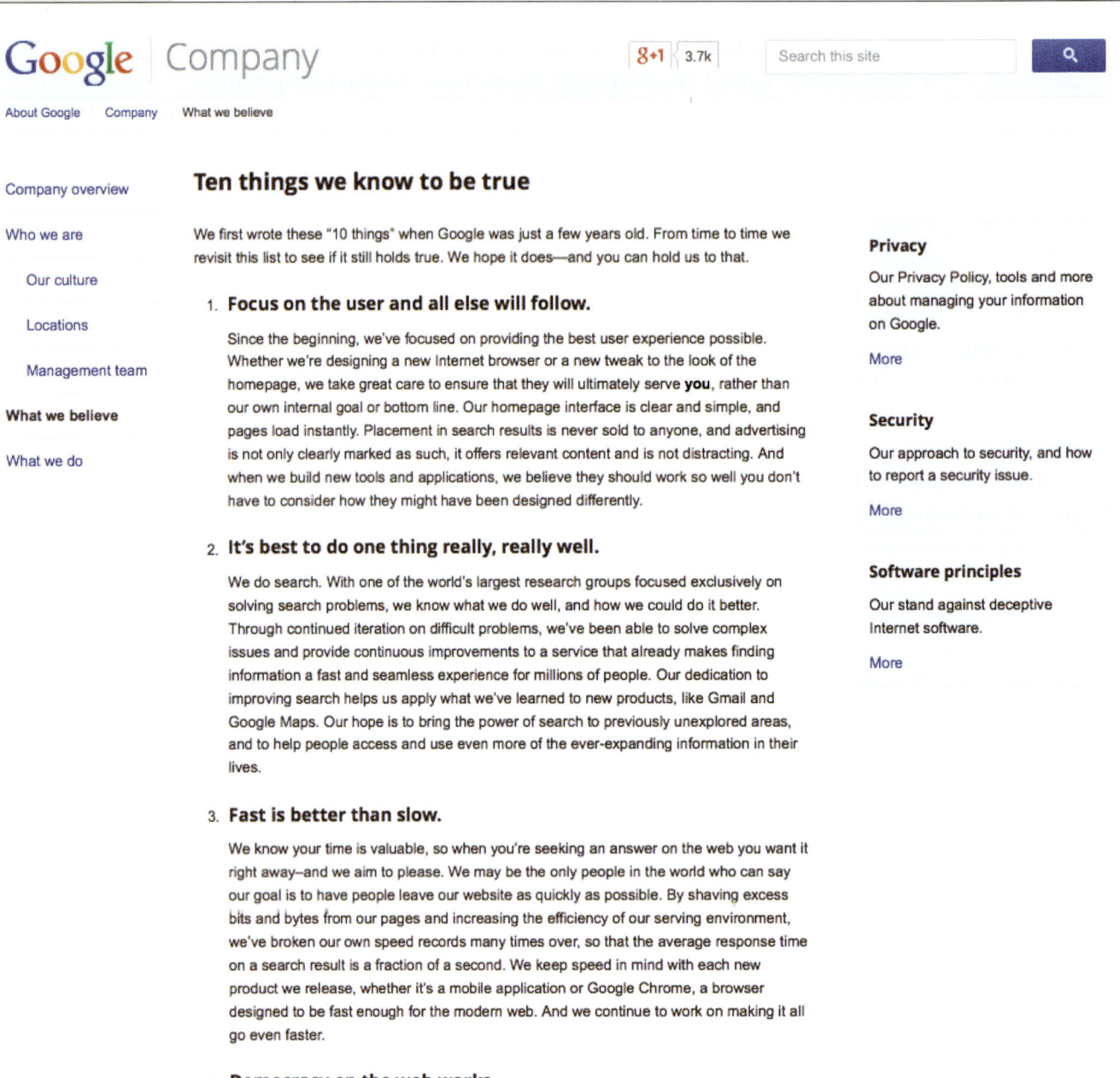

FIGURE 2.3 GOOGLE MISSION STATEMENT

market share changes accurately. Third, a marketing goal should specify a timeframe for its accomplishment. A company that sets a goal of introducing a new product should state the time period in which to do this. Finally, a marketing goal should be consistent with both business-unit and corporate strategy. This ensures that the company's mission is carried out at all levels of the organisation.

Developing corporate, business-unit and marketing strategies

In any organisation, strategic planning begins at the corporate level and proceeds downward to the business-unit and marketing levels. Corporate strategy is the broadest of these three levels and should be developed with the organisation's overall mission in mind. Business-unit strategy should be consistent with the corporate strategy, and marketing strategy should be consistent with both the business-unit and corporate strategies.

Corporate strategy

Corporate strategy determines the means for using resources in the functional areas of marketing, production, finance, research and development, and human resources to reach the organisation's goals. A corporate strategy determines not only the scope of the business but also its resource deployment, competitive advantages and overall coordination of functional areas. It addresses the two questions posed in the organisation's mission statement: Who are our customers? What is our core competency?

Source: © Boeing

corporate strategy
A strategy that determines the means for using resources in the various functional areas to reach the organisation's goals

<< Corporate strategy
Boeing continues to excel in producing innovative new jetliners such as the Dream Liner

The term 'corporate' in this context does not apply solely to corporations; corporate strategy is used by all organisations, from the smallest sole proprietorship to the largest multinational corporation.

Corporate strategy planners are concerned with broad issues such as corporate culture, competition, differentiation, diversification, interrelationships among business units, and environmental and social issues. They attempt to match the resources of the organisation with the opportunities and threats in the environment. Google, for example, purchased YouTube for US$1.65 billion after recognising that the video-sharing website's rapid growth reflected the growing popularity of viewing videos – professional and amateur – on every topic imaginable.[29] Corporate strategy planners are also concerned with defining the scope and role of a company's business units so that they are coordinated to reach the ends desired. A company's corporate strategy may affect its technological competence and ability to innovate.[30]

Business-unit strategy

After analysing corporate operations and performance, the next step in strategic planning is to determine future business directions and develop strategies for individual business

strategic business unit (SBU)
A division, product line or other profit centre within a parent company

units. A strategic business unit (SBU) is a division, product line or other profit centre within the parent company. Australia Post's business units, to name a few, consist of postal services, retail services, distribution and express services, and e-services. The revenues, costs, investments and strategic plans of each SBU can be separated from those of the parent company. SBUs operate in a variety of markets that have differing growth rates, opportunities, degrees of competition and profit-making potential. Recognising this fact in the 1990s, Procter & Gamble implemented business strategies intended to reduce its reliance on two SBUs that accounted for 85 per cent of the value it created during the 1990s. Today, the multinational corporation's portfolio is spread across many categories to balance fast-growing, high-margin businesses, such as home care and beauty products, with foundation businesses including baby care and laundry products.[31] Business strategy is fundamentally focused on the measures required to create value for the company's target markets and achieve greater performance. Marketing research suggests that this requires implementing appropriate strategic actions and targeting appropriate market segments.[32]

Strategic planners should recognise the different performance capabilities of each SBU and carefully allocate scarce resources among those divisions. Several tools allow a company's portfolio of SBUs, or even individual products, to be classified and visually displayed according to the attractiveness of various markets and the business' relative market share within those markets. A market is a group of individuals and/or organisations that have needs for products in a product class and have the ability, willingness and authority to purchase those products. The percentage of a market that actually buys a specific product from a particular company is referred to as that product's (or business unit's) market share. Cadbury dominates market share in Australia and India, whereas Hershey Foods dominates the market for chocolate in the US.[33] Product quality, order of entry into the market and market share have been associated with SBU success.[34]

market
A group of individuals and/or organisations that have needs for products in a product class and have the ability, willingness and authority to purchase those products

market share
The percentage of a market that actually buys a specific product from a particular company

market-growth/ market-share matrix
A strategic planning tool based on the philosophy that a product's market growth rate and market share are important in determining marketing strategy

One of the most helpful tools is the market-growth/market-share matrix, the Boston Consulting Group (BCG) approach, is based on the philosophy that a product's market growth rate and its market share are important considerations in determining its marketing strategy. All a company's SBUs and products should be integrated into a single, overall matrix and evaluated to determine appropriate strategies for individual products and overall portfolio strategies. Managers can use this model to determine and classify each product's expected future cash contributions and future cash requirements. Generally, managers who use this model should examine the competitive position of a product (or SBU) and the opportunities for improving that product's contribution to profitability and cash flow.[35] The BCG analytical approach is more of a diagnostic tool than a guide for making strategy prescriptions.

Figure 2.4, which is based on work by the BCG, enables the strategic planner to classify a company's products into four basic types: stars, cash cows, dogs and question marks.[36] Stars are products with a dominant share of the market and good prospects for growth. However, they use more cash than they generate to finance growth, add capacity and increase market share. An example of a star might be Nintendo's Wii video game system. Cash cows have a dominant share of the market but low prospects for growth; typically, they generate more cash than is required to maintain market share. Dogs have a subordinate share of the market and low prospects for growth; these products are often found in established markets. Portable compact disc (CD) players may be considered dogs at companies like Sony and Panasonic. The increasing popularity and affordability of iPods and other MP3 players has resulted in plummeting profits and market share for portable CD players. Question marks, sometimes called 'problem children', have a small share of a growing market and generally require a large amount of cash to build market share.

The long-term health of an organisation depends on having some products that generate cash (and provide acceptable profits) and others that use cash to support growth. Among the indicators of overall health are the size and vulnerability of the cash cows, the prospects for the stars, if any, and the number of question marks and dogs. Particular attention should be paid to products with large cash appetites. Unless the company has an abundant cash flow, it cannot afford to sponsor many such products at one time. If resources, including debt capacity, are spread too thin, the company will end up with too many marginal products and will be unable to finance promising new-product entries or acquisitions in the future.

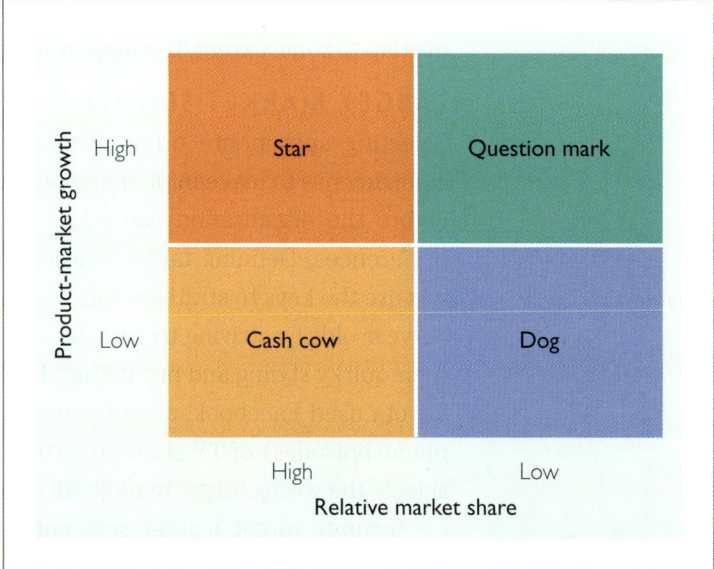

Source: 'Growth-share matrix developed by the Boston Consulting Group', Perspectives, No. 66, 'The Product Portfolio'. © 1970. Reprinted by permission of Boston Consulting Group.

FIGURE 2.4
GROWTH-SHARE MATRIX DEVELOPED BY THE BOSTON CONSULTING GROUP

Marketing strategy

The next phase in strategic planning is the development of sound strategies for each functional area of the organisation. Corporate strategy and marketing strategy must balance and synchronise the organisation's mission and goals with stakeholder relationships. This means that marketing must deliver value and be responsible in facilitating effective relationships with all relevant stakeholders.[37] An effective marketing strategy must gain the support of key stakeholders, including employees, investors and communities, as well as government regulators. If employees and investors, in particular, are not behind a marketing strategy, it is usually doomed to fail. There is a need in marketing to develop more of a stakeholder orientation to go beyond markets, competitors and channel members to understand and address all stakeholder concerns.[38]

Within the marketing area, a strategy is typically designed around two components: (1) the selection of target market segments and (2) the creation of a marketing mix that will satisfy the needs of the chosen target market segment or segments. A marketing strategy articulates the best use of a company's resources and tactics to achieve its marketing goals. It should also match customers' desire for value with the organisation's distinctive capabilities. Internal capabilities should be used to maximise external opportunities. The planning process should be guided by a market-oriented culture and processes in the organisation.[39] A comprehensive strategy involves a thorough search for information, the analysis of many potential courses of action and the use of specific criteria for making decisions regarding strategy development and implementation.[40] When implemented properly, a good marketing strategy also enables a company to achieve its business-unit and corporate objectives. Although corporate, business-unit and marketing strategies all overlap to some extent, the marketing strategy is the most detailed and specific of the three.

TARGET MARKET SEGMENT SELECTION

Selecting appropriate target market segments may be the most important decision a company has to make in planning process because target market segments must be chosen before the organisation can adapt its marketing mix to meet this market's needs and preferences. Defining target market segments and developing an appropriate marketing mix are the keys to strategic success. Toyota, for example, targeted its Yaris sedan at 18- to 34-year-olds by striving to give the compact cars a mischievous personality to complement their quirky styling and promoting them wherever Generation Y consumers could be found. Toyota used Facebook, a user-generated-content website, and 'mobisodes' (short mobile-phone episodes) of TV shows to attract the attention of younger consumers. If a company selects the wrong target market, all other marketing decisions are likely to be made in vain.

Accurate target market segment selection is crucial to productive marketing efforts. Products and even companies sometimes fail because marketers do not identify appropriate customer groups at whom to aim their efforts. If a company selects the wrong target market segment or segments, all other marketing decisions will be a waste of time. Holden, for example, experienced poor sales of its reintroduced Monaro in part because its price tag was too high for the target market segment of younger baby boomers and older Generation Xers. Also, the Monaro could not compete with vehicles such as the BMW M3 and the Audi TT, which offered better road performance and more refined features.

An organisation's marketing management must gather adequate information about the consumers in its target market segments. Marketers of health-food supplements and diet programs, for example, would be very interested in knowing about consumer attitudes and behaviours related to diet and exercise. Identification and analysis of a target market segment provides a foundation on which a company can develop a marketing mix.

Target market selection >> Sports companies such as Nike use different advertising appeals for women and men to market their products

CHAPTER 2: MARKETING PLANNING AND STRATEGY IN A COMPETITIVE ENVIRONMENT

When exploring possible target market segments, marketing managers try to evaluate how entering them would affect the company's sales, costs and profits. Marketing information should be organised to facilitate a focus on the chosen target consumers. Accounting and information systems, for example, can be used to track revenues and costs by customer (or group of customers). In addition, managers and employees need to be rewarded for focusing on profitable customers. Teamwork skills can be developed with organisational structures that promote a customer orientation that allows quick responses to changes in the marketing environment.[41] Marketers should also assess whether a company has the resources to develop the right mix of product, price, promotion and distribution to meet the needs of a particular target market segment. In addition, they determine if satisfying those needs is consistent with a company's overall objectives and mission. When Amazon.com, the number one Internet retailer, began selling electronics on its website, it made the decision that efforts to target various electronics segments in this market would increase profits and be consistent with its objectives to be the largest online retailer. The company believed that reaching a larger target audience through a wider range of products would broaden the company's appeal and result in larger sales. Clearly this was a wise decision, as Amazon.com is now the world's largest online retailer with revenues of over $48 billion annually. Customers can, and do, purchase virtually anything they want via Amazon.com.[42]

CREATING THE MARKETING MIX

The selection of target market segments serves as the basis for creating a marketing mix to serve potential customers in those segments. Considering the elements of the marketing mix as product, promotion, price and place, as well as the extended marketing mix elements of people, process and physical evidence, these need to be constructed in a form most appropriate for the selected target segment needs. The decisions made in creating a marketing mix are only as good as the organisation's understanding of the target market segments. This understanding typically comes from careful, in-depth research into the characteristics of the target market segments. Therefore, while demographic information is important, the organisation should also analyse customer needs, preferences and behaviour with respect to product design, pricing, distribution and promotion. For example, Kimberly-Clark's marketing researchers found that younger, design-conscious consumers are loath to place a run-of-the-mill box of Kleenex tissue even on top of the toilet. Kimberly-Clark, therefore, introduced tissues contained in a contemporary oval package in bright colours and patterns that is stylish enough to place in more places around the house. This product is now sold in many of its international markets successfully.[43]

Marketing-mix decisions could also have two additional characteristics: consistency and flexibility. All marketing-mix decisions should be consistent with the business-unit and corporate strategies. Such consistency allows the organisation to achieve its objectives on all three levels of planning. Flexibility, on the other hand, permits the organisation to alter the marketing mix in response to changes in market conditions, competition and customer needs. Marketing strategy flexibility has a positive influence on organisational performance. Market orientation and strategic flexibility complement each other to help the organisation manage varying environmental conditions.[44]

Whether marketing internationally or domestically, it is very important to ensure that the designed marketing mix for each market segment that is to be targeted entails an element of sustainability. A sustainable competitive advantage is one that the competition cannot easily copy. Aldi, as noted earlier, maintains a sustainable competitive advantage in

sustainable competitive advantage
An advantage that the competition cannot easily copy

staple groceries over other supermarkets because of its very efficient and low-cost sourcing and distribution system. This allows Aldi to offer lower prices and helped it to gain a substantial share of the Australian supermarket business in a very short time after arriving from overseas. Maintaining a sustainable competitive advantage requires flexibility in the marketing mix when facing uncertain competitive environments. Monitoring the broader marketing environment and shifting and shaping the product offer accordingly will enable an established competitive advantage to be sustained (refer to the Sustainable Marketing box below for an example of a business that focuses on broader consumer education in order to maintain a competitive advantage for their products.).

SUSTAINABLE MARKETING | PACKAGING ... THAT DOES NOT COST THE EARTH

In the world of working parents and time-poor executives searching for some form of lifestyle balance, the consumption of plastic packaging is increasing every year. Many consumers and organisations alike, however, are choosing more environmentally friendly packaging options. While some supermarkets and retail stores are beginning to charge for plastic bags at the checkout, any use of plastic bags contributes to the landfill problems of both today and the future. With the aim of supplying packaging with a low carbon footprint, BioPak is biodegradable packaging made from 100 per cent natural resources including sugar cane. But BioPak is not just focused on providing biodegradable packaging to the corporate world for distribution to the business and consumer markets. Unlike most organisations, BioPak has launched their biodegradable packaging product with the deliberate intention of educating the

Source: with Permission BioPak

broader community on the benefits of a world less reliant on oil and fossil fuel. With the goal of changing the way Australians use packaging, BioPak has a focus on educating Australians on what and how to consume in a sustainable manner. Consumers are coached on reducing their carbon emissions by composting and recycling habits, for example, in order to build a better and more sustainable future.[45]

Creating a marketing plan

marketing planning
The process of assessing opportunities and resources, determining objectives, defining strategies and establishing guidelines for implementation and control of the marketing program

A major concern in the strategic planning process is marketing planning, the systematic process of assessing marketing opportunities and resources, determining marketing objectives, defining marketing strategies and establishing guidelines for implementation and control of the marketing program. The outcome of marketing planning is the development of a marketing plan. As noted earlier, a marketing plan is a written document that outlines and explains all the activities necessary to implement marketing strategies. It describes the company's current position or situation, establishes marketing goals for the product or product group and specifies how the organisation will attempt to achieve those goals.

TABLE 2.2 COMPONENTS OF A MARKETING PLAN

Plan component	Component summary	Highlights
Executive summary	One- to two-stage synopsis of the entire marketing plan	
Environmental analysis	Information about the company's current situation with respect to the marketing environment	1 Assessment of marketing environment factors 2 Assessment of target market(s) 3 Assessment of current marketing objectives and performance
SWOT analysis	Assessment of the organisation's strengths, weaknesses, opportunities and threats	1 Strengths 2 Weaknesses 3 Opportunities 4 Threats
Marketing objectives	Specification of the company's marketing objectives	Qualitative measures of what is to be accomplished
Marketing strategies	Outline of how the company will achieve its objectives	1 Target market(s) 2 Marketing mix
Marketing implementation	Outline of how the company will implement its marketing strategies	1 Marketing organisation 2 Activities and responsibilities 3 Implementation timetable
Evaluation and control	Explanation of how the company will measure and evaluate the results of the implemented plan	1 Performance standards 2 Financial controls 3 Monitoring procedures (audits)

Source: VALS/Mediamark Research, Inc., survey, SRI Consulting Business Intelligence, www.sric-bi.com/VALS. Reprinted with permission.

REVISE your knowledge of marketing planning with the Interactive Marketing Plan

Developing a clear, well-written marketing plan, though time-consuming, is important. The plan is the basis for internal communication among employees. It covers the assignment of responsibilities and tasks, as well as schedules for implementation. It articulates goals and specifies how resources are to be allocated to achieve those objectives. Finally, it helps marketing managers monitor and evaluate the performance of a marketing strategy.

Organisations use many different formats when devising marketing plans. Plans may be written for SBUs, product lines, individual products or brands, or specific target market segments. Most plans share some common ground, however, by including many of the same components. Table 2.2 describes the major parts of a typical marketing plan.

Implementing marketing strategies

Marketing planning and implementation are inextricably linked in successful companies. The marketing plan provides a framework to stimulate thinking and provide strategic direction, whereas implementation occurs as an adaptive response to day-to-day issues, opportunities and unanticipated situations – for example, increasing interest rates or an economic slowdown – that cannot be anticipated during the development of the marketing plan.

marketing implementation
The process of putting marketing strategies into action

Marketing implementation is the process of executing marketing strategies. The implementation process determines whether a marketing strategy succeeds.

Customer relationship management

Customer relationship management (CRM) focuses on using information about customers to create marketing strategies that develop and sustain desirable long-term customer relationships in target market segments. Relationship-building efforts have been shown to increase customer value.[46] CRM strives to build satisfying exchange relationships between buyers and sellers by gathering useful data at all customer-contact points – telephone, Internet and personal – and analysing those data to better understand customers' needs, desires and habits. It focuses on analysing and using databases and leveraging technologies to identify strategies and methods that will maximise the lifetime value of each desirable customer to the company.[47] It is imperative that marketers attempt to learn about their customers' expectations in order to satisfy them, for failure to do so can lead to customer dissatisfaction and defection.[48]

CRM technologies enable marketers to identify specific customers, establish interactive dialogues with them to learn about their needs, and combine this information with their purchase histories to customise products to meet those needs. Like many online retailers, Amazon.com stores and analyses purchase data to understand each customer's interests. This information helps the retailer improve its ability to satisfy individual customers and thereby increase sales of books, music, movies and other products to each customer. The ability to identify individual customers allows marketers to shift their focus from targeting groups of similar customers to increasing their share of an individual customer's purchases. Thus, the emphasis shifts from *share of market to share of customer*.

Focusing on share of customer requires recognising that all customers have different needs and that all customers do not have equal value to a company. CRM technologies help marketers analyse individual customers' purchases and identify the most profitable and loyal customers. The most basic application of this idea is the 80/20 rule: 80 per cent of business profits come from 20 per cent of customers. The goal is to assess the worth of individual customers and thus estimate their lifetime value to the company. The concept of *customer lifetime value* (CLV) may include not only an individual's propensity to engage in purchases but also his or her strong word-of-mouth communication about the company's products.[49] Some customers – those who require considerable hand-holding or who return products frequently – may simply be too expensive to retain given the low level of profits they generate. Companies can discourage these unprofitable customers by requiring them to pay higher fees for additional services.

CLV is a key measurement that forecasts a customer's lifetime economic contribution based on continued relationship marketing efforts. It can be calculated by taking the sum of the customer's present value contributions to profit margins over a specific timeframe. For example, the lifetime value of a Jaguar customer could be predicted by how many new cars Jaguar could sell the customer over a period of years and developing a summation of the contribution to margins across the time period. While this is not an exact science, knowing a customer's potential lifetime value can help marketers determine how best to allocate resources to marketing strategies to sustain that customer over a lifetime.

MARKETING IN ACTION | MARKETING NEW PRODUCTS

Have you ever wondered how new products make it in highly competitive, well-established product categories? Non-alcoholic beverages, for example, is traditionally a highly competitive market in Australia. Australia's first non-alcoholic beverage plant goes back to the early European settlement days when colonists and prospectors in the gold fields quenched their thirst with ginger beer and lemonade. Until the 1970s, Australia boasted 450 independent non-alcoholic beverage bottling plants. Today, the industry is much more streamlined with only a few dominant players, but it is equally competitive. Nonetheless, there are more and more newcomers competing for market share by offering unique

product features. Preshafruit, for instance, recently introduced a range of juices that are produced under high pressure processing, rather than heat pasteurisation. The resulting products are part of the company's overall marketing mix (product, price, distribution and promotion) aimed to satisfy the needs of health-conscious customers. ✖

Source: Preshafood Ltd.

Marketing implementation through internal marketing

Just as organisations can achieve their goals by using different marketing strategies, they can implement their marketing strategies by using different approaches. In this section we discuss one fundamental approach to marketing implementation: internal marketing. This approach represents an important mindset that marketing managers should adopt when organising and planning marketing activities.

External customers are the individuals who patronise a business – the familiar definition of customers – whereas internal customers are the company's employees. For implementation to succeed, the needs of both groups of customers must be addressed. If internal customers are not satisfied, it is likely that external customers will not be either. Therefore, in addition to targeting marketing activities at external customers, a company uses internal marketing to attract, motivate and retain qualified internal customers by designing internal products (jobs) that satisfy their wants and needs. Internal marketing is a management philosophy that coordinates internal exchanges between the organisation and its employees to achieve successful external exchanges between the organisation and its target customers. Internal marketing is a process through which leaders instil in employees a sense of oneness with the organisation. Middle managers are especially important in creating the foundation for internal marketing.[50]

Generally speaking, internal marketing refers to the managerial actions necessary to make all members of the marketing organisation understand and accept their respective roles in implementing the marketing strategy. Therefore, marketing managers need to

external customers
Individuals who patronise a business

internal customers
A company's employees

internal marketing
Coordinating internal exchanges between the company and its employees to achieve successful external exchanges between the company and its customers

focus internally on employees as well as externally on customers.[51] This means that all employees, from the president of the company down to the hourly workers on the shop floor, must understand the role they play in carrying out their jobs and implementing the marketing strategy. At Google, employees are reimbursed for taking additional training or even completing degree programs. Google employees are also allocated time to take on projects of their own choice. This employee freedom fosters an organisational culture of innovation. In short, anyone invested in the company, both marketers and those who perform other functions, must recognise the tenets of customer orientation and service that underlies the marketing concept and being market oriented.

As with external marketing activities, internal marketing may involve market segmentation, product development, research, distribution and even public relations and sales promotion.[52] For instance, an organisation may sponsor sales contests to inspire sales personnel to boost their selling efforts. While it has been estimated that two-thirds of companies use sales contests, incentives can vary widely. Most contests offer financial rewards. Such efforts help employees (and ultimately the company) to understand customers' needs and problems, teach them valuable new skills and heighten their enthusiasm for their regular jobs. In addition, many companies use planning sessions, websites, workshops, letters, formal reports and personal conversations to ensure that employees comprehend the corporate mission, the organisation's goals and the marketing strategy. Ethics programs are one such method in educating employees of the organisations ethical standpoint (see Ethical Marketing box below). The ultimate results are more satisfied employees and improved customer relations.

ETHICAL MARKETING | THE PAYOFFS FOR BEING ETHICAL

issue

Is ethics a cost or a benefit to a company?

As companies continue to struggle with 'doing the right thing' for customers, employees and communities, there is an ongoing debate around the costs/benefits of ethics programs. Critics argue that the cost to identify risks, create programs, train employees, implement hotlines and other reporting mechanisms, and establish checks and balances is tremendous for organisations and requires a significant investment. Those who support the cost of ethics programs recognise the benefits in providing employees with the guidance to navigate organisational risks and support the company's ethical culture, create trust in the marketplace that increases customer and employee loyalty, and prevent misconduct that can damage reputations and harm shareholder values. Those who support marketing ethics feel that any short-term costs are overshadowed by long-term gains, including financial performance.[53]

Organising marketing activities

The structure and relationships of a marketing unit, including lines of authority and responsibility that connect and coordinate individuals, strongly affect marketing activities. Companies that truly adopt the marketing concept develop a distinctly market oriented culture: a culture based on a shared set of beliefs that makes the customer's needs the pivotal point of the company's decisions about strategy and operations.[54] Instead of developing products in a vacuum and then trying to persuade customers to purchase them, companies using the marketing concept begin with an orientation toward their customers' needs and desires. A Subaru dealership in Melbourne's Docklands educates customers on how Subaru boxer engines were designed with customer input in order to meet particular needs of drivers. As a result, Subaru believes their engines are better than conventionally designed engines.

If the marketing concept serves as a guiding philosophy, the marketing unit will be closely coordinated with other functional areas, such as production, finance and human resources. Marketing must interact with other departments in a number of key areas. It needs to work with manufacturing in determining the volume and variety of the company's products. Those in charge of production rely on marketers for accurate sales forecasts. Research and development departments depend heavily on information gathered by marketers about product features and benefits desired by consumers. Decisions made by the physical distribution department hinge on information about the urgency of delivery schedules and cost/service trade-offs. Information technology is often a crucial ingredient in managing customer relationships effectively, but successful customer relationship management programs must include every department involved in customer relations.[55]

How effectively a company's marketing management can plan and implement marketing strategies also depends on how the marketing unit is organised. Organising marketing activities in ways that mesh with a company's strategic marketing approach enhances performance.[56] Effective organisational planning can give a company a competitive advantage. The organisational structure of a marketing department establishes the authority relationships among marketing personnel and specifies who is responsible for making certain decisions and performing particular activities. This internal structure helps direct marketing activities. The marketing department's ability to develop connections with customers increases the marketing orientation of the company and is positively correlated to a company's performance.[57]

One crucial decision regarding structural authority is centralisation versus decentralisation. In a centralised organisation, top-level managers delegate very little authority to lower levels. In a decentralised organisation, decision-making authority is delegated as far down the chain of command as possible. The decision to centralise or decentralise the organisation directly affects marketing. Most traditional organisations are highly centralised. In these organisations, most, if not all, marketing decisions are made at the top levels. However, as organisations become more marketing oriented, centralised decision-making proves somewhat ineffective. In these organisations, decentralised authority allows the company to respond to customer needs more quickly.

No single approach to organising a marketing unit works equally well in all businesses. The best approach, or approaches, depends on the number and diversity of the company's products, the characteristics and needs of the people in the target market and many other factors. A marketing unit can be organised according to (1) functions, (2) products, (3) regions or (4) types of customers. Companies often use some combination of these organisational approaches. Product features may dictate that the marketing unit be structured by products,

centralised organisation
A structure in which top management delegates little authority to levels below it

decentralised organisation
A structure in which decision-making authority is delegated as far down the chain of command as possible

whereas customer characteristics may require that it be organised by geographic region or types of customers. By using more than one type of structure, a flexible marketing unit can develop and implement marketing plans to match customers' needs precisely.

Organising by functions

Some marketing departments are organised by general marketing functions, such as marketing research, product development, distribution, sales, advertising and customer relations. The personnel who direct these functions report directly to the top-level marketing executive. This structure is fairly common because it works well for some businesses with centralised marketing operations, such as Coca-Cola and IBM. In more decentralised companies, such as supermarket chains, functional organisation can cause serious coordination problems. However, the functional approach may suit a large, centralised company whose products and customers are neither numerous nor diverse.

Organising by products

An organisation that produces and markets diverse products may find the functional approach inadequate. The decisions and problems related to a single marketing function for one product may be quite different from those related to the same marketing function for another product. As a result, businesses that produce diverse products sometimes organise their marketing units according to product groups. Organising by product groups gives a company the flexibility to develop special marketing mixes for different products. Samsung Group is comprised of numerous subsidiaries including Samsung Electronics and Samsung Heavy Industries. Although organising by products allows a company to remain flexible, this approach can be rather expensive unless efficient categories of products are grouped together to reduce duplication and improve coordination of product management.

Organising by regions

A large company that markets products nationally (or internationally) may organise its marketing activities by geographic regions. Managers of marketing functions for each region report to their regional marketing manager; all the regional marketing managers report directly to the executive marketing manager. This form of organisation is especially effective for an organisation whose customers' characteristics and needs vary greatly from one region to another. Organisations that try to penetrate the national market intensively may divide regions into sub-regions.

Organising by type of customer >>
Marketing is often organised by type of customer. Carlton & United Breweries have established a range of beers and market each beer according to customer type. Crown Lager targets a customer shopping for a more premium or celebratory occasion; specifically focusing on customers prepared to spend a little bit more. Victoria Bitter, by comparison, targets hardworking Australians, focusing more on the 'knock off' or 'after hard work' occasion and representing good value for money

Source: Reprinted with permission from CUB Pty Ltd

Organising by target market segments

Sometimes a company's marketing unit is organised according to target market segments. This form of internal organisation works well for a company that has several groups of customers whose needs and problems differ significantly. For example, Bunnings targets home builders and contractors as well as do-it-yourself customers and consumers who desire installation and service. Retailers may want more rapid delivery of small shipments and more personal selling by the producer than do either wholesalers or institutional buyers. Because the marketing decisions and activities required for these two groups of customers differ considerably, the company may find it efficient to organise its marketing unit by types of customers.

Controlling marketing activities

To achieve both marketing and general organisational objectives, marketing managers must control marketing efforts effectively. The marketing control process consists of establishing performance standards, evaluating actual performance by comparing it with established standards and reducing the differences between desired and actual performance.

Although the control function is a fundamental management activity, it has received little attention in marketing. Organisations have both formal and informal control systems. The formal marketing control process, as mentioned before, involves performance standards, evaluation of actual performance and corrective action to remedy shortfalls (see Figure 2.5). The informal control process involves self-control, social or group control, and cultural control through acceptance of a company's value system. Which type of control system dominates depends on the environmental context of the company.[58] We now discuss these steps in the formal control process and consider the major problems they involve.

marketing control process
Establishing performance standards and trying to match actual performance to those standards

WATCH an interactive animation on the marketing control process

```
        ┌──────────────────────────────────┐
  1  │ Establishment of              │
     │ performance standards         │
        └──────────────────────────────────┘

  3  │ Corrective action,            │        2  │ Evaluation of actual
     │ if necessary                  │           │ performance relative to
                                                 │ established standards
```

FIGURE 2.5 THE MARKETING CONTROL PROCESS

Establishing performance standards

Planning and controlling are closely linked because plans include statements about what is to be accomplished. For purposes of control, these statements function as performance standards. A performance standard is an expected level of performance against which actual performance can be compared. A performance standard might be a reduction of customers' complaints by 20 per cent, a monthly sales quota of $150 000, or a 10 per cent increase per month in new customer accounts. As stated earlier, performance standards should be tied to organisational goals.

Evaluating actual performance

To compare actual performance with performance standards, marketing managers must know what employees within the company are doing and have information about the activities of external organisations that provide the company with marketing assistance. For example, Porsche, like many car makers, evaluates its cars and service levels by how well it ranks on various customer service indexes. These ratings could be used in advertising and sales activities. Records of actual performance are compared with performance standards to determine whether and how much of a discrepancy exists.

Taking corrective action

Marketing managers have several options for reducing a discrepancy between established performance standards and actual performance. They can take steps to improve actual performance, reduce or totally change the performance standard, or do both. When seeking to understand a reduction in the purchases of razor blades in many of its international markets, Gillette found that reduced shaving frequency and better, more durable products were the cause. Gillette had to alter its sales objectives and used advertising public relations to try to increase sales. To improve actual performance, the marketing manager may have to use better methods of motivating marketing personnel or find more effective techniques for coordinating marketing efforts.

Problems in controlling marketing activities

In their efforts to control marketing activities, marketing managers frequently run into several problems. Often the information required to control marketing activities is unavailable or is available only at a high cost. Even though marketing controls should be flexible enough to allow for environmental changes, the frequency, intensity and unpredictability of such changes may hamper control. In addition, the time lag between marketing activities and their results limits a marketing manager's ability to measure the effectiveness of specific marketing activities. This is especially true for all advertising activities.

Because marketing and other business activities overlap, marketing managers often cannot determine the precise costs of marketing activities. Without an accurate measure of marketing costs, it is difficult to know if the outcome of marketing activities is worth the expense. Finally, marketing control may be difficult because it is very hard to develop exact performance standards for marketing personnel.

Incorporating social responsibility and ethics into strategic planning

Although the concepts of marketing ethics and social responsibility are often used interchangeably, it is important to distinguish between them. *Ethics* relates to individual and group decisions – judgements about what is right or wrong in a particular decision-making situation – whereas *social responsibility* deals with the total effect of marketing decisions on society. The two concepts are interrelated because a company that supports socially responsible decisions and adheres to a code of conduct is likely to have a positive effect on society. Because ethics and social responsibility programs can be profitable as well, an increasing number of companies are incorporating these concepts into their overall strategic market planning.

Ethics and codes of conduct

To improve their ethical behaviour, many organisations have developed **codes of conduct** (also called *codes of ethics*) consisting of formalised rules and standards that describe what the company expects of its employees. Without compliance programs and uniform standards and policies regarding conduct, it is hard for a company's employees to determine what conduct, as part of a company strategy, is acceptable. In the absence of such programs and standards, employees will generally make decisions based on their observations of how their peers and superiors behave. Codes of conduct promote ethical behaviour by reducing opportunities for unethical behaviour; employees know both what is expected of them and what kind of punishment they face if they violate the rules. Many stock exchanges around the world now require every member corporation to have a formal code of conduct. Codes help marketers deal with ethical issues or dilemmas that develop in daily operations by prescribing or limiting specific activities. Codes of conduct often include general ethical values such as honesty and integrity, general legal compliance, discreditable or harmful acts, and obligations related to social values, as well as more marketing-specific issues such as confidentiality, responsibilities to employers and clients, obligations to the profession, independence and objectivity and marketing-specific legal and technical compliance issues.[59]

It is important that companies consistently enforce standards and impose penalties or punishment on those who violate codes of conduct. Employees in convenience outlets, clothing stores and food chains are required to maintain a level of service and presentation which is routinely checked and graded by mystery shoppers. In failing to provide customer service to a certain standard, which may entail a degree of upselling, the employee will not receive a monthly bonus. In addition, a company must take reasonable steps in response to violations of standards and, as appropriate, revise the compliance program to diminish the likelihood of future misconduct. Improper hiring practices, discrimination, lying to

codes of conduct
Formalised rules and standards that describe what the company expects of its employees

employees, misreporting hours worked and safety violations are just some commonly observed types of misconduct. To succeed, a compliance program must be viewed as part of the overall marketing strategy implementation. If ethics officers and other executives are not committed to the principles and initiatives of marketing ethics and social responsibility, the program's effectiveness will be in question.

Corporate social responsibility

As we have emphasised throughout this chapter, ethics is one dimension of social responsibility. Being socially responsible, on the other hand, relates to doing what is economically sound, legal, ethical and socially conscious. One way to evaluate whether a specific activity is ethical and socially responsible is to ask other members of the organisation if they approve of it. Contact with concerned consumer groups and industry or government regulatory groups may be helpful. A check to see whether there is a specific company policy about an activity may help resolve ethical questions. If other organisational members approve of the activity, and it is legal and customary within the industry, chances are that the activity is acceptable from both an ethical and a social responsibility perspective.

A rule of thumb for resolving ethical and social responsibility issues is that if an issue can withstand open discussion that results in agreement or limited debate, an acceptable solution may exist. Nevertheless, even after a final decision is reached, different viewpoints on the issue may remain. Openness is not the end-all solution to the ethics problem. However, it creates trust and facilitates learning relationships.[60]

Many of society's demands impose costs. For example, society wants a cleaner environment and the preservation of wildlife and their habitats, but it also wants low-priced products. Consider the plight of the petrol station owner who asked his customers if they would be willing to spend an additional 1 cent per litre if he instituted an air filtration system to eliminate harmful fumes. The majority indicated they supported his plan. However, when the system was installed and the price increased, many customers switched to a lower-cost competitor across the street. Thus, companies must carefully balance the costs of providing low-priced products against the costs of manufacturing, packaging and distributing their products in an environmentally responsible manner.

Balancing society's demands to satisfy all members of society is difficult, if not impossible. Marketers must evaluate the extent to which members of society are willing to pay for what they want. For instance, customers may want more information about a product but be unwilling to pay the costs the company incurs in providing the data. Marketers who want to make socially responsible decisions may find the task a challenge because, ultimately, they must ensure their economic survival.

Study Tools

Chapter review

LO1 UNDERSTAND THE IMPORTANCE OF ENVIRONMENTAL SCANNING AND THE EFFECTS OF COMPETITIVE, ECONOMIC, POLITICAL, LEGAL AND REGULATORY, TECHNOLOGICAL AND SOCIOCULTURAL (PEST) FACTORS ON MARKETING STRATEGIES.

Environmental scanning is the process of collecting information about the forces in the marketing environment; environmental analysis is the process of assessing and interpreting the information gathered through environmental scanning. This information helps marketing managers to minimise uncertainty and threats and to capitalise on opportunities presented by environmental factors.

Marketers need to monitor the actions of competitors to determine what strategies competitors are using and how those strategies affect their own. Economic conditions influence consumers' buying power and willingness to spend. Political decisions are enacted and interpreted by courts. Regulatory agencies are created and operated by elected or appointed officials. Technology determines how members of society satisfy needs and wants and helps to improve the quality of life. Sociocultural forces are the influences in a society that bring about changes in attitudes, beliefs, norms, customs and lifestyles. Changes in any of these forces can create opportunities and threats for marketers.

LO2 DESCRIBE THE STRATEGIC PLANNING PROCESS AND HOW IT IS AFFECTED BY ORGANISATIONAL RESOURCES AND OPPORTUNITIES.

Through the process of strategic planning, a company identifies or establishes its organisational mission and goals, corporate strategy and marketing goals, marketing strategy and marketing plan. To achieve its marketing goals, an organisation must develop a marketing strategy, which includes identifying target market segments and developing a plan of action for developing, distributing, promoting and pricing products that meets the needs of customers in that target market. Customer relationship management (CRM) focuses on using information about customers to create marketing strategies that develop and sustain desirable customer relationships. By increasing customer value over time, organisations try to retain and increase long-term profitability through customer loyalty. The strategic planning process ultimately yields the framework for a marketing plan, which is a written document that specifies the activities to be performed for implementing and controlling an organisation's marketing activities.

When the right combination of circumstances and timing permits an organisation to take action toward reaching a particular target market segment, a market opportunity exists. Strategic windows are temporary periods of optimal fit between the key requirements of a market and the particular capabilities of a company competing in that market. When a company matches a core competency to opportunities it has discovered in the marketplace, it is said to have a competitive advantage.

 **LO3** UNDERSTAND THE PROCESS OF CREATING A MARKETING PLAN.

The outcome of marketing planning is the development of a marketing plan, which outlines all the activities necessary to implement marketing strategies. The plan fosters communication among employees, assigns responsibilities and schedules, specifies how resources are to be allocated to achieve objectives and helps marketing managers monitor and evaluate the performance of a marketing strategy.

 **LO4** DESCRIBE THE MARKETING IMPLEMENTATION PROCESS AND THE MAJOR APPROACHES TO MARKETING IMPLEMENTATION.

Marketing implementation is the process of executing marketing strategies. Marketing strategies do not always turn out as expected. Realised marketing strategies often differ from the intended strategies because of issues related to implementation. Proper implementation requires efficient organisational structures and effective control and evaluation.

One major approach to marketing implementation is internal marketing, a management philosophy that coordinates internal exchanges between the organisation and its employees to achieve successful external exchanges between the organisation and its customers. For marketing implementation to be successful, the needs of both internal and external customers must be met. Integrating socially responsible and ethical behaviours into marketing strategy is also an important approach to marketing implementation.

 **LO5** EXPLAIN HOW TO INCORPORATE ETHICS AND SOCIAL RESPONSIBILITY INTO MARKETING STRATEGY.

Ethics relates to individual and group decisions and judgements about what is right or wrong in a particular situation. *Social responsibility* deals with the total effect of marketing decisions on society. The two concepts are key to a marketing strategy because a company that supports socially responsible decisions and adheres to a code of conduct is likely to have a positive effect on society.

Key concepts

Use these key terms in **Search me! marketing** to find the latest relevant readings from a wide range of world-class journals, e-books and newspapers, including *The Australian*.

- brand competitors
- business cycle
- buying power
- centralised organisation
- codes of conduct
- competition
- competitive advantage
- core competencies
- corporate strategy
- decentralised organisation
- discretionary income
- disposable income
- environmental analysis
- environmental scanning
- external customers
- generic competitors
- internal customers
- internal marketing
- market
- market-growth/market-share matrix
- market opportunity (SBU)
- market share
- marketing control process
- marketing implementation
- marketing objective
- marketing plan
- marketing planning
- marketing strategy
- mission statement
- monopolistic competition
- monopoly
- oligopoly
- performance standard
- product competitors
- pure competition

- sociocultural forces
- strategic business unit
- strategic planning
- strategic windows
- sustainable competitive advantage
- SWOT analysis
- total budget competitors
- willingness to spend

Issues for discussion and review

1 What types of factors are marketers seeking to identify in environmental scanning and analysis?

2 Identify several environmental issues that impact on marketers' planning and describe the impact

3 What are the four types of competition? Which is the most important to marketers?

4 Define *income*, *disposable income* and *discretionary income*.

5 How can economic conditions impact a buyer's willingness to spend?

6 Describe the role of the ACCC. What Acts does is administer?

7 How is the Advertising Standards Bureau, and its role, different to that of the ACCC?

8 What are the two major components of a marketing strategy?

9 What is an organisation's competitive advantage?

10 How is the SWOT analysis used in the marketing planning process?

11 Define a marketing goal and the information it should include.

12 Why is it said that selecting the target market is the most important decision a company makes?

13 How can an organisation make its competitive advantages sustainable over time? How difficult is it to create sustainable competitive advantages?

14 What are the four ways that a marketing unit can be organised within a company?

15 What are the major steps of the marketing control process?

16 What problems are often experienced in controlling marketing activities?

17 Are 'ethics' and 'social responsibility' in marketing the same thing?

Marketing applications

1 Choose an organisation that you think is very successful. Look at the company's website, or conduct an Internet search, to identify their mission statement and their organisational goals. Obtain as much information as possible about these. Discuss how well the statement matches the criteria outlined in the text.

2 Australians and New Zealanders love a good coffee! Imagine that you have sourced some delicious beans from Brazil and decided to import them to roast to make wonderful coffee at your own, new, café. Your new specialty coffee café will open for business in about six months. Write a mission statement for your specialty coffee café, formulate a long-term goal for the company, and then develop short-term goals that will assist you in achieving your long-term goal. Describe the core competencies that will be necessary.

3 Assume that three years have gone by since you opened your new specialty coffee café. You've been very successful – you've started importing coffee beans to sell to both wholesale and retail customers. You sell 20 different coffee blends and you have

opened 30 new specialty coffee cafés in capital cities of Australia, New Zealand and the United Kingdom. You need to sort out your marketing unit.

  a Discuss the ways that you might organise your marketing unit.

  b Discuss how the organisation of your marketing unit might differ from the organisation of the marketing unit of a bank such as ANZ (anz.com.au).

4 Identify an organisation in your community that has a reputation for being ethical and socially responsible. What activities account for this image? How does the company convey this information to its customers and the market?

ONLINE EXERCISE

5 Market Lane Coffee is a small business with a well-organised and informative website. Visit their website at http://www.marketlane.com.au.

  a Based on the information provided on the website, describe Market Lane Coffee's range of products and services.

  b Compare Market Lane Coffee to other coffee retailers and wholesalers (http://www.vittoriacoffee.com, http://www.proudmarycoffee.com.au, http://www.nespresso.com) and describe the company's primary competitive advantage. How does Market Lane Coffee's website support this competitive advantage?

  c Assess the quality and effectiveness of Market Lane Coffee's website. Specifically, perform a preliminary SWOT analysis comparing Market Lane Coffee's website with other high-quality websites you have visited.

Developing your marketing plan

One of the foundations of a successful marketing strategy is a thorough analysis of the company itself. To make the best decisions about what products to offer, which market segments to target and how to reach them, you need to know more about a company's strengths and weaknesses. The information collected in this analysis should be referenced when making many of the decisions in your marketing plan. When thinking about writing the beginning of your plan, the information in this chapter can help you with the following issues.

1 Describe the current competitive market for a product and company of your choice. Can you identify the number of brands or market share that they hold? Expand your environmental analysis to include other products that are similar or could be substituted for yours.

2 Using the business cycle pattern, in which of the four stages is the current state of the economy? Can you identify any changes in consumer buying power that would affect the sale and use of your chosen product?

3 Conduct a brief technology assessment, determining the impact that technology has on your product, its sale or use.

4 Discuss how your product could be affected by changes in social attitudes, demographic characteristics or lifestyles.

5 Can you identify the core competencies of your company? Do they currently contribute to a competitive advantage? If not, what changes could your product's company make in order to establish a competitive advantage?

6 Conduct a SWOT analysis of your product's company in order to identify its strengths and weaknesses. Continue your analysis to include the business environment, discovering any opportunities that exist, or threats that may impact your company.

7 Using the information from your SWOT analysis, have you identified any opportunities that are a good match with your product's company core competencies? Likewise, have you discovered any weaknesses that could be converted to strengths through careful marketing planning?

CengageNOW

Go to http:\\login.cengagebrain.com to link to CengageNOW, your online study tool. First take the Pre-Test for this chapter to get your Personalised Study Plan, and then:

❋ **Revise** your understanding of the key concepts of marketing with the online glossary

❋ **Watch** an interactive animation of strategic marketing to broaden your subject comprehension

❋ **Listen** to an audio summary of the learning objectives covered in this chapter.

After you have completed the activities in your Personalised Study Plan take the Post-Test to determine what concepts you have mastered and what you still need to work on.

Case study

STORMY RIDE FOR QUEENSLAND'S TOURISM INDUSTRY

Tourism businesses in Queensland have experienced a stormy ride in the past few years. First there was the global financial crisis, then a series of cyclones that caused terrible damage in the state's north. For example, in 2011, Cyclone Yasi, together with the worst floods in Queensland in 50 years, resulted in a $590 million fall in tourism revenue alone. The extensive media coverage of the floods and Cyclone Yasi contributed to the mass cancellations and loss of revenue. Unfortunately, tourism businesses in regions not impacted by the disaster also suffered from cancellations and drops in future bookings as well as revenue.[61] In January 2013, the world's media was again distributing images of flood-ravaged Queensland. Tropical Cyclone Oswald hit the Queensland coast, leaving many regions devastated. Some of these communities were still trying to re-build after the floods of

Source: Shutterstock.com

2010/2011, so the impact of the 2013 floods was particularly devastating. The Tourism Industry Council, together with Queensland Tourism, are trying to stop the build-up of a public image of flood-ravaged Queensland with promotional messages featuring the 'Queensland is open to tourists' theme and reminding potential travellers that a vacation in the Sunshine State would be a good idea.[62]

Tropical cyclones are a natural part of Queensland's tropical climate, and according to the Bureau of Meteorology, there are, on average, 4.7 tropical cyclones each year (the cyclone season is between November and April). Unfortunately, the Queensland environment (and economy) has suffered from many major disasters since Cyclone Yasi: multiple instances of serious flooding, bushfires and severe storms (for details and geographical locations see http://disaster.qld.gov.au/Financial%20Support/Activations.html). To improve Queensland's crisis preparedness, a new 'Get Ready' disaster preparedness campaign was launched in October 2013, urging everyone to be more prepared for extreme weather. The aim of this campaign was to reduce the impact of extreme weather as well as help communities bounce back quicker after a disaster.

The materials are available online as well in the high school Business Study curriculum.[63] Furthermore, a mobile phone app 'Ready, Set Go!', designed to help Queensland tourism businesses to be better prepared for extreme weather, was launched in November 2013.[64]

Unfortunately, these natural disasters came at a time when the tourism industry was already struggling due to the strong Australian dollar reducing the competitiveness of Queensland as a travel destination for both domestic as well as overseas visitors.[65] Yet natural disasters are just one of the issues Queensland tourism businesses have to address. For example, campaigners for new all-inclusive casino resorts claim that without the proposed 5–6-star casino resorts, Queensland as a travel product would become marginalised with run-down and eroded facilities.[66] Queensland tourism operators are also learning that their new target market, the Chinese tourists, do not necessarily appreciate travel packages that were originally created for Japanese and Korean visitors.[67] Asian tourists are named as a key target market in the *Future of Tourism in Queensland* plan. Other major trends identified in this plan are that future tourists have high expectations for authentic experiences, and the enhanced importance of electronic word-of-mouth (eWOM) in holiday decision making.[68]

Tourism is one of the four pillars of the Queensland economy (together with agriculture, construction and resources) as well as being a key contributor to Queensland's economy with an estimated total of $22.4 billion in expenditure in the 2012–2013 financial year.[69] This is a 7.0 per cent contribution to Queensland's gross state product (GSP) and the industry employs over 10 per cent of Queenslanders.[70] The Queensland Government prepared a 20-year plan for the state's tourism industry, in consultation with industry stakeholders. The plan is ambitious; the aim is to make Queensland Australia's number one destination and to double overnight visitor expenditure to $30 billion by 2020.[71]

OPRAH'S ULTIMATE AUSTRALIAN ADVENTURE

Oprah Winfrey, a famous TV talk-show host, brought 302 of her ultimate fans, 200 crew members and almost 200 journalists to visit and experience several Australian tourism destinations in late 2010. Over eight days they recorded more than 700 hours' worth of footage and the best scenes were selected for a series of four *Oprah* shows which were screened in the US and Australia in January 2011. To capitalise on the excitement generated, key Australian tourism organisations joined together to produce some Ultimate Australian Adventure holiday packages. The *Oprah* showcase on Australia was very popular in the US, with an audience of 10 million.

From the idea to take a holiday to actually taking the trip takes time. However, Tourism Australia was pleased to report an increase in Americans taking a holiday in Australia, when the 2012 arrival statistics revealed the greatest number of American tourists since the Sydney Olympics.[72]

Outi Niininen, La Trobe University

Outi Niininen, La Trobe University

QUESTIONS FOR DISCUSSION

1 Conduct a SWOT analysis for the Queensland tourism industry.

2 What are some promotions that could reduce the negative image created by the news reports of the natural disasters?

3 The lead time between intention to have a holiday/booking a holiday and the start of the holiday is long.
   a What circumstances could cause tourists to cancel the planned vacation? What could tourism businesses do to reduce the probability of mass cancellations of bookings if a nearby region is impacted by a disaster?
   b How can tourism authorities justify big expenditures like hosting the Oprah Winfrey show when the revenue from this investment is not likely to be evident until a few years later? In your opinion, should tourism authorities or other governmental departments fund such ventures?

4 What are some methods to reduce the negative image created by Twitter and Facebook discussions of natural disasters?

Chapter endnotes

1. Blair Speedy, 'Aldi eyes $2bn expansion as chain outperforms rivals,' *The Australian*, March 30, 2013. Accessed October 28, 2013. http://www .theaustralian.com.au/business/aldi-eyes-2bn -expansion-as-chain-outperforms-rivals/story-e6frg8zx -1226609203004#sthash.YAIzIIT2.dpuf; Lucy Battersby, 'Woolies braced for fight,' *Sydney Morning Herald*, March 5, 2013. Accessed October 28, 2013 http://www .smh.com.au/business/woolies-braced-for-fight-20130304 -2fgwy.html.

2. 'Dotcom Bust,' *Economist*, January 28, 2012, 66.

3. P. Varadarajan, Terry Clark, and William M. Pride, 'Controlling the Uncontrollable: Managing Your Market Environment,' *Sloan Management Review* (Winter 1992): 39–47.

4. 'Carbonated Soft-Drinks Suffer Setback in 2005, Beverage Marketing Corporation Reports,' Beverage Marketing Corporation press release, April 2006, http://www. beveragemarketing.com/news2zz.htm

5. O. C. Ferrell and Michael Hartline, *Marketing Strategy* (Mason, OH: South-Western, 2008), 58; http://online.wsj .com/article/SB10001424127887323783704578245973 076636056.html

6. Ferrell and Hartline, *Marketing Strategy*, 58.

7. Ibid.

8. Andrew Burrell, 'Miners take up fight against tax,' *The Australian*, September 4, 2010. http://www.theaustralian. com.au/national-affairs/miners-take-up-fightagainst-rent -tax-again/story-fn59niix-1225914015218.

9. Sarah Ellison, 'Why Kraft Decided to Ban Some Food Ads to Children,' *The Wall Street Journal*, Octboer 31, 2005. Accessed November 3, 2009. http://www .commercialalert.org/news/archive/2005/10/small -biteswhy-kraft-decided-to-ban-some-food-adsto -children.

10. 'Australia's self-regulated alcohol advertising scheme,' Alcohol Advertising Review Board, accessed October 28, 2013. http://www.alcoholadreview.com.au/key-concerns /australias-current-selfregulatory-system/.

11. 'Values overtake sex in complaints about ads,' Advertising Standards Bureau. http://post.cre8ive.com .au/t/ViewEmail/r/BB87E1CDB3075619.

12. Gwen Moran, 'Top New Marketing Trends,' MSNBC, August 7, 2006, http://www.msnbc.msn.com /id/14231013/.

13. Nick Clayton, 'Social Networks Account for 20% of Time Spent Online,' *The Wall Street Journal*, December 22, 2011, accessed January 13, 2012. http://blogs.wsj.com /techeurope/2011/12/22/social-networks-account-for-20 -of-time-spent-online/.

14. Debbie McAlister, Linda Ferrell, and O. C. Ferrell, *Business and Society* (Mason, OH: South-Western Cengage Learning, 2011), 352–353.

15. Thorne, Ferrell, and Ferrell, *Business and Society*, Third Edition, New York: Houghton Mifflin Co., 2008, 36.

16. Jamin Brophy-Warren, 'The New Examined Life,' *Wall Street Journal* (December 6–7, 2008): W1, W11; Tom Hayes and Michael S. Malone, 'Marketing in the World of the Web,' *Wall Street Journal* (November 29–30, 2008): A13; Jessica E. Vascellaro, 'Facebook Aims to Connect Its Users to Other Sites,' *Wall Street Journal* (December 5, 2008): B4.

17. '3301.0 Births, Summary statistics for Australia,' ABS. http://www.abs.gov.au/ausstats/abs@.nsf/mf/3301.0

18. '3201.0 – Population by Age and Sex, Australian States and Territories, Jun 2010,' ABS.

19. O. C. Ferrell and Michael Hartline, *Marketing Strategy* (Mason, OH: South-Western, 2008), 10.

20. Christian Homburg, Karley Krohmer, and John P. Workman, Jr., 'A Strategy Implementation Perspective of Market Orientation,' *Journal of Business Research* 57 (2004): 1331–1340.

21. Ferrell and Hartline, *Marketing Strategy*, 10.

22. Abraham Lustgarten, 'iPod,' in 'Breakaway Brands,' *Fortune* (October 31, 2005): 154–156.

23. Derek F. Abell, 'Strategic Windows,' *Journal of Marketing* (July 1978): 21

24. Jack Ewing, 'Music Phones Tackle the iPod,' *BusinessWeek Online*, July 11, 2006. http://www.businessweek.com.

25. Ibid.

26. 'Designed to Grow,' *Procter & Gamble Annual Report*, (2007): 5, http://thomson.mobular.net/thomson/7/2481/2810/.

27. Cláudia Simões, Sally Dibb, and Raymond P. Fisk, 'Managing Corporate Identity,' *Journal of the Academy of Marketing Science* 33 (April 2005): 154–168.

28. 'Ben & Jerry's Mission,' accessed January 16, 2012. www.benjerry.com/activism/mission-statement/

29. Jefferson Graham, 'Google Cues Up with YouTube,' *USA Today* (October 10, 2006): 1A.

30. Thomas Ritter and Hans Georg Gemünden, 'The Impact of a Company's Business Strategy on Its Technological Competence, Network Competence and Innovation Success,' *Journal of Business Research* 57 (2004): 548–556.

31. 'Designed to Grow,' *Procter & Gamble Annual Report*, (2007), 4–5, http://thomson.mobular.net/thomson/7/2481/2801.

32. Stanley F. Slater, G. Tomas M. Hult, and Eric M. Olson, 'On the Importance of Matching Strategic Behavior and Target Market Selection to Business Strategy in High-Tech Markets,' *Journal of the Academy of Marketing Science* 35 (2007): 5–17.

33. 'Cadbury officially Australia's favourite chocolate,' *Food Magazine*, March 30, 2012. http://www.foodmag.com.au /news/cadbury-officially-australia-s-favourite-chocolate; 'Cadbury under its new parent Mondelez gets bitter taste of slowdown,' *The Economic Times*, June 7, 2013. http://

articles.economictimes.indiatimes.com/2013-06-07 /news/39815428_1_cadbury-india-toblerone-ceo -irene-rosenfeld

34. Robert D. Buzzell, 'The PIMS Program of Strategy Research: A Retrospective Appraisal,' *Journal of Business Research* 57 (2004): 478–483.

35. Joseph P. Guiltinan and Gordon W. Paul, *Marketing Management: Strategies and Programs* (New York: McGraw-Hill, 1991), 43.

36. George S. Day, 'Diagnosing the Product Portfolio,' *Journal of Marketing* (April 1977): 30–31.

37. Isabelle Maignan, O. C. Ferrell, and Linda Ferrell, 'A Stakeholder Model for Implementing Social Responsibility in Marketing,' *European Journal of Marketing* 39 (September/October 2005): 956–977.

38. Maignan, Ferrell, and Ferrell, 'A Stakeholder Model for Implementing Social Responsibility in Marketing.'

39. G. Tomas, M. Hult, David W. Cravens, and Jagdish Sheth, 'Competitive Advantage in the Global Marketplace: A Focus on Marketing Strategy,' *Journal of Business Research* (January 2001): 1–3.

40. Kwaku Atuahene-Gima and Janet Y. Murray, 'Antecedents and Outcomes of Marketing Strategy Comprehensiveness,' *Journal of Marketing* (October 2004): 33–46.

41. Christian Homburg, John P. Workman, and Ove Jensen, 'Fundamental Changes in Marketing Organization: The Movement Toward a Customer-Focused Organizational Structure,' *Journal of the Academy of Marketing Science* (Fall 2000): 459–478.

42. 'Amazon.com 2011 Annual Report,' Amazon, accessed March 20, 2012, 37. http://phx.corporate-ir.net/phoenix .zhtml?c=97664&p=irol-reportsannual.

43. Jack Neff, 'Tissues Fit for the Toilet,' *Advertising Age* (November 27, 2006): 31.

44. Rajdeep Grewal and Patriya Tansuhaj, 'The Chain of Effects from Brand Trust and Brand Affect to Brand Performance: The Role of Brand Loyalty,' *Journal of Marketing* (April 2001): 67–80.

45. 'About Us,' BioPak. http://www.biopak.com.au/about_us .php?PHPSESSID=c944883c101fcf73bd049d1c1d726d0e

46. Robert W. Palmatier, Lisa K. Scheer, and Jan-Benedict E.M. Steenkamp, 'Customer Loyalty to Whom? Managing the Benefits and Risks of Salesperson-Owned Loyalty,' *Journal of Marketing Research* XLIV (May 2007). http://www .marketingpower.com.

47. V. Kumar, 'Customer Relationship Management,' custom module for William M. Pride and O. C. Ferrell, *Marketing*, 14th ed. (Boston: Houghton Mifflin, 2006), http://www .prideferrell.com.

48. Chezy Ofir and Itamar Simonson, 'The Effect of Stating Expectations on Customer Satisfaction and Shopping Experience,' *Journal of Marketing Research* XLIV (February 2007), http://www.marketingpower.com.

49. V. Kumar, J. Andrew Peterson, and Robert P. Leone, 'The Power of Customer Advocacy,' in Jean L. Johnson and John Hulland (eds.), (2006): AMA Winter Educators' Conference, *Marketing Theory and Applications* 17 (Winter 2006), 81–82.

50. John Wieseke, Michael Ahearne, Son K. Lam, and Rolf von Dick, 'The Role of Leaders in Internal Marketing,' *Journal of Marketing* 73 (March 2009): 123–145.

51. Ian N. Lings, 'Internal Market Orientation: Construct and Consequences,' *Journal of Business Research* 57 (2004): 405–413.

52. Sybil F. Stershic, 'Internal Marketing Campaign Reinforces Service Goals,' *Marketing News* (July 31, 1998): 11.

53. Stefan Ambec and Paul Lanoie, 'Does It Pay to Be Green? A Systematic Overview,' *Academy of Management Perspective* 22, no. 4 (November 2008): 47; Mary K. Pratt, 'The High Cost of Ethics Compliance,' *ComputerWorld*, August 24, 2009, accessed November 21, 2011. www .computerworld.com/s/article/341268/ Ethics_Harder _in_a_Recession.

54. Ferrell and Hartline, *Marketing Strategy.*

55. 'Home Page,' REI, http://www.rei.com.

56. Kathleen Cholewka, 'CRM: Lose the Hype and Strategize,' *Sales & Marketing Management* (June 2001): 27–28.

57. Peter Verhoef and Peter S. H. Leeflang, 'Understanding the Marketing Departments' Influence within the Firm,' *Journal of Marketing* 73 (March 2009): 14–37.

58. Bernard J. Jaworski, 'Toward a Theory of Marketing Control: Environmental Context, Control Types, and Consequences,' *Journal of Marketing* (July 1988): 23–39.

59. Bruce R. Gaumnitz and John C. Lere, 'Contents of Codes of Ethics of Professional Business Organizations in the United States,' *Journal of Business Ethics* 35 (2002): 35–49.

60. Sir Adrian Cadbury, 'Ethical Managers Make Their Own Rules,' *Harvard Business Review* (September/ October 1987): 33.

61. Scott Richardson, Roger March, Jan Lewis, & Kylie Radel, 'Analysing the impact of the 2011 natural disasters on the Central Queensland tourism industry,' *TEAM Journal of Hospitality and Tourism*, 9(1), 1–14. Accessed November 22, 2013. http://teamjournalht.files.wordpress .com/2013/05/team-edsprvrev-p1-14.pdf

62. Ava Benny-Morrison, 'Concerns about Qld tourism industry amid disaster recovery,' *The Chronicle*, February 1, 2013, accessed November 22, 2013. http://www .thechronicle.com.au/news/concerns-about-qld-tourism -industry-amid-disaster/1738686/; 'Flood disaster unfolds as weather wreaks havoc,' updated April 26 2013, accessed November 22, 2013. http://www.abc .net.au/news/2013-01-28/qld-flooding-alert-moves -south/4486666; 'Australia: Tropical Cyclone Oswald /Floods - Information bulletin n° 1,' accessed November 22, 2013. http://reliefweb.int/report/australia /australia-tropical-cyclone-oswaldfloods-information -bulletin-n%C2%B0-1#sthash.O4IrduDE.dpuf; 'Australia: Tropical Cyclone Oswald/Floods, Information

bulletin n° 1,' Red Cross, February 5, 2013, accessed November 22, 2013. http://ifrc.org/docs/Appeals/rpts13 /IBcyOS050213.pdf.

63. Adam Davies, 'Residents urged to 'get ready' as disaster program launches,' October 15, 2013, accessed November 22, 2013. http://www.qt.com.au/news /residents-urged-get-ready-disaster-program -launch/2052226/; 'Get Ready Queensland,' September 11, 2013, accessed November 22, 2013. http://www .stormwise.com.au/tags/get-ready-queensland.

64. 'How prepared is your business for severe weather conditions?' Queensland Tourism Industry Council, October 29, 2013, accessed November 22, 2013. http:// www.qtic.com.au/news/how-prepared-your-business -severe-weather-conditions.

65. 'Editorial: We need more than sun to lure tourists to Queensland, *The Courier-Mail*, October 22, 2013, accessed November 22, 2013. http://www.couriermail.com.au /news/opinion/editorial-we-need-more-than-sun-to-lure -tourists-to-queensland/story-fnihsr9v-1226744099361.

66. Amy Remeikis, 'Queensland tourism 'bleak' without casino vision,' *Brisbane Times*, October 15, 2013, accessed November 22, 2013. http://www.brisbanetimes.com.au /travel/travel-news/queensland-tourism-bleak-without -casino-vision-campbell-newman-20131014-2vj12. html#ixzz2IKIQGNy8.

67. 'Editorial: We need more than sun to lure tourists to Queensland, *The Courier-Mail*.

68. Stefan Hajkowicz, Hannah Cook, and Naomi Boughen, 'Future of Tourism in Queensland plan,' CSIRO Futures, March 18, 2013 | Updated 26 August 2013, accessed November 22, 2013. http://www.csiro.au/en/Portals /Partner/Futures/Future-of-Tourism-in-QLD.aspx.

69. 'Editorial: We need more than sun to lure tourists to Queensland, *The Courier-Mail*.

70 'Tourism and Queensland's economy,' Queensland Government, accessed November 22, 2013. http:// www.business.qld.gov.au/industry/tourism/tourism-in- queensland/queenslands-tourism-industry/tourism-and- queenslands-economy.

71. 'Developing the Queensland Tourism 20 Year Plan,' Destination Q, accessed November 22, 2013. http:// www.destq.com.au/20-year-plan; Stefan Hajkowicz, Hannah Cook, and Naomi Boughen, 'Future of Tourism in Queensland plan.'

72. Angela Saurine, 'Oprah effect pays off with rise in US tourist visiting Australia,' News Corp Australia Network, December 6, 2012, accessed November 22, 2013. http:// www.news.com.au/travel/australian-holidays/oprah-effect -pays-off-with-rise-in-us-tourist-visiting-australia/story -e6frfq89-1226530747845.

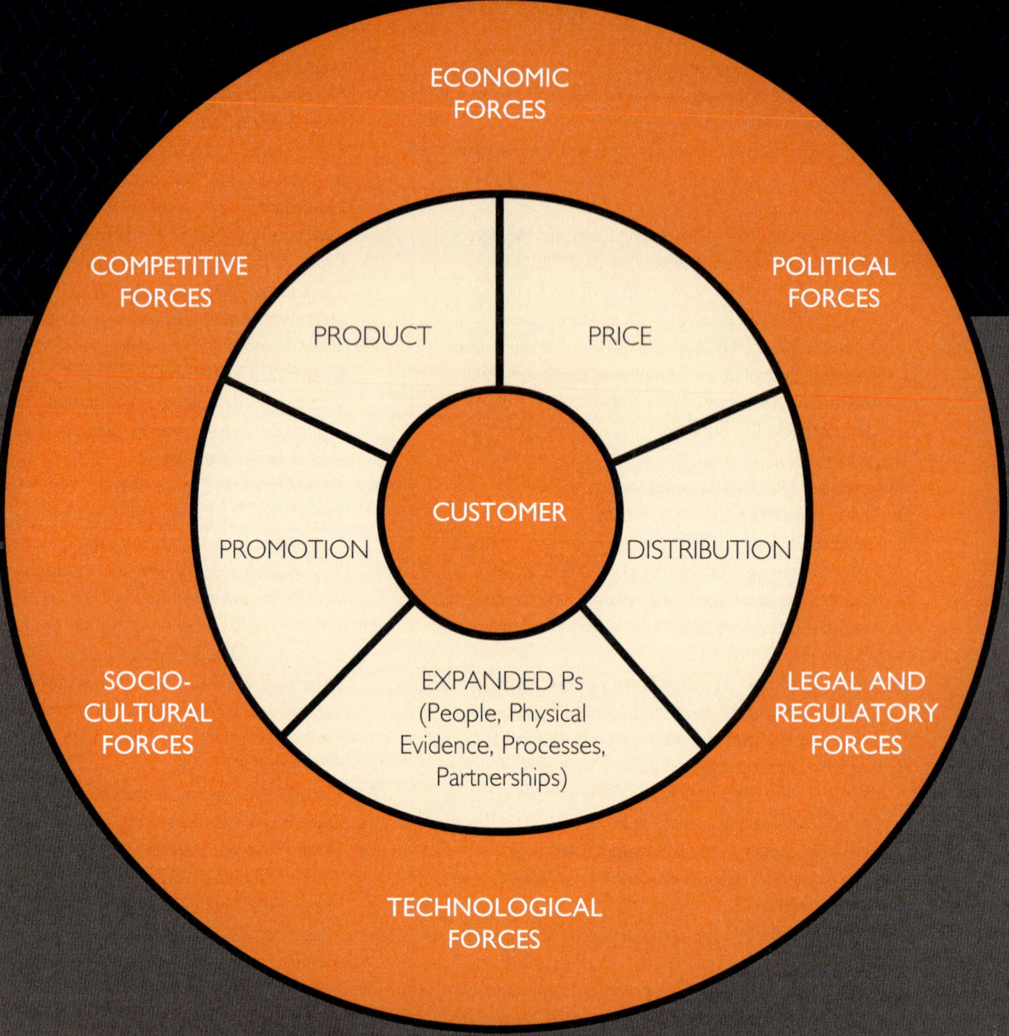

ECONOMIC
FORCES

COMPETITIVE
FORCES

POLITICAL
FORCES

PRODUCT

PRICE

CUSTOMER

PROMOTION

DISTRIBUTION

SOCIO-
CULTURAL
FORCES

EXPANDED Ps
(People, Physical
Evidence, Processes,
Partnerships)

LEGAL AND
REGULATORY
FORCES

TECHNOLOGICAL
FORCES

MARKETING RESEARCH AND INFORMATION SYSTEMS

The importance of marketing research

Marketing research process
Determine the scope
Select the method
Collect and prepare the data
Analyse the data
Transform analysis results into insights

Technology and data analysis
Marketing information systems
Databases
Marketing decision support systems

Issues in marketing research
Ethical marketing research
International issues

Throughout this chapter, Watch, Listen and Revise icons indicate an opportunity for online self-study through CengageNOW, linking you to animated chapter overviews, interactive diagrams, videos, quizzes and more.

3

MARKETING RESEARCH AND INFORMATION SYSTEMS

Learning Objectives

LO1 Define marketing research and understand its importance

LO2 Describe the basic steps in conducting marketing research

LO3 Understand the fundamental methods of gathering data for marketing research

LO4 Describe how tools such as databases, decision support systems and the Internet facilitate marketing information systems and research

LO5 Identify key ethical and international considerations in marketing research.

MARKETING CHALLENGE | SOCIAL MEDIA'S ROLE IN INFORMATION SYSTEMS

Source: Getty Images

Social media has given consumers a powerful new voice with which to communicate directly with businesses about their products, brand and ideas. While many businesses are still using social media as simply another communication channel, for what Avinash Kaushik, Google's Analytics Evangelist, describes as 'shout' marketing, smart businesses have realised that social media provides them with an extraordinary opportunity to better understand their customers.

A recent report by Harvard Business Review Analytics Surveys found that businesses that are effectively using social media are benefitting from a range of information. Businesses' use includes: monitoring what is being said about the business, better understanding customer perceptions of their brand, identifying new product and service opportunities, measuring how frequently the brand is discussed and as an early warning system for product or service issues. One survey respondent explained 'Social media tells you whether people like a TV commercial without waiting for their buying behaviours to show you'.

The principal social media channels being used by businesses are social networks like Facebook (87%), blogs (58%), multimedia sharing websites such as YouTube (58%),

85

micro-blogs like Twitter (53%) and review websites and discussion forums (22%). Businesses who are using social media effectively are likely to use four or more different channels.

The challenge for business marketers is to keep up with the proliferation of social media tools, to understand what they want to accomplish with their use of social media and to effectively capture and measure the benefits to the business of what they are doing.[1]

MARKETING CHALLENGE QUESTION

1   From a businesses' perspective, which social media channel do think is most powerful in generating customer insights? Why?

Introduction

Implementing the marketing concept requires that marketers obtain data about the characteristics, needs and desires of target-market customers. When used effectively, such data helps marketers to focus their efforts on meeting, and even anticipating, the needs of their customers. Marketing research that can provide practical and objective information to help companies develop and implement marketing strategies is essential to effective marketing and being market-oriented.

In this chapter we focus on how marketers gather data needed to make marketing decisions. First, we define marketing research and examine the individual steps of the marketing research process, including various methods of collecting data. Next, we look at how technology aids in collecting, organising and interpreting marketing research data. Finally, we consider ethical and international issues in marketing research.

The importance of marketing research

marketing research
The systematic design, collection and interpretation of data, as well as the reporting of the insights gained to help marketers solve specific marketing problems or take advantage of marketing opportunities

Marketing research is the systematic design, collection and interpretation of marketing-related data, as well as the reporting of the insights that were gained to help marketers solve specific marketing problems or take advantage of marketing opportunities. As the word 'research' implies, it is a process for gathering marketing insights not currently available to decision makers. The purpose of marketing research is to inform an organisation about competitors, customers' needs and desires, marketing opportunities for particular goods and services, and changing attitudes and purchase patterns of customers. Marketing research increases marketers' ability to respond to customer needs, which leads to improved organisational performance.[2] Detecting shifts in buyers' behaviours and attitudes helps companies to stay in touch with the ever-changing marketplace. Strategic planning requires marketing research to facilitate the process of assessing such opportunities or threats.

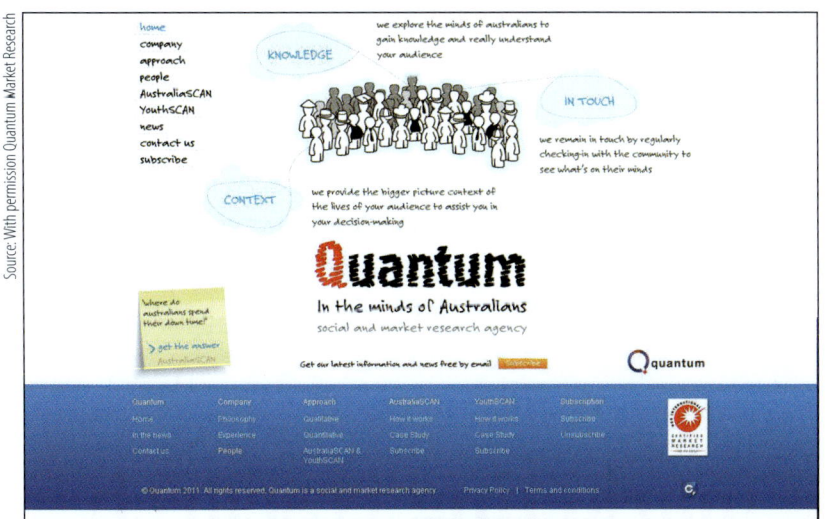

<< **Importance of marketing research**
Quantum provides services to help companies better understand their customers' needs

The real value of marketing research is measured by improvements in a marketer's ability to make decisions. Marketing research conducted for large office-product warehouse stores (often called big box office suppliers; think of OfficeWorks), for example, highlighted problems with many store layouts, which were confusing shoppers, and helped executives to make decisions to improve the layout. As a result, big box office suppliers are replacing grid-like aisles with a less cluttered 'racetrack' layout that gives shoppers a clear view all the way to the back wall and invites them to peruse expensive electronics showcased inside a main aisle that loops inside each store.[3] Marketers should treat data in the same manner as they use other resources, and they must weigh the costs of obtaining insights against the benefits derived (see Marketing in Action box below for one such investment in gaining consumer insights). Information should be judged worthwhile if it results in marketing activities that better satisfy the company's target customers, leads to increased sales and profits or helps the company to achieve some other goal.

MARKETING IN ACTION | THE BILLBOARD OF THE FUTURE

Traditionally, when a person looks at a billboard, information goes one way: from billboard to consumer. However, new marketing research technology now allows information to go two ways. The consumer collects information from the billboard's message, and the billboard in turn collects information about the consumer. In Japan, digital billboards have been invented that estimate a consumer's age and gender. Based on the estimated age and gender, the display then creates advertising tailored to the appropriate demographic. An East

Japan Railway subsidiary introduced vending machines with this technology that use information gleaned from consumers to suggest drinks. Similar billboards are appearing across the world. In the US, marketers are creating displays that recognise gestures and facial expressions of consumers. This data can determine whether the consumer is actually looking at the display. In Australia, Streets ice-cream brand Magnum have launched their new flavoured line through the use of interactive billboards which utilise facial recognition, enabling viewers to interactively eat the ice-cream. For marketers, the technology can help them understand who is attracted to their messages and perhaps create customised messages for each consumer based upon this data collection. However, privacy advocates are wary of this technology. They fear that it can be misused to identify people, a violation of individual privacy. So far there is little regulation to limit how marketers will use information collected from billboards. As this technology becomes more popular, clearer laws will be needed to allow marketers to gather information without abusing consumer privacy.[4]

The marketing research process

To maintain the control needed to obtain accurate information, marketers approach marketing research as a process with logical steps as shown in Figure 3.1: (1) determining the scope for marketing research, (2) selecting the research method, (3) collecting and preparing the data, (4) analysing the data and (5) transforming the analysis results into insights. These steps should be viewed as an overall approach to conducting research rather than as a rigid set of rules to be followed in each project. In planning research projects, marketers must consider each step carefully and determine how they can best adapt them to resolve the particular issues at hand.

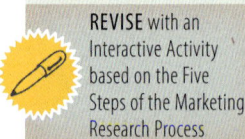

REVISE with an Interactive Activity based on the Five Steps of the Marketing Research Process

FIGURE 3.1 THE FIVE STEPS OF THE MARKETING RESEARCH PROCESS

1 Determining the scope for marketing research → 2 Selecting the research method → 3 Collecting and preparing the data → 4 Analysing the data → 5 Transforming the analysis results into insights

Determine the scope for marketing research

The first step in launching a research study is issue or problem definition, which focuses on uncovering the nature and boundaries of a situation or question related to marketing strategy or implementation. The first sign of a problem is typically a departure from some normal function, such as failure to attain objectives. If a corporation's objective is a 12 per cent sales increase and the current marketing strategy resulted in a six per cent increase, this discrepancy should be analysed to help guide future marketing strategies. Declining sales, increasing expenses and decreasing profits also signal problems. Armed with this knowledge, a company could define a problem as finding a way to adjust for biases stemming from existing customers when gathering data or to develop methods for gathering data to help find new customers. Conversely, when an organisation experiences a dramatic rise in sales or some other positive event, it may conduct marketing research to discover the reasons and maximise the opportunities stemming from them.

Marketing research often focuses on identifying and defining market opportunities or changes in the environment. When a company discovers a market opportunity, it may need to conduct research to understand the situation more precisely so that it can craft an appropriate marketing strategy. For example, Cisco, an international IT company, saw an opportunity to appeal to a $34 billion market of businesses that wished to engage in collaborative projects. Cisco conducted marketing research to determine that it would take three to five years to build a good reputation among businesses that use the Internet and want to collaborate online. Cisco also discovered that it needed to customise software utilised by specific users and to avoid introducing products too similar to ones already sold by competitors.[5] The company can use this information to focus its efforts on specific target markets and to refine its marketing strategy appropriately.

To pin down the specific boundaries of a problem or an issue through research, marketers must define the nature and scope of the situation in a way that requires probing beneath the superficial symptoms. The interaction between the marketing manager and the marketing researcher should yield a clear definition of the research need and a statement of the research question(s). Researchers and decision makers should remain in the scoping stage until they have determined precisely what they want from marketing research and how they will use it. Deciding how to refine a broad, indefinite issue or problem into a precise, researchable question, or set of questions, is a prerequisite for the next step in the research process.

Select the research method

Once the problem or issue has been defined, the next step is research design, an overall plan for obtaining the data needed to address it. This step requires determining what type of research is most appropriate for answering the research question(s).

Types of research

The nature and type of research varies based on the research design and the hypotheses under investigation. Marketers may elect to conduct either exploratory, descriptive or experimental research. While each has distinct purposes, the major differences between them are formalisation and flexibility rather than the specific research methods used.

When marketers need more data about a problem or situation, they may conduct exploratory research. They may also conduct exploratory research to make a tentative hypothesis more specific. A hypothesis is an informed guess or assumption about a certain problem or set of circumstances.

The main purpose of exploratory research is to better understand a problem, situation or hypothesised relationship. Another purpose is to help identify additional data needs or decision alternatives.[6] Consider that until recently there was no research available to help marketers understand how consumers perceive the term 'clearance' versus the term 'sale' in describing a discounted-price event. An exploratory study asked one group of 80 consumers to write down their thoughts about a store window sign that said 'sale' and

research design
An overall plan for obtaining the data needed to address a research problem or issue

exploratory research
Research conducted to gather more data about a problem or to make a tentative hypothesis more specific

hypothesis
An informed guess or assumption about a certain problem or set of circumstances

another group of 80 consumers about a store window sign that read 'clearance'. The results revealed that consumers expected deeper discounts when the term clearance was used, and they expected the quality of the clearance products to be lower than that of products on sale.[7] This exploratory research helped marketers to better understand how consumers view these terms and opened up the opportunity for additional research hypotheses about decision alternatives for retail pricing.

If marketers need to understand the characteristics of certain phenomena to solve a particular problem, descriptive research can aid them. Such studies may range from general surveys of customers' education, occupation or age to specific surveys on how often teenagers eat at fast-food restaurants after school or how often customers buy new pairs of athletic shoes. For example, if Nike and Reebok want to target more young women, they might ask 15- to 35-year-old females how often they work out, how frequently they wear athletic shoes for casual use and how many pairs of athletic shoes they buy in a year. Such descriptive research can be used to develop specific marketing strategies for the athletic shoe market. Descriptive studies generally demand much prior knowledge and assume that the issue or problem is clearly defined. Some descriptive studies require statistical analysis and predictive tools. The marketer's major task is to choose adequate methods for collecting and measuring data.

Descriptive research is limited in providing the evidence necessary to make causal inferences (i.e., that variable x causes a variable y). Experimental research allows marketers to make causal deductions about relationships.[8] Such experimentation requires that an independent variable (one not influenced by or dependent on other variables) be manipulated and the resulting changes in a dependent variable (one contingent on, or restricted to, one value or set of values assumed by the independent variable) be measured. For example, when Coca-Cola introduces new and innovative beverage products (such as Mother or Dasani flavoured waters), managers identify test markets (such as a particular supermarket or city suburb) to estimate sales at various potential price points for the new product. By holding variables such as advertising and shelf position constant, Coca-Cola can manipulate the price variable upward or downward to study its effect on sales. For example, if sales do not increase when prices are reduced in a test market, then managers can make an informed decision about the most effective price point for the new product. Coca-Cola could also use experimental research to manipulate other variables such as advertising or in-store shelf position to determine their effect on sales. Manipulation of the causal variable and control of other variables is what makes experimental research unique. As a result, it can provide much stronger evidence of cause and effect than data collected through descriptive research.

Research reliability and validity

In designing research, marketing researchers must ensure that research techniques are both reliable and valid. A research technique has reliability if it produces almost identical results in repeated trials. But a reliable technique is not necessarily valid. To have validity, the research method must measure what it is supposed to measure, not something else. For example, although a group of customers may express the same level of satisfaction based on a rating scale, the individuals may not exhibit the same repurchase behaviour because of different personal characteristics. This result might cause the researcher to question the validity of the satisfaction scale if the purpose of rating satisfaction was to estimate potential repurchase behaviour.[9] Kellogg's, for example, has found that much research focuses on the wrong measures. In doing research on packaging, Kellogg's discovered that side-by-side comparisons of different packages did not provide a measure of validity as good as shopping behaviour in a virtual supermarket. Using an alternative research method, package alternatives were tested on potential shoppers using a virtual supermarket shelf.[10] Repeated trials generated similar results, which proved the reliability of this alternative measuring technique.

Collect and prepare the data

The next step in the marketing research process is collecting data. The research design must specify what types of data to collect and how they will be collected.

Types of data

Marketing researchers have two types of data at their disposal. Primary data are observed and recorded or collected directly from respondents. These data must be gathered by observing phenomena or surveying people of interest. Secondary data are compiled both inside and outside the organisation for some purpose other than the current investigation. Secondary data include general reports supplied to an enterprise by various data services and internal and online databases. Such reports might concern market share, retail inventory levels and customers' buying behaviour. Secondary data are commonly available in private or public reports or have been collected and stored by the organisation itself. Given the opportunity to obtain data via the Internet, more than half of all marketing research now comes from secondary sources.

Sources of secondary data

Marketers often begin the data-collection phase of the marketing research process by gathering secondary data. They may use available reports and other data from both internal and external sources to study a marketing problem.

Internal sources of secondary data can contribute tremendously to research. An organisation's own database may contain data about past marketing activities, such as sales records and times of the year but also which colours and sizes

WATCH an interactive animation on the market research process

LO3

primary data
Data observed and recorded or collected directly from respondents

secondary data
Data compiled both inside and outside the organisation for some purpose other than the current investigation

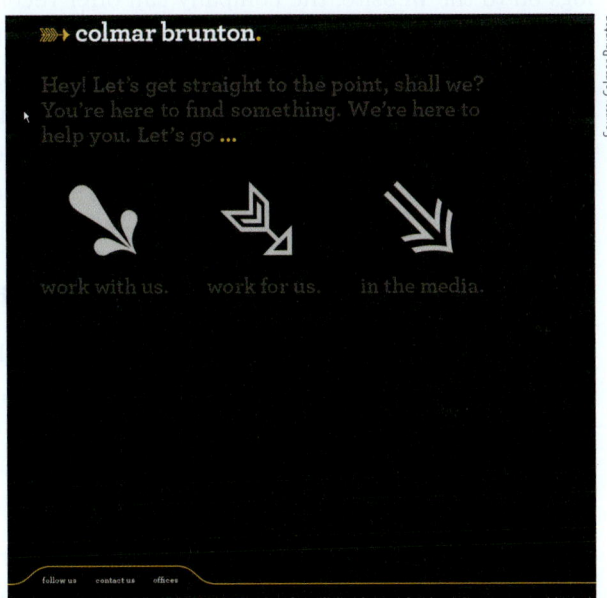

Source: Colmar Brunton

<< Primary data collection
Colmar Brunton works with companies to collect primary data

customers preferred. BMW maintains a corporate intranet system as part of its database collection and access strategy. This system allow field staff to routinely access retailer financials, check vehicle supply and delivery statuses, and view marketing information for such things as advertising and prospecting.[11] Such data may have been gathered using customer relationship management (CRM) tools for marketing, management or financial purposes. Table 3.1 lists some commonly available internal company information that may be useful for marketing research purposes.

TABLE 3.1   INTERNAL SOURCES OF SECONDARY DATA

Sales data, which may be broken down by geographic area, product type or even type of customer
Accounting data, such as costs, prices and profits by product category
Competitive information gathered by the sales force

Accounting records are also an excellent source of data but, strangely enough, are often overlooked. The large volume of data an accounting department collects does not automatically flow to other departments. As a result, detailed data about costs, sales, customer accounts or profits by product category may not be easily accessible to the marketing area. This condition develops particularly in organisations that do not store marketing data on a systematic basis.

External sources of secondary data include periodicals, government publications, unpublished sources and online databases. In addition, companies may subscribe to services such as Nielsen or Roy Morgan Research, which track retail sales and other data.

The Internet can be especially useful to marketing researchers. As we've already seen, search engines such as Google can help marketers locate many types of secondary data or research topics of interest. Of course, companies can mine their own websites for useful data using CRM tools. Amazon.com, for example, has built a relationship with its customers by tracking the types of books, music and other products they purchase. Each time a customer logs on to the website, the company can offer recommendations based on the customer's previous purchases. Such a marketing system helps the company track the changing desires and buying habits of its most valued customers. And marketing researchers are increasingly monitoring blogs to discover what consumers are saying about their products – both positive and negative. Some companies have even established their own blogs in order to monitor consumer dialogue on issues of their choice. Social networking websites have also become an important source of primary marketing research data.

Methods of collecting primary data

The collection of primary data is a more lengthy, expensive and complex process than the collection of secondary data. To gather primary data, researchers use sampling procedures, exploratory methods, survey methods and observation. These efforts can be handled in-house by the company's own research department or contracted to a private research company.

SAMPLING PROCEDURES

population
All the elements, units or individuals of interest to researchers for a specific study

Because the time and resources available for research are limited, it is almost impossible to investigate all the members of a target market or other population. A population, or 'universe', includes all the elements, units or individuals of interest to researchers for a specific study. By systematically choosing a limited number of units – a sample – to represent the characteristics of a total population, researchers can project the reactions of a total market or market segment. Sampling in marketing research, therefore, is the process of selecting representative units from a total population. Sampling techniques allow marketers to predict buying behaviour fairly accurately on the basis of the responses from a representative portion of the population of interest. Most types of marketing research employ sampling techniques.

There are two basic types of sampling: probability sampling and non-probability sampling. With probability sampling, every element in the population being studied has a known chance of being selected for study. Random sampling is a kind of probability sampling. When marketers employ random sampling, all the units in a population have an equal chance of appearing in the sample. The various events that can occur have an equal or known chance of taking place. For example, a specific card in a regulation deck should have a 1 in 52 probability of being drawn at any one time. Sample units ordinarily are chosen by selecting from a table of random numbers statistically generated so that each digit, 0 through 9, will have an equal probability of occurring in each position in the sequence. The sequentially numbered elements of a population are sampled randomly by selecting the units whose numbers appear in the table of random numbers.

Another kind of probability sampling is stratified sampling, in which the population of interest is divided into groups according to a common attribute, and a random sample is then chosen within each group. The stratified sample may reduce some of the error that could occur in a simple random sample. By ensuring that each major group or segment of the population receives its proportionate share of sample units, investigators avoid including too many or too few sample units from each group. Samples are usually stratified when researchers believe that there may be variations among different types of respondents. For example, many political opinion surveys are stratified by gender, race, age and/or geographic location.

The second type of sampling, non-probability sampling, is more subjective than probability sampling because there is no way to calculate the likelihood that a specific element of the population being studied will be chosen. Quota sampling, for example, is highly judgemental because the final choice of participants is left to the researchers. In quota sampling, researchers divide the population into groups and then arbitrarily choose participants from each group. A study of people who wear eyeglasses, for example, may be conducted by interviewing equal numbers of men and women who wear eyeglasses. In quota sampling, there are some controls – usually limited to two or three variables, such as age, gender or race – over the selection of participants. The controls attempt to ensure that representative categories of respondents are interviewed. Because quota samples are not probability samples, not everyone has an equal chance of being selected, and sampling error therefore cannot be measured statistically. Quota samples are used most often in exploratory studies, when hypotheses are being developed. Often a small quota sample will not be projected to the total population, although the findings may provide valuable insights into a problem. Quota samples are useful when people with some common characteristics are found and questioned about the topic of interest. A probability sample used to study people allergic to cats would be highly inefficient.

sample
A limited number of units chosen to represent the characteristics of the population

sampling
The process of selecting representative units from a total population

probability sampling
A sampling technique in which every element in the population being studied has a known chance of being selected for study

random sampling
A type of probability sampling in which all units in a population have an equal chance of appearing in a sample

stratified sampling
A type of probability sampling in which the population is divided into groups according to a common attribute, and a random sample is then chosen within each group

non-probability sampling
A sampling technique in which there is no way to calculate the likelihood that a specific element of the population being studied will be chosen

quota sampling
A non-probability sampling technique in which researchers divide the population into groups and then arbitrarily choose participants from each group

EXPLORATORY METHODS

Often before a survey can be conducted, the marketer or researcher needs to explore what the full breadth of the research issue might be. Basically, the objective is to calibrate a subsequent survey to the extent that all issue-dimensions are uncovered upfront before the survey is designed. A survey is not suitable for exploration; it is more suitable as a descriptive research tool.

Once all the dimensions are revealed, a survey can be designed around what the exploration revealed. This way a survey is most likely to be comprehensive and truly describe all aspects of the research issue. One such exploratory method is a focus group. Other methods include customer advisory boards and telephone depth interviews.

The purpose of a focus group interview is to observe the breadth of group interactions in a focus group when group members are exposed to an idea or a concept. Media companies, including Microsoft and Yahoo, conduct joint focus groups to explore the full range of advertising formats suitable for their purposes. Often focus groups are conducted informally, without a structured questionnaire, in small groups of eight to 12 people. They allow customer attitudes, behaviours, lifestyles, needs and desires to be explored in a flexible and creative manner. Questions are open-ended and stimulate respondents to answer in their own words. Researchers can ask probing questions to clarify something they do not fully understand or something unexpected and interesting that may help to explain ideas. Even the prime minister of Australia uses focus groups to examine ideas.

It may be necessary to use separate focus groups for each major market segment studied – men, women and age groups – and experts recommend the use of at least two focus groups per segment in case one group is unusually idiosyncratic.[12] Focus groups have been found to be especially useful to set new product prices.[13] However, they generally provide only qualitative, not quantitative, data and therefore are best used to uncover issues that can then be explored using quantifiable marketing research techniques. Some criticism of focus groups comes from their failures. After using focus groups to conduct research, Tropicana released a new orange juice package. The new design provoked much negative feedback from loyal consumers who complained via emails and telephone calls. Some believe that utilising social networking websites such as Twitter, which could have gotten the response of hundreds of people nearly instantly, would have been a better and more reliable source of information on the package redesign.[14]

More organisations are starting customer advisory boards, which are small groups of actual customers who serve as sounding boards for new product ideas and offer insights into their feelings and attitudes toward a company's products, promotion, pricing and other elements of marketing strategy. While these advisory boards help companies maintain strong relationships with valuable customers, they also can provide great insight into marketing research questions.[15] Also, Maxine Clark, CEO and founder of the Build-A-Bear Workshop, has run a customer advisory board with the purpose of staying in tune with what her customers want. She highly recommends that startups, in particular, found advisory boards, stating that this technique allows a company to focus immediately on what its consumer base truly wants.[16] In Australia, Coles has run a program where each month up to 2500 consumers across the country quality test products in their homes. A selection of Coles Brand products are tried and compared against other products, with feedback provided through a Coles online forum. As well as feedback on products, consumers tell

focus group interview
A research method involving observation of group interaction when members are exposed to an idea or a concept

customer advisory boards
Small groups of actual customers who serve as sounding boards for new product ideas and offer insights into their feelings and attitudes toward a company's products and other elements of marketing strategy

Coles what the stores, customer service and product packaging are like, and they can share anything else they want about Coles generally.[17]

Still another option is the telephone depth interview, which combines the traditional focus group's ability to probe with the confidentiality provided by telephone surveys. This type of interview is most appropriate for a small targeted group that is difficult to bring together for a traditional focus group because of members' profession, location or lifestyle. Respondents can choose the time and day for the interview. Although this method is difficult to implement, it can yield revealing data from respondents who otherwise would be unwilling to participate in marketing research.[18]

SURVEY METHODS

Marketing researchers often collect primary data through mail, telephone, online or personal interview surveys. The results of such surveys are used to describe buying behaviour. Selection of a survey method depends on the nature of the problem or issue and the data needed to test the hypothesis and the resources, such as funding and personnel, available to the researcher. Marketers may employ more than one survey method depending on the goals of the research. Table 3.2 summarises and compares the advantages of some survey methods.

telephone depth interview
An interview that combines the traditional focus group's ability to probe with the confidentiality provided by telephone surveys

TABLE 3.2 COMPARISON OF THE FOUR BASIC SURVEY METHODS

	Mail surveys	Telephone surveys	Online surveys	Personal interview surveys
Economy	Potentially lower in cost per interview than telephone or personal surveys if there is an adequate response rate.	Avoids interviewers' travel expenses; less expensive than in-home interviews.	The least expensive method if there is an adequate response rate.	The most expensive survey method; shopping centre and focus group interviews have lower costs than in-home interviews.
Flexibility	Inflexible; questionnaire must be short and easy for respondents to complete.	Flexible because interviewers can ask probing questions, but observations are impossible.	Less flexible; survey must be easy for online users to receive and return; short, dichotomous, or multiple-choice questions work best.	Most flexible method; respondents can react to visual materials; demographic data are more accurate; in-depth probes are possible.
Interviewer bias	Interviewer bias is eliminated; questionnaires can be returned anonymously.	Some anonymity; may be hard to develop trust in respondents.	Interviewer bias is eliminated, but email address on the return eliminates anonymity.	Interviewers' personal characteristics or inability to maintain objectivity may result in bias.
Sampling and respondents' cooperation	Obtaining a complete mailing list is difficult; non-response is a major disadvantage.	Sample limited to respondents with telephones; devices that screen calls, busy signals and refusals are a problem.	Sample limited to respondents with computer access; the available email address list may not be a representative sample for some purposes.	Not-at-homes are a problem, which may be overcome by focus group and shopping centre interviewing.

Gathering data through surveys is becoming increasingly difficult because fewer people are willing to participate.[19] Many people believe that responding to surveys takes up too much scarce personal time, especially as surveys become longer and more detailed. Others have concerns about how much data marketers are gathering and whether their privacy is being invaded. The unethical use of selling techniques disguised as marketing surveys has also led to decreased cooperation. These factors contribute to non-response rates for any type of survey. Most researchers consider non-response the greatest threat to valid survey research.[20]

In a mail survey, questionnaires are sent to respondents, who are encouraged to complete and return them. Mail surveys are used most often when the individuals in the sample are spread over a wide area and funds for the survey are limited. A mail survey is potentially the least expensive survey method as long as the response rate is high enough to produce reliable results. The main disadvantages of this method are the possibilities of a low response rate and of misleading results if respondents differ significantly from the population being sampled. Research has found that providing a monetary incentive to respond to a mail survey has a significant impact on response rates for both consumer and business samples. However, such incentives may reduce the cost-effectiveness of this survey method.[21] As a result of these issues, companies are increasingly moving to Internet surveys and automated telephone surveys, as discussed below.

In a telephone survey, an interviewer records respondents' answers to a questionnaire over the phone. A telephone survey has some advantages over a mail survey. The rate of response is higher because it takes less effort to answer the telephone and talk than to fill out and return a questionnaire. If there are enough interviewers, a telephone survey can be conducted very quickly. Thus political candidates or organisations seeking an immediate reaction to an event may choose this method. In addition, a telephone survey permits interviewers to gain rapport with respondents and ask probing questions. Automated telephone surveys, also known as interactive voice response surveys or 'robosurveys', rely on a recorded voice to ask questions while a computer program records respondents' answers. The primary benefit of automated surveys is the elimination of 'bias' introduced by a live researcher.

However, only a small proportion of the population likes to participate in telephone surveys. Moreover, telephone surveys are limited to oral communication; visual aids or observation cannot be included. Many households are excluded from telephone directories by choice (unlisted numbers) or because the residents moved after the directory was published. Potential respondents often use telephone answering machines, voicemail, or caller ID to screen or block calls; many have signed up for 'do not call lists'. Moreover, an increasing number of younger Australians have given up their fixed phone lines in favor of

Source: With permission J W T Melbourne

mobile phones. These issues have serious implications for the use of telephone samples in conducting surveys.

Online surveys are evolving as an alternative to mail and telephone surveys. In an online survey, questionnaires can be transmitted to respondents who have agreed to be contacted and have provided their email addresses. More companies are using their websites to conduct surveys. Online surveys also can make use of online communities – such as chat rooms, Internet-based forums and newsgroups – to identify trends in interests and consumption patterns.

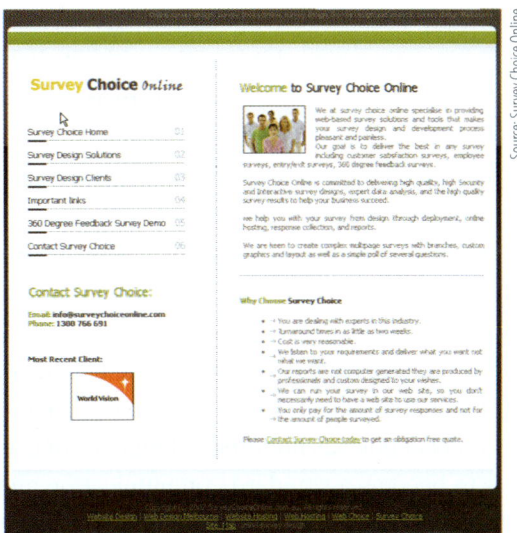

Source: Survey Choice Online

online survey
A research method in which respondents answer a questionnaire via email or on a website

<< Online surveys
surveychoiceonline provides its customers with research delivered by a readily available online survey

Movies, consumer electronics, food and computers are popular topics in many online communities.[22] Indeed, by 'listening in' on these ongoing conversations, marketers may be able to identify new product opportunities and consumer needs. Dell provides employee training in 'social listening', which focuses on listening to online community conversations. Moreover, this type of online data can be gathered at little incremental cost compared with alternative data sources.[23] Evolving technology and the interactive nature of the Internet allow for considerable flexibility in designing questionnaires for online surveys.

One application of online surveys is crowdsourcing. Crowdsourcing combines the words *crowd* and *outsourcing* and takes tasks usually performed by a marketer or researcher and outsources them to a crowd, or potential market, through an open call, usually online. Consider Google, who run an annual 'Doodle for Google' competition, of which the winner has their entry displayed on the Google home page for a day. McDonald's crowdsourced the images that feature on their promotional packaging via online competitions. There are also entire websites dedicated to crowdsourcing. On www.threadless.com, participants can submit and score T-shirt designs. Designs with the highest votes are printed and then sold. Crowdsourcing is a way for marketers to gather input straight from willing consumers and to actively listen to people's ideas and evaluations on products. Dell has used crowdsourcing to tap into consumer insights and to spur innovations in everything from new products to website design and marketing improvements.

crowdsourcing
A research method that combines the words crowd and outsourcing. Crowdsourcing is usually performed by a marketer or researcher who outsources a research question to a crowd, or potential market, through an open call, usually online

Marketing research in the future is likely to rely heavily on online surveys. Furthermore, as negative attitudes toward telephone surveys render that technique less representative and more expensive, the integration of email, fax and voicemail functions into one computer-based system provides a promising alternative for survey research. Email surveys have especially strong potential within organisations whose employees are networked and for associations that publish members' email addresses. University students, in particular, are willing to provide their email address and other personal information in exchange for incentives such as T-shirts and other giveaways.[24] However, there are some ethical issues to consider when using email for marketing research, such as unsolicited email, which could be viewed as 'spam', and privacy, because some potential survey respondents fear that their personal information will be given or sold to third parties without their knowledge or permission.

Social networking websites are a common way for marketers to conduct research. Online social networks function similarly to traditional social networks in that they are often used to gather useful data in understanding consumer decisions. Twitter, Facebook, LinkedIn and Instagram are some of the most popular social networking websites. They reduce the effort and cost of staying in touch with people. Research using online social networking websites can be a good substitute for focus groups (as illustrated in the Marketing in Transition box below). Once a person gathers his or her friends online, they can do the same things they have traditionally done around the neighbourhood. Friends online can share photos, videos, brands they like and even complete product satisfaction evaluations.

Facebook has hundreds of millions of users and continues to grow. The goal of Facebook is to become a standard communication and marketing platform, similar to the telephone, but more interactive and multidimensional. The website can be used for asking about, or providing insights on, desirable features of a new product. Facebook, LinkedIn, Twitter and Pinterest have all become a place from which market researchers can derive useful information.

In a personal interview survey, participants respond to questions face to face. Various audiovisual aids – pictures, products, diagrams or prerecorded advertising copy – can be incorporated in a personal interview. Rapport gained through direct interaction usually permits more in-depth interviewing, including probes, follow-up questions or psychological tests. In addition, because personal interviews can be longer, they may yield more information. Finally, respondents can be selected more carefully, and reasons for non-response can be explored.

One such research technique is the in-home (door-to-door) interview. The in-home interview offers a clear advantage when thoroughness of self-disclosure and elimination of group influence are important. In an in-depth interview of 45 to 90 minutes, respondents can be questioned to reveal their real motivations, feelings, behaviours and aspirations.

The nature of personal interviews has changed. In the past, most personal interviews, which were based on random sampling or prearranged appointments, were conducted in the respondent's home. Today, most personal interviews are conducted outside the home.

social networking websites
Used to gather useful data in understanding consumer decisions

personal interview survey
A research method in which participants respond to survey questions face to face

in-home (door-to-door) interview
A personal interview that takes place in the respondent's home

MARKETING IN TRANSITION | NIELSEN COMPANY OFFERS VALUABLE INSIGHTS FOR MARKETERS

As one of the world's largest global marketing research firms, the Nielsen Company focuses on marketing information; trade shows; and online, television, mobile and other media measurements. Nielsen's Consumer Buy segment collects information on consumer buying patterns through devices such as retail measurements and consumer panels. Nielsen's most well-known device, its people meter, records participating households' TV viewing behaviour.

Such data are important for TV stations and advertisers. As more consumers embrace digital technology, Nielsen is evolving as well. The company has created many online programs to measure user behaviour through digital forums such as blogs and social media. The company has entered into a strategic alliance with MyWebGrocer to measure online supermarket sales in the US. Nielsen believes it will be able to measure approximately 30 per cent of all online supermarket sales in the US, making it an invaluable resource for companies in this industry. It also collects more than 20 million surveys each year related to marketing effectiveness. In addition, Neilson have formed a strategic alliance with Facebook as well as establishing subsidary company SocialGuide, which provides the first ever measure of the total reach of TV-related Twitter conversation. Nielsen's marketing research services provide valuable strategic insights for marketing decisions.[25]

Shopping-centre intercept interviews involve interviewing a percentage of individuals passing by certain 'intercept' points in a centre. As with any face-to-face interviewing method, shopping-centre intercept interviewing has many advantages. The interviewer is in a position to recognise and react to respondents' non-verbal indications of confusion. Respondents can be shown product prototypes, video of commercials and the like and asked for their reactions. The shopping centre environment lets the researcher deal with complex situations. For example, in taste tests, researchers know that all the respondents are reacting to the same product, which can be prepared and monitored from the centre's test kitchen. In addition to the ability to conduct tests requiring bulky equipment, lower cost and greater control make shopping-centre intercept interviews popular.

shopping-centre intercept interviews
A research method that involves interviewing a percentage of persons passing by 'intercept' points in a centre

QUESTIONNAIRE CONSTRUCTION

A carefully constructed questionnaire is essential to the success of any survey. Questions must be clear, easy to understand and directed toward a specific objective; that is, they must be designed to elicit data that meets the study's data requirements. Researchers need to define the objective before trying to develop a questionnaire because the objective determines the substance of the questions and the amount of detail. A common mistake in constructing questionnaires is to ask questions that interest the researchers but do not yield information useful in deciding whether to accept or reject a hypothesis. Finally, the most important rule in composing questions is to maintain impartiality.

The questions are usually of three kinds: open-ended, dichotomous and multiple-choice.

Open-ended question

What is your general opinion about broadband Internet access?

Dichotomous question

Can you imagine not having broadband access at home, work or school?

Yes _____ No _____

Multiple-choice question

What age group are you in?

Under 20   ____

20–35   ____

36 and over ____

Researchers must be very careful about questions that a respondent might consider too personal or that might require an admission of activities that other people are likely to condemn. Questions of this type should be worded to make them less offensive.

OBSERVATION METHODS

In using observation methods, researchers record individuals' overt behaviour, taking note of physical conditions and events. Direct contact with them is avoided; instead, their actions are examined and noted systematically. For instance, researchers might use observation methods to answer the question, 'How long does the average McDonald's restaurant customer have to wait in line before being served?' Observation may include the use of ethnographic techniques, such as watching customers interact with a product in a real-world environment.

To increase its ability to observe consumer behaviour, Time Warner opened a media lab in New York equipped with eye-tracking stations, a home theatre, a mock retail store with a checkout and gaming stations. The lab tries to simulate a real-world environment to test how consumers would react naturally to different forms of media. Researchers can watch the proceedings from observation rooms in the lab. Observation may also be combined with interviews. For instance, during a personal interview, the condition of a respondent's home or other possessions may be observed and recorded. The interviewer can also directly observe and confirm such demographic information as race, approximate age and gender. In addition to observation rooms, the Time Warner lab also has areas for focus group interviews.[26]

Data gathered through observation can sometimes be biased if the person is aware of the observation process. However, an observer can be placed in a natural market environment, such as a supermarket, without biasing or influencing shoppers' actions. If the presence of a human observer is likely to bias the outcome, or if human sensory abilities are inadequate, mechanical means may be used to record behaviour. Mechanical observation devices include cameras, recorders, counting machines, scanners and equipment that records physiologic changes. (See also the Sustainable Marketing box on the next page, which has an example of mechanical observation derived data on consumer recycling habits.) The electronic scanners used in supermarkets are very useful in marketing research. They provide accurate data on sales and customers' purchase patterns, and marketing researchers may obtain such data from the supermarkets.

Observation is straightforward and avoids a central problem of survey methods: motivating respondents to state their true feelings or opinions. However, observation tends to be descriptive. When it is the only method of data collection, it may not provide

Source: JRA Australia

Interpreting research >>
Companies like JRA can help interpret the data collected from market research and offer insights into the areas investigated

insights into causal relationships. Another drawback is that analysis based on observation is subject to the biases of the observer or the limitations of the mechanical device.

Analyse the data

After collecting data, marketers need to analyse their data in order to be able to interpret the data content. Interpretation of the data is easier if marketers carefully plan their data analysis methods early in the research process. They also should allow for continual evaluation of the data during the entire collection period. They can then gain valuable insight into areas that should be probed during the formal interpretation.

The first step in drawing conclusions from most research is to display the data in table format. If marketers intend to apply the results to individual categories of the things or people being studied, cross-tabulation may be quite useful, especially in tabulating joint occurrences. For example, using the two variables gender and purchase rates of car tyres, a cross-tabulation could show how men and women differ in purchasing car tyres.

After the data are tabulated, they must be analysed. Statistical interpretation focuses on what is typical or what deviates from the average. It indicates how widely responses vary and how they are distributed in relation to the variable being measured. When marketers interpret statistics, they must take into account estimates of expected error or deviation from the true values of the population. The analysis of data may lead researchers to accept or reject the hypothesis being studied.

statistical interpretation
Analysis of what is typical or what deviates from the average

SUSTAINABLE MARKETING | MESSAGE IN A BOTTLE: SECONDARY DATA PROVIDE RECYCLING LESSONS

Many marketing problems can be analysed through secondary data. An example of secondary data related to social responsibility and ethical conduct is the branded-water market. Leading companies such as Coca-Cola, Nestlé and PepsiCo are gathering data on the current impact of discarded plastic bottles on the environment. Australians are known for their success in household recycling with, for example, far more than 50 per cent of the beverage containers used at home being recycled. However, Australian consumer behaviour is not the same away from home. The recycling rate in public bins is much lower with public recyclable waste comprising far less than 50 per cent.

In response to this observed consumer behaviour, Coca-Cola has invested significantly in public education and the benefits of recycling, especially in public places. This investment and focus on changing consumer behaviour habits in terms of recycling efforts, however, is slow to take effect. Beverage companies, such as Coca-Cola, must rethink and develop new strategies to deal with the problem that their products are creating. In this case, secondary data are providing information about the issues associated with plastic beverage bottles not only to beverage companies but also to consumer groups, regulatory officials and other stakeholders concerned with ecology and the environment. More recently, and seemingly in contrast to their pro-recycling educational efforts, Coca-Cola has bid to dismantle the existing Northern Territory bottle deposit recycling scheme and they oppose the future construction of similar recycling schemes in other states. Their argument is that it is unfair to Coca-Cola consumers to have to pay the additional 10c in order for the scheme to be operational. In retaliation, protests took to social media channels such as Facebook and Twitter, with Greenpeace releasing an anti-Coca-Cola YouTube clip. It raises the question of corporate responsibility. Is Coca-Cola inclined to protect their customers, or the wider environment?[27]

Transform the analysis results into insights

The final step in the marketing research process is to transform the analysis results into insights that can be reported. Before preparing the report, the marketer must take a clear, objective look at the findings to see how well the gathered facts answer the research question or support or negate the initial hypotheses. In most cases it is extremely unlikely that the study can provide everything needed to answer the research question. Therefore, the researcher must point out the deficiencies, along with the reasons for them, in the report.

The report of research results is usually a formal, written document. Researchers must allow time for the writing task when they plan and schedule the project. Because the report is a means of communicating with the decision makers who will use the research findings, researchers need to determine beforehand how much detail and supporting data to include. They should keep in mind that corporate executives prefer reports that are short, clear and simply expressed. Researchers often give their summary and recommendations first, especially if decision makers do not have time to study how the results were obtained. A technical report allows its users to analyse data and interpret recommendations because it describes the research methods and procedures and the most important data gathered. Therefore researchers must recognise the needs and expectations of the report user and adapt to them.

Using technology to improve data analysis

The ability of marketers to track customer buying behaviour and to discern what buyers want is changing the nature of marketing. Customer relationship management is being enhanced by integrating data from all customer contacts to improve customer retention. Information technology permits internal research and quick information generation to understand and satisfy customers. For example, company responses to email complaints, as well as to communications through mail, telephone and fax, can be used to improve customer satisfaction, retention and value.[28] Armed with such insights, marketers can fine-tune marketing mixes to satisfy the needs of their customers.

Source: © comScore, Inc.

>> **Using technology**
comScore uses advanced marketing research technology to assist clients

The integration of telecommunications and computer technologies is allowing marketers to access a growing array of valuable data sources related to industry forecasts, business trends and customer buying behaviour. Electronic communication tools can be used effectively to gain accurate insights with minimal customer interaction. Most marketing researchers have email, voicemail, teleconferencing and fax machines at their disposal. In fact, many companies use marketing information systems and customer relationship management technologies to network all these technologies and organise all the marketing data available to them. In this next section we look at marketing information systems and specific technologies that are helping marketing researchers obtain and manage marketing research data.

Marketing information systems

A marketing information system (MIS) is a framework for the day-to-day management and structuring of data gathered regularly from data sources both inside and outside an organisation. An MIS provides a continuous flow of data on prices, advertising expenditures, sales, competition and distribution expenses.

The main focus of the MIS is on data storage, data retrieval and data processing, as well as on computer capabilities and management's information requirements. Regular reports of sales by product or market categories, processed data on inventory levels and records of salespeople's activities are examples of data that are useful in making decisions. In the MIS, the means of *gathering* data receive less attention than do the procedures for *processing* the data to create meaningful insights and expediting the *flow* of these insights.

An effective MIS starts by determining the objective of collecting particular data, that is, by identifying decision needs that require certain information. The company can then specify an information system for continuous monitoring to provide regular, pertinent insights on both the external and internal environment. FedEx, for example, has developed interactive marketing systems to provide instantaneous communication between the company and its customers. Through use of the telephone and Internet, customers can track their packages and receive immediate feedback concerning delivery. The company's website provides valuable information about customer usage, and it allows customers to express directly what they think about company services. The evolving telecommunications and computer technology is allowing marketing information systems to cultivate one-to-one relationships with customers.

marketing information system (MIS)
A framework for the management and structuring of data gathered regularly from data sources inside and outside an organisation

Databases

Most marketing information systems include internal databases. They allow marketers to tap into and process an abundance of data useful in making marketing decisions: internal sales reports, newspaper articles, company media releases, government economic reports, bibliographies and more, all typically accessed through a computer system. Information technology has made it possible to develop databases to guide strategic planning and help improve customer services.

Customer relationship management (CRM) employs database marketing techniques to identify different types of customers and to develop specific strategies for interacting with each customer. CRM incorporates three elements:

1 Identifying and building a database of current and potential consumers, including a wide range of demographic, lifestyle and purchase data
2 Delivering differential messages according to each consumer's preferences and characteristics through established and new media channels
3 Tracking customer relationships to monitor the costs of retaining individual customers and the lifetime value of their purchases.[29]

It is important for marketers to distinguish between active customers – those likely to continue buying from the company – and inactive customers – those who are likely to defect, or already have defected. This information should (1) identify profitable inactive customers who can be reactivated (2) remove inactive, unprofitable customers from the customer database, and (3) identify active customers who should be targeted with regular marketing activities.[30]

Many commercial websites require consumers to register and provide personal data to access the website or make a purchase. Frequent-flyer programs permit airlines to ask loyal customers to participate in surveys about their needs and desires and to track their best customers' flight patterns by time of day, week, month and year. Also, supermarkets gain a significant amount of data through checkout scanners tied to store discount cards. In fact, one of the best ways to predict market behaviour is the analysis of data gathered through loyalty programs or other transaction-based processes.[31]

Marketing researchers can also use commercial databases developed by data base companies, such as LexisNexis, to obtain useful insights for marketing decisions. Many of these commercial databases are accessible online for a fee. They can also be obtained in printed form or digitally. In most commercial databases, the user typically does a computer search by keyword, topic or company, and the database service generates abstracts, articles or reports that can be printed out. Accessing multiple reports or a complete article may cost extra.

Regularly and systematically collected data by a research company on household demographics, purchases, television viewing behaviour and responses to promotions such as coupons and free samples are referred to as single-source data.[32] A single-source data base usually monitors consumer household televisions and records the programs and commercials watched. When buyers from these households shop in stores equipped with scanning registers, they present loyalty or store cards (similar to credit cards) to

single-source data
Regularly and systematically collected data by a research company on household demographics, purchases, television viewing behaviour and responses to promotions such as coupons and free samples

cashiers. Using these cards enables each customer to be electronically coded so that the research company can track each product purchased and store the data in a single-source database.

Marketing decision support systems

A marketing decision support system (MDSS) is customised computer software that aids marketing managers in decision making by helping them anticipate the effects of certain decisions. Some MDSSs have a broader range and offer greater computational and modelling capabilities than spreadsheets; they let managers explore a greater number of alternatives. For example, an MDSS can determine how sales and profits might be affected by higher or lower interest rates or how sales forecasts, advertising expenditures, production levels and so on might affect overall profits. For this reason, MDSS software often is a major component of a company's MIS. Customised decision support systems can support a customer orientation and customer satisfaction in business marketing.[33] Some MDSSs incorporate artificial intelligence and other advanced computer technologies.

marketing decision support system (MDSS)
Customised computer software that aids marketing managers in decision-making

LISTEN to this learning objective in an audio summary

Issues in marketing research

Marketers should identify concerns that influence the integrity of research. Ethical issues are a constant risk in gathering and maintaining the quality of information. International issues relate to environmental differences, such as culture, legal requirements, level of technology and economic development.

The importance of ethical marketing research

Marketing managers and other professionals are relying more and more on marketing research, marketing information systems and new technologies to make better decisions. It is therefore essential that professional standards be established by which to judge the reliability of such research. Such standards are necessary because of the ethical and legal issues that develop in gathering marketing research data. In the area of online interaction, for example, consumers remain wary of how the personal data collected by marketers will be used, especially whether it will be sold to third parties. In addition, the relationships between research suppliers, such as marketing research agencies, and the marketing managers who make strategy decisions require ethical behaviour. Organisations such as the Marketing Research Association, Australian Market & Social Research Society and Market Research Society of New Zealand have developed codes of conduct and guidelines to promote ethical marketing research. To be effective, such guidelines must instruct those who participate in marketing research on how to avoid misconduct. Table 3.3 recommends explicit steps interviewers should follow when introducing a questionnaire.

TABLE 3.3   GUIDELINES FOR QUESTIONNAIRE INTRODUCTION

A questionnaire's introduction should
Allow interviewers to introduce themselves by name.
State the name of the research company.
Indicate that this questionnaire is a marketing research project.
Explain that no sales will be involved.
Note the general topic of discussion (if this is a problem in a 'blind' study, a statement such as 'consumer opinion' is acceptable).
State the likely duration of the interview.
Ensure the anonymity of the respondent and the confidentiality of all answers.
State the honorarium if applicable (for many business-to-business and medical studies, this is done up front for both qualitative and quantitative studies).
Reassure the respondent with a statement such as, 'There are no right or wrong answers, so please give thoughtful and honest answers to each question' (recommended by many clients).

Source: Reprinted with permission of The Marketing Research Association, P.O. Box 230, Rocky Hill, CT 06067-0230, (860) 257-4008.

Consumer privacy has also become a significant issue. Firms now have the ability to purchase data on customer demographics, interests, and more personal matters such as bankruptcy filings and past marriages. This information has allowed companies to predict customer behaviour or current life changes more accurately but may also infringe upon consumer privacy.[34] The popularity of the Internet has also enabled marketers to collect data on Internet users who visit their websites. Many companies have been able to use this to their advantage. For instance, Amazon.com and eBay use data to make customised recommendations based on their customers' interests, ratings or past purchases. Companies such as Capital One Financial have used data collected by firms who specialise in tracking consumers' online behaviour. While such data enable companies to offer more personalised services, policy makers fear that it could also allow them to discriminate among consumers who do not appear to make 'valuable' customers.[35] Many consumers also believe that their online behaviour could be used to identify them personally. Google, for instance, collects and stores data from its users' searches. These search queries are kept indefinitely, although Google claims that the data is 'anonymised' after 18 months.[36] Internet privacy concerns have become so great that policy makers in the US have begun proposing a 'Do Not Track' bill for the Internet.

International issues in marketing research

Sociocultural, economic, political and technological forces vary in different regions of the world, and these variations create challenges for organisations attempting to understand foreign customers through marketing research. The marketing research process we describe in this chapter is used globally, but to ensure that the research is valid and reliable, data-gathering methods may have to be modified to allow for regional differences. For example, experts have found that Latin Americans do not respond well to focus groups or in-depth interviews lasting more than 90 minutes. Researchers therefore need to adjust their tactics to generate information useful for marketing products in Latin America.[37] To ensure that global and regional differences are addressed satisfactorily, many companies retain a research company with experience in the country of interest.

Experts recommend a two-pronged approach to international marketing research. The first phase involves a detailed search for and analysis of secondary data to gain greater understanding of a particular marketing environment and to pinpoint issues that must be taken into account in gathering primary research data. Secondary data can be particularly helpful in building a general understanding of the market, including economic, legal, cultural and demographic issues, as well as in assessing the risks of doing business in that market and in forecasting demand.[38] Marketing researchers often begin by studying a country's trade reports, as well as country-specific information from local sources, such as a country's website, and trade and general business publications. These sources can offer insight into the marketing environment in a particular country and can even indicate untapped market opportunities abroad.

The second phase involves field research using many of the methods described earlier, including focus groups and telephone surveys, to refine a company's understanding of specific customer needs and preferences. Specific differences among countries can have a profound influence on data gathering. For example, in-home (door-to-door) interviews are illegal in some countries. In developing countries, few people have regular telephone lines, making telephone surveys both impractical and non-representative of the total population. Furthermore, the collection of data from online sources raises privacy issues, as addressed in the Ethical Marketing box below. Primary data gathering may have a greater chance of success if the company employs local researchers who better understand how to approach potential respondents and can do so in their own language.[39] Regardless of the specific methods used to gather primary data, whether in Australia or abroad, the goal is to understand the needs of specific target market segments and thus craft the best marketing strategy to satisfy the needs of the target customers.

ETHICAL MARKETING   PRIVACY: WHERE DO YOU DRAW THE LINE ONLINE?   issue

Issue: Can online targeting go too far and compromise a person's right to privacy?

When consumers do an online search or download a digital coupon, marketers can follow their electronic movements. The purpose is to better target communications and tailor offers to customers' needs and interests. However, consumers are not always aware of what information is being gathered and how it will be used. 'Imagine that you were walking through a shopping mall, and there was someone that was walking behind you … taking notes on everywhere you went,' says the head of the Federal Trade Commission. Moreover, the data would be available 'to every shop or anyone who was interested, for a small fee'. Privacy advocates also worry about identity theft and whether marketers might restrict access to products based on consumers' online behaviour. As experts debate the limits of online privacy, regulators are formulating new protections and industry groups are developing new ways for consumers to opt out of tracking if they choose.[40]

Study Tools

Chapter review

 **LO1** DEFINE MARKETING RESEARCH AND UNDERSTAND ITS IMPORTANCE.

Marketing research is the systematic design, collection, interpretation and reporting of data to help marketers solve specific marketing problems or take advantage of marketing opportunities. Marketing research can help a company to better understand market opportunities, ascertain the potential for success for new products and determine the feasibility of a particular marketing strategy. The value of marketing research is measured by improvements in a marketer's ability to make decisions.

 LO2 DESCRIBE THE BASIC STEPS IN CONDUCTING MARKETING RESEARCH.

To maintain the control needed to obtain accurate data, marketers approach marketing research as a process with logical steps: (1) determining the scope for marketing research, (2) selecting the research method, (3) collecting and preparing the data, (4) analysing the data and (5) transforming the analysis results into insights. The first step focuses on uncovering the nature and boundaries of a situation or question related to marketing strategy or implementation. The second step involves designing a research project to obtain needed information, formulating a hypothesis and determining what type of research to employ that will test the hypothesis so that the results are reliable and valid. Marketers conduct exploratory research when they need broad data about a problem or want to make a tentative hypothesis; they use descriptive and experimental research to verify insights through an objective procedure. Research is considered reliable if it produces almost identical results in successive repeated trials; it is valid if it measures what it is supposed to measure and not something else. This third step is the data-gathering phase. To apply research data to decision-making, marketers must interpret and report their findings properly – the final two steps in the research process. Statistical interpretation focuses on what is typical or what deviates from the average. After interpreting the research findings, the researchers must prepare a report on the findings that the decision makers can understand and use.

 LO3 UNDERSTAND THE FUNDAMENTAL METHODS OF GATHERING DATA FOR MARKETING RESEARCH.

For the third step in the marketing research process, two types of data are available. Primary data are observed and recorded or collected directly from subjects; secondary data are compiled inside or outside the organisation for some purpose other than the current investigation. Secondary data may be collected from an organisation's database and other internal sources or from periodicals, government publications, online and unpublished sources. Methods for collecting primary data include sampling, surveys, observation and experimentation. Sampling involves selecting representative units from a total population. In probability sampling, every element in the population being studied has a known chance of being selected for study. Non-probability sampling is more subjective because there is no way to calculate the likelihood that a specific element of the population being studied will be chosen. Marketing researchers employ sampling to collect primary data through surveys by mail, telephone and the Internet or through personal or group interviews. A carefully constructed questionnaire is essential to the success of any survey. In using observation methods, researchers record respondents' overt behaviour and take note of physical conditions and events but avoid direct contact with respondents. In an experiment, marketing researchers attempt to maintain certain variables while measuring the effects of experimental variables.

 **LO4** DESCRIBE HOW TOOLS SUCH AS DATABASES, DECISION SUPPORT SYSTEMS AND THE INTERNET FACILITATE MARKETING INFORMATION SYSTEMS AND RESEARCH.

Many companies use computer technology to create a marketing information system (MIS), which is a framework for gathering and managing information from data sources both inside and outside the organisation. A database is a collection of data arranged for easy access and retrieval. A marketing decision support system (MDSS) is customised computer software that aids marketing managers in decision-making by helping them anticipate what effect certain decisions will have. The Internet also enables marketers to communicate with customers and obtain data for information processing.

 **LO5** IDENTIFY KEY ETHICAL AND INTERNATIONAL CONSIDERATIONS IN MARKETING RESEARCH.

Eliminating unethical marketing research practices and establishing generally acceptable procedures for conducting research are important goals of marketing research. International marketing uses the same marketing research process, but data-gathering methods may require modification to address differences.

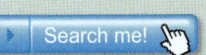

Key concepts

Use these key terms in **Search me! marketing** to find the latest relevant readings from a wide range of world-class journals, e-books and newspapers, including *The Australian*.

- crowdsourcing
- customer advisory boards
- descriptive research
- experimental research
- exploratory research
- focus-group interview
- hypothesis
- in-home (door-to-door) interview
- mail survey
- marketing decision support system (MDSS)
- marketing information system (MIS)

- marketing research
- non-probability sampling
- online survey
- personal interview survey
- population
- primary data
- probability sampling
- quota sampling
- random sampling
- reliability
- research design
- sample
- sampling
- secondary data

- shopping-centre intercept interview
- single-source data
- social networking websites
- statistical interpretation
- stratified sampling
- telephone depth interview
- telephone survey
- validity

Issues for discussion and review

1 What is marketing research? How does marketing research help decision making?

2 Is conducting marketing research always a worthwhile expense?

3 What are the steps in the marketing research process?

4 List several sources of secondary data. What are some key reasons that secondary data is often used by marketers?

5 Describe the different types of approaches to marketing research, and indicate when each should be used.

6 What is the difference between the two basic types of sampling? Describe two variants of probability sampling.

7 Briefly describe the four basic survey methods used to obtain data and the primary advantages and disadvantages of each.

8 What three types of questions are usually used in the construction of surveys?

9 What is a marketing information system, and what should it provide?

10 What is a principal concern that consumers have about market research – particularly where survey data is collected online?

Marketing applications

1 Imagine that, concerned by falling retail sales, David Jones has just gathered together its senior executives to discuss ways to increase sales in struggling departments and locations. What type of customer data (primary or secondary) might the marketing research team need to help understand the problem and inform decision making in the following areas?

a men's clothing

b outer suburban store

c small electrical

d children's toys

2 The university newspaper has asked you to see how political issues are influencing the voting intentions of the university's students at the next federal election. What sampling method will you use and why?

3 Choose a small, local business that you think could benefit from undertaking some marketing research. What do you see as their business problem? From their business problem, develop a research question and outline a method to approach this question. Explain why you think the research question is relevant to the business and why the particular methodology is suited to the question and the business.

4 You've decided to open a boutique Web Development Agency and you will market your services to small businesses (those with fewer than 50 employees). Discuss which database you would use to obtain your marketing information? Explain why you would use it.

5   ESOMAR (The World Association for Market, Social and Opinion Research) is a global, non-profit association for marketing research professionals. The organisation's aim is to encourage, advance and elevate market research worldwide. Visit the association's website at http://www.esomar.org.

   a   What are some examples of research resources that ESOMAR provides to help marketing professionals conduct research?

   b   ESOMAR introduced the first professional code of conduct for marketing research professionals in 1948. The association continues to update the document to address new technology and other changes in the marketing environment. According to ESOMAR's code, what are the specific professional responsibilities of marketing researchers?

   c   What Australian and New Zealand organisations apply the ICC/ESOMAR code?

ONLINE EXERCISE

6   NationMaster is a massive central data source that provides access to compiled data from sources such as the CIA World Factbook, UN and OECD. Imagine that you work for an Internet company looking to establish itself in new markets. You will want information on the level of broadband access in different markets. Go to http://www.nationmaster.com and, in 'Facts & Statistics' select first 'Internet' and then 'Broadband Access'.

   a   Give a summary of the top 15 countries as ranked by their broadband access. From this specified list of markets, include an assessment of the three countries with the most and least access to broadband access. What conclusions can you draw?

Developing your marketing plan

Decisions about which market opportunities to pursue, what customer needs to satisfy and how to reach potential customers are not made in a vacuum. The information provided by marketing research activities is essential in developing both the strategic plan and the specific marketing mix. Focus on the following issues as you relate the concepts in this chapter to the development of your marketing plan.

1   Define the nature and scope of the questions you must answer with regard to your market. Identify the types of data you will need about the market to answer those questions. For example, do you need to know about the buying habits, household income levels or attitudes of potential customers?

2   Determine whether or not this data can be obtained from secondary sources.

3   Choose the appropriate survey method(s) you would use to collect primary data. What sampling method would you use?

CengageNOW

Go to http:\\login.cengagebrain.com to link to CengageNOW, your online study tool. First take the Pre-Test for this chapter to get your Personalised Study Plan, and then:

✳ **Revise** your understanding of the key concepts of marketing with the online glossary

✳ **Watch** an interactive animation of strategic marketing to broaden your subject comprehension

✳ **Listen** to an audio summary of the learning objectives covered in this chapter.

After you have completed the activities in your Personalised Study Plan take the Post-Test to determine what concepts you have mastered and what you still to need work on.

Case study

BOM BOM BOM! RE-IGNITING KMART'S BRAND

Kmart, Australia's first discount department store, has been around for over 40 years. The first store was opened in suburban Victoria in 1969. Since then Kmart has become one of Australia's largest retailers with 190 stores across Australia and New Zealand. Chances are you've been in a Kmart store so you will know that they sell everything from kid's toys to hardware and DVDs.

In 2011, this stalwart of the Australian retail industry was struggling. Kmart was being battered by weakness in the Australian retail sector, competition from online imports and strong local competition. Worse still, over time, perception of Kmart's brand attributes had declined to a point where consumers saw very little difference between both Kmart's quality and price competitiveness and that of its main competitors, Big W and Target. After 10 years of poor financial performance, Wesfarmers, Kmart's parent company, was wondering if it should close Kmart down.

To reinvigorate Kmart, the company's new General Manager of Marketing engaged the creative agency Belgiovane Williams Mackay (BWM) and research partner, Forethought

Source: Reprinted with permission of Kmart Corporate Affairs

Research (Forethought). Ambitious goals were set. The business objectives were to increase:

→ gross margin

→ number of transactions by over 4 per cent

→ store traffic by over 2.5 per cent

→ consumer loyalty (measured as consumers who only shop at Kmart, and not competitors Target or Big W).

There were many fundamental questions that needed to be answered before undertaking any work. One important one was to do with pricing:

→ Was Kmart's pricing strategy the right one? In 2010, in an effort to improve revenue,

Kmart changed its pricing strategy from a high-low pricing model to everyday low prices (EDLP). But this strategy hadn't been as successful as anticipated.

Forethought sought to answer important questions that relate to the rational and emotive drivers of consumers' purchase behaviour:

→ At the explicit, rational level:
- What is the hierarchy of rational drivers of consumption in Kmart's market?
- How well does Kmart and its competitors perform on each of these drivers?

→ At the implicit, emotive level:
- What is the hierarchy of discrete emotions that leads consumers to make a purchase in Kmart's market?
- How well does Kmart and its competitors perform on each of these emotional drivers?
- How well have Kmart's communications generated these discrete emotions?

If price and quality were important to Kmart's consumers, answering these questions would explain:

→ How consumers perceive Kmart on quality in comparison to competitors

→ How competitive consumers perceive Kmart to be on price.

Forethought's proprietary methodology, Prophesy Thoughts & Feelings®, quantitatively measures rational and discrete emotional drivers of consumption.

Consumers' emotional drivers are measured online using animated avatars, known as Prophesy Feelings, to represent discrete emotions. The avatar's degree of emotion is captured visually by the avatar's changing expression. For example, if the emotion being measured is anger, the avatar can be anything from neutral (no anger) to really, really blazing angry. As little as two per cent of emotions are made consciously. This method enables Forethought to measure

an emotion that a consumer has not consciously expressed. Allowing consumers to self-select their level of emotion online also avoids the problems associated with using a moderator to question a survey participant. One such limitation is that participants are less likely to reveal negative emotions than positive ones.

Forethought's consumer insight breaks the communications task into two components. The first is to communicate the rational drivers of consumers' consumption decisions. These should be communicated explicitly. The second is to build communications so that the appropriate implicit consumption emotions are elicited. Explicitly conveying implicit drivers provokes consumers' scepticism and so fails in its objective.

Knowledge of these drivers would enable the creative agency to shape communications that effectively convey the desired rational drivers of consumption with the necessary implicit emotional associations.

Forethought's program of quantitative consumer research surveyed 834 Australian department store shoppers.[41]

Their research showed that Kmart's EDLP strategy was better positioned than its old high-low pricing to achieve market-share growth. The research also indicated that Kmart needed to improve consumers' perception of the quality of its products and consumers' understanding of Kmart's everyday low prices.

Using Forethought's insights into Kmart's consumers, BWM developed the '1000 mums' campaign. One thousand mothers were invited into a closed Kmart store to touch, feel and judge the quality of Kmart's products for themselves. Based on their assessment of the product's quality the mothers were asked to guess the product's price. The mother's were impressed by the product quality and so in most cases they over-estimated the product's price. This was a real-life experiment. BWM filmed the mother's genuinely surprised and delighted reactions to the higher than expected quality and the lower than expected prices of Kmart's products.

This campaign worked by activating select emotions through the creation of a community. The mothers' community was united by common needs, good financial decisions and their shared secret – Kmart's great quality product and low prices. The campaign firmly embedded the select, implicit emotions into the Kmart brand.

Six months after the launch of the '1000 mums' campaign, Kmart was able to announce that it had achieved its business objectives:

→ customer traffic increased by 3 million

→ Earnings Before Interest and Tax (EBIT) increased 5.8 per cent

→ sales increased by 25 million products. Additionally, Kmart had taken market share from both Big W and Target.[42]

Sharon-Lee Lukas, Marketing Consultant, Lukas & Company Pty Ltd

QUESTIONS FOR DISCUSSION

1 What type of data was used by Forethought in their work with Kmart?

2 What survey methods do you think were most likely used by Forethought to collect data? Why?

3 What ongoing research would you recommend to Kmart to avoid the company losing touch with its customers?

Chapter endnotes

1. 'The New Conversation: Taking Social Media From Talk to Action', Harvard Business School Publishing, 2010, Harvard Business Review Analytics Services, viewed online at http://hbr.org/web/slideshows/social-media-what-most-companies-dont-know/1-slide.
2. Anne L. Souchon, John W. Cadogan, David B. Procter, and Belinda Dewsnap, 'Marketing Information Use and Organizational Performance: The Mediating Role of Responsiveness,' Journal of Strategic Marketing (December 2004): 231–242; Bradley Johnson, 'Understanding the Generation Wireless' Demographic,' Advertising Age, March 20, 2006.
3. Kenneth Chang, 'Enlisting Science's Lessons to Entice More Shoppers to Spend More,' The New York Times, September 19, 2006, http://www.nytimes.com.
4. Alex Hayes, 'Magnum launches first Aussie facial recognition billboard,' B&T, May 2, 2012, http://www.bandt.com.au/breaking-campaigns/magnum-launches-first-aussie-facial-reconition-bil; Daisuke Wakabayashi and Juro Osawa, 'Billboard That Can See You,' The Wall Street Journal, September 3, 2010, B5; Emily Steel, 'The Billboard That Knows,' The Wall Street Journal, February 29, 2011, B5.
5. Bobby White, 'Cisco Sets Its Sights on $34 Billion Market,' The Wall Street Journal, (September 24, 2008), B3.
6. A. Parasuraman, Dhruv Grewal, and R. Krishnan, Marketing Research (Boston: Houghton Mifflin, 2007), 63.
7. Ken Manning, O. C. Ferrell, and Linda Ferrell, 'Consumer Expectations of Clearance vs. Sale Prices,' University of Wyoming working paper, 2007.
8. Parasuraman, Grewal, and Krishnan, Marketing Research, 64.
9. Vikas Mittal and Wagner A. Kamakura, 'Satisfaction, Repurchase Intent, and Repurchase Behavior: Investigating the Moderating Effects of Customer Characteristics,' Journal of Marketing Research (February 2001): 131–142.
10. Brian Steel, 'Kellogg's Goes Virtual to Test Real Life Packaging,' Marketing News, January 30, 2009: 13.
11. Nielson Claritas, 'BMW of North America,' http://www.claritas.com/target-marketing/.
12. Peter DePaulo, 'Sample Size for Qualitative Research,' Quirk's Marketing Research Review, (December 2000), http://www.quirks.com.
13. Theodore T. Allen and Kristen M. Maybin, 'Using Focus Group Data to Set New Product Prices,' Journal of Product and Brand Management (January 2004): 15–24.
14. David Armano, 'Rethinking the Focus Group: Tropicana Design Flops,' Logic 1 Emotion, (February 23, 2009), http://darmano.typepad.com/logic_emotion/2009/02/tropicana-html.
15. Sean Geehan and Stacy Sheldon, 'Connecting to Customers,' Marketing Management (November/December 2005): 37–42.
16. Tom Taulli, 'Entrepreneur's Journal: Setting Up a Customer Advisory Board that Gets Results', BloggingStocks, January 24, 2010, www.bloggingstocks.com/2010/01/24/entrepreneurs-journal-setting-up-a-customer-advisoryboard-tha (accessed January 21, 2011).
17. 'Coles Brands,' Coles. http://www.coles.com.au/Products/Our-Brands/Coles-Mums-Panel.aspx.
18. Barbara Allan, 'The Benefits of Telephone Depth Sessions,' Quirk's Marketing Research Review, (December 2000), http://www.quirks.com.

19. Jack Neff, 'Consumers Rebel Against Marketers' Endless Surveys,' *Advertising Age*, (October 2, 2006), http://www.adage.com.

20. Maria Grubbs Hoy and Avery M. Abernethy, 'Nonresponse Assessment in Marketing Research: Current Practice and Suggested Improvements,' in *Marketing Theory and Applications, American Marketing Association Winter Educators' Conference Proceedings*, 2002.

21. David Jobber, John Saunders, and Vince-Wayne Mitchell, 'Prepaid Monetary Incentive Effects on Mail Survey Response,' *Journal of Business Research* (January 2004): 347–50.

22. Robert V. Kozinets, 'The Field Behind the Screen: Using Netnography for Marketing Research in Online Communities,' *Journal of Marketing Research* (February 2002): 61–72.

23. Glen L. Urban and John R. Hauser, "Listening In' to Find and Explore New Combinations of Customer Needs,' *Journal of Marketing* (April 2004): 72–87.

24. Alissa Quart, 'Ol' College Pry,' *Business 2.0*, (April 3, 2001); 'Where the Stars Design the Cars,' *Business 2.0* (July 2005): 32.

25. 'Home Page,' Social Guide, http://www.socialguide.com/; 'Brand and Social,' Nielsen, http://www.nielsen.com/au/en/practices/brand-and-social.html.

26. James Verrinder, 'Time Warner Unveils Hi-Tech Media Lab,' *Research*, January 25, 2012, accessed February 7, 2012. www.research-live.com/news/news-headlines/time-warnerunveils-hi-tech-media-lab/4006765.article.

27. View clip at http://www.youtube.com/watch?v=Q7Uxaw6YoRw; Peter Hannam, 'Greenpeace, Coke's 'recycling war' spills into Google,' *The Sydney Morning Herald*, May 21, 2013, http://www.smh.com.au/environment/greenpeace-cokes-recycling-war-spills-into-google-20130521-2jylr.html; Sarah Whyte, & Nick Toscano, 'Coca-Cola cloud over recycling lobby bid,' *The Age*, September 27, 2013, http://www.theage.com.au/victoria/cocacola-cloud-over-recycling-lobby-bid-20130926-2uh0x.html; 'Anger at Coke's successful bid to abolish Northern Territory recycling deposit,' news.com.au, March 5, 2013, http://www.news.com.au/national-news/anger-at-cokes-successful-bid-to-abolish-northern-territory-recycling-deposit/story-fncynjr2-1226590581256.

28. Judy Strauss and Donna J. Hill, 'Consumer Complaints by E-mail: An Exploratory Investigation of Corporate Responses and Customer Reactions,' *Journal of Interactive Marketing* (Winter 2001): 63–73.

29. D. Aacker, V. Kumar, and G. Day, *Marketing Research*, 8th ed. (New York: Wiley & Sons, 2004).

30. Marlus Wübeen and Florian von Wangenheim, 'Predicting Customer Lifetime Duration and Future Purchase Levels: Simple Heuristics vs. Complex Models,' in Jean L. Johnson and John Hulland, eds., 2006 AMA Winter Educators' Conference: *Marketing Theory and Applications* 17 (Winter 2006): 83–84.

31. Noah Rubin Brier, John McManus, David Myron, and Christopher Reynolds, 'Zero-In' Heroes,' *American Demographics* (October 2004): 36–45.

32. Laurence N. Goal, 'High Technology Data Collection for Measurement and Testing,' *Marketing Research* (March 1992): 29–38.

33. Behrooz Noori and Mohammad Hossein Salimi, 'A Decision-Support System for Business-to-Business Marketing,' *Journal of Business & Industrial Marketing* 20 (2005): 226–236.

34. Chares Duhigg, 'How Companies Learn Your Secrets,' *The New York Times*, February 15, 2012, accessed February 28, 2012. www.nytimes.com/2012/02/19/magazine/shoppinghabits.html?_r=1&pagewanted=all.

35. Emily Steel and Julia Angwin, 'The Web's Cutting Edge, Anonymity in Name Only,' *The Wall Street Journal*, August 4, 2010, accessed February 7, 2012. http://online.wsj.com/article/SB10001424052748703294904575385532109190198.html.

36. Morgan Downs (Producer), *Inside the Mind of Google* [DVD], United States: CNBC Originals, 2010.

37. Carlos Denton, 'Time Differentiates Latino Focus Groups,' *Marketing News* (March 15, 2004): 52.

38. Lambeth Hochwald, 'Are You Smart Enough to Sell Globally?' *Sales & Marketing Management* (July 1998): 52–56.

39. Ibid.

40. Jon Leibowitz, 'FTC Chairman: 'Do Not Track' Rules Would Help Web Thrive,' *U.S. News and World Report*, January 3, 2011, accessed June 21, 2011, www.usnews.com/opinion/articles/2011/01/03/ftc-chairman-do-not-track-rules-would-helpweb-thrive-jon-leibowitz; Wendy Davis, 'Report: Marketers Limit Behavioral Targeting Due to Privacy Worries,' *MediaPost*, May 2, 2010, accessed June 21, 2011, www.mediapost.com/publications/?fa=Articles.showArticle&art_aid=127314; Bob Garfield, 'FTC Privacy Review Could Mean Trouble for Online Marketing,' *Advertising Age*, April 19, 2010, accessed June 21, 2011, http://adage.com/article/bob-garfield/ftc-privacy-review-trouble-onlinemarketing/143343/; Laurie Burkitt, 'Ad Industry to Regulators: We Can Take Care of Ourselves,' *Forbes*, April 14, 2010, accessed June 21, 2011, www.forbes.com/2010/04/14/privacy-advertising-interactive-advertising-networkadvertising-cmo-network-privacy-controls.html; Steve Lohr, 'How Privacy Vanishes Online,' *New York Times*, March 16, 2010, accessed June 21, 2011, www.nytimes.com/2010/03/17/technology/17privacy.html.

41. ARF David Ogilvy Awards 2013, 'Kmart Australia: Revitalising a brand via innovative research & creative collaboration,' page 2, accessed October 28, 2013, http://www.thearf.org/ogilvy-13.php.

42. Ken Roberts, 'So, Tell Me How You Feel…,' *Professional Marketing Magazine*, accessed October 28, 2013, http://www.forethought.com.au/Think-Tank/Papers; ARF David Ogilvy Awards 2013, 'Kmart Australia: Revitalising a brand via innovative research & creative collaboration,' accessed October 28, 2013, http://www.thearf.org/ogilvy-13.php, http://thearf.org/images/uploads/documents/2013_Ogilvy-Awards_Case-Study_Kmart-Australia.pdf; Ken Roberts, 'A Revolution in Advertising Testing,' *Admap*, accessed October 28, 2013, http://www.forethought.com.au/ArticleDocuments/86/Forethought%20White%20Paper%20-%20A%20Revolution%20In%20Advertising%20Testing.pdf.aspx?Embed=Y; 'Kmart,' Wesfarmers, accessed October 28, 2013, http://www.wesfarmers.com.au/our-businesses/kmart.html#kmart-tyre-auto-service.

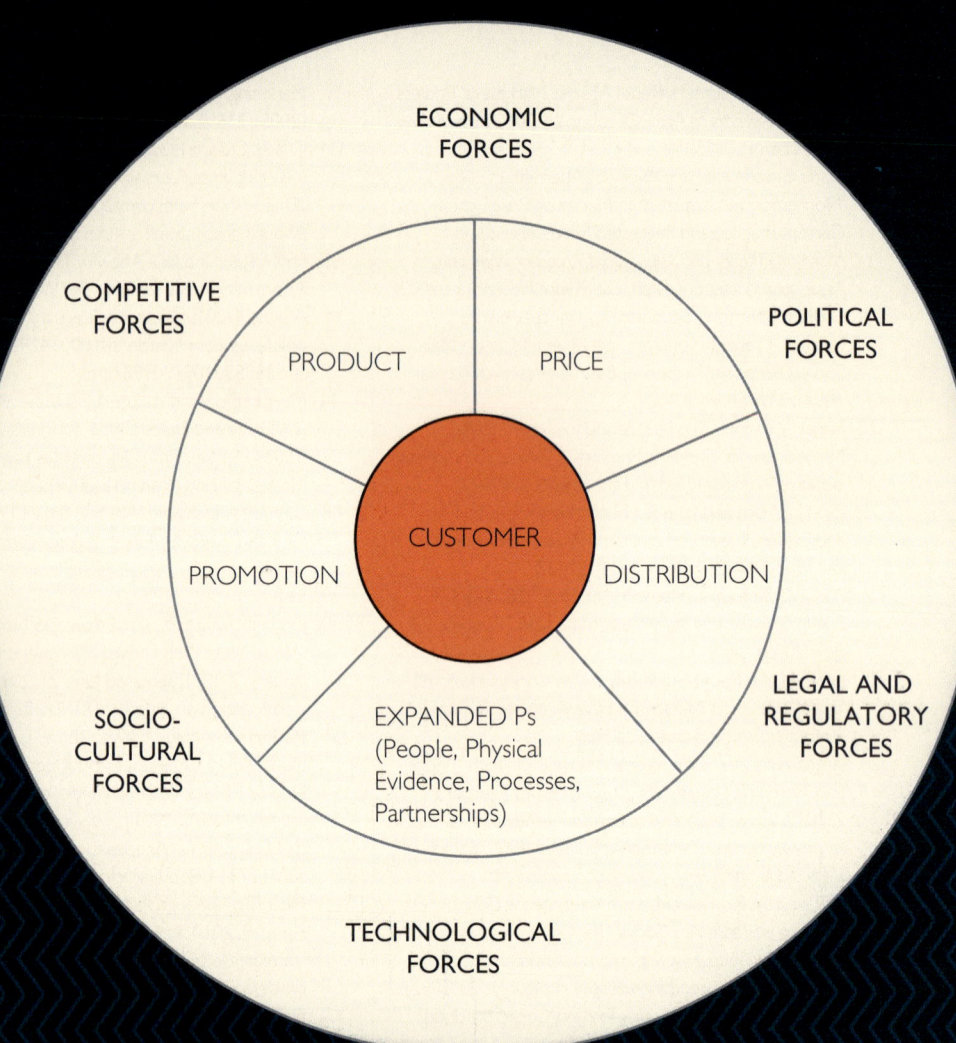

ECONOMIC
FORCES

COMPETITIVE
FORCES

POLITICAL
FORCES

PRODUCT   PRICE

CUSTOMER

PROMOTION   DISTRIBUTION

LEGAL AND
REGULATORY
FORCES

SOCIO-
CULTURAL
FORCES

EXPANDED Ps
(People, Physical
Evidence, Processes,
Partnerships)

TECHNOLOGICAL
FORCES

PART 2

UNDERSTANDING MARKETS

CHAPTER 4   CONSUMER BEHAVIOUR

CHAPTER 5   SEGMENTATION, TARGET MARKETS AND POSITIONING

CHAPTER 6   BUSINESS MARKETS AND BUYING BEHAVIOUR

PART 2 examines how marketers use information and technology to better understand and reach customers. Chapter 4 deals with human action and how customers behave. Understanding elements that affect buying decisions and consumption processes enables marketers to better analyse customers' needs and to evaluate how specific marketing strategies can satisfy those needs. Chapter 5 addresses selecting and analysing target markets, which is one of the major steps in marketing strategy development. Chapter 6 stresses business markets, organisational buyers, the buying centre and the organisational buying decision process.

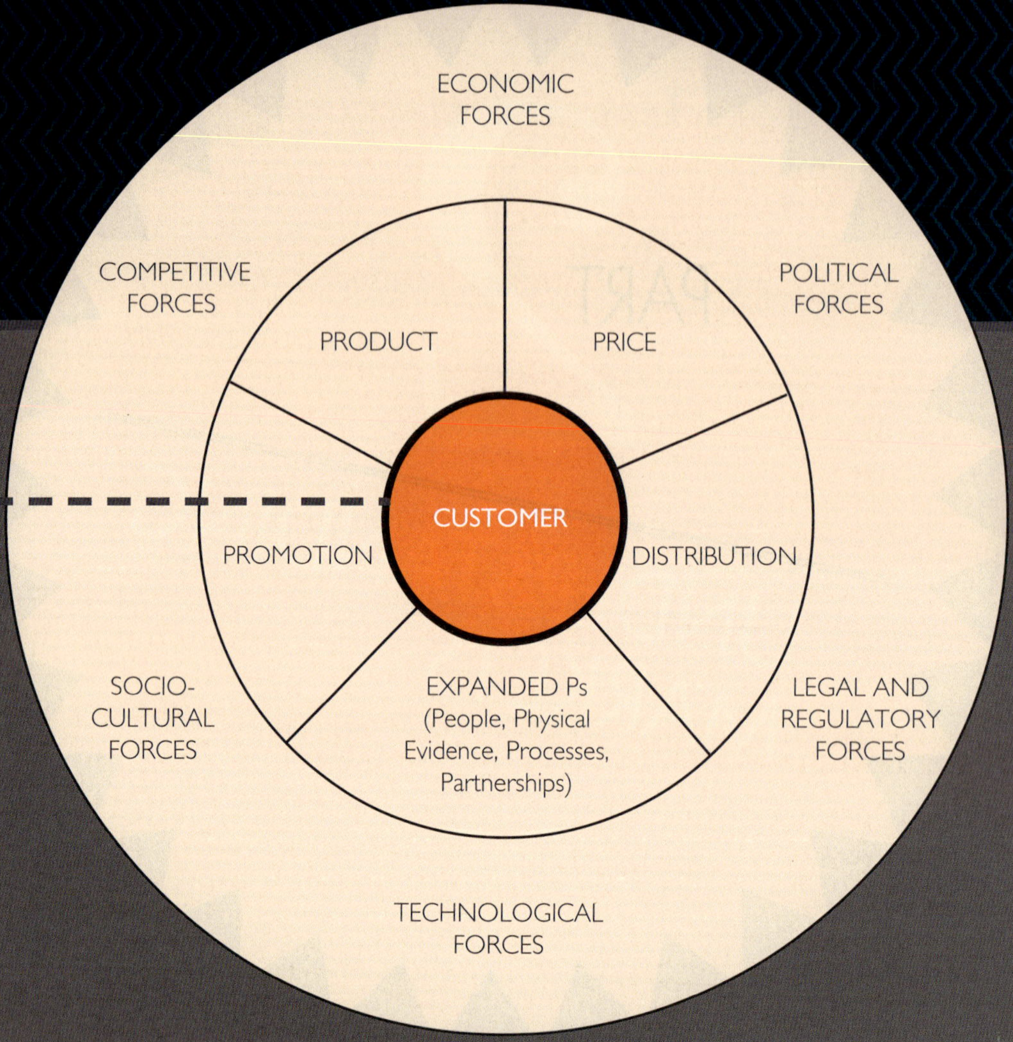

ECONOMIC FORCES

COMPETITIVE FORCES

POLITICAL FORCES

PRODUCT

PRICE

CUSTOMER

PROMOTION

DISTRIBUTION

SOCIO-CULTURAL FORCES

EXPANDED Ps
(People, Physical Evidence, Processes, Partnerships)

LEGAL AND REGULATORY FORCES

TECHNOLOGICAL FORCES

CONSUMER BEHAVIOUR

The importance of understanding consumer behaviour

Consumer buying decision process
  Problem recognition
  Information search
  Evaluation of alternatives
  Purchase
  Post-purchase evaluation

Level of involvement and problem-solving processes

Situational influences

Psychological influences process
  Perception
  Motives

  Learning
  Attitudes
  Self-concept
  Lifestyles

Social influences on the buying decision process
  Roles
  Reference groups
  Opinion leaders
  Digital networks
  Culture and subcultures

Throughout this chapter, Watch, Listen and Revise icons indicate an opportunity for online self-study through CengageNOW, linking you to animated chapter overviews, interactive diagrams, videos, quizzes and more.

CONSUMER BEHAVIOUR

Learning Objectives

LO1 Recognise the importance of understanding consumer behaviour

LO2 Recognise the various stages of the consumer decision process

LO3 Describe the level of involvement and types of consumer problem-solving processes

LO4 Explore how situational influences may affect consumer behaviour

LO5 Explore how psychological influences may affect consumer behaviour

LO6 Explore how social influences may affect consumer behaviour.

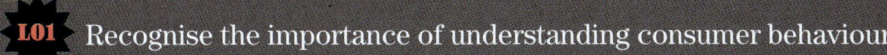

MARKETING CHALLENGE | HIGH FLYING CONSUMERS

Air travel is a popular choice for consumers throughout the Asia-Pacific region, and especially so with the advent of budget airlines. The stated mission for AirAsia (www.airaisa.com) is 'To attain the lowest cost so that everyone can fly with AirAsia'. Part of the way this low-cost strategy is achieved is by

Source: Getty Images

eliminating extras, such as food, service and entertainment in order to profitably offer lower fares. Offering low-cost fares with optional extras broadens the air travel market to those individuals who might not otherwise fly. The International Air Transport Association (IATA) report a continued growth in global air travel demand, and half of that demand (between October 2012 and January 2013) was carried by Asia-Pacific airlines. This identified growth trend is being driven by the acceleration in China's economy combined with the growth in Asian trade. As the demand swells for air travel in Asia, airlines will order more passenger jets and hire thousands more staff within both the airlines and the airports. In turn, more travelling consumers will arrive at their destinations and spend money in hotels, restaurants and retail. More than that, when an airline adds a particular destination to their flight routes, the land values there are boosted.

As an indication of the level of this increase in consumer behaviour, when per-capita gross domestic product (GDP) rises above US$3000 per year, the resident population have enough wealth to travel by air to other destinations. According to the International Monetary Fund (IMF), China, Malaysia and Thailand are currently past that point, Indonesia is almost there and the Philippines is fast approaching. For example, Gilmer Balaba is a rice farmer from the north of the Philippines who travels to see his family once a year. From his rural hometown, Gilmer used to make this journey by boat which was 28 hours each way. However, when competition between airlines lowered the cost of a return ticket from the north to the south to around AU$100, Gilmer began flying. After a bus ride to Manila, that 28-hour boat ride is replaced with a 1.5 hour flight. Much more comfortable![1]

MARKETING CHALLENGE QUESTION	1 How does the behaviour of budget-conscious air travellers differ from the	other travellers when they are waiting at the airport?

Introduction

In this chapter, we discuss the importance of understanding consumer behaviour. This is followed by an analysis of the major stages of the consumer buying decision process, beginning with problem recognition, information search and evaluation of alternatives, then proceed through to purchase and post-purchase evaluation. Then we examine how the customer's level of involvement affects the type of problem solving employed and discuss the types of consumer problem-solving processes. Next, we examine situational influences that affect purchasing decisions: surroundings, time, purchase reason and buyer's mood and condition. We go on to consider psychological influences on purchasing decisions: perception, motives, learning, attitudes, personality and self-concept, and lifestyles. We conclude with a discussion of social influences that affect buying behaviour: roles, family, reference groups and opinion leaders, and culture and subcultures.

The importance of understanding consumer behaviour

A company's ability to establish and maintain satisfying customer relationships requires an understanding of consumer behaviour. Consumer behaviour refers to the decision processes, purchasing and consuming acts of end-user consumers and those consumers who purchase products for personal or household consumption. This does not include consumers who are buying and consuming products for business purposes. As highlighted in the Marketing Challenge box on page 119, budget airlines, such as Air Asia, understand that not all consumers want to pay for in-flight food service. In order to establish and maintain satisfying customer relationships, Air Asia enable budget-conscious consumers to pay a low-priced fare with the option to purchase additional extras such as food and entertainment if they wish. Marketers strive to understand consumer behaviour for several reasons:

* consumers responding to a company's marketing strategy have a great impact on the company's success

* understanding consumer needs means a company can deliver better options than a competitor

* creating a successful marketing mix that satisfies customer needs means examining the main influences on what, where, when and how consumers make consumption decisions

* gaining a better understanding of the factors that affect consumer behaviour means marketers better understand how consumers will respond to marketing strategies.

According to Interbrand, the top three green brands worldwide are Toyota, Ford and Honda as numbers 1, 2 and 3 respectively.[2] Marketers and researchers within the Japanese headquarters of Toyota, for example, go to great lengths to understand the behaviour of their consumers to gain a better understanding of customer needs and wants. Toyota knows that their customers are constantly growing and changing and this recognition of dynamic consumer behaviour is evident in the evolution of the RAV4 models.

Launched in 1994, the first generation RAV4 became a bestseller. It was the world's first crossover SUV (sports utility vehicle), which allowed the comfort of on-road driving to be taken off-road. Launched in 2000, the second generation RAV4 offered further refinements for urban lifestylers, while the third generation RAV4, launched in 2006, was fully remodelled and positioned as the world's top small SUV. With the fourth generation RAV4, Toyota recognised that their customers were seeking a lifestyle that minimises negative environmental impact and therefore the newly released RAV4 redefines and improves these elements.[3] Similarly, Domino's Pizza understands that their hungry and time-poor customers are looking for a fast-food option that offers real pizza at reasonable value. With an emphasis on customer service, Domino's offers more than a basic pizza by offering an extensive menu that includes meal deals and desserts, all of which can be ordered online

consumer behaviour
Behaviour of people who purchase products for personal or household consumption and not for business purposes.

and delivered to your door. Domino's has even developed apps for mobile smart phones for added ordering and payment convenience. One such app offered by Domino's features Hatsune Miku, the latest recent vocal sensation in Japan.

Using Domino's Pizza as an example, the Ethical Marketing box below addresses the consumer behaviour of children and questions whether targeting young consumers' behaviour borders on unethical practice.

Another example of a company seeking to better satisfy consumer needs is Unilever. They repositioned the Pond's skincare brand with an emphasis on consumer love stories. Neil Trinidad, global marketing manager for Pond's states, 'Love and romance have always played a key role in Pond's brand story, but … today's modern woman is no longer a damsel in distress. She can initiate love'.[4] So the Pond's team asked consumers to create short clips 30–60 seconds in length about their own love stories. From 200 000 consumers across 146 countries, the many clips and stories the Pond's marketing team received was ' … an explosion of creativity!'.

ETHICAL MARKETING   ETHICS AND FAST FOOD MARKETING TO CHILDREN   **issue**

Kids get hungry throughout the day and especially at school – they want something fast and tasty. When at school, food choices are limited to what is available at the tuckshop and therefore at-school food consumption decisions are low involvement decisions.

Traditionally, pizza is a fast food that is high in fat and salt. Nevertheless, pizza is often the food of choice for school-aged children. Domino's Pizza is a high-profile Australian brand of pizza that emphasises the nutritional value of their pizza. Introducing Domino's to the school tuckshop menu is highly appealing to children who may not know any better. However, obesity is an increasingly problematic issue for Australian children, who typically grow up to become obese adults. Approximately 25 per cent of Australian children and adolescents are considered overweight or obese and these figures are increasing at an alarming rate. One of the social factors that encourages less healthy food choices is the food advertising aimed at children. Poor food choices and unhealthy eating in the formative years can lead to many serious health problems. Given Domino's Pizza offers a quality product, is it ethical to have pizza available at the school tuckshop?[5]

> *Children make up a large share of the unhealthy food market, and demonstrate behaviours of wanting food that is both easy to attain and tasty; but should advertising be directed toward this segment given the knowledge of childhood obesity problems?*

Consumer buying decision process

consumer buying decision process
A five-stage purchase decision process that includes problem recognition, information search, evaluation of alternatives, purchase and post-purchase evaluation

The consumer buying decision process shown in Figure 4.1 includes five stages: problem recognition, information search, evaluation of alternatives, purchase and post-purchase evaluation. Before we examine each stage, consider these important points:

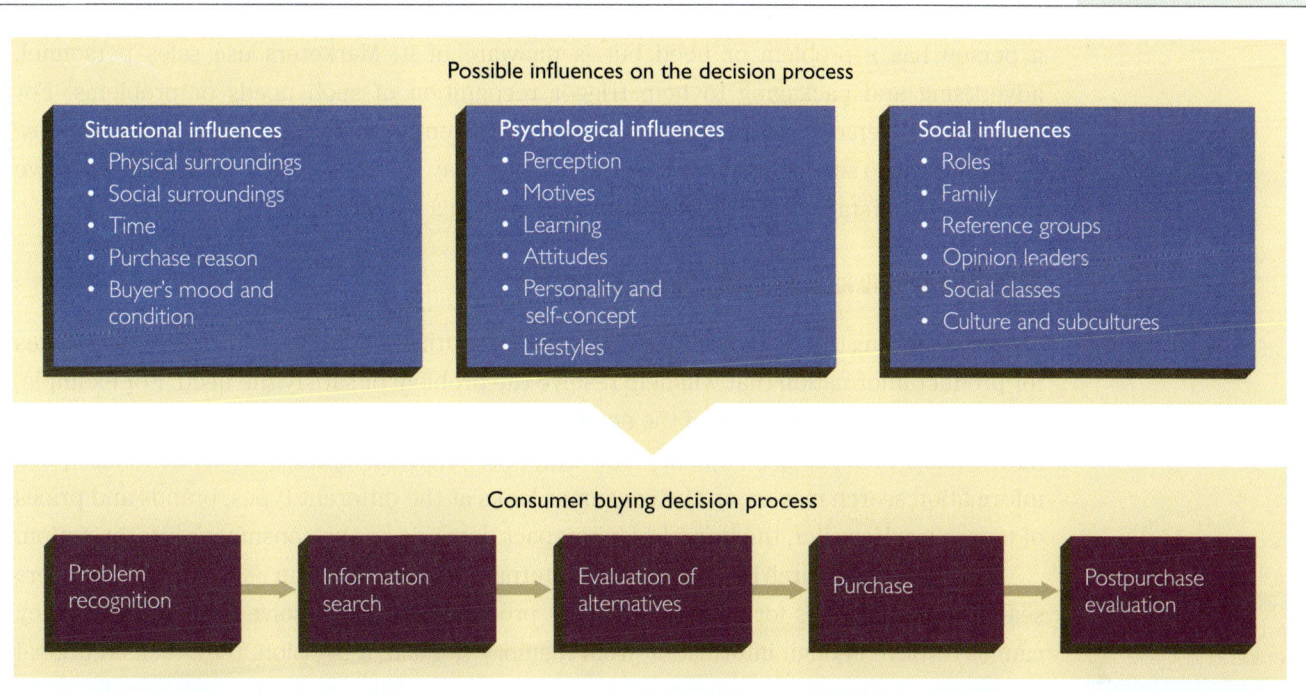

FIGURE 4.1   CONSUMER BUYING DECISION PROCESS AND POSSIBLE INFLUENCES ON THE PROCESS

✳ the act of purchasing is just one stage in the process and usually not the first stage

✳ not all decision processes lead to a purchase and individuals may end the process at any stage

✳ not all consumer decisions include all five stages. People engaged in routine decisions may simply realise the need and skip the info search and the alternative evaluation to go straight to the purchase with little or no post-purchase evaluation. In contrast, those consumers faced with extended problem solving may go through all stages of this decision process, whereas those engaged in limited problem solving may omit some stages.

Problem recognition

Problem recognition occurs when a buyer becomes aware of a difference between a desired state and an actual condition. Consider the situation when you find yourself heading for work and rain unexpectedly begins to fall. Your desired state is to stay dry, but the actual state is that staying dry is unlikely. The difference between your desired state and your actual state is a need or problem recognition. Therefore you decide to stop off at a convenience store to duck out of the rain.

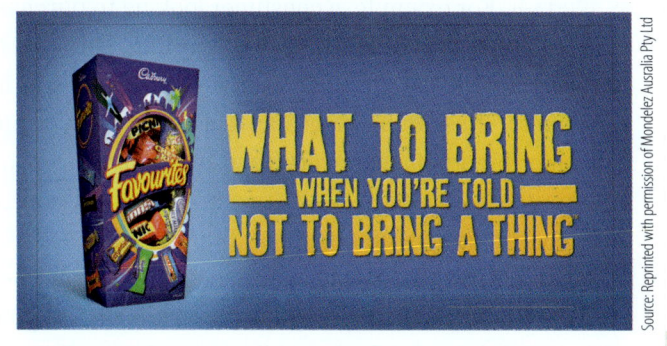

<< Problem recognition
This ad for Cadbury Favourites highlights the problem of what to bring to a social gathering when instructions are to not bring anything. Recognising this problem as a common consumer dilemma, Cadbury positions Cadbury Favourites as the solution. The campaign based around this concept comprised TV, online, radio and outdoor advertising. Repeated exposures means consumers reduce the information search stage of the their buying process

The speed of consumer problem recognition can be quite rapid or rather slow. Sometimes a person has a problem or need but is unaware of it. Marketers use sales personnel, advertising and packaging to help trigger recognition of such needs or problems. For example, convenience stores may choose to prominently display umbrellas on a rainy day. Consumers who see the point-of-purchase display may recognise that an umbrella will solve the problem of staying dry while heading to work on a rainy day.

Information search

After recognising the problem or need, a buyer (if continuing the decision process) searches for product information that will help resolve the problem or satisfy the need. For example, once the problem recognition of the need for an umbrella has been triggered, the consumer may decide to investigate quickly the different umbrella options available. This quick information search may mean the consumer looks at the different types, brands and prices of umbrellas. However, the information's impact depends on the consumer's interpretation.

An information search has two aspects: internal and external. In an internal search, buyers search their memories for information about products that might solve the problem. If they cannot retrieve enough information from memory to make a decision, they seek additional information from outside sources in an external search. The external search may focus on communication with friends or relatives, comparison of available brands and prices, marketer-dominated sources and/or public sources. An individual's personal contacts – friends, relatives and associates – are often influential sources of information because the person trusts and respects them. However, marketing research suggests that consumers may overestimate friends' knowledge about products and their ability to evaluate them.[6] Using marketer-dominated sources of information, such as salespeople, advertising, websites, package labels, in-store demonstrations and point-of-purchase displays, typically requires little effort on the consumer's part. Indeed, the Internet has become a major information source during the consumer buying decision process, especially for product and pricing information. Buyers also obtain information from independent sources – for instance, government reports, news presentations, publications such as *Choice Magazine* (http://www.choice.com.au) and reports from product-testing organisations. Consumers frequently view information from these sources as highly credible because of their factual and unbiased nature.

Evaluation of alternatives

A known group of brands that a buyer views as possible alternatives is referred to as an evoked set. For example, a consumer looking to purchase a new smartphone might know of various brands that include Apple, Samsung, Motorola and Nokia. Consumers are exposed to these brands daily in their everyday activities and interactions with other smartphone consumers. Research suggests that repeated brand exposures favourably influence consumer brand choice, even when that exposure is minimal and incidental. Thus, when attempting to choose between two brands, most consumers will choose the one they are aware of rather than an unfamiliar brand.[7]

To assess the products in an evoked set, the consumer uses both objective and subjective evaluative criteria. Objective evaluation criteria might include the size, weight and dimensions of the smartphone, while the subjective evaluative criteria might include style characteristics.

internal search
An information search in which buyers search their memories for information about products that might solve their problem

external search
An information search in which buyers seek information from outside sources

evoked set
A group of brands that a buyer views as alternatives for possible purchase

evaluative criteria
Objective and subjective characteristics important to a consumer

While one consumer may put a higher importance on the smartphone's capabilities, another consumer may be more interested in a larger screen and a specific colour. Using these various criteria, consumers rate and eventually rank brands in their evoked set. As shown in the Marketing in Action box below, brand evaluation is becoming increasingly easy through the use of technology such as online comparison websites. The evaluation stage may yield no brand the buyer is willing to purchase. In such a case, further information search may be necessary.

Purchase

In the purchase stage, the consumer chooses the product to be bought. Selection is based on the outcome of the evaluation stage and on other dimensions. Product availability may influence which brand is purchased. For example, if a consumer wants a colourful pair of Vans skate shoes and cannot find them in the correct size, a colourful pair of Converse shoes may be chosen as a second preference.

During this stage, consumers also choose the seller from whom they will buy the product. For example, this may involve choosing a car insurance provider from your set of alternatives, as well as determining whether you will purchase the insurance from them in person, or via their online shopping facilities. The choice of seller may affect final product selection – and so may the terms of sale, which, if negotiable, are determined at this stage. Other issues, such as price, delivery, warranties, maintenance agreements, installation and credit arrangements, are also settled. Finally, the actual purchase takes place, unless the consumer decides to terminate the buying decision process.

REVISE your knowledge of the consumer buying decision process with the online crossword

---

MARKETING IN ACTION | TECHNOLOGY IS CHANGING CONSUMPTION HABITS

Technology is playing a more influential role in both the evaluation of alternatives as well as the purchase stages of the consumer buying decision process. Purchases related to a broad range of products, including clothing, cosmetics, cameras and computers, are researched on the Internet before consumers head to the shops. More than that, some consumers are making the buying decision at home. For example, online insurance comparison websites such as iSelect and Compare the Market allow consumers to compare a number of different insurance providers and brands along dimensions such as price and degree of cover. For consumers, this electronic form of pre-shopping is convenient, it easily allows price comparisons and there is less work involved. Furthermore, through technology, consumers also have easy access to what others have to say about a particular product or brand through online customer reviews, discussions and

Source: Shutterstock.com

forums. Popular website TripAdvisor combines both product comparison functions with user reviews for an even more informative pre-purchase evaluation and purchase experience. TripAdvisor users can comment on a product or service and rate it out of 5. Users can also make purchases online as opposed to visiting the service provider in person.

Post-purchase evaluation

After the purchase, the buyer begins evaluating the product to ascertain if the actual performance meets expected levels. Many criteria used in evaluating alternatives are applied again during post-purchase evaluation. The outcome of this stage is either satisfaction or dissatisfaction, which influences whether the consumer complains, communicates with other possible buyers or repurchases the product.

Shortly after the purchase of an expensive product, evaluation may result in cognitive dissonance: doubts in the buyer's mind about whether purchasing the product was the right decision. For example, after buying a $5000 leather lounge suite from Harvey Norman, a person may feel guilty about the purchase or wonder whether he or she purchased the right brand and quality. Cognitive dissonance is most likely to arise when a person has recently bought an expensive, high-involvement product that lacks some of the desirable features of competing brands. A buyer experiencing cognitive dissonance may attempt to return the product or seek positive information about it to justify choosing it. Marketers sometimes attempt to reduce cognitive dissonance by having salespeople contact recent purchasers to make sure that they are satisfied with their new purchases.

The consumer buying decision process is more than just the purchase itself. As discussed in the above section, the process can involve up to five stages, dependant on the consumer and the type of purchase being made. A routine purchase may involve fewer stages than a high risk or expensive purchase. The following section considers further the consumer's level of involvement and how this effects the consumer buying decision process. In doing so, the degree of problem-solving required is also discussed.

Level of involvement and consumer problem-solving processes

In order to acquire and maintain products that satisfy current and future needs, consumers engage in problem solving. People engage in different types of problem-solving processes depending on the nature of the products involved. The amount of effort, both mental and physical, that consumers expend in solving problems varies considerably. A major determinant of the type of problem-solving process employed depends on the customer's level of involvement, the degree of interest in a product and the importance the individual places on this product.

High-involvement products tend to be those that are visible to others (such as clothing, furniture or automobiles) and expensive. Expensive high-tech equipment items, for example, are usually high-involvement products. High-importance issues, such as health care, are also associated with high levels of involvement.

Low-involvement products tend to be those that are less expensive and have less associated social risk, such as many supermarket items. Involvement level, as well as other

cognitive dissonance
A buyer's doubts shortly after a purchase about whether the purchase decision was the right decision or not

level of involvement
An individual's degree of interest in a product and the importance of the product for that person

TABLE 4.1   THREE TYPES OF CONSUMER PROBLEM SOLVING

	Routinised response	Limited problem solving	Extended problem solving
Product cost consideration	Low cost consideration	Low to moderate cost consideration	High cost consideration
Search effort	Minimal search effort	Minimal to moderate search effort	Extensive search effort
Time spent problem solving	Short time spent solving the problem	Short to medium time spent solving the problem	Lengthy time spent solving the problem
Brand preference	More than one brand is acceptable, although one brand may be preferred	Several brands are considered	Varies; usually many brands considered

Source: VALS/Mediamark Research, Inc., survey, SRI Consulting Business Intelligence, http://www.sric-bi.com/VALS. Reprinted with permission.

factors, affects a person's selection of one of three types of consumer problem solving: routinised response behaviour, limited problem solving or extended problem solving. Table 4.1 illustrates the characteristics of these three types of consumer problem solving in terms of product cost, search effort, time spent and brand preference. For example, when a consumer makes a routinised response, the product in question is often of low cost, whereas a high-cost product often calls for extended problem solving.

A consumer uses routinised response behaviour when buying frequently purchased, low-cost items requiring very little search and decision effort. When buying such items, a consumer may prefer a particular brand but is familiar with several brands in the product class and views more than one as being acceptable. Typically, low-involvement products are bought through routinised response behaviour, that is, almost automatically. For example, most buyers spend little time or effort selecting a soft drink or a brand of cereal.

Buyers engage in limited problem solving when buying products occasionally or when they need to obtain information about an unfamiliar brand in a familiar product category. This type of problem solving requires a moderate amount of time for information gathering and deliberation. For example, the iconic Australian cereal, Weet-Bix, produced by Sanitarium, introduces a new and improved version of Weet-Bix called Weet-Bix Bites, and consumers may therefore seek additional information. They might ask a friend who has already tried the new Weet-Bix Bites, or they might notice a new TV ad about it, or they might pick the product up while in the supermarket shelf and read the nutritional details to see how the product is improved. Then they might make a trial purchase.

The most complex type of problem solving, extended problem solving, occurs when purchasing unfamiliar, expensive or infrequently bought products – for instance, a car, home or a university education. The buyer uses many criteria to evaluate alternative brands or choices and spends much time seeking information and deciding on the purchase. Extended problem solving is frequently used for purchasing high-involvement products.

Purchase of a particular product does not always elicit the same type of problem-solving process. In some instances we engage in extended problem solving the first time we buy a certain product but find that limited problem solving suffices when we buy that same product again. On the other hand, if a routinely purchased, formerly satisfying brand no

routinised response behaviour
A type of consumer problem-solving process used when buying frequently purchased, low-cost items that require very little search and decision effort

limited problem solving
A type of consumer problem-solving process that buyers use when purchasing products occasionally or when they need information about an unfamiliar brand in a familiar product category

extended problem solving
A type of consumer problem-solving process employed when purchasing unfamiliar, expensive or infrequently bought products

longer satisfies us, we may use limited or extended problem solving to switch to a new brand. Therefore, if we notice that the brand of detergent or deodorant we normally buy is no longer suitable, we may seek out a different brand through limited problem solving.

Most consumers occasionally make purchases solely on impulse and not on the basis of any of these three problem-solving processes. Impulse buying involves no conscious planning but results from a powerful urge to buy something immediately. These are the items that are not on your shopping list but unexpectedly find their way into your supermarket trolley. Research shows that store environmental elements such as music, lighting, store layout and personnel influence consumer impulse buying behaviour.[8] This research, therefore, suggests that retail managers invest in improving the store environment to encourage impulse buying.

It is now clear that as part of the decision buying process, consumers engage in different forms of problem-solving. The degree of problem solving engaged in is dependent on the nature of the product or service being purchased and the consumer's level of involvement. A consumer's level of involvement and related buying decision process may also be influenced by situation factors. These situational influences are discussed in further detail in the following section.

impulse buying
An unplanned buying behaviour resulting from a powerful urge to buy something immediately

Situational influences on the buying decision process

Situational influences include physical and social surroundings, time and reason considerations as well as the buyer's mood. These influences affect the consumer buying decision process. For example, buying a car tyre after noticing a tyre is badly worn is a different experience from buying a tyre right after a blowout on the freeway spoils your road trip. Situational factors can influence the buyer during any stage of the consumer buying decision process and may cause the individual to shorten, lengthen or terminate the process.

situational influences
Influences from physical and social surroundings, time and reason considerations as well as the buyer's mood, affect the consumer buying decision process

Source: Getty Images

Physical surroundings >>
The Ettamogah Pub in Albury, NSW, is a unique place that encapsulates the essence of Australiana

Situational factors can be classified into five categories: physical surroundings, social surroundings, time perspective, reason for purchase and the buyer's momentary mood and condition.[9] These situational factors are also present within the online context (see the Did you know? box on the next page).

Physical surroundings include store location, atmosphere, aromas, sounds, lighting and other factors in the physical environment, such as the weather, in which the decision process occurs. Research suggests that retail store chains should design their store layout to make browsing as easy as possible for shoppers to spend time choosing and eventually make purchases.[10] The Vanitas Restaurant at Palazzo Versace (http://www.palazzoversace.com) on the Gold Coast presents an opulent dining experience which is reflective of the innovative cuisine, rare and quality cellar, original art and intimate atmosphere that epitomises the luxurious essence that is unmistakably Palazzo Versace. These opulent surroundings tell a very different story to the physical surroundings of the Ettamogah Pub in Queensland. Both of these facilities offer food and beverage options but the physical experience of each differs greatly. Clearly, in some settings, dimensions, such as weather, traffic sounds and odours, are beyond the marketers' control.

Social surroundings include characteristics and interactions of others, such as friends, relatives, salespeople and other customers, who are present when a purchase decision is being made. Buyers may feel pressured to behave in a certain way because they are in public places such as restaurants, stores or sports arenas. Thoughts about who will be around when the product is used or consumed are another dimension of the social setting. An overcrowded store or an argument between a customer and a salesperson may cause consumers to stop shopping or even leave the store.

The *time dimension*, such as the amount of time required to become knowledgeable about a product, to search for it and to buy it, also influences the buying decision process in several ways. For instance, to make an informed decision at their own convenience, more consumers are searching for information online. Quick response times to online enquiries can make or break a sale for vendors. Purchase and consumption can also be influenced by the time of day, day of the week or month, seasons and holidays. Other time dimensions include the possible frequency of product use, the length of time required to consume the product and the amount of time pressure a consumer is under. Time-poor consumers are likely either to make quick purchase decisions or to delay them.

The *purchase reason* raises the questions of what exactly the product purchase should accomplish and for whom. Generally, consumers purchase an item for their own use, for household use or as a gift. For example, people who are buying a gift may buy a different product than if they were purchasing the product for themselves. If you own an engraved Cartier pen, for example, it is unlikely that you bought it for yourself.

The *buyer's momentary moods* (such as anger, anxiety or contentment) or momentary conditions (such as fatigue, illness or being short on cash) may have a bearing on the consumer buying decision process. These moods or conditions immediately precede the current situation and are not chronic. Any of these moods or conditions can affect a person's ability and desire to search for information, receive information, or seek and evaluate alternatives. There is evidence to suggest that sad buyers are more inclined to take risks, whereas happy buyers are more likely to be risk-aversive in buying decisions.[11] Moods can also influence a consumer's post-purchase evaluation significantly.

DID YOU KNOW?

Transferring this theory of situational factors to the online context means understanding what and how each of the five identified situational factors can be considered. The factor of physical surroundings, for example, might translate to the online layout and user friendliness of a particular website. The social surroundings within the online context may translate as interactivity and, importantly, this interactivity might be between both the organisation and the consumer as well as consumer to consumer. Within the virtual world of the Internet, the time dimension to compare alternatives is greatly reduced and similarly expected response times are also greatly reduced. Rapid response by organisations to online enquiries may mean getting the sale or not getting the sale. The purchase reason translated to online may frequently be impulse buying, given that many potential customers may be simply surfing the net and impulsively decide to purchase. And given the convenience and accessibility of online shopping, the buyer's momentary moods may magnify as a considered situational factor. Organisations need to be astute enough to talk to their customers, understand their customers and engage with the customer even before they become a customer.

Psychological influences on the buying decision process

psychological influences
Factors that partly determine people's general behaviour, thus influencing their behaviour as consumers

Psychological influences partly determine people's general behaviour and therefore influence their behaviour as consumers. Primary psychological influences on consumer behaviour are perception, motives, learning, attitudes, personality and self-concept, and lifestyles. Even though these psychological factors operate internally, they are very much affected by social forces outside the individual.

Perception

perception
The process of selecting, organising and interpreting information inputs to produce meaning

information inputs
Sensations received through the sense organs

Different people perceive the same thing at the same time in different ways. When you first look at Figure 4.2, do you see fish or birds? Similarly, an individual at different times may perceive the same item in a number of ways. Perception is the process of selecting, organising and interpreting information inputs to produce meaning. The process of perceiving an image in its entirety, rather than individual lines and curves, suggests the whole is greater than the sum of its parts. This is the principal of Gestalt Psychology, whereby the Gestalt effect relates to our visual perception/recognition of the whole. Information inputs are sensations received through sight, taste, hearing, smell and touch. When we hear an advertisement, see a friend, smell food cooking at a nearby restaurant or touch a product, we receive information inputs. Marketers are increasingly employing perception to help attract consumers who may be in the problem-recognition or information-search stages of the buying decision process For example, a print ad for a Jaguar automobile will stand out more in a magazine about luxury yachting than it will in an upmarket motoring magazine. Similarly, an ad for a Princess luxury yacht will be more noticeable in an upmarket motoring magazine than in a yachting magazine. The Jag stands out amongst the yachts, while the Princess stands out amongst the prestigious cars, yet the target markets of the magazines are appropriate for both the Jag and the Princess.

As the definition indicates, perception is a three-step process of selecting, organising and interpreting information. Although we receive numerous pieces of information at once, only a few reach our awareness.

FIGURE 4.2 FISH OR BIRDS: WHICH DO YOU SEE FIRST?

Selecting some inputs and ignoring others is called selective exposure because an individual selects which inputs will reach awareness. If you are concentrating on this paragraph, you probably are not aware of outside noise, that the room light is on or that you are touching this page. Even though you receive these inputs, they do not reach your awareness until they are pointed out.

An individual's current set of needs affects selective exposure. Information inputs that relate to one's strongest needs at a given time are more likely to be selected to reach awareness. It is not by random chance that many fast-food commercials are aired near mealtimes. Customers are more likely to tune in to these advertisements at these times. This concept of selective exposure is further explored in the example of Clear Shampoo in the Marketing in Transition box below.

selective exposure
The process of selecting inputs to be exposed to our awareness while ignoring others

MARKETING IN TRANSITION | QR CODE HAIRCUTS – CLEAR IN THAILAND

From store windows to magazine ads, the boxy patterns known as QR codes are popping up in many marketing situations to guide consumers toward additional information. As long as the consumer has a smartphone equipped with a QR-reading app, he or she can 'crack the code' and learn more about the product, its manufacturer and its availability, at any time and from anywhere.

To encourage business growth in Thailand, Clear Shampoo needed to establish a strong market position as scalp experts. But in a market where the focus is health and beauty, how do you drive attention to the scalp? Clear decided to let the scalp tell the story by making the invisible, visible. An interactive campaign was introduced that used the scalp as the communication channel. The idea behind this campaign was the QR code haircut. When observers scanned the QR code, they were redirected to the Clear Shampoo website where they could access information about the scalp. 'Guerilla' troops were sent all around Bangkok to raise awareness and generate curiosity. A high-profile Thai TV celebrity was also recruited. By talking about his QR code haircut on his 8 Cable TV program, a massive amount of media coverage was generated. The QR code haircut became cool and immediately went viral. The outcome of the campaign was that the scalp was one of the hottest topics in Thailand. More specifically, with $0 paid

Source: Shutterstock.com

advertising, the QR code haircut campaign generated over 10 million free contacts, which is equivalent to a media value of over AU$1 million. Traffic to the website increased by more than 400 per cent and the idea was replicated by Betfair in the UK and Wayne Rooney's hairdresser.[12]

This campaign is an example of marketers using informational inputs which directly relate to consumer needs and wants. The consumer needs shampoo and wants convenience of information. In targeting consumers who may want a healthier scalp, positioning QR codes on the scalp effectively taps into consumer selective exposure processes.

The selective nature of perception may result not only in selective exposure but also in two other conditions: selective distortion and selective retention. Selective distortion is changing or twisting currently received information; it occurs when a person receives information inconsistent with personal feelings or beliefs. For example, on seeing an advertisement promoting a disliked brand, a viewer may distort the information to make it more consistent with his or her own prior views. This distortion substantially lessens the effect of the advertisement on the individual. In selective retention, a person remembers information inputs that support personal feelings and beliefs and forgets inputs that do not. After hearing a sales presentation and leaving a store, a customer may forget many selling points if they contradict his or her personal beliefs.

The second step in the process of perception is perceptual organisation. Information inputs that reach awareness are not received in an organised form. To produce meaning, an individual must mentally organise and integrate new information with what is already stored in memory. People use several methods to organise information. One method, called *closure*, occurs when a person mentally fills in missing elements in a pattern or statement. In an attempt to draw attention to its brand, an advertiser will capitalise on closure by using incomplete images, sounds or statements in its advertisements.

Interpretation, the third step in the perceptual process, is the assignment of meaning to what has been organised. A person bases interpretation on what he or she expects or what is familiar. Denim jeans for example were originally known as traditional cowboy wear. But, the explosion of denim into mainstream casual fashion has much to do with what jeans have come to symbolise: youthful individualism and rebellion. In the Asia-Pacific region however, jeans are highly symbolic of the Western world. Moving away from traditional Asian dress, middle-class and wealthy Asian consumers are increasingly choosing designer jeans and well-established international brands such as Lee, the second biggest women's jeans brand in the Asia-Pacific region after Levi's. In an innovative move in August 2010, Levi's specifically designed and launched dENiZEN in the Asian markets of South Korea, China, Pakistan, India and Singapore.[13]

Motives

A motive is an internal energising force that orients a person's activities towards satisfying needs or achieving goals. Buyers' actions are affected by a set of motives rather than by just one motive. At a single point in time, some of a person's motives are stronger than others. For example, a person's motives for having a cup of coffee are much stronger right after waking up than just before going to bed. Motives also affect the direction and intensity of behaviour. Some motives may help an individual achieve his or her goals, whereas others create barriers to goal achievement. For example, the prospect of graduating and securing an excellent job may act as a driving force (motive) behind a student studying hard and achieving high grades in their university studies. Whereas, the heavy workload of gaining a degree may create a negative mindset for some, and therefore act as a barrier to completing a degree.

Learning

Learning refers to changes in a person's thought processes and behaviour caused by information and experience. Consequences of behaviour strongly influence the learning

---

selective distortion
An individual's changing or twisting of information when it is inconsistent with personal feelings or beliefs

selective retention
Remembering information inputs that support personal feelings and beliefs and forgetting inputs that do not

motive
An internal energising force that directs a person's behaviour towards satisfying needs or achieving goals

learning
Changes in an individual's thought processes and behaviour caused by information and experience

LISTEN to an Audio Summary that summarises the importance of perception, motives, learning and attitudes

process. Behaviours that result in satisfying consequences tend to be repeated. For example, a consumer who buys a Snickers chocolate bar and enjoys the taste is more likely to buy a Snickers again. In fact, the individual will probably continue to purchase that brand until it no longer provides satisfaction. When effects of the behaviour are no longer satisfying, the person may switch brands or stop eating chocolate bars altogether.

When making purchasing decisions, buyers process information. Individuals have differing abilities to process information. The type of information inexperienced buyers use may differ from the type used by experienced shoppers familiar with the product and purchase situation. Thus two potential purchasers of a piece of artwork may use different types of information in making their purchase decisions. The inexperienced buyer may judge the value of the artwork by the price, whereas the more experienced buyer may seek information about the artist, period and authenticity to judge the quality and value. Consumers lacking experience may seek information from others when making a purchase and even take along an informed 'buying buddy' or shopping friend. More experienced buyers have greater self-confidence and more knowledge about the product and can recognise which product features are reliable cues to product quality. Marketers help customers learn about their products by helping them gain experience with them. Free samples, sometimes coupled with discount vouchers, can successfully encourage trial and reduce purchase risk. In-store demonstrations also allow consumers to taste different food options. In the same way, car dealerships will allow test drives to give potential purchasers some experience with their car of choice. Consumers also learn by experiencing products indirectly through information from salespeople, advertisements, friends and relatives. Through sales personnel and advertisements, marketers offer information before (and sometimes after) purchases to influence what consumers learn and to create more favourable attitudes toward the product.

Attitudes

An attitude is an individual's enduring evaluation of, feelings about and behavioural tendencies towards an object or idea. For example, a positive attitude toward a product may increase the probability of intention to purchase. Attitudes and purchase intentions are closely related. The objects toward which we have attitudes may be tangible or intangible, living or non-living. For example, we have attitudes toward gender, religion, politics and music, just as we do towards cars, football and breakfast cereals. Although attitudes can change, they tend to remain stable and do not vary from moment to moment. However, all of a person's attitudes do not have equal impact at any one time; some are stronger than others. Individuals acquire attitudes through experience and interaction with other people.

Attitudes are similar to beliefs in that both concepts can influence consumer behaviour. But there is much

attitude
An individual's enduring evaluation of feelings about and behavioural tendencies towards an object or idea.

Source: Australian Made, Australian Grown Campaign

<< Attempting to change attitudes
Country of origin is a significant issue for some consumers in making consumption choices

debate in marketing about the connection between consumer attitude and consumer behaviour. While some consider consumer attitude as relatively stable, others consider consumer attitude as a temporary evaluation formed through either memory or context. Argyrior and Melwar provide a review of these debates and conclude that attitudes are indeed evaluative judgement measured as categories on a continuum of several attribute dimensions.[14] Some marketing theorists consider attitude to be formed from beliefs about an object's attributes (e.g. engine size or colour of car) and the categorisation of these beliefs on an affective continuum – from like to dislike, for example.[15]

An attitude consists of three major components: cognitive, affective and behavioural. The cognitive component is the person's knowledge and information about the object or idea. The affective component consists of feelings and emotions towards the object or idea. Affective evaluation influences a person's intentions toward the object or idea. Emotions involve both psychological and biological elements. They relate to feelings and can create visceral responses related to behaviour. Love, hate and anger are emotions that can influence behaviour. For some people, certain brands, such as Apple Inc., Starbucks or their favourite sports franchise, elicit an emotional response. Organisations that create an emotional experience or connection establish a positive brand image and will contribute to customer affinity and loyalty. This means it is important for marketers to generate authentic, genuine messages that consumers can relate to emotionally.

The behavioural component manifests itself in the person's actions regarding the object or idea. Changes in one of these components may or may not alter the other components. Therefore, a consumer may become more knowledgeable about a specific brand without changing the affective or behavioural components of his or her attitude toward that brand.

Consumer attitudes towards a company and its products greatly influence success or failure of the company's marketing strategy. When consumers have strong negative attitudes towards one or more aspect of a company's marketing practices, they not only may stop using its products, but they may also urge relatives and friends to do likewise.

Because attitudes play such an important part in determining consumer behaviour, marketers should seek to identify and understand consumer attitudes toward prices, package designs, brand names, advertisements, salespeople, repair services, store locations, features of existing or proposed products and social responsibility efforts. Several methods help marketers gauge these attitudes. One of the simplest ways is to question people directly. Talking to consumers, staying informed on consumer attitudes and understanding what consumers are looking for enables marketers to better deliver on consumer needs and wants. From an extensive survey of Australian shoppers older than 18 years, Roy Morgan Research reported in 2012 that 98.8 per cent of Australian consumers recognise the Australian Made, Australian Grown (AMAG) logo and that this logo gives 88.6 per cent of Australian consumers' confidence that a product is indeed Australian. More specifically, 68.2 per cent of Australians deliberately choose to purchase products based on country-of-origin.[16]

Self-concept

self-concept
A person's view or perception of himself or herself

Self-concept (sometimes called *self-image*) is a person's view or perception of himself or herself. Individuals develop and alter their self-concepts based on an interaction of psychological and social dimensions. Research shows that a buyer purchases products

Source: Devised by Michele Levine of Roy Morgan Research and Colin Benjamin of the Horizons Network.

FIGURE 4.3 ROY MORGAN VALUES SEGMENTS™

that reflect and enhance their self-concept and that purchase decisions are important to the development and maintenance of a stable self-concept. Consumers' self-concepts may influence whether they buy a product in a specific product category, and where from, and self-concept may also affect brand consumption. Research is increasingly demonstrating that we are what we consume and consumers use brands to demonstrate who they are.[17] Successful business people may choose to drive a BMW, given that this brand is symbolic of success, whereas a Toyota LandCruiser is symbolic of an outdoor lifestyle and, contrastingly, a Porsche symbolises being single and available. As savvy consumers, we carefully construct the self we want to present to the world. Think about what, how and where you consume and how that demonstrates who you are to the outside world.

Lifestyles

Many marketers attempt to segment markets by lifestyle. A lifestyle is an individual's pattern of living expressed through activities, interests and opinions. Lifestyle patterns include the ways people spend time, the extent of their interaction with others and their general outlook on life and living. People partially determine their own lifestyles, but the pattern is also affected by personality, as well as by demographic factors such as age, education, income and social class. Lifestyles are measured through a lengthy series of questions.

lifestyle
An individual's pattern of living, expressed through activities, interests and opinions

Lifestyles have a strong impact on many aspects of the consumer buying decision process, from problem recognition to post-purchase evaluation. Lifestyles influence consumers' product needs, brand preferences, types of media used and how and where they shop.

One of the most popular frameworks for exploring Australian lifestyles is a survey from Roy Morgan Research. This research identifies 10 values segments that are labelled as follows: basic needs, a fairer deal, traditional family life, conventional family life, look at me, something better, real conservatism, young optimism, visible achievement and socially aware. Each of these lifestyle segments are briefly explained in Table 4.2.

TABLE 4.2   A BRIEF DESCRIPTION OF ROY MORGAN VALUES SEGMENTS™

Lifestyle segment	Description of segment	Consumer behaviour
Basic needs	Retired pensioners and social security recipients	Focused on survival. Heavy consumers of free media, daytime soap operas, current affairs and news programs, TV quiz shows.
A fairer deal	Pessimistic and cynical consumers who struggle financially	Heavy consumers of radio and TV, especially reality-TV shows and stories of ordinary people achieving fame and fortune.
Traditional family life	Older, highly conventional consumers; generally empty-nesters	Focused on family and prefer the status quo. They hold a high resistance to change and are heavy consumers of daily newspapers and ABC TV programs.
Conventional family life	Middle mainstream consumers	Focused on family life and lives in suburbia. They seek greater financial security and a higher standard of living. Security and stability are high priorities.
Look at me	Looking for fun and freedom and acceptance in peer groups	Fashion and trend conscious. Socially active with a short-term focus to life and work responsibilities. Music is an important form of expression and a key mechanism for rebellion. Heavy users of iPods and music downloads.
Something better	Competitive, individualist and ambitious	Concerned about acceptance social status and both online and offline networking is a priority. Light readers of newspapers and magazines.
Real conservatism	Cautious and conservative consumers	Focused on value and quality, this 'old school' segment are asset rich and cash poor and typically assume traditional gender roles; male as provider and female as homemaker.
Young optimism	Young and idealistic consumers	Focused on image and style; high-energy consumers who are keen to explore; personally and financially disorganised but highly innovative and takes an international view of the world.
Visible achievement	Successful and confident consumers	Highly individualistic and successful consumers, they look for quality and practicality. Frequent travellers and heavy readers of business and finance magazines.
Socially aware	Community-minded and active with strong sense of social responsibility	Early adopters in design and fashion with a preference for natural and eco options. Heavy consumers of both daily and national newspapers. Heavy support of the arts and so listens to ABC and community radio.

Source: Adapted from Roy Morgan Research, http://www.roymorgan.com/products/values-segments/values-segments.cfm, devised by Michele Levine of Roy Morgan Research and Colin Benjamin of the Horizons Network.

In applying this theory of values segmentation, marketers understand that the market segment that most values 'Basic needs' are senior consumers who are content with what they have and seek nothing more than a simple life. These consumers are highly active in the volunteering movement and they promote a strong work ethic. Whereas the market segment that most values 'A fairer deal' are those consumers who think that everyone else gets all the fun and they miss out. These consumers are angry, disillusioned and self-destructive. Consumption choices for these consumers might include muscle cars, motorbikes and martial arts. In contrast again, the 'Traditional family', along with the younger counterpart 'Conventional family', represent the core of middle Australia. Consumption choices are motivated by security, reliability and providing better opportunities for the family.

While the family segments take a collective view, the 'Look at me' segment is more self-centred and often associated with youth and rebellion. These consumers are highly aware of fashion and other trends and seek to differentiate themselves from their parent's generation but necessarily within the bounds of social desirability among their peers. Rather than focusing on building a career, these youthful consumers are short-term oriented and steer away from responsibility. Those consumers focused on career and responsibility arise from the 'Something better' segment. These consumers want a better deal out of life and are highly ambitious. Consequently, they purchase status symbols that demonstrate their success. Similarly, they choose designer brands, drive the latest-model cars and live in blue-ribbon suburbs. The consumers who choose to save and consume more conservatively are found in the 'Real conservatism' segment. With highly conservative social, moral and ethical values, these consumers willingly pay for products which guarantee consistent value and quality and are particularly attracted to older, well established brands. The consumers who are less risk averse are the 'Young optimists' because these consumers are focused on image and style. These young consumers are long-term thinkers who are busy planning their careers and are perhaps at university. They are people who want to experience all that life has to offer, by way of travel, for example. Moving this segment along a few years, we recognise the 'Visible achievement' segment. These consumers have made it to the top of their field and have the status symbols to show it. However, despite their success, they retain traditional values about home, work and society. With a high emphasis on family, this segment of consumers looks for quality and value for money, rather than the most expensive option. In contrast, the 'Socially aware' market segment is made up of consumers who value highly the community and the environment. These consumers are continually searching for something new and different, as well as opportunities for training, education and knowledge. These consumers are well informed with a strong sense of social responsibility.

Social influences on the buying decision process

Forces that other people exert on buying behaviour are called social influences and include: roles, family, reference groups, opinion leaders, digital networks, and culture and subcultures.

social influences
External social forces on an individual's buying behaviour

Roles

All of us occupy positions within groups, organisations and institutions. Associated with each position is a role, a set of actions and activities. A person in a particular position is supposed to perform based on expectations held by both the individual and surrounding persons. Because people occupy numerous positions, they have numerous roles. For example, a woman may perform the roles of mother, wife, daughter, employee or employer, club member and student. In carrying out these various roles, multiple sets of expectations are placed on each person's behaviour. These various roles depict our multiple selves.

An individual's roles influence both general behaviour and buying behaviour. The demands of a person's many roles may be diverse and even inconsistent. Consider the various types and brands of clothes that you buy and wear depending on whether you are going to class, to work, to a party, to the gym or to your boyfriend's mother's house. You and others involved in these settings have expectations about what is acceptable behaviour and what is acceptable clothing for these events. Therefore the expectations of those around us affect our consumption of clothing as well as many other products.

Family influences have a very direct impact on the consumer buying decision process. Parents (and other household adults) teach children how to cope with various problems, including those dealing with purchase decisions. Consumer socialisation is the process through which a person acquires the knowledge and skills to function as a consumer. Often children gain this knowledge and set of skills by observing parents and older siblings in purchase situations, as well as through their own purchase experiences. Children observe brand preferences, buying and consumption practices in their families. As these children grow into adults, they maintain some of these preferences and practices as they establish households and raise their own families. Buying decisions made by a family are a combination of group and individual decision making.

The extent to which adult family members take part in family decision making varies among families and product categories. Although family structures and roles within the family continually change, women still make buying decisions related to many household items, including health care products, laundry supplies, paper products and foods. It is believed that women make over 80 per cent of all household buying decisions, yet men are increasingly taking on the challenge. Owing to changes in men's roles, a significant proportion of men are now the primary grocery shoppers. Spouses participate jointly in the purchase of several products, especially durable goods. However, some households are single-parent households. Children make many purchase decisions and influence numerous household purchase decisions. The type of family decision making employed depends on the composition of the family as well as on the values and attitudes of family members.

When two or more family members participate in a purchase, their roles may dictate that each is responsible for performing certain purchase-related tasks, such as initiating the idea, gathering information, determining if the product is affordable, deciding whether to buy the product or selecting the specific brand. The specific purchase tasks performed depend on the types of products being considered, the kind of family purchase decision process typically employed and the amount of influence children have in the decision process. Therefore, different family members may play different roles in the family buying process. To develop a marketing mix that meets the needs of target-market members precisely,

marketers must not only know who does the actual buying but also which other family members perform purchase-related tasks.

The family life cycle stage also affects individual and joint needs of family members. For example, consider how the household needs of someone who is in their early 20s differs from those of the same consumer when they are in their late 30s with two young children. Family life cycle changes can affect which family members are involved in purchase decisions and the types of products purchased.

Reference groups

A reference group is any group that positively or negatively affects a person's values, attitudes or behaviour. Reference groups can be large or small. Most people have several reference groups, such as families, work- related groups, local commerce groups, professional associations or religion-related groups.

In general, there are three major types of reference groups: membership, aspirational and disassociative. A membership reference group is one to which an individual actually belongs; the individual identifies with group members strongly enough to take on the values, attitudes and behaviours of people in that group. An aspirational reference group is a group to which one aspires to belong; one desires to be like those group members. A group that a person does not wish to be associated with is a disassociative reference group; the individual does not want to take on the values, attitudes and behaviour of group members.

A reference group may serve as an individual's point of comparison and source of information. A customer's behaviour may change to be more in line with the actions and beliefs of group members. For example, a person might stop buying one brand of clothing and switch to another based on reference group members' advice. Similarly, a consumer may choose a brand of car with a hybrid engine in order to align with a reference group's eco-conscious beliefs (see Sustainable Marketing box 142). An individual may also seek information from the reference group about other factors regarding a prospective purchase, such as where to buy a certain product. Generally, the more conspicuous a product is then the more likely that the purchase decision will be influenced by reference groups.

A product's conspicuousness is determined by whether others can see it and whether it can attract attention. Reference groups can affect whether a person does or does not buy a product at all, buys a type of product within a product category or buys a specific brand. One way that reference groups may influence behaviour is by ridiculing people who violate group norms; researchers have identified this practice among adolescents who admonish, or even shun, peers who deviate from group norms.[18] A marketer sometimes tries to use reference group influence in advertisements by suggesting that people in a specific group buy a product and are highly satisfied with it. For example, beer manufacturer XXXX use a reference group of down-to-earth Aussie blokes who love fishing and BBQ's to advertise XXXX beer in TV ads.

Opinion leaders

In most reference groups, one or more members stand out as opinion leaders. An opinion leader provides information about a specific sphere that interests reference group participants who seek information. Opinion leaders are viewed by other group members as being well informed about a particular area and as easily accessible. An opinion leader is not

reference group
A group that positively or negatively affects a person's values, attitudes or behaviour

opinion leader
A member of a reference group who provides specific information that interests reference group participants

Source: Getty Images

Opinion leaders >>
Toyota's Vice Chairman, Takeshi Uchiyamada

the foremost authority on all issues, but he or she is in a position or has knowledge or expertise that makes him or her a credible source of information on one or more topics. Because such individuals know they are opinion leaders, they may feel a responsibility to remain informed about their sphere of interest and thus seek out advertisements, manufacturers' brochures, salespeople and other sources of information. An opinion leader is likely to be most influential when consumers have high product involvement but low product knowledge, when they share the opinion leader's values and attitudes and when the product details are numerous or complicated.

SUSTAINABLE MARKETING | GREEN CAR SALES UP AND AQUA TOPS PRIUS

As the leader in hybrid engine technology, in 1997 Toyota enjoyed the success of the world's first mass-produced hybrid passenger car. The fuel efficiency of the Prius hybrid engine, delivering nearly 20 kilometres per litre, is highly appealing to the 'socially aware' segment. This market segment is comprised of the more informed consumers who are also eco-conscious and therefore value the low-level carbon footprint that the Prius delivers. But Toyota has continued to evolve this technology with the release of the Aqua (also known as Prius C in some markets). Released in 2012 in Japan, the Aqua is a smaller, more compact model than the Prius and delivers far greater fuel efficiency, with 40 kilometres per litre and nearly $4000 less on the price tag. Impressively, the Aqua hybrid hatchback showed consistently increasing sales with more than 24 000 units sold within the first six months of release, pushing the Prius down into the number two position.

Aimed at younger (female) buyers, the Aqua offers the same 1.5L Toyota Hybrid System II engine. This means performance is not lost at the expense of improved fuel efficiency, nor is the friendliness of the minimal environmental impact, and all this for a lower price tag. More than fuel efficiency and low carbon emissions, however, a 'green car' such as Toyota's Aqua or Prius models makes a statement about the owner.

Source: Getty Images

In other words, those consumers choosing to drive an icon of green are demonstrating to the world their commitment to the environment, and proudly so!

Demonstrating the increasing acceptance of hybrid vehicles, Toyota's hybrid range now comprises 19 passenger car models accounting for 14 per cent of Toyota's global sales and 40 per cent of sales in the Japanese market. Vice Chairman Takeshi Uchiyamada, known as 'the father of the Prius', recalls initial expectations for the Prius were low with only 1000 cars per month planned for production, but with 'opinion leaders', including Hollywood stars, proudly driving a 'green car'.[19]

Digital networks

Although consumers often rely on the recommendations and suggestions from friends and family when making purchasing decisions, they are increasingly turning to electronic network sources during the decision-making process. Some organisations and websites, such as Choice (http://www.choice.com.au/), have established themselves as reliable sources of information for consumers because of their unbiased product comparisons and stringent testing procedures. However, many lesser-known consumer advocate websites and even many individuals are exerting a stronger influence on consumers who are turning to the Internet for product reviews.

Consumers' reliance on the Internet for assistance during the decision-making process can be seen in the proliferation of blogs, social networking websites, online forums, mailing lists and wikis, as well as text messaging and podcasts. Blogs are Internet-based journals in which writers can editorialise and interact with other Internet users. Similarly, wikis are websites that enable users to add or edit content collaboratively (also called wikipages). One of the best-known wikis is Wikepedia (http://www.Wikipedia.org), an online encyclopedia constructed from consumer-generated content. Social networks, such as Facebook, YouTube and Twitter allow members to share personal profiles that include blogs, pictures, audio clips and visual compilations. (See Marketing in Action box on page 142 on the growth of social networking website Facebook.) For example, in 2005 after Jeff Jarvis had an unhappy experience with Dell's ineffective attempts to resolve problems with his new laptop, he wrote about it on his blog. Within days, his blog became one of the most-visited websites triggering a surge of Dell horror stories across the Internet. Soon after, when people typed 'Dell' into search engines, Jarvis's blog and websites with unflattering names would appear on the first listings page.[20]

Culture and subcultures

Culture is the personality of a society. This societal personality is shown in cultural values, knowledge, beliefs, customs, objects and concepts. Examples of objects are foods, furniture, buildings, clothing and tools. Concepts include education, welfare and laws. Culture also includes core values and the degree of acceptability of a wide range of behaviours in a specific society. For example, in Western culture, customers as well as business people are expected to behave ethically. Early research conducted by Geert Hofstede describes culture along a number of dimensions. His cultural dimensions theory examines values of individualism versus collectivism, uncertainty avoidance, power distance, masculinity

<< Social networks
Social network interfaces such as Facebook, YouTube and Twitter allow consumers to create relationships with other individuals or groups in an online context, revealing connections that are otherwise hidden. Social networks overcome traditional communication barriers of distance, language and time

wikis
Websites that enable users to add or edit content collaboratively

blogs
Internet-based journals which can be edited as well as accommodate interactions with other Internet users

MARKETING IN ACTION | THE RITUAL OF FACEBOOK

Source: Shutterstock.com

Are you one of the millions of people who can't go a day – or an hour – without checking Facebook? Facebook started as an online directory for Harvard students, and just two weeks after the website went live over 4000 members had posted their profiles. Soon after that, Facebook was a full-blown social phenomenon connecting people all over the globe. The rest is history. Recent figures show that Brazil and India are in the top three countries of Facebook users, behind the USA, with India and Indonesia placing fourth and fifth respectively.[21] And notably, the nearly 64 million Facebook users in India accounts for less than 6 per cent of the Indian population.

The popularity of social media and social networking websites, such as Facebook, entails a major shift in consumer behaviour. Consumers are increasingly incorporating their online habits as a daily ritual and while consumers are interacting with each other online, they are also interacting with their favourite brands. 'Like' is becoming the new marketing metric because current customers are choosing to note their preference as a something they 'Like'. When consumers 'Like' a brand's photo, post or newsfeed, this announcement appearing in that consumer's Newsfeed raises awareness among that consumer's friends. In this way, the ritual of Facebook gives consumer's increasing power rather than organisations. In understanding this changing consumer behaviour, marketers are faced with a window of opportunity as to how to better engage within the virtual world. ◼

versus femininity and long-term versus short term. Hofstede's theory was one of the first quantifiable theories which could be used in order to measure observed differences between cultures.[22]

Culture influences consumption behaviour because it permeates our daily lives. Our culture determines what we wear and eat and how daily life takes place. Society's interest in the healthiness of food affects food companies' approaches to developing and promoting their products. Culture also influences how we buy and consume products and the satisfaction derived from them.

When marketers sell products into countries other than their own, they realise the tremendous impact different cultures have on product purchases and use. Global marketers find that people in other regions of the world have different attitudes, values and needs, which call for different methods of doing business as well as different types of marketing mixes. Some international marketers fail because they do not or cannot adjust to cultural differences. Throughout Australia and the Asia-Pacific region, there are many success stories of global marketing. An iconic Australian brand that has successfully gone global is R.M. Williams (http://www.rmwilliams.com.au/).

R.M. Williams offers a unique style of Australian bush outfits and achieves annual sales over $50 million. Known as 'the best bootmakers in the world' and operating more than 100 stores in Australia, New Zealand, London and New York, R.M. Williams understands the harsh conditions of the Australian outback and translates that to mainstream consumer (fashion) needs.

A culture consists of various subcultures. Geographic and demographic subcultures are groups of individuals whose characteristic values and behavioural patterns are similar to each other and differ from those of the surrounding culture. Subcultural boundaries are usually based on geographic designations such as district or region and demographic characteristics such as age, religion, race and ethnicity. Our culture is marked by many different subcultures, including the youth subculture, the gay subculture and the various migrant subcultures such as the Vietnamese subculture in western Sydney and the Asian and Pacific Islander subcultures in Auckland, New Zealand.

subcultures
Groups of individuals whose characteristic values and behavioural patterns are similar to each other and different from those of the surrounding culture

Studies show that subcultures can play a significant role in how people respond to advertisements, particularly when pressured to make a snap judgement.[23] To target these groups more precisely, marketers are striving to become increasingly sensitive to and knowledgeable about subcultural differences. Businesses recognise that to succeed, their marketing strategies will have to take into account the values, needs, interests, shopping patterns and buying habits of various subcultures.

The youth subculture

The Australian youth subculture is primarily about interacting with others of a similar age. Whether that interaction is virtual and online or physical and offline, individuals come together to share experiences. Young people thrive on being part of the youth subculture because it gives them a sense of belonging and a common purpose. Teenage behaviour is (heavily) influenced by group norms and peer pressure; alcohol consumption and binge drinking, for example, is increasingly problematic in the Australian youth subculture. Social marketing efforts by the Australian Government highlight the potentially damaging consequences of binge drinking (http://www.australia.gov.au/drinkingnightmare).

In contrast to the Australian youth subculture, the Thai youth subculture are less deviant and resistant consumers. Young Thai consumers have grown up in a time of massive social and cultural transformation and have experienced a high level of urbanisation. Traditionally, the Thai culture is very much focused on rites of passage, such

Source: iStockphoto/fG photography

<< Social promotion focused on youth culture
On average, one in four hospitalisations of people aged 15–24 occur because of alcohol

as courtship practices, but the current Thai youth are more focused on visual cues and symbolism that indicates conspicuous consumption and a deliberate construction of identity that is particularly influenced by the West. Cohen, for example, documents particular groups or subcultures within the Thai youth that include: *dek board/skate* (skateboarders), *dek Vespa* (Vespa scooter riders), *dek B Boy* (breakdancers), *dek bike* (BMX bike riders), *dek punk* (punks) and *kaeng wairun* (violent teenage gangs).[24] These popular youth subcultures illustrate the powerful influence that Western consumer trends have on the formation of youth identities.

Subcultures of consumption

subcultures of consumption
A subculture defined and unified through shared consumption practices

Unlike a traditional subculture that may be defined by geographic boundaries or demographic variables, subcultures of consumption are unified by the element of consumption choice. This means global communities can emerge where age and affluence are not prerequisites. Harley-Davidson, for example, have created a means by which their consumers can socialise together via the Harley Owners' Group (HOGs).[25]

As a social organisation, the HOGs are structured worldwide as local chapters, with a formally elected committee running each one in conjunction with the local Harley dealership. Membership comes through ownership of a Harley-Davidson; there are more than one million global members, and around 23 000 HOG members in Australia and New Zealand. New bikes retail from around AU$14 250, with the average price around AU$25 000. Beyond the bike and the gear, an additional spend to further customise the bike is also not unusual because each bike is considered the signature of a rider. Each year, members travel to the national rally, and given that credibility in this subculture is

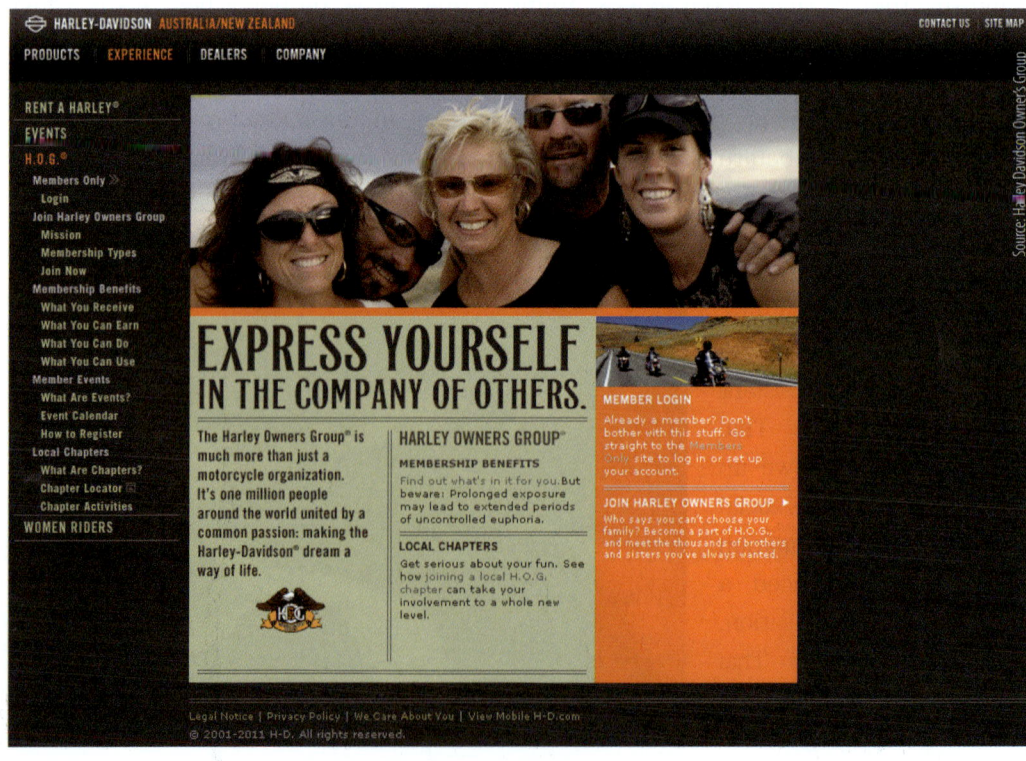

Source: Harley Davidson Owner's Group

HOGs down under >>
Harley-Davidson generates a subcultural following with the HOG brand

generated through participation, members are heavily active in the rallies, rides and other HOG events. A high-profile event in the Asia-Pacific region included the 'Freedom Ride', part of the 110th anniversary celebrations of Harley-Davidson, in 2013.[26] Hence, it takes money to keep up with the unwritten expectations of HOG membership. The economic consideration of the HOGs can also be considered on the other side of the cash register; the small-town vendors receiving a pack of HOGs out for a ride who stop for lunch or overnight, for example, is a lucrative windfall. Annual rallies and rides throughout Australasia bring much needed patronage to struggling businesses. While some business operators might not want this loud crowd, it seems that being biker-friendly is good for business!

MARKETING IN TRANSITION | ARE ALL CONSUMER REVIEWS TRUSTWORTHY?

Some consumers search online for consumer reviews that may help them to evaluate product alternatives and therefore make a purchase decision. However, the integrity of these online consumer reviews is debatable. This is because while some online consumer reviews are unsolicited and user-generated, others are not. It is widely known that some organisations are deliberately engaging consumers to write a positive product review. The problem is that it is not always clear which reviews are unsolicited and which are contrived. Consider this debate about the integrity of online consumer reviews and how effective these reviews may be in persuading a consumer to purchase a particular product.

Study Tools

Chapter review

 **LO1 RECOGNISE THE IMPORTANCE OF UNDERSTANDING CONSUMER BEHAVIOUR.**

Gaining an understanding of consumer behaviour assists in the development of marketing strategies as well as in understanding how consumers will respond to marketing efforts. Understanding consumer needs allows a company to deliver better options than competitors, and create a successful marketing mix that satisfies these needs. An insight into consumer behaviour provides a deeper understanding of the buying process as a whole.

 **LO2 RECOGNISE THE VARIOUS STAGES OF THE CONSUMER DECISION PROCESS.**

The consumer buying decision process includes five stages: problem recognition, information search, evaluation of alternatives, purchase and post-purchase evaluation. Not all decision processes end in a purchase, nor do all consumer decisions include all five stages. Problem recognition occurs when buyers become aware of a difference between a desired state and an actual condition. After recognising the problem or need, buyers search for information about products to help resolve the problem or satisfy the need. A successful search yields a group of brands, called an evoked set, which a buyer views as possible alternatives. To evaluate the product in the evoked set, the buyer establishes certain criteria by which to compare, rate and rank different products. Marketers can influence consumers' evaluation by framing alternatives. In the purchase stage, consumers select products or brands on the basis of results from the evaluation stage and other dimensions. Buyers also choose the seller from whom they will buy the product. After the purchase, buyers evaluate the product to determine if its actual performance meets expected levels.

 **DESCRIBE THE LEVEL OF INVOLVEMENT AND TYPES OF CONSUMER PROBLEM-SOLVING PROCESSES.**

An individual's level of involvement is indicated by the importance and intensity of his or her interest in a product in a particular situation and this involvement level affects the type of problem-solving processes used. Enduring involvement is an ongoing interest in a product class because of personal relevance, whereas situational involvement is a temporary interest stemming from the particular circumstance or environment in which buyers find themselves. There are three kinds of consumer problem solving: routinised response behaviour, limited problem solving and extended problem solving. Consumers rely on routinised response behaviour when buying frequently purchased low-cost items requiring little search and decision effort. Limited problem solving is used for products purchased occasionally or when a buyer needs to acquire information about an unfamiliar brand in a familiar product category. Consumers engage in extended problem solving when purchasing an unfamiliar, expensive or infrequently bought product.

 **EXPLORE HOW SITUATIONAL INFLUENCES MAY AFFECT CONSUMER BEHAVIOUR.**

Situational influences are external circumstances or conditions existing when a consumer makes a purchase decision. Situational influences include surroundings, time, reason for purchase, and the buyer's mood and condition. Surroundings include the physical store location and atmosphere, aromas, sounds, lighting and other factors in the physical environment such as the weather. Socially, surroundings include characteristics and interactions of others, such as friends, relatives, salespeople and other customers who are present when a purchase decision is being made. Another situational influence is the amount of time required to become knowledgeable about a product, to search for it and to buy it. The reason for purchase raises the questions of what exactly the product purchase should accomplish and for whom. Moods also influence behaviour by affecting a person's ability and desire to search for information, receive information, or seek and evaluate alternatives.

 **EXPLORE HOW PSYCHOLOGICAL INFLUENCES MAY AFFECT CONSUMER BEHAVIOUR.**

Psychological influences partly determine people's general behaviour, thus influencing their behaviour as consumers. The primary psychological influences on consumer behaviour are perception, motives, learning, attitudes, self-concept and lifestyles. Perception is the process of selecting, organising and interpreting information inputs (sensations received through sight, taste, hearing, smell and touch) to produce meaning. The three steps in the perceptual process are selection, organisation and interpretation. An individual has numerous perceptions of packages, products, brands and organisations, all of which affect the buying decision process. A motive is an internal energising force that orients a person's activities toward satisfying needs or achieving goals. Learning refers to changes in a person's thought processes and behaviour caused by new information and past experience. Marketers try to shape what consumers learn to influence what they buy. An attitude is an individual's enduring evaluation, feelings and behavioural tendencies toward an object or idea and consists of three major components: cognitive, affective and behavioural. Self-concept, closely linked to personality, is a person's view or perception of himself or herself. Research indicates that a buyer purchases products that reflect and enhance their self-concept. Lifestyle is an individual's pattern of living expressed through activities, interests and opinions.

LO6 EXPLORE HOW SOCIAL INFLUENCES MAY AFFECT CONSUMER BEHAVIOUR.

Social influences are forces that other people exert on buying behaviour. They include roles, family, reference groups, opinion leaders and culture and subcultures. Everyone occupies positions within groups, organisations and institutions, and each position has a role. Each role has a set of actions and activities that a person in a particular position is expected to perform. In a family, children learn from parents (and other household adults) and older siblings how to make purchasing decisions. Consumer socialisation is the process through which a person acquires the knowledge and skills to function as a consumer. The consumer socialisation process is partially accomplished through family influences. A reference group is any group that positively or negatively affects a person's values, attitudes or behaviour. The three major types of reference groups are membership, aspirational and disassociative. In most reference groups, one or more members stand out as opinion leaders by furnishing requested information to reference group participants. Consumers sometimes use Internet networks – especially blogs, wikis and social networks – for information to aid them in buying decisions. Culture is the accumulation of values, knowledge, beliefs, customs, objects and concepts that a society uses to cope with its environment and passes on to future generations. A culture is made up of subcultures. A subculture is a group of individuals whose characteristics, values and behavioural patterns are similar, but differ from those of the surrounding culture.

Key concepts

Use these key terms in **Search me! marketing** to find the latest relevant readings from a wide range of world-class journals, e-books and newspapers, including *The Australian*.

- attitude
- blog
- buying behaviour
- cognitive dissonance
- consumer behaviour
- consumer buying decision
- process
- consumer socialisation
- evaluative criteria

- evoked set
- external search
- extended problem solving
- impulse buying
- internal search
- learning
- level of involvement
- lifestyle
- limited problem solving

- motive
- opinion leader
- perception
- psychological influences
- reference group
- role
- routinised response
  behaviour
- self-concept

- situational influences
- social influences
- social networks
- subcultures
- subcultures of
  consumption
- wikis

Issues for discussion and review

1 Consider your most recent purchase under $10. Describe your decision-making process in terms of the consumer buying decision process shown in Figure 4.1.

2 Consider the most expensive purchase made in your household in the past year. Describe the decision-making process in terms of the consumer buying decision process shown in Figure 4.1.

3 Have you ever bought a high-involvement product on impulse? Compare and contrast your decision-making process in terms of the consumer buying decision process shown in Figure 4.1.

4 How does the Internet impact the consumer decision-making process?

5 What are the categories of situational factors that influence consumer buying behaviour? Explain how each of these factors influences buyers' decisions.

6 What do you consider are the significant situational factors for online shopping?

7 What is selective exposure? Why do people engage in it?

8 How do marketers attempt to shape consumers' learning?

9 Why are marketers concerned about consumer attitudes?

10 In what ways do lifestyles affect the consumer buying decision process?

11 What are reference groups? How do they influence buying behaviour? Name some of your own reference groups.

12 Describe any subcultures of consumption to which you belong. Describe consumption-related behaviour that is unique to one of your subcultures.

Marketing applications

1 Describe three buying experiences you have had – one for each type of problem solving – and identify which problem-solving process you used. Discuss why that particular process was appropriate.

2 Interview someone who is more than 10 years older than yourself about the last purchase he or she made. Ask this person about their attitudes, interests and opinions. Briefly describe any subcultures you are aware of and if values held within this culture influenced this person's consumption choices.

3 Identify two of your roles and give an example of how they have influenced your behaviour as a consumer.

ONLINE EXERCISE

4 Some mass-market e-commerce websites, such as Amazon.com, have extended the concept of customisation to their customer base. Amazon.com has created an affinity group by drawing on certain users' likes and dislikes to make product recommendations to other users. Check out this pioneering online retailer at http://www.amazon.com.

   a What might motivate some consumers to read a 'top selling' list?

   b Is the consumer's level of involvement with an online book purchase likely to be high or low?

   c Discuss the consumer buying decision process as it relates to a decision to purchase from Amazon.com.

Developing your marketing plan

Understanding the process an individual consumer goes through when purchasing a product is essential for developing an effective marketing strategy. Knowledge about potential customers' buying behaviour will become the basis for many of the decisions in the specific marketing plan. Using the information from this chapter, you should be able to determine the following:

* The type of problem solving your customers are likely to use when purchasing your product (see Table 4.1).

* The evaluative criteria that your target market(s) would use when choosing between alternative brands.

* What types of family decision making, if any, would your target market(s) use?

* The reference groups or subcultures that may influence your target market's product selection.

CengageNOW

Go to http:\\login.cengagebrain.com to link to CengageNOW, your online study tool. First take the Pre-Test for this chapter to get your Personalised Study Plan, and then:

 * **Revise** your understanding of the key concepts of marketing with the online glossary

 * **Watch** an interactive animation of strategic marketing to broaden your subject comprehension

 * **Listen** to an audio summary of the learning objectives covered in this chapter.

   After you have completed the activities in your Personalised Study Plan take the Post-Test to determine what concepts you have mastered and what you still need to work on.

Case study

THE IMPORTANCE OF BEHAVIOURAL CHANGE IN SOCIAL MARKETING

Marketing campaigns can focus on more than commercial gain or the interaction between consumers and traditional views of the marketplace. Social marketing looks to improve the lives of individuals or society by encouraging voluntary behavioural change. Many marketing theories, especially those used by consumer behaviourists, can be used to improve the welfare of consumers or society as a whole.

Research has shown that understanding what drives consumers to make decisions can help discourage potentially unhealthy behaviour or encourage healthy behaviours. For example, the influence of reference groups has a significant impact on young adults' decisions to smoke, eat healthily or binge drink. A recent study showed that young adults put a lot of emphasis on gaining approval from their friends. Marketing researchers have been able to use this theory to test if different advertisements are more or less effective in discouraging binge drinking behaviour in university students. In particular, researchers wanted to see if a viable alternative could be found to the traditional health-based messages that are common in Australia and New Zealand. In contrast to traditional public health messages or public service announcements, the focus of these ads was to change behaviour and not just change attitudes. In social marketing, there is a more tenuous relationship between liking an advertisement and actually changing behaviour. One may not like an advertisement, but it will still be an effective means of changing one's behaviour, and vice versa.

Two advertisements were created. The first focused on the adverse health effects of binge drinking (health-based message) and the second focused on the adverse effects binge drinking has on relationships with friends (social approval from reference group message). The health-based advertisement had the tag line 'Binge drinking can cause liver damage, brain damage, impotence and some forms of cancer. Drink responsibly'. The social approval message used the tag line 'Don't let binge drinking ruin a night out for your friends. Drink responsibly'. When shown to over 300 university students, those who saw the social approval message were far less inclined to binge drink – the risk of losing friends was seen as far more serious in the short term than the health risks associated with binge drinking. Interestingly, neither advertisement was liked more than the other, but the one that focused on social disapproval was able to affect behaviour far more.

The key to improving the welfare of consumers and society through marketing is to know what consumers value, because their behaviour (both short- and long-term) is likely to be influenced by these values.

Source: © Roads and Maritime Services (of NSW Australia)

Health-related messages that focus on harmful effects are often ignored by young people, who rarely believe or even notice these messages because the consequences talked about seem so far removed from their everyday lives. For example, encouraging young drivers to keep to the speed limit because speeding can lead to accidents and serious injury, is far less effective than the Road Traffic Authority's multi-award winning 'Pinkie' campaign.

The success of the 'Pinkie' campaign shows that young, male drivers are far more likely to be concerned about how they look to others, especially to young women, than how safe their driving is. The campaign shows young men driving aggressively while onlookers, including friends, wiggle their pinkie fingers, intimating that the driver has a small penis. The campaign's key aim was to make speeding and aggressive driving less 'cool'. It does this by using a universally recognised symbolic gesture to suggest that male drivers who speed are sexually inadequate. The basic premise behind campaigns of this sort is that by using reference groups to raise awareness of antisocial or harmful behaviour, people are more likely to change those attitudes or behaviour in themselves.

The idea is good, but this type of campaign only works if the beliefs are ingrained into society and not just part of a one-off advertising campaign. The success of a campaign relies on people identifying with its message and underpinning ethos. This is where researching and understanding consumer behaviour is of paramount importance to marketers. By understanding the everyday lives of consumers and what motivates them to behave in certain ways, marketers are able to develop more effective campaigns. For example, if the government launched a campaign to discourage online gaming with the tag line 'Only antisocial people play online games!' what effect would that have on young people who may already think they are ostracised by society? My research in the area of online gaming shows that some gamers feel a greater connection with their online communities because this community does not judge them or stigmatise them, like a gamer's offline friends might. As such, any campaign that further validates this sense of stigmatisation could be counterproductive and increase the level of online gaming by some in society.

Campaigns that fail often do so because the marketer focuses too heavily on changing attitudes towards a behaviour and not the behaviour itself. By focusing on creating messages that people can relate to and will affect behaviour has a far greater impact on improving consumer welfare than simply creating cute, funny, scary or beautiful public service announcements. Social marketing is about behaviour – as such, advertising messages need to focus on behaviour.

Ekant Veer, University of Canterbury

1 From a marketing perspective, what do you think are the basic consumer needs in relation to:
   a unhealthy snack foods?
   b a large car with poor fuel efficiency?
   c spending more time with friends online than in person?

2 Thinking about the above three products (unhealthy snack foods, large cars, online connections), what sort of messages would be successful in discouraging their consumption?

3 The case study looked at the impact of 'social approval' in discouraging binge drinking. Would social disapproval have a greater/lesser effect on your behaviour than a health-based message? Why/why not?

Chapter endnotes

1. 'Air passenger market analysis,' IATA Economics, accessed November 2, 2013. http://www.iata.org/publications/economics/market-issues/Pages/demand.aspx; 'Regional Economic Outlook Update Asia and Pacific Department, Fall 2012,' International Monetary Fund, accessed August 11, 2013 from http://www.imf.org/external/pubs/ft/reo/2012/apd/eng/areo1012.pdf; 'Indonesia's per capita GDP expected to rise to USD $5,000 by 2014,' Indonesia Investments, accessed January 29, 2014. http://www.indonesia-investments.com/news/todays-headlines/indonesias-per-capita-gdp-may-rise-to-usd-5-000-by-2014/item1002.

2. 'Best Global Green Brands 2013,' Interbrand, accessed August 11, 2013. http://interbrand.com/en/best-global-brands/Best-Global-Green-Brands/2013/Best-Global-Green-Brands-2013-Brand-View.aspx.

3. 'RAV4 New Generation,' Toyota, accessed January 16, 2014. http://www.toyota-global.com/showroom/vehicle_gallery/special/rav4/.

4. Byravee Iyer, 'Spikes Asia 2012: Unilever brands take lead in co-creation,' Campaign India, September 17, 2012, accessed August 11, 2013. http://www.campaignindia.in/article/315806,spikes-asia-2012-unilever-brands-take-lead-the-in-co-creation.aspx

5. 'Child obesity is quickly beccoming a universal problem,' Child Obesity, accessed January 31, 2014, http://www.child-obesity.info.

6. Andrew D. Gershoff and Gita Venkataramani Johar, 'Do You Know Me? Consumer Calibration of Friends' Knowledge,' Journal of Consumer Research 32 (March 2006): 4961.

7. Rosellina Ferrarim, James R Bettman, and Tanya L Chartrand, 'The Power of Strangers: The effect of incidental consumer brand encounters on brand choice,' Journal of Consumer Research, 35 (5): 729–741.

8. Geetha Mohan, Bharadhwaj Sivakumaran, and Piyush Sharma, 'Impact of store environment on impulse buying behaviour,' European Journal of Marketing, 47 (10): 8.

9. Russell W. Belk, 'Situational Variables and Consumer Behavior,' Journal of Consumer Research (December 1975): 157–164.

10. Nathan Novemsky, Ravi Dhar, Norbert Schwarz, and Itamar Simonson, 'Preference Fluency in Choice,' Journal of Marketing Research 44 (August 2007): 347–356; Law, D., Wong, C. and Yip, J. (2012), 'How does visual merchandising affect consumer affective response? An intimate apparel experience,' European Journal of Marketing, 46: 112–133.

11. Chien-Huang Lin, HsiuJu Rebecca Yen, and Shin-Chieh Chuang, 'The Effects of Emotion and Need for Cognition on Consumer Choice Involving Risk,' Marketing Letters 17 (January 2006): 47–60.

12. B.L. Ochman, B.L., 'Scalped: QR Code haircuts reach 10 million in Thailand,' What's Next? Blog, accessed January 29, 2014, http://www.whatsnextblog.com/2011/05/scalped-qr-code-haircuts-reach-10-million-in-thailand/; Rik Sharma, 'Hair we go! Rooney's hairdresser gets Bromley into shape for the FA Cup,' Daily Mail UK, November 11,

2011, accessed January 29, 2014, http://www.dailymail.co.uk/sport/football/article-2059782/Wayne-Rooney-hairdresser-helps-Bromleys-FA-Cup-cause.html.

13. Zaena Miller, 'Global jeans market recovers but there are challenges ahead for denim,' Euromonitor International, May 13, 2011, accessed August 11, 2013. http://blog.euromonitor.com/2011/05/global-jeans-market-recovers-but-there-are-challenges-ahead-for-denim.html.

14. Evmorfia Argyriou, and T.C. Melewar, 'Consumer attitudes revisited: A review of attitude theory in marketing research,' International Journal of Management Reviews, 13 (4): 431–451.

15. Fishbein, M. and Ajzen, I. (1975). Belief, Attitude, Intention and Behaviour: An Introduction to Theory and Research. Reading, MA: Addison-Wesley.

16. '2012 Consumer Survey – Attitudes towards the AMAG logo, buying Australian,' Roy Morgan Research, accessed August 11, 2013. http://www.australianmade.com.au/resources/research/.

17. Sharon Schembri, Bill Merrilees, and Stine Kristiansen, 'Brand consumption and narrative of the self,' Psychology and Marketing, 27 (6): 623–638.

18. David B. Wooten, 'From Labeling Possessions to Possessing Labels: Ridicule and Socialization Among Adolescents,' Journal of Consumer Research 33 (September 2006): 1881.

19. Yoshio Takahashi, 'Car Sales In Japan Jumped 32% in February,' The Wall Street Journal, March 1, 2012, accessed January 16, 2014. http://blogs.wsj.com/drivers-seat/2012/03/01/car-sales-in-japan-jumped-32-in-february/.

20. Christopher Hart and Pete Blackshaw, 'Internet Inferno,' Marketing Management (January/February 2006): 21.

21. Lim Yung-Hui, 'India is now Facebook Nation No.2, behind the US,' Forbes, February 2, 2012, accessed January 30, 2014, http://www.forbes.com/sites/limyunghui/2012/02/02/india-is-now-facebook-nation-no-2-behind-the-u-s/.

22. Hofstede, Geert (1984). Culture's Consequences: International Differences in Work-Related Values. Thousand Oaks, CA: SAGE Publications.

23. Donnel A. Briley and Jennifer L. Aaker, 'When Does Culture Matter? Effects of Personal Knowledge on the Correction of Culture-Based Judgments,' Journal of Marketing Research 33 (August 2006). http://marketingpower.com.

24. Anjalee Cohen, 'Dek Inter and the 'other': Thai youth subcultures in urban Chiang Mai,' Journal of Social Issues in Southeast Asia, 24 (2): 161–185.

25. Sharon Schembri, 'Reframing brand experience: The experiential meaning of Harley-Davidson,' Journal of Business Research (2009), 62, 1299–1310.

26. L. Mohamad, 'HOG Brunei Chapter to participate in Asia Harley Days,' Borneo Bulletin, July 21, 2013, accessed August 11, 2013. http://borneobulletin.brunei-online.com.bn/index.php/2013/07/21/hog-brunei-chapter-to-participate-in-asia-harley-days/.

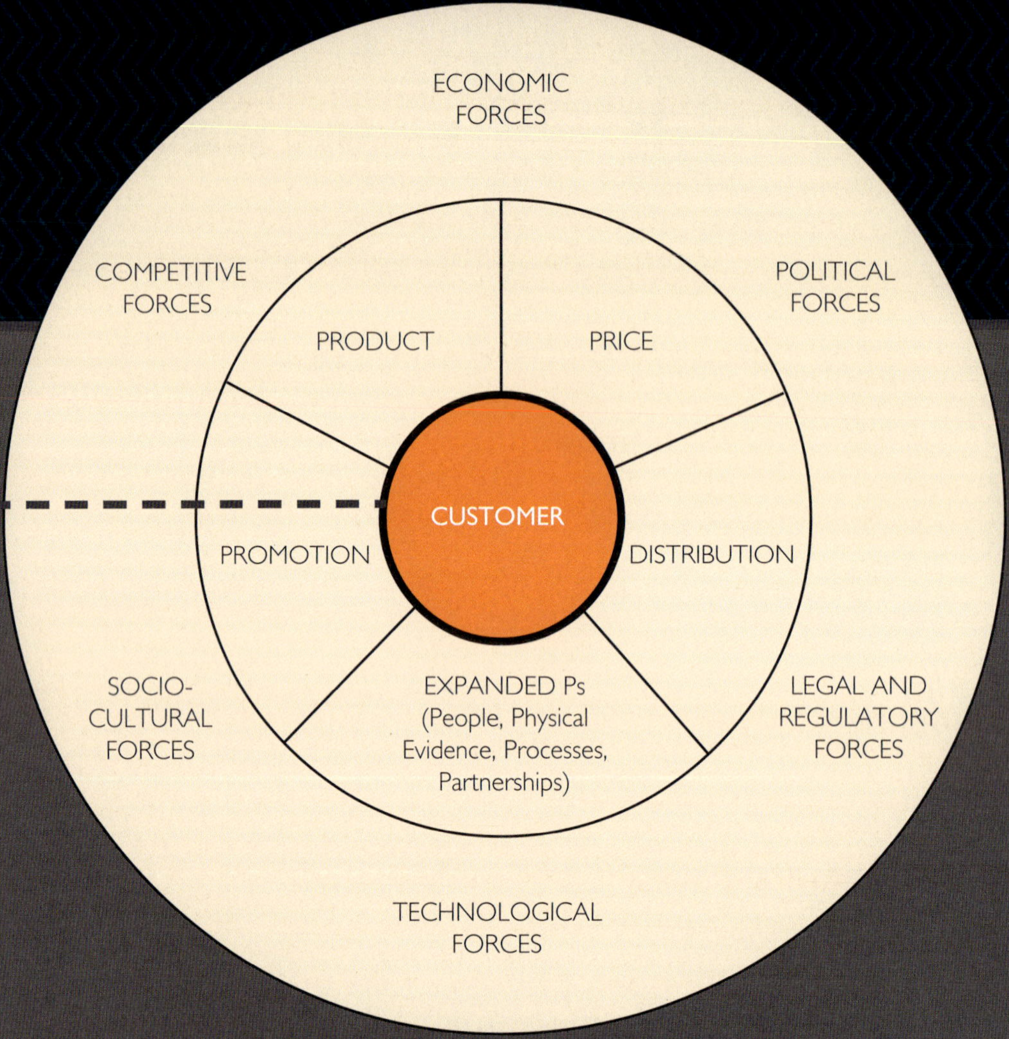
ECONOMIC FORCES
COMPETITIVE FORCES
POLITICAL FORCES
PRODUCT
PRICE
CUSTOMER
PROMOTION
DISTRIBUTION
SOCIO-CULTURAL FORCES
EXPANDED Ps (People, Physical Evidence, Processes, Partnerships)
LEGAL AND REGULATORY FORCES
TECHNOLOGICAL FORCES

SEGMENTATION, TARGET MARKETS AND POSITIONING

What is a market?

Market segmentation

- Variables for consumer markets
- Variables for business markets

Target-market selection process

- Identify the appropriate targeting strategy
- Determine which segmentation variables to use
- Develop market segment profiles
- Evaluate relevant market segments
- Select specific target markets

Product positioning and repositioning

- Perceptual mapping
- Bases for positioning
- Repositioning

Throughout this chapter, Watch, Listen and Revise icons indicate an opportunity for online self-study through CengageNOW, linking you to animated chapter overviews, interactive diagrams, videos, quizzes and more.

5

SEGMENTATION, TARGET MARKETS AND POSITIONING

Learning Objectives

 LO1 Learn what a market is

 LO2 Become familiar with the major segmentation variables

 LO3 Understand the process of selecting and evaluating target market segments

 LO4 Understand the concept of positioning

MARKETING CHALLENGE | THE GREAT GENERATION Y CHALLENGE

Generation Y are sometimes referred to as the 'millennials' because they were born at the turn of the century between 1984 and 2002. Generation Y consumers have posed a challenge for marketers because they are a complicated bunch. This challenge comes about because while Generation Y consumers might be hyper-connected, they are also hard to engage. Generation Y consumers are interested in everything innovative and anything quirky, but at the same time they are very brand savvy, having grown up in a world dominated by marketing messages. They have learnt to discern sometimes dubious messages and therefore Generation Y consumers have very high expectations as to what they need and desire from a consumer–brand relationship. Expectations not only include delivering what is promised, but also creating an engaging experience, catering for user innovation and providing a reward for loyalty. What they are looking for and what Generation Y consumers' value is brands that step up and genuinely involve them in a reciprocal relationship. This means that it is not enough for marketers to say 'buy this [product or that product] because it's the best!' But rather, marketers need to highlight what Generation Y will get from engaging with and consuming a particular brand.[1]

Source: Getty Images

Introduction

In this chapter we explore markets and market segmentation. Initially we introduce the term 'market' and discuss the major requirements of a market. Then we discuss market segmentation and the bases of market segmentation in both consumer and business markets. From there, we look at the steps involved in selecting which market segments to target and we will introduce the basic targeting strategies that can be used. To conclude the chapter, we consider a very important concept in effective marketing – positioning!

What is a market?

In Chapter 2, we defined a market as a group of people who, as individuals or as organisations, have needs for products in a product class and have the ability, willingness and authority to purchase such products. Students, for example, are part of the market for textbooks; they are also part of the markets for computers, books, clothes, food, music and a myriad other products. Individuals can have the desire, the buying power and the willingness to purchase certain products but may not have the authority to do so. For example, teenagers may have the desire, the money and the willingness to buy alcohol, but in countries such as Australia, the Philippines and Taiwan, a hotel does not consider them a market because teenagers under 18 years are prohibited by law from buying alcoholic beverages. A group of people that lacks any one of the four requirements, therefore, does not constitute a market. Here are the four criteria that constitute a market:

1   The potential customers have the desire.
2   The potential customers have the buying power.
3   The potential customers have the willingness to buy.
4   The potential customers have the authority to buy.

Markets fall into one of two categories: consumer markets and business markets. These categories are based on the characteristics of the individuals, groups or organisations that make up a specific market and the purposes for which they buy products. A **consumer market** consists of purchasers and household members who intend to consume or benefit from the purchased products and do not buy products for the main purpose of making a profit. Consumer markets are sometimes also referred to as business-to-consumer (B2C) markets. Each of us as individuals belong to numerous consumer markets. The millions of

consumer market
Purchasers and household members who intend to consume or benefit from the purchased products and do not buy products to make profits

individuals with the desire, ability, willingness and authority to buy make up a multitude of consumer markets for products such as housing, food, clothing, vehicles, personal services, appliances, furniture or recreational equipment and services.

A business market consists of individuals or groups that purchase a specific kind of product for one of three purposes: resale, direct use in producing other products or use in general daily operations. For example, an electrician that buys electrical wire to use in the construction of residential homes is part of a business market for electrical components. This same electrical installation company also buys stationery, computers, photocopiers and filing cabinets. Although these stationery items and office equipment are not used in the direct production of the electrical installation services, they are necessary in the daily operation of the company; thus this electrical installation company is part of a business market for office stationery and equipment. Business markets may also be called business-to-business (B2B), industrial or organisational markets. They can also be classified into producer, reseller, government and institutional markets and each of these B2B segments are discussed later in the chapter.

business market
Individuals or groups that purchase a specific kind of product for resale, direct use in producing other products or use in general daily operations

Source: iStockphoto.com

Source: Fairfax Photos

<< Types of markets
Tiffany & Co aims its diamond rings and jewellery at consumer markets. However, pink diamonds coming from the Argyle Diamond mine are aimed at business target markets

LO2

Market segmentation

Market segmentation is about dividing up the whole mass market into segments or groups of consumers who have similar needs and wants. These segments or groups of consumers who have similar needs and wants are homogenous groups and form homogenous markets as described below. However, when comparing these homogenous groups across the broader market, we see a variation and this is referred to as heterogeneous markets.

When considering the total market as one broad market, marketers are assuming that the potential customers in that market have similar needs and wants. There is no differentiation considered for different types of people, different times of day or even different cultures. This type of market is described as a homogenous market.

In contrast to a homogenous market, markets that are made up of individuals or organisations with diverse product needs are called heterogeneous markets. Not everyone wants the same type of car, furniture or clothes. Consider that some individuals want an economical and fuel efficient car, whereas other consumers desire a status symbol and still others seek the practicality of a utility vehicle. Therefore, the automobile market is heterogeneous. Accordingly, Holden offers the Barina Spark, a compact and fuel efficient model for those consumers focused on economy, the Caprice as a luxury model for the status-oriented consumer, and the SS Ute for the more practically-oriented consumer. However, it is important to note that while the consumer needs are heterogeneous across these automobile segments, within each of these recognised auto segments, the consumer needs are homogenous.

For such heterogeneous markets, market segmentation is appropriate. Market segmentation is the process of dividing a total market into smaller sub-groups, or segments, where each segment consists of people or organisations with relatively similar product needs. The purpose of segmenting the broader homogenous market into smaller heterogeneous segment is to enable a marketer to design a marketing mix that more precisely matches the needs of customers in the selected market segment. A market segment consists of individuals, groups or organisations with one or more similar characteristics that cause them to have relatively similar product needs. In understanding customer needs within a particular or several segments, an organisation will design and implement a marketing mix tailored to meet the needs of that specific segment. A target market is the defined customer segment for which an organisation designs and implements a tailored marketing mix to effectively meet the needs of that segment.

To demonstrate the concept of market segmentation, let's consider the video game market. The popularity of video games is evident throughout the world with total global spending expected to reach $83 billion in 2016.[2] This mass consumer market is driven by the need for social interactivity and the want of entertainment. However, assuming that every consumer who plays video games is seeking social interaction and entertainment is a very simplistic and unsophisticated approach. The total video game market is considered to consist of new console games, computer games, online games and wireless games. So this total market can be segmented in terms of age, gender, geography and/or usage. Here are some examples of gaming segments:

✳ Disney Pixar has designed an online game for kids based on *Brave's* leading character, Merida, the skilled archer and impetuous daughter or King Fergus and Queen Elinor.

✳ Throughout the Philippines, many young men choose to spend hours at Internet cafés where for just a few dollars per hour, they can access fast Internet and play the most popular online games, such as Warcraft III (and by extension DotA) or maybe Star Wars: Battlefront, Counter-Strike and Civilization IV.

✳ China is the world's largest online gaming market with more than 100 million and rising players. But in 2011, one hard-core gamer in Beijing lost his life after a three-day gaming binge. Concern over online addictions in China has led to a proliferation of military-style boot camps for kids.[3]

---

homogeneous market
A market in which a large proportion of customers are considered to have similar needs and wants

heterogeneous markets
Markets made up of individuals or organisations with diverse needs for products in a specific product class

market segmentation
The process of dividing a total market into meaningful groups with relatively similar product needs and wants

market segment
Individuals, groups or organisations with one or more similar characteristics that cause them to have similar product needs

✳ Gamers will gather together to play, and may even choose to share a household so as to save on living costs, enable more time to be spent gaming and engage in collective gaming rituals.[4] Gamers also tend to consume energy-dense low-nutrient food to therefore heighten the hedonistic experience.[5]

In this example of video gaming, we have considered the market segments based on age, gender, geography and usage. These characteristics are referred to as segmentation variables.

Segmentation variables are the characteristics of individuals, groups or organisations used to divide a market into segments. Most marketers use several segmentation variables in combination.

segmentation variables
Characteristics of individuals, groups or organisations used to divide a market into segments

Variables for segmenting consumer markets

A marketer using segmentation to reach a consumer market can choose one of several variables from an assortment of possibilities. As Figure 5.1 shows, segmentation variables can be grouped into four categories: demographic, geographic, psychographic and behaviouristic.

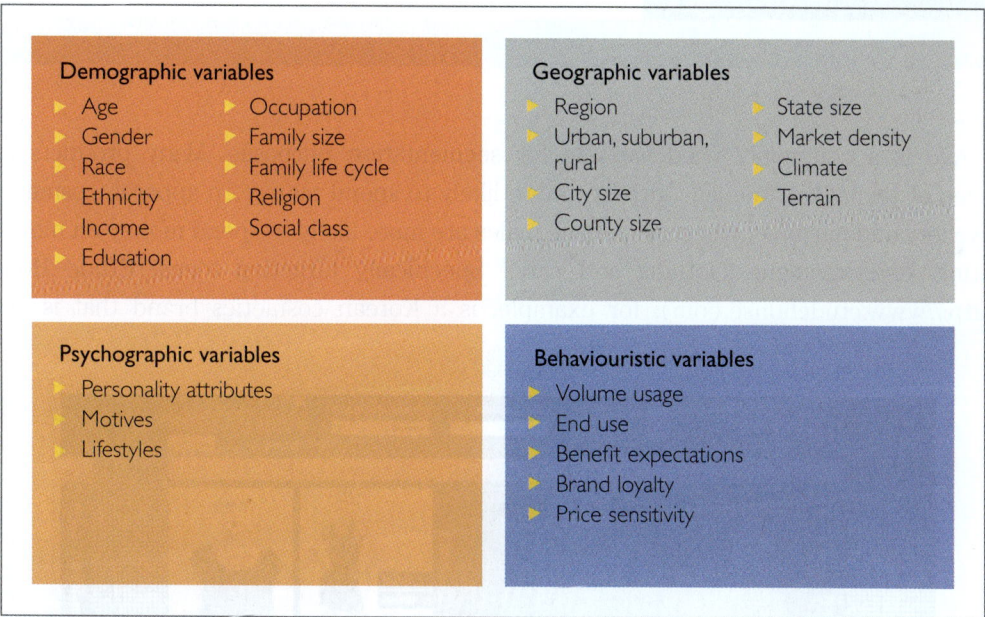

Demographic variables	
▶ Age	▶ Occupation
▶ Gender	▶ Family size
▶ Race	▶ Family life cycle
▶ Ethnicity	▶ Religion
▶ Income	▶ Social class
▶ Education	

Geographic variables	
▶ Region	▶ State size
▶ Urban, suburban, rural	▶ Market density
▶ City size	▶ Climate
▶ County size	▶ Terrain

Psychographic variables
▶ Personality attributes
▶ Motives
▶ Lifestyles

Behaviouristic variables
▶ Volume usage
▶ End use
▶ Benefit expectations
▶ Brand loyalty
▶ Price sensitivity

REVISE your knowledge of market segmentation with the Interactive Activity based on Figure 5.1

FIGURE 5.1
SEGMENTATION VARIABLES FOR CONSUMER MARKETS

Demographic variables

Demographic segmentation is commonly used by marketers. Demographic segmentation variables include age, gender, race, ethnicity, income, education, occupation, family size, family life cycle and religion. Marketers rely on these demographic characteristics because they are often closely linked to customers' needs and purchasing behaviour and can be readily measured. (See Marketing in Transition box on the next page for an example of age-based segmentation.) Like demographers, marketers might at times even use mortality rates. An example is Guardian Insurance, who offers pre-paid funeral packages and therefore targets higher-income suburban areas with an ageing demographic.

demographic segmentation
Market segmentation based on factors such as age, gender, income, education and ethnicity

MARKETING IN TRANSITION | BRAVE GIRL POWER OR FEEBLE FEMALE?

Marketing targeted towards children is being increasingly questioned because children are so impressionable in their formative years. So, when Pixar introduced Merida as the leading character to their movie, *Brave*, social critics applauded because here was a flame-haired princess that did not want to be married and was a skilled archer and horse

Source: Picture Media

rider. Merida does not pine for a prince to rescue her, instead she solves her own problems. However, not all critics agreed because even though Merida is strong, capable and courageous, she is still a princess nevertheless. More than that, when Pixar transported this princess from the big screen into little girl's bedrooms as the latest addition to the Disney Princess doll collection, Merida arrived without her bow and arrow. Some critics argued that Merida had been disempowered and that the feeble female character role had re-emerged.

What do you think? Was Merida disempowered? And is a female carrying a weapon a more powerful statement than a female without a weapon? ✕

Age is a commonly used variable for segmentation purposes. Many products are aimed at teenagers. Teenage girls are more likely to spend money on apparel, cosmetics, jewellery and perfume, whereas teenage males are more likely to spend money on movies, dating, entertainment, clothing and cars.[6] Specifically targeting teens, Etude House (http://www.etudehouse.com), for example, is a Korean cosmetics brand that is very

Age-based segmentation >>
Supré targets teenage girls by advertising in magazines such as *Girlfriend* and by setting up an interactive Facebook page, all of which direct girls to the online shopping website

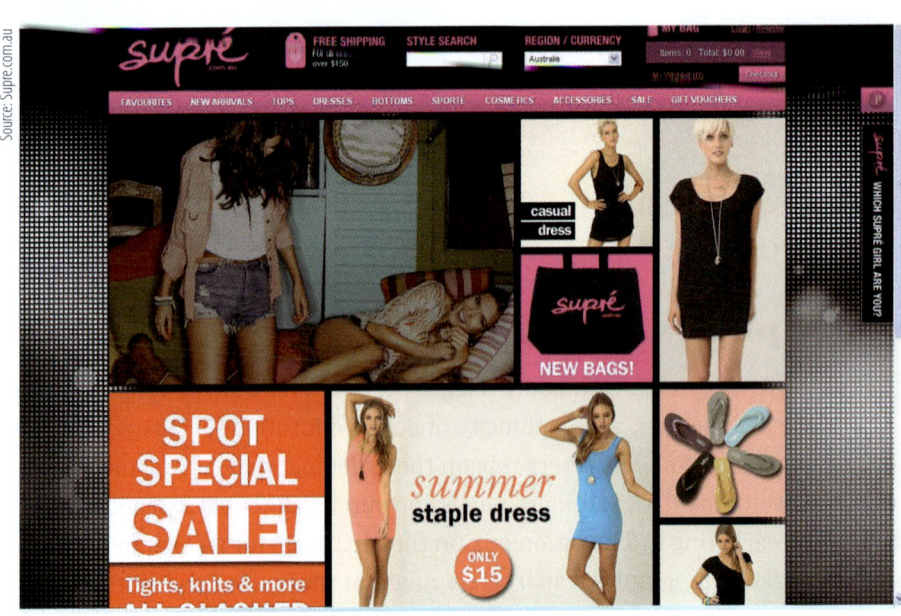

Source: Supre.com.au

ETHICAL MARKETING   TAKING GEEK-CHIC A LITTLE TOO FAR?

issue

Issue: How accountable are marketers when it comes to dangerous consumption trends?

There was a time in a teenager's life that the dreaded visit to the dentist resulted in a mouth full of unwanted steel. However, times have changed and the 'Metal Mouth' effect is in demand! This peculiar fashion trend is evident in Southeast Asia where teens are donning fake braces for the sake of fashion.

This trend was first reported in Thailand in 2006 and authorities were concerned. Young girls with braces were featured in Thai magazines and Thai teens were purchasing do-it-yourself kits that were colour coded with their outfits. The Thai government's Consumer Protection Board considered the trend a potential choking hazard, noting that some of the wires contained lead. By 2013, the trend had spread into China where a black-market trade had emerged. Teens could buy the braces for around AU$100 while real braces cost more than AU$1200. The trend to wear fake braces is driven by the Asian quest to acquire a Western status symbol. Unfortunately, the accessory has been linked to at least two deaths with one 17 year old from Thailand contracting a thyroid infection which resulted in heart failure. Somewhere there are marketers responsible for the manufacture and distribution of this trending product![9]

popular with pretty packaging and store facades that look like massive doll houses. Their deliberate effort to appeal to teenage girls is evident in their stated mission.

The global purchasing power of teens (12–19 years), according to TRU Insights, has reached $819 billion.[7] Breaking this down regionally, 2.2 million Australian teenagers spend a cool $9 billion, and a massive 445 million teenagers across the Asia-Pacific spend $473.7 billion with China ($326 billion) and India ($108 billion) leading the charge.[8]

Source: Advertising Archives

Cracker Barrel

SHARP TASTE FOR MEN OF DISTINCTION

'For a cheese this sharp a toothpick won't cut it. En garde.'

BARON VON ORSÜM

<< Gender-based segmentation
Cracker Barrel Vintage Cheddar is a cheese targeted at affluent men with distinguished taste

So as marketers, what do we need to know about the teenage market? Apart from their spending power, marketers need to know that teenagers are also tech-savvy consumers who challenge the status quo, they are highly discerning and they set the trends. However, such power also comes with responsibility, as discussed below in terms of the questionable ethics of organisations offering fake braces to Asian teens (see Ethical Marketing box on the previous page).

Gender is another demographic variable commonly used to segment markets, including the markets for clothing, soft drinks, nonprescription medications, toiletries, magazines and even cigarettes. The Australian Bureau of Statistics (ABS) reported that as at June 2011, there were 124 700 more females than males in Australia.[10] Some deodorant marketers use gender segmentation: Impulse deodorants are marketed specifically to women, whereas Old Spice deodorants and colognes are directed toward men, with Isiah Mustafa leading the way.[11]

Income often provides a way to divide markets because it strongly influences consumer's product needs. Financial resources affect the consumer's ability to buy and their desires for certain lifestyles. Product markets segmented by income include sporting goods, housing, furniture, cosmetics, clothing, jewellery, home appliances, cars and electronics. While many retailers choose to target consumers with higher incomes, some marketers are instead going after lower-income consumers with new products ranging from prepaid mobile phones and debit cards to budget paper towels.

Among the factors influencing household income and product needs are marital status and the presence and ages of children. These characteristics, often combined and called the *family life cycle*, affect needs for housing, appliances, food and beverages, cars and recreational equipment. Family life cycles can be broken down in a number of ways.

According to the ABS, families are considered as two or more persons (one of whom is 15 years or older), related by blood, marriage (including defacto relationships), adoption, step or fostering, and who usually reside in the same household. More women than men are increasingly living alone and the proportion of people living in group households is decreasing.

The ABS recognises a family can be comprised of:

✵ couples with or without children living in the household

✵ single parents with co-resident children of any age

✵ other family structures of related adults living together where no couple or parent-child relationship exists, for example a brother and sister living together.

This definition of family also includes gay couples living with or without children in the household. Single parent families are equally recognised as family, meaning that the traditional nuclear family of a married man and woman with children is no longer the only accepted family structure. Of the 6.3 million families in Australia in 2009–10, 84 per cent (5.4 million) were couple families, 14 per cent (879 000) were one parent families and 2 per cent (98 000) were other families.

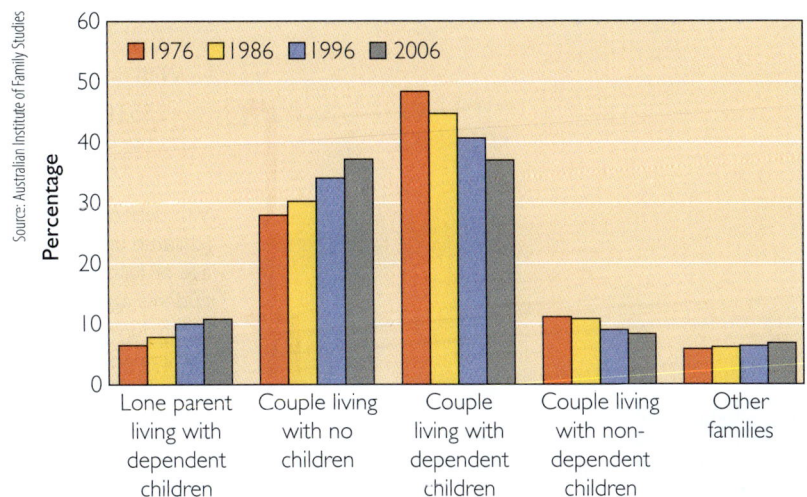

Source: Australian Institute of Family Studies

FIGURE 5.2
FAMILIES THEN AND
NOW: 1976–2006

For couple families, those with co-resident children of any age outnumbered those without children of any age as evidenced in Figure 5.2. The proportion of couple families with children has been decreasing since 1997 (48 per cent of total families in 1997, 46 per cent in 2003, 45 per cent in 2006–07 and 44 per cent in 2009–10), whereas the proportion of couple families without children of any age has been increasing over time (35 per cent of total families in 1997, 38 per cent in 2003, 40 per cent in both 2006–07 and 2009–10). Around Australia, those states or territories with a higher than average proportion of couple families without children of any age were Queensland (42 per cent), South Australia (42 per cent), Western Australia (42 per cent) and Tasmania (44 per cent). The proportion of one-parent families with children of any age declined slightly in 2009–10 compared to previous years (14 per cent in 2006–07; 15 per cent in both 2003 and 1997).[12] Please see Figure 5.2 for a graphical illustration of this changing trend in household structure.

Tracking life changes helps marketers to satisfy the needs of particular target markets through new marketing mixes. For example, companies can choose to specifically target customers according to what life stage the family is at. This can be done by buying a list of names and contact details from a list broker for purposes of developing a direct mail campaign. The list broker can provide marketers with specific lists of people such as those who recently moved, soon-to-be newlyweds, recent high school and university graduates and expectant parents. By focusing on such narrow target markets, the approach is more relevant and communications can be personalised for added impact.

Marketers also use many other demographic variables. For instance, theatres, museums and other providers of the arts use education level as a segmentation variable. Some health insurance companies segment markets using occupation and this segmentation enables them to specifically target university students and single people to encourage them to take out health insurance at an early stage of adult life which is then carried on through the various stages of the family life cycle.

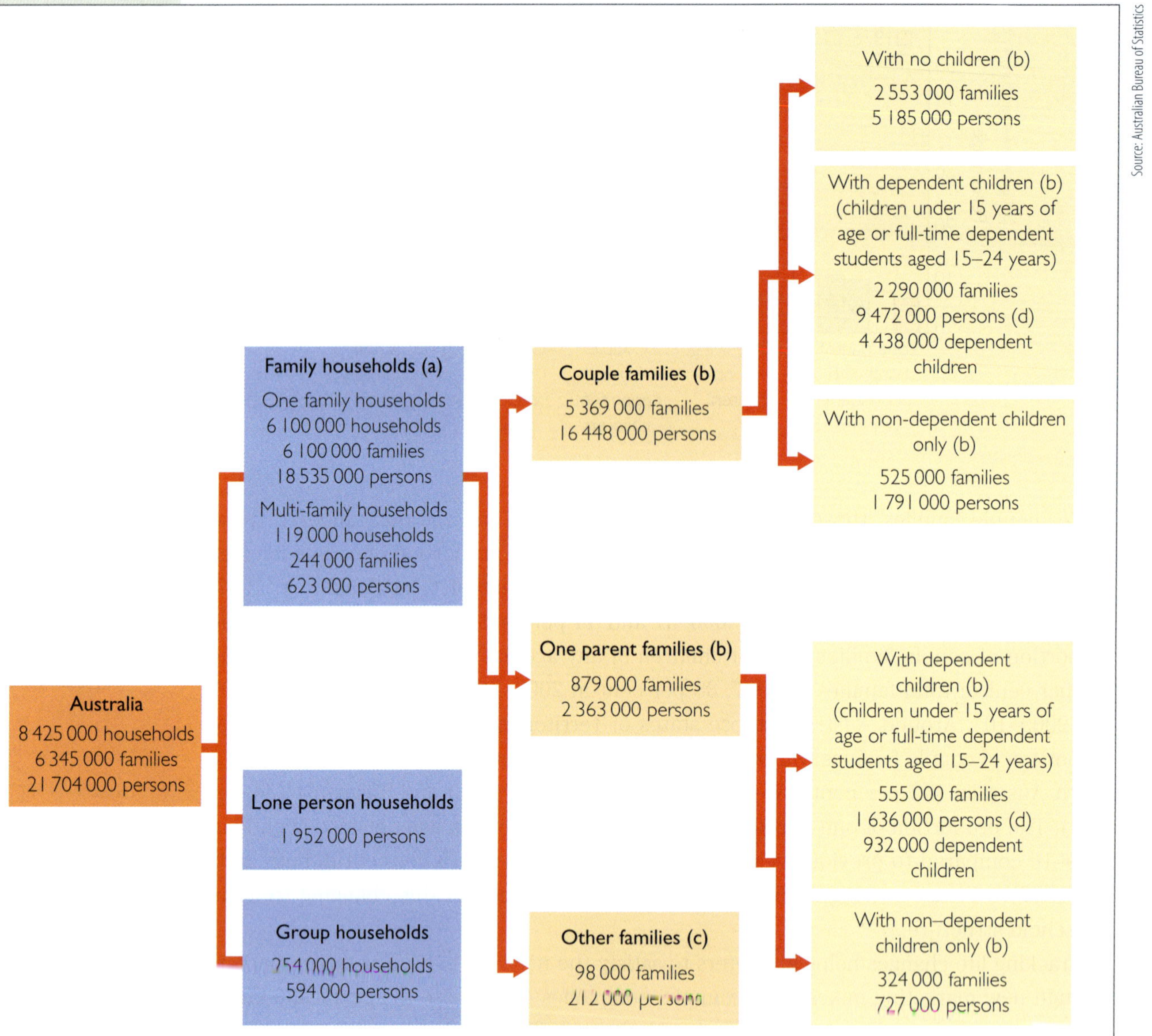

Source: Australian Bureau of Statistics

Australia
8 425 000 households
6 345 000 families
21 704 000 persons

Family households (a)
One family households
6 100 000 households
6 100 000 families
18 535 000 persons

Multi-family households
119 000 households
244 000 families
623 000 persons

Lone person households
1 952 000 persons

Group households
254 000 households
594 000 persons

Couple families (b)
5 369 000 families
16 448 000 persons

One parent families (b)
879 000 families
2 363 000 persons

Other families (c)
98 000 families
212 000 persons

With no children (b)
2 553 000 families
5 185 000 persons

With dependent children (b)
(children under 15 years of
age or full-time dependent
students aged 15–24 years)
2 290 000 families
9 472 000 persons (d)
4 438 000 dependent
children

With non-dependent children
only (b)
525 000 families
1 791 000 persons

With dependent
children (b)
(children under 15 years of
age or full-time dependent
students aged 15–24 years)
555 000 families
1 636 000 persons (d)
932 000 dependent
children

With non–dependent
children only (b)
324 000 families
727 000 persons

(a) In addition to couples, parents, children and other family members, family households may also include unrelated
individuals. Therefore, the number of persons in family households will not equal the number of persons in families.
(b) These families may include 'other related individuals', but excludes 'unrelated individuals', as defined in the Glossary.
(c) Refers to families where there are no partners or children (e.g. adult siblings living together without a parent), but
excludes unrelated individuals.
(d) Includes non-dependent children in families with dependent children as well as other related individuals.

FIGURE 5.3
AUSTRALIAN BUREAU
OF STATISTICS FIGURES
FOR HOUSEHOLDS,
FAMILIES AND PERSONS,
2009–10

**geographic
segmentation**
Market segmenting by
national boundaries, regional
districts or even suburban
postcode

Geographic variables

Geographic segmentation variables such as climate, terrain, city size, population density and urban/rural areas also influence customer product needs. Consumers in Malaysia and Thailand for instance, do not have a need for snow tyres, simply because snow does not fall in that part of the world, Whereas, consumers in certain parts of Australia, as well as mountainous regions of Japan, do require snow tyres during the winter snow season. National geographic markets may be further divided into regions because one or more geographic variable can cause customers to differ from one region to another. A company selling products to the Australian domestic market might divide the nation into states and territories, then add the Pacific Rim region and New Zealand as potential expansion markets. A company operating in one of several states might regionalise its market by cities, postcode areas or other useful units of analysis.

City size can also be an important segmentation variable. Some marketers focus efforts on cities of a certain size. For example, McDonald's aims to situate a franchise operation within each area of a 30 000 population. Other companies actively seek opportunities in smaller towns. A classic example is Australia Post, which is a public service and therefore required to be located in large cities as well as in small towns.

Market density refers to the number of potential customers within a unit of land area, such as a square kilometre. Although market density relates generally to population density, the correlation is not exact. For example, in two different geographic markets of approximately equal size and population, market density for office supplies would be much higher in one area if it contained a much greater proportion of business customers than the other area. Market density may be a useful segmentation variable because low-density markets often require different sales, advertising and distribution activities than high-density markets.

Several marketers use geodemographic segmentation. Geodemographic segmentation clusters people in postcode areas and even smaller neighbourhood units based on lifestyle information and especially demographic data, such as income, education, occupation, type of housing, ethnicity, family life cycle and level of urbanisation. These small, precisely described population clusters help marketers to isolate demographic units as small as neighbourhoods where the demand for specific products is strongest. Geodemographic segmentation allows marketers to engage in micromarketing. Micromarketing is the focusing of precise marketing efforts on very small geodemographic markets, such as community and even neighbourhood markets. Providers of financial and health care services, retailers and consumer products companies use micromarketing. Special advertising campaigns, promotions, retail site-location analyses, special pricing and unique retail product offerings are a few examples of micromarketing facilitated through geodemographic segmentation. Many retailers use micromarketing to determine the merchandise mix for individual stores.

Micromarketing can begin with census data; however, classifying households and geographic segments using census data is too broad for a micromarketing effort. Consequently, some marketing organisations, such as Pacific Micromarketing, have created new and more precisely defined market segmentations. Around the world, neighbourhood classifications (e.g. MOSIAC) perform best within geographies comprised of 15–30 residences. Pacific Mircomarketing, therefore, used residential address information to identify neighbourhoods that contain an average of 22 households, which also aligned exactly with the government-defined Census Collection Districts (CCD). This means that the 7 million residential households in Australia are now segmented into 314 078 micro segments, which are identified by a 10-digit code that includes the government-defined 7-digit CCD code. Microsegments now set the geographic standard for geodemographic classifications and market analysis in Australia.[13]

In the United Kingdom, other segmentation systems specifically based on the census data include the OAC system, CAMEO system and ACORN systems (as well as the GeoSmart

market density
The number of potential customers within a unit of land area

geodemographic segmentation
Market segmentation that clusters people in postcode areas and smaller neighbourhood units based on lifestyle and demographic information

micromarketing
An approach to market segmentation in which organisations focus precise marketing efforts on very small geodemographic markets

system – developed by Australian company RDA Research). Systems such as these are often based on the premise that 'birds of a feather flock together'.

Climate is commonly used as a geographic segmentation variable because of its broad impact on people's behaviour and product needs. Product markets affected by climate include air-conditioning and heating equipment, fireplace accessories, clothing, gardening equipment, recreational products and building materials.

Psychographic variables

Marketers are increasingly using psychographic segmentation variables, such as personality characteristics, motives and especially lifestyles, to segment markets. A psychographic dimension can be used independently to segment a market or can be combined with other types of segmentation variables.

psychographic segmentation
Market segmentation based on factors such as personality and lifestyle

Personality characteristics can be useful for segmentation when a product resembles many competing products and consumers' needs are not significantly related to other segmentation variables. However, segmenting a market according to personality traits can be risky. Although marketing practitioners have long believed consumer choice and product use vary with personality, until recently marketing research had indicated only weak relationships. It is hard to measure personality traits accurately, especially since most personality tests were developed for clinical use, not for market segmentation purposes.

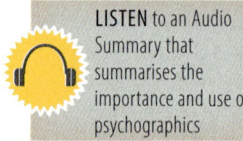
LISTEN to an Audio Summary that summarises the importance and use of psychographics

When appealing to a personality characteristic, marketers almost always select one that many people view positively. Individuals with this characteristic, as well as those who would like to have it, may be influenced to buy that marketer's brand. Marketers taking this approach do not worry about measuring how many people have the positively valued characteristic; they assume that a sizable proportion of people in the target market either have it or want to have it.

When motives are used to segment a market, the market is divided according to consumers' reasons for making a purchase. Personal appearance, affiliation, status, safety and health are examples of motives affecting the types of products purchased and the choice of stores in which they are bought. Marketing efforts based on health and fitness motives can be a point of competitive advantage. For example, Subway, Sizzler and McDonald's each offer a new and healthy menu option to target consumers who are focused on health consciousness and weight-loss resolutions. While Subway is well positioned as the healthy choice among the fast-food options, the company also diligently introduced a number of menu items that contain only six grams of fat.

Lifestyle segmentation groups individuals according to how consumers spend time, the importance of things in their surroundings (homes or jobs, for example), beliefs about themselves and broad issues, and some demographic characteristics, such as income and education.[14] Lifestyle analysis provides a broad view of buyers because it encompasses numerous characteristics related to people's activities (work, hobbies, entertainment and sports), interests (family, home, fashion, food and technology) and opinions (politics, social issues, education and the future).

Behaviouristic variables

Companies can divide a market according to some feature of consumer behaviour toward a product, commonly involving some aspect of product use. For example, a market may be separated into users – classified as heavy, moderate or light – and non-users. To satisfy a specific group, such as heavy users, marketers may create a distinctive product, set special prices, or initiate special promotion and distribution activities. Per capita consumption data help to identify different levels of usage.[15]

EXPLORE SCULPTURES 60 MILLION YEARS IN THE MAKING

THERE'S NOTHING LIKE AUSTRALIA

DISCOVER THE BUNGLE BUNGLE RANGES AT AUSTRALIA.COM

Source: © Tourism Australia, reproduced with permission

<< Lifestyle segmentation This Tourism Australia ad is designed to encourage travellers to 'go walkabout down under'

How customers use or apply products may also determine segmentation. To satisfy customers who use a product in a certain way, a product feature such as the packaging, size, texture or colour, may be designed precisely to make the product easier to use, safer or more convenient to consumers with a particular lifestyle. (See Sustainable Marketing box below for an example of a product designed specifically for consumers who have chosen environmentally conscious consumption practices.)

SUSTAINABLE MARKETING | IT'S NOT EASY BEING GREEN?

If you are making green claims in your marketing efforts in Australia, then you are required to abide by the *Competition and Consumer Act 2010*. The **Australian Competition and Consumer Commission (ACCC)** provides a guide to educate businesses about their green obligations. The ACCC guidelines were designed to counter those businesses who inaccurately claim their products and operations are green. Penalties apply for those found to be guilty of misleading conduct, or **greenwashing**. The ACCC therefore advises marketers to steer away from using words such as 'green', 'environmentally friendly' or 'environmentally safe'. The key message is that sustainability is important but ensuring the accuracy of any green advertising or marketing is equally important. The following tips are highly recommended.

Source: Shutterstock.com

Tips for green advertising and marketing

→ Ensure you are 100 per cent honest in your claims – There is more than reputation at stake, after the

ACCC launched a crackdown on green claims with the release of its guidelines, *Green Marketing and the Trade Practices Act*. Under the Act, the maximum fine can be as high as $1.1 million for organisations and $220 000 for individuals.

→ Check and double-check your claims – To ensure the accuracy of your claims, it can be helpful to use a (credible) third party to objectively measure what you are saying.

→ Collect data – Substantiate your claims, and make them publicly available; for example, by putting this evidence up on the organisation's website. If unsure, seek legal advice – this is the only way to ensure the accuracy of your claims.

→ Steer clear of overused phrases – As advised by the ACCC, phrases such as environmentally friendly, green, carbon neutral and CFC-free can be misleading and open to an individual's interpretation. Ensure you research appropriate terminology and educate your staff to prevent misuse.

→ Avoid 'green' imagery – Pictures of leaves, dolphins, pandas and other 'green' imagery are often overused. For instance, a picture of a dolphin on packaging infers that the product is dolphin friendly – but are these claims substantiated? Use clear language as an alternative.

→ Use your website – Promote your commitment to sustainability. Sometimes not all the information you want to convey will fit in a brochure or on a product.

→ Consider your use of marketing materials – Ensure you carefully consider printing brochures and flyers – could you put this information on your website to minimise paper use? Also, where possible, use recycled materials for printing and only print quantities you require.

→ Promote green-friendly options for consumers – You may like to consider providing an accredited carbon offset scheme for your consumers or encourage consumers to use public transport or to adopt green practices, such as reusing towels in their room. Packaging can support a product's green positioning. Unilever, for example, has repackaged their Omo laundry liquid into an ultra-concentrated 475 ml recyclable bottle. This new packaging is an easy way for consumers to reduce environmental impact without sacrificing washing performance. Unilever also promises that Omo Small & Mighty gives excellent washing results even though it contains low sodium levels and no phosphate. The concentrated form of laundry liquid means less packaging, less energy required to transport the product and less waste. Unilever, therefore, offers consumers a smart and green choice in the laundry liquid category.

Australian Competition and Consumer Commission (ACCC)

The ACCC promotes competition and fair trade in the market place to benefit consumers, businesses and the community. Its primary responsibility is to ensure that individuals and businesses comply with the Commonwealth competition, fair trading and consumer protection laws.

benefit segmentation
The division of a market according to benefits that customers want from the product

Benefit segmentation involves the division of a market according to benefits that consumers want from the product. Although most types of market segmentation assume a relationship between the variable and customers' needs, benefit segmentation differs because the benefits customers seek are their product needs. For example, a customer who purchases toothpaste may be interested in cavity protection, whiter teeth, natural ingredients or sensitive gum protection. Therefore, individuals are segmented directly according to their needs and/or desired benefits. By determining the desired benefits, marketers may be able to divide people into groups seeking certain sets of benefits. For example, Kellogg's cereals have recently repackaged two of their favourite breakfast cereals (Coco Pops and Nutri-Grain) in a liquid format. This investment in product development delivers the benefit of convenience in a user-friendly form for those consumers seeking a breakfast on the go.

The effectiveness of benefit segmentation depends on three conditions:

* the benefits sought must be identifiable

* using these benefits, marketers must be able to divide people into recognisable segments

* one or more of the resulting segments must be accessible to the company's marketing efforts.

Variables for segmenting business markets

Like consumer markets, business markets are frequently segmented, often by multiple variables in combination. Marketers segment business markets according to geographic location, type of organisation, customer size and product use.

Geographic location

We noted earlier that the demand for some consumer products varies considerably among geographic areas because of differences in climate, terrain, customer preferences and other similar factors. Demand for business products also varies according to geographic location. For example, producers of certain types of timber and wood divide their markets geographically because their customers' needs vary from region to region. Geographic segmentation may be especially appropriate for reaching industries concentrated in certain locations. Furniture and textile producers, for example, are concentrated on the east coast of Australia. However, Western Australia has some quite unique timbers and therefore there are specialist producers in the west that cater for a niche market.

Type of organisation

A company sometimes segments a market by types of organisations within that market. Different types of organisations often require different product features, distribution systems, price structures and selling strategies. Given these variations, a company may either concentrate on a single segment with one marketing mix (concentration strategy) or focus on several groups with multiple mixes (a differentiated targeting strategy). A carpet producer, for example, could segment potential customers into several groups, such as car manufacturers, commercial carpet contractors (companies that lay carpet in large commercial buildings), property developers (companies who build high-rise apartment buildings), carpet wholesalers and large retail carpet outlets.

Customer size

An organisation's size may affect its purchasing procedures and the types and quantities of products it wants. Size, therefore, can be an effective variable for segmenting a business market. To reach a segment of a particular size, marketers may have to adjust one or more marketing-mix components. For example, customers who buy in extremely large quantities are sometimes offered discounts. In addition, marketers must often expand personal selling efforts to serve large organisational buyers properly. Because the needs of large and small buyers tend to be quite distinct, marketers frequently use different marketing practices to reach various customer groups.

Product use

Certain products, especially basic raw materials such as steel, petroleum, plastics and timber, are used in numerous ways. How a company uses products affects the types and amounts of products purchased, as well as the purchasing method. For example, computers are used for engineering purposes, basic scientific research and business operations, such as word processing, accounting and telecommunications. A computer manufacturer, therefore, may segment the computer market by types of use because organisational needs for computer hardware and software depend on the purpose for which products are purchased.

Target-market selection process

WATCH an interactive animation on the target-market selection process

To begin the process of developing an effective marketing strategy, marketers need to select an appropriate target market. Although marketers may employ several methods for target market selection, generally they use a five-step process. This process is shown in Figure 5.4, and we discuss this process in the following sections.

FIGURE 5.4
TARGET-MARKET SELECTION PROCESS

Step 1: Identify the appropriate targeting strategy

A target market is a group of people or organisations for which a business creates and maintains a marketing mix specifically designed to satisfy the needs of group members. The strategy used to select a target market is affected by target-market needs and characteristics, product attributes and the organisation's objectives and resources. Figure 5.5 illustrates the three basic targeting strategies: undifferentiated, concentrated and differentiated.

Undifferentiated targeting strategy

undifferentiated targeting strategy
A strategy in which an organisation designs a single marketing mix and directs this strategy at the entire market for a particular product

An organisation sometimes defines an entire market for a particular product as its target market. When a company designs a single marketing mix and directs it at the entire market for a particular product, it is using an undifferentiated targeting strategy. As Figure 5.5 shows, an undifferentiated targeting strategy assumes that all customers in the market for a specific kind of product have similar needs. This assumption enables the organisation to satisfy most customers with a single marketing mix, which is a very cost-efficient way to market. But how effective is an undifferentiated targeting strategy? An undifferentiated strategy simply targets

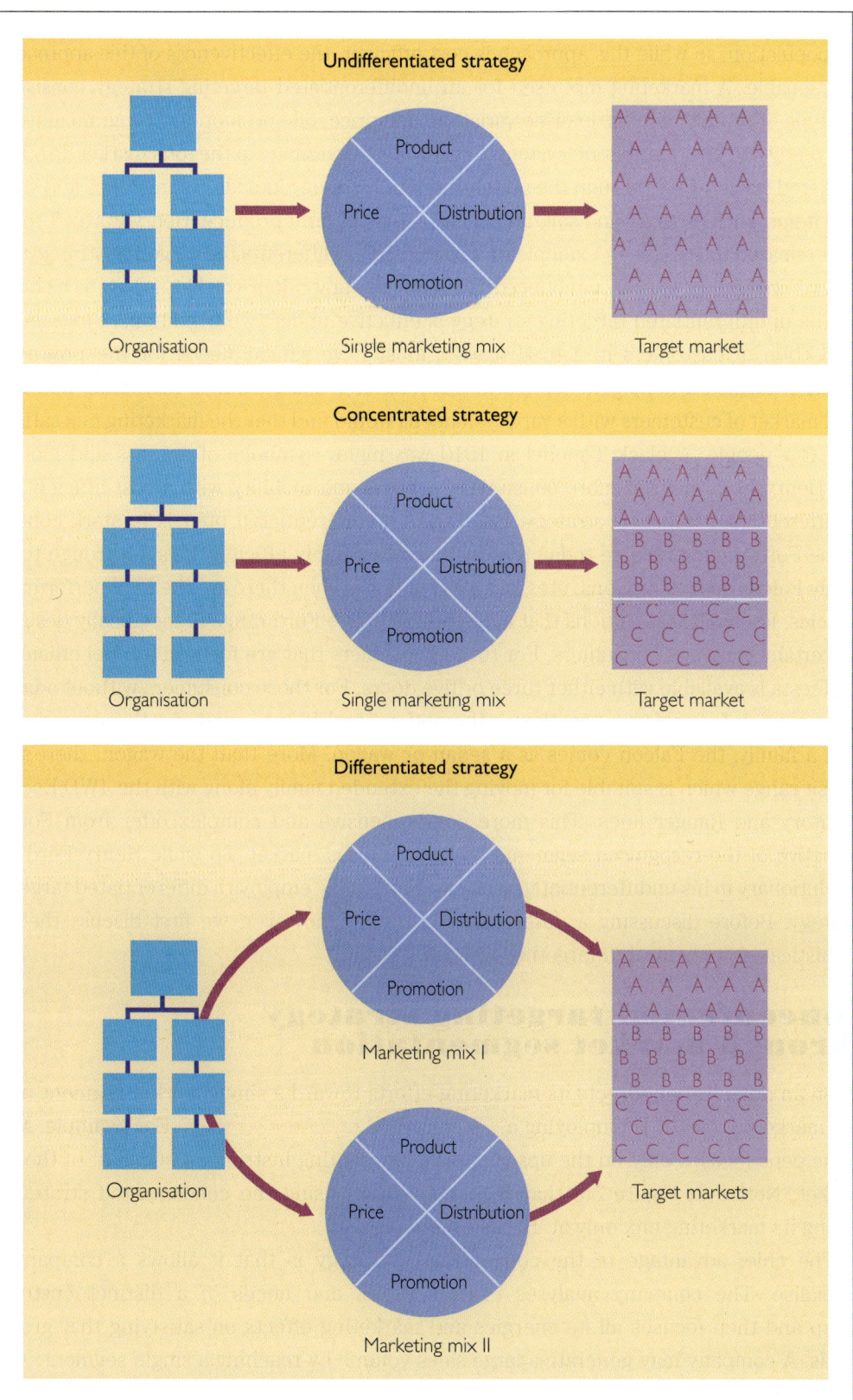

FIGURE 5.5
TARGETING STRATEGIES

Note: The letters in each target market represent potential customers. Customers with the same letters have similar characteristics and similar product needs.

the masses without any effort to address different needs and wants of various segments in the population, so while this approach is cost efficient, the effectiveness of this approach is questionable. A marketing mix used for an undifferentiated targeting strategy consists of one type of product with little or no variation, one price, one promotional program aimed at everybody and one distribution system to reach most customers in the total market. Products marketed successfully through the undifferentiated strategy include commodities and staple food items, such as sugar and salt, and certain kinds of farm produce. Henry Ford's T-model Ford released in 1910 is an example of a successful undifferentiated targeting strategy – as Henry Ford himself proudly announced: 'You can have any colour you like as long as its black!'

The undifferentiated targeting strategy is effective under two conditions. First, a large proportion of customers in a total market must have similar needs for the product, a situation termed a homogeneous market. A marketer using a single marketing mix for a total market of customers with a variety of needs would find that the marketing mix satisfies very few people. A black T-model in 1910 was highly symbolic of success and mobility and Henry Ford enabled more consumers' success and mobility with a cost efficient and undifferentiated targeting strategy. But Ford's undifferentiated offer is in stark contrast to the Ford range available today that includes the highly efficient Fiesta, through to the family Falcon sedans, wagons, utes and 4WD options. Then there are the FPV performance vehicles. Each of these options that make up the entire Ford range is specifically designed for certain groups of consumers. For those consumers that are focused on fuel efficiency, the Fiesta is available with either three or five doors. For those consumers without a family and a passion for performance, there's the option of a FPV ute, while for those consumers with a family, the Falcon comes as a sedan or wagon. More than the wagon, there's the transit range which is suitable for moving the extended family along with the 4WD Escape, Territory and Ranger lines. This more comprehensive and complex offer from Ford is reflective of the recognised segments within the mass market. So while Henry Ford was revolutionary in his undifferentiated strategy, Ford today employs a differentiated targeting strategy. Before discussing a differentiated strategy, however, we first discuss the less sophisticated concentrated targeting strategy.

Concentrated targeting strategy through market segmentation

When an organisation directs its marketing efforts toward a single market segment using one marketing mix, it is employing a concentrated targeting strategy. For example, Mont Blanc pens focuses only on the upscale, premium writing instrument segment of the pen market. Notice in Figure 5.5 that the organisation using the concentrated strategy is aiming its marketing mix only at 'B' customers.

The chief advantage of the concentrated strategy is that it allows a company to specialise. The company analyses characteristics and needs of a distinct customer group and then focuses all its energies and marketing effects on satisfying that group's needs. A company may generate a large sales volume by reaching a single segment. Also, concentrating on a single segment permits a company with limited resources to compete with larger organisations that may have overlooked smaller segments. (The Marketing in Transition box on the next page illustrates a successful concentrated targeting strategy.)

concentrated targeting strategy
A strategy in which an organisation targets a single market segment using one marketing mix for each

Specialisation, however, means that a company puts all its eggs in one basket, which can be risky. If a company's sales depend on a single segment and the segment's demand for the product declines, the company's financial strength also declines. When a company penetrates one segment and becomes well entrenched, its popularity may keep it from moving into other segments. For example, it is very unlikely that Bentley could or would want to compete with Ford in the family sedan and/or the performance vehicle market segment. That would be inconsistent for Bentley and the prestige that Bentley represents in the luxury auto market.

MARKETING IN TRANSITION | FACEBOOK GEO-TARGETING DELIVERS GOATS AND 500 000 FANS

Organisations delving into the world of social media and Facebook are delighted when their marketing efforts begin to work. Website traffic grows and sales start to roll in. But for Alex Morrisey of JamaicansMusic.com, the turning point was when a party happening in Indonesia ran out of goats! When a launch party invite went out to 200 Indonesian fans, they had enough rice and peas, but needed more goats. The goats arrived along with 1000 partyers thanks to Morrissey, a 22-year-old tech-savvy music enthusiast from Jamaica. The venture came about because he could not find a website that accommodated his music tastes and so he built his own. As the traffic has grown, JamaicansMusic.com has evolved into a multimedia company that allows consumers to not only listen to relevant radio shows, watch clips and read about artists, but they are now hosting live events, its own Internet radio and magazine. Here is how Morrissey achieved this growth: rich content on Facebook, attractive giveaways and geographic targeting.

Regular updates that give customers fresh and engaging content brings people to your Facebook page.

JamaicansMusic.com does this daily by posting new music clips. More than that, once a week Morrissey will run a hot promotion that again brings people to the website. These hot promos are conducted in partnership with radio stations and record labels, which compounds the effect. For example, JamaicansMusic.com launched the Song Writa game on Facebook but deliberately drove traffic to the Facebook page by offering smartphones and JM$5000 phone credit. The launch itself attracted 218 participants, but the promotion helped drive Facebook traffic up to the tune of 7000 new fans and 15 000 users of the new game. This is low cost, effective marketing. Geographically, JamaicansMusic.com fans come from more than 230 countries and surprisingly, more than 65 000 fans come from Indonesia. By sharing the demographic and geographic breakdown of the fan base with sponsors, JamaicansMusic.com can target specific countries with a relevant offer without alienating other fans and this is very appealing to sponsors and partners because sponsors are able to get really specific by geography and type of music.[16]

Differentiated targeting strategy through market segmentation

With a differentiated targeting strategy, an organisation directs its marketing efforts at two or more segments by developing a marketing mix for each (see Figure 5.5). After a company uses a concentrated strategy successfully in one market segment, it sometimes expands its efforts to include additional segments. For example, Bonds singlets traditionally have been

differentiated targeting strategy
A strategy in which an organisation targets two or more segments by developing a marketing mix for each

aimed at one segment: men. However, the company now markets underwear for women and children as well, with a tailored marketing mix for each of these segments. Marketing mixes for a differentiated strategy may vary according to product features, distribution methods, promotion methods and prices.

A company may increase sales in the aggregate market through a differentiated strategy because its marketing mixes are aimed at more people. For example, rather than offering one style and form of airline travel, Qantas offers First Class, Business Class and Economy. These different offers in airline travel are specifically designed for different types of travellers. Those consumers seeking a high-end premium service will opt for the more expensive First Class option. Those consumers who may travel frequently for business purposes may choose the Business Class option, whereas those consumers who seek standard service and reasonably priced air travel will opt for Economy. Each of these options are made available on most flights which means Qantas aircraft seating is arranged so as to accommodate the more sophisticated and affluent traveller in First Class by sectioning off that area of the plane. Dedicated staff will attend to the needs of First Class travellers and a choice of gourmet menu options is also made available. This differentiated strategy works because the sale of products to additional segments may absorb excess capacity. On the other hand, a differentiated strategy often demands more production processes, materials and people. Therefore, production and costs may be higher for a differentiated strategy than is the case with a concentrated strategy.

Differentiated targeting strategy >>
Many companies employ the differentiated targeting strategy by focusing on more than one market segment, using multiple marketing mixes. Snack food company, Smiths Crisps, produces multiple marketing mixes and aims them at multiple market segments. The Smiths Crisps range includes Twisties, Doritos, Nobbys and others, including the new Grain Waves and Sakata Gourmet Bites product lines. These different options are designed to meet the needs of different market segments

Source: d.library.com.au

Step 2: Determine which segmentation variables to use

For market segmentation to succeed, five conditions must exist. First, customers' needs for the product must be heterogeneous. That is, there must be enough variation across the market to segment, otherwise there is little reason to group within the market. Second, segments must be identifiable and divisible. The company must find a characteristic or variable for effectively separating individuals in a total market into groups containing people with relatively uniform needs for the product. Third, the total market should be divided so that segments can be compared with respect to estimated sales potential, costs and profits. Fourth, at least one segment must have enough profit potential to justify developing and maintaining a special marketing mix for that segment. Finally, the company must be able to reach the chosen segment with a particular marketing mix. Some market segments may be difficult or impossible to reach because of legal, social or distribution constraints. In the

Marketing in Action box that follows, the customer is a do-it-yourself (DIY) renovator and this market has specific needs compared to the rest of the renovations market. They have, for example, a limited budget to complete their renovations and are therefore unable to hire a contractor to complete the work for them. Or, they could have a high level of skill and ample time to complete the renovation. These factors differentiate this segment and make the DIY market a viable segment to target. In understanding the needs and wants, and more specifically the lifestyle, of the DIY renovators market, astute marketers can further understand their media habits and therefore effectively communicate with this consumer segment. The following Marketing in Action box demonstrates how Bunnings targets the Australian DIY lifestyle segments.

MARKETING IN ACTION | THE AUSTRALIAN DIY LIFESTYLE SEGMENTATION

Bunnings Warehouse is one of Australia's favourite brands with their low-priced hardware and outdoor goods. Bunnings celebrate their people, including customers and workers. Their narrative style of advertising shows frontline personnel telling stories of DIY accomplishments; ordinary people, relating to other ordinary people, with similar lifestyles. Customers come to Bunnings because there is always someone to help them find what they are looking for in the large and sometimes overwhelming warehouse.

Source: Getty Images

This level of excellence in customer service is also evident in the children's workshops that Bunnings hold in-store. Children can learn how to pot a plant or how to build a box. The adult version of this kind of education happens in their weekend DIY workshops, as well as in the aisles where the retail assistants give comprehensive explanations at the point of purchase. In hosting such in-house workshops, Bunnings is demonstrating a connection with consumers' lifestyle and behaviour. Rather than just showing the consumer the location of a certain product in a certain aisle, the frontline personnel have a conversation about which tools are best for the job at hand, how to use the tools and how to ensure the project is completed in an optimal manner. ◼

To select an appropriate segmentation variable, several factors are considered. The segmentation variable should relate to customers' needs for, uses of, or behaviour towards the product.

Marketers offering 3D TVs might segment the market based on customer income and age, but not religion because people's TV needs do not usually differ due to religion.[17] If individuals or organisations in a total market are to be classified accurately, the segmentation variable must be measurable. Age, location and gender are measurable because such information can be obtained through observation or questioning. Segmenting a market on the basis of a variable such as intelligence, however, would be extremely difficult because this attribute is harder to measure accurately. Another option would be to segment on education rather than intelligence. Furthermore, a company's resources and capabilities affect the number and size of segment variables used. The type of product and degree of variation in customers' needs also dictate the number and size of segments targeted. In short, there is no best way to segment markets.

Marketers segment markets in ways that may help them to build and manage relationships with targeted customers. Marketing research is often necessary to acquire information about customers' preferences and interests; basic demographic information about target customers' age, income, employment status, household structure and family roles may be revealing but it may not be enough. Astute marketers talk to consumers and are increasingly using customer relationship management techniques to track their customers' purchases over time. By tracking purchase behaviour over time, marketers are able to develop databases, where the data held within those databases can be analysed, or mined, in order to identify trends and develop more appropriate marketing mixes for repeat customers.

Choosing one or more segmentation variables is a critical step in targeting a market. Selecting inappropriate variables limits the chances of developing a successful marketing strategy. Once segmentation variables have been identified, marketers further develop a profile of the typical customer they are aiming to target. This process is described as developing market segment profiles.

Step 3: Develop market segment profiles

A market segment profile describes the similarities among potential customers within a segment and explains the differences between people and organisations in different segments. A profile may cover aspects such as demographic characteristics, geographic factors, product benefits sought, lifestyles, brand preferences and usage rates. Individuals and organisations within segments should be quite similar with respect to several characteristics and product needs and differ considerably from those within other market segments. Marketers use market segment profiles to assess the degree to which the organisation's possible products can match or fit potential customers' product needs. Market segment profiles help marketers to understand how a business can use its capabilities to serve potential customer groups.

The use of market segment profiles benefits marketers in several ways. Such profiles help a marketer determine which segment or segments are most attractive to the organisation relative to the organisation's strengths, weaknesses, objectives and resources. While marketers initially may believe that certain segments are quite attractive, development of market segment profiles may yield information that indicates the opposite. For the market segment or segments chosen by the organisation, the information included in market segment profiles can be highly useful in making marketing decisions.

Step 4: Evaluate relevant market segments

After analysing the market segment profiles, a marketer is likely to identify several relevant market segments that require further analysis and to eliminate certain other segments from consideration. To assess relevant market segments further, several important factors, including sales estimates, competition and estimated costs associated with each segment should be analysed.

Sales estimates

Potential sales for a segment can be measured along several dimensions, including product level, geographic area, time and level of competition.[18] With respect to product level, potential sales can be estimated for a specific product item (for example, Diet Coke) or an entire product line (for example, Coca-Cola, Coke Zero, Diet Coke, Vanilla Coke and Diet Vanilla Coke). A marketer must also determine the geographic area to be included in the estimate. In relation to time, sales estimates can be short range (one year or less), medium range (one to five years) or long range (longer than five years). The competitive level specifies whether sales are being estimated for a single company or for an entire industry.

Market potential is the total amount of a product, for all companies in an industry, that customers will purchase within a specified period at a specific level of industry-wide marketing activity. Market potential can be stated in terms of dollars or units. A segment's market potential is affected by economic, sociocultural and other environmental forces. Marketers must assume a certain general level of marketing effort in the industry when they estimate market potential. The specific level of marketing effort varies from one company to another, but the sum of all the marketing activities by companies equals industry-wide marketing efforts. A marketing manager must also consider whether and to what extent industry marketing efforts will change.

Company sales potential is the maximum percentage of market potential that an individual company within an industry can expect to obtain for a specific product. Several factors influence company sales potential for a market segment. First, the market potential places absolute limits on the size of the company's sales potential. Second, the magnitude of industry-wide marketing activities has an indirect but definite impact on the company's sales potential. Those activities have a direct bearing on the size of the market potential. When Eagle Boys Pizza advertises home-delivered pizza, for example, it indirectly promotes pizza in general; its commercials may also help to sell Pizza Hut's and other competitors' home-delivered pizza. Third, the intensity and effectiveness of a company's marketing activities relative to those of its competitors affect the size of the company's sales potential. If a company spends twice as much as any of its competitors on marketing efforts and if each dollar spent is more effective in generating sales, the company's sales potential will be quite high compared with the competition.

There are two general approaches to measuring company sales potential: breakdown and buildup. In the breakdown approach the marketing manager first develops a general economic forecast for a specific time period. Next, market potential is estimated on the basis of this economic forecast. The company's sales potential is then derived from the general economic forecast and estimate of market potential. In the buildup approach the

market potential
The total amount of a product that customers will purchase within a specified period at a specific level of industry-wide marketing activity

company sales potential
The maximum percentage of market potential that an individual company can expect to obtain for a specific product

breakdown approach
Measuring company sales potential based on a general economic forecast for a specific period and the market potential derived from it

buildup approach
Measuring company sales potential by estimating how much of a product a potential buyer in a specific geographic area will purchase in a given period, multiplying the estimate by the number of potential buyers and adding the totals of all the geographic areas considered

<< **Understanding your segment profile**
According to a recent national Bank of Queensland (BOQ) study, Australian consumers have a longer relationship with their bank than with other major services, such as doctors and lawyers. Those consumers surveyed reported banking with the same financial institution for an average of 16 years. This finding enables BOQ to better understand the conservative nature of the Australian banking customer. Jon Sutton, BOQ Chief Operating Officer, said 'The BOQ Professional Partnerships Survey revealed that Australians stay with their main financial institution for an average of 16 years, with those over 35 years old remaining with their bank for nearly two decades. These figures certainly reflect the importance that many of us place on choosing a trustworthy financial institution'[19]

marketing manager begins by estimating how much product a potential buyer in a specific geographic area, such as a sales territory, will purchase in a given period. The manager then multiplies that amount by the total number of potential buyers in that area. The manager performs the same calculation for each geographic area in which the company sells products and then adds the totals for each area to calculate market potential. To determine company sales potential, the manager must estimate, based on planned levels of company marketing activities, the proportion of the total market potential the company can obtain.

Competitive assessment

Besides obtaining sales estimates, it is crucial to assess competitors already operating in the segments being considered. Without competitive information, sales estimates may be misleading. A market segment that seems attractive based on sales estimates may prove to be much less so following a competitive assessment. Such an assessment should ask several questions about competitors: How many exist? What are their strengths and weaknesses? Do several competitors have major market shares and together dominate the segment? Can our company create a marketing mix to compete effectively against competitors' marketing mixes? Is it likely that new competitors will enter this segment? If so, how will they affect our company's ability to compete successfully? Answers to such questions are important for proper assessment of the competition in potential market segments.

Cost estimates

To fulfill the needs of a target segment, an organisation must develop and maintain a marketing mix that precisely meets the wants and needs of individuals and organisations in that segment. Developing and maintaining such a mix can be expensive. Distinctive product features, attractive package design, generous product warranties, extensive advertising, attractive promotional offers, competitive prices and high-quality personal service consume considerable organisational resources. Indeed, to reach certain segments, the costs may be so high that a marketer may see the segment as inaccessible. Another cost consideration is whether the organisation can reach a segment effectively at costs equal to or below competitors' costs. If the company's costs are likely to be higher, it will be unable to compete in that segment in the long run.

Step 5: Select specific target markets

An important initial issue to consider in selecting a target market is whether customers' needs differ enough to warrant the use of market segmentation. If segmentation analysis shows customer needs to be fairly homogeneous, the company's management may decide to use the undifferentiated approach, discussed earlier. However, if customer needs are heterogeneous, which is much more likely, one or more target markets must be selected. On the other hand, marketers may decide not to enter and compete in any of the segments.

Assuming that one or more segments offer significant opportunities for the organisation to achieve its objectives, marketers must decide in which segments to target. Ordinarily, information gathered in the previous step – information about sales estimates, competitors and cost estimates – requires careful consideration in this final step to determine long-term profit opportunities. Also, the company's management must investigate whether the organisation has the financial resources, managerial skills, employee expertise and facilities to enter and compete effectively in selected segments. Furthermore, the requirements of some market segments may be at odds with the company's overall objectives, and the possibility of legal problems, conflicts with stakeholders and technological advances could make certain segments unattractive. In addition, when prospects for long-term growth are taken into account, some segments may appear very attractive and others less desirable.

Selecting appropriate target markets is important to an organisation's adoption and use of the marketing concept philosophy. Identifying the right target market is the key to implementing a successful marketing strategy, whereas failure to do so can lead to low sales, high costs and severe financial losses. A careful target market analysis places an organisation in a better position both to serve customers' needs and to achieve organisational and marketing objectives.

Product positioning and repositioning

Once the target market has been selected, the product offering can be strategically positioned in order to align with the selected target markets characteristics and needs. Determining a product's position prior to selecting a target market may lead to a misalignment or weak position in comparison to competitors. Product positioning refers to the decisions and activities intended to create and maintain a certain concept of the company's product (relative to competitors' products) in customers' minds. When marketers introduce a product, the product is positioned to ensure characteristics most desired by the target market are highlighted. This projected image is crucial. For example, Toyota have positioned their Landcruiser Troop Carrier as tough and durable, whereas Rolls Royce position their cars as refined luxury. Colgate Total is positioned as a fluoride toothpaste that fights cavities, whereas White Glo is positioned as whitening toothpaste and packaged with a complimentary toothbrush.

product positioning
Creating and maintaining a certain concept of a product in customers' minds

Perceptual mapping

A product's position is the result of customers' perceptions of the product's attributes relative to those of competing brands. Buyers make numerous purchase decisions on a regular basis. To avoid a continuous re-evaluation of numerous products, buyers tend to group, or 'position', products in their minds to simplify buying decisions. Rather than allowing customers to position products independently, marketers often try to influence and shape consumers' concepts or perceptions of products through advertising. Marketers sometimes analyse product positions by developing perceptual maps, as shown in Figure 5.6. Perceptual maps are created by considering the two primary evaluative criteria, such as price and quality as per the horizontal and vertical axis in Figure 5.6. Customer surveys can be done to establish the primary evaluative criteria and maybe for hotels, customers would respond with service and location as the ways in which they evaluate hotels. In which case, service and location would form the horizontal and vertical axis and the perceptual map would be rearranged accordingly. Then marketers can see how their brand is perceived compared with the ideal points. Perceptual mapping is also good to identify any gaps in the market as bases for positioning.

Bases for positioning

Marketers can use several bases for product positioning. A product can be positioned on various aspects, such as a prominent or unique product feature, a benefit and/or advantage, such as price, quality or maybe brand reputation, as we can see, for example, with Apple

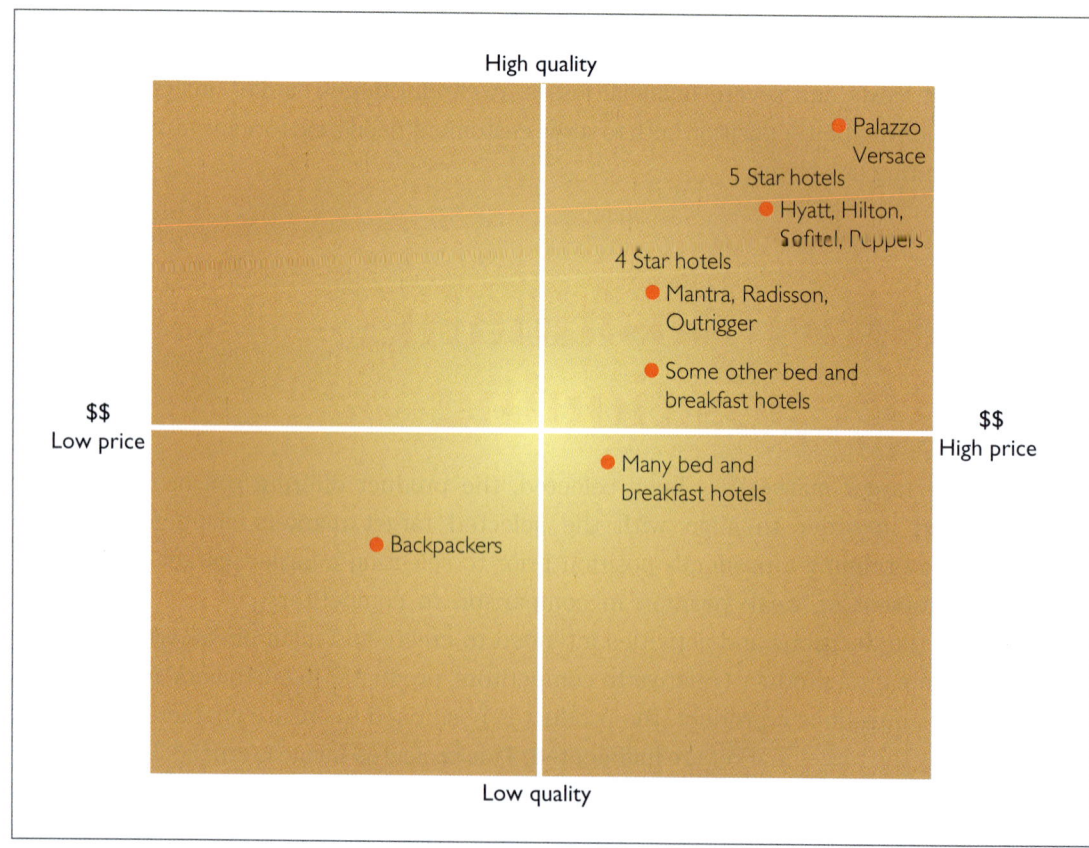

FIGURE 5.6
HYPOTHETICAL
PERCEPTUAL MAP FOR
HOTELS IN AUSTRALIA

iPhone 5. Nike position their range of sports apparel and accessories as cutting edge, performance enhancing and innovative. To maintain this market position they invest heavily in research and development in order to remain at the forefront of sports apparel technology (see the Did you know? box on page 182).

Another common basis for positioning products is to use competitors. A company can position a product to compete head-on with another brand, as Pepsi has done against Coca-Cola, or to avoid competition, as carbonated energy drinks have done relative to other soft drink producers. Head-to-head competition may be a marketer's positioning objective if the product's performance characteristics are at least equal to those of competitive brands and if the product is priced lower. Head-to-head positioning may be appropriate when the evaluative criteria within a certain segment are well established. Beer, for example, is typically positioned as a masculine symbol and targeted at men who are proud and thirsty due to a strong work ethic. In contrast, wine is positioned as a more sophisticated beverage that has become increasingly popular, especially so in New Zealand given the quality of the wines produced. DB Export Breweries recognised this dilemma and therefore positioned their Export Dry product as 'the beer that saves men from wine'. The DB Export Dry 'The Wine is Over' campaign won multiple awards at the 2012 Cannes International Festival of Creativity.

Similarly in the auto market, Volvo has for years positioned itself away from competitors by focusing on the safety characteristics of their cars. Some car manufacturers do mention safety issues in their ads, but many focus instead on style, fuel efficiency, performance or terms of sale.

A product's position can be based on specific product attributes or features. For example, the Apple's iPhone is positioned based on product attributes such as its unique shape, easy-to-use touch screen and access to iTunes. If a product has been planned properly, its features will give it the distinct appeal needed. Style, shape, construction and colour help to create the image and the appeal. If buyers can easily identify the benefits, they are, of course, more likely to purchase the product. When the new product does not offer certain preferred attributes, there is room for another new product.

Other bases for product positioning include price, quality level and benefits provided by the product. For example, Colgate-Palmolive's Cold Power liquid laundry detergent provides the advantage of washing with cold rather than hot water. By positioning on cold water usage, Colgate–Palmolive is emphasising a customer benefit.

Also, the target market can be a positioning basis for marketing. This type of positioning relies heavily on promoting the types of people who 'use' the product. Sonia Kruger, a well-known television presenter, suggesting 'you'll feel better on Swisse' is an example of this. Using Sonia to front this ad suggests that if you want to feel as good as Sonia looks, take the Swisse brand of multivitamins.

Repositioning

Positioning decisions are not just for new products. Evaluating the positions of existing products is important because a brand's market share and profitability may be strengthened by product repositioning. An excellent example is found in the Australian airline industry, which is

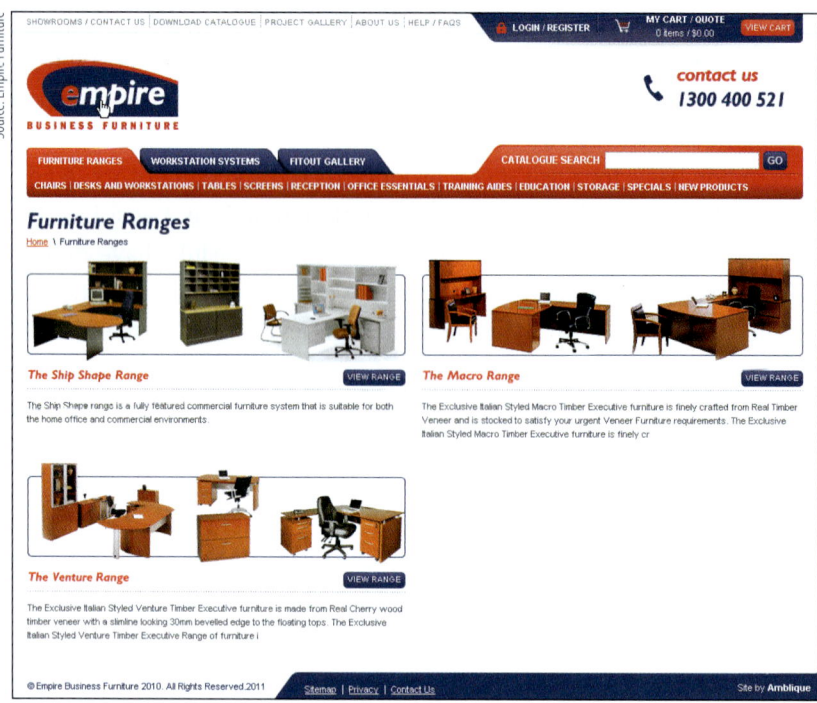

Source: Empire Furniture

currently dominated by Qantas along with JetStar (a Qantas-owned budget priced subsidiary) and Virgin Australia (previously branded Virgin Blue). Qantas is positioned on premium service, whereas both Virgin and JetStar are positioned on price. As a premium service airline, Qantas was unable to adequately contend with the fierce price penetration strategy by Virgin Blue in 2000. So JetStar, owned by Qantas but positioned on price like Virgin, was introduced in 2004. After 10 years it is Virgin Australia who is seeking to reposition from a low-cost carrier to a premium-service operator.[20] Virgin Australia now also holds a 60 per cent stake in Tigerair, another low-budget carrier.[21] This corporate structure allows Virgin to compete effectively with Qantas on service, and to use Tigerair to compete with JetStar on price.

Qantas suffered some loss of market share when JetStar was introduced. This is referred to as cannabilisation. Similarly, Virgin will be cannabilised to some extent by Tigerair. However, the benefit for Virgin in repositioning on premium service is the gain in market share within the business market, estimated to be between AU$3 billion to AU$4 billion. With an extensive network of airport lounges specifically designed for the business traveller, Qantas is well placed and well versed in this market and holds 84 per cent market share.[22] However, repositioning efforts by Virgin have included the introduction of business class to commuter flights, new airport lounges and refurbishing others, an in-flight wi-fi system and frequent flyers can now go through a dedicated entrance to check-in and security that leads straight into the lounge.

When introducing a new product into a product line, one or more existing brands may have to be repositioned to minimise cannibalisation of established brands, as seen in the above airline example. Qantas introduced JetStar to halt the need for Qantas to reposition from service to price. In the process, JetStar did cannabilise some Qantas market share but Qantas minimised their loss to Virgin, so the cannabilisation was worth it for Qantas. Tigerair will also cannabilise some Virgin market share, but Virgin is effectively working to keep the price-sensitive traveller while at the same time aiming to take a bite of the business-traveller market.

Repositioning can also be accomplished by physically changing the product, its price or its distribution. Rather than making any of these changes, however, marketers sometimes reposition a product by changing its image through promotional efforts. Finally, a marketer may reposition a product by aiming it at a different target market.

Source: Getty Images; Getty Images

<< Product repositioning
Virgin is repositioning from a price positioning to a premium service positioning as evidenced by the introduction of business class, airport lounges and other service augmentations

Study Tools

Chapter review

LO1   LEARN WHAT A MARKET IS.

A market is a group of people who, as individuals or as organisations, have needs for products in a product class and have the ability, willingness and authority to purchase such products.

LO2   BECOME FAMILIAR WITH THE MAJOR SEGMENTATION VARIABLES.

Segmentation variables are the characteristics of individuals, groups or organisations used to segment a total market. The variable(s) used should relate to customers' needs for, uses of or behaviour toward the product. Segmentation variables for consumer markets can be grouped into four categories: demographic (age, gender, income, ethnicity and family life cycle), geographic (population, market density and climate), psychographic (personality traits, motives and lifestyles) and behaviouristic (volume usage, end use, expected benefits, brand loyalty and price sensitivity). Variables for segmenting business markets include geographic location, type of organisation, customer size and product use.

LO3   UNDERSTAND THE PROCESS OF SELECTING AND EVALUATING TARGET MARKET SEGMENTS.

Marketers select and evaluate relevant market segments by understanding the market needs. There are five steps to target-market selection, beginning with the identification of an appropriate targeting strategy. From there, the task is to determine which segmentation variables are to be used, then to develop the market segment profiles. An evaluation of relevant market segments is then carried out, followed by the selection of specific target markets. When the market or segment is homogenous, an undifferentiated strategy is effective. An undifferentiated strategy uses the same marketing mix across the homogeneous market or segment. When there are heterogeneous segments across the market, a differentiated strategy is effective. A differentiated strategy targets two or more market segments with a marketing mix that is customised according to the consumer needs and wants within the targeted segments. A concentrated strategy involves targeting a single market with one marketing mix.

 **LO4** UNDERSTAND THE CONCEPT OF POSITIONING.

Product positioning refers to the decisions and activities that create and maintain a certain concept of the company's product in the customer's mind. Organisations can position a product and/or brand to compete head-to-head with another brand if the product's performance is at least equal to the competition's brand and if the product is priced lower. When a brand possesses unique characteristics that are important to some buyers, positioning it to avoid competition is appropriate. Companies also increase an existing brand's market share and profitability through product repositioning.

Key concepts

Use these key terms in **Search me! marketing** to find the latest relevant readings from a wide range of world-class journals, e-books and newspapers, including *The Australian*.

- benefit segmentation
- breakdown approach
- buildup approach
- business market
- company sales potential
- concentrated targeting strategy
- consumer market
- differentiated targeting strategy

- demographic segmentation
- geodemographic segmentation
- geographic segmentation
- psychographic segmentation
- heterogeneous markets
- homogeneous market
- market density
- market potential

- market segment
- market segmentation
- micromarketing
- product positioning
- segmentation variables
- undifferentiated targeting strategy

Issues for discussion and review

1 Outline the five major steps in the target-market selection process.

2 What is market segmentation? Describe the basic conditions required for effective segmentation.

3 Identify and describe a consumer segment in terms of demographic, geographic and psychographic variables. Identify and describe this same consumer segment in terms of their needs and wants.

4 What is a differentiated strategy? Under what conditions is a differentiated strategy most useful? Describe a present market situation where a differentiated strategy is evident. Is the business successful? Why or why not?

5 Identify and describe four major categories of variables that can be used to segment consumer markets. Give examples of product markets that are segmented by variables in each category.

6 What dimensions are used to segment business markets?

7 What is a market segment profile? Why is developing a market segment profile an important step in the target market selection process?

8 What are the important factors that marketers should analyse when evaluating market segments?

9 What is positioning? Why is positioning important?

10 Describe your favourite brand in terms of market positioning.

Marketing applications

1 The free-to-air TV channel SBS offers different news programs from the Asia-Pacific region and Europe. These various news programs target members of those nationalities who now reside in or are visiting Australia. Identify another product, which may be a service like the SBS news service, that is marketed to a distinct target market. Describe the target market, and explain how the marketing mix appeals specifically to that group.

2 Locate a print ad that includes a picture of one or more individuals. Describe the target market and explain the strategy being used to reach that market.

3 The stereo market may be segmented according to income and age. Name two ways the market for each of the following products might be segmented.

a running shoes
b education services
c bicycles
d hair spray

ONLINE EXERCISE

4 iExplore is an Internet company that offers a variety of travel and adventure products. Visit their website at http://www.iexplore.com.

a Based on the information provided on the website, what are some of iExplore's basic products?
b What market segments does iExplore appear to be targeting with its website? What segmentation variables are being used to segment these markets?
c How does iExplore appeal to comparison shoppers?

Developing your marketing plan

Identifying and analysing a target market is a major component of formulating a marketing strategy. A clear understanding and explanation of a product's target market is crucial to developing a useful marketing plan. References to various dimensions of a target market are likely to appear in several locations in a marketing plan. To assist you in understanding how information in this chapter relates to the creation of your marketing plan, focus on the following considerations:

1   What type of targeting strategy is being used for your product and should a different targeting strategy be employed?

2   Select and justify the segmentation variables that are most appropriate for your product. If your product is a consumer product, use Figure 5.1 for ideas regarding the most appropriate segmentation variables. If your marketing plan focuses on a business product, review the information in the section entitled 'Variables for segmenting business markets'.

3   How is your product or brand positioned? Construct a perceptual map for the industry or category that you are planning to operate in.

CengageNOW

Go to http:\\login.cengagebrain.com to link to CengageNOW, your online study tool. First take the Pre-Test for this chapter to get your Personalised Study Plan, and then:

* **Revise** your understanding of the key concepts of marketing with the online glossary

* **Watch** an interactive animation of strategic marketing to broaden your subject comprehension

* **Listen** to an audio summary of the learning objectives covered in this chapter.

    After you have completed the activities in your Personalised Study Plan take the Post-Test to determine what concepts you have mastered and what you still need to work on.

Case study

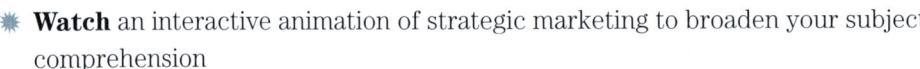

IS THERE A TREK BICYCLE FOR EVERYBODY?

Trek Bicycle, founded in 1976, gets a marketing boost whenever high-profile professional racers speed off on their Trek bikes or world-class cyclists power through dirt-bike races. Trek has US$800 million in annual sales and a worldwide network of 1000 dealers in 90 countries. Knowing it can't be all things to all cyclists, Trek focuses its marketing efforts on satisfying the needs of serious cyclists seeking top-quality, high-performance bicycles for athletic training and competition, recreation or commuting. For example, Trek has found that the lifestyles and

Source: Shutterstock.com

behaviour of consumers who like mountain biking are distinctly different from those of consumers who ride in city streets. Even among mountain bikers, some consumers prefer to feel the rough terrain under their wheels, while others want a smoother ride. Similarly, some urban riders are interested in style, while others care about a bike's environmental impact. Professional athletes want the very best performance, whether they're competing in a fast-paced triathlon or the gruelling Tour de France.

Targeting the segments it can satisfy most effectively, Trek now offers two separate lines of mountain bikes, 'hardtails' for feeling the ride and 'full-suspension' for comfort. For urban riders, it markets seven models of pedal-power bikes and five bikes equipped with electric motors. For consumers who wheel around on bike paths or take a spin on city streets, Trek offers a wide variety of options, including one tandem model. The company's triathlon bicycles are designed with aerodynamics in mind, to help speed cyclists on their way to victory or through a high-powered workout.

Because one size does not fit all cyclists, Trek also designs bikes specifically for women. In addition, customers can design and equip their own bikes online using Trek's Project One configuration tool. To ensure proper fit, customers must visit a local dealer to be measured before their bikes are manufactured and delivered.

Trek's choices of product names reflect the interests of each targeted segment. For example, the Madone product line, for dedicated athletes, is named for Col de la Madone, a French mountain famously known for testing cyclists' strength. Some of the commuter models are named after cities where cyclists can be seen pedalling along, such as the Soho (New York). Prices for Trek's high-end Madone models can top $14000, depending on exact specifications and customising touches. The urban bikes range in price from $500 to more than $1500. Many of its children's bicycles are priced above $200. These are well-made bicycles for people who want advanced engineering, stylish looks and a great riding experience – and are willing to pay for it.

Just as Trek tailors its bikes to the needs of each customer group, it also tailors its promotional efforts. These include targeted advertising, training programs to help cyclists build their skills, and product demonstrations at parks and sporting events. Trek uses Facebook, blogs, Twitter, online videos, and email newsletters to stay in touch with customers, answer questions and gather feedback.

Supporting charitable groups, such as the Breast Cancer Research Foundation, helps the company show its commitment to social responsibility. Trek also funds DreamBikes, a non-profit organisation that recycles used bikes and trains teenagers in repair and retail sales techniques. DreamBikes asks for donations of bicycles that are unwanted or in disrepair and hires high school students to refurbish and resell the bikes, which are priced for affordability. Currently, DreamBikes has two stores in the US, with more in the planning stage.

Trek started with the mission of building the world's best bicycle. Today, it markets the bicycle as a way to be fit, reduce traffic and make the world a greener place. Its Eco Design bicycles incorporate environmentally friendly materials and can be disassembled to recycle the parts at the end of their useful lives. The company practices what it preaches about environmental issues, using renewable power to run its manufacturing plant and providing convenient parking for employees who bicycle to work. Green targeting helps Trek attract like-minded customers as well as employees. Employees – cycling enthusiasts, like their customers – often come up with new product ideas and enjoy testing new products along the way. Where will targeting take Trek next?[24]

1 How is Trek positioning in the marketplace?

2 Is Trek using an undifferentiated, concentrated or differentiated strategy for targeting? How do you know?

3 Identify the segmentation variables that Trek is applying to consumer markets. What additional variables would you suggest that it apply, and why?

Chapter endnotes

1. Christopher Schroeder, *Creating Customer Value for Generation Y* (GRIN Verlag, 2012).
2. 'Global entertainment and media outlook 2013-2017' PriceWaterhouseCoopers, accessed January 31, 2014. http://www.pwc.com/gx/en/global-entertainment-media-outlook/segment-insights/video-games.jhtml.
3. Hannah Gardner, 'Latest death of Chinese online addict brings calls for net games clampdown,' *The National*, May 20, 2011, accessed January 17, 2014. http://www.thenational.ae/news/world/asia-pacific/latest-death-of-chinese-online-addict-brings-calls-for-net-games-clampdown#ixzz2sHmiBUd9.
4. Frans Mayra, *An Introduction to Game Studies* (London: Sage Publications, 2008).
5. James Cronin, and Mary McCarthy, 'Fast Food and Fast Games: An ethnographic exploration of food consumption complexity among the videogames subculture,' *British Food Journal* 113 (6): 720–743.
6. S.A. Yusof, R. M. Amin, M. A. M. Haneef, and H. M. Noon, 'Formation of desired values: the role of parent,' *International Journal of Social Economics*, 26 (6): 468–479.
7. 'Website Showcase,' TRU, http://www.tru-insight.com/.
8. Christina Sommer, 'Purchase power of global teens tops $819 Billion,' Mastercard, 2012, http://insights.mastercard.com/2012/11/21/purchase-power-of-global-teens-tops-819-billion/
9. Alexander Quince, 'What's Hot: Fake braces for teens,' *10 News*, accessed January 17, 2014. http://www.wtsp.com/news/watercooler/story.aspx?storyid=24456; Lauren Hanson, 'Fake braces: Asia's curious teenage fashion trend,' *The Week*, January 2, 2013, accessed January 17, 2014. http://theweek.com/article/index/238327/fake-braces-asias-curious-teenage-fashion-trend.
10. 'Populations by age and sex, regions of Australia, 2011 (Cat. # 3235.0),' ABS, http://www.abs.gov.au/Ausstats/abs@.nsf/mf/3235.0.
11. 'Isiah Mustafa: Old Spice,' Know Your Meme, accessed Janaury 17, 2014. http://knowyourmeme.com/memes/events/isaiah-mustafa-old-spice.
12. '4442.0 – Family Characteristics and Transitions, Australia, (2006-07),' ABS, http://www.abs.gov.au/AUSSTATS/abs@.nsf/Lookup/4442.0Main+Features12006-07.
13. 'Homepage,' Experian Marketing Services, www.pacificmicromarketing.com.au.
14. Joseph T. Plummer, 'The Concept and Application of Life Style Segmentation,' *Journal of Marketing* (January 1974): 33.
15. 'Energy Statistics,' *NationMaster*, data from CIA (June 14, 2007), www.nationmaster.com/graph/ene_ele_con_percap-energy-electricity-consumption-per-capita.
16. Casey Hibbard, 'Facebook geotargeting draws 500,000 fans for small biz,' *Social Media Examiner*, accessed August 11, 2013. http://www.socialmediaexaminer.com/facebook-geotargeting-draws-500000-fans-for-small-biz/
17. People of the Amish religion usually choose not to have a TV in their household due to their value system. According to Amish values, having a TV in the house reduces the quality time spent with children (http://voices.yahoo.com/5-fascinating-aspects-amish-beliefs-practices-6525340.html).
18. Philip Kotler, *Marketing Management: Analysis, Planning, Implementation, and Control*, 7th ed. (Englewood Cliffs, NJ: Prentice Hall, 2003): 144.
19. The BOQ Professional Partnerships Survey was commissioned by BOQ and conducted by D&M research in June 2013. 1024 respondents took part in the survey resulting in a +-error rate of 5.5 at a 95% confidence level. The sample was randomly selected from the Research Now Permission Panel of over 170000 panellists. A boost was conducted among Bank of Queensland Customers (n=34 BoQ as Main Financial Institution). This information was sourced from BOQ Media Resources, 11 August 2013 from http://www.boq.com.au/aboutus_media_20130703.htm.
20. Michael Bleby, 'Updated: Qantas, Virgin battleground shifts to business travel,' *Business Review Weekly*, February 21, 2013, accessed January 17, 2014. http://www.brw.com.au/p/business/updated_qantas_virgin_battleground_eitdDU6yG40qzgcJuwAPzK.
21. John Walton, 'Virgin Australia buys into Tiger, pits it against Qantas' Jetstar,' *Australian Business Traveller*, October 30, 2012, accessed January 17, 2014. http://www.ausbt.com.au/virgin-australia-buys-tiger-pits-it-against-qantas-jetstar.

22. John Walton, 'Virgin Australia buys into Tiger, pits it against Qantas' Jetstar,' *Australian Business Traveller*, October 30, 2012.

23. Austin Carr, 'Nike: The no.1 most innovative company of 2013,' Fast Company, February 11, 2013, accessed August 11, 2013. http://www.fastcompany.com/most-innovative-companies/2013/nike.

24. 'Tim's Travels: Building a Better Bike,' *NBC 15* (Madison, WI), February 29, 2012, www.nbc15.com; 'Trek's John Burke Testifies in Congress,' *Bicycle Retailer*, March 31, 2011, www.bicycleretailer.com; Tom Held, 'DreamBikes Opens a Store and Opportunities in Milwaukee,' *Journal Sentinel*, April 7, 2010, www.jsonline.com; 'Trek Announces Title Sponsorship of 2010 Dirt Series,' *Mountain Bike Review*, February 3, 2010, http://reviews.mtbr.com/; Joe Vanden Plas, 'CIO Leadership: Trek's Brent Leland Cycles through Business-IT Alignment,' Wisconsin Technology Network FusionCIO, February 24, 2009, http://wistechnology.com; www.trekbikes.com.

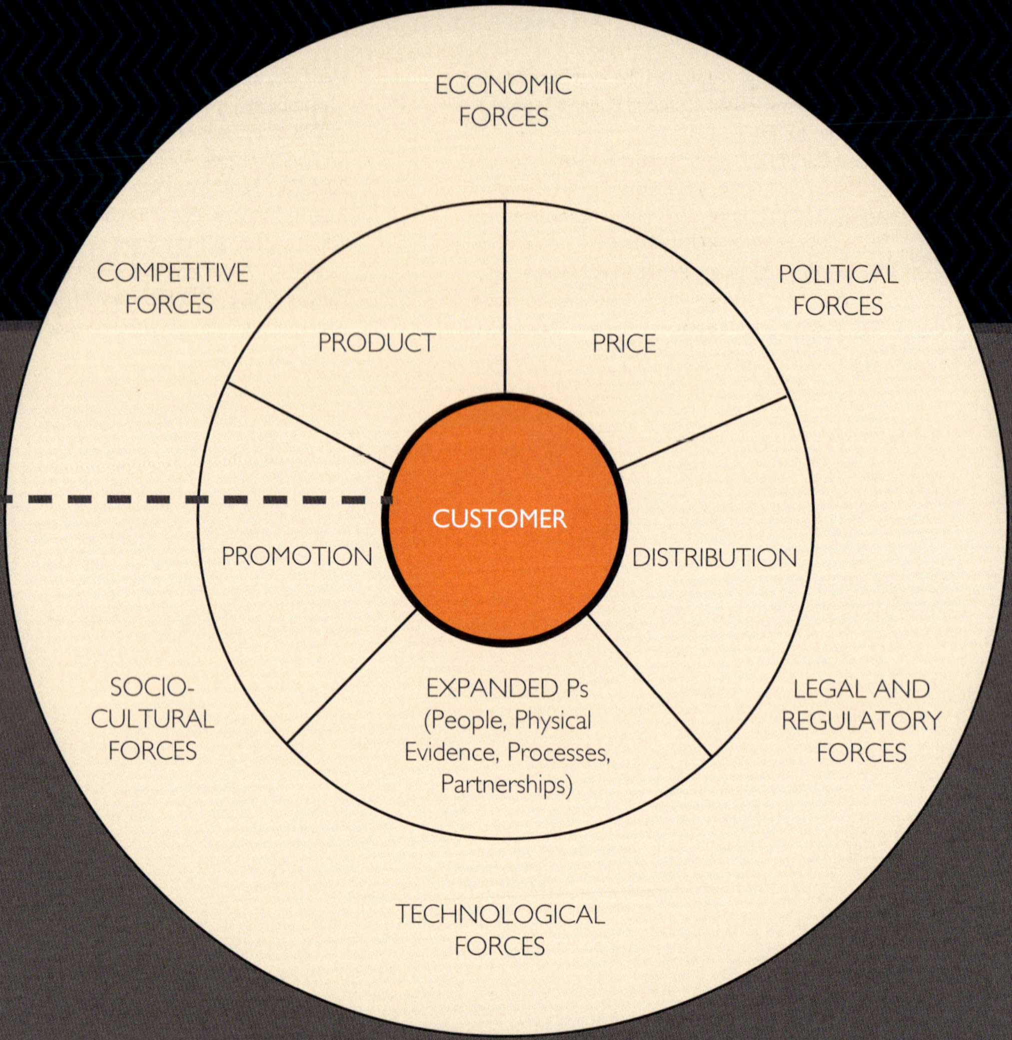
ECONOMIC FORCES
POLITICAL FORCES
LEGAL AND REGULATORY FORCES
TECHNOLOGICAL FORCES
SOCIO-CULTURAL FORCES
COMPETITIVE FORCES
PRODUCT
PRICE
DISTRIBUTION
EXPANDED Ps (People, Physical Evidence, Processes, Partnerships)
PROMOTION
CUSTOMER

BUSINESS MARKETS AND BUYING BEHAVIOUR

Business markets
- Producer
- Reseller
- Government
- Institutional

Marketing to business customers
- Characteristics of transactions
- Attributes
- Primary concerns
- Methods of buying
- Types of purchases

Demand for business products
- Derived demand
- Inelastic demand
- Joint demand
- Fluctuating demand

Business buying decisions
- The buying centre

Stages of the business buying decision process

Throughout this chapter, Watch, Listen and Revise icons indicate an opportunity for online self-study through CengageNOW, linking you to animated chapter overviews, interactive diagrams, videos, quizzes and more.

6 BUSINESS MARKETS AND BUYING BEHAVIOUR

Learning Objectives

L01 Be able to distinguish among the various types of business markets

L02 Identify the major characteristics of business customers and transactions

L03 Understand several attributes of the demand for business products

L04 Understand the characteristics of business buying behaviour and become familiar with the major components of a buying centre

L05 Understand the stages of the business buying decision process and the factors that affect this process.

MARKETING CHALLENGE | BUSINESS MARKETERS AND CUSTOMERS RELY ON VIRTUAL MARKETING

Many business customers try to look online for virtual product demonstrations or to visit virtual trade shows as they search for goods and services to solve problems or satisfy business needs. Small wonder that virtual marketing is a key activity for many companies seeking to reach business buyers across the country or around the world.

IBM is using virtual marketing to sell sophisticated information technology systems. 'As we looked at our market segmentation, we knew that 30 to 60 per cent of the purchase decision is based on buzz', explains the company's vice president for Service-Oriented Architecture and WebSphere Marketing. To create buzz, she used virtual marketing to help 'reach an audience we hadn't reached before and help us reach it in a very effective way.'

Source: © AFP PHOTO DDP/NIGEL TREBLIN GERMANY OUT/NEWSCOM

191

First, IBM posted a product demonstration on Yahoo! Video, which proved so popular that the team planned a 30-minute movie about service-oriented architecture, promoted by trailers uploaded to YouTube and Yahoo! Video. Next, the company invited prospects to screenings around the world and then posted the movie online for buyers to watch at their convenience. The result: tens of thousands of new sales leads for IBM.

All kinds of businesses are turning to virtual marketing. For example, one way Visa markets credit card services to small businesses is by sponsoring online networking tools and pages on Facebook. In less than three months, Visa's Facebook community attracted 20 000 small business members and is aiming to bring its services to thousands as the community expands.[1]

MARKETING CHALLENGE QUESTION

1 Why do so many businesses like Visa have a Facebook page? What advantages does digital marketing offer to businesses?

TEST your comprehension by taking the Pre- and Post-Test

Introduction

Serving business markets effectively requires business marketers like IBM to understand business customers. Business marketers go to considerable lengths to understand and reach their customers so that they can provide better services and develop and maintain long-term customer relationships. Like consumer marketers, business marketers are concerned about satisfying their customers.

In this chapter we look at business markets and business buying decision processes. We first discuss various kinds of business markets and the types of buyers making up these markets. Next, we explore several dimensions of business buying such as characteristics of transactions, attributes and concerns of buyers, methods of buying, and distinctive features of demand for products sold to business purchasers. We then examine how business buying decisions are made and who makes the purchases. Finally, we consider how business markets are analysed.

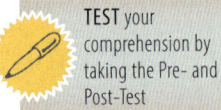

Business markets

A business market (also called a *business-to-business* or *B2B* market) consists of companies doing business with each other, as opposed to a consumer market (also called a *business-to-consumer* or *B2C* market) where organisations do business with consumers. Although B2B marketing employs the same concepts as marketing to consumers, such as defining target markets, understanding buying behaviour and developing effective marketing mixes, there are structural and behavioural differences in business markets. A company marketing to other companies must recognise how its product will influence other associated companies such as wholesalers, retailers and even other manufacturers. Business products can be technically complex, and the market often consists of sophisticated buyers. Because the business market consists of relatively small customer–company populations, a segment of the market could be as small as one customer company. The market for navy submarine components in Australia, for example, is limited to only one shipyard which builds navy submarines. On the other hand, a business product can be a commodity, such as corn or a bolt or screw, but the quantity purchased and the buying methods differ significantly from the consumer market, as we shall see. Business marketing is often based on long-term mutually profitable relationships across members of the marketing channel. Networks of suppliers and customers recognise the importance of building strong alliances based on cooperation, trust and collaboration. Manufacturers may even co-develop new products with business customers, sharing marketing research, production, scheduling, inventory management and information systems. One form of B2B collaboration is outsourcing, which is addressed in the Ethical Marketing box below. Although business marketing can be based on collaborative long-term buyer–seller relationships, there are also transactions based on timely exchanges of basic products at highly competitive market prices. For most business marketers, the goal is understanding customer needs and providing a value-added exchange that shifts from attracting customers to keeping customers and developing favourable customer relationships.

ETHICAL MARKETING | WHEN OUTSOURCING GOES BAD

issue

Who should be held responsible for outsourcing?

Over the last decade, many manufacturers have joined the widely publicised trend of outsourcing to foreign countries for cheaper products to cut their costs, particularly in China. Many of the products made in China have an acceptable quality level, but some products do not and may even be unsafe. Can the country to which work is outsourced influence the consumers' ultimate purchasing decision?

A classic and well-publicised case is Mattel Toys who, in 2007, had to recall nearly 1 million toys because the products were covered in paint that contained lead, a potential health hazard. Once the news hit the media, Mattel had to make countless public relations moves to try and maintain consumer confidence in its products. The products were made in factories in China, and public opinion regarding Chinese products has become rather shaky after several product recalls.

Similarly, Australian toy company Moose Enterprises outsourced the manufacturing of their 'Bindeez' bead craft toy to China. The 'Bindeez' toy won Australian Toy of the Year in 2007, however after children were hospitalised with seizure and overdose-like symptoms

it was discovered that the wrong chemical had been used in the manufacturing process. Instead of using the non-toxic chemical pentanediol, the chemical butanediol was used, which metabolises into the party drug known as GHB, an anesthetic used for recreational use. It was feared that people may intentionally ingest the toy in order to experience the chemical effects, which could potentially lead to a 'Bindeez' black market. The 'Bindeez' toy was recalled and later re-released under the new brand name 'Beados' in an attempt to extinguish links to the previous product.

When manufacturing is outsourced to producers in another country, who should take responsibility? Should the Chinese or the government of the country in which in the company is based share some of the blame? How much is the cost of losing a good reputation worth to companies that want to cut costs through outsourcing? Can the cost of a tarnished reputation more than offset the cost savings associated with outsourcing production?[2]

The four categories of business markets are producer, reseller, government and institutional. In the remainder of this section we discuss each of these types of markets.

Producer markets

Individuals and business organisations that purchase products for the purpose of making a profit by using them to produce other products or using them in their operations are classified as producer markets. Producer markets include buyers of raw materials, as well as purchasers of semi-finished and finished items used to produce other products. For example, manufacturers buy raw materials and component parts for direct use in product production. Supermarkets are part of producer markets for numerous support products such as paper and plastic bags, shelves, counters and scanners. Farmers are part of producer markets for farm machinery, fertiliser, seed and livestock. Producer markets include a broad array of industries, ranging from agriculture, forestry, fisheries and mining to construction, transportation, communications and utilities.

Manufacturers are geographically concentrated. This concentration sometimes enables businesses that sell to producer markets to serve them more efficiently. Within certain states, production in a specific industry may account for a sizable proportion of that industry's total production.

Our shredders have to be tough to wear our name.

When you shred with a Fellowes, you get more than a tough machine. You get a shredder built with premium components and rigorously tested to ensure years of reliable performance. No wonder it's the brand chosen by more businesses worldwide. Learn more about the Fellowes difference at fellowes.com

THE WORLD'S TOUGHEST SHREDDERS® Fellowes.

Reseller markets

Reseller markets consist of intermediaries, such as wholesalers and retailers, who buy finished goods and resell them for profit. Aside from sometimes making minor alterations, resellers do not change the physical characteristics of the products they handle. Wholesalers purchase products for resale to retailers. Retailers purchase products for resale to final consumers. Some retailers – Bunnings and David Jones, for example – carry a large number of items.

When making purchase decisions, resellers consider several factors. They evaluate the level of demand for a product to determine in what quantity and at what prices the product can be resold. Retailers assess the amount of space required to handle a product relative to its potential profit. In fact, they sometimes evaluate products on the basis of sales per square metre of selling area. Because customers often depend on resellers to have products available when needed, resellers typically appraise a supplier's ability to provide adequate quantities when and where wanted. Resellers also take into account the ease of placing orders and the availability of technical assistance and training programs from the producer. These types of concerns distinguish reseller markets from other markets.

Government markets

Federal, state and local governments make up government markets. These markets spend billions of dollars annually for a variety of goods and services – ranging from office supplies and health care services to vehicles, heavy equipment and weapons – to support their internal operations and provide citizens with products such as highways, education, water, energy and national defence. The federal government spends billions of dollars annually on national defence alone. The amount spent by federal, state and local government units over the last 30 years has increased rapidly because the total number of government units and the services they provide have both increased. Costs of providing these services also have risen.[3]

Although it is common to hear of large corporations being awarded government contracts, in fact businesses of all sizes market to government agencies. In recent years, the Internet has helped small businesses earn more government contracts than ever before by providing venues for small businesses to learn about and bid on government contracting opportunities. For example, ZANA Network is an online marketplace and business development resource for small and medium enterprises (SMEs) worldwide. ZANA Network provides selling, buying and partnering opportunities, along with trade resources, business guidance and essential services. It also enables entrepreneurs, inventors, professionals and other SME business people to come together in a community for mutual benefit. Along with the new government contracts feature, ZANA Network provides a one-stop menu of online services that enables businesses to buy and sell products.[4] Because government agencies spend public funds to buy the products needed to provide services, they are accountable to the public. This accountability explains their relatively complex set of buying procedures. Some companies do not even try to sell to government buyers because they want to avoid the tangle of red tape. However, many marketers have learned to deal efficiently with government procedures and do not find them to be a stumbling block. For certain products, such as defence-related items, the government may be the only customer.

Institutional markets

Organisations with charitable, educational, community or other non-business goals constitute institutional markets. Members of institutional markets include churches, some hospitals, charitable organisations and private education institutions. Institutions purchase millions of dollars' worth of products annually to provide goods, services and ideas to congregations, students, patients and others. Because institutions often have different goals and fewer resources than other types of organisations, marketers may use special marketing efforts to serve them.

government markets
Federal, state and local governments that buy goods and services to support their internal operations and provide products to their constituencies

institutional markets
Organisations with charitable, educational, community or other non-business goals

Source: Bionic Vision Australia

Dimensions of marketing to business customers

Having considered different types of business customers, we now look at several dimensions of marketing to them, including transaction characteristics, attributes of business customers, primary concerns of business customers, buying methods, major types of purchases and the characteristics of demand for business products. (See Figure 6.1.)

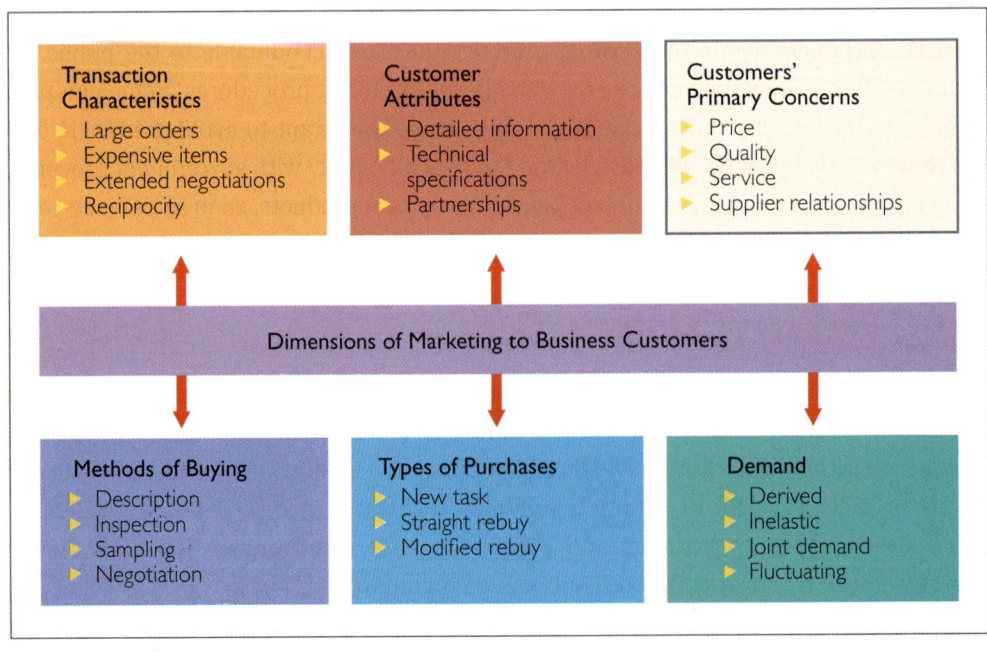

FIGURE 6.1
DIMENSIONS OF MARKETING TO BUSINESS CUSTOMERS

Characteristics of transactions with business customers

Transactions between businesses differ from consumer sales in several ways. Orders by business customers tend to be much larger than individual consumer sales. Consider that Ireland's Ryanair, one of the largest discount airlines in Europe, once placed a single order for 32 Boeing 737-800 jet aircraft at an estimated cost of US$2.25 billion to add to its fleet of 281 Boeing 737 aircraft.[5] Also consider that Turkish Airlines recently placed an order for 15 of Boeing's 737 aircraft. In total, the order was worth more than $1.2 billion.[6]

Suppliers frequently must sell products in large quantities to make profits; consequently, they prefer not to sell to customers who place small orders. Some business purchases involve expensive items, such as computer systems. Other products, such as raw materials and component items, are used continuously in production and the supply may need frequent replenishing. The contract regarding terms of sale of these items is likely to be a long-term agreement.

Discussions and negotiations associated with business purchases can require considerable marketing effort. Purchasing decisions are often made by committee. Orders frequently are large and expensive. Products may be custom-built. Several people or departments in the purchasing organisation may be involved.

One practice unique to business markets is reciprocity, an arrangement in which two organisations agree to buy from each other. Reciprocal agreements that threaten competition are illegal. Many governments take action to stop anticompetitive reciprocal practices. Nonetheless, a certain amount of reciprocal activity occurs among small businesses and, to a lesser extent, among larger companies. Because reciprocity influences purchasing agents to deal only with certain suppliers, it can lower morale among agents and lead to less than optimal purchases.

reciprocity
An arrangement unique to business marketing in which two organisations agree to buy from each other

Attributes of business customers

Business customers differ from consumers in their purchasing behaviour because they are better informed about the products they purchase. They typically demand detailed information about products' functional features and technical specifications to ensure that the products meet the organisation's needs. Personal goals, however, may also influence business buying behaviour. Most purchasing agents seek the psychological satisfaction that comes with organisational advancement and financial rewards. Agents who consistently exhibit rational business buying behaviour are likely to attain these personal goals because they help their companies achieve organisational objectives. Today, many suppliers and their customers build and maintain mutually beneficial relationships, sometimes called *partnerships*. Even in a partnership between a small vendor and a large corporate buyer, a strong partnership exists because high levels of interpersonal trust can lead to higher levels of commitment to the partnership by both organisations.[7]

Primary concerns of business customers

When making purchasing decisions, business customers take into account a variety of factors. Among their chief considerations are price, product quality, service and supplier relationships. Obviously, price matters greatly to business customers because it influences operating costs and costs of goods sold, which, in turn, affect selling price, profit margin and, ultimately, the ability to compete. When purchasing major equipment, a business customer views price as the amount of investment necessary to obtain a certain level of return or savings. A business customer is likely to compare the price of a product with the benefits the product will provide to the organisation, often over a period of years.

Most business customers try to achieve and maintain a specific level of quality in the products they buy. To achieve this goal, most companies establish standards (usually stated as a percentage of defects allowed) for these products and buy them on the basis of a set of expressed characteristics, commonly called *specifications*. A customer evaluates the quality of the products being considered to determine whether they meet specifications. If a product fails to meet specifications or malfunctions for the ultimate consumer, the customer may drop that product's supplier and switch to a different supplier. On the other hand, business customers are ordinarily cautious about buying products that exceed specifications because such products often cost more, thus increasing the organisation's overall costs. Specifications are designed to meet a customer's wants, and anything that does not contribute to meeting those wants may be considered wasteful.

Business buyers value service. Services offered by suppliers directly and indirectly influence customers' costs, sales and profits. In some instances the mix of customer services is the major means by which marketers gain a competitive advantage. WaterFurnace, an international manufacturer of geothermal energy equipment for residential and commercial markets, recently launched a web-based platform just for businesses. WeDoGeo.com provides business customers with information on equipment selection and pricing, ordering, and answers to construction questions. The platform improves communication and ease of ordering, and attracts customers looking for strong customer service.[8] Typical services desired by customers are market information, inventory maintenance, on-time delivery, repair services and online communication capabilities. Business buyers are likely to need technical product information, data regarding demand, information about general economic conditions or supply and delivery information. Maintaining adequate inventory is critical because it helps to make products accessible when a customer needs them and reduces customer inventory requirements and costs. Because business customers are usually responsible for ensuring that products are on hand and ready for use when needed, on-time delivery is crucial. Furthermore, reliable, on-time delivery saves business customers money because it enables them to carry less inventory. Purchasers of machinery

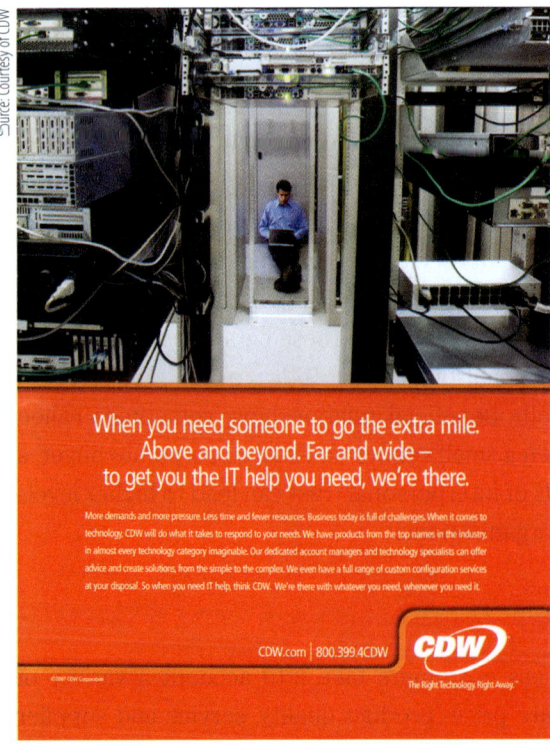

Concerns of business customers >>
In this ad, CDW promises excellent and timely service, one of the primary concerns of business customers

are especially concerned about obtaining repair services and replacement parts quickly because inoperable equipment is costly. Caterpillar Inc., manufacturer of earth-moving, construction and materials-handling machinery, has built an international reputation, as well as a competitive advantage, by providing prompt service and replacement parts for its products around the world. Business customers are likely to resist a supplier's effort to implement a new technology if there are questions about the technology's compatibility, reliability or other factors that could cause the supplier to fail to deliver on promises.[9]

Communication channels that allow customers to ask questions, voice complaints, submit orders and trace shipments are indispensable components of service. Marketers should strive for uniformity of service, simplicity, truthfulness and accuracy. Marketers should develop customer service objectives and monitor customer service programs. Companies can monitor service by formally surveying customers or informally calling on customers and asking questions about the quality of the services they receive. Expending the time and effort to ensure that customers are happy can greatly benefit marketers by increasing customer retention.

Finally, business customers are concerned about the costs of developing and maintaining relationships with their suppliers. By developing relationships and building trust with a particular supplier, buyers can reduce their search effort and uncertainty about monetary price. Business customers have to keep in mind the overall fit of a purchase, including its potential to reduce inventory and carrying costs, as well as to increase inventory turnover and ability to move the right products to the right place at the right time. The entire business can be affected by a single supplier failing to be a good partner.

Methods of business buying

Although no two business buyers do their jobs the same way, most use one or more of the following purchase methods: *description, inspection, sampling* and *negotiation*. When products are standardised according to certain characteristics (such as size, shape, weight and colour) and graded using such standards, a business buyer may be able to purchase simply by describing or specifying quantity, grade and other attributes. Agricultural products often fall into this category. Sometimes buyers specify a particular brand or its equivalent when describing the desired product. Purchases on the basis of description are especially common between a buyer and seller with an ongoing relationship built on trust.

Certain products, such as industrial equipment, used vehicles and buildings, have unique characteristics and may vary with regard to condition. For example, a particular used truck may have a bad transmission. Consequently, business buyers of such products must base purchase decisions on inspection.

Sampling entails taking a specimen of the product from the lot and evaluating it on the assumption that its characteristics represent the entire lot. This method is appropriate when the product is homogeneous – for instance, grain – and examining the entire lot is not physically or economically feasible.

Some purchases by businesses are based on negotiated contracts. In certain instances, buyers describe exactly what they need and ask sellers to submit bids. They then negotiate with the suppliers who submit the most attractive bids. This approach may be used when acquiring commercial vehicles, for example. In the case of IBM, suppliers are required to comply with environmental guidelines (see Sustainable Marketing box below). In other cases, the buyer may be unable to identify specifically what is to be purchased but can provide only a general description, such as might be the case for a piece of custom-made equipment. A buyer and seller might negotiate a contract that specifies a base price and provides for the payment of additional costs and fees. These contracts are used most commonly for one-time projects such as buildings, custom-made equipment and special projects.

SUSTAINABLE MARKETING | GO GREEN – PASS IT ALONG

Just as many consumers are concerned about the environmental impact of the goods and services they buy, more companies are checking that suppliers have the credentials to do business in an eco-friendly manner. In fact, IBM and a growing number of business buyers are even insisting that suppliers of suppliers have the right green credentials in place. In 1998, IBM asked its suppliers to consider complying with international green operating standards. By 2004, it had drafted its own environmental guidelines for suppliers. Today, IBM requires its 28 000 primary suppliers to take four steps: (1) measure their environmental impacts, (2) set specific goals for improvement, (3) publicly announce their environmental results and (4) 'cascade' these green requirements to their main suppliers. Although some companies may find these requirements challenging, IBM believes that establishing green credentials is a smart and profitable business decision.[10]

WATCH an online video activity exploring the types of business purchases

new-task purchase
An initial purchase by an organisation of an item to be used to perform a new job or solve a new problem

straight-rebuy purchase
A routine purchase of the same products under approximately the same terms of sale by a business buyer

Types of business purchases >>
When purchasing this type of equipment, business customers are prone to use a modified rebuy

Types of business purchases

Most business purchases are one of three types: new-task, straight-rebuy or modified-rebuy purchase. Each type is subject to different influences and therefore requires business marketers to modify their selling approach appropriately.[11] In a new-task purchase, an organisation makes an initial purchase of an item to be used to perform a new job or solve a new problem. A new-task purchase may require development of product specifications, vendor specifications and procedures for future purchases of that product. To make the initial purchase, the business buyer usually needs much information. For example, if Heineken were introducing a salty, spicy beer-flavoured snack and were purchasing automated packaging equipment, that would be a new-task purchase.

A straight-rebuy purchase occurs when buyers purchase the same products routinely under approximately the same terms of sale. Buyers require little information for these routine purchase decisions and tend to use familiar suppliers that have provided

Twice the impact. Half the cost.

Source: Courtesy of Hewlett-Packard

satisfactory service and products in the past. These suppliers try to set up automatic reordering systems to make reordering easy and convenient for business buyers.

In a modified-rebuy purchase, a new-task purchase is changed the second or third time it is ordered, or requirements associated with a straight-rebuy purchase are modified. A business buyer might seek faster delivery, lower prices or a different quality level of product specifications. A modified-rebuy situation may cause regular suppliers to become more competitive to keep the account because other suppliers could obtain the business. When a company changes the terms of a service contract, such as for telecommunication services, it has made a modified purchase.

Demand for business products

Unlike consumer demand, demand for business products (also called *industrial demand*) can be characterised as (1) derived, (2) inelastic, (3) joint or (4) fluctuating.

Derived demand

Because business customers, especially producers, buy products for direct or indirect use in the production of goods and services to satisfy consumers' needs, the demand for business products derives from the demand for consumer products. It is therefore called derived demand. Business marketers at different levels are affected by a change in consumer demand for a particular product. For instance, consumers have become concerned with health and good nutrition and as a result are purchasing more products with less fat, cholesterol and sodium. When consumers reduced their purchases of high-fat foods, a change occurred in the demand for products marketed by food processors, equipment manufacturers and suppliers of raw materials associated with these products. Similarly, increased emphasis on workplace health and safety and workplace efficiency has led to an increase in the purchase of ergonomic products (this issue is further explored in the Marketing in Action box on the next page). When consumer demand for a product changes, it sets in motion a wave that affects demand for all companies involved in the production of that product.

Inelastic demand

Inelastic demand means that a price increase or decrease will not significantly alter demand for a business product. Because some business products contain a number of parts, price increases affecting only one or two parts may yield only a slightly higher per-unit production cost. When a sizable price increase for a component represents a large proportion of the product's cost, demand may become more elastic because the

modified-rebuy purchase
A new-task purchase that is changed on subsequent orders or when the requirements of a straight-rebuy purchase are modified

derived demand
Demand for industrial products that stems from demand for consumer products

inelastic demand
Demand that is not significantly altered by a price increase or decrease

Source: © iStockphoto.com/4kodiak

price increase in the component causes the price at the consumer level to rise sharply. For example, if aircraft engine manufacturers substantially increase the price of engines, forcing Boeing to raise the prices of the aircraft it manufactures, the demand for airliners may become more elastic as airlines reconsider whether they can afford to buy new aircraft. An increase in the price of windshields, however, is unlikely to greatly affect either the price of or the demand for airliners.

Inelasticity applies only to industry demand for business products, not to the demand curve that an individual company faces. Suppose that a spark plug producer increases the price of spark plugs sold to small-engine manufacturers, but its competitors continue to maintain lower prices. The spark plug company will probably experience reduced unit sales because most small-engine producers will switch to lower-priced brands. A specific company is vulnerable to elastic demand, even though industry demand for a specific business product is inelastic.

Joint demand

joint demand
Demand involving the use of two or more items in combination to produce a product

Demand for certain business products, especially raw materials and components, is subject to joint demand. Joint demand occurs when two or more items are used in combination to produce a product. For example, a company that manufactures axes needs the same number of axe handles as it does axe blades. These two products are therefore demanded jointly. If a shortage of axe handles exists, the producer buys fewer axe blades. Understanding the effects of joint demand is particularly important for a marketer selling multiple, jointly demanded items. Such a marketer realises that when a customer begins purchasing one of the jointly demanded items, a good opportunity exists to sell related products.

MARKETING IN ACTION | STEELCASE WANTS TO KEEP BUSINESS CUSTOMERS HEALTHY

International office furniture company Steelcase received its first patent in 1914 for a steel wastepaper basket, marketed as a solution to the common business problem of straw wastepaper baskets catching on fire. Today they are finding solutions to help businesses create office environments that enhance efficiency. Knowing that employee health is a growing concern, Steelcase's marketing experts worked with a doctor at Mayo Clinic to develop a line of office furniture that helps office workers get (or stay) in shape. The Walkstation consists of an adjustable desk and computer workstation attached to a treadmill (matching chair is optional). More recently, after conducting a global

posture study, Steelcase revealed new postures that have evolved from the use of new technologies including texting on smart phones and swiping iPads. The research findings led to the development of the Gesture Chair, an office chair that is designed to provide better ergonomics to support interactions with today's technologies. Steelcase's CEO asks one key question over and over again of his marketing experts: 'What's the user insight that led to this product?'[12]

Fluctuating demand

Because the demand for business products is derived from consumer demand, it may fluctuate enormously. In general, when particular consumer products are in high demand, their producers buy large quantities of raw materials and components to ensure meeting long-run production requirements. In addition, these producers may expand production capacity, which entails acquiring new equipment and machinery, more workers and more raw materials and component parts. Conversely, a decline in demand for certain consumer goods significantly reduces demand for business products used to produce those goods. Sometimes price changes lead to surprising temporary changes in demand. A price increase for a business product initially may cause business customers to buy more of the item because they expect the price to rise further. Similarly, demand for a business product may be significantly lower following a price cut because buyers are waiting for further price reductions. Fluctuations in demand can be substantial in industries in which prices change frequently.

Business buying decisions

LO4

Business (organisational) buying behaviour refers to the purchase behaviour of producers, government units, institutions and resellers. Although several factors affecting consumer buying behaviour (discussed in Chapter 4) also influence business buying behaviour, several factors are unique to the latter. We first analyse the buying centre to learn who participates in business purchase decisions. We then focus on the stages of the buying decision process and the factors affecting it.

The buying centre

Relatively few business purchase decisions are made by just one person; often they are made through a buying centre. A buying centre is a group of people within an organisation

business (organisational) buying behaviour
The purchase behaviour of producers, government units, institutions and resellers

buying centre
The people within an organisation, including users, influencers, buyers, deciders and gatekeepers, who make business purchase decisions

who make business purchase decisions. They include users, influencers, buyers, deciders and gatekeepers.[13] One person may perform several roles.

Users are the organisation members who actually use the product being acquired. They frequently initiate the purchase process and generate purchase specifications. After the purchase, they evaluate product performance relative to the specifications. *Influencers* are often technical personnel, such as engineers, who help develop the specifications and evaluate alternative products. Technical personnel are especially important influencers when products being considered involve new, advanced technology. *Buyers* select suppliers and negotiate terms of purchase. They may also become involved in developing specifications. In the case of Costco buyers, specifications may include the packaging (as illustrated in the Marketing in Transition box below). Buyers are sometimes called purchasing agents or purchasing managers. Their choices of vendors and products, especially for new-task purchases, are heavily influenced by people occupying other roles in the buying centre. *Deciders* actually choose the products. Although buyers may be deciders, it is not unusual for different people to occupy these roles. For routinely purchased items, buyers are commonly deciders. However, a buyer may not be authorised to make purchases exceeding a certain dollar limit, in which case higher-level management personnel are deciders. *Gatekeepers*, such as secretaries and technical personnel, control the flow of information to and among people occupying other roles in the buying centre. Buyers who deal directly with vendors may also be gatekeepers because they can control information flows.

MARKETING IN TRANSITION | PARTNERING FOR PROFIT

Large or small, the companies that supply large discount retailers benefit enormously from partnering with them. For example, Costco – whose Australian stores in Melbourne and Sydney are generating more sales than the average North American Costco – has

insisted that some companies repackage their products so that they can supply products in larger sizes, and so that more can fit in every truck and on store shelves.

When Costco's buyers ask for something, even the biggest companies pay close attention because the retailer is such a big customer. Iconic brands in Australia that supply Costco include Pantene, OMO, Kleenex, Finish and Napisan.

Costco's US parent has sketched out ambitious plans for the retailer in the Asia-Pacific region, recently discovering it could reap faster growth rates from its offshore supermarkets than those in its home market. Seven out of Costco's 10 most profitable stores are in the Asia-Pacific region.[14]

The number and structure of an organisation's buying centres are affected by the organisation's size and market position, the volume and types of products being purchased and the organisation's overall managerial philosophy regarding exactly who should be involved in purchase decisions. The size of a buying centre is influenced by the stage of the buying decision process and the type of purchase (new task, straight rebuy or modified rebuy). A marketer attempting to sell to a business customer should determine who is in the buying centre, the types of decisions each individual makes and which individuals are most influential in the decision process. Because in some instances many people make up the buying centre, marketers cannot feasibly contact all participants. Instead, they must be certain to contact a few of the most influential participants.

Stages of the business buying decision process

Like consumers, businesses follow a buying decision process. This process is summarised in the lower portion of Figure 6.2. In the first stage, one or more individuals recognise that a problem or need exists. Problem recognition may arise under a variety of circumstances – for instance, when machines malfunction or a company modifies an existing product or introduces a new one. Individuals in the buying centre, such as users, influencers or buyers, may be involved in problem recognition, but it may be stimulated by external sources, such as sales representatives or advertisements.

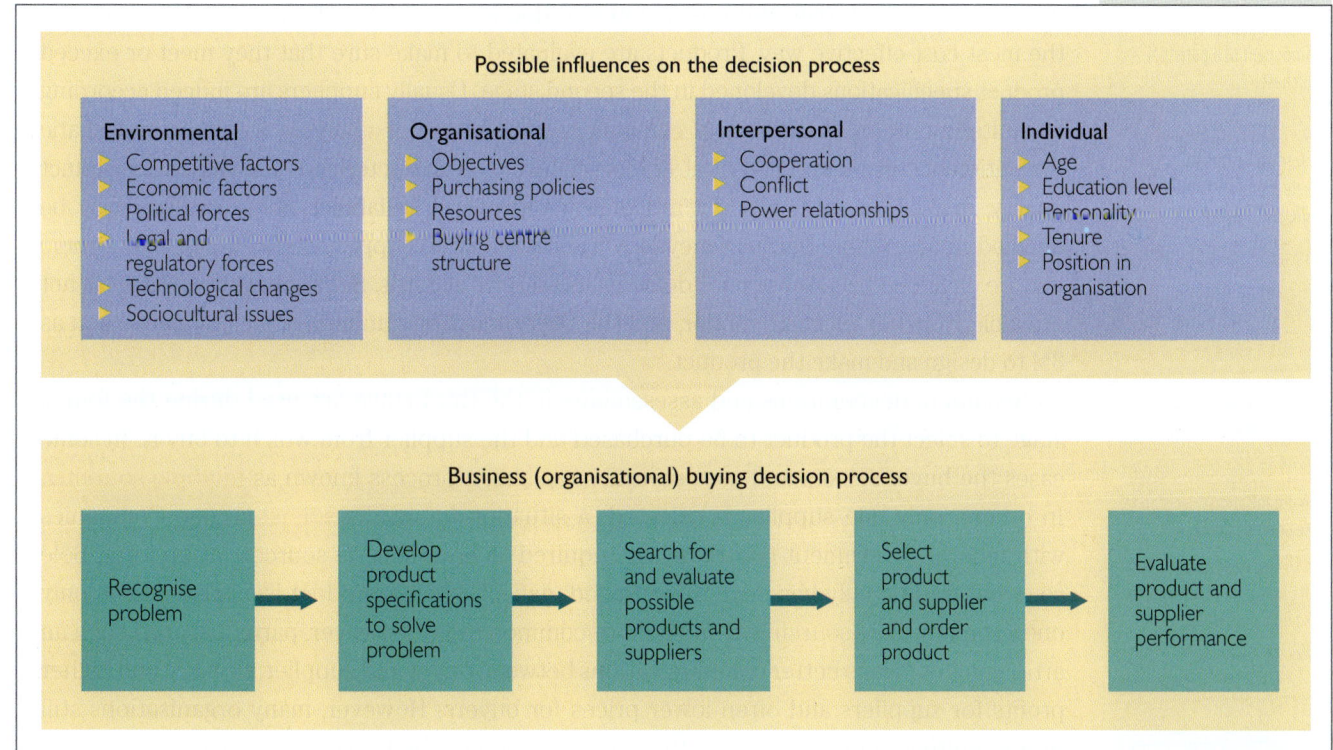

FIGURE 6.2 BUSINESS (ORGANISATIONAL) BUYING DECISION PROCESS AND FACTORS THAT MAY INFLUENCE IT

The second stage of the process, development of product specifications, requires that buying centre participants assess the problem or need and determine what is necessary to resolve or satisfy it. During this stage, users and influencers, such as engineers, often provide information and advice for developing product specifications. By assessing and describing needs, the organisation should be able to establish product specifications.

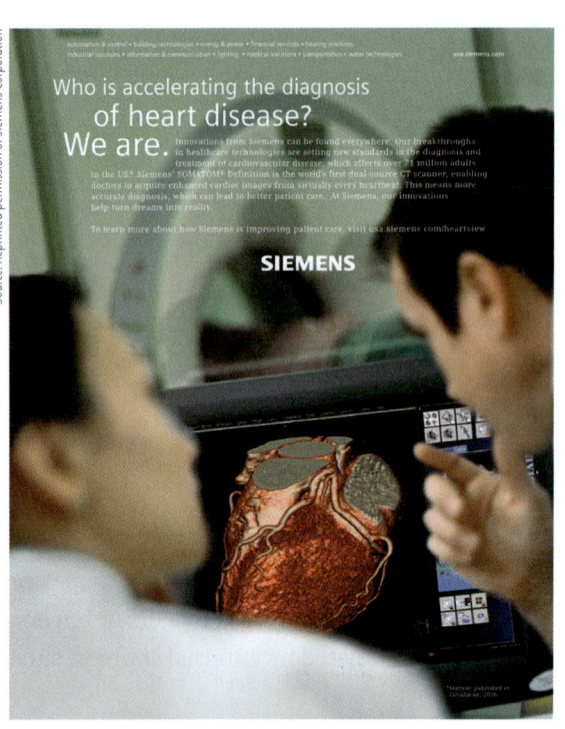

Source: Reprinted permission of Siemens Corporation

Source: Reprinted permission of Siemens Corporation

Problem recognition >>
This ad aimed at health care providers focus on problem recognition. Some health care providers may want to update equipment to improve diagnostic capabilities

value analysis
An evaluation of each component of a potential purchase

vendor analysis
A formal, systematic evaluation of current and potential vendors

multiple sourcing
An organisation's decision to use several suppliers

sole sourcing
An organisation's decision to use only one supplier

Searching for and evaluating potential products and suppliers constitutes the third stage in the decision process. Search activities may involve looking in company files and trade directories, contacting suppliers for information, soliciting proposals from known vendors and examining websites, catalogues and trade publications. To facilitate vendor searches, some organisations advertise their desire to build partnerships with specific types of vendors, such as those that adhere to environment-friendly production practices. During this stage, some organisations engage in value analysis, an evaluation of each component of a potential purchase. Value analysis examines quality, design, materials and possibly item reduction or deletion to acquire the product in the most cost-effective way. Products are evaluated to make sure that they meet or exceed product specifications developed in the second stage. Usually suppliers are judged according to multiple criteria. A number of companies employ vendor analysis, a formal, systematic evaluation of current and potential vendors focusing on characteristics such as price, product quality, delivery service, product availability and overall reliability. Some vendors may be deemed unacceptable because they lack the resources to supply needed quantities. Others may be excluded because of poor delivery and service records. Sometimes the product is not available from any existing vendor, and the buyer must find an innovative company such as 3M to design and make the product.

Results of deliberations and assessments in the third stage are used during the fourth stage to select the product to be purchased and the supplier from which to buy it. In some cases the buyer selects and uses several suppliers, a process known as multiple sourcing. In others, only one supplier is selected, a situation known as sole sourcing. Companies with federal government contracts are required to have several sources for an item. Sole sourcing traditionally has been discouraged, except when a product is available from only one company. Sole sourcing is much more common today, however, partly because such an arrangement means better communications between buyer and supplier, stability and higher profits for suppliers and often lower prices for buyers. However, many organisations still prefer multiple sourcing because this approach lessens the possibility of disruption caused by strikes, shortages or bankruptcies. The actual product is ordered in this fourth stage, and specific details regarding terms, credit arrangements, delivery dates and methods, and technical assistance are finalised.

During the fifth stage, the product's performance is evaluated by comparing it with specifications. Sometimes the product meets the specifications, but its performance does not solve the problem adequately or satisfy the need recognised in the first stage. In such a case, product specifications must be adjusted. The supplier's performance is also evaluated during this stage. If supplier performance is inadequate, the business purchaser seeks corrective action from the supplier or searches for a new supplier. Results of the evaluation become feedback for the other stages in future business purchase decisions.

This business buying decision process is used in its entirety primarily for new-task purchases. Several stages, but not necessarily all, are used for modified-rebuy and straight-rebuy situations.

Influences on the business buying decision process

Figure 6.2 also lists four major categories of factors that influence business buying decisions: environmental, organisational, interpersonal and individual.

Environmental factors include competitive factors as well as the so-called PEST factors: political (P) forces, economic (E) factors, sociocultural (S) issues and technological (T) changes. These competitive and PEST factors generate considerable uncertainty for an organisation, which can make individuals in the buying centre apprehensive about certain types of purchases. Changes in one or more environmental force can create new purchasing opportunities and threats. For example, changes in competition and technology can make buying decisions difficult in the case of products such as software, computers and telecommunications equipment. On the other hand, many business marketers believe that the Internet can reduce their customer service costs and allow companies to improve relationships with business customers.[15]

Source: Light Eco is a registered trademark of Ilum-a-lite Pty Ltd

Organisational factors influencing the buying decision process include the company's objectives, purchasing policies and resources, as well as the size and composition of its buying centre. An organisation may have certain buying policies to which buying centre participants must conform. For instance, a company's policies may mandate unusually long- or short-term contracts, perhaps longer or shorter than most sellers desire. An organisation's financial resources may require special credit arrangements. Any of these conditions could affect purchase decisions.

Interpersonal factors are the relationships among people in the buying centre. Trust among all members of collaborative partnerships is crucial, particularly in purchases involving customised products.[16] Use of power and level

<< **Influences on the business buying decision process** Numerous business purchases are influenced by environmental forces. Energy savings result in lower costs which, in turn, allow organisations to be more competitive

of conflict among buying centre participants influence business buying decisions. Certain individuals in the buying centre may be better communicators than others and may be more persuasive. Often these interpersonal dynamics are hidden, making them difficult for marketers to assess.

Individual factors are personal characteristics of participants in the buying centre, such as age, education, personality and tenure and position in the organisation. For example, a 55-year-old manager who has been in the organisation for 25 years may affect decisions made by the buying centre differently than a 30-year-old person employed only two years. How influential these factors are depends on the buying situation, the type of product being purchased and whether the purchase is new task, modified rebuy or straight rebuy. Negotiating styles of people vary within an organisation and from one organisation to another. To be effective, marketers must know customers well enough to be aware of these individual factors and the effects they may have on purchase decisions.

Study Tools

Chapter review

 **LO1**   BE ABLE TO DISTINGUISH AMONG THE VARIOUS TYPES OF BUSINESS MARKETS.

Business (B2B) markets consist of individuals and groups that purchase a specific kind of product for resale, direct use in producing other products or use in day-to-day operations. Producer markets include those individuals and business organisations purchasing products for the purpose of making a profit by using them to produce other products or as part of their operations. Intermediaries that buy finished products and resell them to make a profit are classified as reseller markets. Government markets consist of federal, state and local governments, which spend billions of dollars annually for goods and services to support internal operations and to provide citizens with services. Organisations with charitable, educational, community or other non-profit goals constitute institutional markets.

 **LO2**   IDENTIFY THE MAJOR CHARACTERISTICS OF BUSINESS CUSTOMERS AND TRANSACTIONS.

Transactions involving business customers differ from consumer transactions in several ways. Such transactions tend to be larger and negotiations occur less frequently, although they are often lengthy when they do occur. They often involve more than one person or department in the purchasing organisation. They may also involve reciprocity, an arrangement in which two organisations agree to buy from each other. Business customers are usually better informed than ultimate consumers and more likely to seek information about a product's features and technical specifications.

UNDERSTAND SEVERAL ATTRIBUTES OF THE DEMAND FOR BUSINESS PRODUCTS.

Business customers are particularly concerned about quality, service, price and supplier relationships. Quality is important because it directly affects the quality of products the buyer's company produces. To achieve an exact level of quality, organisations often buy products on the basis of a set of expressed characteristics, called *specifications*. Because services have such a direct influence on a company's costs, sales and profits, matters such as market information, on-time delivery, availability of parts and communication capabilities are crucial to a business buyer. Although business customers do not depend solely on price to decide which products to buy, price is of prime concern because it directly influences profitability.

Business buyers use several purchasing methods, including description, inspection, sampling and negotiation. Most organisational purchases are new task, straight rebuy or modified rebuy. In a new-task purchase, an organisation makes an initial purchase of items to be used to perform new jobs or to solve new problems. A straight-rebuy purchase occurs when a buyer purchases the same products routinely under approximately the same terms of sale. In a modified-rebuy purchase, a new-task purchase is changed the second or third time it is ordered, or requirements associated with a straight-rebuy purchase are modified.

Industrial demand differs from consumer demand along several dimensions. Industrial demand derives from demand for consumer products. At the industry level, industrial demand is inelastic. Some business products are subject to joint demand, which occurs when two or more items are used in combination to make a product. Finally, because organisational demand derives from consumer demand, the demand for business products can fluctuate widely.

UNDERSTAND THE CHARACTERISTICS OF BUSINESS BUYING BEHAVIOUR AND BECOME FAMILIAR WITH THE MAJOR COMPONENTS OF A BUYING CENTRE.

Business purchase decisions are made through a buying centre, the group of people involved in making such purchase decisions. Users are those in the organisation who actually use the product. Influencers help to develop specifications and evaluate alternative products for possible use. Buyers select suppliers and negotiate purchase terms. Deciders choose the products. Gatekeepers control the flow of information to and among individuals occupying other roles in the buying centre.

UNDERSTAND THE STAGES OF THE BUSINESS BUYING DECISION PROCESS AND THE FACTORS THAT AFFECT THIS PROCESS.

The stages of the business buying decision process are problem recognition, development of product specifications to solve problems, search for and evaluation of products and suppliers, selection and ordering of the most appropriate product, and evaluation of the product's and supplier's performance.

Four categories of factors influence business buying decisions. Environmental factors include competitive forces as well as the so-called PEST factors: political (P) forces, economic (E) conditions, sociocultural (S) factors and technological (T) changes. Organisational factors include the company's objectives, purchasing policies and resources, as well as the size and composition of its buying centre. Interpersonal factors are the relationships among people in the buying centre. Individual factors are personal characteristics of members of the buying centre, such as age, education, personality, tenure and position in the organisation.

Key concepts

Use these key terms in **Search me! marketing** to find the latest relevant readings from a wide range of world-class journals, e-books and newspapers, including *The Australian*.

- business (organisational) buying behaviour
- buying centre
- derived demand
- government markets
- inelastic demand
- institutional markets
- joint demand
- modified-rebuy purchase
- multiple sourcing
- new-task purchase
- producer markets
- reciprocity
- reseller markets
- sole sourcing
- straight-rebuy purchase
- value analysis
- vendor analysis

Issues for discussion and review

1   What type of business market are the following companies primarily examples of:
    a   The Salvation Army
    b   Australian Taxation Office
    c   Woolworths
    d   South Gippsland Eggs.

2   In what ways are business customer's transactions different to those of consumer transactions?

3   What are the primary concerns of business customers? Think about how these concerns are different to those of a consumer

4   What are the commonly used methods of business buying?

5   Describe the three types of business purchases.

6   How does demand for business products differ from consumer demand?

7   What is an organisation's buying centre? What are the buying centre's major components?

8   Explain the stages of the business buying decision process.

9   How do environmental, business, interpersonal and individual factors affect business purchases?

Marketing applications

1   Think about your four most recent purchases. Maybe that was sushi, a train ticket, a coffee and new jeans. How did those items get to you? The sushi started as rice, chicken and seaweed (producers), which went to a cafe that made the

sushi (reseller). Categorise each business in the supply chain of your most recent purchases as either – producer, reseller, government and institutional. Explain your classifications.

2 Indicate the method of buying (description, inspection, sampling or negotiation) an organisation would be most likely to use when purchasing each of the following items. Defend your selection.

  a Premises for the opening of your specialist coffee shop.
  b Denim for a clothing manufacturer.
  c A hotel for a football club's end-of-season getaway, assuming a regular travel agency is used.
  d Photocopy paper for a University library.

3 Categorise the following purchase decisions as new task, modified-rebuy or straight-rebuy and explain your choice.

  a Dan has purchased napkins from Smiths Restaurant Supply for 25 years and recently placed an order for blue napkins rather than the usual white ones.
  b Julie's investment company has been purchasing envelopes from AAA Office Supply for a year and now needs to purchase boxes to mail year-end portfolio summaries to clients. Julie calls AAA to purchase these boxes.
  c Reliance Insurance has been supplying its salespeople with small personal computers to assist in their sales efforts. The company recently agreed to begin supplying them with faster, more sophisticated computers.

ONLINE EXERCISE

1 The Saudi Basic Industries Corporation (SABIC) is a highly diversified, global corporation with many divisions. SABIC Innovative Plastics is the online website for SABIC's resins and plastics business. Visit the website at http://www.sabic-ip.com.

  a At what type of business markets are SABIC's resin products targeted?
  b How does SABIC's website address some of the concerns of business customers?
  c What environmental factors do you think affect the demand for SABIC resin products?

Developing your marketing plan

When developing a marketing strategy for business customers it is essential to understand the process the business goes through when making a buying decision. Knowledge of business buying behaviour is important when developing several aspects of the marketing plan. To assist you in relating the information in this chapter to the creation of a marketing plan for business customers, consider the following issues:

1 What are the primary concerns of business customers? Could any of these concerns be addressed with strengths of your company?

2 Determine the type of business purchase your customer will likely be using when purchasing your product. How would this impact the level of information required by the business when moving through the buying decision process?

3 Discuss the different types of demand that the business customer will experience when purchasing your product.

CengageNOW

Go to http:\\login.cengagebrain.com to link to CengageNOW, your online study tool. First take the Pre-Test for this chapter to get your Personalised Study Plan, and then:

* **Revise** your understanding of the key concepts of marketing with the online glossary

* **Watch** an interactive animation of strategic marketing to broaden your subject comprehension

* **Listen** to an audio summary of the learning objectives covered in this chapter.

After you have completed the activities in your Personalised Study Plan take the Post-Test to determine what concepts you have mastered and what you still need to work on.

Case study

THE EVOLUTION OF BUSINESS BANKING – THE IMPACT OF TECHNOLOGY

When dealing with business customers, relationships have been considered the most important component of marketing. It is important to build trust and commitment, to strengthen this relationship. In the past, this meant that business customers often received birthday cards from the businesses they dealt with and phone calls asking how everyone in the family was going. The business and its business customer developed a business relationship that was more like a friendship. With the fast-paced nature of business and the use of technology, this has shifted.

Customer relationships have been considered essential in business banking for some time. However, more recently, with the increased use of technology, many businesses have said that they'd prefer a fast transaction and see no need to get to know their business banker.

The banking industry is well known for its innovation in service delivery and distribution and this has been a method of differentiation in the industry for decades. The use of the Internet in business banking has given customers the opportunity to have greater control over their financial information and transactions, with added convenience. For the bank, this leads to cost reductions and a better ability to compete. For the customer, it adds convenience.

Joe, the finance manager of a large Australian golf course, believes that for his business, nothing in banking has really changed. Although Joe uses Internet banking every day, to manage his transactions and check on his account, he says he needs to know his business banker. His business banker, Susan, understands his business requirements, so whenever the golf course needs additional funds, or wants to move investments, she doesn't require a long story about why this is the case. He said it's rare that a week would pass without him talking to Susan and every year in September, he receives a birthday card from the bank he does his business banking with. Although Joe is very satisfied with the bank he works with, he said that if Susan moved to another bank, he would move the golf course's bank accounts, because his loyalty is with his banker, rather than his bank.

Source: Getty Images

Caleb, a young Generation Y business owner in Sydney, operates as a sole trader in the IT sector. Very tech-savvy, Caleb prefers to do his banking at arm's length. He can't remember the last time he went into a branch, however he prefers to bank with a bank with branches 'just in case'. He says he doesn't even know his bank manager's name and doesn't care about that. In fact, he is annoyed when the bank does contact him unnecessarily.

David is the finance manager of a medium-sized non-profit organisation, operating in Melbourne. A few years ago, David knew his business' bank manager, but more recently the bank has urged the organisation to do most of their transactions online. When he does need to visit a branch, David has to queue up like personal bankers and no one knows him or his business. He feels quite unhappy that his organisation isn't treated the way it had been treated in the past. Although he thinks online banking is a convenience, he is frustrated by the way he feels forced out of the branches. The organisational structure means that if David wants to change the bank the organisation banks with, a board meeting needs to be held and the majority of the members of the board need to agree to the change.

Here are three different business structures and three different business banking relationships. In the past, relationships ruled in business banking, but with the use of the Internet, relationships are no longer as important for some businesses. It's become very important for all businesses to understand their business customers, rather than trying a 'one size fits all' model.[17]

Raechel Johns, Univeristy of Canberra

QUESTIONS FOR DISCUSSION

1 Why have relationships been so important in business banking in the past? What has changed? Joe and Caleb are both quite happy with their banking relationship, but David is not. What are some of the issues here?

2 What is derived demand? How would this work in a business banking context?

3 Discuss the role of the buying centre. How does the buying centre impact on David's satisfaction or dissatisfaction with his bank?

Chapter endnotes

1. Jacqueline Renerow, 'Small Business Owners Get Intimate with Visa's New Network,' *Response* (December 2008): 32; Charlotte Woolard, 'Virtual Events Keep Down Costs,' *B to B* (April 23, 2007): 31; Maggie Rauch, 'Virtual Reality: How IBM Uses Web 2.0 to Grow Its Brand, from Wikis to Viral Video to Second Life,' *Sales and Marketing Management* (January–February 2007): 181.2.

2. David Rood, 'Recall ordered for toy that turns into drug,' *The Age*, November 7, 2007, http://www.theage.com.au/news/national/recall-for-toy-that-turns-int-drug/2007/11/06/1194329225773.html; 'Bindeez banned over GHB fears,: *ABC News*, November 6, 2007, http://www.abc.net.au/news/2007-11-06/bindeez-banned-over-ghb-fears/717180;

3. William M. Pride and O. C. Ferrell, *Marketing*, 2010 edition, p. 226 (Mason, OH: South-Western Cengage Learning).

4. 'ZANA Network Members Get Access to Thousands of Government Contracts,' *PR Newswire*, New York (December 5, 2007).

5. 'Boeing, RyanAir Agree to Order for 32 Additional 737-800s,' Boeing press release, September 29, 2006. http://www.boeing.com/news/releases/2006/q3/060929a_nr.html.

6. 'Boeing, Turkish Airlines Sign Order for 15 Planes,' *Reuters*, April 1, 2011, www.reuters.com/article/2011/04/01/us-boeing-turkishairlinesidUSTRE7300ZV20110401.

7. Das Narayandas and V. Kasturi Rangan, 'Building and Sustaining Buyer-Seller Relationships in Mature Industrial Markets,' *Journal of Marketing* (July 2004): 63.

8. 'WaterFurnace Introduces WeDeGeo.com, a Comprehensive B2B Selection Software for Applied Commercial Representatives,' *Market-Watch*, January 25, 2012, www.marketwatch.com/story/waterfurnaceintroduces-wedogeocom-a-comprehensive-b2b-selection-software-forapplied-commercial-representatives-2012-01-25?refl ink=MW_news_stmp.

9. Alex R. Zablah, Wesley J. Johnston, and Danny N. Bellenger, 'Transforming Partner Relationships Through Technological Innovation,' *Journal of Business & Industrial Marketing* 20 (August 2005): 355–363.

10. Based on information in Melissa Hincha-Ownby, 'Newsweek Names IBM Greenest Company in America,' *Forbes*, October 18, 2011, www.forbes.com; Susan Campriello, 'IBM Is Environmental Leader,' *Poughkeepsie Journal* (New York), June 11, 2011, www.poughkeepsiejournal.com; Todd Woody, 'IBM Suppliers Must Track Environmental Data,' *The New York Times*, April 14, 2010, www.nytimes.com; 'IBM, Accenture Lead Responsible Government Suppliers,' *Environmental Leader*, July 21, 2011, www.environmentalleader.com.

11. Leonidas C. Leonidou, 'Industrial Buyers' Influence Strategies: Buying Situation Differences,' *Journal of Business & Industrial Marketing* 20 (January 2005): 33–42.

12. 'Gesture by Steelcase,' Steelcase, http://www.steelcase.com/en/products/category/seating/task/gesture/pages/overview.aspx; Maha Atal, 'Sustaining the Dream,' *BusinessWeek* October 15, 2007: 60; Kristen Gerencher, 'Treadmill Desks Let Employees Feel the Burn,' *Boston Globe*, March 26, 2006: n.p.; Reena Jana, 'Exercise More Than Just Your Options,' *BusinessWeek* October 29, 2007: 24; 'Making the Tough Call,' *Inc.* November 2007: 361.

13. Frederick E. Webster, Jr., and Yoram Wind, 'A Generic Model for Understanding Organizational Buyer Behavior,' *Marketing Management* (Winter/Spring 1996): 52–57.

14. 'How Costco Australia will change Australian retail,' Smart Company, http://www.smartcompany.com.au/retail/20090507-how-costco-australia-will-change-australian-retail/2.html?ml=5&mlt=system&tmpl=component; Eli Greenblat, 'Costco wheels out aggressive expansion plans,' *The Sydney Morning Herald*, February 12, 2011, http://www.smh.com.au/business/costco-wheels-out-aggressive-expansion-plans-20110220-1b105.html; Jena McGregor, 'Costco's Artful Discounts,' *BusinessWeek* (October 20, 2008): 58; Jim Wyss, 'Local Vendors Audition for Retail Giant,' *Miami Herald* (May 30, 2008): http://www.herald.com.

15. George S. Day and Katrina J. Bens, 'Capitalizing on the Internet Opportunity,' *Journal of Business & Industrial Marketing* 20 (2005): 160–168.

16. Niklas Myhr and Robert E. Spekman, 'Collaborative Supply-Chain Partnerships Built upon Trust and Electronically Mediated Exchange,' *Journal of Business & Industrial Marketing* 20 (2005): 179–186.

17. James G Barnes, 'Closeness, Strength, and Satisfaction: examining the nature of relationships between providers of financial services and their retail customers,' *Psychology and Marketing*, 14: 765–790; Mark Colgate, N. Auckland, and Nicholas Alexander, 'Banks, retailers and their customers: a relationship marketing perspective,' *International Journal of Bank Marketing*, 144 (1998): 152; Raechel Johns, 'Relationship Marketing in a Self-Service Context: No Longer Applicable? *Journal of Relationship Marketing* 11 (2012): 91; R. Johns, and B. Perrott, 'The Impact of Internet Banking on Business-Customer Relationships (are you being self-served?),' *International Journal of Bank Marketing*, 26 (2008): 465–482; Tero Pikkarainen, Kari Pikkarainen, Heikki Karjaluoto, and Seppo Pahnila, 'Consumer acceptance of online banking: an extension of the technology acceptance model, *Internet Research*, 14 (2004): 224–235; Siriluck Rotchanakitumnuai, and Mark Speece, 'Barriers to Internet Banking Adoption: a qualitative study among corporate customers in Thailand,' *International Journal of Bank Marketing* (2003): 312–323; Katherine Tyler and Edmund Stanley, 'Marketing financial services to businesses: a critical review and research agenda,' International Journal of Bank Marketing, 98 (1999): 115.

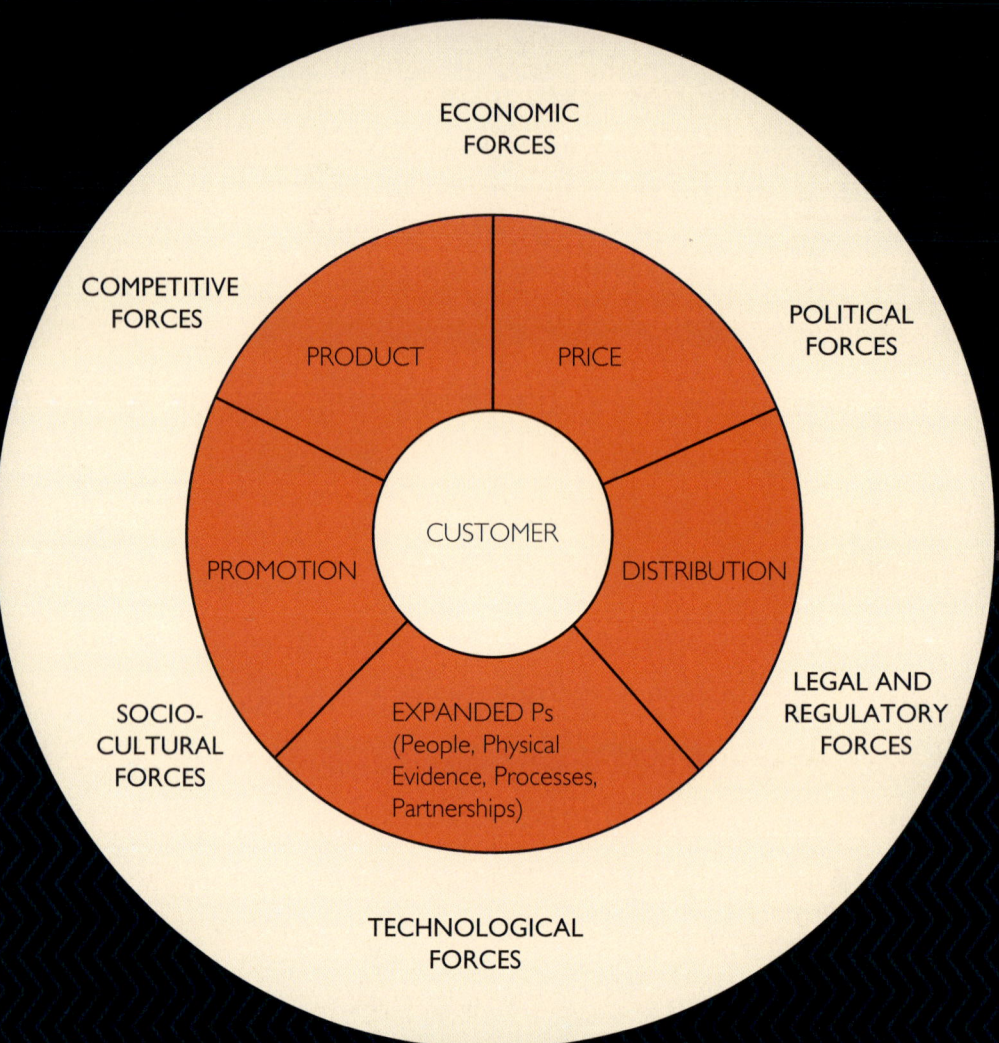

The diagram shows concentric circles. The outer ring labels (clockwise from top):

ECONOMIC FORCES

POLITICAL FORCES

LEGAL AND REGULATORY FORCES

TECHNOLOGICAL FORCES

SOCIO-CULTURAL FORCES

COMPETITIVE FORCES

Inner circle segments:

PRODUCT

PRICE

DISTRIBUTION

EXPANDED Ps (People, Physical Evidence, Processes, Partnerships)

PROMOTION

Centre: CUSTOMER

CHAPTER 7	THE POWER OF BRANDING
CHAPTER 8	PRODUCT DECISIONS
CHAPTER 9	DEVELOPING AND MANAGING GOODS AND SERVICES
CHAPTER 10	PRICING DECISIONS
CHAPTER 11	DISTRIBUTION DECISIONS
CHAPTER 12	INTEGRATING MARKETING COMMUNICATIONS: DESIGNING PROMOTIONAL CAMPAIGNS
CHAPTER 13	MARKETING COMMUNICATIONS MIX VARIABLES: APPLICATION
CHAPTER 14	EXPANDING THE MARKETING MIX
CHAPTER 15	DIGITAL MARKETING AND SOCIAL NETWORKING

PART 3

THE EXPANDED MARKETING MIX

THIS FINAL section of the book provides a comprehensive look at how to apply the theory outlined to this point and, essentially, how to 'do' marketing. As we have highlighted, the environment of marketing is dynamic in nature, both as a concept and in its tasks/activities. A conventional approach to marketing might include an application of the 4Ps: product, price, place and promotion. However, in this text, we present the extended marketing mix that goes beyond the standard conventions.

We begin Part 3 with a chapter on the power of branding. Brands, as the interface between producers and consumers, are a powerful transformational tool of the times. The six chapters that follow focus on the 4Ps of marketing. Chapter 14 then explores how an understanding of an additional 4ps (people, physical evidence/ assets, processes and partnerships) can help organisations to achieve greater competitiveness in today's business environment. The final chapter discusses the developments in internet and mobile technologies and how these are changing the business of marketing.

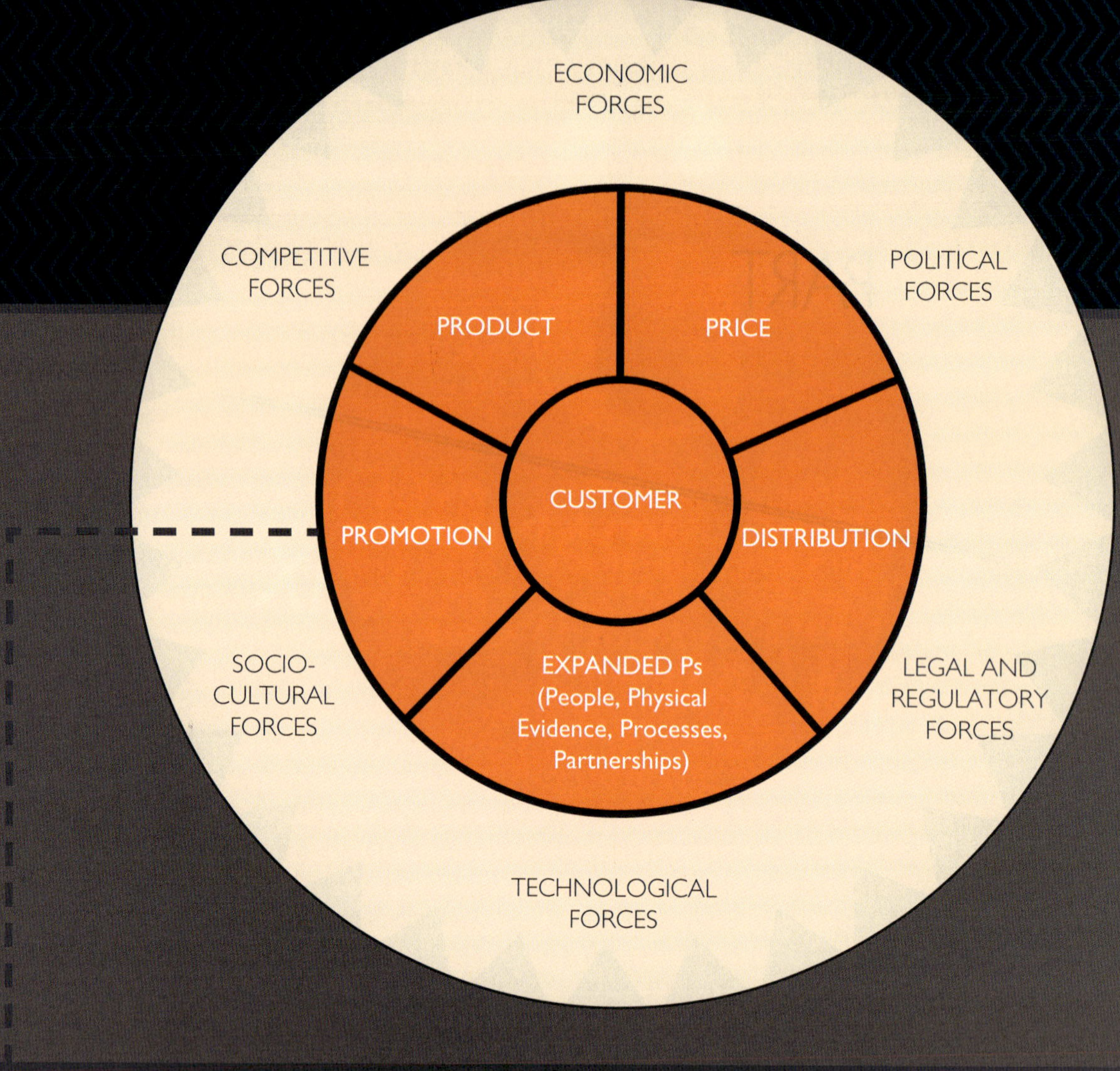

ECONOMIC
FORCES

COMPETITIVE
FORCES

POLITICAL
FORCES

PRODUCT

PRICE

CUSTOMER

PROMOTION

DISTRIBUTION

SOCIO-
CULTURAL
FORCES

EXPANDED Ps
(People, Physical
Evidence, Processes,
Partnerships)

LEGAL AND
REGULATORY
FORCES

TECHNOLOGICAL
FORCES

THE POWER OF BRANDING

The strategic power of branding

Value of branding

Brand equity

How brand names are selected and protected

Branding policies, brand extensions, co-branding and brand licensing

Building and sustaining brands
  Brand vision
  Organisational culture

Brand objectives
Auditing the brandsphere
Brand essence
Internal implementation
Brand resourcing
Brand evaluation

Connecting the marketing mix and brands
  Brands and pricing
  Branding and physical distribution
  Branding and promotion
  Branding and products

   Throughout this chapter, Watch, Listen and Revise icons indicate an opportunity for online self-study through CengageNOW, linking you to animated chapter overviews, interactive diagrams, videos, quizzes and more.

THE POWER OF BRANDING

Learning Objectives

LO1 Identify and describe the strategic power of branding

LO2 Explain the value of branding

LO3 Define brand equity and the discuss the major components of brand equity

LO4 Recognise how brand names are selected and protected

LO5 Identify two types of branding policies, and explain brand extensions, co-branding and brand licensing

LO6 Explore different strategies for building and sustaining brands

LO7 Examine brands and the marketing mix.

MARKETING CHALLENGE | PRISTINE RAINFOREST EXPERIENCE

Mossman Gorge is a spectacular rainforest and waterfall environment nestled in the World Heritage listed Daintree Rainforest. Considered to be 135 million years old, this magnificent place contains one of the oldest continuously surviving rainforests on earth. However, one of the major problems in protecting Mossman Gorge is its popularity and the heavy level of tourist traffic visiting the area. Branding and packaging the Mossman Gorge as the Mossman Gorge Centre enabled both effective marketing and protection of the beautiful landmark for future generations.

The Mossman Gorge Centre is positioned as a world class eco-tourism visitor and interpretive centre situated at the entrance to the iconic Mossman Gorge north of Cairns, in Queensland, Australia. Steeped in Aboriginal heritage and history, the Mossman Gorge Centre is an Aboriginal development designed to better serve visitors to the Mossman Gorge World Heritage site. It is an iconic Aboriginal cultural experience, and it means jobs and training opportunities for the local Aboriginal people.

Source: Image courtesy of Mossman Gorge Centre

Source: Image courtesy of Mossman Gorge Centre

The Mossman Gorge Centre includes an array of services to help consumers organise their adventure through the Gorge. There is a visitor information desk, a contemporary café and restaurant, an art gallery, a retail gift shop and shuttle bus services to and from the Gorge. The visitor information desk is staffed by culturally sensitive local residents with a breadth of knowledge on the area. Their task is to assist visitors in planning their journey through the Gorge and take bookings for the Dreamtime Walk. The Dreamtime Gorge Walk begins with a smoking ceremony by the Kuku Yalanji people, who guide visitors along private, gentle tracks to culturally significant sites, past traditional bark shelters and over meandering cool rainforest streams. The Centre also offers visitors the cuisine experience of the Mayi Café and Restaurant. The menu features locally sourced produce infused with local bush ingredients. Continuing this consistency of a culturally rich experience, the Indigenous Art gallery showcases the art of the local Kuku Yalanji people and other leading Aboriginal artists from throughout far north Queensland. These authentic works reflect the traditional lore and culture through vibrant pieces of art that can be admired and purchased. The gallery also stocks and sells a range of jewellery, cards, small artefacts and clothing. Similarly, the gift shop offers a range of items designed and produced by the local Aboriginal community. As a means to reduce the environmental impact of the heavy tourist traffic to and from the Gorge, the Mossman Gorge Centre also offers an eco-friendly shuttle service which departs every 15 minutes and transports visitors on an open-air low emission shuttle bus from the Centre to the heart of the Gorge.

MARKETING CHALLENGE QUESTION

1 Visit http://www.mossmangorge.com and observe the consistent brand message of the Mossman Gorge Centre as a pristine rainforest and culturally rich experience. Do you think branding this spectacular area is an effective tourism and environmental protection strategy?

Introduction

In this chapter, we explore brands, branding and the strategic power of branding. According to Shawn Parr of Bulldog Drummond, 'Brand' as a concept is misunderstood, underappreciated and many times under-utilised.[1] Red hot irons pressed into cow hides, brand name tattoos, Nike's 'swoosh' and the spectacle of a Lady Gaga concert are all examples of branding, and demonstrate how branding, has evolved over time. Brand experiences are powerful statements and it is essential to understand how to use branding as an effective business and marketing tool.

To develop our understanding about the power of branding, we look at the value of branding and the most valuable brands in Australia and the Asia-Pacific region. From there we consider the different ways to brand a product and how a brand name might be selected and protected. Another important consideration addressed in this chapter is the strategic issue of building and sustaining brands. Bold brands and branding efforts are not delivered as a whole, but created and shaped over time through strategic marketing efforts.

The strategic power of branding

Brands are the interface through which producers can communicate with consumers about their service or product offering. For this reason, brands are increasingly regarded as a powerful tool, often influencing product- and service-development decisions. For example, in order to align with the well-established Porsche brand, the luxury car manufacturer makes new product-related decisions that favour performance, high quality and luxury, as these characteristics are symbolised by the brand. With this in mind, and in contrast to a traditional marketing approach, this text addresses the brand prior to determining market-oriented product decisions.

Marketers must make many decisions about products, including choices about brands, brand names, brand marks, trademarks and trade names. In the most basic form, a **brand** is a name, term, design, symbol or any other feature that identifies one marketer's product as distinct from those of other marketers. A brand may identify a single item, a family of items or all items of that seller.[2] Some have defined a brand as not just the physical good, name, colour, logo or ad campaign but everything associated with the product, including its symbolism and experiences.[3] For example, Rolex watches are defined by their symbolism of luxury and timeless quality. Founded in 1905, the Rolex brand is distinct within the larger watch market, and embodies history, fine craftsmanship and reliability. As stated on the Rolex website, consumers do not merely wear a Rolex, they 'Experience Rolex' (http://www.rolex.com).

A **brand name** is the part of a brand that can be spoken – including letters, words and numbers – such as the Apple brands of iPod and iPad. A brand name is often a product's only distinguishing characteristic. Without the brand name, a company could not differentiate

brand
A name, term, design, symbol or any other feature that identifies one marketer's product as distinct from those of other marketers

brand name
The part of a brand that can be spoken

its products. To consumers, a brand name is as fundamental as the product itself. Indeed, many brand names have become synonymous with the product, such as Google, McDonald's and Coke.

The element of a brand that is not made up of words – often a symbol or design – is a brand mark. Examples of brand marks include Qantas' flying kangaroo, Nike's 'swoosh' and the stylised apple and leaf silhouette of the Apple brand. A trademark is a legal designation indicating that the owner has exclusive use of a brand or a part of a brand and that others are prohibited by law from using it. To protect a brand name or brand mark, an organisation must register it as a trademark. Notably, a trade name is the full and legal name of an organisation, such as International Business Machines Corporation, rather than the short-hand name IBM.

brand mark
The part of a brand not made up of words, but symbols

trademark
A legal designation of exclusive use of a brand

trade name
Full legal name of an organisation

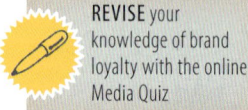
REVISE your knowledge of brand loyalty with the online Media Quiz

Value of branding

The value of branding begins with branding being a differentiating factor whereby both buyers and sellers benefit. Brands help buyers to identify specific products that they do and do not like, which, in turn, facilitates the purchase of items that satisfy their needs and reduces the time required to purchase the product. Without brands, product selection would be quite random because buyers could have no assurance that they were purchasing what they preferred. The move by the Australian Government to enforce plain packaging for cigarettes was based on this understanding. The purchase of certain brands can be a form of self-expression. For example, the Kia, Daewoo and Chery brand of cars may not be as prestigious as the Mercedes-Benz and Porsche brands. More than that, the brand of car you drive makes a statement about who you are. While the Kia, Daewoo and Chery indicate a budget-oriented consumer, the Mercedes-Benz indicates elegance and the Porsche indicates a wealthy consumer, probably without a family, who is focused on speed and status. Similarly, in the fashion field, clothing brand names are important to many consumers. Names such as Tommy Hilfiger, Polo Ralph Lauren, Burberry and Nike give manufacturers an advantage in the marketplace. When a customer is unable to judge a product's quality, a brand may symbolise a certain level of quality to the customer, and the customer lets that perception of quality represent the quality of the item. A brand helps to reduce a buyer's perceived risk of purchase. In addition, a psychological reward may come from owning a brand that symbolises status, as mentioned above with the Porsche brand and what that brand means in the marketplace.

Source: Shutterstock.com

Brand mark >>
The widely recognised flying kangaroo is the brand mark for Australian airline Qantas

Sellers benefit from branding because the brand identifies their products, which makes repeat purchasing easier for customers. Branding helps a company to introduce a new product that carries the name of one or more of its existing products because buyers are already familiar with the company's existing brands. It facilitates promotional efforts because the promotion of each branded product indirectly promotes all other similarly branded products. Branding also fosters brand loyalty. To the extent that buyers become loyal to a specific brand, the company's market share for that product achieves a certain level of stability, allowing the organisation to use its resources more efficiently. Once a company develops some degree of customer loyalty for a brand, it can maintain a fairly consistent price rather than continually cutting the price to attract customers.

There is also a cultural dimension to branding. Brand experience is relative to the individual and each consumer confers his or her own social meaning onto brands. A brand's appeal is largely at an emotional level based on its symbolic image and key associations.[4] For some brands, such as Harley-Davidson, Google and Apple, this can result in an almost cult-like following.[5] These brands often develop a community of loyal customers that communicate through get-togethers, online forums, blogs, podcasts and other means. These brands may even help consumers to develop their identity and self-concept and serve as a form of self-expression. The term *cultural branding* has been used to explain how a brand conveys a powerful myth that consumers find useful in cementing their identities.[6] It is also important to recognise that because a brand exists independently in the consumer's mind, it is not controlled directly by the marketer. Every aspect of a brand is subject to a consumer's emotional involvement, interpretation and memory. By understanding how branding influences purchases, marketers can foster customer loyalty.[7]

Brand equity

A well-managed brand is an asset to an organisation. The value of this asset is often referred to as brand equity. Brand equity is the marketing and financial value associated with a brand's strength in a market. Besides the actual proprietary brand assets, such as patents and trademarks, four major elements underlie brand equity: brand name awareness, brand loyalty, perceived brand quality and brand associations[8] (see Figure 7.1).

Brand awareness is the extent to which a brand is recognised by potential customers, and correctly associated with a particular product or service. Being aware of a brand leads to brand familiarity, which, in turn, results in a level of comfort with the brand. A familiar brand is more likely to be selected than an unfamiliar brand because the familiar brand is often viewed

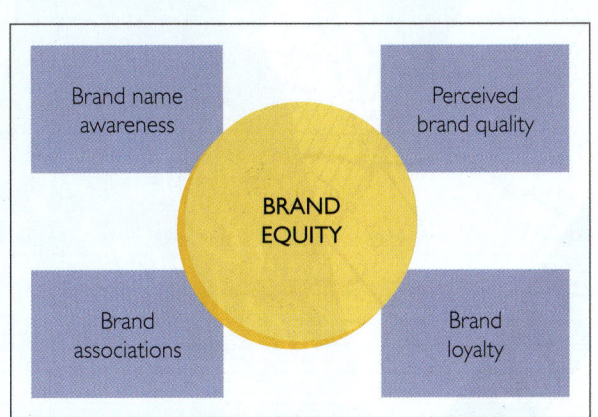

brand equity
The marketing and financial value associated with a brand's strength in a market

brand awareness
The extent to which a brand is recognised by potential customers, and correctly associated with a particular product or service

WATCH an interactive animation on the major types of brand equity

FIGURE 7.1 MAJOR ELEMENTS OF BRAND EQUITY

as more reliable and of more acceptable quality. The familiar brand is likely to be in a customer's consideration set, whereas the unfamiliar brand is not.

brand loyalty
A customer's favourable attitude toward a specific brand

Brand loyalty is a customer's favourable attitude toward a specific brand. If brand loyalty is strong enough, customers may purchase this brand consistently when they need a product in that product category. Customer satisfaction with a brand is the most common reason for loyalty to that brand.[9] Development of brand loyalty in a customer reduces his or her risks and shortens the time spent buying the product. However, the degree of brand loyalty for products varies from one product category to another. It is challenging to develop brand loyalty for some products, such as bananas, because customers can readily judge the quality of these products and do not need to refer to a brand as an indicator of quality. Brand loyalty also varies by country. Customers in France, Germany and the UK tend to be less brand-loyal than US-based customers.

brand recognition
A customer's awareness that the brand exists and is an alternative purchase

brand preference
The degree of brand loyalty in which a customer prefers one brand over competitive offerings

brand insistence
The degree of brand loyalty in which a customer strongly prefers a specific brand and will accept no substitute

There are three degrees of brand loyalty: recognition, preference and insistence. Brand recognition occurs when a customer is aware that the brand exists and views it as an alternative purchase if the preferred brand is unavailable or if the other available brands are unfamiliar. This is the mildest form of brand loyalty. The term *loyalty* is clearly used very loosely here. Brand preference is a stronger degree of brand loyalty.[10] A customer definitely prefers one brand over competitive offerings and will purchase this brand if it is available. However, if the brand is not available, the customer will accept a substitute brand rather than expending additional effort finding and purchasing the preferred brand. When brand insistence occurs, a customer strongly prefers a specific brand, will accept no substitute and is willing to spend a great deal of time and effort to acquire that brand. If a brand-insistent customer goes to a store and finds the brand unavailable, he or she will seek the brand elsewhere rather than purchase a substitute brand. Brand insistence can also apply to service products, for example consumers choosing only to stay at Hilton Hotels and Resorts or fly with Qantas. When travelling the world for either business or pleasure, these consumers insist on brands such as Hilton and Qantas because the brands promises a certain standard of service.

Source: Alamy

Brand equity >>
Since 1919, Hilton Hotels and Resorts have gained considerable brand equity by demonstrating worldwide brand consistency, thereby generating brand insistence

Hello Kitty branded products include stationery gifts and accessories, with a focus on the 'cute' segment of popular Japanese culture. Through the use of the Kitty White brand character, the marketing of the Hello Kitty brand has been a global success. Sanrio have since partnered with Fender to release the 'Hello Kitty Stratocaster' and with EVA Airways to release the 'Hello Kitty Jet', among many other branded products.

Brand loyalty is an important component of brand equity because it reduces a brand's vulnerability to competitors' actions. It allows an organisation to keep its existing customers and avoid spending significant resources to gain new ones. Loyal customers provide brand visibility and reassurance to potential new customers. Customers expect their brands to be available when and where they shop and retailers strive to carry the brands known for their strong customer following.

Source Shutterstock.com

<< **Stimulating brand associations** Japanese company Sanrio developed the brand Hello Kitty in 1974, using the cute character Kitty White as the central favourable brand association

Customers associate a particular brand with a certain level of overall quality. **Perceived brand quality** is an intangible, overall brand evaluation. As mentioned above, a brand name may be used as a substitute for actual judgement of quality. Perceived high brand quality helps to support a premium price, allowing a marketer to avoid severe price competition. Also, favourably perceived brand quality can ease the introduction of brand extensions because the high regard for the brand will likely translate into high regard for the related products.

perceived brand quality
An intangible, overall brand evaluation

Brand association is the set of associations linked to a brand and is another key component of brand equity, as evidenced in the Marketing in Action box below. At times, a marketer works to connect a particular lifestyle or, in some instances, a certain personality type with a specific brand. For example, customers associate a Tiffany & Co. diamond with sophistication, glamour and romantic love. In the famous song 'Diamond's Are A Girl's Best Friend', the lyrics sung by Marilyn Monroe actually mention the brand Tiffany's. These types of brand associations contribute significantly to the brand's equity. Brand associations are sometimes facilitated by using trade characters, such as Cadbury's Freddo Frog, Kraft's Tiger Energy biscuits and Kellog's Coco the Monkey (Coco-Pops). Placing these trade characters in ads and on packages helps consumers to link the ads and packages with the brands.

brand association
The set of associations linked to a brand which connect a particular lifestyle or, in some instances, a certain personality type with a specific brand

MARKETING IN ACTION | WEET-BIX BRAND CULTURE

The Weet-Bix brand associates itself with young Australian kids and sport. Weet-Bix managers have positioned the Weet-Bix brand as a kids' cereal, emphasised through the tag line 'I'm a Weet-Bix kid'.

The Australian culture and climate is well suited to the traditional outdoor lifestyle and part of that tradition is the emphasis on sport. In building on this strong Australian sporting culture, the Weet-Bix brand commissions sporting heroes such as cricket fast bowler

Brett Lee and Socceroos player Tim Cahill to endorse the brand and encourage a connection between the Weet-Bix brand and the strength of the Australian sporting culture. Young Australian kids look up to sporting heroes and associate the Weet-Bix brand with the brand endorser. Weet-Bix is represented as a part of the Australian outdoor lifestyle and growing up healthy. Accordingly, the Weet-Bix brand integrates this message consistently throughout the Weet-Bix marketing messages. For example, specific (child-focused) sporting events profile the Weet-Bix brand such as the Weet-Bix TRYathon, a triathlon for kids. The children who participate in Weet-Bix branded events and consume the Weet-Bix product are in essence generating and sustaining the Weet-Bix brand positioning as a healthy kids' cereal.

Branded cereals are a popular breakfast option for kids. However, some breakfast cereal brands are not a healthy option for kids. Many cereals marketed to children contain excessive amounts of sugar and salt and consumer group Choice reports that among the wide variety of breakfast cereal brands, only Weet-Bix and Vita Brits are suitable for daily consumption. Breakfast cereal brand managers are wizards of spin, and have been spruiking vitamins and dietary fibre for

years, and there is no shortage of new health claims for various cereals.[11] ▨

Although difficult to measure, brand equity represents the value of a brand to an organisation. Table 7.1 lists the top 10 retail brands in the Asia-Pacific region with the highest economic value. Any company that owns a brand listed in Table 7.1 would agree that the economic value of that brand is likely to be the greatest single asset in the organisation's possession. For Woolworths, brand value is well ahead at AU$4015 million, with the nearest competitor being Japan's UNIQLO at $2606 million. Established in 1984 in Hiroshima by Tadashi Yanai, UNIQLO is a clothing brand that transcends standard product categories and social groups. Positioned as simple and essential, yet universal, UNIQLO encourages

TABLE 7.1   INTERBRAND TOP 10 ASIA-PACIFIC RETAIL BRANDS: 2011

Rank	Brand	Brand value AUD$ million	Country
1	Woolworths	4015	Australia
2	UNIQLO	2606	Japan
3	Harvey Norman	897	Australia
4	David Jones	613	Australia
5	Myer	529	Australia
6	Suning	489	China
7	Meters/bonwe	401	China
8	Yamada	240	Japan
9	OME	208	China
10	Ito Yokado	202	Japan

Source: Interbrand, via http://dragonbuzz.blogspot.com.au/2011/07/top-brands-retail-global-or-regional.html.

TABLE 7.2   TOP 10 GLOBAL BRANDS: 2012

Rank	Brand	Country	Sector	Brand value (US$ million)	Change in brand value
1	Coca-Cola	United States	Beverages	77 839	+8%
2	Apple	United States	Electronics	76 568	+129%
3	IBM	United States	Business Services	75 532	+8%
4	Google	United States	Internet Services	69 726	+26%
5	Microsoft	United States	Computer Software	57 835	−2%
6	GE	United States	Diversified	42 682	+2%
7	McDonald's	United States	Restaurants	40 062	+13%
8	Intel	United States	Electronics	39 385	+12%
9	Samsung	South Korea	Electronics	32 893	+40%
10	Toyota	Japan	Automotive	30 280	+9%

Source: http://www.interbrand.com/en/best-global-brands/2012/Best-Global-Brands-2012-Brand-View.aspx

freedom of individual style. Notably, the UNIQLO brand has evolved from a chain of roadside retail stores to an international leader in style, quality and fun.

As highlighted in Table 7.2, the most successful global brands include brands that are relevant and active across the Asia-Pacific region. More specifically, the top 10 global brands listed in Table 7.2 are successfully marketed both internationally and throughout the Asia-Pacific region. While Coca-Cola maintains the number one spot, Apple has jumped ahead from number 17 in 2009 to second position. For Apple this has meant a brand equity increase from US$21 143 million in 2009 to $76 568 million in 2012 – an increase of 129 per cent (from previous year) and is noted by Interbrand as the top riser of this group of global brands. The common denominator across these successful globally marketed brands, and regardless of the economic conditions, is that each of the brands on the list represent a brand that consumers trust.

As the world's biggest car manufacturer and Asia's biggest manufacturer, Toyota has beaten off auto rivals Nissan, Ford and Honda in overall performance to hold the number 10 position globally and number one spot on the list of global green brands. Toyota is well positioned in terms of being environmentally friendly, given the success of the Prius and Toyota's hybrid engine design. The Prius sold more than 2.9 million units worldwide in 2012 and has achieved top-of-the-mind positioning as the eco-friendly brand of car.

International branding and marketing entails more fierce competition because more is at stake. Market share is a precious commodity and marketers will fight to the death to protect their brand. Astute marketers looking to enter international markets, therefore, must ensure they have done their homework. Mistakes are expensive.

Manufacturer brands are initiated by producers and ensure that producers are identified with their products at the point of purchase – for example, Toyota, Ford and Holden are manufacturer brands and consumers are very familiar with them. A manufacturer brand usually requires a producer to become involved in distribution, promotion and, to some

manufacturer brands
Brands initiated by producers

ETHICAL MARKETING | THE POPULARITY OF HOUSE BRANDS AND THE EFFECT ON COMPETITION

Ethical consumption can be an expensive option. Supermarkets are realising the sales potential of house brands and are therefore increasingly spurning outside suppliers in favour of their own house brands: 'Homebrand' and 'Select' at Woolworths and 'Coles Smartbuy' at Coles. Another bare-bones house brand is 'Black & Gold'. House brands take up an increasingly large share of the average supermarket shelf which means less choice for consumers and less competition to keep the price down. With minimal packaging and minimal prices, supermarkets are slowly but surely taking over their own shelf space, and market share translates to market power. With this in mind, do you think supermarkets should be regulated in the use of house brands? Are you prepared to pay more to consume in an ethical way? ▨

Is the expansion of house brands anti-competitive behaviour, and do supermarkets have an ethical responsibility to equally promote products from outside suppliers?

house brands
Brands initiated and owned by resellers

extent, pricing decisions. For example, on the interface of production and consumption, consumers see the brands showcased in the car dealerships.

House brands (also called store brands or generic brands) are initiated and owned by resellers – wholesalers or retailers. The major characteristic of house brands is that the manufacturers are not identified on the products. This is a no-frills product that is packaged in a low-budget manner, to reflect the low cost of the house brand products. Effectively, this is an unbranded product with a price-focused strategy. However, given that brands enable consumer trust, many consumers have voiced concerns regarding the quality of house brands. In an attempt to reduce this negative brand association, supermarket chain Woolworths have introduced the additional house brands 'Select' and 'Macro' to target different consumers segments. Their 'Homebrand' brand competes with a price-focused strategy, 'Select' branded products must pass a stringent quality assurance process, and their 'Macro' branded products focus on nutritional value and target the health conscious consumer. By diversifying their house brand range, the association between house brand and low quality is weakened (the impact of house brands on the market is explored in the Ethical Marketing box above). While there may still be some form of stigma towards house

Source: Newspix/News Ltd/Jeff Herbert

House brands >>
More consumers are buying house brands each year

brands, the recent global financial crisis has meant consumers have become more price conscious. Consumers are therefore turning to supermarket home brands, which are not only cheaper, but equally ranked in quality.[12]

How brand names are selected and protected

The brand name is the spoken part of the brand, and must be carefully selected in order to be unique, memorable and to align with the brand itself. Once a brand name is selected, marketers can take certain measures in order to protect the brand from infringement and counterfeiting.

Selecting a brand name

Marketers consider several factors in selecting a brand name. They are outlined below.

1 The name should be easy for customers (including foreign buyers if the company intends to market its products in other countries) to say, spell and recall. Short and simple brand names, such as Google and Apple, often satisfy this requirement.

2 The brand name should indicate the product's major benefits and, if possible, should suggest in a positive way the product's uses and special characteristics; negative or offensive references should be avoided. For example, the brand names of confectionary such as Kinder Surprise and Fantales allude to their special characteristics, whereas Chomp and Crunchie connote the experiential aspects of consumption. There is evidence that consumers are more likely to recall and evaluate favourably names that convey positive attributes or benefits.[13]

3 To set it apart from competing brands, the brand should be distinctive. If a marketer intends to use a brand for a product line, that brand must be compatible with all products in the line.

4 A brand should be designed so that it can be used and recognised in all types of media. Finding the right brand name has become a challenging task because many obvious product names have already been used.

5 Cultural interpretations need to be considered in order to avoid branding mistakes. The popular Japanese brand of mayonnaise, Kewpi, uses the image of a Kewpi doll as part of its brand logo, as well as on the product's packaging. Kewpi released their branded mayonnaise to the Malaysian market in 2010. When introducing Kewpi Mayonnaise to a predominantly Islamic culture, the product was ill received after consumers perceived the angel-winged Kewpi doll logo as un-Islamic.

How are brand names devised? Brand names can be created from single or multiple words – for example, Louis Vuitton. Letters and numbers are used to create brands such as Hyundai's i30. Words, numbers and letters are combined to yield brand names such as Apple's iPhone5 or BMW's M3 Convertible. To avoid terms that have negative connotations, marketers sometimes use fabricated words that have absolutely no meaning when created – for example, Kodak and Exxon.

Who actually creates brand names? Brand names can be created internally by the organisation. Sometimes a name is suggested by individuals who are close to the development of the product. Some organisations have committees that participate in brand name creation and approval. Large companies that introduce numerous new products annually are likely to have an in-house department that develops brand names. Another option is working with outside consultants and companies that specialise in brand name development.

Protecting a brand

REVISE your knowledge of Brand Selection and Protection with the Online Revision Quiz

A marketer should also design a brand so that it can be protected easily through registration. The *Trade Marks Act 1995* defines a trademark as a *sign* which distinguishes goods or services from any other person's goods or services. Trademark registration requires goods or services to be distinctive, in that the sign must be inherently capable of being distinguished from another person's goods or services. Distinctiveness is established when the trademark is unlike other goods or services used by another in the course of business. Where a trademark is similar to another in trade then it is not distinctive and incapable of registration. Surnames and descriptive, geographic or functional names, for example, are difficult to protect.[14] However, research shows that overall, consumers prefer descriptive and suggestive brand names and find them easier to recall compared with fanciful and arbitrary brand names.[15] Because of their designs, some brands can be legally infringed on more easily than others. Although registration protects trademarks and trademarks can be renewed, a company should develop a system for ensuring that its trademarks are renewed as needed, because brands evolve and change over time to keep up with changing consumer needs.

To protect its exclusive rights to a brand, a company must ensure that the brand is not likely to be considered an infringement on any brand already registered. Consider that after Apple launched the iPhone to much fanfare, it was sued by Cisco, which owns the trademark name iPhone, after the two companies failed to reach agreement on Apple's use of the name. This task may be complex because infringement is determined by the courts, which base their decisions on whether a brand causes consumers to be confused, mistaken or deceived about the source of the product. McDonald's is one company that aggressively protects its trademarks against infringement; it has successfully brought charges against a number of companies with *Mc* names because it fears that use of the prefix will give consumers the impression that these companies are associated with or owned by McDonald's.

A company can also indicate that the brand is a registered trademark by using the symbol ®.

Many companies that try to protect a brand in a foreign country frequently encounter problems. In many countries, brand registration is not possible; the first company to use and/or register a brand in such a country automatically has the rights to it. In some instances, companies aiming to enter a particular country may have actually had to buy their own brand rights from a company in a foreign country because the foreign company was the first user in that country. In some instances, other companies register the name and the originator is left with nowhere to go!

Protecting a brand >>
Companies register brand names and feature the ® logo to protect the brand from unauthorised use

Source: Pacific Brands Limited

Marketers trying to protect their brands must also contend with brand counterfeiting. Consumers know they can purchase counterfeit Rolex watches, Louis Vuitton handbags and Chanel accessories. The maker of high-end shoes and handbags, Christian Louboutin, prides itself on the quality of its product, which is priced at a premium, usually more than AU$600 for a pair of shoes, for example. However, luxury brands such as Christian Louboutin are being forced to react to counterfeiters, with both an offline and online strategy. Christian Louboutin has taken to listing those websites that sell counterfeit copies of its product in the hope of shaming those involved.[16] Other luxury brands are striking back, too. Versace recently won AU$20 million in damages in a case involving fake goods.[17] Closer to home, the Australian Competition and Consumer Commission (ACCC) ordered the Designer Brand Outlet website to be shut down (for a time in 2010). This suspension was ordered due to false, misleading and deceptive representations made on the website as deemed by the ACCC. As well, some of the clothing being promoted on the website was counterfeit.[18]

Branding policies, brand extensions, co-branding and brand licensing

There are a number of approaches available to the marketer when branding a product or service. An individual branding policy, a family branding policy, or combination of both, may be appropriate. A brand extension approach applies an existing brand to a new product. Conversely, co-branding capitalises on the brand equity of multiple brands, and brand licensing is a brand use agreement between organisations.

Branding policies

Before establishing branding policies, an organisation must decide whether to brand its products at all. If a company's product is homogeneous and is similar to competitors' products, it may be difficult to brand in a way that will generate brand loyalty. Raw materials such as coal, sand and farm produce are hard to brand because of the homogeneity of such products and their physical characteristics. However, Australian coal is well received throughout the world as are Australian fruit and vegetables; country-of-origin preferences works well for Australian producers. Commodities that have been branded successfully include fuel, timber and water. Consumers have preferences for BP fuel rather than Shell for example, or Evian bottled water rather than the Pump or Aqua water brands.

If a company chooses to brand its products, it may use individual branding, family branding or a combination. Individual branding is a policy of naming each product differently. Unilever Australasia, for example, produces a range of food brands, personal care brands and home care brands. Unilever food brands include well-known brands such as Lipton and Walls (also known as Streets). These food brands are stand-alone brands, independent of Unilever. Unilever personal care brands include Dove, Rexona and Ponds, which are also

individual branding
A policy of naming each product differently

branded individually and they each hold a strong position within the personal care industry. Unilever home care brands include Domestos, Jif and Omo, each branded individually and not dependent on the Unilever brand for their viability even though Unilever is one of the most successful consumer goods companies in the world. The branding is strategically individual.

A major advantage of individual branding is that if an organisation introduces an inferior product, the negative images associated with it do not contaminate the company's other products. An individual branding policy may also facilitate market segmentation when a company wishes to enter many segments of the same market. Separate, unrelated names can be used, and each brand can be aimed at a specific segment.

Australian ice-cream manufacturer, Streets, has a number of product lines that target specific segments. Streets' Paddle Pop and Bubble O' Bill brands are targeted toward younger consumers, and symbolise childhood fun. On the other hand, Streets' Magnum brand is a more rich, indulgent 'adult' ice-cream, targeted toward pleasure seekers. By branding individually, Streets achieves a breadth of coverage across the consumer markets with tailored brands designed to meet the needs of specific segments.

family branding
Branding all of a company's products with the same name

When using family branding, all of a company's products are branded with the same name or at least part of the name, such as Kellogg's Coco-Pops, Kellogg's Special K and Kellogg's Corn Flakes. In some cases, a company will use both individual branding and family branding strategies within the company's brand portfolio, as does the Coca-Cola Company. A company that uses primarily individual branding for many of its products may also use family branding for a specific product line. The Coca-Cola Company, for example, includes the beverage brands of Powerade, Nestea, Mount Franklin and Sprite. Across these brands, the Coca-Cola Company takes a back seat as the products are individually branded. Within the Coca-Cola Company brand portfolio, however, is the Coca-Cola brand as well, which in itself includes ranges of soft drink, such as Coca-Cola Zero and Diet Coca-Cola.

An organisation is not limited to a single branding policy. Branding policy is influenced by the number of products and product lines the company produces, the characteristics of its target markets, the number and types of competing products available, and the size of the company's resources.

Brand extensions

brand extension
Using an existing brand to brand a new product in a different product category

A brand extension occurs when an organisation uses one of its existing brands to brand a new product in a different product category. Honda for example, is a well know car and motorcycle manufacturer brand, but Honda also manufacturers marine engines, jet engines and generators. A more recent brand extension from Honda is the introduction of lawn mowing and gardening equipment, such as trimmers and blowers.

However, a brand extension should not be confused with a line extension. A line extension refers to using an existing brand on a new product in the same product category, such as Honda's line extension into sedans as the Accord and Civic models. A soft drink company might introduce a brand extension in the form of a probiotic yogurt drink whereas a line extension would be a new flavour of soft drink or a different size option. For example, Pepsi introduced Pepsi Max and Pepsi Next, and these new products are argued to be a line extension because they are in the same category as the originating brand.

Diversification within the brand portfolio is well demonstrated within the many and varied Virgin brands. The Virgin brand is a marker of quality and value in industries where a challenge can be made to the status quo and add an element of fun and informality. In Australia, for example, the

Source: AAP Image/Torsten Blackwood

<< Virgin consolidates
The Virgin brand is repositioning to better compete on a global scale by consolidating Virgin Blue, V Australia and Pacific Blue as Virgin Australia

Virgin brand portfolio includes the airline Virgin Australia, the financial services company Virgin Money and the telecommunications company Virgin Mobile. Virgin Australia entered the Australian airline industry in 2000 as Virgin Blue with just two aircraft, one route and 200 employees. At that time, the Australian airline industry was ruled by a duopoly between Qantas and Ansett. Using aggressive marketing, a highly differentiated offer and a hard-line pricing strategy, Virgin Blue revolutionised air travel in Australia. Virgin Blue halved the cost of flying for consumers by offering a less formal service and electronic ticketing. As a consequence of a fiercely intense price war, Ansett was knocked out of play. The collapse of Ansett was the most emotionally charged corporate collapse in Australian history, leaving Qantas to battle Virgin Blue alone. As a premium service and high-priced airline, Qantas was fast losing ground to Virgin Blue because of their informal and low-cost airline service. More than gaining market share, Virgin Blue was expanding the market by enabling many consumers who previously could not afford to fly to travel by air. To counteract this in a strategic and competitive move, Qantas launched JetStar and offered a similarly low-budget, less formal airline that could directly compete with Virgin Blue. Today, we see the Virgin brand hold a strong position throughout the Asia-Pacific region with the branding consolidated as Virgin Australia. This branding consolidation is designed to enable Virgin to better compete on a global scale.

Co-branding

Rather than developing a portfolio of brands, another option is to use a co-branding strategy. Co-branding is the use of two or more brands on one product. Marketers employ co-branding to capitalise on the brand equity of multiple brands. Co-branding is popular in several processed-food categories and in the credit-card industry. The brands used for co-branding can be owned by the same company, such as McCafé, or be a collaborative effort between two different companies. For example, Italian car manufacturer Fiat teamed up with toy manufacturing company and Barbie brand owner Mattel to create the Fiat 500 Barbie. The model comes in nail-polish pink with a Barbie branded key cover, makeup holder and pink-trimmed Barbie floor mats. Complete with Swarovski-crystal-encrusted hubcaps, the Fiat model was created in celebration of the Barbie brand's 50th birthday.

co-branding
Using two or more brands on one product

Source: Newspix/News Ltd/Bob Finlayson [Caltex]; Getty Images [Nike]

Supermarkets have teamed up with fuel brands, such as Woolworths' co-branding with Caltex. Consumers benefit with the fuel discount offered with every grocery purchase over $30 and, similarly, Woolworths and Caltex benefit with an effective tracking system on the behaviour of consumers. Analysis of Woolworths grocery receipts can be correlated with consumer fuel purchases to identify those consumers who are consistently spending higher amounts or shopping more often at both the supermarket and at the bowser. In this effective and strategic move to co-brand, Woolworths and Caltex have distinct offers and distinct brands that combine well together. It is important for marketers to understand that when a co-branded product is unsuccessful, both brands are implicated in the product failure. To gain customer acceptance, the brands involved must represent a complementary fit in the minds of buyers. The essential combination of music during fitness training is strategically demonstrated with the co-branding between Nike and Apple. Nike and iPod co-brand the 'Nike + iPod sports kit'; a range of running shoes and apparel featuring sensors and ports which connect to an Apple iPod Nano.

Brand licensing

brand licensing
An agreement whereby a
company permits another
organisation to use its brand
on other products for a
licensing fee

A popular branding strategy involves brand licensing, an agreement in which a company permits another organisation to use its brand on other products for a licensing fee. Royalties may be as low as two per cent of wholesale revenues or higher than 10 per cent. Kellogg's licensed the Hannah Montana brand from Disney for use on the cereal product, Hannah Montana Cereal. Toys R Us licensed the Cars brand from Disney for the use on a wide range of children's toys. And, in the perfume product category, Elizabeth Arden Inc. holds the license to brand celebrity names including Brittany Spears, Mariah Carey and Taylor Swift fragrances.

Under a brand license, the licensee is responsible for all manufacturing, selling and advertising functions. On the upside, the advantages of brand licensing range from extra revenues and low-cost or free publicity to new images and trademark protection. On the downside however, the major disadvantages of brand licensing are a lack of manufacturing control, which could hurt the company's name, and bombarding consumers with too many unrelated products bearing the same name. The licensee also bears the costs if the licensed product fails.

MARKETING IN TRANSITION | R.M. WILLIAMS BRAND IDENTITY

Within the highly competitive and constantly changing fashion market, brands need to take measures in order to stay current, whilst still remaining true to the brands identity. The R.M. Williams Company was founded in 1932 by Australian legend, Reginald Murray Williams. Much has changed in the fashion industry since those depression years and, yes, the R.M. Williams brand has managed to survive as an excellent example of sustainable marketing. The iconic Australian brand is renowned for high-quality bush wear ranging from solid-hide work belts, oilskin coats, grazier shirts, moleskin jeans and leather elastic-sided boots. The brand communicates to consumers an identity of the Australian outback, hard work, tough wear and rugged country. Representing more than leather and stitching, the brand reflects the life of R.M. Williams who was a drover, digger, miner and swagman. R.M. Williams' legendary status imbues the brand with rich layers of emotional meaning. The identity of the brand is enacted through Australian stockmen, drovers and farmers who wear the brand.

Successful brand management means R.M. Williams has remained competitive within the fashion industry, both within Australia and internationally, and they have retained the authenticity of the brand while broadening the brand target from farming to mainstream culture. In extending the original niche target to the broader mainstream target, R.M. Williams has achieved sustainability by reading the macro environment in an effective manner. Remaining with the narrow niche of farming as the primary target, the R.M. Williams brand may not have survived or experienced the growth it has. In a sustainable manner, the brand still symbolises the Australian identity while it adapts to the dynamic fashion industry through seasonal ranges. Transferring the romance of the rugged outback into modern fashion, the R.M. Williams brand is now worn by movie stars, political figures, sporting champions and the everyday mainstream consumer.

Building and sustaining brands

LO6

Some brands work better than others. R.M. Williams (explored in the Marketing in Transition box above) is an iconic Australian brand and many other brands strive for this status. Marketers aiming to build and sustain a strong and successful brand necessarily have to take small steps to ensure the brand is sustainable in the long term. Leslie de Chernatony proposes that the stages in building and sustaining brands involves complex coordination of many people across various functions of the organisation.[19] Through a planning process, the organisation identifies a specific approach and brand objectives are formulated according to the specific approach. Stating this organisational direction and these brand objectives in organisational documents helps to ensure that everyone involved is on the same page. Brands are enacted and performed by various people and the role they play in supporting the brand needs to be clearly understood and explicitly stated. The strategic process for building integrated brands, proposed by de Chernatony, begins with a brand vision that is integrated with the organisational culture and brand objectives (see Figure 7.2). Astute marketers are continuously monitoring what's going on within the 'brandsphere' in order to bring out the brand's essence. There is an internal implementation process that happens in and around this process which naturally involves resources. This process feeds into a brand evaluation process that loops back into the brand vision in an iterative manner. Therefore, the process of building and sustaining brands is an ongoing and integrated strategic process.

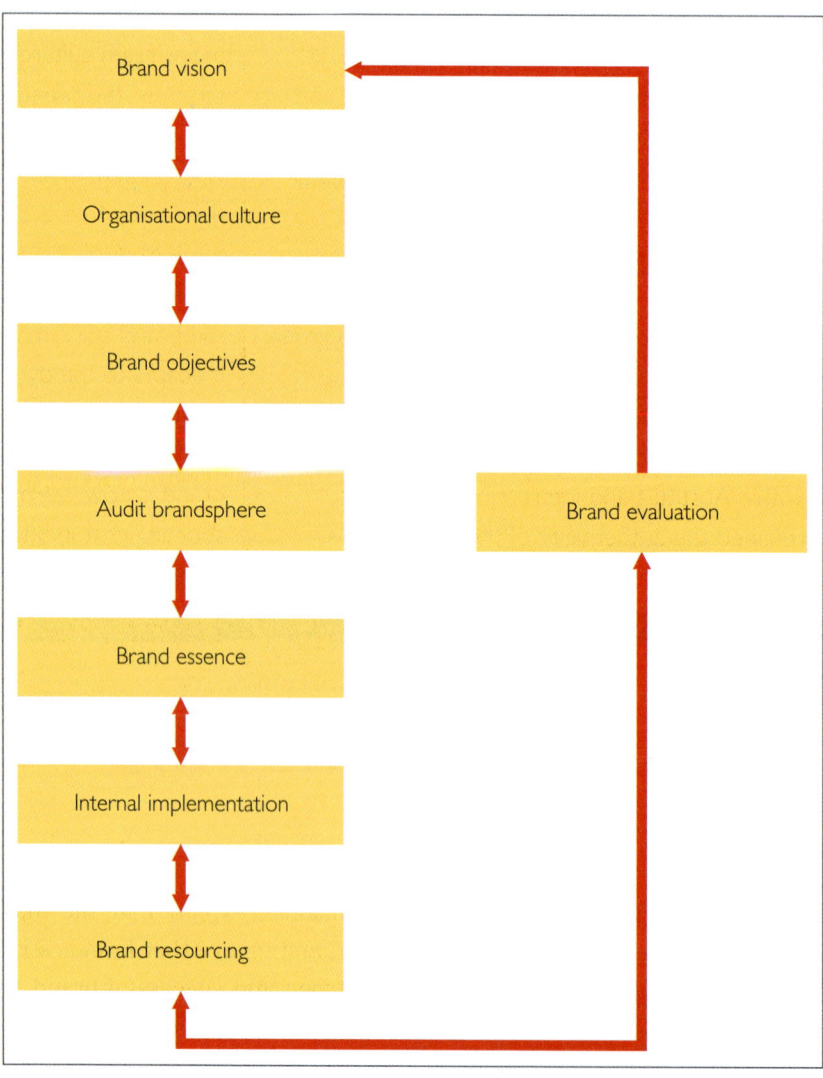

FIGURE 7.2
PROCESSES FOR
BUILDING AND
SUSTAINING BRANDS

Source: de Chernatony, L, *From Brand Vision to Brand Evaluation: The strategic process of growing and strengthening brands,* 2nd edition, Butterworth-Heinemann/Elsevier, 2007, p. 87.

Brand vision

The process of building and sustaining brands begins with the brand vision. In this stage of building and sustaining brands, establishing a brand vision is about identifying a strategic future for the brand. The three elements of the brand vision are:

* a strategic future for the brand
* the purpose of the brand
* the brand values.

A future cosmetics brand might strategically establish a point of differentiation by positioning on the therapeutic value of the brand rather than on the standard promise of enhancing beauty. A designer label of jeans might establish a point of differentiation by positioning on their innovative military design rather than the standard promise of durability, fit and wear. A local volunteering organisation might establish a point of differentiation by positioning on global welfare projects rather than the standard transport and volunteering services. The latter organisation may consider that a small, local operation expanding globally is not necessarily viable and clearly one of the challenges is to develop the cross-cultural expertise and connections that might facilitate such an expansion.

While many organisations exist to make a profit, the purpose of the brand is *not* just to be profitable. The purpose of the brand might, for example, be to reinforce the image of the organisation as an innovative leader in the field. The purpose of the brand might be to make the world a better place, as is the case with The Body Shop or Oxfam, for example. Or, the

purpose of the brand might be to strengthen the organisational portfolio and presence in a particular area of expertise.

Source: The Body Shop

Brand values need to be aligned with the organisation's values. For example, if the brand values include committing to a low carbon footprint, then all the company's products and processes, including production and distribution, will ideally be ecologically safe and environmentally friendly. Brand values usually include both functional values and emotional values; for example, a high-end furniture retailer will promote the functional value of comfort while also promoting the emotional value of opulence. Ideally, brand values align to the overall brand vision, which sets the strategic direction for the brand.

<< **Brand values**
The Body Shop campaigns against sex trafficking of young people

Organisational culture

When the brand vision is clearly stated and understood, then management and employees will appreciate the action and behaviour suited to this vision. Appropriate action and behaviour can create a competitive advantage for a brand, as the brand experience is not just about what the customer gets, but how. The elements that comprise *how* the customer receives the brand include the brand values, the people that deliver the brand experience and the environment in which that happens. These elements characterise organisational culture. The organisational culture of legal firm Shine Lawyers is associated with Erin Brockovich, and demonstrates a culture of integrity, honesty, and a belief in standing up for the rights of ordinary people. Alternatively, the organisational culture of Google encourages an open and sharing environment, thereby encouraging loyalty and creativity. Unlike a traditional corporate culture, Google facilitates a creative and unique organisatonal culture through, for example, holding conferences in diner booths instead conference rooms, structuring its office more like a campus and allowing employees to follow creative interests ranging from cycling to beekeeping.

Brand objectives

Brand objectives guide management and employees towards (a) clear and measurable target(s). For example, a jeans designer has a long-term objective of providing designs representative of a specific lifestyle and fashion statement. This then leads to a range of military-style designs which reach all sales targets. If the brand's objective is to offer an experience of being at the cutting edge of fashion, then a mechanism *must* be in place to monitor fashion trends (thereby encouraging appropriate jean designs). Keeping in touch with what the market demands and what customers are looking for is a standard requirement in seeking to achieve brand objectives. By continuously monitoring the environmental trends, the brand objectives can be shifted and shaped as needed to stay relevant to the marketplace. Put simply, this means talk to the customers to keep the brand on track.

Auditing the brandsphere

Keeping a close watch on the shifting sands that make up the big picture of a company's industry, an effective and sustainable brand means continuously auditing five key forces, which are the:

* organisation
* distributors
* customers
* competitors
* macro-environment (political, economic, social, technological).

By continuously monitoring these factors in the brandsphere, critical forces are identified which may enable or prohibit a brand's vision. In order to handle any brand shortcomings and challenges, astute marketers need to be aware of them as they arise.

Brand essence

When brand managers and marketers are in touch with the relevant factors and forces influencing the brandsphere, ideas will begin to emerge about what the essence of the brand might be or could be. At this stage of the brand evaluation, the goal is to identify the central characteristics that define the brand. By looking at and analysing the features and benefits that differentiate the brand from other brands, thinking about brand positioning and brand personality can be clarified and advanced. What do customers understand as the essence of this brand and how do they action this understanding?

Internal implementation

When the essence of the brand is identified and understood, a system of internal implementation needs to be established, developed and monitored. A key issue, for example, is what form the various systems will take. Systems that need to be considered include the customer service system, the frontline management system, operational systems, support systems and delivery systems. This range of necessary systems needs to reinforce the brand's functional and emotional values and capitalise on what the organisation is known for and good at. Internal systems that empower staff and frontline personnel have more chance of accurately representing the essence of the brand, the brand values and vision. However, everything costs money and organisations usually operate with limited resources which need to be allocated appropriately.

Brand resourcing

Establishing, developing and implementing internal systems means looking at the finer details of resource allocation. A strong brand will demand more organisational resources, but brands have to build up to that point in order to sustain that status. On the way up, brand resourcing can be a hot debate. Essentially, evidence needs to be collected to justify investment of resources, where meeting brand objectives is a basic requirement to justify sustained investment. The key to this process of justification is continual brand evaluation, and so the feedback loop continues.

Brand evaluation

Brand evaluation must be carried out on a regular basis and brand performance needs to be measured against key criteria (objectives). This continual monitoring of brand performance against key criteria identifies whether the brand is on track or not. Favourable or unfavourable results provide guidance for future action and strategic direction. This process of continual brand evaluation shifts and shapes how branding is translated at the tactical level of the (extended) marketing mix.

Connecting the marketing mix and brands

While much of marketing is common sense, the relationship between marketing mix elements and marketing outcomes is not always immediately apparent. The population of many countries, including Australia, is recognised as an ageing population, given birth rates are decreasing and life expectancy is increasing. Many older and elderly members of our communities are active consumers with an accessible disposable income and time to spare. Recognising this segment as a lucrative target, Nature Bound Australia offers

LISTEN to an Audio Summary that connects the marketing mix and brands

holiday packages for the over 50s, travel options for seniors and soft adventure tours. As a resilient and resourceful generation who have worked hard for what they have attained in life, the over 50s are looking for value for money but price is not necessarily the primary purchasing criteria. The brand holder's position on environmental matters may act as a motivation to purchase one brand over another. For example, Japanese brand Suntory are known for their corporate social responsibility, promoting recycling, and reducing energy and water consumption in the production of their beverages (see the Sustainable Marketing box on the next page). We will now briefly examine the connections between brands and the marketing mix elements of price, place, promotion and product.

Brands and pricing

Consumers will pay higher prices for strong brands than for weaker brands. Branding is key to creating a competitive advantage that absolutely overrides the competition and generates excessive profit. A strong brand enables consumers to take short cuts in their decision-making process to purchase a particular product and/or brand. Consumers will opt for the reassurance of a brand they know and trust. A high price might be part of this reassurance, given the widely held belief that you get what you pay for. A low price might be interpreted by consumers to indicate a cheap and nasty product and/or brand. A strong brand, therefore, enables a strategically higher price.

Branding and physical distribution

Placing an offer in front of a customer involves, at times, a complex logistical effort. Distribution considerations include the shelf-life and durability of the product. Fruit and vegetables are best offered fresh and therefore the produce markets begin their trading day before dawn. Fresh produce growers readily greet the retail and wholesale buyers who then busily transport this produce to the everyday consumer. A banana might have a shelf life of a few days while a car can sit on the dock for weeks. Consumers trust brands and therefore trust that Cavendish Bananas will not be sold when over-ripe and that imported Japanese cars are safe for Australian conditions.

Distribution channels might be short or long depending on the product offered for sale. A short distribution channel occurs when manufacturers sell direct to consumers, as do Dell Computers for example. Efficient distribution is a platform of the Dell brand. Manufacturers selling direct to consumers has become a more viable method of distribution with the evolution of the Internet negating the need for manufacturers to engage with intermediaries. Skipping the intermediaries strategically shortens the distribution channel and also skips the margin that would otherwise be pocketed by a wholesaler and/or retailer. A direct-to-consumer distribution strategy gives the manufacturer full control over price, margin and merchandising. However, in many cases it is strategically smart for the manufacturer to hand over to a wholesaler and/or a retailer in order to effectively get the product to market. In this case, the manufacturer's brand is not targeted towards consumers but to the intermediaries.

Manufacturers using a long distribution channel target one or many intermediaries. Most fast moving consumer goods (FMCGs), for example, will usually be produced by a manufacturer in a low-cost capital environment and then shipped in bulk to a wholesaler

SUSTAINABLE MARKETING | BRANDING AND CORPORATE SOCIAL RESPONSIBILITY

Consumers may choose a certain brand for the company's underlying environmental stance. Suntory is a Japanese brand world-renowned for whisky and liquor. But the Suntory Group is also well known for their corporate social responsibility and as the 'Bringing Water to Life' corporation. A traditional Japanese organisation, this corporate social responsibility vision statement was adopted with an eye to Suntory becoming a truly valuable company that will achieve coexistence with nature and society.

Established in 1899, by founder Shinjiro Torii, in Osaka, Japan, Suntory began manufacturing and selling grape wine. Since that time, Suntory has grown into several global organisations, including various food and beverage companies, but the Suntory brand is best known for wine and liquor. Aiming to maintain the original spirit of their founder, Suntory willingly considers the societal impact of its corporate efforts and continuously strives for a mutually beneficial relationship with 'Kaizen' philosophy, which means continuously improving business operations. Environmental efforts include reducing energy, water usage and waste as well as promoting recycling. Other stakeholder considerations include relations with customers, employees, suppliers and the local community. More specifically, Suntory's mission statement reads, 'In Harmony with People and Nature'.

who then repacks and distributes to nominated (large and small) retailers who might be dispersed across a nation. In this long distribution chain, the manufacturer is only dealing with the wholesaler, and from there the wholesaler negotiates with the range of many and varied retailers. This can be a simpler and less expensive strategic option for a manufacturer because there is no need to establish elaborate and expensive marketing efforts. Using intermediaries can have other advantages. Local distributors have local market insight and well-established connections and networks with a regular client base.

Branding and promotion

Successful promotional campaigns can have powerful, profitable and long-term effects, including the generation of strong brand equity. Communicating to a particular target market with an appropriate combination of promotional efforts can generate a strong following, even to the extent of a consumer 'tribe'. A good example of this is the commercial-free Australian radio station, triple j, which is the centrepiece of the triple j brand that targets young Australians who love music.

Listeners to the triple j radio station are so dedicated to the brand that regional communities have erected and funded their own triple j transmitters in order to receive the triple j broadcasts. The triple j brand has also expanded into a television show (triple j tv), a magazine (triple j magazine), an online space (http://www.triplej.net.au) and a range of triple j

Source: ABC

branded events including triple j Hottest 100, triple j Unearthed, triple j One Night Stand and triple j Impossible Music Festival.

The strength of the youth market following triple j is demonstrated in their participation and interaction: consumers of the triple j brand produce music, engage in talk-back radio and participate in triple j events. The triple j Unearthed initiative alone involves over 23 000 Australian musicians. Connected through their shared passion for Australian music, triple j consumers form meaningful social relationships with fellow brand consumers, both online and offline, on-air and off-air.

Branding and products

In today's world it seems as if people are consuming not just products, but brands. Consumer behaviour is complex and not always rational as effective brand management steers us towards thinking a certain way about an organisation and what they can offer to the market place. Maintaining a strong presence in the highly competitive field of sportswear, Nike has released an innovative product and brand that incorporates technology with the growing culture of barefoot running (see the Marketing in Transition box overleaf).

Product offers that predominantly involve services are equally viable for branding strategies. Given that services involve some combination of people, physical evidence and processes, branding services is an effective marketing strategy (for further discussion on the expanded marketing mix variables, see Chapter 15). For example, Disneyland is the ultimate branded space and unique brand experience. The parks consist of numerous themed lands such as adventureland, tomorrowland and fantasyland. The Disneyland space is subtly branded with 'hidden mickeys', whereby the architectural design of buildings, right down to the shape of plants reflect the famous Mickey Mouse ears. Disneyland employees are referred to as cast

Source: Getty Images

members, adding to the idea that the Disney brand is a consumption experience. The Disneyland brand was established by Walt Disney in 1953, in Anaheim, California. Today, the Disneyland brand has many brand extensions, including the Disney Cruise Line, Disney Weddings, Disney Visa Cards and Disney Parks, scattered throughout the world, including Hong Kong.

MARKETING IN TRANSITION | NIKE BRAND INNOVATION

To remain competitive within the marketplace and to stay true to the Nike brand's characteristics of innovation, the company turned to science for inspiration. Biomechanical studies have revealed many benefits of running barefoot, including decreased impact on the knees and ankles, as well as strength building and natural stance improvement. Taking an innovative approach to footwear design, sports apparel brand Nike have released a new line of running shoes branded Nike Free. Recognising the growing fitness trend of barefoot running, Nike Free runners are designed to allow multidirectional movement and superior flexibility. Combined with lightweight technology, the Nike Free aims to emulate the motion of running barefoot. As a brand that is committed to technological innovation, Nike Free runners are marketed as an evolutionary shoe that will 'Free your run'. Consumers can choose from a scale of sole flexibility ratings,

Source: Getty Images

whereby the Nike Free 5.0 indicates the shoe to be halfway between barefoot and a traditional running shoe. The scale ranges from a 2.0 upwards, and the lower the number, the closer to a barefoot feel. Through identification of the barefoot running trend and strategic branding of the new shoe line, Nike has harnessed technology to produce brand innovation.

Another good example of a brand and an experience is the Red Bull Flugtag, which is a German term for flying day and pronounced floog-tag. In this competition, entrants attempt to fly home-made human powered flying machines off a 6.7 metre high platform over water. The Red Bull brand is highly visible at this wacky event. This Red Bull-branded event is so popular it now takes place annually in over 35 cities globally, with each event attracting up to 200 000 spectators. In Singapore, for example, the first Red Bull Flugtag held at Siloso Beach saw 35 000 people attend and 38 teams who were judged on creativity, showmanship and flight distance.[20]

MARKETING IN TRANSITION | POWER SHIFT FROM ORGANISATIONS TO CONSUMERS

Contemporary marketing professionals now concede that they no longer own the brand and that the most important brand conversations are not the conversations taking place between the brand and consumers but among consumers. That is, consumer to consumer conversations. Facebook, eBay and Instagram, for example, are social media websites where the active participation of the consumer generates the product on offer. This evident power shift means that organisations have to let go of the control of marketing communications that they had in the past. How do you see this power shift away from organisations and towards consumers in your own brand consumption?

Study Tools

Chapter review

 **LO1** IDENTITY AND DESCRIBE THE STRATEGIC POWER OF BRANDING.

Branding is the key to creating a competitive advantage that absolutely overrides the competition and generates excessive profit. A strong brand enables consumers to take short-cuts in their decision-making process to purchase a particular product and/or brand. Successful promotional campaigns can have powerful, profitable and positive long-term effects. Consumers will pay higher prices for strong brands than for weaker brands. Consumers will opt for the reassurance of a brand they know and trust. A strong brand, therefore, enables a strategically higher price. It seems that in today's world, what people consume are not products, but brands.

 **LO2** EXPLAIN THE VALUE OF BRANDING

A brand is a name, term, design, symbol or any other feature that identifies one seller's goods or service and distinguishes it from those of other sellers. Branding helps buyers to identify and evaluate products, helps sellers to facilitate product introduction and repeat purchasing, and fosters brand loyalty.

 **LO3** DEFINE BRAND EQUITY AND THE DISCUSS THE MAJOR COMPONENTS OF BRAND EQUITY.

Brand equity is the marketing and financial value associated with a brand's strength. It represents the value of a brand to an organisation. The four major elements underlying brand equity include brand name awareness, brand loyalty, perceived brand quality and brand associations.

 **LO4** RECOGNISE HOW BRAND NAMES ARE SELECTED AND PROTECTED.

When selecting a brand name, a marketer should choose one that is easy to say, spell and recall and that alludes to the product's uses, benefits or special characteristics. Brand names can be devised from words, letters, numbers, nonsense words or a combination of these. Companies protect ownership of their brands through registration with IP Australia (http://www.ipaustralia.gov.au).

 **LO5** IDENTIFY TWO TYPES OF BRANDING POLICIES, AND EXPLAIN BRAND EXTENSIONS, CO-BRANDING AND BRAND LICENSING.

Individual branding designates a unique name for each of a company's products. Family branding identifies all of a company's products with a single name. A brand extension is the use of an existing name on a new or improved product in a different product category. Co-branding is the use of two or more brands on one product. Through a licensing agreement and for a licensing fee, a company may permit another organisation to use its brand on other products. Brand licensing enables producers to earn extra revenue, receive low-cost or free publicity and protect their trademarks.

 **EXPLORE DIFFERENT STRATEGIES FOR BUILDING AND SUSTAINING BRANDS.**

Building and sustaining a strong and successful brand is a strategic process involving the coordination of various functions within an organisation. The process begins with establishing a brand vision, organisational culture and brand objectives. Through continuous observation of the brandsphere, the brand's essence is derived. Once a brand's essence is determined, a system of internal implementation is developed and monitored, including the management of brand resourcing. The final stage of building and sustaining process involves brand evaluation: measuring the brands performance against key criteria. This process is an ongoing and integrated strategic process.

 **EXAMINE BRANDS AND THE MARKETING MIX.**

Branding is connected to each element of the marketing mix. In relation to pricing, consumers will pay a higher price for strong brands over weaker brands. A brand's strength provides price reassurance, and pricing can be used as a strategic branding tool. Distribution considerations include shelf life, durability and length of distribution channels. The promotion element of the marketing mix can generate strong brand equity. Increasingly, people are not only consuming products, but brands.

 # Key concepts

Use these key terms in **Search me! marketing** to find the latest relevant readings from a wide range of world-class journals, e-books and newspapers, including *The Australian*.

- brand
- brand association
- brand awareness
- brand equity
- brand extension
- brand insistence
- brand licensing
- brand loyalty
- brand mark
- brand name
- brand preference
- brand recognition
- co-branding
- family branding
- home brands
- individual branding
- manufacturer brands
- perceived brand quality
- trademark
- trade name

Issues for discussion and review

1 Explain the strategic power of branding across the extended marketing mix.

2 What is the value of branding in relation to differentiation? Explain the cultural dimension of a brand.

3 What is brand equity? Identify and explain the major elements of brand equity.

4 What are the three major degrees of brand loyalty?

5 Compare and contrast manufacturer brands, private distributor brands and generic brands.

6 Identify the factors a marketer should consider when selecting a brand name.

7 What is brand vision? What are the three key elements of brand vision?

Marketing applications

1   Identify two brands for which you are brand loyal. What keeps you loyal to this brand? How did you begin using these brands? Why do you no longer use other brands?

2   Mercedes-Benz introduced the sub-compact and fuel efficient A-class series. Invent a brand name for a line of luxury sports cars that would also appeal to an international market. Suggest a name that implies quality, luxury and value.

3   For each of the following product categories, choose an existing brand. Then, for each selected brand, suggest a co-brand and explain why the co-brand would be effective.

   a   ice-cream
   b   pizza
   c   telecommunications
   d   soft drink.

ONLINE EXERCISE

4   The evolution of technology is changing the way we consume and the way marketing is conducted. A daily routine for many consumers online today is a visit to Facebook and Twitter. The implication for marketers is the need to join this online conversation. The following questions address the consumer perspective and the business perspective.

   a   For consumers, what do brands such as Facebook and Twitter mean to people? How have these brands become part of our daily routine? How do consumers access these brands as part of their daily routine?
   b   For businesses, how might brands such as Facebook and Twitter become part of the organisational mode of operation? How have these brands become part of the business and marketing world? What do marketers need to monitor in terms of online consumer action and behaviour? How can this behaviour be monitored?

Developing your marketing plan

A company's branding strategy must be in line with the overall marketing strategy. When developing a marketing plan, the company must decide how to brand a particular product and how to establish that brand in the marketplace. Ensuring a consistent branding message throughout your marketing material is a strategic priority. The strategic value of branding is found in every element of the extended marketing mix (price, place, promotion, product, people, physical evidence, processes and, potentially, partnerships). Consistency is the key.

Here are some questions to help develop an effective branding strategy.

1   Who are your target consumers and what brand characteristics make them brand loyal?
   ■   Demonstrate that the brand encourages brand loyalty through promotional efforts.

2   What is the perceived brand quality?
   ■   Communicate with consumers in a manner that aligns with the perceived brand quality.

3   How do stakeholders (other than customers) develop opinions about your brand?
   ■   Communicate with stakeholders in a manner that suits their interaction habits.

4   Check all elements of the extended marketing mix are reinforcing a consistent message.
   ■   Does all brand communication reinforce the brand's core values?

5 What roles do people and technology play in communicating your branded offer?
- Do the people and technology involved support the brand's core values?
6 What mechanisms are in place to reinforce the brand's value after the exchange?
- What mechanisms need to be put in place to reinforce the brand's values after an initial exchange?

CengageNOW

Go to http:\\login.cengagebrain.com to link to CengageNOW, your online study tool. First take the Pre-Test for this chapter to get your Personalised Study Plan, and then:

* **Revise** your understanding of the key concepts of marketing with the online glossary

* **Watch** an interactive animation of strategic marketing to broaden your subject comprehension

* **Listen** to an audio summary of the learning objectives covered in this chapter.

After you have completed the activities in your Personalised Study Plan take the Post-Test to determine what concepts you have mastered and what you still need to work on.

Case study

BRANDING STRATEGY WITHIN AN UNBRANDED MARKET: A CASE OF THE AUSTRALIAN TOBACCO INDUSTRY

Tobacco control has long been on the Australian government's legislation agenda. In an attempt to curb rising tobacco consumption, and the associated detrimental health effects, the avenues available for advertising, marketing and distributing tobacco products have been increasingly controlled. Tobacco companies have had to compete with the introduction of restrictions, such as an Australia-wide ban on all formats of tobacco advertising, as well as a ban on the retail display of tobacco products. In 2006, legislation enforced cigarette packets to feature large Government health warnings on the packaging, whereby 30 per cent of the front of the packet and 90 per cent of the back of the packet is now taken up by a selection of health warnings and images.[21] Since December 2012, the *Tobacco Plain Packaging Act* states that it is mandatory for all cigarette packaging to be a uniform brownish-green colour, also known as Pantone 448C, and with no distinguishing features between different brands, such as symbols, logos, colours or fonts.[22] Legislation has now effectively removed all marketing and branding devices available to tobacco companies.

The implementation of these extreme measures illustrates the understood power of branding. Prior to packaging and branding control, marketing and branding efforts allured consumers to one brand over another. Cigarette brand Benson & Hedges' gold packaging, sponsorship of major sporting events and premium price imparted notions of luxury, status and quality. Vogue cigarettes targeted women through distinctive decorative and slim-line packaging, symbolising elegance, class and refinement. Marlboro, once recognised for the product's red and white box and distinct typeface, deliberately enhanced their branding with the distinct personality of the Marlboro Man as a symbol of independence, masculinity and success.[23] Research suggests that without exposure to these brand associations and images, and through the implementation of plain packaging laws, smoking adoption will decrease and quitting smoking will be encouraged.[24] One study concluded that by removing brand elements such as colour, branded fonts and imagery, positive cigarette brand associations were reduced among adolescents. A similar study on plain packaging concluded that cigarette packs with fewer branding design elements were perceived as increasingly unfavourable in terms of the inferred experience of smoking in comparison to smoking from full-branded packs.[25] However, with the implementation of plain packaging, where does that leave tobacco manufacturers in differentiating their brand from competing brands in an otherwise unbranded market?

Strategies adopted by major cigarette companies include reconsidering the product name, investing in product innovation, altering the packaging content and focusing marketing efforts toward retailers. These strategies are adopted with the goal of maintaining strong brand presence, brand differentiation, and fostering brand loyalty. Brands such as Peter Jackson have changed the name of their various cigarette blends to reduce any potential consumer confusion with the introduction of plain packaging laws. What were once labelled as 'Peter Jackson Rich', which came in a gold-coloured pack, are now known as 'Peter Jackson Rich Gold', in their new Pantone 448C packaging. Incorporating the brand's previous packaging characteristics into the brand name helps consumers to identify the brand despite the uniform packaging. Cigarette manufacturers are also competing in terms of product innovation. For example, new cigarette blends have been introduced that allow users to change the flavour from normal to menthol by simply pressing on the filter. Winfield have introduced the Optimum Crush, Peter Jackson have released a new hybrid range and Dunhill have released the Dunhill Switch. Another effort in retaining brand loyalty, as well as encouraging brand switching behaviour, is made by altering the packaging content. Cigarette packets traditionally contained 20, 25 or 30 cigarettes. Now consumers are being offered a little extra, for example Peter Stuyvesant's 20 pack is now rebranded as a 20 pack with one 'Loosie'. Similarly, John Player Special is now a 26-pack, rather than a traditional 25-pack, imparting the notion that consumers are getting an extra cigarette for free. This repackaging of unbranded goods is designed to stimulate positive brand associations, and increased brand loyalty. Furthermore, tobacco companies are focusing their efforts in increasing brand awareness toward retailers, investing time in brand education, as well as offering sales incentives. Effectively, the tobacco companies are shifting from a consumer focus, to an intermediary focus, given the recognition that retailers are a powerful marketing device.

Lorien Latimer, Freelance Consultant, Queensland Australia

QUESTIONS
FOR
DISCUSSION

1 Consider and discuss the ethics of companies advertising a product which is potentially harmful. How does this situation apply to the fast emerging (and largely unregulated) product category of e-cigarettes?

2 Should governments have the power to control a private company's branding efforts?

3 Apart from diversifying into the e-cigarettes market, describe another strategy cigarette manufacturers could implement in order to increase brand loyalty?

4 Comment on the power of branding and whether or not legislating against branding is an effective government policy.

Chapter endnotes

1. Shawn Parr, '5 smart ways to building your brand the right way,' *Fast Company*, accessed November 16, 2013. http://www.fastcompany.com/3018334/how-to-be-a-success-at-everything/5-smart-steps-to-building-your-brand-the-right-way.

2. 'Dictionary of Marketing Terms,' American Marketing Association, http://www.marketingpower.com/_layouts/Dictionary.aspx.

3. Sharon Schembri, 'Reframing brand experience: The experiential meaning of Harley-Davidson,' *Journal of Business Research* 62 (2009): 1299–1310.

4. C. D. Simms and P. Trott, 'The Perception of the BMW Mini Brand: The Importance of Historical Associations and the Development of a Model,' *Journal of Product & Brand Management* 15 (2006): 228–238.

5. R. W. Belk, and G. Tumbat, 'The cult of Macintosh,' *Consumption, Markets & Culture* 8 (3) (2005): 205–217.

6. Douglas B. Holt, *How Brands Become Icons: The Principles of Cultural Branding* (Boston: Harvard Business School Press, 2004).

7. David C. Edelman, 'Branding in the digital age,' *Harvard Business Review* 88 (12) (2010): 14–18.

8. David A. Aaker, *Managing Brand Equity: Capitalizing on the Value of a Brand Name* (New York: Free Press, 1991): 16–17.

9. Bernd Schmitt, Lia Zarantonello, and J. Brakus, 'Brand experience: what is it? How is it measured? Does it affect loyalty?,' *Journal of Marketing* 73.3 (2009): 52–68.

10. Jean-Noel Kapferer, *The new strategic brand management: Advanced insights and strategic thinking* (Kogan Page, 2012).

11. D. Oakenfull, 'Breakfast cereal review. CHOICE finds most cereals have too much sugar to be healthy choices,' *Choice online* (2009): http://www.choice.com.au/Reviews-and-Tests/Foodand-Health/Food-and-drink/Groceries/Breakfast-cereal-reviewand-compare/Page/Introduction.aspx.

12. Blair Speedy, 'Home brands lose their stigma,' *The Australian*, September 13, 2010. http://www.theaustralian.com.au/business/industry-sectors/home-brands-lose-their-stigma/story-e6frg9h6-1225919825501.

13. Kohli S. Chiranjeev, Katrin R. Harich, and Lance Leuthesser, 'Creating Brand Identity: A Study of Evaluation of New Brand Names,' *Journal of Business Research* 58 (2005): 1506–1515.

14. Dorothy Cohen, 'Trademark Strategy,' *Journal of Marketing* (January 1986): 63.

15. R. D. Petty, 'Naming names: Trademark strategy and beyond: Part one – selecting a brand name,' *Journal of Brand Management* (2008): 15: 190–197.

16. Barry Silverstein, 'New Counterfeit Gambit: Knock-off Cheaper Brands,' *Brand Channel*, August 3, 2010. http://www.brandchannel.com/home/post/2010/08/03/New-Counterfeit-Gambit-Knock-Off-Cheaper-Brands.aspx.

17. Ibid.

18. Ibid.; 'Designer Brand Outlet' website suspended,' ACCC, September 9, 2008, http://www.accc.gov.au/content/index.phtml/itemId/842259.

19. Leslie de Chernatony, *From Brand Vision to Brand Evaluation*, (Butterworth-Heinemann: Oxford, UK, 2006).

20. 'Team of commercial pilots wins the inaugural Red Bull Flugtag in Singapore,' Redbull.com, October 28, 2012, http://www.redbull.com/cs/Satellite/en_SG/Red-Bull-Flugtag-Singapore/001243205610299.

21. M. M. Scollo, and M. H. Winstanley, *Tobacco in Australia: Facts and issues* (4th ed. Melbourne: Cancer Council Victoria, 2012). http://www.tobaccoinaustralia.org.au/a12-1-1-history-health-warnings.

22. 'Tobacco Plain Packaging Regulations 2011,' Australian Government, http://www.comlaw.gov.au/Details/F2011L02644; 'Tobacco Plain Packaging Act 2011,' Australian Government, http://www.comlaw.gov.au/Details/C2011A00148.

23. N. Hafez, and Pamela M. Ling, 'How Philip Morris Built Marlboro into a global brand for young adults: implications for international tobacco control,' *Tobacco Control* 14(4) (2005). http://tobaccocontrol.bmj.com/content/14/4/262.full.

24. M. M. Scollo, and M. H. Winstanley, *Tobacco in Australia: Facts and issues.*

25. Daniella Germain, Melanie A. Wakefield, and Sarah J. Durkin, 'Adolescents' Perceptions of Cigarette Brand Image: Does Plain Packaging Make a Difference?,' *Journal of Adolescent Health*, 46 (4) (2010): 385–392. Centre for Behavioural Research in Cancer, The Cancer Council Victoria, Victoria, Australia.

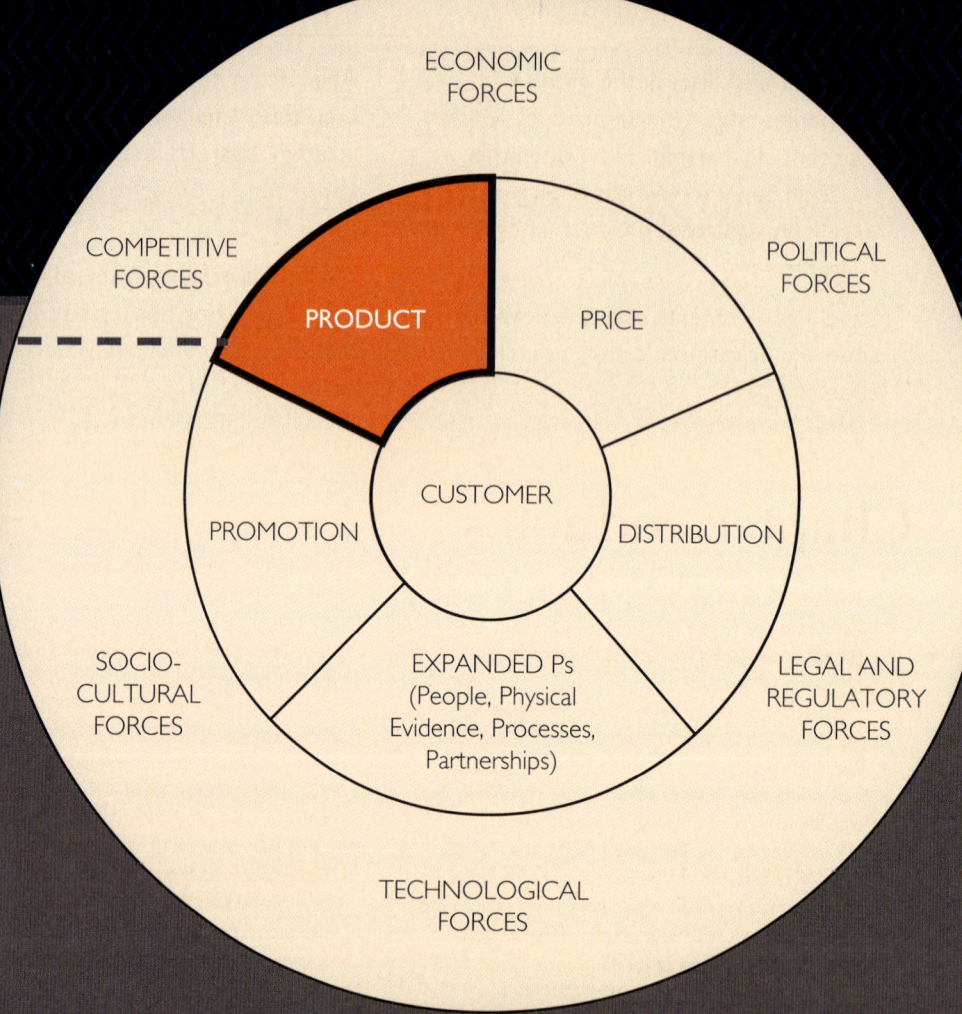

ECONOMIC FORCES

COMPETITIVE FORCES

POLITICAL FORCES

PRODUCT

PRICE

CUSTOMER

PROMOTION

DISTRIBUTION

SOCIO-CULTURAL FORCES

EXPANDED Ps
(People, Physical Evidence, Processes, Partnerships)

LEGAL AND REGULATORY FORCES

TECHNOLOGICAL FORCES

PRODUCT DECISIONS

What is a product?
Classifying products
Consumer products
Business products

Product line and product mix

Product life cycles and marketing strategies
Introduction stage
Growth stage

Maturity stage
Decline stage

Product adoption process
Consumer adoption categories

Packaging functions, design consideration and strategy

Labelling and legal issues

   Throughout this chapter, Watch, Listen and Revise icons indicate an opportunity for online self-study through CengageNOW, linking you to animated chapter overviews, interactive diagrams, videos, quizzes and more.

Learning Objectives

LO1 ▸ Understand the concept of a product and how products are classified

LO2 ▸ Understand the connection between the concepts of product line and product mix

LO3 ▸ Understand the concept of product life cycle and its impact on marketing strategies

LO4 ▸ Understand the consumer adoption process and the connection to the product life cycle

LO5 ▸ Understand the major packaging functions and design considerations as used in marketing strategies

LO6 ▸ Understand the functions of labelling and selected legal issues.

MARKETING CHALLENGE | WELCOME TO THE WONDERFUL WORLD OF LEGO®

Source: Getty Images

LEGO is an iconic brand that targets the primary market of boys aged 7–12 years, and many consumers who have fond memories of LEGO from their childhood. LEGO hit the market some 80 years ago and continues to rejuvenate and expand in the digital world of today. Based in Denmark, and founded in 1932, LEGO aims to develop children's creativity through playing and learning. But, the LEGO brand is more than simply plastic bricks and the logo; it is symbolic of creative kids, playing, learning and having fun.

LEGO now offers an array of products and games that range from the Marvel Super Heroes product line to the newly released Architecture line. The Marvel Super Heroes products include 10 play-set variations, and online interactivity is encouraged with eight online games and videos depicting, for example, the heroic tales of Iron Man, Spiderman and the Avengers. To date, LEGO has deliberately tailored their product

251

offer to young children, even showcasing the wonderful world of LEGO in LEGOLAND Parks and Discovery Centres located around the world, including Malaysia and Tokyo. However, LEGO is now reaching out to the adult market with the recent release of the Architecture product line. The Architecture line focuses on design and allows the practice of techniques, such as creating surfaces, symmetry, modules and repetition. The aim of the product line is to encourage younger and older consumers to explore architecture, engineering and construction.[1]

MARKETING CHALLENGE QUESTION

1   The Architecture product line from LEGO is designed for adult consumers. How could this new product line be explained in terms of a market-oriented product decision?

Introduction

As introduced in Chapter 7, the brand is an interface between the organisation and the consumer. If a company's products do not meet customers' desires and needs, the company will fail unless adjustments are made. Developing successful products and keeping the product relevant to the current market requires knowledge of fundamental product concepts. So the product is the manifestation of the brand and this chapter discusses the concepts of product, product line and various other product strategies. We first define a product and discuss how products are classified. Next, we examine the concepts of product line and product mix. We then explore the stages of the product life cycle and the effect of each life cycle stage on marketing strategies. Next, we outline the consumer adoption process and connect that process to the product life cycle concept. From there, we look at the critical role packaging plays as part of the product. We then explore the functions of packaging, issues to consider in packaging design and how the package can be a major element in the marketing strategy. We conclude with a discussion of labelling.

What is a product?

A product is a good, a service or an idea received in an exchange. A product can be tangible and/or intangible and include functional, social and psychological benefits. Products also include supporting services, such as installation, guarantees, product information and promises of repair or maintenance. Therefore, the four-year/100 000 km warranty received by buyers of a new car is a supplementary part of the product offer.

    A **good** is a tangible physical entity, such as a can of Red Bull, an android tablet or a functional chair. Unlike a good, a **service** is mostly intangible. The intangibility of a service is the result of the application of human and/or mechanical efforts to people or objects. Examples of services include a music festival, online booking agencies, medical

good
A tangible physical entity

service
A mostly intangible result of the application of human and mechanical efforts to people or objects

services and martial arts lessons. An idea is a concept, philosophy, image or issue. Ideas provide the psychological stimulation that aids in solving problems or adjusting to the environment. For example, Mothers Against Drunk Driving (MADD) promotes safe consumption of alcohol and stricter enforcement of laws against drink driving.

Products can be a combination of various components that might include a goods component, a services component and even ideas or symbolism. In others words, every product has multiple aspects, which can be referred to as product attributes or product features. Some highly tangible products, such as a gym, are packaged as a service where members pay a fee that may or may not include the services of a personal trainer. Similarly, when you buy a can of Red Bull, you are buying the aluminium can filled with an energy drink; this is the tangible component of the product. You are also buying the intangible idea or symbolic image of Red Bull as extreme sportsmanship, as per Red Bull Racing and X Games. Also, the idea or symbolism behind Red Bull is that 'Red Bull gives you wings'.

Whether a product is predominantly a tangible good, as is the case with Red Bull, an intangible service, as is the case with medical services, or a concept or idea such as MADD, each requires packaging. The Red Bull product is packaged in a slim, lightweight aluminium can with a user-friendly ring-pull top and vivid colours in the branding. Medical services are packaged differently according to what type of health care they are providing, the pricing and the positioning of the service being offered. For example, a government-owned public service general practice (GP) clinic may be presented as a functional design with inexpensive plastic/vinyl chairs, whereas a neurosurgeon specialist will be located in an expensive suburb and furnished with designer décor and leather sofas.

Think of a total product offering as having three interdependent elements: the core product, supplementary features (such as a warranty) and symbolic or experiential benefits. Consider that some people buy headphones for the basic utility of quality sound, such as Pioneer stereo headphones. According to Jamie Carter of techradar.av[2], the Grado Prestige SR125i (around AU$150) are the functional choice for home that have a comfortable retro style and fit but lack the noise-cancelling capabilities of other choices. Some consumers look for reliability and style and Jamie Carter suggests the Klipsch Image X71 (around AU$230). This teardrop-style of tiny inserts work best with the iPhone and the sound quality is described as 'warm, lively and full with pin-sharp detail'. The manufacturer claims 'noise isolation' so be careful when crossing roads! Other consumers seeking the high-end, lightweight option, might choose the Sennheiser Momentum (AU$400). These headphones are a closed-dynamic model weighing

Source: Shutterstock.com

idea
A symbolic concept, philosophy, image or issue

<< What is a product?
The Red Bull product offer includes a tangible component of an energy drink in an aluminium can, the intangible component of the image of extreme sports and the symbolism that somehow Red Bull gives you enhanced performance and even wings

DID YOU KNOW?
Do you know the Bubble O'Bill ice-cream? This fun-loving product is a packaged ice-cream cowboy made of strawberry, chocolate and caramel ice confection with a bubble gum nose and a bullet through his hat. Adding a digital dimension, Bubble O' Bill has attracted over 1.2 million Facebook fans by posting silly photo-shopped images and initiating quirky, nostalgic challenges. Not bad for a Neapolitan cowboy on a stick. See http://www.streetsicecream.com.au/.

just 190 g. The sound quality is reported as detailed and crystal clear and on par with the Grabo Labs Prestige Series ST125i. With little sound spillage, these headphones are great for the office and for travelling and come with an adaptor and carry-case accessories. The product is described by Jamie Carter in his review as 'truly brilliant'.

In the case of headphones, the core product consists of a fundamental utility or main benefit of sound and sound quality, which addresses a need of the consumer. Supplementary features, such as noise cancelling innovations, provide added value or attributes in addition to the core utility or benefit. Supplementary products can also include various adaptors, cables and a carry case. These supplementary product attributes are not required to make the core product function effectively, but they help to differentiate one product brand from another. Adding the attribute of a six-month warranty or financing, for example, can be described as a service augmentation. In this way, the product as a whole entails multiple components that include tangible, intangible and symbolic aspects.

Moving to a more mundane example, Woolworths and Coles supermarkets have stepped into the world of online shopping and now offer consumers the opportunity to place their orders online. This flexibility enables shoppers the convenience of doing the weekly grocery shop in the comfort of their home, and either collect at their convenience or request delivery at their preferred time and day.

Many smaller supermarket competitors, however, do not offer the online shopping option, given the cost of establishing and maintaining the online purchase mechanisms as well as the offline collection and delivery systems involved. For some consumers, the simple act of shopping has symbolic value and the human interaction is highly valued. Some retail stores are understanding this important point and aim to strategise and capitalise on this symbolic value. Giving shoppers a high level of customer service, for example, is something that is not necessarily easy to achieve in the online environment. By striving to create a special shopping experience for customers, smaller independent supermarkets effectively achieve a competitive advantage. This product strategy is a potential point of differentiation for the smaller supermarkets over the larger chain supermarkets. Unlike the major stores, many smaller stores are independently owned. The owners of these stores are quite often found in the aisles interacting with customers in a more personalised manner than that found in the larger chain operations. In line with this thinking, IGA has positioned their stores with a 'Local heroes' campaign. This promotional campaign shows IGA owners talking with customers and deliberately ordering in specific products to cater to individual customer needs. In this way, the product of IGA is positioned on the idea or symbolism of community connection and involvement.

Supermarkets are also seeking to differentiate on technology. Standard inclusions are the self-serve checkouts and the in-aisle price kiosks. Supermarket giants, such as the UK's Tesco and Yihaodian (China's largest line food retailer), have announced plans to open 1000 virtual supermarkets. Just like Tesco's trial in Korean subway stations, Yihaodian is proposing to use augmented reality technology to present virtual products on virtual shelves inside a physical space that smartphone users can select as if in an actual store. The selected items will then be shipped to the consumer. Effectively, the supermarket is considered the entire product offer, which combines the convenience, speed and lightweight nature of online shopping with the intuitive experience of browsing a physical store.[3]

Another example of a unique store experience is provided by coffee-bean and coffee-accessory retailer Nespresso. In order to provide consumers with an immersive retail experience, Nespresso provide in-store complimentary tasting facilities, allowing customers to try various blends of their take home coffee pods. The retail space is modern, stylish and comfortable, featuring an in-store café, lounges and highly-personalised service. Once leaving the Nespresso store, customers can remain in contact with Nespresso via their coffee boutique app, allowing online ordering, as well as access to the Nespresso club. Collectively, these experiential aspects contribute to the special event of the Nespresso product purchase and consumption.

When consumers purchase a product, they are really buying the benefits and satisfaction they think the product will provide. Christian Louboutin shoes, for example, are easily recognised by the red sole and are a symbolic statement of success. Services, in particular, are purchased on the basis of expectations. Expectations, suggested by images, promises and symbols, as well as processes and delivery, help consumers to make judgements about tangible and intangible products. Products are formed by the activities and processes that help to satisfy expectations. For instance, NapoleanPerdis did not invent cosmetics, but this highly innovative Australian organisation has certainly had a great impact on the global cosmetics industry. Rather than being dictated by fashion, the NapoleanPerdis philosophy emphasises natural beauty achieved with confidence-enhancing cosmetic products. Beginning with a flagship store in Oxford Street, Sydney in 1995, NapoleanPerdis Cosmetics are now available in more than 50 concept stores around Australia, as well as 28 exclusive David Jones counters and 400 independent stockists. In 2005, NapoleanPerdis launched in SAKS Fifth Avenue and in 2007 opened a flagship store and academy in Hollywood. Part of what makes the NapoleanPerdis Cosmetics brand so different to other cosmetics brands is the dynamic new take on make-up education. As the largest make-up and cosmetics training facility in the southern hemisphere, NapoleanPerdis has seven Australian campuses and the new one in Hollywood. Now available throughout Target stores in the US, the NapoleanPerdis Cosmetics product has grown because of a very different approach to the beauty industry. NapoleanPerdis Cosmetics is based on the idea that glamour is sourced from within and according to the NapoleanPerdis philosophy, the customer is understood to be women who want wearable empowerment. This corporate philosophy is very much in the foreground of the NapoleanPerdis brand and product offerings.

Classifying products

Products fall into one of two general categories. Products purchased to satisfy personal and family needs are consumer products. Those bought to use in a company's operations, to resell or to make other products are business products. Consumers buy products to satisfy their personal wants, whereas business buyers seek to satisfy the goals of an organisation. Product classifications are important because they may influence pricing, distribution and promotion decisions. In this section we examine the characteristics of consumer and business products and explore the marketing activities associated with some of these products.

consumer products
Products purchased to satisfy personal and family needs

business products
Products bought to use in an organisation's operations, to resell or to make other products

Consumer products

The most widely accepted approach to classifying consumer products is based on characteristics of consumer buying behaviour. This approach classifies consumer products into four categories: convenience, shopping, speciality and unsought products. However, not all buyers behave in the same way when purchasing a specific type of product. Thus a single product can fit into several categories. To minimise this problem, marketers think in terms of how buyers *generally* behave when purchasing a specific item. Examining the four traditional categories of consumer products can provide further insight. The discussion that follows introduces the four categories of consumer products as: Convenience products, Shopping products, Specialty products and Unsought products. The Marketing in Action box below gives you a brief showcase of Surfer Girl clothing line as a shopping product.

MARKETING IN ACTION | SUMMER THE SURFER GIRL!

Surfer Girl is everything for girls in the surf. Promoted as the best all-girls surf shop in the world, the Surfer Girl product is a shopping product available through Surfer Girls retail stores and online stores. In the summer of 1998, Surfer Girl began in the surfing paradise of Bali where the surf is fabulous and the girls are beautiful, and very talented on the waves. From just one small room in Kuta, the Surfer Girl brand has now developed to include production of a full clothing line. The brand face is Summer the Surfer Girl! Summer and her friends rock the surfing scene. The product offer entails stylish street, surf and lifestyle collections.

With a strong online presence and social media strategy, this brand holds the attention of more than 2.9 million fans.[4] The brand success is geographically concentrated in Indonesia, and distribution has recently commenced in Malaysia, the Philippines, South Korea and Singapore. ✖

Source: © Surfer Girl International Pty Ltd &™ Surfer Girl Head Logo is a trade mark of Surfer Girl International Pty Ltd, used with permission

Convenience products

convenience products
Relatively inexpensive, frequently purchased items for which buyers exert minimal purchasing effort

Convenience products are relatively inexpensive, frequently purchased items for which buyers exert only minimal purchasing effort. They range from bread, soft drinks and chewing gum to petrol and newspapers. The buyer spends little time planning the purchase or comparing available brands or sellers. Even a buyer who prefers a specific brand will readily choose a substitute if the preferred brand is not conveniently available. A convenience product is normally marketed through many retail outlets, such as

Woolworths supermarkets, 7-Eleven outlets and suburban corner stores. As a convenience strategy, for example, The Coffee Club has opened locations inside airports, hotels and grocery stores to ensure that customers can get coffee whenever or wherever the desire strikes. Because sellers experience high inventory turnover, per-unit gross margins can be relatively low. Producers of convenience products, such as Cadbury's Freddo Frog, expect little promotional effort at the retail level and thus must conduct advertising and sales promotion dedicated to the product. Packaging is also important because many convenience items are available only on a self-service basis at the retail level and thus the package plays a major role in selling the product.

Shopping products

Shopping products are items for which buyers are willing to expend considerable effort in planning and making the purchase. Buyers spend much time comparing stores and brands with respect to prices, product features, qualities, services and perhaps warranties. The Surfer Girl brand story presented earlier is an example of a shopping product. Department stores such as Myer carry shopping products and are often found in the same shopping centres with competitors so that consumers can shop and compare products and prices. Appliances, bicycles, furniture, stereos, cameras and shoes exemplify shopping products. These products are expected to last a fairly long time and are therefore purchased less frequently than convenience items. Even though shopping products are more expensive than convenience products, few buyers of shopping products are particularly brand loyal. If consumers were brand loyal, they would be unwilling to shop and compare among brands. Shopping products require fewer retail outlets than convenience products. Because shopping products are purchased less frequently, inventory turnover is lower, and marketing channel members expect to receive higher gross margins. In certain situations, both shopping products and convenience products may be marketed in the same location.

shopping products
Items for which buyers are willing to expend considerable effort in planning and making purchases

Source: The Skinny Cow®

Source: Shutterstock.com

<< Convenience product and shopping product
An ice cream is a convenience product. Hotels and up-market restaurants are shopping products

Specialty products

specialty products
Items with unique characteristics that buyers are willing to expend considerable effort to obtain

Specialty products possess one or more unique characteristics and generally consumers are willing to expend considerable effort to obtain them. Consumers actually plan the purchase of a specialty product, as they know exactly what they want and will not accept a substitute. Examples of specialty products include the Apple iPhone and an authentic piece of Aboriginal or Torres Strait Islander art. When searching for specialty products, buyers do not compare alternatives. They are concerned primarily with finding an outlet that has the preselected product available. With the continued migration of Muslim consumers throughout the world, for example, halal products are increasingly in demand in traditionally non-Muslim markets. While halal products may be readily available in many Asian countries, finding halal products in Western countries is more difficult. Halal products are considered specialty products in this context. Once a reputable outlet is identified, the information spreads throughout the relevant community. More specifically, and from a marketing perspective, Asian producers of halal products need to recognise that Western non-Muslim markets are viable and potentially lucrative. With the increasing number of Muslims choosing to reside in non-Muslim countries, as well as the rise in the 'foodies' segment and the conscious consumer markets, halal has the potential as a preferred product.[5]

Unsought products

unsought products
Products purchased to solve a sudden problem, products of which customers are unaware and products that people do not necessarily think about buying

Unsought products are products purchased when a sudden problem must be solved, products of which customers are unaware and products that people do not necessarily think of purchasing. Emergency medical services and vehicle towing are examples of products needed quickly to solve a problem. A consumer who is sick or injured has little time to plan to go to an emergency medical centre or hospital. Likewise, in the event of a broken fan belt on the highway, a consumer will likely seek the closest tow truck and the nearest mechanic to get back on the road as quickly as possible. In such cases, speed and problem resolution are far more important than price and other features that consumers might normally consider if they had more time for making decisions. Companies such as Australian Disaster Recovery specialise in the recovery and restoration of fire- and water-damaged property and content losses. Specialising in a field such as disaster recovery makes the purchases of these unsought products more bearable by building trust with consumers through recognisable brands and superior functional performance.

Business products

Business products are usually purchased on the basis of organisational goals and objectives. Generally, the functional aspects of the product are more important than the psychological rewards sometimes associated with consumer products. Business products can be classified into seven categories according to characteristics and intended uses: installations; accessory equipment; raw materials; component parts; process materials; maintenance, repair and operating (MRO) supplies; and business services. In effect, business products across these seven categories constitute the exchange between businesses and the business-to-business market as discussed in Chapter 6.

Also increasingly important in the business context, is the consideration of sustainability. Sustainable practices may be part of organisational goals and objectives and, therefore, will hold some bearing across the seven categories of business products discussed below. Deliberately designing a building to be environmentally friendly, National Australia Bank, in Docklands, Melbourne, has set a new global benchmark for sustainable workplace design.[6] The Sustainable Marketing box (overleaf) discusses maintenance, repair and operating supplies, such as cleaning supplies, which highlights one way businesses can choose to go green. Also, with regard to raw materials and process materials, organisations can choose more sustainable options, as Cadbury has done, in choosing to use fair trade cocoa. In 2009, Cadbury invested $2.1 million to ensure that the cocoa ingredient, used in 300 million chocolate bars sold each year, is certified as fair trade.[7] The cocoa in Cadbury chocolate is sourced from Ghana, and this move has benefitted Ghanaian cocoa farmers in terms of pay, working conditions and a tripling of the country's fair trade cocoa production. Nice work Cadbury!

source: Copyright © Boeing

<< Business product
Boeing aircraft offer specifically designed products for business customers

Installations

Installations include facilities, such as office buildings, factories and warehouses, and major equipment that are immobile, such as production lines and very large machines. Normally, installations are expensive and intended to be used for a considerable length of time. Because they are so expensive and typically involve a long-term investment of capital, purchase decisions often are made by high-level management. Marketers of installations frequently must provide a variety of services, including training, repairs, maintenance assistance and even aid in financing such purchases.

installations
Facilities and immobile major equipment

SUSTAINABLE MARKETING | DIGGING DEEPER INTO GREEN CLAIMS

In recent years, many businesses have boarded the environmental bandwagon to ride on its growing popularity. The fast-growing green products sector offers consumers an environmentally responsible product alternative and offers businesses an opportunity to gain a competitive advantage. But how do we know if a product is really green? Many consumer products ranging from toothpaste, to printers, to cleaning products make false, confusing or vague green claims (also known as green washing – see Chapters 5 and 12). Shampoos claim to be certified organic with no verifiable certification, and cleaning products claim to be 100 per cent natural, even if they contain naturally occurring hazardous substances. With the growth of false green claims, marketers need to provide consumers with clear information regarding the relevant environmental benefits of the product.

The Earth Choice brand highlights the superior environmental benefits of their cleaning products over traditional cleaning products through commercials featuring aquatic animals being used for household cleaning. The commercials for Earth Choice depict a starfish being used as a dish scrubber, an octopus serving as a mop and a duck being used as a toilet cleaner with confronting realism. The tortuous use of aquatic life in Earth Choice commercials highlights the benefits of using Earth Choice over alternative products, and at a broader level creates an awareness of the impact cleaning products have on aquatic life. The commercials prompt consumers to consider where their waste water goes after it leaves their home, effectively positioning Earth Choice products as an environmentally conscious alternative. ☒

Source: dLibrary.com.au

Accessory equipment

accessory equipment
Equipment that does not become part of the final physical product but is used in production or office activities

Accessory equipment does not become part of the final physical product but is used in production or office activities. Examples include filing cabinets, calculators and tools. Compared with major equipment, accessory items usually are much cheaper, purchased routinely with less negotiation, and treated as expense items rather than capital items because they are not expected to last as long. More outlets are required for distributing accessory equipment than for installations, but sellers do not have to provide the multitude of services expected of installations marketers.

Raw materials

raw materials
Basic natural materials that become part of a physical product

Raw materials are the basic natural materials that actually become part of a physical product. They include minerals, chemicals, agricultural products and materials from forests and oceans. Sugar, for example, is a raw material found in many different products, including food, beverages and even fuel, as ethanol. Indeed, the growing popularity of ethanol as

LISTEN to the Audio Summary for a recap of the product types introduced in this chapter

an alternative fuel has to some extent rescued the struggling agricultural crop of sugar cane. Raw materials are usually bought and sold according to graded specifications and in relatively large quantities.

Component parts

Component parts become part of the physical product and are either finished items ready for assembly or products that need little processing before assembly. Although they become part of a larger product, component parts can often be identified and distinguished easily. Spark plugs, tyres, clocks, brakes and electronics are all component parts of an automobile. Industrial buyers purchase such items according to their own specifications or industry standards. They expect the parts to be of a specified quality and delivered on time so that production is not slowed or stopped. Producers that are primarily assemblers, such as most lawn mower and computer manufacturers, depend heavily on suppliers of component parts.

component parts
Items that become part of the physical product and are either finished items ready for assembly or products that need little processing before assembly

Process materials

Process materials are used directly in the production of other products. Unlike component parts, however, process materials are not readily identifiable. For example, a salad dressing manufacturer includes vinegar in its salad dressing. The vinegar is a process material because it is included in the salad dressing but is not identifiable. As with component parts, process materials are purchased according to industry standards or the purchaser's specifications. A larger scale example of process materials is found in road infrastructure. To construct the road systems we use everyday, the government will call for tenders for bitumen and asphalt work, for example.

process materials
Materials that are used directly in the production of other products but are not readily identifiable

Servicing all three levels of government (local, state and federal), Rock & Road Bitumen offers full-service bitumen and asphalt contracting, road profiling and road rehabilitation. This innovative and versatile specialist organisation has the experience and equipment to patch and seal, as well as deliver on major highway projects. Importantly, in delivering on government projects, such as road and highway infrastructure, Rock & Road is registered with Main Roads as a Quality Assured supplier in compliance with AS/NZS ISO 9001:2000.

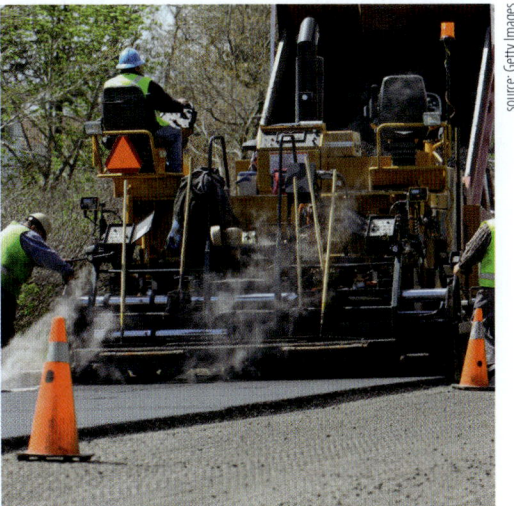
source: Getty Images

Process Materials
The process of spraying bitumen and asphalt is a highly specialised business service with expertise that is significant to road safety, but may be taken for granted by everyday road users

Maintenance, repair and operating (MRO) supplies

MRO supplies are maintenance, repair and operating items that facilitate production and operations but do not become part of the finished product. Paper, pencils, oils, cleaning agents and paints are in this category. While you might be familiar with such consumables

MRO supplies
Maintenance, repair and operating items that facilitate production and operations but do not become part of the finished product

as Reflex paper and Bostick Blu-Tack, to offices, restaurants and hotels, these light consumable products are MRO supplies needed to conduct business in the commercial market. Australian organisations, such as Rubbedin (http://www.rubbedin.com.au), who provide innovative cleaning and surface protection solutions, such as the Magic range, are increasingly targeting business customers in the commercial cleaning market. MRO supplies are commonly sold through numerous outlets and are purchased routinely. To ensure supplies are available when needed, buyers often deal with more than one seller.

Business services

business services
The intangible products that many organisations use in their operations

Business services are the intangible products that many organisations use in their operations. They include financial, legal, marketing research, information technology and cleaning services. Companies must decide whether to provide their own services internally or obtain them externally. This decision depends on the costs associated with each alternative and how frequently the services are needed. For example, few companies have the resources to provide global overnight delivery services efficiently, so most companies rely on FedEx, DHL and other service providers.

Product line and product mix

product item
A specific version of a product that can be designated as a distinct offering among a company's products

Marketers must understand the relationships among all the products of their organisation to coordinate the marketing of the total group of products. The following concepts help to describe the relationships among an organisation's products. A product item is a specific version of a product that can be designated as a distinct offering among an organisation's products. Havaiana sandals (or thongs in Australian terms), for example, offer many variations of havaianas with each version of havaianas considered a product item. More specifically, havaianas' Aquabumps Black for men, retailing at AU$29.99, is a product item in the men's line. However, havaianas also offers a line of products for men, women, boys, girls and even babies. The men's line also includes 12 Top options in various colors, 10 Original options in various colours, 20 Rubber Logo options in various colours, six Top Mix options in various colours, four Top Flip options in various colours, six Tred Mix options in various colours, 34 Trend options in various colours, eight Flag options in various colours, four Teams options, seven Metal Logo options, five Casual options, one Aero option, three Tradicional options and two options as a limited edition – and that is just the men's line!

product line
A group of closely related product items viewed as a unit because of marketing, technical or end-use considerations

A product line is a group of closely related product items that are considered to be a unit because of marketing, technical or end-use considerations.

To develop the optimal product line, marketers must understand buyers' goals. Specific product items in a product line usually reflect the desires of different target markets or the different needs of consumers.

product mix
The total group of products that an organisation makes available to customers

A product mix is the composite, or total, group of products that an organisation makes available to customers.

Continuing with the havaianas example, the product mix is more than just sandals. The havaianas product mix includes inflatables, Gummy lights, phone accessories, table cases,

USB drives, magnets, keyrings, towels and beach umbrellas. The width of product mix is measured by the number of product lines a company offers. The depth of product mix is the average number of different product items offered in each product line. Figure 8.1 shows the width and depth of the havaianas product mix.

width of product mix
The number of product lines a company offers

depth of product mix
The average number of different product items offered in each product line

Men	Women	Boys	Girls	Babies	Make your own	Havaianas®
Inflatables	Jelly inflatables	Print inflatables	Fluro inflatables	Flags	Mini inflatables	
Gummy lights	Gummy lights	Gummy Glow				
Phone accessories	Phone Case 4	Phone Bumper 4	9700 Cases	Phone Case 3	Mobile charms	
Tablet Cases	Table Case 2	Table Case 1				
USB Drives	Colour USB Drives	Print USB Drives	4GB Colour USB Drives			Accessories
Magnets	Magnets Pack	Magnets Clip				
Keyrings	Colour Thong Keyrings	Print Thong Keyrings	Crystal Keyrings	Keystraps	Metal Thong Keyrings	
Towels	Beach Towels					
Beach Umbrellas	Red Beach Umbrella					

DEPTH ↕   WIDTH ↔

FIGURE 8.1 THE CONCEPTS OF PRODUCT MIX, WIDTH AND DEPTH APPLIED TO THE HAVAIANAS RANGE

Source: Granted Courtesy Rubbedin Pty. Ltd.

<< Product lines
Rubbedin has developed several product lines including the 'Magic' range of innovative cleaning products, the 'Clean Green' range of environmentally responsible cleaning products and the 'Fuel Stove' range of maintenance products

Product life cycles and marketing strategies

Just as biological cycles progress from birth through growth and decline, so do product life cycles. As Figure 8.2 shows, a product life cycle has four major stages: introduction, growth, maturity and decline. As a product moves through its cycle, the strategies relating

L03

product life cycle
The progression of a product through four stages: introduction, growth, maturity and decline

to competition, pricing, distribution, promotion and market information must be evaluated periodically and possibly changed. Astute marketing managers use the life cycle concept to make sure that the introduction, alteration and deletion of a product are timed and executed properly. By understanding the typical life cycle pattern, marketers can maintain profitable product mixes.

Introduction stage

The introduction stage of the product life cycle begins at a product's first appearance in the marketplace, when sales start at zero and profits are negative. Profits are below zero because initial revenues are low and the company generally must cover large expenses for product development, promotion and distribution. Notice in Figure 8.2 how sales should move upward from zero, and profits also should move upward from a position in which they are negative because of high expenses.

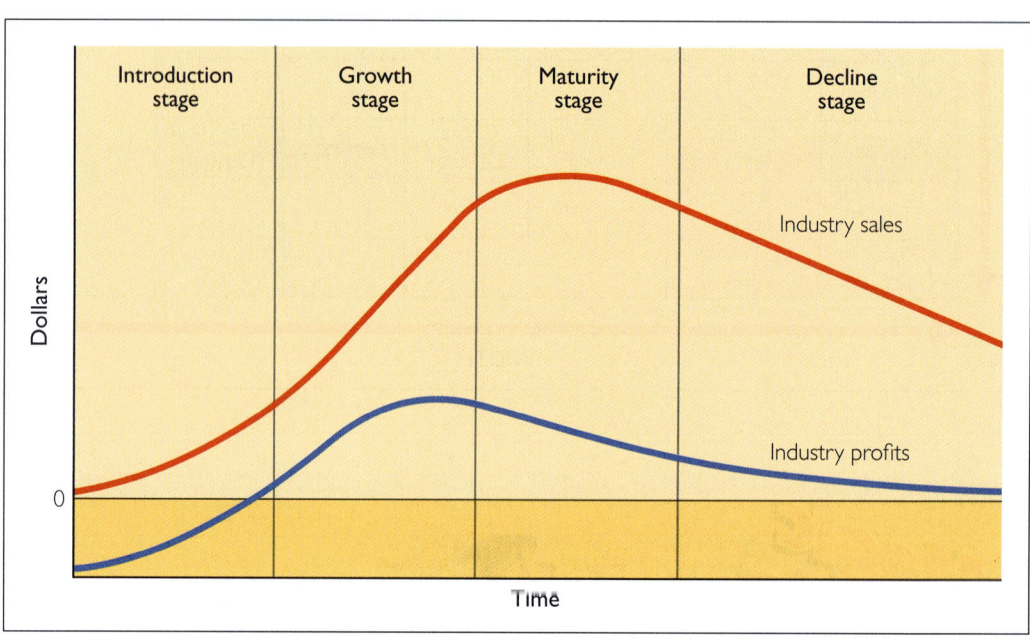

During the introduction stage of the product life cycle, potential buyers must be made aware of new product features, uses and advantages. San Remo utilised a successful partner already established in the market, combined with heavy investment in promotions, to introduce pasta to a predominantly noodle-consuming Indonesian market (see Did you know? on the next page). Efforts to highlight a new product's value can create a foundation for building brand loyalty and customer relationships.[8] Two difficulties may arise at this point.

✳ Sellers may lack the resources, technological knowledge and marketing know-how to launch the product successfully. Entrepreneurs without large budgets can still attract attention, however, by giving away free samples, as Kosmea does with its organic rose hip oil and other skin care products. Another technique is to gain visibility through public relations, such as editorial coverage and media appearances. Mia Freedman began blogging in 2007, writing about women and the issues that women face. From that humble beginning, Mamamia is now a high-profile Australian online community with more than 1.3 million members. Controversial issues are tackled both online and in traditional media vehicles

such as TV morning shows. As a recent expansion to this strong online presence, Mamamia now incorporates iVillage.com.au.

✳ The initial product price may have to be high to recoup expensive marketing research or development costs. For example, 1Above is an innovative product currently available at select airports in Australia and New Zealand. The product promises optimal hydration on long-haul flights. The tangible component of the product includes a vitamin B boost along with the active ingredient of Pycnogenol, which has been shown to reduce both the length and severity of jet lag, while supporting circulation. However, the investment involved in getting this product offer to market must be recouped, and therefore the online price is currently at $7.50 per 100 ml (in concentrate form). Given these difficulties, it is not surprising that many products never get beyond the introduction stage.

Most new products start off slowly and seldom generate enough sales to bring immediate profits. As buyers learn about the new product, marketers should be alert for product weaknesses and make corrections quickly to prevent the product's early demise. As the sales curve moves upward, the break-even point is reached, where competitors enter the market and the growth stage begins.

Growth stage

During the growth stage, sales rise rapidly and profits reach a peak, but then start to decline (see Figure 8.2). The growth stage is critical to a product's survival because competitive reactions to the product's success during this period will affect the product's life expectancy. Profits begin to decline late in the growth stage as more competitors enter the market, driving prices down. However, even though margins might be squeezed, overall sales will continue to increase and therefore management must support the momentum by adjusting the marketing strategy. The growth phase is the exciting phase but also a little dangerous. The goal in the growth phase is to not only meet the increasing demand but also to establish and fortify the product's market position by encouraging brand loyalty. To achieve greater market penetration, segmentation may have to be used more intensely. This requires developing product variations to satisfy the needs of people in several different market segments.

growth stage
The stage of a product's life cycle when sales rise rapidly and profits reach a peak and then start to decline

One of India's oldest and most respected brands is TATA, currently valued at US$10 907 million by Interbrand.[9] The TATA Group started as an iron and steel manufacturer in 1907 and by 1939 was operating the largest steel plant in the British Empire. By understanding the needs of the community were shifting, TATA moved towards providing crucial infrastructure, especially electrical power. TATA Power commissioned the first hydroelectricity project near Mumbai. From there, TATA Group recognised that consumer needs were again shifting towards vehicles and TATA Motors was set up as a collaboration with Daimler-Benz. Now the group had a focus on steel, power and transport – sectors that account for a major portion of infrastructure. However, beyond independence (from British rule), the changing Indian consumer has been matched by changes in TATA Group's composition. The world and India alike moved towards a service-led economy and TATA Consultancy Services was launched in 1968, which provided supplementary services to TATA Steel and has now grown to be one of the world's leading information technology organisations. Managing a century-old brand in a way that continues to be relevant today has involved many reinventions and a depth of understanding of market dynamics. TATA Group is also one of India's most philanthropic and environmentally responsible organisations, having been awarded the Carnegie Medal of Philanthropy in 2007.

During the growth phase, sales volume increases and efficiencies in production may result in lower costs, thus providing an opportunity for lower prices. For example, when flatscreen TVs were introduced, the price was AU$5000 or more. As demand soared, manufacturers of both liquid crystal display (LCD) and plasma technologies were able to take advantage of economies of scale to reduce production costs and lower prices to less than AU$1000 within several years. If price cuts are feasible, they can help a brand gain market share and discourage new competitors from entering the market. Gaps in geographic market coverage should be filled during the growth period. As a product gains market acceptance, new distribution outlets usually become easier to obtain. Promotion expenditures may be slightly lower than during the introductory stage but are still quite substantial. As sales increase, promotion costs should drop as a percentage of total sales. The advertising messages should stress brand benefits. Discount vouchers and samples may be used to increase market share.

Maturity stage

maturity stage
The stage of a product's life cycle when the sales curve peaks and starts to decline as profits continue to fall

During the maturity stage, the sales curve peaks and starts to decline and profits continue to fall (see Figure 8.2). This stage is characterised by intense competition because many brands are now in the market. Competitors emphasise improvements and differences in their versions of the product. As a result, during the maturity stage, weaker competitors are squeezed out of the market. The producers who remain in the market are likely to change their promotional and distribution efforts. Advertising and dealer-oriented promotions are typical during this stage of the product life cycle. Marketers must also take into account that as the product reaches maturity, buyers' knowledge of it attains a high level. Consumers are no longer inexperienced generalists. Instead, they are experienced specialists. Marketers of mature products sometimes expand distribution into global markets. Often the products have to be adapted to fit differing needs of global customers more precisely.

 WATCH an online video activity describing the product life cycle

Because many products are in the maturity stage of their life cycles, marketers must know how to deal with these products and be prepared to adjust their marketing strategies. There are many approaches to altering marketing strategies during the maturity stage. To increase the sales of mature products, marketers may suggest new uses for them. Bicarbonate soda is traditionally used as a cooking and baking ingredient for cakes and such but McKenzie's Bi-Carb Soda has boosted demand for its bicarbonate soda by promoting the highly environmentally responsible deodorising and cleaning properties of this product. By adding a bi-carb component to the cleaning agent, marketers were able to promote the product as a greener option for cleaning, hence repositioning the cleaning product and encouraging growth rather than maturity or decline.

During the maturity stage, three objectives are sometimes pursued, including generating cash flow, maintaining share of market and increasing share of customers. Generating cash flow is essential for recouping the initial investment and generating excess cash to support new products. For example, Elken Malaysia has a stronghold across the Asia-Pacific region within the health and beauty industry. With a direct to consumer business model, Elken offers a broad product mix that includes product lines in health care, beauty, fast moving consumer goods (FMCGs) and home appliances. With more than 300000 independent distributors in seven countries (Malaysia, Singapore, Indonesia, Thailand, Brunei, Hong Kong and India) Elken is now in the maturity phase of the product life cycle and must consider their future organisational direction. Elken has grown up with this community of independent distributors and created a strong foundational network. But what now? Further technological innovation is one option, as per Elken's development of Reverse Osmosis water treatment. The goal is to keep the innovations up to steer clear of decline.[10]

To avoid decline, some companies, such as Elken and Coca-Cola, simply strive to maintain their current market shares through aggressive promotions and new-product introductions. Companies with marginal market shares must decide whether they have a reasonable chance to improve their position or whether they should drop out. Companies can also focus on boosting individual customer's purchases. For example, many banks have added new services (brokerage, financial planning, car leasing, etc.) to cross-sell banking products, gain more of each customer's financial services business and increase the amount of business done with individual customers. Likewise, many supermarkets are seeking to increase share of customers by adding services such as restaurants, movie rentals and dry cleaning to provide one-stop shopping for their customers' household needs.[11]

Thinnovation.

The world's thinnest notebook. 13.3-inch widescreen display. Full-size keyboard. MacBook Air

Source: Image courtesy of The Advertising Archives

<< Product life cycle
Notebook and laptop computers are in the maturity stage of the product life cycle. Consumers are now choosing tablets and smartphones rather than a cumbersome laptop or notebook

A greater mixture of pricing strategies is used during the maturity stage. Strong price competition is likely and may ignite price wars. Companies also compete in other ways besides price, such as through product quality or services. In addition, marketers develop price flexibility to differentiate offerings in product lines. Markdowns and price incentives are common. Prices may have to be increased, however, if distribution and production costs rise.

During the maturity stage, marketers go to great lengths to serve dealers and to provide incentives for selling their brands. Maintaining market share during the maturity stage requires moderate, and sometimes large, promotion expenditures. Advertising messages focus on differentiating a brand from the field of competitors and sales promotion efforts may be aimed at both consumers and resellers.

Decline stage

During the decline stage, sales fall rapidly (see Figure 8.2). When this happens, the marketer considers pruning items from the product line to eliminate those not earning a profit. The marketer also may cut promotion efforts, eliminate marginal distributors and, finally, plan to phase out the product. But facing the reality of decline and exit is a serious challenge and many organisations remain in denial for far too long and sometimes the realisation that repositioning

decline stage
The stage of a product's life cycle when sales fall rapidly

and reinvention is required comes too late. Often, a long-term chart is required to see what is going on. Microsoft, for example, as the dominant player in the personal computer industry, has long enjoyed the benefits of that dominance. But taking a long-term view of connected devices since 2009 raised the alarm bells. Figure 8.3 shows this decline in sales graphically.

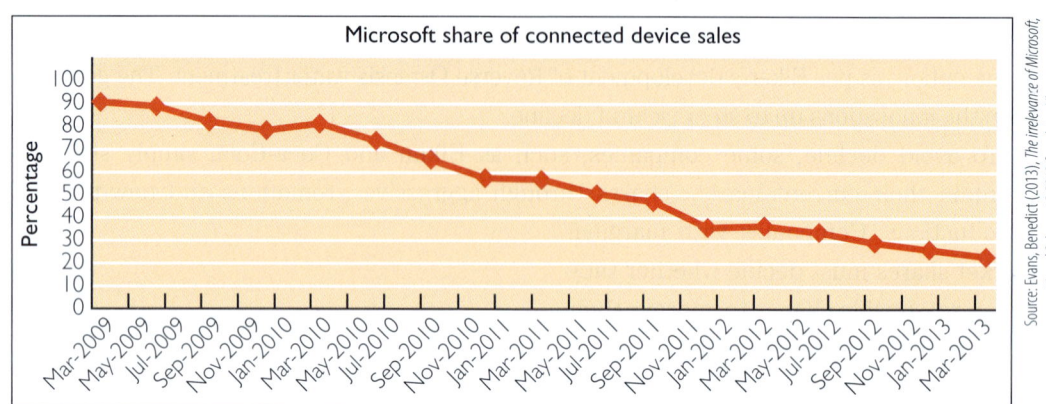

FIGURE 8.3 EVIDENCE THAT MICROSOFT IS IN DECLINE

Source: Evans, Benedict (2013), *The irrelevance of Microsoft,* retrieved 3 August 3 2013 from http://ben-evans.com /benedictevans/2013/7/20/the-irrelevance-of-microsoft

In the decline stage, marketers must determine whether to eliminate the product or try to reposition it to extend its life. While Microsoft will aim to reposition, Volkswagen has officially decided to end the production of the iconic Kombie van.[12] Usually, a declining product has lost its distinctiveness because similar competing products have been introduced. Competition engenders increased substitution and brand switching as buyers become insensitive to minor product differences. For these reasons, marketers do little to change a product's style, design or other attributes during its decline. New technology or social trends, product substitutes, such as e-cigs in the tobacco industry (refer to the Ethical Marketing box below), or environmental considerations may also indicate that the time has come to delete the product. In the music industry, we have seen vinyl come and go, superseded by digital technology. Vinyl recordings, however, are making a comeback as the 'retro' option among up-and-coming musicians and DJs.

ETHICAL MARKETING | REINVENTING TOBACCO PRODUCTS AS ELECTRONIC

According to Euromonitor International, smoking rates are in decline in most developed economies, such as North America and Australia, but not so in many emerging markets such as China, Indonesia and Saudi Arabia. Given this state of global decline in cigarette sales, tobacco giants such as Phillip Morris are reinventing the traditional cigarette as an electronic cigarette (e-cig). Electronic cigarettes are promoted as an effective means to quit smoking. However, given this product is not a food, manufacturers are not required to include ingredients on the labelling.

Therefore, exactly what is in e-cigs is unknown. In the Philippines, for example, e-cigs have been gaining favour given recent tax increases imposed on tobacco products. A basic e-cig kit in the Phillipines costs as little as AU$24 and features a battery-powered vaporiser that delivers a nicotine-laced mist. Food and Drug Administrators dispute the claim that e-cigs help smokers kick the habit and the Philippine health department suggests this tobacco substitute could turn children into smokers. What do you think? Is the e-cig an ethical or unethical product?[13]

During a product's decline, outlets with strong sales volumes are maintained and unprofitable outlets are weeded out. An entire marketing channel may be eliminated if it does not contribute adequately to profits. An outlet not used previously, such as a factory outlet or Internet retailer, sometimes will be used to liquidate remaining inventory of an obsolete product. As sales decline, the product becomes more inaccessible, but loyal buyers seek out dealers who still carry it. Spending on promotion efforts is usually reduced considerably. Advertising of special offers may slow the rate of decline. Sales promotions, such as vouchers and two-for-one offers, may regain buyers' attention temporarily. As the product continues to decline, the sales staff shifts its emphasis to more profitable products.

Product adoption process

Acceptance of new products — especially new-to-the-world products — usually doesn't happen overnight. In fact, it can take a very long time. People are sometimes cautious or even sceptical about adopting new products, as indicated by some of the remarks quoted in Table 8.1.

TABLE 8.1   MOST NEW IDEAS HAVE THEIR SCEPTICS

'I think there is a world market for maybe five computers.' – Thomas Watson, chairman of IBM, 1943.
'We don't like their sound, and guitar music is on the way out.' – Decca Recording Company rejecting The Beatles, 1962.
'Everything that can be invented has been invented.' – Charles H. Duell, Commissioner, US Office of Patents, 1899.
'Heavier-than-air flying machines are impossible.' – Lord Kelvin, president, Royal Society, 1895.
'If I had thought about it, I wouldn't have done the experiment. The literature was full of examples that said you can't do this.' – Spencer Silver on the work that led to the unique adhesives for 3M 'Post-It' notepads.

Customers who eventually accept a new product do so through an adoption process. The stages of the product adoption process are as follows:

* *Awareness.* The buyer becomes aware of the product.
* *Interest.* The buyer seeks information and is receptive to learning about the product.
* *Evaluation.* The buyer considers the product's benefits and decides whether to try it.
* *Trial.* The buyer examines, tests or tries the product to determine if it meets his or her needs.
* *Adoption.* The buyer purchases the product and can be expected to use it again whenever the need for this general type of product arises.[14]

product adoption process
The stages buyers go through in accepting a product

In the first stage, when individuals become aware that the product exists, they have little information about it and are not concerned about obtaining more. Consumers enter the interest stage when they are motivated to get information about the product's features, uses, advantages, disadvantages, price or location. During the evaluation stage, individuals consider whether the product will satisfy certain criteria that are crucial to meeting their specific needs. In the trial stage, they use or experience the product for the first time, possibly by purchasing a small quantity, taking advantage of free samples or borrowing the product from someone. Individuals move into the adoption stage by choosing a specific product when they need a product of that general type. Entering the adoption process does not mean that the person will eventually adopt the new product. Rejection may occur at any stage, including the adoption stage. Both product adoption and product rejection can be temporary or permanent.

Consumer adoption categories

When an organisation introduces a new product, people do not begin the adoption process at the same time, nor do they move through the process at the same speed. This variance is because some consumers are more risk averse than others, while some are willing to try a new product before others in the market. Of those who eventually adopt the product, some enter the adoption process rather quickly, whereas others start considerably later. For most products, there is also a group of non-adopters who never begin the process.

Depending on the length of time it takes them to adopt a new product, consumers fall into one of five major adopter categories: innovators, early adopters, early majority, late majority and laggards.[15] Figure 8.4 illustrates each consumer adopter category and the percentage of total adopters it typically represents. Innovators are the first to adopt a new product; they enjoy trying new products and tend to be more adventurous consumers. When introducing a new product to the market, the marketing strategies are focused on raising awareness of that new product and therefore marketers will deliberately target the innovators. Early adopters choose new products carefully and are quite typically well informed, opinion leaders within the segment of interest. Those consumers in the remaining adopter categories will tend to follow these early adopters and therefore move the product life cycle from the growth phase of the product life cycle towards the maturity phase. Consumers in the early majority adopt just prior to the average person. Early majority consumers are deliberate and cautious in trying new products. Individuals in the late majority are quite sceptical of new products but eventually adopt them because of economic necessity or social pressure. Laggards are the last to adopt a new

innovators
First adopters of new products

early adopters
Careful choosers of new products

early majority
Those adopting new products just before the average person

late majority
Sceptics who adopt new products when they feel it is necessary

laggards
The last adopters, who distrust new products

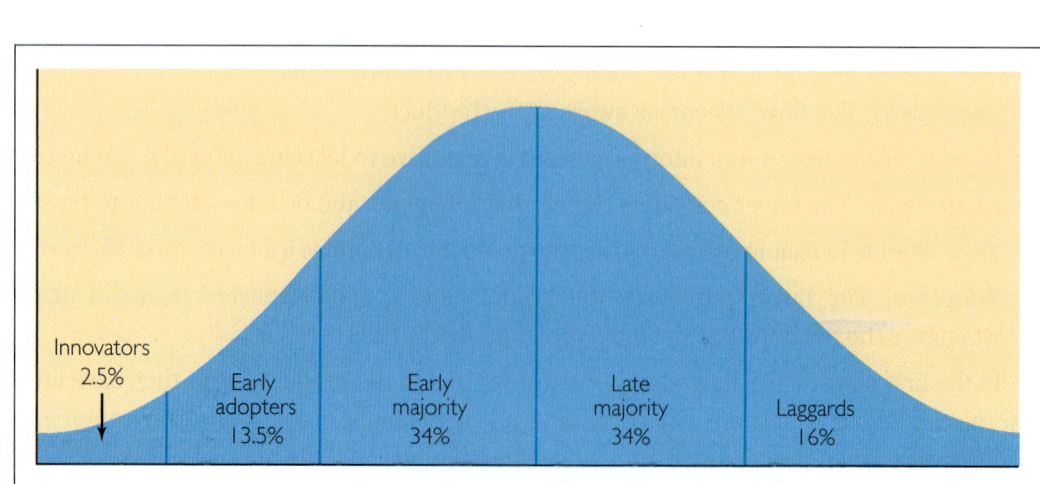

FIGURE 8.4
DISTRIBUTION OF CONSUMER ADOPTION CATEGORIES

Source: Reprinted with permission of The Free Press, a division of Simon & Schuster Adult Publishing Group, from *Diffusion of Innovations*, Fourth Edition, by Everett M. Rogers. Copyright © 1995 by Everett M. Rogers. Copyright © 1962, 1971, 1983 by The Free Press. All rights reserved.

product and are predominantly risk averse and oriented toward the past. They are highly suspicious of new products and when they finally adopt the innovation, the product may have already moved into the decline phase of the product life cycle. Laggards are last and may even miss the boat entirely by waiting until the product is so well established in the marketplace that the product may have been replaced by a new product or reinvented with an incremental innovation that repositions the product and hence extends the product life cycle. The laggards will choose the original version of the product because they will consider the improved version untrusted. Unlike the laggards, the early adopters will again choose the new and improved product and hence the cycle begins again moving from the introduction of the product, through to the growth stage and so on.

REVISE your understanding of product adoption by taking the Online Revision Quiz

Packaging functions, design consideration and strategy

Packaging involves the development of a container and a graphic design for a product. A package can be a vital part of a product, making it more versatile, safer and easier to use. Like a brand name, a package can influence customers' attitudes toward a product and so affect their purchase decisions. For example, several producers of jams, sauces and yoghurts have packaged their products in squeezable plastic containers to make usage and storage more convenient, whereas several paint manufacturers have introduced easy-to-open-and-pour paint cans. Other manufacturers are striving towards more sustainable packaging options, as shown in the Sustainable Marketing box below. Package characteristics help to shape buyers' impressions of a product at the time of purchase or during use. In this section we examine the main functions of packaging and consider several major packaging decisions. We also analyse the role of the package in a marketing strategy.

SUSTAINABLE MARKETING | SUSTAINABLE PACKAGING AT GUCCI

Gone are the plastic laminated fashion bags for Gucci. Demonstrating their stand on corporate social responsibility, Gucci now offers their range of products packaged in the subtle luminosity of beater-dyed paper prominently labelled with the de-bossed GG logo. The new packaging for the Gucci brand was created by Frida Giannini and it is 100 per cent recyclable. Cotton ribbons replace polyester and the paper itself is certified by the Forest Stewardship Council® to ensure that no paper is sourced from endangered forests. As a further step towards being environmentally friendly, Gucci is considering using other biodegradable packaging materials such as corn, bamboo and cotton.

Source: Getty Images

Packaging functions

Effective packaging involves more than simply putting products in containers and covering them with wrappers. First, packaging materials serve the basic purpose of protecting the product and maintaining its functional form. Fluids such as milk and orange juice need packages that preserve and protect them. The packaging should prevent damage that could affect the product's usefulness and thus lead to higher costs. Since product tampering has become a problem, several packaging techniques have been developed to counter this danger and hence comply with governmental regulations. Some packaging is also designed to deter shoplifting.

Another function of packaging is to offer convenience to consumers. For example, small, individual-size boxes or plastic bags that contain liquids and do not require refrigeration strongly appeal to children and young adults with active lifestyles. The size or shape of a package may relate to the product's storage, convenience of use or replacement rate. Small, single-serving packages of sliced vegetables, for instance, may prevent waste and make storage easier. A third function of packaging is to promote a product by communicating its features, uses, benefits and image. Sometimes a reusable package is developed to make the product more desirable. For example, the Australian-owned food company Outback Spirit packages herbs in reusable tins.

Source: Robins Foods Pty. Ltd.

Reusable and convenient packaging >> Outback Spirit are relying on these reusable tins to make their product more desirable to consumers

Major packaging considerations

When developing packages, marketers must take many factors into account. Obviously, one major consideration is cost. Although a number of different packaging materials, processes and designs are available, costs vary greatly. In recent years, buyers have shown a willingness to pay more for improved packaging, but there are limits.

Marketers should consider how much consistency is desirable among an organisation's package designs. No consistency may be the best policy, especially if a company's products are unrelated or aimed at vastly different target markets. To promote an overall company image, a company may decide that all packages should be similar or include one major element of the design. This approach is called family packaging. All Nespresso coffee blends come in identically sized individual metallic pods, designed to fit perfectly with Nespresso brand coffee machines.

A package's promotional role is an important consideration. Through verbal and non-verbal symbols, the package can inform potential buyers about the product's content, features, uses, advantages and hazards. A company can create desirable images and associations by its choice of colour, design, shape and texture. Many cosmetics manufacturers, for example, design their packages to create impressions of richness, luxury and exclusiveness. To develop a package that has a definite promotional value, a designer must consider size, shape, texture, colour and graphics. Beyond the obvious limitation that the package must be large enough to hold the product, a package can be designed to appear taller or shorter. Light-coloured packaging may make a package appear larger, whereas darker colours may minimise the perceived size.

Colours on packages are often chosen to attract attention, and colour can positively influence customers' emotions. People often associate specific colours with certain feelings and experiences. Blue is soothing and associated with wealth, trust and security. Grey is associated with strength, exclusivity and success. Orange can stand for low cost. Red connotes excitement and stimulation. Purple is associated with dignity and stateliness. Yellow connotes cheerfulness and joy. Black is associated with being strong and masterful. When opting for colour on packaging, marketers must judge whether a particular colour will evoke positive or negative feelings when linked to a specific product. Rarely, for example, do processors package meat or bread in green materials because customers may associate green with mould. Marketers also must determine whether a specific target market will respond favourably or unfavourably to a particular colour. Packages designed to appeal to children often use primary colours and bold designs.

Packaging also must meet the needs of resellers. Wholesalers and retailers consider whether a package facilitates transportation, storage and handling. Resellers may refuse to carry certain products if their packages are cumbersome. Concentrated versions of laundry detergents and fabric softeners aid retailers in offering more product diversity within the existing shelf space.

Packaging and marketing strategy

Packaging can be a major component of a marketing strategy. A new cap or closure, a better box or wrapper, or a more convenient container may give a product a competitive advantage. The right type of package for a new product can help it to gain market recognition very quickly. Mini Babybel cheese, for example, had this in mind when packaging their cheese products. Designed to target consumers who live a busy lifestyle, Babybel cheese

family packaging
Using similar packaging for all of a company's products or packaging that has one common design element

are bite-sized ellipsoid portions, encased in red wax for which the product is now famous. This style of packaging keeps the product fresh and makes it portable enough for the lunchbox or desk. In the case of existing brands, marketers should re-evaluate packages periodically. Marketers should view packaging as a major strategic tool, especially for consumer convenience products. For instance, in the food industry, jumbo and large package sizes for products such as hot dogs, pizzas, English muffins, frozen dinners and biscuits have been very successful. When considering the strategic uses of packaging, marketers must also analyse the cost of packaging and package changes. Some packaging decisions are out of the marketer's control, as is the case of tobacco products (see Did you know? box at left). In this section we examine several ways in which packaging can be used strategically.

Altering the package

At times, a marketer changes a package because the existing design is no longer in style, especially when compared with the packaging of competitive products. Goulburn Valley now packages fruit in plastic screw top containers rather than in an aluminum tin, keeping fruit fresher after opening and eliminating the need for customers to transfer contents to a sealable container. A package may be redesigned because new product features need to be highlighted or because new packaging materials have become available.

For example, Australian and New Zealand wines are widely recognised throughout the world as being of good quality. While Europe offers traditional styles of wines and a traditional approach to wine-making, Australia and New Zealand are more technologically driven. The success of Australian bottled wine continues to rise, with the current overall volume of Australian wine being exported at 698 million litres, which is an export value of $1.82 billion.[17] In terms of value, Australian wine accounts for the highest importation of wine in the United Kingdom as well as New Zealand and is second highest in the US. In keeping with the technological focus on wine production, Australia also has a history of leading innovations within wine packaging. Thomas Angove created cask wine in 1970 and more recently Lupé Wines have launched The Single Serve concept in both 187 ml and 150 ml volumes. The idea behind the concept is that this single-serve packaging offers a user-friendly design for both consumers and service providers of outdoor events and venues. Using an injection mold technique the wine is served in a no-glass, recyclable, sophisticated package that is fast to chill, fast to serve and tamper resistant.

Source: Courtesy of Lupé Single Serve Packaging

Altering the package >>
The Single Serve was named one of BRW's top 10 start-ups of 2012 and they are now expanding their single-serve concept outside of the wine industry[18]

Secondary-use packaging

A secondary-use package is one that can be reused for purposes other than its initial function. For example, a margarine container can be reused to store leftovers, and a jam jar can serve as a drinking glass. Customers often view secondary-use packaging as adding value to products, in which case its use should stimulate unit sales. Some promotions even deliberately design the packaging to serve as a second use, such as a jam jar being used as an everyday kitchen glass.

Category-consistent packaging

With category-consistent packaging, the product is packaged in line with the packaging practices associated with a particular product category. Some product categories – for example, mayonnaise, mustard, tomato sauce and peanut butter – have traditional package shapes. Other product categories are characterised by recognisable colour combinations, such as red and white for soup and red, blue, green and yellow for cleaning products, and purple for chocolate. When an organisation introduces a brand in one of these product categories, marketers often will use traditional package shapes and colour combinations to ensure that customers will recognise the new product as being in that specific product category.

Innovative packaging

Sometimes a marketer employs a unique cap, design, applicator or other feature to make a product distinctive. Such packaging can be effective when the innovation makes the product safer or easier to use or provides better protection for the product. In some instances, marketers use innovative or unique packages that are inconsistent with traditional packaging practices to make the brand stand out from its competitors. Unusual packaging sometimes requires spending considerable resources not only on package design but also on making customers aware of the unique package and its benefits. Moreover, the research findings suggest that uniquely shaped packages that attract attention are more likely to be perceived as containing a higher volume of product.[19]

Multiple packaging

Rather than packaging a single unit of a product, marketers sometimes use twin-packs, tri-packs, six-packs or other forms of multiple packaging. For certain types of products, multiple packaging may increase demand because it increases the amount of the product available at the point of consumption (in one's house, for example). It also may increase consumer acceptance of the product by encouraging the buyer to try the product several times. Multiple packaging can make products easier to handle and store, as in the case of six-packs for soft drinks.

Handling-improved packaging

A product's packaging may be changed to make it easier to handle in the distribution channel – for example, by changing the outer carton or using special bundling, shrink-wrapping or pallets. In some cases, the shape of the package is changed. Outer containers for products are sometimes changed so that they will proceed more easily through automated warehousing systems.

L06

labelling
Providing identifying, promotional or other information on package labels

Labelling and legal issues

Labelling is very closely interrelated with packaging and is used for identification, promotional, informational and legal purposes. Labels can be small or large relative to the size of the product and carry varying amounts of information. Pacific Coast Eco Bananas are distinguished from other bananas by a red wax tip. Grown in North Queensland, Pacific Coast Eco Bananas promote a better taste and healthier option for both consumers and the environment. Using an ecologically sensitive farming system, these red-tipped bananas are sweeter and creamier with a longer shelf life. As well as these bananas being a healthier option for consumers, this form of banana farming is an ecologically sensitive farming system that improves the environmental health of the farm, soil fertility and the surrounding ecosystem, including the World Heritage listed Great Barrier Reef. The red wax tip is, therefore, a highly visible label indicating a healthy option for both consumers and the environment.

A label can also be part of the package itself or a separate feature attached to the package. The label on a can of Coca-Cola is actually part of the can, whereas the label on a 2-litre bottle of Coca-Cola is separate and can be removed. Information presented on a label may include the brand name and mark, the registered trademark symbol, package size and content, product features, nutritional information, potential presence of allergens, type and style of the product, number of servings, care instructions, directions for use and safety precautions, the name and address of the manufacturer, expiration dates, seals of approval and other facts.

A product label is a direct means of communicating product information between buyers and sellers. From a public policy perspective, the purpose of a product label is to maximise public confidence in product safety by enabling consumers to make informed choices. For consumers then, a product label can provide basic product information including ingredients and nutritional information, manufacturer details and promotional messages. Labels are a source of information regarding a product's association with environmental organisations (refer to the Marketing in Transition box below). For marketers and manufacturers, a product label is also a means to differentiate between individual products and brands and therefore facilitate an informed choice.

MARKETING IN TRANSITION | HOW GREEN IS THAT PRODUCT? CHECK THE LABEL

The eco industry is booming with products using labels such as 'eco-friendly', 'environmentally friendly', 'sustainable' and 'green' in order to more effectively satisfy environmentally conscious customers. As a consequence, codes and guidelines are being developed to create standards which dictate what these terms actually mean and who can use them on their products. Some widely used green certification labels and designations include:

→ *Energy rating labels.* An Australian government-initiated mandatory label found on electrical appliances including dishwashers, televisions, clothes washers, refrigerators and air conditioners. The energy rating label features a star rating and estimates the annual energy consumption of the product, enabling consumers to compare the energy efficiency of domestic appliances. The label provides an incentive for manufacturers to improve

Source: FSC Australia used with permission of FSC Australia Trademark Services Unit

the energy performance of appliances (http://www.energyrating.gov.au).

→ *Forest Stewardship Council® (FSC®).* An international non-profit organisation promoting environmentally appropriate, socially beneficial and economically viable management of the world's forests. FSC® labelled products may include furniture, office paper, toilet tissue, building materials and stationery. The label provides recognition for responsible forest management throughout the product's production process (http://www.au.fsc.org).

→ *Good Environmental Choice.* An Australian voluntary eco-label program awarding a mark of recognition for products and services that meet standards of environmental, quality and social performance. The

label is designed to give manufacturers, distributors and marketers the financial benefits of dealing in and producing environmentally preferable products (http://www.geca.org.au).

→ *Marine Stewardship Council (MSC).* The MSC is the leading global non-profit certification and eco-labelling program for sustainable seafood, providing environmental standards for sustainable and well-managed fishery practices. In order to achieve MSC certification, fisheries must demonstrate – through a scientifically robust, independent assessment process – that the seafood stocks being targeted are healthy, the fishing practices being used have minimal impact on the marine eco-system and overall the fishery is well managed. Around 120 fisheries worldwide have already been certified to the MSC environmental standard, and more are on the way all the time (http://www.msc.org).

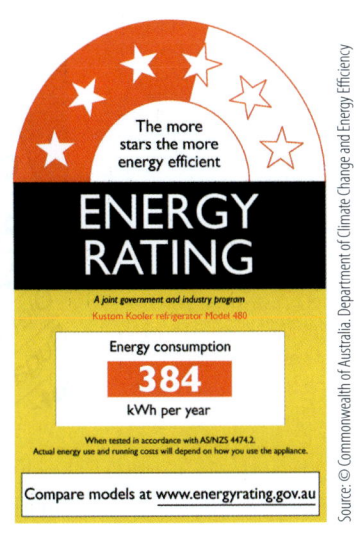

Source: © Commonwealth of Australia, Department of Climate Change and Energy Efficiency

In Australia and New Zealand, labelling is not regulated by either Commonwealth or State governments. Rather, each industry in each Australian state and territory has to look to more than one law to ensure compliance with relevant packaging and labelling requirements. This becomes very complicated when products are marketed in more than one state or territory because the number of regulations increases and requires constant monitoring to comply with changes.

At the federal level, no single Australian agency has taken responsibility for the development of a national labelling policy. There are actually several agencies responsible for developing labelling requirements. This arrangement does mean unnecessary costs for both businesses and consumers, and an increasing complexity of poorly coordinated

Source: Shutterstock.com

Food labelling >>
The information provided on nutrition panels helps us choose healthier food

obligations. Businesses are, therefore, required to make contact with a number of different agencies at both state and federal levels to obtain information, which at times might be incomplete, contradictory and frequently changing. The goal is, however, to ensure that consumers are provided with the information required to make an informed decision.

Food Standards of Australia and New Zealand (FSANZ) is the governing body responsible for the development and administration of the *Australia New Zealand Food Standards Code*. This code lists labelling requirements for food additives, food safety and genetically modified foods. The enforcement and interpretation of the Code is not the responsibility of any one agency, but rather, this responsibility is spread across various state and territory government departments and food agencies. Any food product for which a nutritional claim is made must have nutrition labelling that follows a standard format. Food product labels must state the number of servings per container, serving size, number of calories per serving, number of calories derived from fat, number of carbohydrates and amounts of specific nutrients such as vitamins. In addition, new nutritional labelling requirements focus on the amounts of trans-fatty acids in food products. Although consumers have responded favourably to this type of information on labels, evidence as to whether they actually use it has been mixed. Another governing body responsible for labelling regulations is the Therapeutic Goods Administration (TGA), which is the primary regulatory body for medical drugs and devices. This administrative body was formulated in 1983 to limit the availability of many products of concern to the US-based Food and Drug Administration (FDA).

The use of new technology in the production and processing of food has led to additional food labelling issues. Of concern to many manufacturers, especially those outsourcing to countries other than their own, are the increasingly complex labelling requirements related to country of origin. Manufacturers are increasingly competing in global markets and a product's country of origin becomes an important cue in evaluating the quality and value of the product. A consumer's perception on country of origin plays a role in influencing a consumer's product choice.

In some cases, consumers associate certain products with country of origin. Consider products such as Swiss watches, Italian fashion, German cars and French wine as opposed to Australian wine. The country of origin plays a role in consumers' perceptions of quality. In recognition of the effect country of origin has on consumer perceptions of value and quality, some products are foreign branded. Foreign branding is a marketing strategy whereby product naming, packaging and advertising implies superiority through the adoption or association with foreign-sounding names. Foreign branding directs consumers to desirable product or brand associations. The following brands are examples of foreign branding:

* Häagen-Dazs premium ice-cream – European-sounding name, Oakland California manufacturer
* Le Tigre Clothing – French-sounding name, American clothing brand
* Dolmio Italian Pasta Sauce – Italian name, Australian brand now owned by Mars
* Ginsu knives – Japanese-sounding name, American brand.

Study Tools

Chapter review

LO1 UNDERSTAND THE CONCEPT OF A PRODUCT AND HOW PRODUCTS ARE CLASSIFIED.

A product is a good, a service, an idea or any combination of the three received in an exchange. A product can be tangible and/or intangible and includes functional, social and psychological utilities or benefits. When consumers purchase a product, they are buying the benefits and satisfaction they think the product will provide. Products can be classified on the basis of the buyer's intentions. Consumer products are those purchased to satisfy personal and family needs. Business products are purchased for use in a company's operations, to resell or to make other products. Consumer products can be subdivided into convenience, shopping, specialty and unsought products. Business products can be classified as installations, accessory equipment, raw materials, component parts, process materials, maintenance, repair and operating (MRO) supplies and business services.

LO2 UNDERSTAND THE CONNECTION BETWEEN THE CONCEPTS OF PRODUCT LINE AND PRODUCT MIX.

A product item is a specific version of a product that can be designated as a distinct offering among an organisation's products. A product line is a group of closely related product items that are considered a unit because of marketing, technical or end-use considerations. The composite, or total, group of products that an organisation makes available to customers is called the product mix. The product mix is considered in terms of both width and depth. The width of the product mix is measured by the number of product lines the company offers. The depth of the product mix is the average number of different products offered in each product line.

LO3 UNDERSTAND THE CONCEPT OF PRODUCT LIFE CYCLE AND ITS IMPACT ON MARKETING STRATEGIES.

The product life cycle is depicted as a graph that plots sales over time. The plotted curve describes how product items in an industry move through four stages: introduction, growth, maturity and decline. The curve is at zero at introduction because sale of the product is yet to begin and consumer awareness is low. At the introduction stage, therefore, marketing strategy is focused on raising consumer awareness. Following the introduction phase, the curve rises at an increasing rate during growth, given more and more consumers are becoming aware of the product and sales are increasing. Profits peak toward the end of the growth stage of the product life cycle. Once the majority of the market have chosen to consume the product and sales have peaked, the product life cycle moves into maturity where a plateau in the sales curve is observed. From there, unless the product is repositioned, with a new technological innovation for example, the sales will begin to decline and the product will fade from the marketplace.

 **UNDERSTAND THE CONSUMER ADOPTION PROCESS AND THE CONNECTION TO THE PRODUCT LIFE CYCLE.**

Not all consumers move through the product adoption process at the same speed. Some consumers are more willing to try a new product than others. Those consumers most willing to adopt a new product is the smallest percentage group of consumers in a market and are labelled innovators. Astute marketers will deliberately target innovators at the introduction phase of the product life cycle. To move the product into the growth phase of the product life cycle, marketing strategy will focus on raising awareness within the early majority consumers. The early majority consumers are typically well informed opinion leaders. Once the early majority choose to adopt the product, the late majority will follow and sales will peak, thus moving the product into the maturity phase of the product life cycle. From there, laggards finally opt in when the product life cycle is in decline.

 UNDERSTAND THE MAJOR PACKAGING FUNCTIONS AND DESIGN CONSIDERATIONS AS USED IN MARKETING STRATEGIES.

Packaging involves the development of a container and a graphic design for a product. Effective packaging offers protection, economy, safety and convenience. Effective packaging options can influence a customer's purchase decision by promoting features, uses, benefits and image. When developing a package, marketers must consider the value to the customer of efficient and effective packaging, offset by the price the customer is willing to pay. Other considerations include how to make the package tamper-resistant, whether to use multiple packaging and family packaging, how to design the package as an effective promotional tool, and how to best accommodate resellers. Packaging can be an important part of an overall marketing strategy and can be used to target certain market segments. Modifications in packaging can revive a mature product and extend its product life cycle. Producers alter packages to convey new features or to make them safer or more convenient. If a package has a secondary use, the product's value to the consumer may increase. Category-consistent packaging makes products more easily recognised by consumers. Innovative packaging enhances a product's distinctiveness.

 **UNDERSTAND THE FUNCTIONS OF LABELLING AND SELECTED LEGAL ISSUES.**

Labelling is closely interrelated with packaging and is used for identification, promotional and informational and legal purposes. Various federal and state laws and agency regulations require that certain products be labelled or marked with warnings, instructions, nutritional information, manufacturer's identification and perhaps other information.

Key concepts

 Search me!

Use these key terms in **Search me! marketing** to find the latest relevant readings from a wide range of world-class journals, e-books and newspapers, including *The Australian*.

- accessory equipment
- business products
- business services
- component parts
- consumer products
- convenience products
- decline stage
- depth of product mix
- early adopters
- early majority
- family packaging
- good
- growth stage
- idea
- innovators
- installations
- introduction stage
- labelling
- laggards
- late majority
- maturity stage
- MRO supplies
- process materials
- product adoption process
- product item
- product life cycle
- product line
- product mix
- raw materials
- service
- shopping products
- specialty products
- unsought products
- width of product mix

Issues for discussion and review

1 Describe your mobile phone in terms of the product concept, encompassing the multiple good/service/symbolism components.

2 Consider the impact of technology in the following product categories:
   a shoes
   b cameras
   c lingerie.

3 Adoption of tablet technology is evident in both consumer markets and business markets. Discuss the different needs of these two markets.

4 Choose three products and analyse these three products in terms of product mix.

5 What is the difference between product mix depth and product mix width? Provide examples.

6 How do marketing efforts change as a product moves through the four stages of the product life cycle?

7 Describe the consumer adoption process categories and how these categories relate to the product life cycle.

8 Describe how a product can be packaged to encourage consumer adoption. Give an example from your recent consumption choices.

9 How can packaging be used as a strategic tool?

Marketing applications

1 Choose a familiar clothing store. Describe the range this clothing store carries in terms of product lines and product mix, including the depth and width of that product mix. Evaluate the product mix and make suggestions to the owner.

2 Tobacco is a product that has entered the maturity stage of the product life cycle and government regulations and taxation law is designed to further discourage tobacco

consumption. However, tobacco giants are now venturing into the e-cigarette market. Describe this technological innovation in terms of the product life cycle.

3   When do you choose to buy a new product? Are you at the front of the market with the innovators and the early adopters or at the back end with the laggards? How does marketing impact your decision whether or not to adopt a product?

4   Dog food in tubes, Coca-Cola in a plastic bag, education online. Discuss the innovative ways that products can be packaged.

5   Many goods and services are encouraging consumer co-creation in the product design process. Consider the advantages and disadvantages with co-creation.

ONLINE EXERCISE

6   Beginning Boutique (http://beginningboutique.com.au/) is an online fashion website founded by Sarah Timmerman in 2008. Now beyond the introduction stage of the product life cycle, Beginning Boutique could be described as currently in the growth phase and social media strategies are key. Facebook advertising spend achieved a 70 per cent return on investment and an 11 per cent increase in sales during 2012. Research is indicating that four in 10 consumers who share or favourite a post on Facebook, Twitter or Pinterest will make a purchase. More specifically, Pinterest is the social media network most likely to drive sales.[20]

    a   How does Beginning Boutique communicate information to consumers on social media about product offers?

    b   How does Beginning Boutique's website demonstrate product and design features?

    c   What social media activity has Beginning Boutique used to position itself in the marketplace?

Developing your marketing plan

Identifying the needs of consumer groups and developing products that satisfy those needs is essential when creating a marketing strategy. Successful product development begins with a clear understanding of fundamental product concepts. The product concept is the basis on which many of the marketing plan decisions are made. When relating the information in this chapter to the development of your marketing plan, consider the following:

1   Using Figure 8.1 as a guide, create a matrix of the current product mix for your company.

2   Discuss how the marketing strategy for your product will change as it moves through each of the phases of the product life cycle.

3   Create a brief profile of the type of consumer who is likely to represent each of the product adopter categories for your product.

4   Outline the packaging design, function and colour. Explain why you have chosen each element of the packaging.

5   Discuss the factors that could contribute to the failure of your product. How will you define product failure?

CengageNOW

Go to http:\\login.cengagebrain.com to link to CengageNOW, your online study tool.
First take the Pre-Test for this chapter to get your Personalised Study Plan, and then:

* Revise your understanding of the key concepts of marketing with the online glossary

* Watch an interactive animation of strategic marketing to broaden your subject comprehension

* Listen to an audio summary of the learning objectives covered in this chapter.

After you have completed the activities in your Personalised Study Plan take the Post-Test to determine what concepts you have mastered and what you still need to work on.

Case study

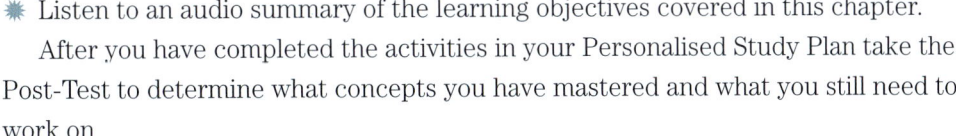

PRODUCT STRATEGY AND INNOVATION AT GLACÉAU VITAMINWATER

Feeling thirsty, run-down and bored? Chances are you're part of the consumer trend towards more thirst-quenching, new-age beverages (typically non-alcoholic, non-carbonated, innovative, single-serve drinks).[21] Do you prefer your new-age drink to be coffee-based, tea-based, water-based, dairy-based, juice-based, energy or sports? Within each of these categories is a dazzling array of brands – 1500 new-age beverage brands in the United States alone.[22] Water is the most popular new-age beverage, attracting nearly one-third of spending.[23] Within this category, enhanced, flavoured and essence water has been doing particularly well, driven by growing consumer concern about health and wellness, as well as an interest in trying something new.[24]

The world's leading non-alcoholic beverage producer, The Coca-Cola Company (TCCC) is driven to successfully adapt to the rapidly changing non-alcoholic beverage business environment – 'a result of changes in consumer preferences, including changes based on health and nutrition considerations and obesity concerns; shifting consumer tastes and needs; changes in consumer lifestyles; and competitive product and pricing pressures'.[25] In 2013, the company's website claimed TCCC is 'refreshing consumers with more than 500 sparkling and still brands', 'bringing more innovation, information and choices to everyone', and has four 'commitments to address obesity' (smaller portions, low kilojoule beverage options, transparent nutritional labelling and activity programs).

Pioneering a response to these consumer trends since 1996 is Energy Brands Inc., also trading as Glacéau. Feeling run-down and on his way to a yoga class, Glacéau founder, Darius Bikoff, ate a vitamin C lozenge and chased it with a swig of water. The combination of flavour and nourishment inspired Bikoff to develop and launch Glacéau Vitaminwater. He initially introduced a line of enhanced waters

Source: fdilibrary.com.au

to smaller independent natural food stores in New York, gradually expanding nationally. Eventually, the company came to the attention of TCCC. In an effort to grow its product portfolio for still beverage offerings, TCCC acquired Energy Brands in 2007 for approx. US$4.1 billion.[26]

As a TCCC subsidiary, Glacéau continues to operate under the direction of Bikoff. Its aim is to satisfy demand worldwide (via retailers or to distributors, wholesalers and bottling partners in 26 countries) for its 'active lifestyle' beverages. With its slogan 'hydrate responsibly', Glacéau currently has two main product lines within the enhanced or premium bottled water segment, each subtly different:

→ *Smartwater* – vapour-distilled water with added electrolytes.

→ *Vitaminwater* – Smartwater plus added vitamins and natural flavours.
  ■ There are over 10 variations of Vitaminwater (depending on location) – all related to one health benefit or another, e.g. Vitaminwater XXX (triple antioxidants). In the UK, Truvia (a Stevia-based sugar substitute, developed jointly by TCCC and Cargill) was introduced in 2012 to reduce the sugar levels by 30 per cent.
  ■ Vitaminwater Zero (calorie-free with Truvia).

Ranked the number one beverage by a US industry beverage source, trademarked Vitaminwater is considered the most successful of the two.[27] It is touted as 'a nutrient-packed, great-tasting water with added electrolytes' (http://www.Glacéau.com) or, more soberly, as a nutrient-enhanced water beverage which hydrates responsibly without sodium and artificial ingredients (no artificial sweeteners, no artificial colours) (http://www.thecoca-cola company.com).

The vibrancy of Vitaminwater's brand positioning is manifest in the colours of the drink, matching colour-blocked labels, as well as energetic, quirky names and product descriptions. Compared with competitors, such as Gatorade, the tone of Glacéau's communication with consumers is friendlier and more cerebral, and the focus is on health and lifestyle, rather than performance. Glacéau's Facebook page states: 'Each Glacéau Vitaminwater is packed full of 10 life-loving vitamins and minerals plus a hero vitamin or two'. These product characteristics mirror the imagery and verbiage (e.g. 'Make boring brilliant') that today's internet generation – a primary Glacéau target market – are familiar with and interact with on a daily basis.

Vitaminwater is at the forefront of interactive brand promotion. This helps TCCC, which acknowledges that 'changes in consumer's media preferences, such as the shift away from traditional mass media to the Internet, may undermine the effectiveness of our media advertising campaigns in reaching consumers and may increase our marketing costs'.[28] Glacéau Vitaminwater successfully uses mobile and SMS media as a promotional tool, especially in regard to Generation Y consumers.[29] Glacéau also routinely interacts with customers via Facebook, fostering discussion among product fans, such as 'what's the next flavour to be discontinued?, 'side effects' and 'why is there no Vitaminwater in Germany?', thereby increasing the product's word-of-mouth attributes and building consumer brand awareness.[30]

In addition, Glacéau has used its website and Facebook page to crowdsource and co-create product innovation with consumers. Notably, in September 2009, the Flavour Generator competition created a new variant 'Connect'. The video call to action was a classic six to eight week 'contest' cycle, which many FMCGs use as a best practice time period to focus people's attention. In

November, Glacéau announced the flavour and the top three recipes. The winners and the package design were announced in January 2010. By March 2010, the product was on the shelves. This contest not only increased consumer-brand interaction but also provided immense market research data and is an example of sophisticated crowdsourcing.

Similarly, Glacéau's website for Vitaminwater provides a platform for its community of consumers to share designs and ideas with the tantalising invitation: 'We haven't made this brilliant yet because we think you can. Correct, you can fight boredom. You can tame it with your brilliant touch. Tickle its furry belly. Just tweet your brilliant videos, gifs, pics, and comments to @vitaminwater and be sure to c'mon back. (especially if you're bored.) One up it.' While these Internet and Facebook pages don't give the ability to mix flavours together to create a new one, they allow the monitoring of social media buzz on the top flavours in contention. They pull in social chatter from sources such as Google News, Twitter, Flickr and Foodgawker, which means that tweets, blogposts, searchers and images could contribute toward a range of marketing decisions, including product design. The more chatter on a flavour, for instance, the more likely it will make the final top 10 list.[31]

Despite Vitaminwater's success, some issues loom. Its credibility as a health drink is at stake in the face of criticism from the US Food and Drug Administration and the UK Advertising Standards Authority that it is just a sugary snack food.[32] Further, consumer beverage preferences are fickle and fast-changing. The biggest trend is now toward low-/no-calorie drinks. In 2010, Glacéau's Vitaminwater sales plunged 22 per cent, with sales being cannibalised by the launch of Truvia-sweetened Vitaminwater 10 (since repositioned as a zero-calorie line) and Vitaminwater Zero.[33] Hence, the response in the UK to reformulate the original Vitaminwater with Truvia. TCCC is also expanding its still-water brand portfolio, which now includes Oasis, Capri-Sun and 5 Alive, in addition to Vitaminwater. TCCC is also adding new categories to its product range, such as non-alcoholic 'adult socialising', for which Cascade was acquired in Australia in 2012 and relaunched in 2013. Another issue facing Glacéau is how best to manage its Vitaminwater portfolio across the globe, given the global marketing imperative 'standardise where possible' to achieve efficiencies, and 'adapt where necessary' to address local market needs. Clearly, ensuring its product strategy is contemporary and effective remains one of Glacéau's key challenges.

Tania von der Heidt, Southern Cross University

QUESTIONS FOR DISCUSSION

1 What are the product line and mix issues at Glacéau? Make some recommendations for improvement.

2 Define the concepts 'crowdsourcing' and 'co-creation'. What are their pros and cons? Do you think that digital crowdsourcing and co-creation are effective ways for Glacéau to undertake product innovation? What are some alternatives?

3 Go to websites hosted by Glacéau, e.g. its Facebook page http://www.facebook.com/Glacéauvitaminwateranz, its home page http://www.Glacéau.com and http://www.vitaminwater.com/ and check out the latest discussion topics. To what extent does this consumer feedback provide value to the company, e.g. provide impetus for product innovation?

Chapter endnotes

1. Michael Bleby, 'Lego ups the ante for an unforgiving crowd of architects', *Business Review Weekly*, August 2, 2013, accessed August 3, 2013, http://www.brw.com.au/p/professions/lego_ups_the_ante_for_an_unforgiving_0buYUxJxx18CM1WGqjEncl

2. Jamie Carter, 'Best headphones: 10 top headphones for sound quality', *techradar.av*, May 21, 2013, accessed November 16, 2013, http://www.techradar.com/us/news/audio/portable-audio/best-headphones-10-top-headphones-for-sound-quality-1153023.

3. 'Chinese retailer plans to open 1,000 virtual supermarkets', Peer1 hosting Ping & People, October 18, 2012, accessed November 16, 2013, http://www.peer1hosting.co.uk/industry-news/chinese-retailer-plans-open-1000-virtual-supermarkets.

4. 'Surfer Girl Facebook Page Statistics in Indonesia', Socialbakers, accessed November 16, 2013, http://www.socialbakers.com/facebook-pages/9095464410-surfer-girl/in-indonesia.

5. R. J. Whitehead, 'Halal ready for export to a growing number of non-Muslim markets', Foodnavigator-asia.com, accessed November 16, 2013, http://www.foodnavigator-asia.com/Markets/Halal-ready-for-export-to-a-growing-number-of-non-Muslim-markets.

6. Norman Day, (2005), 'National Australia Bank', *The Age*, http://www.theage.com.au/news/Reviews/National-Australia-Bank/2005/02/20/1108834654243.html.

7. Bonnie Alter, (2009), 'Cadbury's Dairy Milk chocolate bar goes fair trade', Mother Nature Network, http://www.mnn.com/money/sustainable-business-practices/stories/cadburys-dairy-milk-chocolate-bar-goes-fair-trade#.

8. Michael D. Johnson, Andreas Herrmann, and Frank Huber, 'Evolution of Loyalty Intentions', *Journal of Marketing* 70 (April 2006): http://www.marketingpower.com.

9. Ashish Mishra, 'Best Indian Brands 2013', accessed August 3, 2013, http://www.interbrand.com/en/best-global-brands/region-country/best-indian-brands/indias-top-30-brands.aspx.

10. 'Company Profile', Elken, accessed November 16, 2013, http://www.elken.com/my/en/company-profile.

11. O. C. Ferrell and Michael Heartline, *Marketing Strategy* (Mason, OH: South-Western, 2008): 172–173.

12. Liam Ducey, 'Kombi van officially at the end of the (production) line', *WA Today*, August 16, 2013, accessed August 17, 2013, http://www.watoday.com.au/wa-news/kombi-van-officially-at-the-end-of-the-production-line-20130816-2s0ws.html.

13. 'Lighting up or putting out? Global trends in smoking prevalence', Euromonitor International, accessed August 3, 2013, http://blog.euromonitor.com/tobacco/; 'Tobacco in Asia-Pacific: Driver of the global marketing – will it remain the tobacco market powerhouse?', Euromonitor International, accessed August 3, 2013, http://www.euromonitor.com/tobacco-in-asia-pacific-driver-of-the-global-market-will-it-remain-the-tobacco-market-powerhouse-/report; 'Philippines warns against e-cigarette use', *Channel NewsAsia*, accessed August 3, 2013, http://www.channelnewsasia.com/news/asiapacific/philippines-warns-against/636408.html.

14. Adapted from Everett M. Rogers, *Diffusion of Innovations* (New York: Macmillan, 1962): 81–86.

15. Ibid., 247–250.

16. 'Reducing the appeal of smoking – first experiences with Australia's plain tobacco packaging law', World Health Organization, accessed August 17, 2013, http://www.who.int/features/2013/australia_tobacco_packaging/en/.

17. 'Australian wine exports continue to grow at higher price points', Australian Government, Wine Australia, July 15, 2013, accessed August 6, 2013, http://www.wineaustralia.com/en/News%20and%20Events/~/media/0000Industry%20Site/Documents/News%20and%20Media/News/Media%20Releases/2013/MR%20%20WEAR%20report%20June13%20150713%2031.ashx

18. Andrew Heathcote, 'The 10 start-ups to watch', Business Review Weekly, February 8, 2012, accessed August 6, 2013, http://brw.com.au/p/lists/the_start_ups_to_watch_fOix6pBtoxG5zBRAUf8ajM.

19. Valerie Folkes and Shashi Matta, 'The Effect of Package Shape on Consumers' Judgment of Product Volume: Attention as a Mental Contaminant', *Journal of Consumer Research* (September 2004): 390.

20. Kath Walters, 'Five ways social media can help drive sales', *Business Review Weekly*, July 17, 2013, accessed August 16, 2013, http://www.brw.com.au/p/business/mid-market/five_ways_social_media_can_help_DSfeli8vY9SXp3vYpp4zCL.

21. Jennifer Gitlitz, and Pat Franklin, 'Water, water everywhere: The growth of non-carbonated beverages in the United States', Container Recycling Institute, February, www.container-recycling.org; 'The 2010 Nielsen wider beverages report (Australia)', Nielsen, August, http://au.nielsen.com/site/documents/NielsenWiderBeverageReport_PressRelease10Aug10.pdf; Jorge Olson, 'Why are energy drinks & new age beverages the new hot companies?', July 15, 2008, http://www.articlesbase.com/business-opportunities-articles/why-are-energy-drinks-new-age-beverages-the-new-hot-companies-101990.html.

22. 'Reviews', Bevnet, http://www.bevnet.com/reviews

23. 'New age beverages in the U.S. 2010 Edition', Beverage Marketing Corporation, November, 2010, http://www.beveragemarketing.com/?service=publications&section=newageus.

24. F. Glazer, 'New flavour options drive noncarbonated drink growth', *Nation's Restaurant News*, February 26, p. 16, http://www.nrn.com; Jorge Olson, 'Why are energy drinks & new age beverages the new hot companies?'.

25. '2009 Annual report', The Coca-Cola Company, http://www.thecoca-colacompany.com/investors/pdfs/form_10K_2009.pdf

26. Ibid.

27. 'Reviews', Bevnet, http://www.bevnet.com/reviews

28. '2009 Annual report', The Coca-Cola Company, http://www.thecoca-colacompany.com/investors/pdfs/form_10K_2009.pdf, p. 17.

29. Giselle Tsirulnik, 'Coca-Cola's Vitaminwater turns to SMS for branding', *Mobile Marketer*, May 21, 2010, http://www.mobilemarketer.com/cms/news/messaging/6333.print.

30. F. Duden, 'Whose marketing mix reigns supreme: Glacéau's Vitaminwater vs Innocent's smoothies', unpublished student assignment (2010), Southern Cross University, Lismore, Australia

31. J. Bell, 'Beyond the campaign: Crowdsourcing and co-creation with Glacéau', *Social Media Today*, January 11, 2010, http://socialmediatoday.com/SMC164642.

32. 'Lawsuit over deceptive Vitaminwater claims to proceed', Centre for Science in the Public Interest, http://cspinet. org/new/201007231.html; J. Coyle, 'Ad ban', October 10, 2009, http://www.lawdit.co.uk/reading_room/room /view_article.asp?name=../articles/3328-ad-ban-asa.htm.

33. 'Strategies in enhanced water: Analysis and case studies from the US market', New Nutrition Business, May, 2010, http://www.marketresearch.com/product/display .asp?productid=2765189.

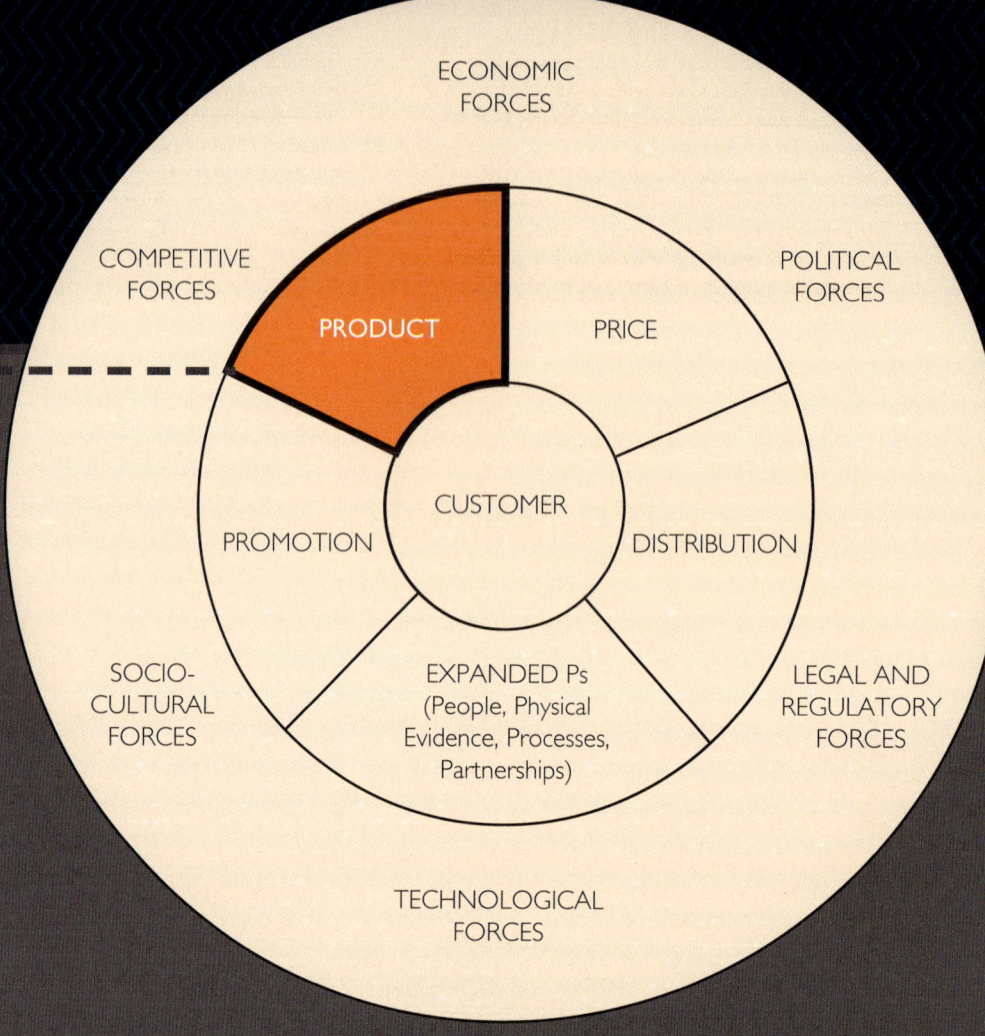

ECONOMIC FORCES

COMPETITIVE FORCES

POLITICAL FORCES

PRODUCT

PRICE

COMPETITIVE FORCES

CUSTOMER

PROMOTION

DISTRIBUTION

SOCIO-CULTURAL FORCES

EXPANDED Ps (People, Physical Evidence, Processes, Partnerships)

LEGAL AND REGULATORY FORCES

TECHNOLOGICAL FORCES

DEVELOPING AND MANAGING GOODS AND SERVICES

Developing new products
Idea generation
Screening
Concept testing
Business analysis
Product development
Test marketing
Commercialisation

Managing existing products
Line extensions
Product modifications

Quality modifications
Functional modifications
Aesthetic modifications
Product deletions

Nature and importance of services
Traditional characteristics of services

Managing intangible (service) product components
Creating marketing mixes for services

Product differentiation through quality, design and service components

   Throughout this chapter, Watch, Listen and Revise icons indicate an opportunity for online self-study through CengageNOW, linking you to animated chapter overviews, interactive diagrams, videos, quizzes and more.

9

DEVELOPING AND MANAGING GOODS AND SERVICES

Learning Objectives

LO1 Understand how businesses develop new products

LO2 Understand how organisations manage existing products

LO3 Understand the nature and importance of services

LO4 Understand how intangible (service) product components are managed

LO5 Understand the elements of product differentiation.

MARKETING CHALLENGE | WET 'N' WILD IN THE WEST

Source: Getty Images

Village Roadshow Limited provides a range of fantastical experiences across Australia in various theme parks. Village Roadshow owns such well-known attractions as SeaWorld, Movie World and Wet 'n' Wild, all located within the number one tourist destination in Australia, the Gold Coast in Queensland. Also located on the Gold Coast, and owned and operated by Village Roadshow, are SeaWorld Resort and the Australian Outback Spectacular. In the Sydney area, other Village Roadshow theme parks include the Sydney Aquarium, Sydney Wildlife World, Sydney Tower Sky Walk and Ocean World Manly. This range of theme parks from Village Roadshow constitutes their product mix.

Adding to this product mix, Village Roadshow in December 2013 launched an AU$80 million investment on a new Wet 'n' Wild theme park in western Sydney. Expected return on this investment is more than AU$500 million in the first 10 years. For the local economy, this translates to a turbo boost of 700 jobs, approximately AU$320 million and 900 000 visitors (including 175 000 international tourists) to the area during that time.[1]

The significant investment by Village Roadshow in western Sydney is an economic boost to the area, especially with regard to the 700 jobs on offer. Ideally, local western Sydney teenagers and young adults would be taking up those jobs. However, Village Roadshow has a certain organisational culture and all employees must fit that culture to hold their jobs for any length of time. Similarly, employees perform a role in working at a theme park like Wet 'n' Wild. People and their performances are part of the product being offered to the marketplace by Village Roadshow.

Analysing Sydney's new Wet 'n' Wild in terms of product decisions, the 150 m surf pool and 70 m wave pool as well as 42 slides and rides, including the Aqua Loop, Mar Racer, Double Skycoaster, The Python, Rattler and Constrictor, form the tangible aspects of this Village Roadshow product. However, this product also has intangible components such as the Wet 'n' Wild experience and the service delivered by the frontline employees. This theme park is a great example of how products are comprised of both tangible – goods – components as well as intangible – service – components.[2]

| MARKETING CHALLENGE QUESTION | 1 New frontline service employees of Wet 'n' Wild' Sydney will be required to deliver the Wet 'n' Wild experience. | What are the tangible and intangible components of this new Wet 'n' Wild product? |

Introduction

Bringing in new customers, delivering a memorable experience and encouraging repeat visits is important when a new theme park costs millions of dollars and competition is fierce. Just as Disney continues to add new attractions to Disneyland, Village Roadshow is constantly refreshing and expanding its attractions. To compete effectively and achieve their goals, organisations such as Village Roadshow must be able to adjust their product mixes in response to changes in customers' needs. A company often has to introduce new products, modify existing products or delete products that were successful perhaps only a few years ago. One way that a product can be modified is to change the tangible components or improve the intangible components, such as service, that comprise the product as a whole. Because customers' attitudes and product preferences change over time, their desire for certain products may wane. Smart marketers are on top of these trends.

In this chapter we examine several ways to improve an organisation's product mix. First, we discuss the stages of new-product development. Then we discuss how to manage existing products through effective line extension and product modification. We then examine the traditional characteristics of services and how these characteristics present challenges when developing marketing mixes for service products and intangible product components. To finish the chapter, we consider the importance of product differentiation and the potential way, shape and form of differentiating products in the marketplace.

Developing new products

A company develops new products as a means of enhancing its product mix. Developing and introducing new products is frequently expensive and risky. However, failure to introduce new products is also risky.

The term *new product* can have more than one meaning. A genuinely new product offers innovative benefits. Enviga, a green-tea product offered by a joint venture of Coca-Cola and Nestlé, purports to be calorie deficient, meaning drinking Enviga causes individuals to burn more calories than consumed per can of drink.[3] But products that are different and distinctly better are often viewed as new. Cascade Lacrosse, for example, introduced a new sports helmet that reduces shock sustained by the brain in an injury by 40 per cent. Since 40 per cent of pro hockey players get at least one concussion a year, this represents a significant new product.[4] The following items are product innovations of the last 30 years: Post-it Notes, fax machines, mobile phones, personal computers, digital music players, satellite radio and digital video recorders. A new product can be an innovative product that has never been sold by any organisation, such as the digital camera when it was first introduced. A radically new product involves a complex developmental process, including an extensive business analysis to determine the possibility of success.[5] A new

Source: Powerade

<< **New products**
Some marketers would consider Powerade Isotonic to be a new product while others would view it as a line extension. Both arguments can be made because Powerade has come up with this new idea and developed this concept as a new product, but Powerade is already an established brand and therefore Powerade Zero could also be considered as a line extension

product can also be one that a company is currently launching even though other companies are already producing and marketing similar products. Honda, for example, released the Honda Insight car model into the hybrid car market, already established by Toyota with their Toyota Prius model. A product can also be viewed as new when it is brought to one or more markets from another market. For example, making the Holden Cruze available in Japan is viewed as a new-product introduction in Japan. Similarly, making Powerade Zero available to those concerned about their sugar intake is a market extension strategy.

Before a product is introduced, it goes through the seven phases of the new-product development process shown in Figure 9.1: (1) idea generation, (2) screening, (3) concept testing, (4) business analysis, (5) product development, (6) test marketing and (7) commercialisation. A product may be dropped – and many are – at any stage of development. In this section we look at the process through which products are developed from idea inception to fully commercialised product.

new-product development process
A seven-phase process for introducing products

Idea generation

Businesses and other organisations seek product ideas that will help them to achieve their objectives. This activity is idea generation. The fact that only a few ideas are good enough to be successful commercially underscores the challenge of the task. Although some organisations get their ideas almost by chance, companies that try to manage their product mixes effectively usually develop systematic approaches for generating new-product ideas. At the heart of innovation is a purposeful, focused effort to identify new ways to serve a market.

idea generation
Seeking product ideas to achieve objectives

WATCH an interactive animation on the phases of product development

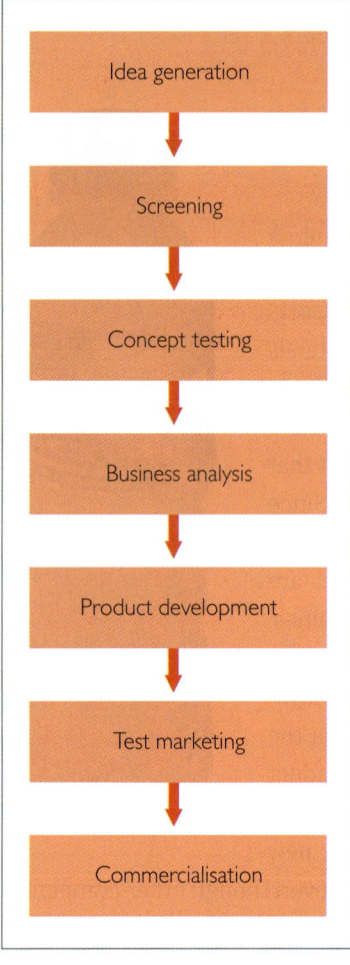

FIGURE 9.1 PHASES OF NEW-PRODUCT DEVELOPMENT

New-product ideas can come from several sources. They may come from internal sources – marketing managers, researchers, sales people, engineers or other organisational personnel. Brainstorming and incentives or rewards for good ideas are typical intra-company devices for stimulating development of ideas. For example, the idea for 3M Post-it Notes came from an employee. As a church-choir member, he used slips of paper to mark songs in his hymnal. Because the pieces of paper fell out, he suggested developing an adhesive-backed note. In the restaurant industry, ideas may come from franchisees. A more recent platform for new ideas comes from crowdsourcing. Kickstater.com, for example, offers the opportunity for community members to post ideas and ask for funding. In the watch industry sales have been in decline since 2006. But, on Kickstarter, the story is very different. Innovative watches on Kickstarter have reportedly netted US$15 million. One example of a watch generated via Kickstarter crowdsourcing funding is the CST-01, which has raised US$1million and is noted as the world's thinnest personal timepiece.[6]

New-product ideas also may arise from sources outside the company, such as customers, competitors, advertising agencies, management consultants and research organisations, as well as brand communities. LEGO, for example, is now working with various partners including customers and outside consultants. Focusing on education solutions, LEGO has deliberately collaborated with global leaders in software, engineering and education to develop specific products.

Consultants are often used as sources for stimulating new-product ideas. When outsourcing new-product development activities to outside organisations, the best results are achieved from spelling out the specific tasks with detailed contractual specifications.[7] A significant portion of this money is used to assess customers' needs. Asking customers what they want from products and organisations has helped many companies become successful and remain competitive. Indeed, as the prominent author and researcher Gary Hamel advises, much of what an organisation needs to know is better observed from outside the organisation.[8] By engaging those people, including customers, who are outside of the organisation, the ideas and processes have a better chance of remaining relevant and current. In a heavily networked world, the opportunity to engage with customers and others outside of the organisation is increasing, but not all organisations are taking on this challenge and opportunity. However, engaging with the community and stakeholders outside of the organisation is often a strategic opportunity for smaller organisations as it may be more difficult for larger organisations to achieve.

One form of inviting customers to contribute to new product development is through engaging brand communities. Kraft, for example, is widely known as the creator of powerhouse brands such as Twisties. As an American organisation, Kraft is also the owner of the iconic (Australian) Vegemite brand. The success of Kraft is closely linked to their being on the cutting edge of consumer insights. More specifically, Kraft has deliberately built an online community that involves consumers every step of the way in terms of product design. This co-creation strategy has enabled Kraft to develop a line of South Beach Diet branded meal, snacks and frozen foods. By engaging with customers, Kraft was able to develop 48 products for this new line and accordingly sales in the first six months was reported at US$100 million.[9]

While Kraft is focused on food products, governments are focused on public services and the process of strategically engaging with those outside the organisation similarly applies. Government services are increasingly taking on a customer orientation and more than that, they are seeking to engage with the customer as an agent.[10] This form of strategic policy direction aims to develop and design consumer-friendly services that respond to individual needs as well as being relevant to their circumstances. In essence, reforming the public service administration is a systematic pursuit of sustained collaboration between government, agencies, non-government organisations, communities and individual citizens. The Australian Government's (2010) report *Ahead of the Game*, presents the blueprint for such reform.[11]

Understanding how consumers consume products is another key in the quest to identify new product ideas. In 1998, LEGO released a new product called LEGO Mindstorm that was a 727-part set with a microchip-enabling movement. Mindstorm was an instant success with more than 80 000 units sold in the first 90 days. However, buyers were not children but adults. These adult consumers were not consuming Mindstorm in the way that LEGO had intended and LEGO was not impressed. What took LEGO by surprise was that consumers cracked the electronic code and created many new applications that were far more sophisticated than what LEGO had developed. The LEGO consumers were effectively producing rather than consuming the LEGO product, and in doing so forming an online LEGO brand community. LEGO did nothing for a year in response to this consumer activity, then, initial communication between LEGO and the LEGO online brand communities consisted mainly of legal threats with the claim that the communities used the LEGO logo without authorisation. Then after much tension and conflict, LEGO relented and the Senior Vice President of LEGO posted a message on the (fan-created) LEGO users' online group network. Importantly, this message was posted with the permission of the website administrators (i.e. consumers).[12]

ETHICAL MARKETING BUILDING BLOCKS AND INNOVATIVE COMMUNITIES issue

The LEGO example above should not be considered an isolated case but rather a blueprint for product development and innovation. Brand communities are innovative because they use the product and can customise the product according to their needs while conversing with other consumers who are also customising. In this way, brand communities change the way innovation takes place. In other words, brand communities move organisations from a closed system to an open

Who should profit from brand community innovation?

model of innovation. This shift is quite challenging for some marketers and organisations. Some organisations are highly resistant to allowing such an open system where the customer, not the organisation, has control. LEGO initially wanted to sue their customers for using the LEGO brand without authorisation but then realised the value in what the customers were doing in their consumption and customisation of the LEGO product. So, if new product development requires significant investment, is it ethical for organisations to market a product developed by the customer? Do these customers and brand communities need to be appropriately compensated for their innovations?

Screening

screening
Choosing the most promising ideas for further review

In the process of screening, the ideas with the greatest potential are selected for further review. During screening, product ideas are analysed to determine whether or not they match the organisation's objectives and resources. If a product idea results in a product similar to the company's existing products, marketers must assess the degree to which the new product could cannibalise the sales of current products. The company's overall abilities to produce and market the product are also analysed. Other aspects of an idea to be weighed are the nature and wants of buyers and possible environmental changes. At times, a checklist of new-product requirements is used when making screening decisions. This practice encourages evaluators to be systematic and therefore reduces the chances of overlooking some pertinent fact. The greatest numbers of new-product ideas are rejected during the screening phase; however, the screening phase is not the only phase where new product ideas can be rejected.

Concept testing

concept testing
Seeking potential buyers' responses to a product idea

To evaluate ideas properly, it may be necessary to test product concepts. In concept testing, a small sample of potential buyers is presented with a product idea through a written or oral description (and perhaps a few drawings) to determine their attitudes and initial buying intentions regarding the product. For a single product idea, an organisation can test one or several concepts of the same product. Concept testing is a low-cost procedure that allows a company to determine customers' initial reactions to a product idea before it invests considerable resources in research and development. Input from online communities may also be beneficial in the product-development process.[13] The results of concept testing can help product development personnel better understand which product attributes and benefits are most important to potential customers.

During concept testing, the concept is described briefly and then a series of questions is presented to test subjects. The questions vary considerably depending on the type of product being tested. Typical questions are: In general, do you find this proposed product attractive? Which benefits are especially attractive to you? Which features are of little or no interest to you? Do you feel that this proposed product would work better for you than the product you currently use? Compared with your current product, what are the primary advantages of the proposed product? If this product were available at an appropriate price, would you buy it? How often would you buy this product? How could this proposed product be improved?

Another way to do this form of research is to study what and how consumers consume, just as the Marketing in Action box below explains with the new Spanx concept.

Business analysis

During the business analysis stage, the product idea is evaluated to determine its potential contribution to the company's sales, costs and profits. In the course of a business analysis, evaluators ask various questions: Does the product fit with the organisation's existing product mix? Is demand strong enough to justify entering the market and will the demand endure? What types of environmental and competitive changes can be expected and how will these changes affect the product's future sales, costs and profits? Are the organisation's research, development, engineering and production capabilities adequate to develop the product? If new facilities must be constructed, how quickly can they be built and how much will they cost? Is the necessary financing for development and commercialisation on hand or obtainable at terms consistent with a favourable return on investment?

In the business analysis stage, companies seek market information. The results of consumer polls, along with secondary data, supply the specifics needed to estimate potential sales, costs and profits. For many products in this stage (when they are still just product ideas), forecasting sales accurately is difficult. This is especially true for innovative and completely new products. Organisations sometimes employ break-even analysis, involving the calculation of expenses, to determine how many units they would have to sell to begin making a profit. At times, an organisation also uses payback analysis, in which marketers compute the time period required to recover the funds that would be invested in developing the new product. Because break-even and payback analyses are based on estimates, they are usually viewed as useful but not particularly precise tools.

business analysis
Evaluating the potential contribution of a product idea to the company's sales, costs and profits

Product development

Product development is the phase in which the organisation determines if it is technically feasible to produce the product and if it can be produced at costs low enough to make the final price reasonable. To test its acceptability, the idea or concept is converted into a prototype or working model. The prototype should reveal tangible and intangible attributes associated with the product in consumers' minds. The product's design, mechanical features and intangible aspects must be linked to wants in the marketplace. Through marketing research and concept testing, product attributes and, maybe more importantly, the benefits that are important to buyers are identified. These characteristics must be communicated to customers through the design of the product.

Developing a prototype allows the product to be brought to life for the first time and taken to the market on a trial and/or limited basis. This prototype development step therefore enables a measure of market response. This prototype investment also enables preparation for full market entry. As an exercise, taking a prototype to market highlights any flaws in the product itself as well as any adjustments that need to be made in terms of the process and marketing at launch. The prototype is a valuable investment.

After a prototype is developed, its overall functioning must be tested. Its performance, safety, convenience and other functional qualities are tested both in a laboratory and in the field. Functional testing should be rigorous and lengthy enough to test the product thoroughly. Manufacturing issues that come to light at this stage may require adjustments. For example, chocolate brands Cadbury and Nestlé faced performance problems when releasing their products in warmer, tropical climates where the chocolate would melt. By adjusting the ingredients and method of manufacturing, non-melting chocolates have been developed and patented.[15]

A crucial question that arises during product development is how much quality to build into the product. For example, a major dimension of quality is durability. Higher quality often calls for better materials and more expensive processing, which increase production costs and, ultimately, the product's price. In determining the specific level of quality, a marketer must ascertain approximately what price the target market views as acceptable. In addition, a marketer usually tries to set a quality level consistent with that of the company's other products. Obviously, the quality of competing brands is also a consideration.

The development phase of a new product is frequently lengthy and expensive; therefore a relatively small number of product ideas are put into development. If the product appears sufficiently successful during this stage to merit test marketing, then during the latter part of the development stage marketers begin to make decisions regarding branding, packaging, labelling, pricing and promotion for use in the test marketing stage.

Test marketing

A limited introduction of a product in specific geographic areas chosen to represent the intended market is one example of test marketing. Launching a new product is exciting and daunting at the same time given that many new products fail, and cutting through the highly competitive clutter that consumers experience every day is a complex task. Research organisations such as AC Nielsen, for example, can test and measure whether or not your proposed advertising will work, how many prospective buyers are expected to be repeat buyers and can, therefore, indicate if the product needs to be adjusted prior to release.

The aim of test marketing is to determine the extent to which potential customers will buy the product. Test marketing is not an extension of the development stage, it is a sample launching of the entire marketing mix. Ideally, test marketing should be conducted only after the product has gone through development and initial plans regarding the other marketing-mix variables. However, the ideal does not always happen and may be for the better in some cases.

In the Australian marketplace, Adelaide is well known for being one of the most difficult markets for entry, even though as a smaller market, there is less risk in terms of an entry point. As a relatively small city combined with a conservative community, the toughness of the market is great as a testing ground. Some innovative food and innovative hospitality products that have launched in Adelaide include Boost Juice, Wendy's and Haigh's, each of which has gone on to interstate and/or international success.[16] From the humble beginnings of the Adelaide test market, Boost Juice is now global and expanding on average to four new countries and 30 stores each year for the past four years.[17]

Companies use test marketing to lessen the risk of product failure. The dangers of introducing an untested product include undercutting already profitable products and, should the new product fail, loss of credibility with distributors and customers. Selection of appropriate test areas is very important because the validity of test market results depends heavily on selecting test sites that provide accurate representation of the intended target market.

Test marketing provides several benefits. It lets marketers expose a product in a natural marketing environment to measure its sales performance. While the product is being marketed in a limited area, the company can strive to identify weaknesses in the product or in other parts of the marketing mix. A product weakness discovered after a nationwide introduction can be expensive to correct. If consumers' early reactions are negative, marketers may be unable to persuade consumers to try the product again. Therefore, making adjustments after test marketing can be crucial to the success of a new product. On the other hand, testing results may be positive enough to accelerate introduction of the new product. Test marketing also allows marketers to experiment with variations in advertising, pricing and packaging in different test areas and to measure the extent of brand awareness, brand switching and repeat purchases resulting from these alterations in the marketing mix.

Test marketing is not without risks. It is expensive and competitors may try to interfere. A competitor may attempt to 'jam' the test program by increasing its own advertising or promotions, lowering prices and offering special incentives, all to

Source: Newspix/Alan Pryke

<< Test marketing
Boost Juice will deliberately test a market and/or new product before full scale launch

combat the recognition and purchase of the new brand. Any such tactics can invalidate test results. Sometimes, too, competitors copy the product in the testing stage and rush to introduce a similar product. This is the time to conduct research to identify issues that might drive potential customers to market-leading competitors instead.[18] It is desirable to move to the commercialisation phase as soon as possible after successful testing. On the other hand, some companies have been known to promote new products heavily long before they are ready for the market to discourage competitors from developing similar new products.

Because of these risks, many companies use alternative methods to measure customer preferences. One such method is simulated test marketing. Typically, consumers at shopping centres are asked to view an advertisement for a new product and are given a free sample to take home. These consumers are interviewed subsequently over the phone and asked to rate the product. The major advantages of simulated test marketing are greater speed, lower costs and tighter security, which reduce the flow of information to competitors and reduce jamming. However, not all products that are test marketed are launched. At times, problems discovered during test marketing cannot be resolved. Smart marketers have to know when to quit. If a product is at the stage of test marketing, significant investment has been made and to walk away from that can be difficult. Test marketing showing a favourable result is encouraging but, just as importantly, test marketing showing an unfavourable result also needs to be heeded. Moving into the next stage beyond test marketing is commercialisation, which requires much more investment.

Commercialisation

commercialisation
Deciding on full-scale manufacturing and marketing plans and preparing budgets

During the commercialisation phase, plans for full-scale manufacturing and marketing must be refined and settled and budgets for the project prepared. Early in the commercialisation phase, marketing management analyses the results of test marketing to find out what changes in the marketing mix are needed before the product is introduced. The results of test marketing may tell marketers to change one or more of the product's physical attributes, modify the distribution plans to include more retail outlets, alter promotional efforts or change the product's price. However, as more and more changes are made based on test marketing findings, the test marketing projections may become less valid.

During the early part of this stage, marketers not only must gear up for larger-scale production but must also make decisions about warranties, repairs and replacement parts. The type of warranty a company provides can be a critical issue for buyers, especially when expensive, technically complex products are involved. Establishing an effective system for providing repair services and replacement parts is necessary to maintain favourable customer relationships. Although the producer may furnish these services directly to buyers, it is more common for the producer to provide such services through regional service centres. Regardless of how services are provided, it is important to customers that they be performed quickly and correctly.

The product enters the market during the commercialisation phase. When introducing a product, a company may spend enormous sums for advertising, personal selling and other types of promotion, as well as for plant and equipment. Such expenditures may not be recovered for several years. Smaller companies may find this process difficult but, even so, they may use press releases, blogs, podcasts and other tools to capture quick feedback as well as promote the new product. Another low-cost promotional tool is product reviews in newspapers and magazines, which can be especially helpful when they are positive and target the same customers.

Products are not usually launched nationwide overnight but are introduced through a process called a *rollout*. In a rollout, a product is introduced in stages, starting in one geographic area or with one retail distribution point, and then gradually expanding into adjacent areas and/or other stores. Cadbury, for example, released their new addition to the Marvellous Creations range (banana candy, peanut drops and chocolate biscuit) exclusively at Woolworths. Cadbury are inviting the consumer to vote whether to keep this new range or not via the Cadbury website, before rolling it out nationally through more channels.[19] It may take several years to market the product nationally. Sometimes the test cities are used as initial marketing areas, and introduction of the product becomes a natural extension of test marketing. Gradual product introduction is desirable for several reasons. It reduces the risks of introducing a new product. If the product fails, the company will experience smaller losses if it introduced the item in only a few geographic areas than if it marketed the product nationally. Furthermore, a company cannot introduce a product nationwide overnight because a system of wholesalers and retailers necessary to distribute the product cannot be established so quickly. The development of a distribution network may take considerable time. Also, the number of units needed to satisfy national demand for a successful product can be enormous, and a company usually cannot produce the required quantities in a short time. Finally, gradual introduction allows for fine-tuning of the marketing mix to better satisfy target customers.

Despite the good reasons for introducing a product gradually, marketers realise that this approach creates some competitive problems. A gradual introduction allows competitors to observe what the company is doing and to monitor results, just as the company's own marketers are doing. If competitors see that the newly introduced product is successful, they may quickly enter the same target market with similar products. In addition, as a product is introduced region by region, competitors may expand their marketing efforts to offset promotion of the new product.

Managing existing products

An organisation can benefit by capitalising on its existing products. By assessing the composition of the current product mix, a marketer can identify weaknesses and gaps. This analysis then can lead to improvement of the product mix through line extensions and product modifications. Analysing the current product mix can be done several ways, including analysis of the product offer relative to competitors' product offers. An outcome of this analysis is identification of opportunities and gaps in the market. Existing products can be also be analysed in terms of features and benefits. This is a useful and insightful analytical process because the product is looked at from the customer's perspective. Another important analysis of existing products comes from market research. Talking to customers informally or formally surveying customers provides an important insight on what products are valued in the marketplace and why. This insight then provides direction on what and where to invest future time and efforts.

REVISE your knowledge of product management by taking the Media Quiz

New product development is an expensive exercise, so investing in the analysis of existing products is a sound investment when the outcome is an insight on the needs and wants of consumers. More than 80 per cent of new products fail fairly quickly and therefore the investment in new product development and line extensions is continuous. A global survey by AC Nielsen of New Product Sentiment showed that consumers in emerging markets (e.g. Latin America) were more eager to try new products, whereas consumers in the Asia-Pacific region were most likely to wait to see if the product works. Similarly, 60 per cent of consumers worldwide prefer to wait until a new innovation is proven, 60 per cent are willing to buy a new brand from familiar brand, 50 per cent will willingly switch brands and only 39 per cent are willing to pay a premium price.[20] Many product failures may occur but one successful product will usually counteract the costs. Sometimes the analytical process indicates that a line extension, rather than developing a completely new product, is the best investment option.

Source: © Arnotts, used with permission

Line extensions

A line extension is the development of a product closely related to one or more products in the existing product line but designed specifically to meet somewhat different customer needs.

Coca-Cola Australia, for example, has launched an extension to their highly successful Powerade line, Powerade Zero. Powerade Zero is closely related to the current Powerade products, but with the defining characteristic of being sugar free. Powerade is the market leader in the sports drink category and continues to drive innovation with the Powerade Zero line extension. Individuals exercising twice each week (or more) are the target market for Powerade Zero, which is more than 6.7 million Australians.[21] The launch of Powerade Zero was supported by a multi-million dollar integrated marketing campaign, which included extensive out-of-home digital, mobile and social-media advertising, as well as print advertising, sporting event sponsorships and point of sale displays.[22]

Many of the so-called new products introduced each year are in fact line extensions. Line extensions are more common than new products because they are a less expensive, lower-risk alternative for increasing sales. A line extension may focus on a different market segment or may be an attempt to increase sales within the same market segment by more precisely satisfying the needs of people in that segment. However, one side effect of employing a line extension is that it may result in a less positive evaluation of the core product if customers are less satisfied with the line extension.

Product modifications

Product modification means changing one or more characteristics of a product. A product modification differs from a line extension because the original product does not remain in the line. For example, car manufacturers use product modifications each year when they create new models of the same car brand. Once the new models are introduced,

Line extension >> Arnotts treat packs are a line extension of the original Tim Tam product. The package size has been modified and the product flavours expanded

line extension Development of a product that is closely related to existing products in the line but meets different customer needs

product modification Change in one or more characteristics of a product

the manufacturers stop producing last year's model, which is then sold at a discounted price. Like line extensions, product modifications entail less risk than developing new products.

Product modifications can indeed improve a company's product mix, but only under certain conditions:

* the product must be modifiable
* customers must be able to perceive that a modification has been made
* the modification should make the product more consistent with customers' desires so it provides greater satisfaction.

One drawback to modifying a successful product is that the consumer who had experience with the original version of the product may view a modified version as a riskier purchase.[23]

There are three major ways to modify products: quality, functional and aesthetic modifications.

Quality modifications

Quality modifications are changes relating to a product's dependability and durability. The changes are usually executed by altering the materials or the production process. For example, Omega, manufacturer of prestige Swiss watches, offer a range of high quality time keeping devices including sports and dive watches, limited-edition timepieces and luxury collections. The Omega brand continues to evolve through technical innovation in order to remain at the forefront of time-keeping accuracy and watch durability. The Omega brand is the official time-keeping device of the Olympic Games, it was the first watch to be worn on the moon and is the watch worn by James Bond in the Bond films. Omega also offer additional services, including maintenance and vintage Omega restoration. The Omega Tourbillion model is made by hand from start to finish by one watchmaker. When the Tourbillion model wristwatch requires servicing, it is serviced by the same watchmaker who initially produced the watch. These additional services enhance the emotional experience that makes the consumer passionate and loyal to the Omega brand, and reinforce the dependability and durability of the Omega product.

Car manufacturers employ quality, functional and aesthetic modifications. Holden, for example, has announced the interior design of the next-generation Holden Cruze to be released in 2016.[24] Quality modifications on the new model include an 'Eco' mode, parking aids and a neater steering wheel. Functional modifications include an overhauled instrument cluster on the dash and a large display screen positioned between the speedometer and tachometer. Aesthetic modifications include frontal style more akin to the Holden Barina than the first-generation Cruze. The second-generation Cruze is expected to be released globally in 2015 with Australian production scheduled for the latter half of 2016. However, given Holden has since announced Australian production of the Holden is to cease in 2016, this promise is now questionable.[25]

Reducing a product's quality may allow an organisation to lower its price and direct the item at a different target market. In contrast, increasing the quality of a product may give a company an advantage over competing brands. Higher quality may enable a

quality modifications
Changes relating to a product's dependability and durability

Source: Getty Images

company to charge a higher price by creating customer loyalty and lowering customer sensitivity to price, just as Omega has done in offering consumers superior workmanship and additional service options. However, higher quality may require the use of more expensive components and processes, thus forcing the organisation to cut costs in other areas. In facing this challenge, companies are finding ways to increase quality while reducing costs.

Functional modifications

Changes that affect a product's versatility, effectiveness, convenience or safety are called functional modifications; they usually require that the product be redesigned. Functional modifications can make a product useful to more people and thus enlarge its market. Product categories that have undergone considerable functional modification include office and farm equipment, appliances, cleaning products and consumer electronics. In terms of functional labelling, modifications are being ethically debated in the product category of energy drinks. Various health advocacy groups, such as the Obesity Policy Coalition, are calling for functional modifications to be mandated with labelling of caffeine and sugar content in energy drinks.[26] This argument is reinforced with research that highlights the rising concern over energy drink producers failing to adequately disclose potential health risks associated with high-level caffeine consumption, which is best countered with functional modifications in labelling.[27]

Functional modifications can place a product in a favourable competitive position by providing benefits that competing brands do not offer. Functional modifications can also help an organisation achieve and maintain a progressive image. With Samsung, for example (and as discussed in the Marketing in Transition box overleaf), regularly introducing new and innovative functional modifications means that consumers come to understand that Samsung is an excellent choice in the mobile phone product category. A point to note regarding functional modifications is that sometimes functional modifications are made to reduce the possibility of product liability lawsuits, such as warning labels on toxic products.

Positioned around the world as an aspirational product for young consumers, Samsung engages the millennial market segment with celebrity endorsements that include Alexander Wang, LeBron James, Usher and Jay Z. Samsung markets the Galaxy S4 as a 'life companion' and it includes features such as navigating without touching the screen and built-in health monitoring. Connectivity features enable tech-savvy refrigerators and smart TVs to communicate via the S4. In this way, Samsung is evolving and differentiating the brand by enhancing the lives of consumers. This example shows how an organisation enacts the stated Samsung vision of 'inspire the world, create the future'.

In tremendous innovative style, Samsung surpassed Apple in smartphone sales in 2013. The brand net worth went up 20 per cent and is now estimated at US$39 610 million. In the handsets market alone, for example, Samsung has snatched more than 30 per cent of the market share, generating a profit of more than US$5.2 billion – and that was just in the second quarter of 2013.[28]

The key for Samsung is innovation and innovative products, such as the Galaxy S4 and Galaxy Note II. In launching and marketing these innovative products, Samsung has invested more than US$4 billion, which is approximately four times the Apple marketing spend. ☒

Aesthetic modifications

Aesthetic modifications change the sensory appeal of a product by altering its taste, texture, sound, smell or appearance. A buyer making a purchase decision is swayed by how a product looks, smells, tastes, feels or sounds. Camera manufacturer Leica, for example, has released the Leica M3, a compact digital camera inside, with the aesthetics of a classic vintage film camera on the outside. Coming in a wooden camera box, the Leica M3 features textured leather, metal levers and an old-style flash. This approach to retro-style aesthetic modification has been adopted by other camera brands including Fujifilm, Pentax and Lomography. Furthermore, Leica have released the Leica A La Carte model which invites consumers to design their own styling and technical nuances. An aesthetic modification may strongly affect purchases. Camera manufacturers rely on both quality and aesthetic modifications.

Through aesthetic modifications, a company can differentiate its product from competing brands and thus gain a sizeable market share. The major drawback in using aesthetic modifications is that their value is determined subjectively. Although a company may strive to improve the product's sensory appeal, customers may actually find the modified product less attractive. Some consumers may find the addition of too many decals unappealing, for example.

aesthetic modifications
Changes to the sensory appeal of a product

Source: © Leica Camera Australia Pty Ltd, used with permission

<< Product modification
Leica offers the A La Carte model digital camera which, as the name suggests, allows consumers to customise the product to their liking

Product deletions

Generally, a product cannot satisfy target market customers and contribute to the achievement of an organisation's overall goals indefinitely. Product deletion is the process of eliminating a product from the product mix, usually because it no longer satisfies a sufficient number of customers. A declining product reduces an organisation's profitability and drains resources that could be used to modify other products or develop new ones. Sony, for example,

product deletion
Eliminating a product from the product mix

discontinued production of cassette Walkmans in 2010, 31 years after they were first released to the market. This discontinuation was due to declining sales and newer portable music technology being introduced by Apple and Samsung by way of iPods and smartphones. A questionable or marginal product therefore may require shorter production runs, which can increase per-unit production costs. When a dying product completely loses favour with customers, the negative feelings may transfer to some of the company's other products.

Most organisations find it difficult to delete a product. A decision to drop a product may be opposed by managers and other employees who believe that the product is necessary to the product mix. Sales people who still have some loyal customers are especially upset when a product is dropped. Considerable resources and effort are sometimes spent trying to change a slipping product's marketing mix to improve its sales and thus avoid having to eliminate it. In the case of iconic products such as the Ford Ranger and the Holden Ute being discontinued, the community backlash can be highly damaging.[29]

Some organisations delete products only after the products have become heavy financial burdens. A better approach is some form of systematic review in which each product is evaluated periodically to determine its impact on the overall effectiveness of the company's product mix. Such a review should analyse the product's contribution to the company's sales for a given period, as well as estimate future sales, costs and profits associated with the product. It also should gauge the value of making changes in the marketing strategy to improve the product's performance. A systematic review allows an organisation to improve product performance and ascertain when to delete products.

There are three basic ways to delete a product: phase it out, run it out or drop it immediately (see Figure 9.2). A *phase out* allows the product to decline without a change in the marketing strategy; no attempt is made to give the product new life. Nikon, for example, simply allowed sales of its discontinued film cameras to continue until their supplies ran out. A *run out* exploits any strengths left in the product. Intensifying marketing efforts in core markets or eliminating some marketing expenditures, such as advertising, may cause a sudden jump in profits. This approach is commonly taken for technologically obsolete products, such as older models of computers and calculators. Often the price is reduced to get a sales spurt. The third alternative, an *immediate drop* of an unprofitable product, is the best strategy when losses are too great to prolong the product's life.

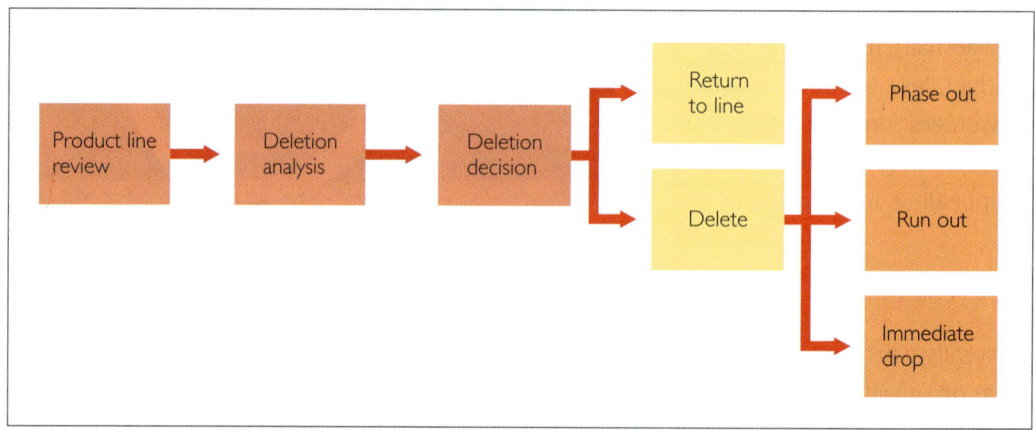

FIGURE 9.2 PRODUCT DELETION PROCESS

Source: Martin L. Bell, *Marketing: Concepts and Strategy*, 3rd ed., p. 267; copyright 1979, Houghton Mifflin Company; used by permission of Marcellette Bell Chapman.

Nature and importance of services

The services sector is broad ranging and fast growing. Services include, for example, retail, transport, professional, labour/trade, technological and maintenance services. All products, whether goods, services or ideas, comprise to some extent both tangible and intangible components. The implication therefore is that all products are marketed with this combination in mind. Services are usually provided through the application of human and/or mechanical efforts directed at people or objects. For example, educational services involve the efforts of service providers (teachers) directed at people (students), whereas cleaning services and interior-decorating services are service performances directed at objects. Services can also involve the use of mechanical efforts directed at people (air or mass transportation) or objects (freight transportation). A wide variety of services, such as health care and landscaping, involve both human and mechanical efforts. Although many services entail the use of tangibles such as tools and machinery, the primary difference between a service and a good is that a service is dominated by the intangible portion of the total product. Services, as products, should not be confused with the related topic of customer services. While customer service is part of the marketing of goods, service marketers also provide customer service.

One way to consider the structure of an economy is to look at the contribution from three main sectors: agriculture, industry and services. In most industrialised countries, including Germany, Japan, Australia and Canada, services account for about 70 per cent of the country's gross domestic product (GDP).[90] In terms of total GDP, a major contribution from agriculture indicates a developing economy. In an emerging economy, agriculture gives way to the industrial sector and from there the industrial sector gives way to the service sector in an industrialised economy. These economic and structural changes can be explained in terms of consumer demand and the relative productivity in each of the three main sectors.

When a nation becomes industrialised as is currently the case with China (See Figure 9.3), more than half of new businesses are service businesses and,

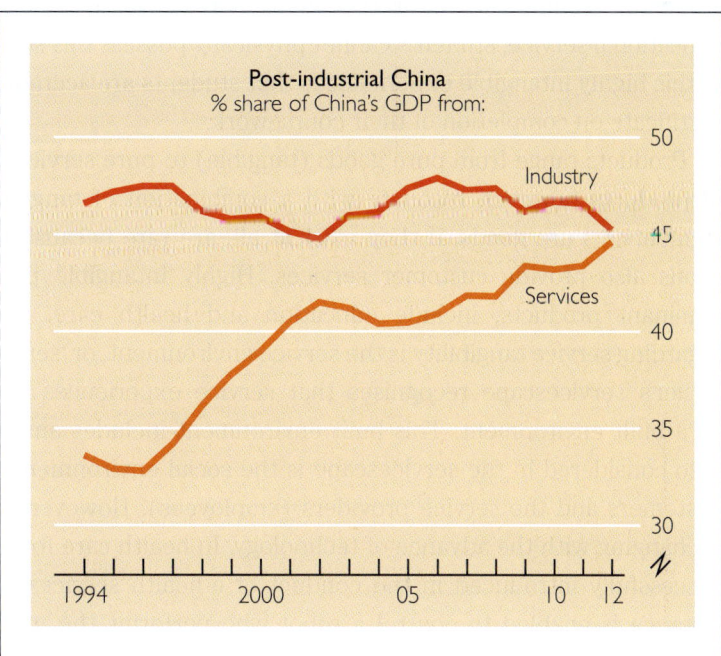

Source: S.C Hong Kong, 'The post-industrial future is nigh', *The Economist*, December 12, 2013, http://www.economist.com/blogs/analects/2013/02/services-sector.

FIGURE 9.3 THE RISE OF SERVICES IN CHINA

accordingly, service employment takes on a steep growth curve. This increase in businesses and opportunities absorbs much of the influx of women and minorities into the workforce, with many taking an entrepreneurial approach and starting their own businesses.[31] In a rising service economy such as China, another emergent trend is service workers, such as people working in child care and bookkeeping, working from home rather than having to commute to an office or work environment.

In Malaysia, for example, the government is taking an aggressive approach to expand the services sector with expectations that services will contribute 70 per cent of GDP by 2015, as stated by Malaysia's Deputy International Trade and Industry Minister Mukhriz Mahathir.[32]

Traditional characteristics of services

Traditionally, the issues associated with marketing service products are considered different to those associated with marketing goods. To understand these considered differences, it is first necessary to outline the traditional characteristics of services. Services have six assumed characteristics: intangibility, inseparability of production and consumption, perishability, heterogeneity, client-based relationships and customer contact.[33] However, as shown in the discussion that follows, these traditional characteristics are somewhat challenged in the information age.[34]

Intangibility

intangibility
An aspect that is not physical and cannot be touched

Many services are highly intangible. Intangibility means a service is not physical and therefore cannot be touched. For example, the production of educational services entails a teacher teaching and students learning and attending classes. The intangible benefit for students is gaining a degree and becoming more knowledgeable. Effectively, in consuming an educational service, students cannot physically possess this service. However, the outcome of this highly intangible experience is that students are accredited a degree officiated by a certificate on completion of their coursework.

Products range from pure goods (tangible) to pure services (intangible). The majority of products however, resonate with a combination of tangible elements and intangible elements.[35] Pure goods, if they exist at all, are rare because practically all marketers of goods also provide customer services. Highly intangible products, which are service-dominant products, include education and health care. An important consideration regarding service tangibility is the service environment, or 'servicescape' in Bitner's terms.[36] Bitner's servicescape recognises that service experiences are surrounded and shaped by a built environment. This built environment includes ambience, function and design. Also considered in the servicescape is the social environment, or people, including other customers and the service providers (employees). However, the intangibility of services is changing with the advance of technology. In health care for example, robotics are being successfully introduced in the conduct of e-health services. A doctor operating from a distance is enabled to control a robot who performs the medical procedure at another location. Similarly, the servicescape of many services is now digital or even virtual. For example, the servicescape of eBay is the website platform and the servicescape of Facebook is the social network individualised by the user. Taken a step further, the servicescape of the online game World of Warcraft is the virtual world of mighty heroes and limitless adventure. One step further again, the commercial world of Second Life entails virtual service experiences created by user-generated content.

Inseparability

Another traditional characteristic of services that creates challenges for marketers is inseparability, which refers to the production of a service being inseparable from its consumption by customers. For example, airline services are produced and consumed simultaneously; once the aircraft is in flight, the inflight service can only be produced for those consumers on the flight. In other words, services are often produced, sold and consumed at the same time. In goods marketing, a customer can purchase a good, take it home and store it until he or she is ready to use it. The manufacturer of the good may never see an actual customer. Customers, however, must often be present at the production of a service (such as marriage counselling or surgery) and cannot take the service home for the purpose of consuming at a later convenient time. Indeed for some services, both the service provider and the customer must work together to provide the service's full value.[37] For instance, when getting a new haircut, the customer is required to be present and the hairdresser will ask for what style the customer wants. The outcome is a negotiated outcome between what the customer wants and what the hairdresser can deliver. Further customer participation is required for other services such as an automated car wash. Customers who wash their car at the local car wash must keep the machine fed with coins while they brush, soap, scrub and rinse the body and wheels of their car. This high level of physical effort on the part of the customer implies that a share of responsibility for the quality of this service falls on the consumer's shoulders. In this way, inseparability implies a shared responsibility between the customer and service provider. As a result, marketing material needs to clearly indicate the customer's role in the service experience to reinforce shared responsibility and positive feelings.[38]

In considering the traditional service characteristic of inseparability of production and consumption, there are also many services where this does not apply. When a car needs work, for example, it is dropped off at the mechanic's workshop, and then picked up later when the tune-up is complete. There is no need for the customer to be present when consuming a mechanic's service and, more than that, customers are not permitted to enter the mechanic's workshop due to occupational health and safety regulations. Similarly, a dry-cleaning service is separable in the production and consumption: the soiled suit is left to be laundered and the customer returns at a later date. Technology has progressed the potential separability of services. An online application for a home loan, for example, is produced by the bank at an earlier date and made available to consumers 24/7. Once the application is complete, the customer might submit the application online and the processing of that application is handled by a home-loans officer within the bank over several different days. After identifying a suitable home, the consumer will then seek the services of an insurance company, where the policy is purchased online and the customer consumes that insurance policy for many years without ever actually physically meeting with the insurer.

inseparability
An aspect that is produced and consumed at the same time

Perishability

perishability
The inability of unused service capacity to be stored for future use

Services are traditionally characterised by perishability because the unused service capacity of one time period cannot be stored for future use. For example, empty seats on an air flight today cannot be stored and sold to passengers at a later date. Other examples of service perishability include unsold football tickets, unscheduled dentists' appointment times and empty hotel rooms. Although some goods, such as meat, milk and fruit, are perishable in terms of shelf life, services are also perishable and to a large extent simply cannot be stored.

Perishability >>
Experiences need to be consumed at the same time as they are offered. However, technology is changing the perishability of services

Source: Shutterstock.com

If a pair of jeans has been sitting on a department store shelf for a week, someone can still buy them the next day; the jeans as goods are not perishable. Goods marketers can handle the supply–demand problem through production scheduling and inventory techniques. Service marketers do not have the same advantage because live rock concert tickets, for example, are only valid for that night and once the concert is over the opportunity is gone for both the vendor to sell more tickets and/or the consumer to attend the concert. There may be a repeat performance the following night, but it won't be (exactly) the same performance: it might be raining, for example, and many consumers might choose not to attend, hence the ambience is not as inviting; whereas the night before, the concert rocked, there was a packed audience and the experience will be talked about for years afterwards. A service's perishability, therefore, presents many challenges for services marketers when trying to balance supply and demand.

The implication for marketers, therefore, is to recognise that demand may fluctuate according to the day of the week, time of day or season. Australian ski resorts that are popular in winter have successfully encouraged conferences and conventions to be held at their facilities in the summer. Similarly, Canadian ski slopes are converted to mountain biking and BMX tracks in summer. This means the usual drop in demand during summer for ski resorts is counteracted in some way. Cinemas might offer Tuesday night as 'two for one' entry and the Saturday afternoon matinee is also offered at a discounted price in order to encourage demand to flow away from peak periods. Similarly, restaurants might offer lunch for half price or early bird specials to encourage daytime or early dinner patronage rather than a queue at 7 p.m.

Technology, however, is changing the way we consume services as there are now options to store certain services for future consumption. There are, therefore, new challenges faced by the marketers of such services. A live recording of a successful rock concert, for example, can be made available online for consumers to download (for a price). This is an example of storage of an entertainment service. This live recording can be downloaded to be consumed on an iPod while out for a walk the next day and the day after. In this context, the producer's output is durable and replicable.[39]

Heterogeneity

Services delivered by people are susceptible to heterogeneity, or variation in quality. Quality of manufactured goods is easier to control with standardised procedures, and mistakes are easier to isolate and correct. Because of the nature of human behaviour, however, it is very difficult for service providers to maintain a consistent quality of service delivery. This variation in quality can occur from one organisation to another, from one service person to another within the same service facility and from one service facility to another within the same organisation. For example, the retail assistant in one bookstore may be more knowledgeable and therefore more helpful than those in another bookstore owned by the same chain. Heterogeneity usually increases as the degree of labour intensiveness increases. Many services, such as medical, education and hairstyling, rely heavily on human labour. Other services, such as telecommunications, health clubs and public transportation, are more equipment-intensive. People-based services are often prone to fluctuations in quality from one time period to the next. For example, a hair stylist that gives a customer a good haircut today cannot absolutely guarantee that customer a haircut of equal quality at a later date. However, if the hairstylist provides an excellent cut then the customer is more likely to return. Equipment-based services, in contrast, suffer from this problem to a lesser degree than people-based services. For instance, automated teller machines (ATMs) have less inconsistency than the quality of teller services at banks, and barcode scanning has improved the accuracy of service at checkout counters in supermarkets. To some extent, therefore, technological advances have enabled better quality-control procedures through higher levels of standardisation and automation.

heterogeneity
Variation in quality

Client-based relationships

The success of many services depends on creating and maintaining client-based relationships. Ideally, client-based relationships are interactions with customers that result in satisfied customers who use a service repeatedly over time. In seeking to provide a service, some service providers, such as lawyers, accountants and financial advisers, develop and maintain close long-term relationships with their clients. For professional service providers like doctors, lawyers and accountants, they are successful only to the degree to which they can maintain a group of clients who use their services on an ongoing basis. For example, an accountant may serve a family in his or her area for decades. If the members of this family like the quality of the accountant's services, they are likely to recommend the accountant to other families. If several families repeat this positive word-of-mouth communication, the accountant will likely acquire a long list of satisfied clients. Indeed, research has found that word-of-mouth communication plays a key role in services.[40] This process of interaction and communication is the key to creating and maintaining client-based relationships. To encourage client-based relationships, the service provider must take steps to build trust, demonstrate customer commitment and satisfy customers so well that they become very loyal to the provider and are unlikely to switch to competitors.

client-based relationships
Interactions that result in satisfied customers who use a service repeatedly over time

Customer contact

Not all services require a high degree of customer contact, but many do. Customer contact refers to the level of interaction that is necessary between the service provider and the customer, to deliver the service. High-contact services include health care, legal and hair care services.

customer contact
The level of interaction between provider and customer needed to deliver the service

Examples of low-contact services are telecommunications, insurance and dry cleaning. Some service-oriented businesses are reducing their level of customer contact through technology. Woolworths supermarkets, for example, introduced self-service checkouts, where customers can scan their own goods and pay via EFTPOS. Similarly, fuel stations allow customers to pump their own fuel and pay at the pump via EFTPOS, requiring no direct contact with the service personnel. Note that high-contact services generally involve actions directed toward people, who must be present during production. A hairstylist's customer, for example, must be present during the styling process. When the customer must be present, the process of production may be just as important as its final outcome. Although it is sometimes possible for the service provider to go to the customer, high-contact services typically require that the customer go to the production facility. Thus the physical appearance of the facility, the servicescape, may be a major component of the customer's overall evaluation of the service. When the physical setting fosters customer-to-customer interactions, it can lead to greater loyalty to an establishment and positive word-of-mouth communications.[41]

Employees of high-contact service providers are a very important ingredient in creating satisfied customers. A fundamental precept of customer contact is that satisfied employees lead to satisfied customers. Research indicates that employee satisfaction is the single most important factor in providing high service quality. Therefore, to minimise the problems that customer contact can create, service organisations must take steps to understand and meet the needs of employees by training them adequately, empowering them to make more decisions and rewarding them for customer-oriented behaviour.[42]

Managing intangible (service) product components

As we have mentioned, many products are a combination of intangible services and tangible goods. However, some products are comprised of mostly an intangible service component. For example, the primary product offered by a medical professional is the knowledge and skill of a trained physician, but essential to any medical service are the tools and implements and even the office or surgery where the service is administered. Similarly, the primary product of a local restaurant is the culinary cuisine served in an ambient atmosphere created with lighting and music but essential to any quality restaurant is the décor and furnishings as well as the frontline personnel who interact with the customers. If the restaurant is offering high-end French cuisine, the décor and furnishings might be chic Parisian style teamed with dimmed lighting and soft romantic music. Whereas, a Japanese noodle house might have wooden chairs and tables combined with brighter lighting and a more energetic style of music. Whether the intangible service components are the predominant component of the product or not, the intangible service components are managed to reflect the essence of the product as a whole.

In this section we initially focus on the growing importance of service industries in our economy. Then we address the traditional characteristics of services. We also discuss the challenges these characteristics pose in developing and managing marketing mixes for services.

Creating marketing mixes for services

The characteristics of services create a number of challenges for service marketers (see Table 9.1). These challenges are especially evident in the development and management of marketing mixes for services. Although such mixes contain the four major marketing-mix variables – product, price, distribution and promotion – the characteristics of services require that marketers consider additional issues.

Bundling services

A service offered by an organisation is generally a package, or bundle, of services consisting of a core service and one or more supplementary services. A *core service* is the basic service experience or commodity that a customer expects to receive. A *supplementary service* is a supportive one related to the core service that is used to differentiate the service bundle from that of competitors.

The mobile phones market demonstrates the concept of bundling services, where the core service is telecommunications but this service is delivered via the tangible product of the handset. So the telecommunications service is bundled with a Samsung S4 or Apple iPhone, for example, but sold by the telecommunications service provider. Other complementary services associated with this same bundle include the apps that enable various other services to be accessed via the same handset and customised as per the consumer's choice and lifestyle. While many Generation Y consumers might choose to access Facebook via an app on their mobile phone, international travellers might choose to use the Viber (enables free international calls) app to keep in contact with those at home. Banking and/or Paypal apps might also be used, as well as a pedometer while walking, or the many other options that are continuously being released.

Other bundling examples can be seen in the hospitality industry, with the Hyatt Regency Sanctuary Cove, for example, providing a hotel room as a core service, but this core service is bundled with other supplementary services such as free local phone calls, free wi-fi and a complimentary bottle of champagne on arrival. This standard room package is then adjusted as required by particular customers. Adjusting this standard room package means the marketers meet the challenge of heterogeneity in services. Not all customers are alike or want the same service. Some customers require a king room with a lagoon view, others want the manor suite and some are more interested in the day spa facilities than the golf course. While heterogeneity results in variability in service quality and makes it difficult to standardise services, heterogeneity is valuable to service marketers because this aspect of services allows the service to be customised to match the specific needs of individual customers.

Health care is another example of a predominately customised service. Necessarily, health care services provided differ from one patient to the next. Such customised services can be expensive for both provider and customer, and some service marketers therefore face a dilemma: how to provide service at an acceptable level of quality in an efficient and economic manner and still satisfy individual customer needs. To cope with this problem, some service marketers offer standardised packages. For example, a rehab facility may offer a package at a specified price for one week and another priced differently for a four-week package.

LISTEN to the Audio Summary to check your understanding of managing product components

When service bundles are standardised, the specific actions and activities of the service provider are usually highly specified. Even car mechanics frequently offer a service bundle for a single price; the specific actions to be taken are quite detailed about what will be done to a customer's car. Various other equipment-based services are also often standardised into packages. For instance, pay-TV service providers frequently offer several different monthly packages.

Revisiting Wet 'n' Wild at west Sydney, the product offer is more than a water theme park. The offer is a bundle of services as well. The core product is the water theme park, but the ticket price at the door includes life guards on duty throughout the park, cleaners who are continuously attending to the hygiene of the park, access to food and beverage facilities while in the park, as well as other (background support) services that contribute to the smooth running of the park and the overall experience of Wet 'n' Wild. There is also a serious lighting arrangement that enables the park to be open at night and an educational component, given that the Surf Life Saving Association has established a Nippers club at the park. In this way, the youngest visitors to the park will be developing their water skills and life-saving skills and all the while developing a strong consumer-brand relationship not only with the Surf Life Saving Association but also with Wet 'n' Wild. Effectively, the park becomes part of their life, their daily routine and their preferred destination.

TABLE 9.1 SERVICE CHARACTERISTICS AND MARKETING CHALLENGES

Service characteristics	Resulting marketing challenges
Intangibility	Difficult for customer to evaluate
	Customer does not take physical possession
	Difficult to advertise and display
	Difficult to set and justify prices
	Service process usually not protectable by patents
Inseparability	Service provider cannot mass produce services
	Customer must participate in production
	Other consumers affect service outcomes
	Services are difficult to distribute
Perishability	Services cannot be stored
	Balancing supply and demand is very difficult
	Unused capacity is lost forever
	Demand may be very time-sensitive
Heterogenetity	Service quality is difficult to control
	Service delivery is difficult to standardise
Client-based relationships	Success depends on satisfying and keeping customers over the long term – generating repeat business is challenging
	Relationship marketing becomes critical
Customer contact	Service providers are critical to delivery
	Requires high levels of service employee training and motivation
	Changes a high-contact service into a low-contact service to achieve lower costs without reducing customer satisfaction

Sources: K. Douglas Hoffman and John E. G. Bateson, *Essentials of Services Marketing* (Mason, OH: South-Western, 2001); Valarie A. Zeithaml, A. Parasuraman and Leonard L. Berry, *Delivering Quality Service: Balancing Customer Perceptions and Expectations* (New York: Free Press, 1990); Leonard L. Berry and A. Parasuraman, *Marketing Services: Competing through Quality* (New York: Free Press, 1991), p. 5.

MARKETING IN TRANSITION | @SBYUDHOYONO – INDONESIAN PRESIDENT TWITTER SUCCESS!

With more than 4 million followers, Indonesia's President Susilo Bambang Yudhoyono is a star in the Twitterverse. Even beyond Twitter, President Yudhoyono is developing his online presence via Facebook, YouTube and Google Plus. As recently as July 2013, President Yudhoyono wrote his first Facebook status expressing his gratitude to Indonesian citizens. In December 2013, he had 1.4 million Facebook likes. And most impressively, reportedly, these social media accounts are managed by President Yudhoyono himself. However, this success can be somewhat attributed to the success of social media within Indonesia. For example, as of July 2013, Indonesia had 64 million active Facebook users – and accordingly, Facebook recognises Indonesia as one of the key countries that will fuel Facebook's growth and achievement of the next billion in its user-base.[43]

Source: Getty Images

The social media strategy demonstrated by the Indonesian President in the Marketing in Transition box above is an example of tangibilising the intangible. Politicians, such as President Susilo Bambang Yudhoyono and US President Barack Obama are increasingly using social media to develop an online presence. Just as the entertainment service provided by Sydney's Wet 'n' Wild is tangibilised by the exciting and innovative slides and rides, President Yudhoyono is tangibilising in terms of a brand personality. In this way, politicians develop customer (i.e. public and community) relationships. Social media gives the politician a direct line of communication with the broader community and this communication vehicle is a platform for promises. Consumers and citizens come to know and trust the political brand and effectively the political career is born or advanced along. However, as we are all aware, political promises are sometimes empty promises, which demonstrates the difficulty in evaluating intangible service products.

For the more mundane and everyday services, the characteristic of intangibility makes services difficult for customers to evaluate prior to purchase. Intangibility requires service marketers, such as hairstylists, to market promises to customers. The customer is forced to place some degree of trust in the service provider to perform the service in a manner that meets or exceeds those promises. Service marketers must guard against making promises that raise customer expectations beyond what they can provide. To cope with the problem of intangibility, marketers employ tangible cues, such as well-groomed, professional-appearing contact personnel and clean, attractive physical facilities, to help assure customers about the quality of the service. Most service providers provide a uniform for at least some of their high customer-contact employees. Uniforms help make the service experience more tangible, and they serve as physical evidence to signal quality, create consistency and suggest a desired image.[44] Consider the professionalism, experience and competence conveyed by an airline pilot's uniform. In contrast, character uniforms worn by Disneyland employees convey fantasy, humour and fun.

The inseparability of production and consumption and the level of customer contact also influence the development and management of services. Given that customers are present during the production of a service means that other customers can affect the outcome of the service. For instance, if a couple out for a romantic evening dine in a restaurant next to a table of mum, dad and an unsettled baby, the overall quality of service experienced by the couple declines. Service marketers can reduce these problems by encouraging customers to share the responsibility of maintaining an environment that allows all participants to receive the intended benefits of the service. Keeping noise levels to a minimum in public libraries is ingrained in service participants from a young age, as is the requirement of customers in fast-food restaurants to dispose of packaging and other waste when leaving the dining areas. Service marketers can also seek to meet this challenge by encouraging different customer segments to dine/visit/buy at different times. Marketers can tailor their service to meet the needs of different segments of the market and in doing so can segregate incompatible groups.

Pricing of services

Services should be priced so as to reflect consumer price sensitivity, the nature of the transaction and its costs.[45] Prices for services can be established on several different bases. The prices of pest-control services, dry cleaning, carpet cleaning and a doctor's consultation are usually based on the performance of specific tasks. Other service prices are based on time. For example, legal attorneys, management consultants, psychologists, piano teachers and plumbers often charge by the hour or day.

Some services use demand-based pricing. When demand for a service is high, the price is also high; when demand for a service is low, so is the price. The perishability of services means that when demand is low, the unused capacity cannot be stored and is therefore lost forever. Every empty seat on an air flight or in a movie theatre represents lost revenue. Some services are very time-sensitive because a significant number of customers desire the service at a particular time. This point in time is called *peak demand*. A provider of time-sensitive services brings in most of its revenue during peak demand. For an airline, peak demand is usually the early red-eye flights and then again later in the evening whereas for a nightclub peak demand is on Friday and Saturday nights. Providers of time-sensitive services often use demand-based pricing to manage the problem of balancing supply and demand. They charge top prices during peak demand and lower prices during off-peak demand to encourage more customers to use the service. This is why the price of a matinee movie is often half the price of the same movie shown at night.

When services are offered to customers in a bundle, marketers must decide whether to offer the services at one price, price them separately, or use a combination of the two methods. For example, some hotels offer a package of services at one price, whereas others charge separately for the room, phone service and breakfast. Some service providers offer a one-price option for a specific bundle of services and make add-on bundles available at additional charges. For example, telephone services, such as call waiting and caller ID, are frequently bundled and sold as a package for one price. Some budget-priced airlines will sell just the basic airline ticket but then charge extra for luggage, food/drink and in-flight entertainment. Whereas, premium-priced airlines will sell within the ticket price an all-inclusive package.

Because of the intangible nature of services, customers rely heavily at times on price as an indicator of quality. If customers perceive the available services in a service category as being similar in quality, and if the quality of such services is difficult to judge even after these services are purchased, customers may seek out the lowest-priced provider. For example, many customers seek car insurance providers with the lowest rates. If the quality of different service providers is likely to vary, customers may rely heavily on the price–quality association. For example, if you have to have an appendectomy, will you choose the surgeon who charges an average price of $1500 or the surgeon who will take your appendix out for $399?

Intangibility of services as well as the inseparability of services means that potential customers must experience the service to evaluate the service, and even then it may be difficult or near impossible, as is the case with education or health care for example. Some services therefore will seek to induce trial of services to encourage customer adoption of the service. A 30-day trial might be offered for a particular service, such as a gym membership. Offering a free trial period encourages potential customers to engage with the service provider with nominal risk. This encourages uptake and sales.

Distribution of services

Marketers deliver services in various ways. In some instances customers go to a service provider's facility. For example, most health-care, dry-cleaning and spa services are delivered at the service providers' facilities. Some services are provided at the customer's home or business. Lawn care, air-conditioning and heating repair and carpet cleaning are examples. Some services are delivered primarily at 'arm's length', meaning that no face-to-face contact occurs between the customer and the service provider. Several equipment-based services are delivered at arm's length, including electric, Internet, cable television and telephone services. Providing high-quality customer service at arm's length can be costly but essential in keeping customers satisfied and maintaining market share.

To give an example of distribution of service, we can look at Domain, an Australian provider of aged care services. With 55 facilities and 4500 beds across NSW, Queensland, Victoria and Western Australia, they are Australia's largest private provider of residential aged care services. Demonstrating the current value and growth expectations of aged care services, Singaporean tycoon Goh Geok Khim has purchased a 47.62% stake in Domain for a cool $136.7 million. Domain is an example of direct distribution to the consumer, because they, as the aged care service provider, are directly interacting with the consumer within their facilities.[47]

Marketing channels for services are usually short and direct, meaning that the producer delivers the service directly to the end user. Some services, however, use intermediaries. For example, online reservation systems such as Webjet (http://webjet.com.au) facilitate the delivery of e-ticketing for airline services and independent insurance agents participate in the marketing of various insurance policies and financial planners market investment services.

Service marketers are less concerned with warehousing and transportation than are goods marketers. They are very concerned, however, about inventory management, especially balancing supply and demand for services. The service characteristics of inseparability and level of customer contact contribute to the challenges of demand management. In some instances service marketers use appointments and reservations as approaches for scheduling the delivery of services. Health care providers, legal attorneys, accountants, mechanics and

Source: Getty Images

restaurants often use reservations or appointments to plan and pace the delivery of their services. To increase the supply of a service, marketers use multiple service sites and also increase the number of contact service providers at each site. National and regional eye-care and hair-care services are examples.

To make delivery more accessible to customers and to increase the supply of a service, as well as reduce labour costs, some service providers have decreased the use of contact personnel and replaced them with equipment. In other words, they have changed a high-contact service into a low-contact one. The banking industry is an example. By installing ATMs and encouraging Internet banking, banks have increased production capacity and reduced customer contact. Such services have helped to lower costs by reducing the need for customer-service representatives. Changing the delivery of services from human to technical has created some problems, however. Talking to a machine or running into a problem when doing online banking damages the trust a customer may hold. Hence Suncorp Bank's advertising that emphasises honesty and the promise that when you call, you will speak to an actual person; a leading ad that promoted Suncorp Bank as genuine featured brand-ambassador Adam Gilchrist rolling up his sleeves, opening the door for someone and saying hello to passersby.

MARKETING IN ACTION | DELIVERY BY DRONES…!

While still illegal in other countries (such as the US), Australia is set to be the first country in the world to see commercial courier deliveries conducted by drones. Developed by students (of course!) for purposes of textbook rental deliveries, from March 2014, Zookal will offer a service to students where they can order books via a smartphone app and have one of six Flirtey drones deliver them to their door. Sydney is the planned point of market entry. During transit, the app enables the delivery to be tracked via Google Maps. Following this initial planned launch, Flirtey is planning to expand the drone delivery service to other products and locations. While this idea is not new, there are many concerns and obstacles to making it work. Amazon.com founder and CEO Jeff Bezo, for example, admits Amazon.com has considered the idea of small electric and autonomous octocopters is appealing but years away from realistic implementation.[48] ✖

Promotion of services

The intangibility of services results in several promotion-related challenges to service marketers. Because it may not be possible to depict the actual performance of a service in an ad or to display it in a store, explaining a service to customers can be a difficult task. Promotion of services typically includes tangible cues that symbolise the service, just as the advertising did for Suncorp Bank.

To make a service more tangible, ads for services often show pictures of facilities, equipment and service personnel. Marketers may also promote their services as a tangible expression of consumers' lifestyles. The weight loss service provided by Jenny Craig expresses a healthy lifestyle with the weight loss stories of comedian Magda Szubanski and Masterchef's Matt Preston.

Compared with goods marketers, service providers are more likely to promote price, guarantees, performance documentation, availability and training and certification of contact personnel. Car and home insurance provider Youi offers service price flexibility. With Youi car insurance, for example, you only pay for how much you use your car rather than a flat rate. The telecommunications service provider, Dodo, competes in a fierce industry led by Telstra but plagued with customer service problems. Therefore, Dodo Australia seeks to rise above the competition by promoting a customer service guarantee. This guarantee specifies timeframes for the connection of services, the repair of faults and the making and keeping of appointments. A point to note, however, is that all Australian telecommunications service providers are required to comply with these customer service standards as set out in the *Telecommunications Act 1999*.

When preparing ads, service marketers are careful to use concrete, specific language to help make services more tangible in the minds of customers. Virgin Australia advertising for example, highlights the fun and informal nature of the Virgin Australia offer through symbolic images and language. Through their actions, service contact personnel can be directly or indirectly involved in the personal selling of services. Virgin Australia personnel perform on the frontline of Virgin Australia production by helping to deliver a fun and informal airline service. Visual cues in services can help the customer recognise the benefits of a given service. Because service contact personnel are interacting with customers and this interaction weighs heavily in the customer's evaluation of the service, some companies invest heavily in training.

What other people say about a service provider can have a tremendous impact on whether an individual decides to use that provider. Some service marketers attempt to stimulate positive word-of-mouth communication by asking satisfied customers to tell their friends and associates about the service and may even provide incentives for doing so.

Product differentiation through quality, design and service components

Some of the most important characteristics of products are the elements that distinguish them from one another. **Product differentiation** is the process of creating and designing products so that customers perceive them as different from competing products. The Marketing in Action box (next page) illustrates how Cirque du Soleil differentiates itself from other circuses by providing a unique circus experience. Customer perception is critical

product differentiation
Creating and designing products so that customers perceive them as different from competing products

in differentiating products. Perceived differences might include quality, features, styling, price and image. A crucial element used to differentiate one product from another is the brand. In this section we examine three aspects of product differentiation that companies must consider when creating and offering products for sale: product quality, product design and features, and product support services. These aspects involve the company's attempt to create real differences among products. Later in this chapter we discuss how companies position their products in the marketplace based on these three aspects.

MARKETING IN ACTION | THIS IS NOT YOUR GRANDMOTHER'S CIRCUS!

When Guy Laliberté founded Cirque du Soleil in 1984, his goal was to reinvent the circus. Starting with a handful of street performers, today he employs thousands of performers, choreographers, artists, trainers and planners who concurrently stage 19 distinctly different shows each year. Cirque's scouts travel the world searching for talent to fill the roles for each show. Cast members receive months of training to fine-tune every aspect of their performance before taking the stage.

Meanwhile, Cirque's marketing experts consider the image they want to project as they plan their marketing mix, including print ads and merchandise. These tangible elements help to convey Cirque's innovative approach to the circus concept and hint at the memorable experiences that await audience members at every performance. [49]

Product quality

quality
Characteristics of a product that allow it to perform as expected in satisfying customer needs

Quality refers to the overall characteristics of a product that allow it to perform *as expected* in satisfying customer needs. The words *as expected* are very important to this definition because quality usually means different things to different customers. For some, durability signifies quality. For other customers, a product's ease of use may indicate quality.

The concept of quality also varies between consumer and business markets. For business markets, technical suitability, ease of repair and company reputation are important characteristics. Unlike consumers, most businesses place far less emphasis on price than on product quality.

level of quality
The amount of quality a product possesses

One important dimension of quality is **level of quality**, the amount of quality a product possesses. The concept is a relative one because the quality level of one product is difficult to describe unless it is compared with that of other products. For example, most consumers would consider the quality level of Timex watches to be good, but when they compare Timex watches with Rolex watches, most consumers would say that Rolex's level of quality is higher. How high should the level of quality be? It depends on the product and the costs and consequences of a product failure.

consistency of quality
The degree to which a product has the same level of quality over time

A second important dimension is consistency. **Consistency of quality** refers to the degree to which a product has the same level of quality over time. Consistency means giving customers the quality they expect every time they purchase the product. As with level of quality, consistency is a relative concept. It implies a quality comparison within the same brand over time. The quality level of McDonald's french fries is generally consistent from one location to another throughout the world. While the language may vary a little, the consistency of the McDonald's product quality is something that travellers might turn to in foreign lands. The consistency of product quality can also be compared across competing products, where consistency in product quality can be the competitive advantage. At this stage, consistency becomes critical to a company's success. Companies that can provide quality on a consistent basis have a major competitive advantage over rivals.

Source: Courtesy of Rolex

<< Product quality
Select products are designed to have very high quality and to use quality as a major competitive tool

Product design and features

Product design refers to how a product is conceived, planned and produced. Design is a very complex topic because it involves the total sum of all the product's physical characteristics. Many companies are known for the outstanding designs of their products: Sony for personal electronics, Hewlett Packard for printers and Apple for computers and music players, for example. Good design is one of the best competitive advantages any brand can possess.

One component of design is **styling**, or the physical appearance of the product. The style of a product is one design feature that can allow certain products to sell very rapidly. Good design, however, means more than just appearance; it also involves a product's functionality and usefulness. For example, a pair of jeans may look great, but if they fall apart after three washes, clearly the design was poor. Most consumers seek products that both look good and function well.

Product features are specific design characteristics that allow a product to perform certain tasks. By adding or subtracting features, a company can differentiate its products from those of the competition. Chrysler promotes its line of minivans as having more features related to passenger safety – dual air bags, steel-reinforced doors and integrated child safety seats – than any other car company. Product features can also be used to differentiate products within the same company. For example, Nike offers both a walking shoe and a running shoe for specific consumer needs. In these cases, the company's products are sold with a wide range of features, from low-priced 'base' or 'stripped-down' versions to high-priced, prestigious, 'feature-packed' ones. The automotive industry regularly sells products with a wide range of features. In general, the more features a product has, the higher is its price and, often, the higher is the perceived quality. For a brand to have a sustainable competitive advantage, marketers must determine the product design that customer's desire. Information from marketing research efforts and from databases can help in assessing customers' product design preferences. Being able to meet customers' desires for product design style and features at prices they can afford is crucial to a product's long-term success. Organisations might choose to incorporate and promote a product's sustainability features, as does Foster's Australia.

product design
How a product is conceived, planned and produced

styling
The physical appearance of a product

product features
Specific design characteristics that allow a product to perform certain tasks

SUSTAINABLE MARKETING | QUALITY GREEN BEER

Differentiating products as green has generated big profits for Australian businesses such as Foster's Australia. Foster's Brewery, located at Yatala in southeast Queensland, produces 25 per cent of Australia's annual beer consumption – approximately 430 million litres of beer. Water is one of the four main ingredients used in the production process of brewing beer. To produce a litre of beer would require 4.5 litres of water and in times of drought this amount of water is significant. However, green initiatives introduced by Fosters have upgraded their industrial processes with the intention of reducing water consumption and the outcome is very green beer. Foster's Brewery is now the world's most water-efficient brewery using just 2.3 litres of water to make one litre of beer.

Fosters has achieved this massive reduction in water consumption via a $14 million investment in a

Source: Shutterstock.com

water conservation and recycling plant featuring 1.2 million-litre water tanks. A consistent supply of water is vital to maintaining the quality of beer for which the Foster's brand is known.[50]

Product support services

customer services
Human or mechanical efforts or activities that add value to a product

Many companies differentiate their product offerings by providing support services. Usually referred to as customer services, these services include any human or mechanical efforts or activities a company provides that add value to a product.[51] Examples of customer services include delivery and installation, financing arrangements, customer training, warranties and guarantees, repairs, convenient hours of operation, adequate parking, and information through free-call numbers and websites. For example, small businesses who provide personalised product support are able to gain an advantage on big business by taking this part of their business and the service they offer seriously. To reinforce this point, more than 95 per cent of businesses in Australia are small businesses (less than 10 employees) and Rod Drury and Hamish Edwards recognised that these small businesses did not have adequate accounting systems, and so Xero was born in 2006. Based in New Zealand, Xero offers a cloud accounting system. Doubling in growth since 2012, Xero now has revenue of AU$39 million and 157 000 clients. The basic premise of the Xero offer made to small business owners was about flexibility and 'making life easier'. Popular accounting systems were described as clunky, not user-friendly and expensive. Xero enables small business owners to focus on their business rather than time-consuming administrative tasks. Cloud computing and systems like Xero mean that new systems are installed online and therefore seamlessly integrated with other business information. The support they offered small business owners was simplicity and reliability.[52]

Whether as a major or minor part of the total product offering, all marketers of goods sell customer services. Providing good customer service may be the only way that a company can differentiate its products when all products in a market have essentially the same quality, design and features. This is especially true in the fruit retailing industry. When buying apples for example, the quality of Granny Smith's is relatively similar among different retailers, so fruit retailers differentiate themselves by offering a friendly personalised service, free grocery delivery, take-home recipe ideas and specials. Through research, a company can discover the types of services customers want and need. The level of customer service a company provides can profoundly affect customer satisfaction.

Study Tools

Chapter review

 **LO1** UNDERSTAND HOW BUSINESSES DEVELOP NEW PRODUCTS.

Before a product is introduced, it goes through a seven-phase new-product development process. In the idea-generation phase, new-product ideas may come from internal or external sources. In the process of screening, ideas are evaluated to determine whether they are consistent with the company's overall objectives and resources. Concept testing, the third phase, involves having a small sample of potential customers review a brief description of the product idea to determine their initial perceptions of the proposed product and their early buying intentions. During the business analysis stage, the product idea is evaluated to determine its potential contribution to the company's sales, costs and profits. In the product development stage, the organisation determines if it is technically feasible to produce the product and if it can be produced at a cost low enough to make the final price reasonable. Test marketing is a limited introduction of a product in areas chosen to represent the intended market. Finally, in the commercialisation phase, full-scale production of the product begins, and a complete marketing strategy is developed.

 **LO2** UNDERSTAND HOW ORGANISATIONS MANAGE EXISTING PRODUCTS.

Organisations must be able to adjust their product mixes to compete effectively and achieve their goals. Using existing products, a product mix can be improved through line extension and through product modification. A line extension is the development of a product closely related to one or more products in the existing line but designed specifically to meet different customer needs. Product modification is the changing of one or more characteristics of a product. This approach can be achieved through quality modifications, functional modifications and aesthetic modifications. Another consideration in managing existing products is the deletion of products that are no longer aligned with organisational goals, have not performed in some way or no longer meet consumer needs.

 **LO3**   UNDERSTAND THE NATURE AND IMPORTANCE OF SERVICES.

Services are highly intangible products involving deeds, performances or efforts that cannot be physically possessed. They have six fundamental characteristics: intangibility, inseparability of production and consumption, perishability, heterogeneity, client-based relationships and customer contact. Intangibility means that a service cannot be seen, touched, tasted or smelled. Inseparability refers to the production of a service being inseparable from its consumption. Perishability means that unused service capacity of one time period cannot be stored for future use. Heterogeneity is variation in service quality. Client-based relationships are interactions with customers that lead to the repeated use of a service over time. Customer contact is the interaction needed to deliver a service between providers and customers.

 **LO4**   UNDERSTAND HOW INTANGIBLE (SERVICE) PRODUCT COMPONENTS ARE MANAGED.

Products comprise both tangible (goods) components and intangible (services) components; some have more of one than the other. What we as consumers see as predominantly a 'good', such as a can of baked beans, is purchased from a corner store or a supermarket, which is a retail service. More than that, there is a complex distribution and logistics system that delivered that can to that store just in time for you to purchase for your breakfast. Similarly, the retail store is a service that is predominantly intangible; but without the building, the shelves and the can of baked beans on the shelf along with the range of other goods available for purchase, the retail product is incomplete. Therefore, products are always usually some combination of tangible elements and intangible elements.

Products that are predominantly intangible, such as medical services or legal services, also have important tangible elements. The doctor's surgery, for example, requires the stethoscope, the thermometer and the prescription script pad. Without these tangible elements, the medical service is incomplete and may even be questionable. The legal service located on the 34th floor overlooking Sydney Harbour, with red cedar desks and leather chairs, uses the tangible elements of their service to demonstrate what it is they are offering.

 LO5   UNDERSTAND THE ELEMENTS OF PRODUCT DIFFERENTIATION.

Product differentiation is the process of creating and designing products so that customers perceive them as different from competing products. Product quality, product design and features, and product support services are three dimensions of product differentiation that companies consider when creating and marketing products.

Key concepts

Use these key terms in **Search me! marketing** to find the latest relevant readings from a wide range of world-class journals, e-books and newspapers, including *The Australian*.

- aesthetic modifications
- business analysis
- client-based relationships
- commercialisation
- concept testing
- consistency of quality
- customer contact
- customer services
- functional modifications
- heterogeneity

- idea generation
- inseparability
- intangibility
- level of quality
- line extension
- new-product development process
- perishability
- product deletion
- product design

- product development
- product differentiation
- product features
- product modification
- quality
- quality modifications
- screening
- styling
- test marketing

Issues for discussion and review

1 Describe the steps involved in new product development.

2 What is the difference between concept testing and test marketing?

3 What is a line extension, and how does it differ from a product modification?

4 What is a good reason to delete a product from a product line?

5 Describe the three major approaches to modifying a product. Give an example of each.

6 What are the traditional characteristics of services?

7 How has technology impacted the five traditional characteristics of services?

8 What is test marketing and how is this concept part of the new product development?

9 What are the fundamental differences between goods and services?

10 Discuss how to manage and market the intangible components of products.

11 Why is product development a cross-functional activity within an organisation? That is, why must finance, engineering, manufacturing and other functional areas be involved?

12 How can product differentiation be achieved through quality, design and services?

13 Explain how a product can comprise both tangible goods components and intangible service components.

Marketing applications

1 What product innovations do you think are missing in the marketplace? That is, what is on your wish list? Describe how you would market this new product or line extension.

2 Choose a product (good and/or service) and analyse the product in terms of features and benefits. Now look at how this product is positioned in the market place. What alternative positioning strategies could this product use?

3 Identify a product that is in decline. Some say McDonald's is in decline and even Microsoft is in decline. What do you think?

ONLINE EXERCISE

4 Retailers face the current daunting challenge of competing with the online shopping phenomenon. The key for retailers in facing this challenge is to focus on and enhance the in-store experience. In line with this strategic approach, General Pants have met this challenge with an in-store digital integration. Within 50 retail stores throughout Australia, web kiosks have been installed with the intention of engaging the 16–30 year old target market. The digital kiosks are designed as tables with six, four or two iPads on a spinnable mount. The idea is that customers can browse fashion trends, select music to play in the store and take photos of outfits they try on to get instant opinions from people inside the store, as well as from their friends and social networks. With 320 installed kiosks around the country, General Pants has effectively created an intra-store social media network. The goal is a 10 per cent life in retail sales; online sales are currently at 8 per cent, but a total sales increase is the goal.[53]

   a Given that General Pants have now incorporated in-store digital kiosks as part of their retail product, how would you describe this product? Consider the tangible goods components and the intangible services components

   b What role does the customer play in this in-store digital kiosk integration? What role do non-customers play who are interacting with in-store customers from outside and online social media sites?

   c Does this in-store digital kiosk strategy enhance the General Pants retail experience?

Developing your marketing plan

A company's marketing strategy may be revised to include new products as it considers its internal strengths and weaknesses and the impact of environmental factors on its product mix. When developing a marketing plan, the company must decide whether new products are to be added to the product mix, or if existing ones should be modified. The information in this chapter will assist you in the creation of your marketing plan as you consider the following:

1 Identify whether your product will be the modification of an existing one in your product mix, or the development of a new product.

2 If the product is an extension of one in your current product mix, determine the type(s) of modifications that will be performed.

3 Using Figure 9.1 as a guide, discuss how your product idea would move through the stages of new-product development. Examine the idea using the tests and analyses included in the new-product development process.

4 Discuss how the management of this product will fit into your current organisational structure.

CengageNOW

Go to http:\\login.cengagebrain.com to link to CengageNOW, your online study tool. First take the Pre-Test for this chapter to get your Personalised Study Plan, and then:

* **Revise** your understanding of the key concepts of marketing with the online glossary

* **Watch** an interactive animation of strategic marketing to broaden your subject comprehension

* **Listen** to an audio summary of the learning objectives covered in this chapter.

After you have completed the activities in your Personalised Study Plan take the Post-Test to determine what concepts you have mastered and what you still need to work on.

Case study

PILATES STUDIO

INTRODUCTION

The Pilates Studio is a small gym located in the Anglesea Health Centre on the corner of Anglesea and Thackeray Streets, Hamilton, New Zealand. It is owned and run by Dennis and Samantha Reddy. The Health Centre provides a range of medical and therapeutic services including an emergency doctor service open seven days a week. The gym is open five and a half days a week (weekdays and Saturday mornings) and provides classes in a form of exercise devised by

Josef Pilates in the middle of the twentieth century.

BACKGROUND

Dennis and Samantha Reddy are both immigrants from England where they trained as physiotherapists, doing both graduate and post-graduate work to develop their skills. In 1998, Samantha came into contact with Pilates via an American company called Polestar which had established a Pilates clinic in Auckland. She began to use Pilates in her work as a physiotherapist and then established a Pilates studio at Contours (a gym exclusively for women). This was so successful that in 2002 she set up a separate gym at the Anglesea Health Centre, initially downstairs for about a year and then moved to the present site in the complex. Dennis also began to do Pilates with clients and now spends around two-thirds of his time at the gym, the rest being spent doing physiotherapy work with sports teams (particularly the Waikato Chiefs rugby team) and on administration.

Specialist areas where they differ from other Pilates studios include dancers (Samantha has a dance background), rehabilitation (both Dennis and Samantha are physiotherapists and Samantha has an advanced certificate for rehabilitation and spinal injuries), pregnant women (Samantha has an advanced certificate in pregnancy Pilates) and Samantha is a mentor for other Pilates instructors. They work with elite New Zealand athletes including rowers, cyclists and, as mentioned above, they have a contract with the Chiefs rugby team.

CURRENT SITUATION

The Pilates Studio has been established at the Anglesea Health Centre for around 11 years and in that time has established a regular clientele.

STAFF

Aside from Dennis and Samantha, there are two staff members employed at the Pilates Studio. First there is Rachel Smart, who works around seven hours per day, five days a week, helping people doing their exercise routines and conducting group classes. Second there is Sarah Jones who does administrative work for about four hours per day. Unfortunately, neither of these staff members is a physiotherapist but Rachel is fully certified in all studio work with a 20-year history of exercise training. However only Dennis and Samantha are able to do intensive work with patients.

OPENING HOURS

As stated previously, the gym is open five and a half days per week. Sessions vary between group sessions, individual sessions and mat and specialist classes, so the gym may not be open all day depending on what classes are scheduled.

CUSTOMERS

Most of the customers fall into the 35+ age bracket and around three quarters are women. Generally they are too expensive for most students and younger people but student dancers who need quality training form part of the client base. Also, younger people sometimes find the discipline and focus quite hard unless they are dedicated or have specific goals.

Around 35 per cent of the clients are symptomatic, in other words, they have come to try and deal with existing physical problems that they suffer from. Of the total clients currently attending classes, around 70 per cent are beginners, 20 per cent are at an intermediate level and 10 per cent are classified as advanced. On any given day, the gym has approximately 17 individual clients (people who have one-on-one sessions with either Dennis or Samantha), and around 20 to 25 clients who come to group sessions.

COMPETITION

Since they first opened, a number of other Pilates gyms have opened in Hamilton. There are now three other Pilates gyms in Hamilton. They offer group classes, with people joining groups and then being led by an instructor as they advance through a typical Pilates program. There are also other gyms in Hamilton that offer Pilates, including Les Mills, Contours, the YMCA and the University recreation studio. Given the nature of Dennis and Samantha's training, it is possible that other physiotherapists could also be viewed as being in competition with the Pilates Studio.

Some physiotherapy clinics have physiotherapists who have completed very short Pilates courses and teach mat classes. However to be a Pilates instructor you need to have completed many hours as an apprentice and be able to perform a full repertoire of work. The public are generally unaware of the distinction between partial Pilates classes and a full program, and the fact that many gyms offer the 'exercises' without their instructors understanding the method and its principles.

PROMOTION

Currently, very little promotional activity is carried out. In the past, ads for mat classes have been placed in the local paper

The Waikato Times two or three times, but this was discontinued as the effectiveness of this type of advertising was difficult to measure.

Most promotion is from word of mouth, and referrals from doctors, osteopaths, chiropractors and other physiotherapists.

FUTURE PROSPECTS

At the moment, the Pilates Studio has as many individual clients as its staff can handle, and only Dennis and Samantha can provide this service. They have tried in the past to employ another staff member trained in physiotherapy but this has proved to be very difficult due to a lack of trained people. There is, however, room to double the number of group clients from around 20–25 per day up to 40–50. There is also the possibility of going into merchandising gym gear, and increasing referrals from other professionals, such as doctors.

Mark Kilgour and Quentin Somerville, University of Waikato
This case was made possible through the cooperation of the Pilates Studio.

*Note while this case is based on a real company, names have been changed for commercial reasons.

QUESTIONS FOR DISCUSSION

1 This case highlights the product life cycle concept and how, as a market expands and competition increases, the market needs to be segmented, with new products and services being offered and the organisational offerings augmented. In what other additional ways may the market be segmented?

2 How would you develop the service to take into account existing market conditions?

3 What service aspects, and additional complimentary service areas, would you develop given your target market selection (i.e. 24/7, individual personal trainers, spa and sauna services, etc.)?

4 Consider how relevant technology and social media can be incorporated into this current service design and explain how this innovation will enable the management of demand for the Pilates Studio.

Chapter endnotes

1. Simon Black, 'Wet 'n' Wild in Sydney's West,' *The Daily Telegraph*, April 26, 2013, accessed October 16, 2013, http://www.dailytelegraph.com.au/wetnwild-in-sydneys-west/story-e6freuy9-1226629587193.

2. Evan Sief, 'Gold season pass holders get sliding at Wet 'n' Wild Sydney,' *thetelegraph.com.au*, accessed December 10, 2013, http://www.dailytelegraph.com.au/newslocal/west/gold-season-pass-holders-get-sliding-at-wetnwild-sydney/story-fngr8i5s-1226778983802.

3. Kate Macarthur, 'Coke, Nestlé Offer a Workout in a Can,' *Advertising Age* (October 16, 2006): 8.

4. 'Making Headway with Helmets,' *BusinessWeek* (January 15, 2007): 75.

5. Lee G. Cooper, 'Strategic Marketing Planning for Radically New Products,' *Journal of Marketing* (January 2000): 1–16.

6. 'Want to design the perfect watch? Kickstarter has the answers,' *Fast Company* (2013), accessed December 10, 2013, http://www.fastcompany.com/3014882/want-to-design-the-perfect-watch-kickstarter-has-the-answers.

7 Stephen J. Carson, 'When to Give Up Control of Outsourced New Product Development,' *Journal of Marketing* 71 (January 2007): 49–66.

8. G. Hamel, *Leading the revolution: How to thrive in turbulent times by making innovation a way of life* (Harvard Business Press, 2002).

9. 'Customers co-create 48 products they want to buy,' Communispace (2013), accessed December 10, 2013, http://www.communispace.com/kraft-south-beach-diet-case-study/.

10. Brenton Holmes, 'Citizens engagement in policymaking and the design of public services,' Research Paper No. 1 2011–12, Parliament of Australia, Department of Parliamentary Services.

11. 'Ahead of the Game: Blueprint for Reform of Australian Government Administration,' Department of the Prime Minister and Cabinet, (DPMC), 2010, accessed December 10, 2013, http://www.dpmc.gov.au/publications/aga_reform/aga_reform_blueprint/index.cfm.

12. Martin Kornberger, *Brand Society* (Cambridge University Press: Cambridge, 2010).

13. Dennis A. Pitta and Danielle Fowler, 'Online Consumer Communities and Their Value to New Product Developers,' *Journal of Product & Brand Management* 14 (2005): 283–291; Füller et al., 'Community Based Innovation: How to Integrate Members of virtual Communities into New Product Development,' *Electronic Commerce Research* 6(1) (2006); Füller et al., 'Innovation creation by online basketball communities,' *Journal of Business Research* 60 (1): (2007) 60–71; J. Füller, K. Matzler and M. Hoppe, 'Brand community members as a source of innovation,' *Journal of Product Innovation Management* 25, 6 (2008): 608–619.

14. 'Spanx,' http://www.spanx.com; Meredith Bryan, 'Spanx Me, Baby!,' *The New York Observer* (December 4, 2007): http://www.observer.com/2007/spanx-me-baby?page=1.

15. Oliver Nieberg, 'Nestlé's answer to melting chocolate,' Confectionery news.com, June 18, 2013, http://www.confectionerynews.com/R-D/Nestle-s-answer-to-non-melting-chocolate; 'Cadbury invents non-melting chocolate,' Fox News, November 26, 2012, http://www.foxnews.com/leisure/2012/11/26/cadbury-invents-non-melting-chocolate/.

16. Amelia Pinna, 'Testing the market: is Adelaide still the state for new business?,' On the Record, 2012, accessed December 30, 2013, http://www.ontherecord-unisa.com.au/?p=3501.

17. 'Boost Global,' Boost Juice Bars (2013), accessed December 11, 2013 from http://www.boostjuice.com.au/boost_global.

18. Alexander E. Reppel, Isabelle Szmigin, and Thorsten Gruber, 'The iPod Phenomenon: Identifying a Market Leaders's Secrets through Qualitative Marketing Research,' *Journal of Product & Brand Management* 15 (2006): 239–249.

19. 'Cadbury/Woolies Joyville TVC,' CB Australia, 2013, http://www.youtube.com/watch?v=XvIRoHVpBsQ.

20. 'Every breakthrough product needs an audience: Find yours in all corners of the world,' The Nielsen Company (Jan 2013), accessed October 16, 2013, http://es.nielsen.com/news/NielsenGlobalNewProductsReport.pdf.pdf.

21. '4102.0 - Australian Social Trends, Jun 2011,' ABS, http://www.abs.gov.au/AUSSTATS/abs@.nsf/Lookup/4102.0Main+Features30Jun+2011.

22. 'Zero excuses for new Powerade Zero campaign,' Coca-Cola, February 5, 2013, http://www.coca-cola.com.au/mediaroom/assets/Press_Release.pdf.

23. Maria Sääksjärvi and Minuttu Lampinen, 'Consumer Perceived Risk in Successive Product Generations,' *European Journal of Innovation Management* 8 (June 2005): 145–156.

24. Tim Beissman, '2016 Holden Cruze interior revealed,' *Car Advice*, 2013, accessed October 16, 2013, http://www.caradvice.com.au/254950/2016-holden-cruze-interior-revealed/.

25. Nick Jaynes, 'Bugger! Holden ending the 'Ute' in 2016 and all hopes for a new El Camino,' *Digital Trends*, 2013, accessed December 12, 2013, http://www.digitaltrends.com/cars/bugger-holden-ending-ute-2016-hopes-new-el-camino/#ixzz2nDh6I3RF.

26. Ankush Chibber, 'Labels on energy drinks inadequate, say Australian health group,' *Foodnavigator-asia.com*, 2013, accessed October 16, 2013, http://www.foodnavigator-asia.com/Policy/Labels-on-energy-drinks-inadequate-says-Australian-health-group.

27. Evan A. Peterson, 'Caffeine Catastrophe: Energy Drinks, Products Liability and Market Strategy,' *International Journal of Marketing Studies*, 5 (2) (2013): 50–58.

28. 'Best global brands 2013,' Interbrand (2013), accessed December 10, 2013, http://www.interbrand.com/en/best-global-brands/2013/Samsung.

29. Nick Jaynes, 'Bugger! Holden ending the 'Ute' in 2016 and all hopes for a new El Camino.'

30. B. Eichengreen, and P. Gupta, 'The two waves of service-sector growth,' *Oxford Economic Papers*, 65(1) (2013): 96–123.

31. S. T. Rahman, M. K. Alam, and S. Kar, 'Factors Considered Important for Establishing Small and Medium Enterprises by Women Entrepreneurs—A Study on Khulna City,' *Business and Management Horizons*, 1(1) (2013): 171; S. Mahmood, 'Microfinance and women entrepreneurs in Pakistan. *International Journal of Gender and Entrepreneurship*, 3(3) (2011): 265–274.

32. Intan Farhana Zainul, 'Services to drive M'sian economic growth and expected to be 70% of GDP by 2015,' The Star online, 2013, accessed December 12, 2013, http://www.thestar.com.my/Business/Business-News/2013/02/20/Services-to-drive-Msian-economic-growth-and-expected-to-be-70-of-GDP-by-2015.aspx.

33. The information in this section is based on K. Douglass Hoffman and John E. G. Bateson, *Essentials of Services Marketing* (Mason, OH: South-Western, 2001); and Valarie A. Zeithaml, A. Parasuraman, and Leonard L. Berry, *Delivering Quality Service: Balancing Customer Perceptions* (New York: Free Press, 1990).

34. C. Lovelock and E. Gummesson, 'Whither Services Marketing: In Search of a New Paradigm and Fresh Perspectives,' *Journal of Service Research* 7, 20 (2004): 20–41.

35. G. Lynn Shostack, 'Breaking Free from Product Marketing,' *Journal of Marketing* 44 (April 1977): 73-80.

36. Mary Jo Bitner, 'Servicescapes: The Impact of Physical Surroundings on Customers and Employees,' *Journal of Marketing* 56 (April 1992): 57-71; Mary Jo Bitner, 'The Servicescape,' *Handbook of Services Marketing and Management* T. A. Swartz and D. Iacobucci, eds. (Thousand Oaks, CA: Sage, 2000), 37-50.

37. Don E. Schultz, 'Lost in Transition,' *Marketing Management* (March/April 2007): 10–11.

38. Jeremy J. Sierra and Shaun McQuitty, 'Service Providers and Customers: Social Exchange Theory and Service Loyalty,' *Journal of Services Marketing* 19 (October 2005): 392–400.

39. C. Lovelock and E. Gummesson (2004).

40. Sabin Im, Charlotte H. Mason, and Mark B. Houston, 'Does Innate Consumer Innovativeness Relate to New Product/Service Adoption Behavior? The Intervening Role of Social Learning via Vicarious Innovativeness,' *Journal of the Academy of Marketing Science* 35 (2007): 63–75.

41. Robert Moore, Melissa L. Moore, and Michael Capella, 'The Impact of Customer-to-Customer Interaction in a High Personal Contact Service Setting,' *Journal of Services Marketing* 19 (July 2005): 482–491.

42. Michael D. Hartline and O. C. Ferrell, 'Service Quality Implementation: The Effects of Organization and Managerial Actions of Customer Contact Employee Behavior,' *Marketing Science Institute Report* 93–122 (Cambridge, MA: Marketing Science Institute, 1993).

43. Dewi Yulini, 'After Twitter Success, Indonesia's President Goes Crazy for Social Media,' TechinAsia, July 6, 2013, accessed December 12, 2013, http://www.techinasia.com /twitter-success-indonesias-president-crazy-social-media /; Enrico Luckman, 'With 64 Million Monthly Facebook Users in Indonesia, Is it Opening an Office Soon?' TechinAsia, June 19, 2013, accessed December 12, 2013, http://www.techinasia.com/facebook-64-million-monthly -users-indonesia-answers-question-open-jakarta-office/.

44. Raymond P. Fisk, Stephen J. Grove, and Joby John, *Interactive Services Marketing* (Boston: Houghton Mifflin, 2003), 91.

45. Ahmed Taher and Hanan El Basha, 'Hetergeneity of Consumer Demand: Opportunities for Pricing of Services,' *Journal of Product & Brand Management* 15 (2006): 331–340.

46. Darren Quick, 'Samoa Air becomes first airline to implement 'pay as you weigh' system,' *Gizmag*, April 2, 2013, accessed August 17, 2013, http://www .gizmag.com/samoa-air-pay-weigh-airline/26906/.

47. Ben Wilmot, 'Tycoon Goh Geok Khim takes stake in Domain Principal Group,' *The Australian*, August 17, 2013, http://www.theaustralian.com.au/business/property/ tycoon-goh-geok-khim-takes-stake-in-domain-principal- group/story-fn9656lz-1226698904970.

48. Ben Grubb, 'Push for lift-off on drone deliveries in Australia,' *The Sydney Morning Herald*, October 15, 2013, accessed December 15, 2013, http://www.smh.com.au /technology/sci-tech/push-for-liftoff-on-drone-deliveries -in-australia-20131014-2vixx.html; Jason Paur, 'Why Amazon's drone delivery service won't fly any time soon,' accessed December 15, 2013, http://www.wired.com /autopia/2013/12/amazon-drone-delivery/.

49. Cirque du Soleil, http://www.cirquedusoleil.com; Douglas Belkin, 'Talent Scouts for Cirque du Soleil Walk a Tightrope,' *The Wall Street Journal* (September 8, 2007): A1; Forrest Glenn Spencer, 'It's One Big Circus,' *Information Outlook* (Oct. 2007): 22–23.

50. Jason Oxenbridge, 'It pays to be green,' *Gold Coast Business News* (June, 2007): http://www .goldcoastbusinessnews.com.au/article502/It%20pays%20 to%20be%20green.html

51. Adapted from Michael Levy and Barton A. Weitz, *Retailing Management* (Burr Ridge, IL: Irwin/McGraw-Hill, 2001), 585.

52. Jane Lindhe, 'Winning with SMEs: Why big business is thinking small,' *Business Review Weekly*, accessed December 14, 2013, http://brw.com.au/p /marketing/winning_with_smes_why_big_business _aAAImkzNK2jVUrHpUdWQjL.

53. Caitlin Fitzsimmons, 'How General Pants is bringing digital into the in-store-experience,' *Australian Financial Review*, (2013), http://www.afr.com/p/tech-gadgets/how_general _pants_experience_bringing_ajDw71m92cAoG8Jpe1B1K L?noMobileRedirect.

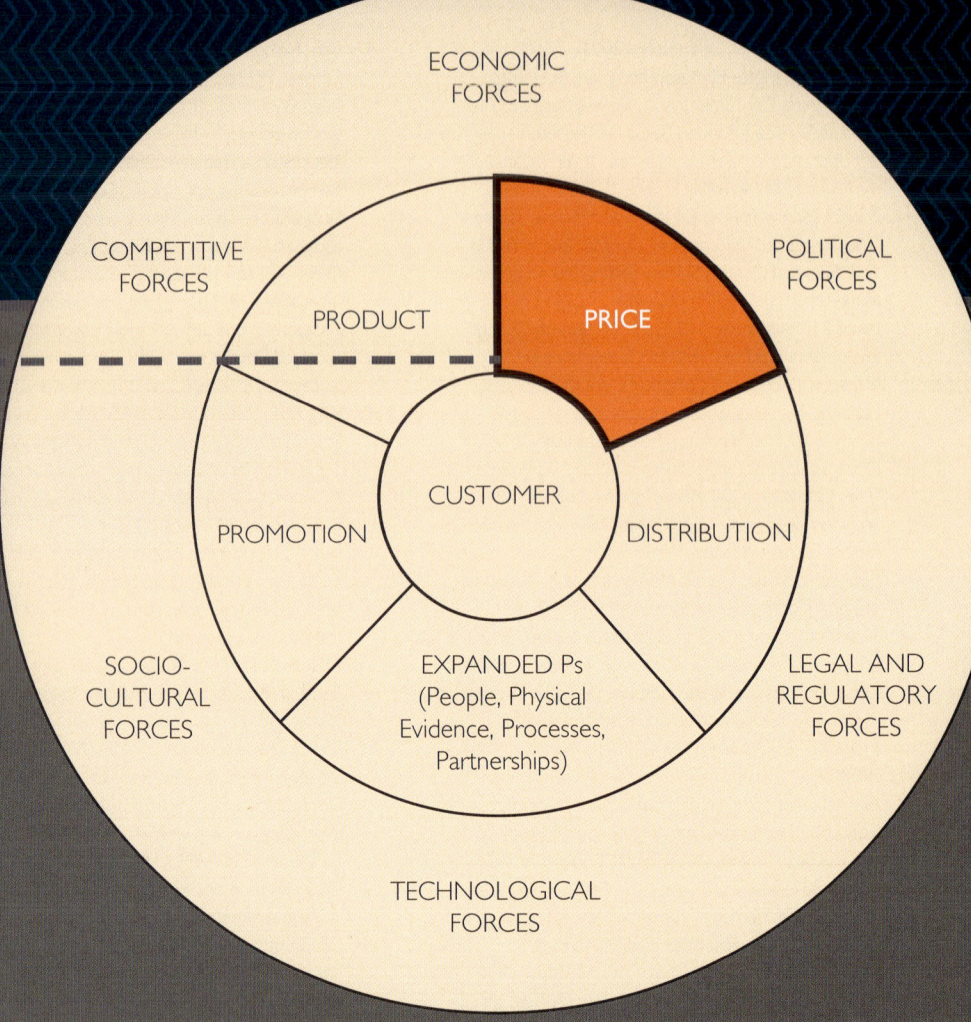

ECONOMIC FORCES

COMPETITIVE FORCES

POLITICAL FORCES

PRODUCT

PRICE

PROMOTION

CUSTOMER

DISTRIBUTION

SOCIO-CULTURAL FORCES

EXPANDED Ps (People, Physical Evidence, Processes, Partnerships)

LEGAL AND REGULATORY FORCES

TECHNOLOGICAL FORCES

PRICING DECISIONS

The role of price

Price and non-price competition

Factors affecting pricing decisions and objectives
Organisational and marketing objectives
Types of pricing objectives
Costs
Marketing mix variables other than price
Customer interpretations of, and responses to, a price
Customer perceptions of the product
Demand

Setting prices
Development of pricing objectives
Assessment of the target market's evaluation of price

Evaluation of competitors' prices
Selection of a basis for pricing

Selection of a pricing strategy
Differential pricing
New-product pricing
Product-line pricing
Psychological pricing
Professional pricing
Price discounting

   Throughout this chapter, Watch, Listen and Revise icons indicate an opportunity for online self-study through CengageNOW, linking you to animated chapter overviews, interactive diagrams, videos, quizzes and more.

10 PRICING DECISIONS

Learning Objectives

LO1 To understand the role of price

LO2 Identify the characteristics of price and non-price competition

LO3 To explore issues related to developing pricing objectives and understand the importance of identifying the target market's evaluation of price

LO4 Be familiar with the bases used for setting prices

LO5 Explain the different types of pricing strategies.

MARKETING CHALLENGE | AMAZON.COM'S BEST-SELLING PRICING IDEAS

Source: Getty Images

Amazon.com is the world's largest online retailer. It is a profitable billion-dollar business. Founded as a web-based bookstore selling both new and used books, Amazon.com has expanded into dozens of product categories, services and countries, including Australia. Amazon.com is now much more than just a bookstore.

Underpinning all areas of Amazon.com's business is its core value proposition, 'to be the Earth's most customer-centric company' and 'to offer its customers the lowest possible prices'. While Amazon.com does sell direct to customers using a traditional markup strategy, the organisation has pioneered an innovative retail strategy whereby Amazon.com provides a marketplace for other retailers. Amazon.com's innovative model ensures that its margins are high because Amazon.com keeps very little inventory itself and the costs to buy and store inventory are low. Additionally, Amazon.com does not carry product risk; superseded products and unsold stock are the concern of Amazon.com's retailers. Amazon.com also has business units catering to web-services and direct publishing.

Amazon.com's pricing model is tailored to be appropriate for each of its different business units:

* Every purchase from the Amazon Marketplace earns Amazon.com a small fee that is calculated as a percentage of the sale. Most of us are familiar with Amazon.com's fixed-price marketplace.
* Amazon.com's web services provide in-the-cloud access to infrastructure services. This service is charged as a fee for usage.
* Authors using Amazon.com's digital publishing pay 30 per cent of sales as a fee. Authors retain 70 per cent of sales as a royalty. Amazon.com provides authors with a global audience, access to its Kindle readers and speedy publishing.

Amazon.com is committed to continuing investment to keep its technology and Kindle reading device updated and customer-relevant. For example, Amazon.com have launched a local eBook store that features Australian authors, in addition to a new Kindle Fire tablet range. Thus Amazon.com ensures an ongoing market for its own products and services and protects its competitive advantage.[1]

MARKETING CHALLENGE QUESTION

1 Even if the company is willing to accept a tiny profit margin on a high volume of download purchases, can the Kindle generate the kind of profitability Amazon.com needs to continue growing?

Introduction

Many companies use pricing as a tool to compete against major competitors. However, their rivals may also employ pricing as a major competitive tool. In some industries, companies are very successful even if they don't have the lowest prices. The best price is not always the lowest price.

In this chapter we focus first on the role of price. We then consider some characteristics of price and non-price competition. Next, we explore issues related to developing pricing objectives and the importance of identifying the target market's evaluation of price, followed by a discussion of some pricing-related concepts, including demand. Then we examine in some detail the numerous factors that can influence pricing decisions. Finally, we discuss the main stages in setting a price.

LO1

price
Value exchanged for products in a marketing transaction

The role of price

Price is a key element in the marketing mix because it relates directly to the generation of total revenue. The following equation is an important one for the entire organisation:

$$Profit = total\ revenue - total\ costs$$

or

$$Profits = (price \times quantity\ sold) - total\ costs$$

Prices affect an organisation's profits in several ways because price is a key component of the profit equation and can be a major determinant of the quantities sold. For example, price is a top priority for Hewlett-Packard in gaining market share and improving financial performance.[2] Furthermore, total costs are influenced by quantities sold.

Price and non-price competition

The competitive environment strongly influences the marketing mix decisions associated with a product. Pricing decisions often are made according to the price or non-price competitive situation in a particular market. Price competition exists when consumers have difficulty distinguishing competitive offerings, and marketers emphasise low prices. Non-price competition involves a focus on marketing mix elements other than price.

Price competition

When engaging in price competition, a marketer emphasises price as a competitive issue and matches or beats the prices of competitors. To compete effectively on a price basis, a company should be the low-cost seller of the product. If all companies producing the same product charge the same price for it, the company with the lowest costs is the most profitable. Companies that stress low price as a key marketing mix element tend to market standardised products. A seller competing on price may change prices frequently or at least must be willing and able to do so.

Price competition gives a marketer flexibility. Prices can be altered to account for changes in the company's costs or in demand for the product. If competitors try to gain market share by cutting prices, an organisation competing on a price basis can react quickly to such efforts. However, a major drawback of price competition is that competitors also have the flexibility to adjust prices. If they quickly match or beat a company's price cuts, a price war may ensue.

© AP Images/AP Photo/Nick Ut

price competition
Emphasising price and matching or beating competitors' prices

<< Price competition
Consumer electronics stores compete on the basis of price

Non-price competition

Non-price competition occurs when a seller decides not to focus on price and instead emphasises distinctive product features, service, product quality, promotion, packaging or other factors to distinguish its product from competing brands. A major advantage of non-price competition is that a company can build customer loyalty toward its brand. If customers

non-price competition
Emphasising factors other than price to distinguish a product from competing brands

prefer a brand because of non-price factors, they may not be easily lured away by competing companies and brands. In contrast, when price is the primary reason customers buy a particular brand, a competitor is often able to attract these customers through price cuts.

Non-price competition is effective only under certain conditions. A company must be able to distinguish its brand through unique product features, higher product quality, promotion, packaging or excellent customer service. Buyers not only must be able to perceive these distinguishing characteristics, but they also must view them as important. The distinguishing features that set a particular brand apart from competitors should be difficult, if not impossible, for competitors to imitate. Finally, the organisation must extensively promote the distinguishing characteristics of the brand to establish its superiority and set it apart from competitors in the minds of buyers.

Even a marketer that is competing on a non-price basis cannot ignore competitors' prices. It must be aware of them and sometimes be prepared to price its brand near or slightly above competing brands. Therefore, price remains a crucial marketing-mix component even in environments that call for non-price competition.

Factors affecting pricing decisions and objectives

Pricing decisions can be complex because of the number of factors to be considered. Frequently, there is considerable uncertainty about the reactions to price among buyers, distribution-channel members and competitors. Price is also an important consideration in marketing planning, market analysis and sales forecasting. It is a major issue when assessing a brand's position relative to competing brands. Most factors that affect pricing decisions can be grouped into one of the seven categories shown in Figure 10.1. In this

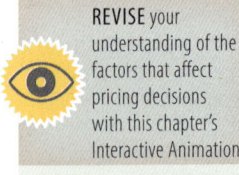

REVISE your understanding of the factors that affect pricing decisions with this chapter's Interactive Animation

FIGURE 10.1 FACTORS THAT AFFECT PRICING DECISIONS

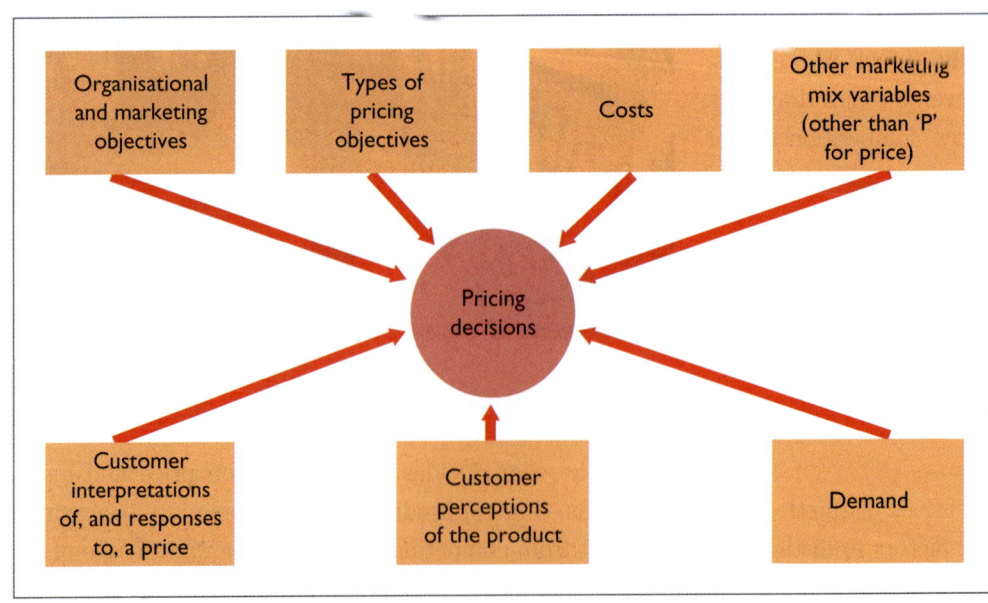

section, we explore how each of these six factor categories enters into price decision making.

Organisational and marketing objectives

Marketers should set prices that are consistent with the organisation's goals and mission. For example, a retailer trying to position itself as value-oriented may wish to set prices that are quite reasonable relative to product quality. In this case a marketer would not want to set premium prices on products but would strive to price products in line with this overall organisational goal.

Pricing decisions also should be compatible with the organisation's marketing objectives. For instance, suppose that one of a producer's marketing objectives is a 12 per cent increase in unit sales by the end of the next year. Assuming that buyers are price-sensitive, increasing the price or setting a price above the average market price would not be in line with this objective.

Types of pricing objectives

The types of pricing objectives a marketer uses obviously have considerable bearing on the determination of prices. For example, an organisation that uses pricing to increase its market share likely would set the brand's price below those of competing brands of similar quality to attract competitors' customers. A marketer sometimes uses temporary price reductions in the hope of gaining market share. If a business needs to raise cash quickly, it likely will use temporary price reductions such as sales, rebates and special discounts.

Costs

Clearly, costs must be an issue when establishing price. A company temporarily may sell products below cost to match competition, to generate cash flow or even to increase market share, but in the long run it cannot survive by selling its products below cost. Even when a company has a high-volume business, it cannot survive if each item is sold slightly below what it costs. A marketer should be careful to analyse all costs so that they can be included in the total cost associated with a product.

To maintain market share and revenue in an increasingly price-sensitive market,

Source: Courtesy of The Advertising Archives

<< Price affects promotion decisions
Most fragrance advertisements do not include prices

many marketers have concentrated on reducing costs such as those shared with other products in the product line, including costs of research and development, production and distribution. Most marketers view a product's cost as a minimum, or floor, below which the product cannot be priced.

Marketing mix variables other than price

All marketing mix variables are highly interrelated. For instance, buyers associate better product quality with a high price, and poorer product quality with a low price. This perceived price–quality relationship is a cornerstone of Sony's promotion activities because the relationship influences customers' overall image of products or brands. Sony, for example, prices its TVs higher than average to help communicate that Sony TVs are high-quality electronic products. Consumers recognise the Sony brand name, its reputation for quality and the prestige associated with buying Sony products.

The price of a product is linked to several dimensions of its distribution. Premium-priced products – a Bentley or a Rolls-Royce car, for example – are often marketed through selective or exclusive distribution. Lower-priced products in the same product category may be sold through intensive distribution. For example, Parker pens are distributed in Australia through selective distribution and Bic pens through intensive distribution. Moreover, an increase in physical distribution costs, such as shipping, may have to be passed on to customers. When setting a price, the profit margins of marketing channel members, such as wholesalers and retailers, must be considered. Channel members must be compensated adequately for the functions they perform.

Price may determine how a product is promoted. Bargain prices are often included in advertisements. Premium prices are less likely to be advertised, although they are sometimes included in ads for upscale items such as luxury cars or fine jewellery. Higher-priced products are more likely than lower-priced ones to require personal selling. Furthermore, the price structure can affect a salesperson's relationship with customers. A complex pricing structure takes longer to explain to customers, is more likely to confuse potential buyers and may cause misunderstandings that result in long-term customer dissatisfaction. For example, the pricing structures of many airlines are complex and frequently confuse ticket sales agents and travellers alike.

Customer interpretations of, and responses to, a price

When making pricing decisions, marketers should be concerned with a vital question: How will our customers interpret our prices and respond to them? *Interpretation* in this context refers to what the price means or what it communicates to customers. Does the price mean 'high quality', 'low quality' or 'great deal', 'fair price' or 'rip-off'? Customer *response* refers to whether the price will move customers closer to the purchase of the product and the degree to which the price enhances their satisfaction with the purchase experience and with the product after purchase. The ethical issue of fine print pricing can have a negative impact on the purchase experience, as discussed in the Ethical Marketing box below.

ETHICAL MARKETING   TRAVEL PRICES AND FINE PRINT

issue

Should customers have to check the fine print to know how much travel services cost?

What is the real price of a room at a resort hotel or a seat on a plane? In many cases, customers don't know until they follow the asterisk in an ad or read the fine print at the bottom of the screen or page. Because many travel services are subject to taxes and fees that are not always prominently disclosed, customers may be surprised when a bargain turns out to not be as good as it appeared at first glance.

Airlines and travel websites often promote low fares to grab attention and boost sales in a hurry. After customers complained about 'hidden' fees and taxes added at the end of a purchase, US regulators began requiring airlines to disclose the full price at the start. Some airlines objected,

saying that fees and taxes should be disclosed separately, because they're imposed by the government and not under the airline's pricing control. A growing number of resort hotels are adding mandatory all-in-one fees to cover parking, fitness centre facilities, Internet access and other services, saying that bundled pricing is more convenient for guests. However, guests who don't take advantage of these services sometimes grumble about the higher price, especially when they aren't aware of the extra fees at the time of booking.

Should fees be in the fine print or in the price?[3]

Customers' interpretation of and response to a price are determined to some degree by their assessment of value, or what they receive compared with what they give up to make the purchase. In evaluating what they receive, customers will consider product attributes, benefits, advantages, disadvantages, the probability of using the product, and possibly the status associated with the product. In assessing the cost of the product, customers likely will consider its price, the amount of time and effort required to obtain it and perhaps the resources required to maintain it after purchase.

At times, customers interpret a higher price as an indication of higher product quality. They are especially likely to make this price–quality association when they cannot judge the quality of the product themselves. This is not always the case, however. Whether price is equated with quality depends on the types of customers and products involved. Obviously, marketers who rely on customers making a price–quality association and who provide moderate- or low-quality products at high prices will be unable to build long-term customer relationships.

When interpreting and responding to prices, how do customers determine if the price is too high, too low or about right? In general, they compare prices with internal or external reference prices. An internal reference price is a price developed in the buyer's mind through experience with the product. It is a belief that a product should cost approximately a certain amount. To arrive at an internal reference price, consumers may consider one or more values, including what they think the product 'ought' to cost, the price usually charged for it, the last price they paid, the highest and lowest amounts they would be

internal reference price
A price developed in the buyer's mind through experience with the product

Source: © Green Stock Media/Alamy

Source: © Green Stock Media/Alamy

willing to pay, the price of the brand they usually buy, the average price of similar products, the expected future price and the typical discounted price.[4] Research has found that less-confident consumers tend to have higher internal reference prices than consumers with greater confidence, and frequent buyers – perhaps because of their experience and confidence – are more likely to judge high prices unfairly.[5] As consumers, our experiences have given each of us internal reference prices for several products. For example, most of us have a reasonable idea of how much to pay for a six-pack of soft drinks, or a loaf of bread. For the product categories with which we have less experience, we rely more heavily on external reference prices. An external reference price is a comparison price provided by others, such as retailers or producers. Customers' perceptions of prices are also influenced by their expectations about future price increases, by what they paid for the product recently and by what they would like to pay for the product. Other factors affecting customers' perception of whether the price is right include time or financial constraints, the costs associated with searching for lower-priced products and expectations that products will go on sale.

Customer perceptions of the product

Customers' perceptions of a product (goods or services) relative to competing products may allow the company to set a price that differs significantly from rivals' prices. If the product is deemed superior to most of the competition, a premium price may be feasible. However, even products with superior quality can be overpriced. Strong brand loyalty sometimes provides the opportunity to charge a premium price. On the other hand, if buyers view a product less than favourably (although not extremely negatively), a lower price may generate sales.

In the context of price, customers can be characterised according to their degree of value consciousness, price consciousness and prestige sensitivity. Marketers who understand these characteristics are better able to set pricing objectives and policies. Value-conscious consumers are concerned about both price and quality of a product.[6] These consumers may perceive value as quality per unit of price or as not only economic savings but also the additional gains expected from one product over a competitor's brand. The first view is appropriate for commodities such as bottled water, bananas and petrol. If value-conscious consumers perceive the quality of petrol to be the same for Mobil, they will go to the station

Customer interpretation and response >>
Over the past few years, a number of airlines have imposed additional charges for baggage, food, fuel and video. Many travelers have interpreted these add-on charges as excessive and unfair.

external reference price
A comparison price provided by others

value-conscious
Concerned about price and quality of a product

with the lower price. For consumers looking not just for economic value but additional gains they expect from one brand over another, a product differentiation value could be associated with benefits and features that are believed to be unique.[7] Price-conscious individuals strive to pay low prices.[8] Prestige-sensitive buyers focus on purchasing products that signify prominence and status. It is important to recognise that some consumers vary in their degree of value, price and prestige consciousness. In some segments, moreover, consumers are increasingly 'trading up' to higher-status products in categories such as cars, home appliances, restaurants and even pet food; yet they remain price conscious regarding cleaning and grocery products.

price-conscious
Striving to pay low prices

prestige-sensitive
Drawn to products that signify prominence and status

Demand

Before a particular price point can be decided on, demand for a product at various potential price points also has to be established. Determining the demand for a product is the responsibility of marketing managers, who are aided in this task by marketing researchers and forecasters. Marketing research and forecasting techniques yield estimates of sales potential, or the quantity of a product that could be sold during a specific period. These estimates are helpful in establishing the relationship between a product's price and the quantity demanded.

For most products, the quantity demanded goes up as the price goes down, and as the price goes up, the quantity demanded goes down. Intel, for example, knows that lowering prices boosts demand for its processors. Thus an inverse relationship exists between price and quantity demanded. As long as the marketing environment and buyers' needs, ability (purchasing power), willingness and authority to buy remain stable, this fundamental inverse relationship holds.

Figure 10.2 illustrates the effect of one variable – price – on the quantity demanded. The classic demand curve (D_1) is a graph of the quantity of a product taken by buyers in the market at various prices, given that all other factors are held constant.[9] It illustrates that as price falls, the quantity demanded usually rises. Demand depends on other factors in the marketing mix, including product quality, promotion and distribution. An improvement in any of these factors may cause a shift to, say, demand curve D_2. In such a case, an increased quantity (Q_2) will be sold at the same price (P).

There are many types of demand, and not all conform to the classic demand curve shown in Figure 10.2. Prestige products, such as select perfumes and

demand curve
A graph of the quantity of a product taken by buyers in the market at various prices, given that all other factors are held constant

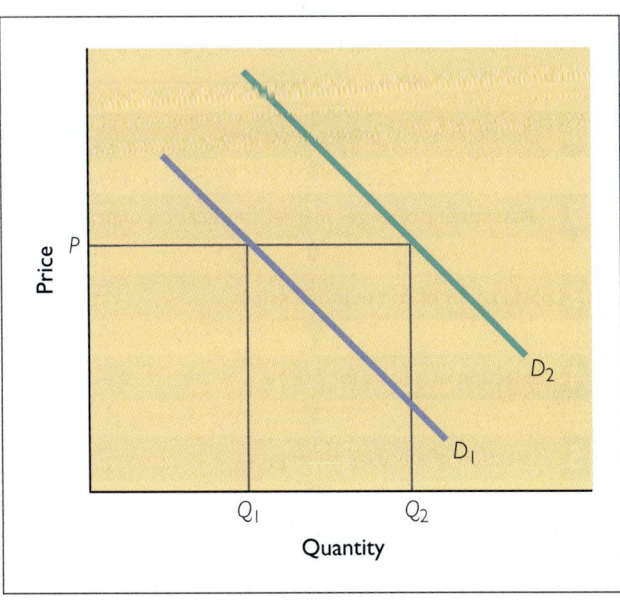

FIGURE 10.2 DEMAND CURVE ILLUSTRATING THE PRICE–QUANTITY RELATIONSHIP AND INCREASE IN DEMAND

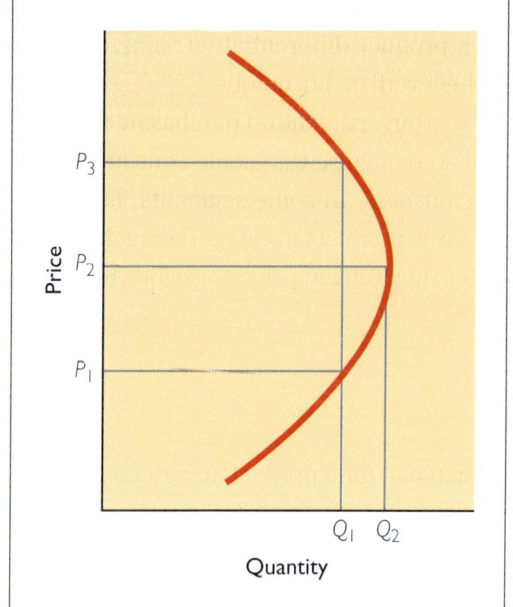

FIGURE 10.3 DEMAND CURVE ILLUSTRATING THE RELATIONSHIP BETWEEN PRICE AND QUANTITY FOR PRESTIGE PRODUCTS

jewellery, seem to sell better at high prices than at low ones. These products are desirable partly because their expense makes buyers feel elite. If the price fell drastically and many people owned these products, they would lose some of their appeal.

The demand curve in Figure 10.3 shows the relationship between price and quantity demanded for prestige products. Quantity demanded is greater, not less, at higher prices. For a certain price range – from P_1 to P_2 – the quantity demanded (Q_1) goes up to Q_2. After a certain point, however, raising the price backfires. If the price goes too high, the quantity demanded goes down. The figure shows that if the price is raised from P_2 to P_3, the quantity demanded goes back down from Q_2 to Q_1.

Setting prices

In the remainder of this chapter we examine six stages of a process marketers can use when setting prices (Figure 10.4). Stage 1 is the development of a pricing objective that is compatible with the organisation's overall objectives and its marketing objectives. Stage 2 entails assessing the target market's evaluation of price. For example, regarding the price of mobile apps, a freemium pricing strategy may be most effective in reaching the target market, as discussed in the Marketing in Transition box on the next page. Stage 3 involves evaluating competitors' prices, which helps to determine the role of price in the marketing strategy. Stage 4 involves choosing a basis for setting prices. Stage 5 is the selection of a pricing strategy, or the guidelines for using price in the marketing mix. Stage 6, determining the final price, depends on environmental forces and marketers' understanding and use of a systematic approach to establishing prices. These stages are not rigid steps that all marketers must follow; rather, they are guidelines that provide a logical sequence for establishing prices.

1 Development of pricing objectives

2 Assessment of target market's evaluation of price

3 Evaluation of competitors' prices

4 Selection of a basis for pricing

5 Selection of a pricing strategy

6 Determination of a specific price

FIGURE 10.4 STAGES FOR ESTABLISHING PRICES

Development of pricing objectives

The first step in setting prices is developing pricing objectives which are goals that describe what a company wants to achieve through pricing. Developing pricing objectives is an important task because pricing objectives form the basis for decisions about other stages of pricing. Thus pricing objectives must be stated explicitly, and the statement should include the time frame for accomplishing them.

Marketers must make sure that the pricing objectives are consistent with the organisation's marketing objectives and with its overall objectives because pricing objectives influence decisions in many functional areas, including finance, accounting and production. A marketer can use both short- and long-term pricing objectives and can employ one or multiple pricing objectives. For instance, a company may wish to increase market share by 18 per cent over the next three years,

pricing objectives
Goals that describe what a company wants to achieve through pricing

Source: Image courtesy of the advertising archives

THAT
UNIQUE
KELLOGG'S QUALITY

If it doesn't say Kellogg's on the box, then it won't be Kellogg's in the box. As it's been since 1906, when W. K. Kellogg started making cereal from only the finest ingredients.

Kellogg's   Bringing our best to you.

<< Product quality
This ad for Kellogg's Corn Flakes focuses on high product quality. A part of Kellogg's message in many of its ads is 'bringing our best to you'

TABLE 10.1   PRICING OBJECTIVES AND TYPICAL ACTIONS TAKEN TO ACHIEVE THEM

Objective	Possible action
Survival	Adjust price levels so that the company can increase sales volume to match organisational expenses
Profit	Identify price and cost levels that allow the company to maximise profit
Return on investment	Identify price levels that enable the company to yield targeted return on investment
Market share	Adjust price levels so that the company can maintain or increase sales relative to competitors' sales
Cash flow	Set price levels to encourage rapid sales
Status quo	Identify price levels that help stabilise demand and sales
Product quality	Set prices to recover research and development expenditures and establish a high-quality image

achieve a 15 per cent return on investment, and promote an image of quality in the marketplace. Table 10.1 examines some of the pricing objectives that companies might set for themselves.

Assessment of the target market's evaluation of price

After developing pricing objectives such as those discussed in Table 10.1, marketers next need to assess the target market's evaluation of price. Despite the general assumption that price is a major issue for buyers, the importance of price depends on the type of product, the type of target market and the purchase situation. For example, buyers are probably more sensitive to petrol prices than to luggage prices. With respect to the type of target market, adults may have to pay more than children for certain products. The purchase

SUSTAINABLE MARKETING | HOME-MADE ENERGY

From energy-generating solar panels to nature-friendly building materials, new homes are getting greener. However, cutting-edge products such as solar panels and decking made from recycled plastics are often marketed using a price-skimming strategy. As a result, even people who want to own a green home hesitate when they see the price tag of these extra features. For instance, the cost of installing solar panels to generate electricity when the sun shines can range from $8000 to $40 000 per home.

Fortunately, a solar investment will pay for itself by reducing the owner's energy costs in the long run.

Some homeowners pay less than $30 monthly for electricity – sometimes they even receive money back from the energy companies – thanks to solar panels and other energy-efficient house improvements.

Little by little, prices are starting to move lower as more competitors enter the market. In addition, state and federal government–sponsored incentives are making green home features more affordable for buyers. Finally, no matter how high the price tag, builders and buyers in many communities will soon have no choice but to go greener to comply with local building codes.[11]

situation also affects the buyer's view of price. In other situations, most movie goers would never pay the prices charged for soft drinks, popcorn and lollies at the kiosks. By assessing the target market's evaluation of price, a marketer is in a better position to know how much emphasis to put on price in the overall marketing strategy. Information about the target market's price evaluation also may help a marketer to determine how far above the competition the company can set its prices.

Because some consumers today are seeking less expensive products and shopping more selectively, some manufacturers and retailers are focusing on the value of their products. Value combines a product's price and quality attributes.

Evaluation of competitors' prices

In most cases marketers are in a better position to establish prices when they know the prices charged for competing brands, the third step in establishing prices. Discovering competitors' prices may be a regular function of marketing research. Some grocery and department stores, for example, have full-time comparative shoppers who systematically collect data on prices. However, uncovering competitors' prices is not always easy, especially in producer and reseller markets. Competitors' price lists are often closely guarded. Even if a marketer has access to competitors' price lists, these lists may not reflect the actual prices at which competitive products are sold because those prices may be established through negotiation.

Knowing the prices of competing brands can be very important for a marketer. Competitors' prices and the marketing-mix variables they emphasise partly determine how important price will be to customers. A marketer in an industry in which price competition prevails needs competitive price information to ensure that its prices are the same as, or lower than, competitors' prices. In some instances an organisation's prices are designed to be slightly above competitors' prices to give its products an exclusive image. In contrast, another company may use price as a competitive tool and price its products below those of competitors.

Selection of a basis for pricing

The fourth step involves selecting a basis for pricing: cost, value and/or competition. The choice of the basis to use is affected by the type of product, the market structure of the industry, the brand's market share position relative to competing brands, and customer characteristics. Although we discuss each basis separately in this section, an organisation generally considers two or all three of these dimensions, even though one may be the primary dimension on which it bases prices. For example, if a company is using cost as a basis for setting prices, marketers in that firm are also aware of and concerned about competitors' prices. If a company is using value as a basis for pricing, those making pricing decisions still must consider costs and competitors' prices.

Pricing based on cost

When setting a price based on cost, a dollar amount or percentage is added to the cost of the product. The most common approach to determining a price based on cost is cost-plus pricing, also known as markup pricing. This approach involves calculations of desired profit margins. Cost-plus pricing does not necessarily take into account the economic aspects of

TEST your knowledge of pricing with the online Crossword

cost-plus pricing
Adding a specified dollar amount or percentage to the seller's cost. Also known as markup pricing

markup pricing
Adding to the cost of the product a predetermined percentage of that cost

supply and demand, nor must it relate to just one pricing strategy or pricing objective. Cost-plus pricing is straightforward and easy to implement.

With cost-plus pricing, the seller's costs are determined (usually during a project or after a project is completed), and then a specified dollar amount or percentage of the cost is added to the seller's cost to establish the price. Cost-plus pricing is one of the *most* commonly used bases for pricing all sorts of products, including professional services.[12] Projects involving custom-made equipment and commercial construction are often priced by this technique. Refer to the Marketing in Action box below for an example of a unique product with minimal competition which has adopted a cost-plus pricing strategy. The government frequently uses such pricing in granting defense contracts. When production costs are difficult to predict, cost-plus pricing is also appropriate.

MARKETING IN ACTION | REINVENTING THE WHEELIE BIN

Australian company Wheelie Bin Sound Systems reinvented the everyday wheelie bin into a portable, environmentally friendly sound system. Branded Sunny Bins, the wheelie bins are fitted internally with a speaker system, which runs off solar power. The solar power is generated from solar panels attached to the lid of the bin, and the system can also be charged through a 240-volt wall charger. The Sunny Bin can simply be wheeled into position for both indoor and outdoor events, with each bin individually decorated and customisable. ✖

One pitfall of cost-plus pricing for the buyer is that the seller may increase costs to establish a larger profit base. Furthermore, some costs, such as overhead, may be difficult to determine. In periods of rapid inflation, cost-plus pricing is popular, especially when the producer must use raw materials that are fluctuating in price.

A common approach to cost-plus pricing is when a product's price is derived by adding a predetermined percentage of the cost, called *markup*, to the cost of the product. Although the percentage markup in a retail store for instance varies from one category of goods to another – 35 per cent of cost for hardware items and 100 per cent of cost for greeting cards, for example – the same percentage often is used to determine the price on items within a single product category, and the percentage markup may be largely standardised across an industry at the retail level. Using a standard percentage markup for a specific product category reduces pricing to a routine task that can be performed quickly. This is one of the major reasons that many retailers use cost-plus pricing.

A markup can be stated as a percentage of the cost or as a percentage of the selling price. The following example illustrates how percentage markups are determined and points out the differences in the two methods. Assume that a retailer purchases a pencil at 45 cents, adds 15 cents to the cost, and then prices the pencil at 60 cents. Here are the figures:

$$\text{Markup as percentage of cost} = \frac{\text{markup}}{\text{cost}}$$

$$= \frac{15}{45}$$

$$= 33.3 \text{ per cent}$$

$$\text{Markup as percentage of selling price} = \frac{\text{markup}}{\text{selling price}}$$

$$= \frac{15}{60}$$

$$= 25.0 \text{ per cent}$$

Obviously, when discussing a percentage markup, it is important to know whether the markup is based on cost or selling price.

Pricing based on value

Marketers sometimes base prices on customers' willingness to pay for the particular benefits that the product offers. This method is called value-based pricing. Companies that are able to offer goods and services which are unique or special, and to that end offer valuable benefits, are more likely to benefit from value-based pricing than companies with undifferentiated and undistinguished offerings.

When value-based pricing is used, customers pay a higher price if demand for the product is strong and a lower price if demand is weak. To use this pricing basis, a marketer must be able to estimate how much consumers will pay for a product's perceived benefits before choosing to purchase from a competitor or seeking a substitute. The marketer then selects the price that generates the highest total revenue. Obviously, the effectiveness of value-based pricing depends on the marketer's ability to estimate demand accurately. Compared with cost-plus pricing, value-based pricing places a firm in a better position to reach higher profit levels, assuming that buyers value the product at levels sufficiently above the product's cost. One downside of applying value-based pricing too rigorously and without exception is that customers may feel that they are being constantly squeezed for their last dollar which, over time, may lead to consumer resentment towards the company using the pricing method.

value-based pricing
Pricing based on the level of benefits the product offers

Pricing based on competition

Marketers also sometimes base prices on what their competitors are charging for a similar or identical product. This method is called competition-based pricing, whereby an organisation considers its costs as secondary to competitors' prices. The importance of this method increases when competing products are relatively homogeneous, and the organisation is serving markets in which price is a key purchase consideration. A company that uses competition-based pricing may choose to price below competitors' prices, above competitors' prices or at the same level. Airlines use competition-based pricing, often charging identical fares on the same routes. Also, many online travel services employ competition-based pricing.

competition-based pricing
Pricing influenced primarily by competitors' prices

Although not all introductory marketing texts have exactly the same price, they do have similar prices. The price the bookstore paid to the publishing company for this textbook was determined on the basis of competitors' prices. Competition-based pricing can help a company achieve the pricing objective of increasing sales or market share. Competition-based pricing may necessitate frequent price adjustments. For example, for many competitive airline routes, fares are adjusted often.

Selection of a pricing strategy

The next step after choosing a basis for pricing is to select a particular pricing strategy, an approach or a course of action designed to achieve pricing and other marketing objectives. Generally, pricing strategies help marketers to solve the practical problems of establishing prices.

Differential pricing

differential pricing
Charging different prices to different buyers for the same quality and quantity of product

Differential pricing means charging different prices to different buyers for the same quality and quantity of product. For differential pricing to be effective, the market must consist of multiple segments with different price sensitivities, and the method should be used in a way that avoids confusing or antagonising customers. Customers paying the lower prices should not be able to resell the product to the individuals and organisations paying higher prices, unless that is the intention of the seller. Differential pricing can occur in several ways, including negotiated pricing and secondary-market discounting.

Negotiated pricing

negotiated pricing
Establishing a final price through bargaining

Negotiated pricing occurs when the final price is established through bargaining between seller and customer. If you buy a house, for example, you are likely to negotiate the final price with the seller. Negotiated pricing occurs in numerous industries and at all levels of distribution. During an economic downturn, there is a greater use of negotiated pricing.[13] Even when there is a predetermined stated price or a price list, manufacturers, wholesalers and retailers still may negotiate to establish the final sales price.

Secondary-market pricing

secondary-market pricing
Setting one price for the primary target market and a different price for another market

Secondary-market pricing means setting one price for the primary target market and a different price for another market. Often the price charged in the secondary market is lower. However, when the costs of serving a secondary market are higher than normal, secondary-market customers may have to pay a higher price. Examples of secondary markets include a geographically isolated domestic market, a market in a foreign country, and a segment willing to purchase a product during off-peak times. For example, some restaurants offer special 'early bird' prices during the early evening hours, cinemas offer senior-citizen discounts, and some textbooks and pharmaceutical products are sold for considerably less in certain foreign countries than in Australia or New Zealand. Secondary markets give an organisation an opportunity to use excess capacity and to stabilise the allocation of resources.

New-product pricing

Setting the base price for a new product is a necessary part of formulating a marketing strategy. The base price is easily adjusted (in the absence of government price controls), and its establishment is one of the most fundamental decisions in the marketing mix. When a marketer sets base prices, it also considers how quickly competitors will enter the market, whether they will mount a strong campaign on entry and what effect their entry will have on the development of primary demand. Two strategies used in new-product pricing are price skimming and penetration pricing.

LISTEN to the Audio Summary to check your understanding of pricing strategy

Price skimming

Price skimming is charging the highest possible price that buyers who most desire the product will pay. A skimming policy can generate much-needed initial cash flows to help offset sizeable developmental costs. When introducing a new pharmaceutical, most drug makers such as Merck and Pfizer often use a skimming price to defray large research and development costs and to help fund further research and development into other drugs. Price skimming protects the marketer from problems that arise when the price is set too low to cover costs. When a firm introduces a product, its production capacity may be limited. A skimming price can help to keep demand consistent with the firm's production capabilities. The use of a skimming price may attract competition into an industry because the high price makes that type of business appear to be quite lucrative.

price skimming
Charging the highest possible price that buyers who most desire the product will pay

Penetration pricing

In penetration pricing, prices are set below those of competing brands to penetrate a market and gain a large market share quickly. This approach is less flexible for a marketer than price skimming because it is more difficult to raise a penetration price than to lower or discount a skimming price. It is not unusual for a firm to use a penetration price after having skimmed the market with a higher price.

Penetration pricing can be especially beneficial when a marketer suspects that competitors could enter the market easily. If penetration pricing allows the marketer to gain a large market share quickly, competitors may be discouraged from entering the market. In addition, because the lower per-unit penetration price results in lower per-unit profit, the market may not appear to be especially lucrative to potential new entrants.

penetration pricing
Setting prices below those of competing brands to penetrate a market and gain a significant market share quickly

Product-line pricing

Rather than considering products on an item-by-item basis when determining pricing strategies, some marketers employ product-line pricing. Product-line pricing means establishing and adjusting the prices of multiple products within a product line. When marketers use product-line pricing, their goal is to maximise profits for an entire product line rather than focusing on the profitability of an individual product. Product-line pricing can provide marketers with flexibility in price setting. For example, marketers can set prices so that one product is quite profitable, while another increases market share by virtue of having a lower price than competing products. When marketers employ product-line

product-line pricing
Establishing and adjusting prices of multiple products within a product line

Image courtesy of The Advertising Archives

SHOW THE WORLD
HOW PHENOMENAL YOU CAN BE.

captive pricing
Pricing the basic product in a product line low while pricing related items at a higher level

Captive pricing >>
The Gillette razor is inexpensive. To use this razor on a regular basis, customers must buy the replacement blade cartridges. The annual cost of the replacement blade cartridges is significant. Gillette is using captive pricing

premium pricing
Pricing the highest-quality or most versatile products higher than other models in the product line

bait pricing
Pricing an item in the product line low with the intention of selling a higher-priced item in the line

price lining
Setting a limited number of prices for selected groups or lines of merchandise

pricing, they have several strategies from which to choose, including captive pricing, premium pricing, bait pricing and price lining.

Captive pricing

With captive pricing, the basic product in a product line is priced low, whereas the price on the items required to operate or enhance it may be higher. Printer companies such as Hewlett-Packard and Canon have used this pricing strategy, providing relatively low-cost, low-margin printers and selling ink cartridges to generate significant profits. Likewise, theme parks such as Movie World and Dream World set competitive yearly VIP pass prices for locals which start from AU$69, then capitalise by charging higher than average prices for in-park experience add-ons such as memorabilia, photos, food and beverages.

Premium pricing

Premium pricing is often used when a product line contains several versions of the same product; the highest-quality products or those with the most versatility are given the highest prices. Chevrolet, for example, set an initial price of $100 000 for its fastest, most powerful Corvette ZR1. The company expects the muscle car, with its hand-built 620-horsepower V8 engine, to compete with the performance of a Ferrari.[14] Other products in the line are priced to appeal to price-sensitive shoppers or to those who seek product-specific features.

Bait pricing

To attract customers, marketers may put a low price on one item in a product line, with the intention of selling a higher-priced item in the line; this strategy is known as bait pricing. For example, a computer retailer might advertise its lowest-priced computer model, hoping that when customers come to the store, they will purchase a higher-priced one. This strategy can facilitate sales of a line's higher-priced products. As long as a retailer has sufficient quantities of the advertised low-priced model available for sale, this strategy is considered acceptable. However, *bait and switch* is an activity in which retailers have no intention of selling the bait product; they use the low price merely to entice customers into the store to sell them higher-priced products. Bait and switch is considered unethical.

Price lining

When an organisation sets a limited number of prices for selected groups or lines of merchandise, it is using price lining. A retailer may have various styles and brands of similar-quality men's shirts that sell for $15 and another line of higher-quality shirts that sell for $22. Price lining simplifies customers' decision-making by holding constant one key variable in the final selection of style and brand within a line. Another type of price lining is subscription services. Cable and satellite TV subscribers choose different packages or groupings of channels with different prices.

The basic assumption in price lining is that the demand for various groups or sets of products is inelastic. If the prices are attractive, customers will concentrate their purchases without responding to slight changes in price. Thus a women's dress shop that carries dresses priced at $85, $55 and $35 may not attract many more sales with a drop to, say, $83, $53 and $33. The 'space' between the price of $85 and $55, however, can stir changes in consumer response.

Psychological pricing

Learning the price of a product is not always a pleasant experience for customers. It can sometimes be surprising (as at a movie concession stand) and sometimes downright horrifying. Most of us have been afflicted with 'sticker shock'. Psychological pricing attempts to influence a customer's perception of price to make a product's price more attractive. In this section we consider several forms of psychological pricing.

Reference pricing

Reference pricing means pricing a product at a moderate level and displaying it next to a more expensive model or brand in the hope that the customer will use the higher price as an external reference price (i.e. a comparison price). Because of the comparison, the customer is expected to view the moderate price favourably. Reference pricing is based on the 'isolation effect', meaning an alternative is less attractive when viewed by itself than when compared with other alternatives. When you go to an electronic retailer to buy a DVD player, a moderately priced DVD player may appear especially attractive because it offers most of the important attributes of the more expensive alternatives on display and at a lower price. It is not unusual for an organisation's moderately priced private brands to be positioned alongside more expensive, better-known manufacturer brands.

Bundle pricing

Bundle pricing is packaging together two or more products, usually complementary ones, to be sold for a single price. Bundle pricing is often used to help a company drive business to its slow-moving products, for example when slow-moving products are bundled with products with higher turnover. To attract customers, the single price is usually considerably less than the sum of the prices of the individual products. Many fast-food restaurants, for example, offer combination meals at a price that is lower than the combined prices of each item priced separately. Most telephone and cable television providers bundle local telephone service, broadband Internet access, and digital cable or satellite television for one monthly fee.

Multiple-unit pricing

Multiple-unit pricing occurs when two or more identical products are packaged together and sold for a single price. This normally results in a lower per-unit price than the one regularly charged. Multiple-unit pricing is used commonly for twin-packs of potato chips,

psychological pricing
Pricing that attempts to influence a customer's perception of price to make a product's price more attractive

reference pricing
Pricing a product at a moderate level and displaying it next to a more expensive model or brand

bundle pricing
Packaging together two or more complementary products and selling them for a single price

multiple-unit pricing
Packaging together two or more identical products and selling them for a single price

Source © Telstra, used with permission from Telstra Legal Services

four-packs of light bulbs, and six- and 12-packs of soft drinks. Customers benefit from the cost saving and convenience this pricing strategy affords. A company may use multiple-unit pricing to attract new customers to its brand and, in some instances, to increase consumption of its brands. When customers buy in larger quantities, their consumption of the product may increase. For example, multiple-unit pricing may encourage a customer to buy larger quantities of snacks, which are likely to be consumed in higher volume at the point of consumption simply because they are available. However, this is not true for all products. For instance, greater availability at the point of consumption of light bulbs, bar soap and table salt is not likely to increase usage.

Discount stores and especially warehouse clubs, such as Costco, are major users of multiple-unit pricing. For certain products in these stores, customers receive significant per-unit price reductions when they buy packages containing multiple units of the same product, such as an eight-pack of canned tuna fish.

Everyday low prices (EDLP)

To reduce or eliminate the use of frequent short-term price reductions, some organisations use an approach referred to as everyday low prices (EDLP). With EDLP, a marketer sets a low price for its products on a consistent basis rather than setting higher prices and frequently discounting them. Everyday low prices, though not deeply discounted, are set far enough below competitors' prices to make customers feel confident they are receiving a fair price. A company that uses EDLP benefits from reduced losses from frequent markdowns, greater stability in sales and reduced promotional costs.

A major problem with EDLP is that customers have mixed responses to it. Over the last several years, many marketers have 'trained' customers to seek and expect deeply discounted prices. In some product categories, such as apparel, finding the deepest discount has become almost a national consumer sport. Thus failure to provide deep discounts can be a problem for certain marketers. In some instances customers simply don't believe that everyday low prices are what marketers claim they are but are instead a marketing gimmick.

everyday low prices (EDLP) Setting a low price for products on a consistent basis

Odd-even pricing

Through odd even pricing – ending the price with certain numbers – marketers try to influence buyers' perceptions of the price or the product. Odd pricing assumes that more of a product will be sold at $99.95 than at $100. Theoretically, customers will think, or at least tell friends, that the product is a bargain – not $100, but $99 and change. Also, customers will supposedly think that the store could have charged $100 but instead cut the price to the last cent, to $99.95. Some claim, too, that certain types of customers are more attracted by odd prices than by even ones. Research indicates that women are more likely to respond to odd ending prices than men.[15] Nonetheless, odd prices are far more common today than even prices.

Even prices are often used to give a product an exclusive or upscale image. An even price supposedly will influence a customer to view the product as being a high-quality premium brand. A shirt maker, for example, may print on a premium shirt package a suggested retail price of $42.00 instead of $41.95; the even price of the shirt is used to enhance its upscale image.

odd-even pricing Ending the price with certain numbers to influence buyers' perceptions of the price or product

Customary pricing

In customary pricing, certain goods are priced primarily on the basis of tradition. Recent economic uncertainties have made most prices fluctuate fairly widely, but the classic example of the customary, or traditional, price is the price of a chocolate bar. For years, the price of a chocolate bar has more or less stayed the same relative to what the average Australian consumer is able to spend on chocolate. A new chocolate bar has to be something very special to sell for more. One way to keep the price proportionately the same has been to increase or decrease the size of the chocolate bar itself as chocolate prices fluctuate. Customary pricing remains the standard for the Australian chocolate market.

customary pricing Pricing on the basis of tradition

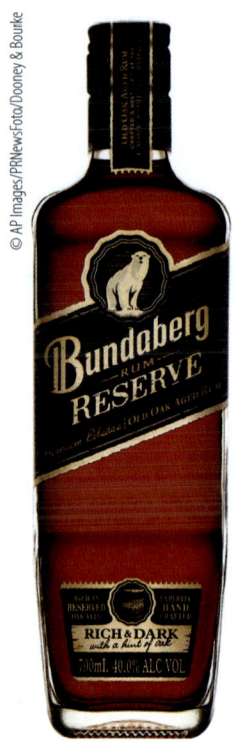

Prestige pricing

prestige pricing
Setting prices at an artificially high level to convey prestige or a quality image

In prestige pricing, prices are set at an artificially high level to convey prestige or a quality image. Prestige pricing is used especially when buyers associate a higher price with higher quality. Pharmacists report that some consumers complain when a prescription does not cost enough; apparently some consumers associate a drug's price with its potency. Research confirms that many consumers believe a more expensive medicine works better than a less costly one.[16]

Typical product categories in which selected products are prestige priced include perfumes, alcohol, jewellery and cars. Although traditionally appliances have not been prestige priced, upscale appliances have appeared in recent years to capitalise on the willingness of some consumer segments to 'trade up' for high-quality products. These consumers do not mind paying extra for a Gaggenau kitchen appliance because this product brand offers high quality and prestige. If producers who use prestige pricing lowered their prices dramatically, the new prices would be inconsistent with the perceived high-quality images of their products. From golf clubs to handbags, prestige products are selling at record levels.

Prestige pricing >>
Organisations employ prestige pricing to help support and communicate a premium, high-quality product

Price leader

Sometimes a firm prices a few products below the usual markup, near cost or below cost, which results in prices known as price leaders. This type of pricing is used most often in supermarkets and restaurants to attract customers by giving them especially low prices on a few items. Management hopes that sales of regularly priced products will more than offset the reduced revenues from the price leaders.

price leader
Product priced below the usual markup, near cost or below cost

Comparison pricing

Comparison pricing sets the price of a product at a specific level and simultaneously compares it with a higher price. The higher price may be the product's previous price, the price of a competing brand, the product's price at another retail outlet or a manufacturer's suggested retail price.

comparison pricing
Setting a price at a specific level and comparing it with a higher price

Professional pricing

Professional pricing is used by people who have great skill or experience in a particular field. Professionals often believe their fees (prices) should not relate directly to the time and effort spent in specific cases; rather, a standard fee is charged regardless of the problems involved in performing the job. Some doctors' and lawyers' fees are prime examples.

professional pricing
Fees set by people with great skill or experience in a particular field

Determination of a specific price

A pricing strategy will yield a certain price point. However, this price may need some refinement, often temporarily, to make it consistent with market circumstances such as aggressive competitor pricing practices. Keep in mind that, in the absence of government price controls, pricing remains a flexible and convenient way to adjust the marketing mix. In many situations, prices can be adjusted quickly by competitors – in a matter of minutes or over a few days. Such flexibility is unique to this component of the marketing mix and makes it a highly competitive marketing variable.

Therefore, in this final section of the chapter, we turn to price discounting. As a form of price promotion, to stimulate sales, producers, intermediaries and resellers often operate with price discounts, or reductions from list prices. Although there are many types of price discounts, they usually fall into one of the categories discussed below. Such discounts can be an important booster of sales volume and an important element in a marketing strategy.

Regardless of which form of price discount is employed, retailers often employ tensile pricing when putting products on sale. Tensile pricing refers to a broad statement about price reductions as opposed to detailing specific price discounts. Examples of tensile pricing would be statements such as '20 to 50 per cent off', 'up to 75 per cent off' and 'save 10 per cent or more'. Generally, using and advertising the tensile price that mentions only the maximum reduction (such as 'up to 50 per cent off') generates the highest customer response.[17]

tensile pricing
Refers to a broad statement about price reductions as opposed to detailing specific price discounts

Trade discounts

A reduction off the list price given by a producer to an intermediary (e.g. a wholesaler) for performing certain distribution functions is called a trade, or functional, discount. A trade discount is usually stated in terms of a percentage or series of percentages off the list price. Intermediaries are given trade discounts as compensation for performing distribution functions, such as selling, transporting and storing. Although certain trade discounts are often a standard practice within an industry, discounts vary considerably among industries. It is important that a manufacturer provide a trade discount large enough to offset the intermediary's costs, plus a reasonable profit, to entice the reseller to carry the product.

trade (functional) discount
A reduction off the list price given by a producer to an intermediary for performing certain functions

Quantity discounts

Deductions from list price that reflect the economies of purchasing in large quantities are called quantity discounts. Quantity discounts are used in many industries and pass on to the buyer cost savings gained through economies of scale.

quantity discounts
Deductions from list price for purchasing large quantities

Cash discounts

A cash discount, or price reduction, is given to a buyer for prompt payment or cash payment. Accounts receivable are an expense and a collection problem for many organisations. A policy to encourage prompt payment is a popular practice and sometimes a major concern in setting prices.

cash discount
Price reduction given to buyers for prompt payment or cash payment

Seasonal discounts

A price reduction to buyers who purchase goods or services out of season is a seasonal discount. These discounts let the seller maintain steadier production during the year.

seasonal discount
A price reduction given to buyers for purchasing goods or services out of season

For example, car rental agencies offer seasonal discounts in winter and early spring to encourage companies to use cars during the slow months of the car rental business.

Allowances

allowance
A concession in price to achieve a desired goal

Another type of reduction from the list price is an allowance, or a concession in price to achieve a desired goal. Trade-in allowances, for example, are price reductions granted for turning in a used item when purchasing a new one. Allowances help to make the buyer better able to make the new purchase. This type of discount is popular in the aircraft industry.

Special-event pricing

special-event pricing
Advertised sales or price cutting linked to a special event

Special-event pricing involves advertised sales discounts linked to a special event. If the pricing objective is survival, special sales events may be designed to generate the necessary operating capital. A special event might be the 10-year anniversary of a firm, or a limited production run of a product. Whenever a sales lag occurs, special-event pricing is an alternative that some marketers consider.

Periodic discounts

periodic discounts
Temporary reduction of prices on a patterned or systematic basis

Periodic discounts involve the temporary reduction of prices on a patterned or systematic basis. For example, most retailers have annual holiday sales. Car dealers regularly discount prices on current models when the next year's models are introduced. From the marketer's point of view, a major problem with periodic discounting is that because the discounts follow a pattern, customers can predict when the reductions will occur and may delay their purchases until they can take advantage of the lower prices.

Random discounts

random discounts
Temporary reduction of prices on an unsystematic basis

To alleviate the problem of customers knowing when discounting will occur, some organisations employ random discounts; that is, they temporarily reduce their prices on an unsystematic basis. When price reductions of a product occur randomly, current users of that brand are likely to be unable to predict when the reductions will occur and so will not delay their purchases. However, in the car industry, with its increasing dependence on sales, rebates and incentives such as zero per cent financing, random discounting has become nearly continuous discounting, and some analysts have warned that car manufacturers will find it increasingly difficult to cease generous incentives that consumers have come to expect. Marketers also use random discounting to attract new customers.

© Jeff Greenberg/PhotoEdit

Random discounting >>
Retailers use random discounting to attract customers to its stores. Consumers cannot predict when discounts will be available

Study Tools

Chapter review

 **LO1 TO UNDERSTAND THE ROLE OF PRICE.**

Price is the value paid for a product in a marketing exchange. Price is a key element in the marketing mix, because it relates directly to generation of total revenue. The profit factor can be determined mathematically by multiplying price by quantity sold to get total revenue and then subtracting total costs. Price is the only variable in the marketing mix that can be adjusted quickly and easily to respond to changes in the external environment.

 **LO2 IDENTIFY THE CHARACTERISTICS OF PRICE AND NON-PRICE COMPETITION.**

Price competition emphasises price as the major product differential. Prices fluctuate frequently, and price competition among sellers is aggressive. Non-price competition emphasises product differentiation through distinctive features, services, product quality or other factors. Establishing brand loyalty by using non-price competition works best when the product can be physically differentiated and the customer can recognise these differences.

 **LO3 EXPLORE ISSUES RELATED TO DEVELOPING PRICING OBJECTIVES AND UNDERSTAND THE IMPORTANCE OF IDENTIFYING THE TARGET MARKET'S EVALUATION OF PRICE.**

Assessing the target market's evaluation of price tells the marketer how much emphasis to place on price and may help to determine how far above the competition the firm can set its prices. Understanding how important a product is to customers relative to other products, as well as customers' expectations of quality, helps marketers to correctly assess the target market's evaluation of price.

 **LO4 BE FAMILIAR WITH THE BASES USED FOR SETTING PRICES.**

The three major dimensions on which prices can be based are cost, value and competition. When using cost-plus pricing, the company determines price by adding a dollar amount or percentage to the cost of the product. Value-based pricing is based on the perceived benefits a product offers consumers. To use this method, a marketer must be able to estimate buyers' willingness to pay for a product at different prices. Value-based pricing results in a high price when demand for a product is strong and a low price when demand is weak. In the case of competition-based pricing, costs and revenues are secondary to competitors' prices.

L05   EXPLAIN THE DIFFERENT TYPES OF PRICING STRATEGIES.

A pricing strategy is an approach or a course of action designed to achieve pricing and marketing objectives. The major categories of pricing strategies are differential pricing, new-product pricing, product-line pricing, psychological pricing, professional pricing and promotional pricing. When marketers employ differential pricing, they charge different buyers different prices for the same quality and quantity of products. Negotiated pricing, secondary-market pricing, periodic discounting and random discounting are forms of differential pricing. Two strategies used in new-product pricing are price skimming and penetration pricing. With price skimming, the organisation charges the highest price that buyers who most desire the product will pay. A penetration price is a low price designed to penetrate a market and gain a significant market share quickly. Product-line pricing establishes and adjusts the prices of multiple products within a product line. This category of strategies includes captive pricing, premium pricing, bait pricing and price lining. Psychological pricing attempts to influence customer's perceptions of price to make a product's price more attractive. Psychological pricing strategies include reference pricing, bundle pricing, multiple-unit pricing, everyday low prices, odd-even pricing, customary pricing and prestige pricing. Professional pricing is used by people who have great skill or experience in a particular field, therefore allowing them to set the price. As an ingredient in the marketing mix, price is often coordinated with promotion. The two variables are sometimes so interrelated that the pricing policy is promotion-oriented. Promotional pricing includes price leaders, special-event pricing and comparison discounting. Price leaders are products that are priced below the usual markup, near cost or below cost. Special-event pricing involves advertised sales or price-cutting linked to a special event. Marketers who use a comparison-discounting strategy price a product at a specific level and compare it with a higher price.

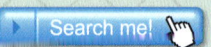

Key concepts

Use these key terms in **Search me! marketing** to find the latest relevant readings from a wide range of world-class journals, e-books and newspapers, including *The Australian*.

- allowance
- bundle pricing
- captive pricing
- cash discount
- comparison pricing
- competition-based pricing
- cost-plus pricing
- customary pricing
- demand curve
- differential pricing
- everyday low prices (EDLP)
- external reference price
- internal reference price

- multiple-unit pricing
- negotiated pricing
- non-price competition
- odd-even pricing
- penetration pricing
- periodic discounts
- premium pricing
- prestige pricing
- prestige-sensitive
- price
- price competition
- price lining
- price skimming
- price-conscious

- pricing objectives
- product-line pricing
- professional pricing
- psychological pricing
- quantity discounts
- random discounts
- reference pricing
- seasonal discount
- secondary-market pricing
- special-event pricing
- tensile pricing
- trade (functional) discount
- value-based pricing
- value-conscious

Issues for discussion and review

1 What features characterise price competition?

2 What factors affect pricing decisions?

3 Under what conditions is non-price competition effective?

4 Describe the stages that are involved in setting prices.

5 What are the benefits of cost-plus pricing?

6 Under what conditions is cost-plus pricing most appropriate?

7 A café can make a coffee for 80 cents. The café then sells the coffee for $4.00. Calculate the markup as a percentage of cost and as a percentage of selling price.

8 What is differential pricing? In what ways can it be achieved?

9 What are the advantages and disadvantages of using everyday low prices?

10 Why do customers associate price with quality? When should prestige pricing be used?

11 Are price leaders a realistic approach to pricing? Explain your answer.

Marketing applications

1 How aware are you of the strategy being used to price products and services that you buy every day? Think about the things you regularly buy, or situations you've recently observed, to identify examples of the following pricing strategies:

a multiple-unit pricing

b special-event pricing

c odd-even pricing

d secondary-market pricing.

How appropriate was the pricing strategy? How is your perception of the companies and/or their products influenced by their choice of pricing strategy?

2 Customers' interpretations and responses regarding a product and its price are an important influence on marketers' pricing decisions. Perceptions of price are affected by the degree to which customers are value conscious, price conscious or prestige sensitive. Discuss how these factors influence the buying decision process for the following products:

a a new house

b weekly groceries for a family of five

c an airline ticket.

d a soft drink from a vending machine.

3 Browse the shelves of a local retail store to find examples of price lining. Report your observations. For what types of products and stores is this practice most common? For what products and stores is price lining not typical or usable?

4 Explain whether price skimming or penetration pricing is the more appropriate pricing strategy for the following products:

a the next book in a bestselling vampire series.

b an upgraded mobile phone

   c a backpack or book bag with a lifetime warranty

   d season tickets for a newly franchised rugby team.

ONLINE EXERCISE

5 Find two online examples of services that reflect a professional-pricing policy. How do you think the price is established? Are there any restrictions on the services offered at that price?

Developing your marketing plan

Setting the right price for a product is a crucial part of marketing strategy. Price helps to establish a product's position in the mind of the consumer and can differentiate a product from its competition. Several decisions in the marketing plan will be affected by the pricing strategy that is selected. To assist you in relating the information in this chapter to the development of your marketing plan, focus on the following:

1 Does your company currently compete based on price or non-price factors? Should your new product continue with this approach?

2 Select a basis for pricing your product (cost, demand and/or competition). How will you know when it is time to revise your pricing strategy?

    The information obtained from these questions should assist you in developing various aspects of your marketing plan.

CengageNOW

Go to http:\\login.cengagebrain.com to link to CengageNOW, your online study tool. First take the Pre-Test for this chapter to get your Personalised Study Plan, and then:

 ✳ **Revise** your understanding of the key concepts of marketing with the online glossary

 ✳ **Watch** an interactive animation of strategic marketing to broaden your subject comprehension

 ✳ **Listen** to an audio summary of the learning objectives covered in this chapter.

    After you have completed the activities in your Personalised Study Plan take the Post-Test to determine what concepts you have mastered and what you still need to work on.

SPA CEYLON

Case study

COMPANY AND PRODUCT OVERVIEW

Spa Ceylon manufactures and distributes luxury Ayurvedic products while operating premium Ayurvedic spas in Sri Lanka. Ayurvedic medicine is a complementary and alternative medicine originating from India. Ayurveda has been in practice for more than 3000 years, and its success as a medicine is often attributed to its natural application and whole-body approach. Ayurveda is known as 'the science of life'; it incorporates our individual characteristics – physical, emotional and environmental – that are rooted in the energies of the universe. The central value proposition is to provide consumers with rejuvenation in the setting of an ancient Ceylonese spa. Value is communicated in different ways from product features and quality to the service mix.

Spa Ceylon launched its first product range in 2010 and its first spa in 2011. Their goods and service offerings fall within two of the sub-sectors on India's wellness market (see Table 10.2). Spa Ceylon's business portfolio is made up of products sold through exclusive lifestyle channels, covering over 300 products for skin, body, hair care, home aroma blends, spa accessories and 25 spa treatments. Currently there are twenty domestic spa and retail outlets in operation. Spa Ceylon exports to 11 locations and has an online retail website. Spa Ceylon is the largest premium spa operator in Sri Lanka, with recent sales across the total business of over US$15 million.

TABLE 10.2 AN OVERVIEW OF INDIA'S WELLBEING INDUSTRY

Segment	Products	Services
Beauty services and cosmetic products	Cosmetic products (skincare, hair care, colour cosmetics and fragrances)	Salons and beauty centres Cosmetic treatments (invasive and non-invasive)
Fitness and cosmetic products	Fitness equipment Slimming products	Fitness centres Slimming centres
Nutrition	Health and wellness food, beverages Dietary supplements	
Alternate therapy	Ayurveda, homeopathy, unani, etc.	Treatment centres for Ayurveda, homeopathy, unani, naturopathy, etc.
Rejuvenation		Spas

Source: 'Riding the growth wave', PWC/India, 3rd Annual Wellness Conference, September 2011, p.9.

INDUSTRY OVERVIEW

The wellness industry in India is estimated to be worth US$8.9 billion, approximately two per cent of the global industry according to a study conducted by the Federation of Indian Chambers of Commerce and Industry. Forty per cent of the Indian wellness sector is made up of wellness services, of which the rejuvenation or spa category accounts for US$9.1 million. Traditional massages continue to drive growth. The total industry is estimated to grow at an average annual rate of 20 per cent, stimulated by high growth sectors, including spas.

TARGET MARKET

Typically, a female consumer dominates this market, with a significant share of cosmetics and skincare. Traditional beauty archetypes, which emphasise fairness, eyes and haircare over skincare, and the prevalence of traditional beauty treatments, are responsible for this slightly skewed market structure. Per capita consumption is one of the lowest in the world yet is growing at 16 per cent per annum.

By 2016, it is estimated that 40–50 million women in the age group of 20–40 in urban India will be working. In 2011, 11 per cent of CEOs were women, compared to 3 per cent for *Fortune* 500 companies in the US. Income of women living and working in cities in India has increased and will continue to grow.

PRICING AT SPA CEYLON

Spa Ceylon's products and services are priced at a premium, catering to a niche market. The pricing strategy that Spa Ceylon pursues aims to build strong brand equity, generate consumer awareness and perceived value for the brand and therefore directly compete with other premium domestic and international spa operators. Affluent Indian consumers inherently perceive the value of a brand by its pricing; this is driving demand for premium-priced products in Mumbai as more consumers move towards the upper-middle income bracket. Table 10.3 depicts price point comparisons among the industry competitors.[18]

TABLE 10.3   COMPARATIVE PRICING IN INDIA'S WELLNESS MARKET (US$)

Brand	Basic massages	Full body rituals	Product prices
Spa Ceylon	$45	$250	$40–80
L'Occitane	$50	$200	$20–70
Quan Spa	$40	$220	$30–80
Tahaa Spa	$20	$65	
The Palms Spa	$20	$100	
Aura Thai Spa	$18	$90	
Four Seasons Spa	$60	$200	
Antara Spa	$15	$70	

Nicholas Grigoriou, Monash University

QUESTIONS FOR DISCUSSION

1 Identify the pricing objective(s) pursued by Spa Ceylon for the skincare products. How does this pricing objective support the organisation's value proposition?

2 What pricing strategies should Spa Ceylon implement for the sale of their products to India? Give reasons for your answer.

3 What market forces are likely to impact on Spa Ceylon's price setting? Suggest approaches that Spa Ceylon can use to address these market-based concerns.

Chapter endnotes

1. Chris Griffith, 'Amazon opens Aussie eBook store, appstore, releases three models of Kindle Fire locally,' *The Australian*, November 13, 2013, http://www .theaustralian.com.au/technology/personal-tech /amazon-opens-aussie-ebook-store-appstore-releases -three-kindle-fires-locally/story-e6frgazf-1226758697051; Amazon.com, various pages accessed October 17, 2013: 'About Amazon,' http://www.amazon.com/Careers -Homepage/b?ie=UTF8&node=239364011, 'Amazon Web Services,' http://aws.amazon.com; 'Welcome to Amazon's Kindle Direct Publishing,' https://kdp.amazon .com/self-publishing/signin.

2. 'Hewlett-Packard,' Professional Pricing Society Case Study, http://members.pricingsociety.com/articles/ not_free.pdf.

3. Based on information in Christopher Elliott, 'Bill Aims to Scuttle New Airfare Pricing Rule,' *Chicago Tribune*, February 7, 2012, www.chicagotribune.com; 'Rule Takes Surprises Out of Airfares,' *San Francisco Chronicle*, February 14, 2012, www.sfgate.com; Rob Lovitt, 'Mandatory Resort Fees Frustrate Hotel Guests,' *MSNBC*, January 10, 2011, www.msnbc.com; David Segal, 'Name Your Price, Then Get Ready for the Fees,' *The New York Times*, September 10, 2011, www.nytimes.com.

4. Donald Lichtenstein, Nancy Ridgway, and Richard Netemeyer, 'Price Perceptions and Consumer Shopping Behavior: A Field Study,' *Journal of Marketing Research* (May 1993): 234–245.

5. Manoj Thomas and Geeta Menon, 'Internal Reference Prices and Price Expectations,' *Journal of Marketing Research* XLIV (August 2007).

6. Lichtenstein, Ridgway, and Netemeyer, 'Price Perceptions and Consumer Shopping Behavior: A Field Study,' *Journal of Marketing Research* (May 1993): 234–245.

7. Gerald E. Smith and Thomas T. Nagle, 'A Question of Value,' *Marketing Management* (July/August 2005): 39–40.

8. Donald Lichtenstein, Nancy M. Ridgway, and Richard G. Netemeyer, 'Price Perceptions and Consumer Shopping Behavior: A Field Study,' *Journal of Marketing Research* (May 1993), 234–245.

9. 'Dictionary of Marketing Terms,' American Marketing Association, http://www.marketingpower.com/_layouts /Dictionary.aspx.

10. Phil Libin, 'Four Lessons from Evernote's First Week on the Mac App Store,' *TechCrunch*, January 19, 2011, http://techcrunch.com/2011/01/19/evernotemac-app -store/; Ari Levy and Greg Bensinger, 'LinkedIn Joins ESPN, Skype in Shifting from Free to 'Freemium,'' *Business Week Online*, December 21, 2009, www.businessweek.com; Rita Chang and Michael Learmonth, 'Are Your Ads Being Used to Drive Consumers to Ad-free Services?' *Advertising Age*, September 21, 2009, p. 3; Dan Macsai, 'Evernote CEO Phil Libin's 3 Steps to 'Freemium' Success,' *FastCompany*, July 1, 2010, accessed July 12, 2011, www.fastcompany .com/magazine/147/next-tech-remember-the-money.html.

11. Lisa Rein, 'Maryland Couple Basks in Savings from a 19-Year-Old Solar System,' *Washington Post* (March 12, 2009): B1; 'Green as Houses: Environmentalism and Building,' *The Economist* (September 15, 2007): 42; Christopher Palmeri, 'Green Homes: The Price Still Isn't Right,' *BusinessWeek* (February 12, 2007): 67.

12. George J. Avlonitis and Kostis A. Indounas, 'Pricing Objectives and Pricing Methods in the Services Sector,' *Journal of Services Marketing* 19 (January 2005): 45–47.

13. 'Five Actions CPOs Should Take Now to Address an Economic Downturn,' *Marketwire*, April 23, 2008, http://www.marketwire.com/press-release/Emptoris -847780.html.

14. Mark Phelan, '$100,000 Corvette Supercar Aims to Best Exotic Rivals,' *USA Today* (December 20, 2007): http://usatoday.com/money/autos/2007-12-20-corvette -zr1_N.htm.

15. Christine Harris and Jeffery Bray, 'Price Endings and Consumer Segmentation,' *Journal of Product & Brand Management* 16 (March 2007): 200–205.

16. Rita Rubin, 'Placebo Tests 'Costlier is Better' Notion,' *USA Today*, March 4, 2008, http://www.usatoday.com/news /health/2008-03-04-placebo- effect_N.htm.

17. 'Dictionary of Marketing Terms,' American Marketing Association, http://www.marketingpower.com/_layouts /Dictionary.aspx.

18. 'Riding the Growth Wave: Wellness 3rd Annual Wellness Conference - September 2011, Proceedings,' PricewaterhouseCoopers Private Limited, http://www .pwc.in/en_IN/in/assets/pdfs/publications-2011 /wellness-report-15-sept.pdf.

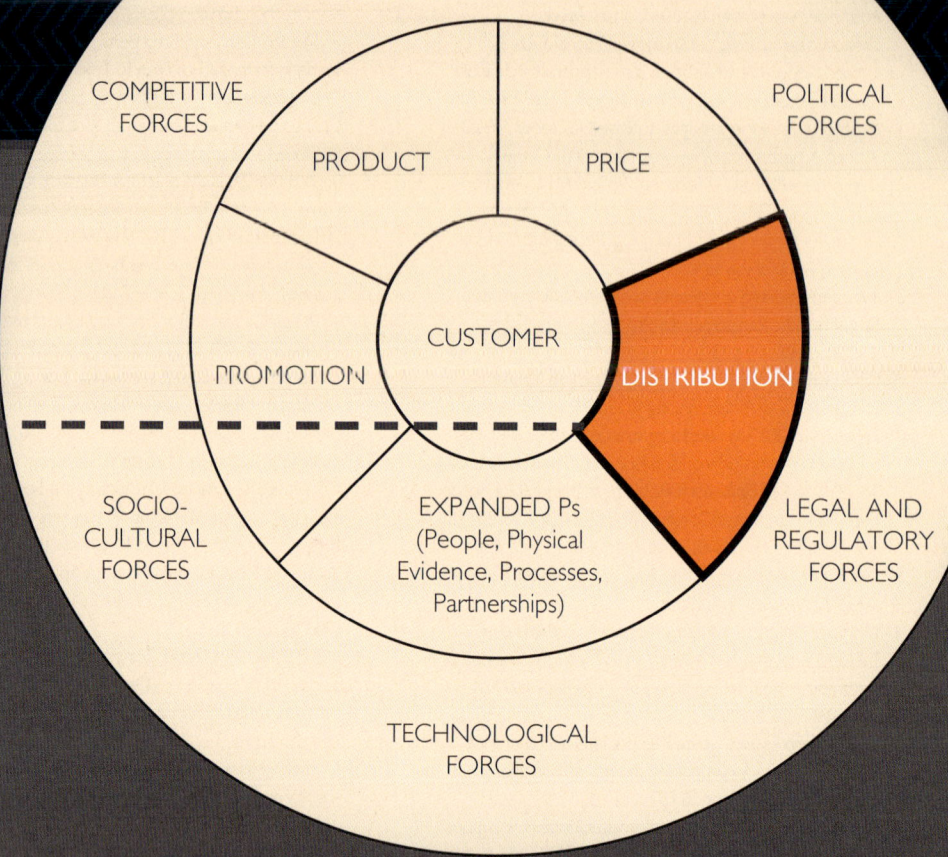

ECONOMIC FORCES

COMPETITIVE FORCES

POLITICAL FORCES

PRODUCT

PRICE

PROMOTION

CUSTOMER

DISTRIBUTION

SOCIO-CULTURAL FORCES

EXPANDED Ps (People, Physical Evidence, Processes, Partnerships)

LEGAL AND REGULATORY FORCES

TECHNOLOGICAL FORCES

DISTRIBUTION DECISIONS

The role of marketing channels
Types of marketing channels

Distribution in supply-chain management and marketing strategies
Order processing
Inventory management
Materials handling
Warehousing
Transportation

Types of retailers and strategic issues in retailing

Direct marketing
Catalogue marketing
Direct response marketing

Telemarketing
Television home shopping
Online retailing
Direct selling

Wholesaling
Services provided by wholesalers
Types of wholesalers

Strategic issues in marketing channels
Selecting marketing channels
Channel leadership, cooperation and conflict

Throughout this chapter, Watch, Listen and Revise icons indicate an opportunity for online self-study through CengageNOW, linking you to animated chapter overviews, interactive diagrams, videos, quizzes and more.

11 DISTRIBUTION DECISIONS

Learning Objectives

LO1 Describe the role of marketing channels

LO2 Recognise the importance of the role of physical distribution activities in supply-chain management and overall marketing strategies

LO3 Identify the major types of retailers and explore strategic issues in retailing

LO4 Recognise the various forms of direct marketing and selling

LO5 Understand the nature and functions of wholesalers

LO6 Examine strategic issues in marketing channels, including the factors that influence marketing channel selection, and leadership, cooperation and conflict.

MARKETING CHALLENGE | TARGET REINVIGORATES ITS BRAND

Rather than trying to be all things to all shoppers, Target has chosen to differentiate itself on the basis of great design at low prices. The retailer's red-and-white bull's-eye logo has come to stand for 'cheap chic'.

Target has had success with its strategy of producing ranges of clothes designed especially for Target by high-end fashion designers. Designers to partner with Target have included Stella McCartney (2007 and 2010), Zac Posen (2008) and Roberto Cavalli (2012). In a move likely to have further enhanced Target's fashion credibility and relevance to a younger generation, the Roberto Cavalli campaign featured supermodel Karolina Kurkova. This designer strategy has also been used effectively by H&M, a Swedish multinational retail-clothing company – bringing them coveted coverage in *Vogue*.

Source: Getty Images

363

Continuing to deliver what customers want is vital. Target Australia's managing director says, 'Our customers have told us that they love Target, but they want more from us. They want more style, more quality, more excitement instore – and they expect to pay less'. In response, Target have introduced Gok Wan as their style and quality ambassador. Gok is a high-profile, international fashion consultant and television presenter of *How to Look Good Naked*. Gok's job is to make Target's fashion and homewares 'hot' – creating 'must-have' fashion.

Social media is also allowing Target to engage with its customers. Posts on Target Australia's Facebook page promote fashion staples and invite valuable feedback from consumers. These posts are given relevancy and credibility by the inclusion of Gok as the new style ambassador. Pinterest is creating a visual dialogue with lifestyle quotes, competitions and desirable product images – including the Roberto Cavalli range. Gok features in a series of YouTube videos looking to bring Target's fashion vision to life. Meanwhile, the company's Twitter account (@Targetaus) generates excitement around new product launches and events.

Target is demonstrating the steps that a market-oriented retailer needs to undertake to continue to compete. Evolving their brand and strategy to suit changing consumer needs, listening to customer feedback and engaging with customers to ensure they remain relevant.[1]

MARKETING CHALLENGE QUESTIONS	1 What is Target hoping to achieve with these tactics and choice of communication channels?	2 How does Target's strategy reinforce its mission statement 'It's our aim to provide stylish living, at an affordable price, for all Australians'?

Introduction

Developing products that satisfy customers is important, but it is not enough to guarantee successful marketing strategies. Products must also be available in adequate quantities in accessible locations at the times when customers desire them. Marketing channels fulfil this distribution function. Retailers such as Target or Big W are the most visible and accessible marketing-channel members to consumers. They are an important link in the marketing channel because they are both marketers for, and customers of, producers and wholesalers. They perform many channel functions, such as buying, selling and developing and maintaining information databases about customers.

This chapter covers the distribution of products and addresses the 'P' for place in the marketing mix. Chapter discussions are centred on the decisions and activities associated with the physical distribution of products; and the role of marketing channels and the types of marketing channels available for business and consumer products are explored. The chapter also explores retailing and wholesaling, including types of retailers and wholesalers, direct marketing and selling and strategic retailing issues.

distribution
The decisions and activities that make products (goods and services) available to customers when and where they want to purchase or access them

WATCH a video exploring the real-world implications of marketing channels

The role of marketing channels

A marketing channel is a group of individuals and organisations that direct the flow of products from producers to customers. A marketing channel is referred to as 'P' for 'place' in the marketing mix. A marketing channel is one part of a supply chain. Another separate part of a supply chain is production, which consists of the individuals and organisations that transform raw materials, and resources in general, into the products destined for distribution by the marketing channel. Managing production and, therefore, the transformation of resources into products is called operations management – it is not part of managing a marketing channel. The process of managing the marketing channel is called channel management.

Buyers' needs and behaviour are important concerns of channel members. The major role of marketing channels is to make existing products available at the right time at the right place in the right quantities. Therefore, a marketing channel plays an important role in enabling a company to be market-oriented.

Some marketing channels are direct, meaning that the product goes directly from the producer to the end customer. A mail-order business would be an example of a direct channel. Similarly, any manufacturer offering online ordering is a direct-to-consumer channel. The Internet offers manufacturers the opportunity to skip the middlemen and avoid the margins charged by intermediaries. However, manufacturers hold a core competence in manufacturing, but not marketing or direct-to-consumer sales. Most channels, therefore, have one or more marketing intermediaries that link producers to ultimate consumers through contractual arrangements or through the purchase and resale of products. Marketing intermediaries perform the activities described in Table 11.1. They also play key roles in customer relationship management, not only through their distribution activities but also by maintaining databases and

TABLE 11.1   MARKETING CHANNEL ACTIVITIES PERFORMED BY INTERMEDIARIES

Marketing activities	Sample activities
Marketing information	Analyse sales data and other information in databases and information systems
	Perform or commission marketing research
Marketing management	Establish strategic and tactical plans for developing customer relationships and organisational productivity
Facilitating exchanges	Choose product assortments that match the needs of customers
	Cooperate with channel members to develop partnerships
Promotion	Set promotional objectives.
	Coordinate advertising, personal selling, sales promotion, publicity and packaging
Price	Establish pricing policies and terms of sales
Physical distribution	Manage transportation, warehousing, materials handling, inventory control and communication

marketing channel
The aggregate of all individuals and organisations that direct the flow of products from producers to customers; marketing channels are referred to as 'place' in the marketing mix

supply chain
All the activities associated with the flow and transformation of products from raw materials through delivery to the end customer

operations management
The total set of managerial activities used by an organisation to transform resource inputs into products; primarily concerned with production

channel management
The total set of managerial activities used by an organisation to distribute products in the right quantities to the right locations at the right time

marketing intermediaries
The middlemen between producers and customers in a marketing channel linking producers to consumers

information systems to help all members of the marketing channel maintain effective customer relationships. Wholesalers and retailers are examples of intermediaries. Wholesalers buy and resell products to other wholesalers, to retailers and to industrial customers. Retailers purchase products and resell them to the end consumers. Auction houses are also intermediaries, eBay is such an example as it serves as a marketing intermediary between Internet sellers and buyers. It not only provides a forum for these exchanges, but also helps facilitate relationships among eBay channel members and eases payment issues through its PayPal subsidiary.

The significance of marketing channels

Although marketing-channel decisions do not need to precede other marketing decisions, they are a powerful influence on products, how products are promoted and how products are priced. Channel decisions are critical because they determine a product's market presence and buyers' accessibility to the product. Without effective marketing channel operations, even the best goods and services will not be successful. Consider that small businesses are more likely to purchase computers from chain specialty stores such as OfficeMax, putting computer companies without distribution through these outlets at a disadvantage. In fact, even Dell – which pioneered the direct sales model in the computer industry – is now selling its computers through chain speciality stores. The option of buying Dell systems directly from Dell or in retail stores means that customers can purchase what they need when and where they want while also allowing customers to 'test drive' a computer system of their choice.

Marketing channels generally entail long-term commitments among marketing intermediaries. Therefore, it is usually easier to change prices or promotional strategies than to change marketing channels. Marketing channels serve many functions, including creating utility and facilitating exchange efficiencies. Although some of these functions may be performed by a single channel member, most functions are accomplished through both independent and joint efforts of channel members.

Marketing channels create utility

Marketing channels create four types of utility: time, place, possession and form. *Time utility* is having products available when the customer wants them. *Place utility* is created by making products available in locations where customers wish to purchase them. Possession utility means that the customer has access to the product to use or to store for future use. *Possession utility* can occur through ownership or through arrangements that give the customer the right to use the product, such as a lease or rental agreement. Channel members sometimes create *form utility* by assembling, preparing or otherwise refining the product to suit individual customer needs.

Marketing channels facilitate exchange efficiencies

Marketing intermediaries can reduce the costs of exchanges by performing certain services or functions efficiently. Even if producers and buyers are located in the same city, there are costs associated with exchanges. As Figure 11.1 shows, when four buyers seek products from four producers, 16 transactions are possible. If one intermediary serves both producers and buyers, the number of transactions can be reduced to eight. Intermediaries are specialists in facilitating exchanges. They provide valuable assistance because of their access to and control over important resources used in the proper functioning of marketing channels.

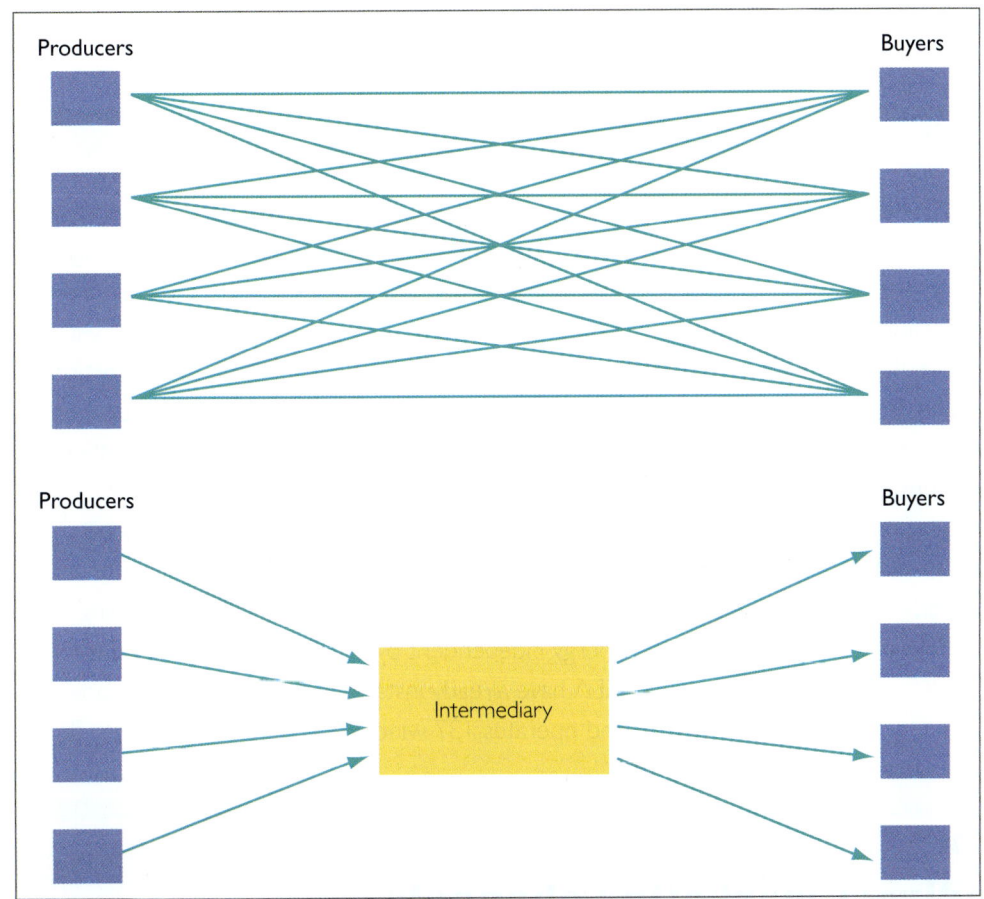

FIGURE 11.1
EFFICIENCY IN
EXCHANGES PROVIDED
BY AN INTERMEDIARY

Types of marketing channels

Because marketing channels appropriate for one product may be less suitable for others, many different distribution paths have been developed. The various marketing channels can be classified generally as direct channels, indirect channels, multiple channels and hybrid channels.

Direct marketing channels

A direct marketing channel combines all stages of the marketing channel, from producers to consumers, under a single owner, to serve a target market segment. Thus, in direct channel marketing, most or all stages of the marketing channel are under common control. The advantage is that marketing activities can be coordinated for maximum effectiveness and economy without duplication of channel functions. The main disadvantages are the high expenses of maintaining the entire channel and the often limited reach of the channel. Supermarkets that own their own food-processing plants and large retailers

direct marketing channel
A marketing channel owned and managed by a single channel member to supply a target market segment

that purchase wholesaling and production facilities are examples of direct channels. An example of a successful direct channel is IKEA, who oversee material supply, production, distribution and promotion on a global scale. This strategy enables the furniture retailing giant to offer low product prices, and furthermore, add to their value offering through implementing a range of environmentally sustainable initiatives (refer to Sustainable Marketing box below).

SUSTAINABLE MARKETING | IKEA'S SUSTAINABLE GEOTHERMAL ENERGY INITIATIVE

Although we rarely equate large-scale retailers with sustainability, IKEA takes the topic to heart. As a global furniture supplier, IKEA maintain a competitive advantage by investing in highly automated production, producing large quantities and optimising the entire value chain. As a result the company has a large carbon footprint, thanks in part to global shipping. To counteract this, IKEA leads a number of sustainable initiatives. One such initiative is running stores on geothermal energy. All of its Swedish stores are going geothermal, and IKEA has already transformed other European locations. Its first US location is Denver, Colorado, with their Merriam Kansas store geothermal system currently underway.

Geothermal energy uses heat pumps to bring the fairly consistent moderate temperature found roughly 150 metres below ground to the surface via a liquid loop. The heat pump then heats or cools the air within the store. According to the Environmental Protection Agency, geothermal heat pumps eliminate 72 per cent of energy used and emissions created by conventional systems. In Denver, IKEA has partnered with the National Renewable Energy Laboratory, which will monitor the project. The implementation of geothermal systems is part of the global retailer's goal of being energy independent by 2020. Consistent with this goal, IKEA have already installed over 300 000 solar panels and operates 137 wind turbines in Europe alone.[2]

Indirect marketing channels

indirect marketing channel
A marketing channel comprised of several independently owned channel members who work together to serve a target market segment

In an indirect marketing channel, several independently owned channel members work together to serve a target market segment. Most grocery manufacturers, for example, rely on indirect channels for the distribution of their products. The main advantages of such a channel are the low channel management costs and greater reach and flexibility. The disadvantages are that marketing activities cannot be always controlled and sometimes channel functions are duplicated.

Multiple marketing channels

multiple marketing channel
A marketing channel that is a combination of direct and indirect channels whereby each channel is used to reach a different target market segment

A multiple marketing channel is a combination of direct and indirect channels whereby each channel is used for different target market segments. For example, textbook publishers sell textbooks to students through their own online shops and independent bookshops, but sell books to university professors through their own sales representatives. One disadvantage of multiple marketing channels is their complex coordination and different degrees of control. The main advantage of such a channel type is its differentiated approach to serving different target market segments.

Hybrid marketing channels

A hybrid marketing channel is a combination of direct and indirect channels whereby different channels are used for the same target market segment. An example of a hybrid marketing channel is a company that sells products through retail outlets and its own mail-order catalogue or website, in each case targeting the same consumers. Many airlines have such a channel structure to reach a consumer, selling the same tickets directly from their websites and through independent travel agencies. The main advantage of a hybrid marketing channel is its comprehensive reach into target market segments. The main disadvantage of such a channel type is its complex coordination and different degrees of control.

IF IT DOESN'T SAY *Kellogg's* ON THE BOX ... IT ISN'T *Kellogg's* IN THE BOX

Kellogg's

CRUNCHY NUT

...It's Ludicrously Tasty!

Source: Photolibrary.com

hybrid marketing channel
A marketing channel that is a combination of direct and indirect channels whereby different channels are used to reach the same target market segment

LISTEN to the Audio Summary to check your understanding of marketing channels

<< Using multiple marketing channels
Major food companies such as Kellogg's employ multiple marketing channels

Physical distribution in supply-chain management and marketing strategies

LO2

Physical distribution, also known as *logistics*, refers to the activities used to move products from producers to consumers and other end users. Physical distribution systems must meet the needs of both the supply chain and customers. Distribution activities are thus an important part of supply-chain planning and require the cooperation of all partners.

Within the marketing channel, physical distribution activities may be performed by a producer, a wholesaler or a retailer, or they may be outsourced. In the context of distribution, outsourcing is the contracting of physical distribution tasks to third parties who do not have managerial authority within the marketing channel. Most physical distribution activities can be outsourced to third-party firms that have special expertise in areas such as warehousing, transportation, inventory management and information technology. Some manufacturing firms, for example, outsource delivery services to LinFox Logistics. Cooperative relationships with third-party organisations, such as trucking companies, warehouses and data-service providers, can help to reduce marketing-channel costs and boost service and customer satisfaction for all supply-chain partners. When choosing companies through

physical distribution
Activities used to move products from producers to consumers and other end users

outsourcing
The contracting of physical distribution tasks to third parties who do not have managerial authority within the marketing channel

which to outsource, marketers must be cautious and use efficient firms that help the outsourcing company provide excellent customer service. They need to recognise as well the importance of logistics functions such as warehousing and information technology in reducing physical distribution costs associated with outsourcing.[3]

Planning an efficient physical distribution system is crucial to developing an effective marketing strategy because it can decrease costs and increase customer satisfaction (refer to Marketing in Transition box below for an example of extreme physical distribution efficiency). Speed of delivery, flexibility and quality of service are often as important to customers as costs. Companies that have the right goods, in the right place, at the right time, in the right quantity and with the right support services are able to sell more than competitors that do not. Even when the demand for products is unpredictable, suppliers must be able to respond quickly to inventory needs. In such cases, physical distribution costs may be a minor consideration when compared with service, dependability and timeliness.

Customer relationship management systems exploit the information from supply-chain partners' database systems to help logistics managers identify and root out inefficiencies in the supply chain for the benefit of all marketing-channel members – from the producer to the ultimate consumer. Indeed, technology is playing a larger and larger role in physical distribution within marketing channels. Technology has transformed physical distribution by facilitating just-in-time delivery, precise inventory visibility and instant shipment tracking capabilities,

MARKETING IN TRANSITION | STREAMLINING PHYSICAL DISTRIBUTION TO PROFIT FROM YOUR GROCERY SHOP

Supermarket chain Woolworths partnered with Network Ten to deliver an innovative TV series called *Recipe to Riches*. The TV reality show featured people from all over Australia competing to have their home recipes become branded products sold on supermarket shelves. Each episode concluded with a new winning branded product, which consumers could then purchase from Woolworths the very next day.

The innovative notion of being able to watch the TV show in the evening and then purchase the winning product the next day relied on the efficiency of physical distributions channels. The branded products are fresh in customer's minds, therefore they have a competitive advantage over similar products in the same category. Furthermore, the products are new, unique and only available for a limited time, which further entices shoppers to purchase. Consequently, Woolworths' partnership with the Network Ten and Recipe to Riches has proven to be a profitable one. A similar example of efficient physical distribution as a competitive advantage includes the reality TV show *Fashion Star* in the US.[4]

Source: Getty Images

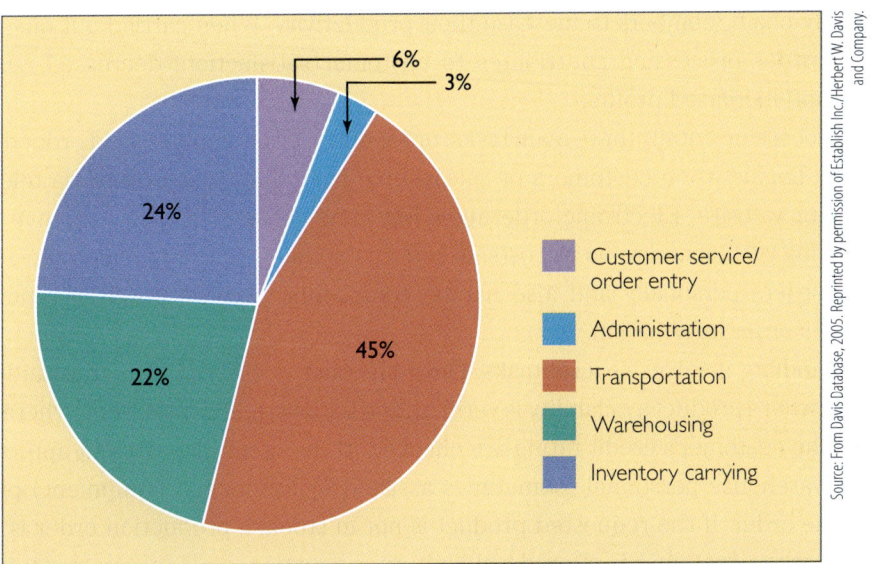

Source: From Davis Database, 2005. Reprinted by permission of Establish Inc./Herbert W. Davis and Company.

FIGURE 11.2
PROPORTIONAL COST OF EACH PHYSICAL DISTRIBUTION FUNCTION AS A PERCENTAGE OF TOTAL DISTRIBUTION COSTS

which help companies to avoid expensive mistakes, reduce costs and even generate revenues. Information technology brings visibility to the supply chain by allowing all marketing-channel members to see precisely where an item is within the supply chain at any time.[5]

Although physical distribution managers try to minimise the costs associated with order processing, inventory management, materials handling, warehousing and transportation, decreasing the costs in one area often raises them in another. Figure 11.2 shows the percentage of total costs that physical distribution functions represent. A total-cost approach to physical distribution enables managers to view physical distribution as a system rather than a collection of unrelated activities. This approach shifts the emphasis from lowering the separate costs of individual activities to minimising overall distribution costs.

Physical distribution managers must be sensitive to the issue of cost trade-offs. Higher costs in one functional area of a distribution system may be necessary to achieve lower costs in another. Trade-offs are strategic decisions to combine (and recombine) resources for greatest cost-effectiveness. When distribution managers regard the system as a network of integrated functions, trade-offs become useful tools in implementing a unified, cost-effective distribution strategy.

Another important goal of physical distribution involves cycle time, the time needed to complete a process. For example, reducing cycle time while maintaining or reducing costs and/or maintaining or increasing customer service is a winning combination in supply chains, ultimately leading to greater end-customer satisfaction.

In the rest of this section, we take a closer look at a variety of physical distribution activities, including order processing, inventory management, materials handling, warehousing and transportation.

Order processing

Order processing is the receipt and transmission of sales-order information. Although management sometimes overlooks the importance of these activities, efficient order processing facilitates product flow. Computerised order processing provides a database

cycle time
The time needed to complete a process

order processing
The receipt and transmission of sales order information

for all supply-chain members to increase their productivity. When carried out quickly and accurately, order processing contributes to customer satisfaction, decreased costs and cycle time and increased profits.

Order processing entails three main tasks: order entry, order handling and order delivery. Order entry begins when customers or salespeople place purchase orders via telephone, mail, email or website. Electronic ordering is less time-consuming than a manual, paper-based ordering system and reduces costs. In some companies, sales representatives receive and enter orders personally and also handle complaints, prepare progress reports and forward sales order information.

Order handling involves several tasks. Once an order is entered, it is transmitted to a warehouse, where product availability is verified, and to the credit department, where prices, terms and the customer's credit rating are checked. If the credit department approves the purchase, warehouse personnel (sometimes assisted by automated equipment) pick and assemble the order. If the requested product is not in stock, a production order is sent to the factory, or the customer is offered a substitute.

When the order has been assembled and packed for shipment, the warehouse schedules delivery with an appropriate carrier. If the customer pays for rush service, overnight delivery by FedEx or another overnight carrier is used. The customer is sent an invoice, inventory records are adjusted and the order is delivered.

Whether to use a manual or an electronic order-processing system depends on which method provides the greater speed and accuracy within cost limits. Manual processing suffices for small-volume orders and is more flexible in certain situations. Most companies, however, use electronic data interchange (EDI), which uses computer technology to integrate order processing with production, inventory, accounting and transportation. Within the supply chain, EDI functions as an information system that links marketing-channel members and outsourcing firms together. It reduces paperwork for all members of the supply chain and allows them to share information on invoices, orders, payments, inquiries and scheduling. Consequently, many companies have pushed their suppliers toward EDI to reduce distribution costs and cycle times.[6] Kmart and Bunnings for example, strongly urge their suppliers to use EDI systems which focus on developing EDI software for medium-sized suppliers.

electronic data interchange (EDI)
A computerised means of integrating order processing with production, inventory, accounting and transportation

inventory management
Developing and maintaining adequate assortments of products to meet customers' needs

Inventory management >>
This handheld inventory management device allows employees to have an instant overview of every item – and its price – in the warehouse at any given time

Source: © AP IMAGES/KEVIN RIVOLI

Inventory management

Inventory management involves developing and maintaining adequate assortments of products to meet customers' needs. It is a key component of any effective physical distribution system. Inventory decisions have a major impact on physical distribution costs and the level of customer service provided. When too few products are carried in inventory, the result is stock-outs, or shortages of products, which, in turn, can result in brand switching, lower sales and loss of customers. When too many products (or too many slow-moving products) are carried, costs increase, as do risks of product obsolescence, pilferage and damage. The objective of inventory management is to minimise inventory costs while maintaining an adequate supply of goods to satisfy customers. To achieve this objective, marketers focus on two major issues: when to order and how much to order.

To determine when to order, a marketer calculates the *reorder point*, the inventory level that signals the need to place a new order. To calculate the reorder point, the marketer must know the order lead time, the usage rate and the amount of safety stock required. The *order lead time* refers to the average time lapse between placing the order and receiving it. The *usage rate* is the rate at which a product's inventory is used or sold during a specific time period. *Safety stock* is the amount of extra inventory a firm keeps to guard against stockouts resulting from above-average usage rates and/or longer-than-expected lead times. The reorder point can be calculated using the following formula:

$$\text{Reorder point} = (\text{order lead time} \times \text{usage rate}) + \text{safety stock}$$

Thus, if order lead time is 10 days, usage rate is 3 units per day and safety stock is 20 units, the reorder point is 50 units.

Efficient inventory management with accurate reorder points is crucial for firms that use a just-in-time (JIT) approach, in which supplies arrive just as they are needed for use in production or for resale. When using JIT, companies maintain low inventory levels and purchase products and materials in small quantities whenever they need them. Usually there is no safety stock, and suppliers are expected to provide consistently high-quality products. JIT inventory management requires a high level of coordination between producers and suppliers, but it eliminates waste and reduces inventory costs significantly. This approach has been used successfully by many well-known firms, including Chrysler, Harley-Davidson and Dell, to reduce costs and boost customer satisfaction. When a JIT approach is used in a supply chain, suppliers often move close to their customers.

just-in-time (JIT)
An inventory-management approach in which supplies arrive just when needed for production or resale

Materials handling

Materials handling, the physical handling of tangible goods, supplies and resources, is an important factor in warehouse operations, as well as in transportation from points of production to points of consumption. Efficient procedures and techniques for materials handling minimise inventory management costs, reduce the number of times a good is handled, improve customer service and increase customer satisfaction. Systems for packaging, labelling, loading and movement must be coordinated to maximise cost reduction and customer satisfaction. RFID greatly improves the tracking of shipments and reduces cycle times. Hundreds of RFID tags can be read at a time, which represents an advantage over bar codes. RFID has many applications, from tracking inventory to paying for goods and services, and even asset management.

materials handling
Physical handling of tangible goods, supplies and resources

Product characteristics often determine handling. For example, the characteristics of bulk liquids and gases determine how they can be moved and stored. Internal packaging is also an important consideration in materials handling; goods must be packaged correctly to prevent damage or breakage during handling and transportation. Most companies employ packaging consultants during the product design process to help them decide which packaging materials and methods will result in the most efficient handling.

Unit loading and containerisation are two common methods used in materials handling. With *unit loading*, one or more boxes are placed on a pallet or skid; these units then can be loaded efficiently by mechanical means such as forklifts, trucks or conveyer systems. *Containerisation* is the consolidation of many items into a single, large container that is sealed at its point of origin and opened at its destination. Containers are usually 2.5 metres wide, 2.5 metres high and 3 to 12 metres long. They can be conveniently stacked and shipped via train, barge, or ship. Once containers reach their destinations, wheel assemblies can be added to make them suitable for ground transportation. Because individual items are not handled in transit, containerisation greatly increases efficiency and security in shipping.

Warehousing

warehousing
The design and operation of facilities for storing and moving goods

Warehousing, the design and operation of facilities for storing and moving goods, is another important physical distribution function. Warehousing provides time utility by enabling firms to compensate for dissimilar production and consumption rates. When mass production creates a greater stock of goods than can be sold immediately, companies may warehouse the surplus until customers are ready to buy. Warehousing also helps to stabilise prices and the availability of seasonal items.

distribution centres
Large, centralised warehouses that focus on moving rather than storing goods

Distribution centres are large, centralised warehouses that receive goods from factories and suppliers, regroup them into orders, and ship them to customers quickly, the focus being on movement of goods rather than storage.[7] Distribution centres are specially designed for rapid flow of products. They are usually one-storey buildings (to eliminate elevators) with access to transportation networks such as major highways and/or railway lines. Many distribution centres are highly automated, with computer-directed robots, forklifts and hoists that collect and move products to loading docks. Efficiency and creativity in distribution operations helps the firm to keep up with a high volume of merchandise moving through the centres and stay on top of busy holiday seasons.[8] Although some public warehouses offer such specialised services, most distribution centres are privately owned. They serve customers in regional markets and, in some cases, function as consolidation points for a company's branch warehouses.

Transportation

transportation
The movement of products from where they are made to intermediaries and end users

Transportation, the movement of products from where they are made to intermediaries and end users, is the most expensive physical distribution function. Because product availability and timely deliveries depend on transportation functions, transportation decisions directly affect customer service. A firm even may build its distribution and marketing strategy around a unique transportation system if that system can ensure on-time deliveries and thereby give the firm a competitive edge. Companies may build their own transportation fleets (private carriers) or outsource the transportation function to a common or contract carrier.

Transportation modes

There are five basic transportation modes for moving physical goods: railways, trucks, waterways, airways and pipelines. Each mode offers distinct advantages. Many companies adopt physical handling procedures that facilitate the use of two or more modes in combination.

Railways carry heavy, bulky freight that must be shipped long distances over land. Railways commonly haul minerals, sand, lumber, chemicals and farm products, as well as low-value manufactured goods and an increasing number of cars. They are especially efficient for transporting full carloads, which can be shipped at lower rates than smaller quantities because they require less handling. Many companies locate factories or warehouses near rail lines for convenient loading and unloading.

Trucks provide the most flexible schedules and routes of all major transportation modes because they can go almost anywhere. Because trucks have a unique ability to move goods directly from factory or warehouse to customer, they are often used in conjunction with other forms of transport that cannot provide door-to-door deliveries. Trucks are more expensive and somewhat more vulnerable to bad weather than trains. They are also subject to size and weight restrictions on the products they carry. Trucks are sometimes criticised for high levels of loss and damage to freight and for delays caused by the rehandling of small shipments.

Waterways are the cheapest method of shipping heavy, low-value, non-perishable goods such as ore, coal, grain and petroleum products. Water carriers offer considerable capacity. Powered by tugboats and towboats, barges that travel along intra-coastal canals, inland rivers and navigation systems can haul at least 10 times the weight of one rail car, and ocean-going vessels can haul thousands of containers. More than 95 per cent of international cargo is transported by water. However, many markets are inaccessible by water transportation unless supplemented by rail or truck. Droughts and floods also may create difficulties for users of inland waterway transportation. Nevertheless, the extreme fuel efficiency of water transportation and the continuing globalisation of marketing likely will increase its use in the future.

Source: © AP IMAGES/SETH PERLMAN

<< **Transportation**
Waterway transportation is used to move heavy, non-perishable products, such as large equipment, grain, motor vehicles and chemicals

Air transportation is the fastest but most expensive form of shipping. It is used most often for perishable goods, for high-value, low-bulk items, and for products requiring quick delivery over long distances, such as emergency shipments. Some air carriers transport combinations of passengers, freight and mail. Despite its expense, air transit can reduce warehousing and packaging costs and losses from theft and damage, thus helping to lower total costs (but truck transportation needed for pickup and final delivery adds to cost and transit time). Although air transport accounts for less than one per cent of total goods carried, its importance as a mode of transportation is growing. In fact, the success of many businesses is now based on the availability of overnight air delivery service provided by organisations such as FedEx and Australia Post. Amazon.com, for example, ships many products ordered online via UPS within a day of order.

Choosing transportation modes

Logistics managers select a transportation mode based on the combination of cost, speed, dependability, load flexibility, accessibility and frequency that is most appropriate for their products and generates the desired level of customer service.

Marketers compare alternative transportation modes to determine whether benefits from a more expensive mode are worth higher costs. Companies like Port Logistics can assist marketers in analysing various transportation options. Port Logistics is a supply chain logistics consulting firm that offers a wide range of services, such as determining the best channels and transportation options. Port Logistics even helps firms with considerations such as sustainability through reducing transportation fuel outputs, increasing renewable energy usage and reducing waste. The company demonstrated its commitment to the environment by converting its own fleet of trucks to clean power.[9]

Coordinating transportation

intermodal transportation
Two or more transportation modes used in combination

To take advantage of the benefits offered by various transportation modes and compensate for deficiencies, marketers often combine and coordinate two or more modes. Intermodal transportation, as this integrated approach is sometimes called, has become easier because of new developments within the transportation industry. Several kinds of intermodal shipping are available. All combine the flexibility of trucking with the low cost or speed of other forms of transport. Containerisation facilitates intermodal transportation by consolidating shipments into sealed containers for transport by *piggyback* (shipping that uses both truck trailers and railway flatcars), *fishyback* (truck trailers and water carriers) and *birdyback* (truck trailers and air carriers). As transportation costs have increased, intermodal shipping has gained popularity.

freight forwarders
Organisations that consolidate shipments from several firms into efficient lot sizes

Specialised outsource agencies provide other forms of transport coordination. Known as freight forwarders, these firms combine shipments from several organisations into efficient lot sizes. Small loads (less than 225 kilos) are much more expensive to ship than full carloads or truckloads, which frequently require consolidation. Freight forwarders take small loads from various marketers, buy transport space from carriers and arrange for goods to be delivered to buyers. Freight forwarders' profits come from the margin between the higher, less-than-carload rates they charge each marketer and the lower carload rates they themselves pay. Because large shipments require less handling, use of freight forwarders can speed delivery. Freight forwarders also can determine the most efficient carriers and routes and are useful for shipping goods to foreign markets. Some companies prefer to outsource their shipping to freight forwarders because the latter provide door-to-door service.

Another transportation innovation is the development of megacarriers, freight transportation companies that offer several shipment methods, including rail, truck and air service. CSX, for example, has trains, barges, container ships, trucks and pipelines, thus offering a multitude of transportation services. In addition, air carriers have increased their ground-transportation services. As they expand the range of transportation alternatives, carriers too put greater stress on customer service.

Types of retailers and strategic issues in retailing

Retailers are important channel members of channels designed to distribute consumer products. The practice of retailing includes all transactions in which the buyer intends to consume the product through personal, family or household use. Buyers in retail transactions are therefore the ultimate consumers. A retailer is an organisation that purchases products for the purpose of reselling them to ultimate consumers. Although most retailers' sales are made directly to the consumer, non-retail transactions occur occasionally when retailers sell products to other businesses. Retailing often takes place in stores or service establishments, but it also occurs through direct selling, direct marketing and vending machines outside stores.

Retailers add value, provide services and assist in making product selections. They can enhance the value of products by making buyers' shopping experiences more convenient, as in home shopping. Through their locations, retailers can facilitate comparison shopping; for example, car dealerships often cluster in the same general vicinity, as do furniture stores. Product value is also enhanced when retailers offer services, such as technical advice, delivery, credit and repair. Finally, retail sales personnel can demonstrate to customers how products can satisfy their needs or solve problems.

The value added by retailers is significant for both producers and ultimate consumers. Retailers are the critical link between producers and ultimate consumers because they provide the environment in which exchanges with ultimate consumers occur. Ultimate consumers benefit through retailers' performance of marketing functions that result in the availability of broader arrays of products. Retailers play a major role in creating time, place and possession utility and, in some cases, form utility.

Leading retailers such as David Jones and Myer offer consumers a place to browse and compare merchandise to find just what they need. However, such traditional retailing is being challenged by direct marketing channels that provide home shopping through catalogues, television and the Internet.

New store formats and advances in digital technologies are making the retail environment highly dynamic and competitive. Instant-messaging technology is enabling online retailers to converse in real time with customers so that they don't click away to another website. For example, shoppers in Australia and New Zealand interested in buying clothes from Lands'

megacarriers
Freight transportation firms that provide several modes of shipment

retailing
All transactions in which the buyer intends to consume the product through personal, family or household use

retailer
An organisation that purchases products for the purpose of reselling them to ultimate consumers

End, a US-based online retailer of clothes, can go to the Lands' End website and click to chat, via keyboard, directly with a customer-service representative about sizes, colours or other product details. The key to success in retailing is to have a strong customer focus with a retail strategy that provides the level of service, product quality and innovation that consumers desire. Partnerships among non-competing retailers and other marketing-channel members are providing new opportunities for retailers. For example, airports are leasing space to retailers such as Sunglass Hut and The Body Shop. David Jones and Myer have developed joint co-branded credit cards that offer rebates to customers at participating stores.

Retailers are also finding global opportunities. For example, Gap Inc. is now opening stores in Australia. Starbucks has opened hundreds of stores in Japan and Southeast Asia.

Major types of retail stores

Many types of retail stores exist. One way to classify them is by the breadth of products offered. Two general categories include general merchandise retailers and specialty retailers.

General merchandise retailers

A retail establishment that offers a variety of product lines stocked in considerable depth is referred to as a general merchandise retailer. The types of product offerings, mixes of customer services and operating styles of retailers in this category vary considerably. The primary types of general merchandise retailers are department stores, discount stores, convenience stores, supermarkets, superstores, hypermarkets, warehouse clubs and warehouse showrooms (see Table 11.2).

TABLE 11.2   GENERAL MERCHANDISE RETAILERS

Type of retailer	Description	Examples
Department store	Large organisation offering wide product mix and organised into separate departments	David Jones, Myer
Discount store	Self-service general merchandise store offering brand name and private brand products at low prices	Target, Kmart
Convenience store	Small self-service store offering narrow product assortment in convenient locations	7-Eleven
Supermarket	Self-service store offering complete line of food products and some non-food products	Aldi, Coles, Woolworths
Superstore	Giant store offering all food and non-food products found in supermarkets, as well as most routinely purchased products	Mainly in Europe, North America and South America
Hypermarket	Giant store that combines supermarket and discount store; larger than a superstore	Mainly in Europe, North America and South America
Warehouse club	Large-scale members-only establishments combining cash-and-carry wholesaling with discount retailing	Costco
Warehouse showroom	Facility in a large, low-cost building with large on-premises inventories and minimal service	IKEA

DEPARTMENT STORES

Department stores are large retail organisations characterised by wide product mixes and organised into separate departments, such as cosmetics, housewares, apparel, home furnishings and appliances, to facilitate marketing and internal management. Often each department functions as a self-contained business, and buyers for individual departments are fairly autonomous. Typical department stores, such as David Jones and Myer, obtain a large proportion of sales from apparel, accessories and cosmetics. Other products that these stores carry include gift items, luggage, electronics, home accessories and sports equipment. Some department stores offer services such as haircare and optical services. In some cases, space for these specialised services is leased out, with proprietors managing their own operations and paying rent to the department store. Some department stores also sell products through their websites.

Department stores are highly service-oriented. Their total product may include credit, delivery, personal assistance, merchandise returns and a pleasant atmosphere. Although some so-called department stores are actually large, departmentalised specialty stores, most department stores are shopping stores. Consumers can compare price, quality and service at one store with those at competing stores. Along with large discount stores, department stores are often considered retailing leaders in a community.

Source: AAP Images/Tracey Nearmy

<< **Department store**
Because of its size, wide product mix and services provided, Myer is classified as a department store

department stores
Large retail organisations characterised by wide product mixes and organised into separate departments to facilitate marketing and internal management

DISCOUNT STORES

In recent years, department stores have been losing market share to discount stores. Discount stores are self-service, general merchandise outlets that regularly offer brand name and private brand products at low prices. Discounters accept lower margins than conventional retailers in exchange for high sales volume. To keep inventory turnover high, they carry a wide but carefully selected assortment of products, from appliances to housewares and clothing. Major discount establishments also offer food products, toys, garden supplies and sports equipment. Walmart, based in the US, is the largest discount store in the world. Discount stores usually offer everyday low prices rather than relying on sales events.

discount stores
Self-service, general merchandise stores offering brand name and private brand products at low prices

CONVENIENCE STORES

A convenience store is a small self-service store that is open long hours and carries a narrow assortment of products, usually convenience items such as soft drinks and other beverages, snacks, newspapers and petrol, as well as services such as automated teller machines (ATMs). The primary product offered by the 'corner store' is convenience. They are open 24 hours a day, 7 days a week, and stock about 500 items. In addition to many national chains, there are many family-owned independent convenience stores in operation.[10]

convenience store
A small self-service store that is open long hours and carries a narrow assortment of products, usually convenience items

SUPERMARKETS

Supermarkets are large self-service stores that carry a complete line of food products, as well as some non-food products such as cosmetics and non-prescription drugs. Supermarkets are arranged in departments for maximum efficiency in stocking and handling products but have central checkout facilities. They offer lower prices than smaller neighbourhood grocery stores and usually provide free parking. Today, consumers make more than three-quarters of all food purchases in supermarkets. Even so, supermarkets' total share of the food market is declining because consumers now have widely varying food preferences and buying habits, and in many communities, shoppers can choose from several convenience stores, discount stores and specialty food stores, as well as a wide variety of restaurants.

SUPERSTORES

Superstores, which originated in Europe, are giant retail outlets that carry not only food and non-food products ordinarily found in supermarkets but also routinely purchased consumer products. Superstores combine features of discount stores and supermarkets. Examples include Walmart Supercentres in the US and Costco in Australia.

Besides a complete food line, superstores sell housewares, hardware, small appliances, clothing, personal-care products, garden products and tyres – about four times as many items as supermarkets. Services available at superstores include dry cleaning, car repairs, cheque cashing, bill paying and snack bars. To cut handling and inventory costs, they use sophisticated operating techniques and often have tall shelving that displays entire assortments of products. Sales volume is two to three times that of supermarkets partly because locations near good transportation networks help to generate the in-store traffic needed for profitability. Millions of people pass through the doors of Walmart each week.[11]

HYPERMARKETS

Hypermarkets combine supermarket and discount store shopping in one location. They are larger than superstores and offer 45 000 to 60 000 different types of low priced products. They commonly allocate 40 to 50 per cent of their space to grocery products and the remainder to general merchandise, including athletic shoes, designer jeans and other apparel, refrigerators, televisions and other appliances, housewares, cameras, toys, jewellery, hardware, and automotive supplies. Many lease space to non-competing businesses such as banks, optical shops and fast-food restaurants. All hypermarkets focus on low prices and vast selections. Although Walmart and Carrefour (a French retailer) have operated hypermarkets in the US, most of these stores were unsuccessful and closed. Such stores may be too big for time-constrained US shoppers. However, hypermarkets are more successful in Europe and South America.

Hypermarkets are not present in Australia. Coles did try to set up a hypermarket concept with the introduction of Super Kmarts in the 1980s. Those stores effectively combined a Coles supermarket with a Kmart outlet. The result was not particularly positive so the Super Kmarts were discontinued in the 1990s.[12]

WAREHOUSE CLUBS

Warehouse clubs, an emerging form of mass merchandising in Australia, are large-scale members-only selling operations combining cash-and-carry wholesaling with discount retailing. Sometimes called buying clubs, warehouse clubs offer the same types of products as discount stores but in a limited range of sizes and styles. Whereas most discount stores carry around 40 000 items, a warehouse club handles only 3500 to 5000 products, usually acknowledged brand leaders. Some warehouse clubs can also be classified as superstores. Costco, a superstore, also leads the warehouse club industry in Australia, offering a broad product mix, including food, beverages, books, appliances, housewares, car parts, hardware and furniture.

<< **Warehouse club**
Costco is a warehouse club that markets many product lines. Most of Costco product lines have limited depth

To keep prices lower than those of supermarkets and discount stores, warehouse clubs provide few services. They generally do not advertise, except through direct mail. Their facilities, often located in industrial areas, have concrete floors and aisles wide enough for forklifts. Merchandise is stacked on pallets or displayed on pipe racks. Customers must transport purchases themselves. Warehouse clubs appeal to many price-conscious consumers and small retailers unable to obtain wholesaling services from large distributors. The average warehouse club shopper has more education, a higher income and a larger household than the average supermarket shopper.

WAREHOUSE SHOWROOMS

Warehouse showrooms are retail facilities with five basic characteristics: large, low-cost buildings; warehouse materials-handling technology; vertical merchandise displays; large on-premises inventories; and minimal services. IKEA sells furniture, household goods and kitchen accessories in warehouse showrooms and via catalogues around the world, including China and Russia. These high-volume, low-overhead operations have fewer personnel and services. Lower costs are possible because some marketing functions have been shifted to consumers, who must transport, finance and perhaps store larger quantities of products. Most consumers carry away purchases in the manufacturer's carton, although stores will deliver for a fee.

warehouse showrooms
Retail facilities in large, low-cost buildings with large on-premises inventories and minimal services

Specialty retailers

In contrast to general merchandise retailers with their broad product mixes, specialty retailers emphasise narrow and deep assortments. Despite their name, specialty retailers do not sell specialty items (except when specialty goods complement the overall product mix). Instead, they offer substantial assortments in a few product lines. We examine three types of specialty retailers: traditional specialty retailers, category killers and off-price retailers.

Traditional specialty retailers are stores that carry a narrow product mix with deep product lines. Sometimes called *limited-line retailers*, they may be referred to as *single-line retailers* if they carry unusual depth in one main product category. Traditional specialty retailers commonly sell shopping products such as apparel, jewellery, sporting

traditional specialty retailers
Stores that carry a narrow product mix with deep product lines

goods, fabrics, computers, toys and pet supplies. Gap Inc. and OPSM are examples of retailers offering limited product lines but great depth within those lines. Many traditional specialty retailers are small businesses with just one or a few outlets.

Because they are usually small, specialty stores may have high costs in proportion to sales, and satisfying customers may require carrying some products with low turnover rates. However, these stores sometimes obtain lower prices from suppliers by purchasing limited lines of merchandise in large quantities. Successful traditional specialty stores understand their customer types and know what products to carry, thus reducing the risk of unsold merchandise. Traditional specialty stores usually offer better selections and more sales expertise than department stores, their main competitors. By capitalising on fashion, service, personnel, atmosphere and location, these retailers position themselves strategically to attract customers in specific market segments.

Over the last 15 years, a new breed of specialty retailer, the category killer, has evolved. A category killer is a very large specialty store that concentrates on a major product category and competes on the basis of low prices and enormous product availability. These stores are referred to as category killers because they expand rapidly and gain sizeable market shares, taking business away from smaller, high-cost retail outlets. Examples of category killers include Bunnings (a home-improvement chain) and OfficeMax (an office-supply chain).

Off-price retailers are stores that buy manufacturers' seconds, overruns, returns and off-season production runs at below-wholesale prices for resale to consumers at deep discounts. Unlike true discount stores, which pay regular wholesale prices for goods and usually carry second-line brand names, off-price retailers offer limited lines of national-brand and designer merchandise, usually clothing, shoes or housewares. Off-price stores charge 20 to 50 per cent less than do department stores for comparable merchandise but offer few customer services. They often feature community dressing rooms and central checkout counters. Some of these stores do not take returns or allow exchanges. Off-price stores may or may not sell goods with the original labels intact. They turn over their inventory nine to 12 times a year, three times as often as traditional specialty stores. They compete with department stores for the same customers: price-conscious customers who are knowledgeable about brand names.

Source: Shutterstock.

Traditional specialty store >>
Traditional specialty stores, like Foot Locker, have narrow but deep product mixes

category killer
A very large specialty store concentrating on a major product category and competing on the basis of low prices and product availability

off-price retailers
Stores that buy manufacturers' seconds, overruns, returns and off-season merchandise for resale to consumers at deep discounts

Strategic issues in retailing

Whereas most business purchases are based on economic planning and necessity, consumer purchases may result from social and psychological influences. Because consumers shop for various reasons – to search for specific items, escape boredom or learn about something new – retailers must do more than simply fill space with merchandise. They must make desired products available, create stimulating shopping environments and develop marketing strategies that increase store patronage. In this section we discuss how store location, store image and category management are used to help achieve retailing objectives.

Location

Location, the least flexible of the strategic retailing issues, is one of the most important because location dictates the limited geographic trading area from which a store draws its customers. Retailers consider various factors when evaluating potential locations, including location of the company's target market within the trading area, kinds of products being sold, availability of public transportation, customer characteristics and competitors' locations. Retailers may even opt for a solely online-based location (refer to Marketing in Action box below). If a physical location is preferable, a retailer evaluates the relative ease of movement to and from the site, including factors such as pedestrian and vehicular traffic and parking. Retailers also evaluate the characteristics of the site itself: types of stores in the area; size, shape and visibility of the lot or building under consideration; and rental, leasing or ownership terms. Retailers look for compatibility with nearby retailers because stores that complement one another draw more customers for everyone.

Many retailers choose to locate in central business districts, whereas others prefer sites within various types of planned shopping centres. Some retailers, including Bunnings and many fast-food restaurants, opt for freestanding structures that are not connected to other buildings, but many chain stores are found in planned shopping centres. Some retailers choose to locate in less orthodox settings. For example, McDonald's, one of the world's largest franchising operations, has opened several stores inside hospitals such as the Royal Children's Hospital in Melbourne. Planned shopping centres include neighbourhood, community, regional, super-regional and lifestyle shopping centres.

franchising
An arrangement in which a supplier (franchiser) grants a dealer (franchisee) the right to sell the franchiser's products in exchange for some type of consideration such as a percentage of the franchisee's sales or an annual fee. Some of the benefits that the franchisee receives from the franchiser, apart from the right to sell the franchiser's products (goods or services), include furnishing equipment, management know-how and marketing assistance.

MARKETING IN ACTION | ETSY CREATES A CRAFTY CHANNEL

Since 2005, makers of handcrafted items have had a dedicated online channel for distributing their works: Etsy. Photographer/carpenter Rob Kalin co-founded Etsy with two friends as an Internet marketplace where he and other artisans could connect with buyers seeking creative crafts and artwork. Under Etsy's rules, all items must be handmade by the seller. The exceptions are vintage goods, which must be at least 20 years old to be offered for sale on the website.

Today, Etsy serves as a convenient yet global virtual storefront for 800 000 crafts entrepreneurs who offer a total of 13 million handmade and vintage products and ring up US$526 million in annual sales. It provides apps for buyers who want to browse or search offerings via mobile phone, apps for sellers who want to promote their shops, and support services like payment processing and accounting services for its craft shopkeepers.

Going beyond channel functions, Etsy encourages a sense of community among crafts lovers through social media, such as blogs, Facebook, Tumblr, Twitter, and Meetup. 'It's not just handcrafted goods, but it's a handcrafted experience,' explains CEO Chad Dickerson. 'You can get a real message from a real seller. That's different than Walmart.'[13]

**local shopping
centres**
Shopping centres usually
consisting of several small
convenience and specialty
stores

**community
shopping centres**
Shopping centres with one
or two department stores,
some specialty stores and
convenience stores

**regional shopping
centres**
A type of shopping centre
with the largest department
stores, the widest product mix
and the deepest product lines
of all shopping centres

**super-regional
shopping centres**
A type of shopping centre
with the widest and deepest
product mixes that attracts
customers from many
kilometres away

**lifestyle shopping
centre**
A type of shopping centre
that is typically open air and
features upscale specialty,
dining and entertainment
stores

Retail location >>
Many retailers, like
Hungry Jack's, spend
considerable time
and resources to
place stores in the
right locations

Local shopping centres usually consist of several small convenience and specialty stores, such as small grocery stores, service stations and fast-food restaurants. Many of these retailers consider their target markets to be consumers who live within two to three kilometres of their stores, or 10 minutes' driving time. Because most purchases are based on convenience or personal contact, there is usually little coordination of selling efforts within a local shopping centre. Generally, product mixes consist of essential products, and depth of the product lines is limited.

Community shopping centres include one or two department stores and some specialty stores, as well as convenience stores. They draw consumers looking for shopping and specialty products not available in local shopping centres. Because these centres serve larger geographic areas, consumers must drive longer distances to community shopping centres than to local centres. Community shopping centres are planned and coordinated to attract shoppers. Special events, such as art exhibits and automobile shows stimulate traffic. Managers of community shopping centres look for tenants that complement the centres' total assortment of products. Such centres have wide product mixes and deep product lines.

Regional shopping centres usually have the largest department stores, the widest product mixes and the deepest product lines of all shopping centres. Many shopping malls are regional shopping centres, although some are community shopping centres. With 150 000 or more consumers in their target market, regional shopping centres must have well-coordinated management and marketing activities. Target markets may include consumers travelling from a distance to find products and prices not available in their hometowns. Because of the expense of leasing space in regional shopping centres, tenants are more likely to be national chains than small, independent stores. Large centres usually advertise, have special events, furnish transportation to some consumer groups, maintain their own security forces and carefully select the mix of stores. The largest of these centres, sometimes called super-regional shopping centres, have the widest and deepest product mixes and attract

Source: Photolibrary/Alamy/Z J Urbanski

customers from many kilometres away. Super-regional centres often have special attractions beyond stores, such as upscale restaurants.

With traditional shopping centre sales declining, some shopping centre developers are looking to new formats that differ significantly from traditional shopping centres. A lifestyle shopping centre is typically an open-air shopping centre that features upscale specialty, dining and entertainment stores, usually owned by national chains. They are often located near affluent neighbourhoods and may have fountains, benches and other amenities that encourage 'casual browsing'. Indeed, architectural design is an important aspect of these 'mini-cities', which may include urban streets or parks, and is intended to encourage consumer loyalty by creating a sense of place. Some lifestyle centres are designed to resemble traditional 'Main Street' shopping centres or may have a central theme evidenced by architecture.[14]

Factory outlets feature discount stores carrying traditional manufacturer brands, such as Quicksilver and Reebok. Some outlet centres feature upscale products. Manufacturers own these stores and make a special effort to avoid conflict with traditional retailers of their products. Manufacturers claim that their stores are in non-competitive locations; indeed, most factory outlet centres are located outside metropolitan areas. Not all factory outlets stock closeouts and irregulars, but most avoid comparison with discount houses. Factory outlet centres attract value-conscious customers seeking quality and major brand names. They operate in much the same way as regional shopping centres but usually draw customers, some of which may be tourists, from a larger shopping radius. Promotional activity is at the heart of these shopping centres. Craft and antique shows, contests and special events attract a great deal of traffic.

Store image

To attract customers, a retail store must project an image – a functional and psychological picture in the consumer's mind – that appeals to its target market. Store environment, merchandise quality and service quality are key determinants of store image.

Atmospherics, the physical elements in a store's design that appeal to consumers' emotions and encourage buying, help to create an image and position a retailer (see Chapter 14 for further discussion). Supermarkets, for example, should use cooler colours and simple layout and presentations because their customers tend to be task-motivated, whereas specialty retailers may be able to use more complex layouts and brighter colours to stimulate their more recreationally motivated customers.[15]

Exterior atmospheric elements include the appearance of the storefront, display windows, store entrances and degree of traffic congestion. Exterior atmospherics are particularly important to new customers, who tend to judge an unfamiliar store by its outside appearance and may not enter if they feel intimidated by the building or inconvenienced by the parking lot. Interior atmospheric elements include aesthetic considerations such as lighting, wall and floor coverings, dressing facilities and store fixtures (how environmentally friendly these physical distribution channels are in comparison to inline distribution is discussed in the Ethical Marketing box on the next page). Interior sensory elements contribute significantly to atmosphere. Colour can attract shoppers to a retail display. Many fast-food restaurants use bright colours, such as red and yellow, because these have been shown to make customers feel hungrier and eat faster, which increases turnover. Sound is another important sensory component of atmosphere and may range from silence to subdued background music. Some department stores, for example, vary the music across the store – even within departments – based on local demographics.[16] Many retailers employ scent, especially food aromas, to attract customers. Research suggests that consumer evaluations of a product are affected by scent, but only when the scent employed is congruent with the product.[17]

Category management

Category management is a retail strategy of managing groups of similar, often substitutable products produced by different manufacturers. For example, supermarkets such as

atmospherics
The physical elements in a store's design that appeal to consumers' emotions and encourage buying

category management
A retail strategy of managing groups of similar, often substitutable products produced by different manufacturers

ETHICAL MARKETING   WHICH ARE MORE EARTH-FRIENDLY: ONLINE OR TRADITIONAL CHANNELS?

On two of the biggest shopping days of the year in the US – Black Friday and Cyber Monday, the first Friday and Monday after Thanksgiving – the outdoor apparel marketer Patagonia ran online and newspaper ads headlined, 'Don't Buy This Jacket'. Patagonia, known for its environmental protection policies, wanted consumers to stop and think before they buy, even when choosing products made from recycled materials. The ads rekindled debates over marketing's environmental impact, including the question of whether online channels (the focus of Cyber Monday promotions) are more earth-friendly than traditional channels (the focus of most Black Friday promotions).

In Australia, online sales spike on what is termed Cyber Boxing Day which begins Christmas eve. When customers buy online in order to get in first on the Boxing Day sales, their purchases have to be wrapped for shipment and delivered by mail or by package carrier. Shipping containers are often recyclable but still consume natural resources when manufactured. Most deliveries of online purchases rely on gasoline-powered vehicles or even jet fuel, adding to pollution.

Moreover, online marketers consume considerable energy, keeping their websites and warehouses running around the clock. Traditional channels use lots of energy in lighting, heating and cooling local stores. Their many employees use fuel commuting to and from store locations, and their many customers use fuel when they visit different stores. Transporting merchandise to warehouses and then individual stores eats up fuel and adds to pollution – as does returning unsold inventory to the manufacturer or sending it to other outlets for sale.[18]

Are online channels of distribution easier on the environment than traditional channels?

Source: © Patagonia, US, used with permission from Patagonia Legal Department

Woolworths use category management to determine space for products such as cosmetics, cereals and soups. An assortment of merchandise is both customer and strategically driven to improve performance. Category management developed in the food industry because supermarkets were concerned about highly competitive behaviour among manufacturers. Category management is a move toward a collaborative supply-chain initiative to enhance customer value. Successful category management requires the acquisition, analysis and sharing of sales and consumer information between the retailer and manufacturer.

The development of information about demand, consumer behaviour and optimal allocations of products should be available from one source. Companies such as the software company SAS provide software to manage data associated with each step of the category management decision cycle. The key is cooperative interaction between the manufacturers of category products and the retailer to create maximum success for all parties in the supply chain.

Direct marketing

Although retailers are the most visible members of the supply chain, many products are retailed outside the confines of a retail store. Direct marketing accounts for an increasing percentage of retail sales and is a form of retailing. Direct marketing is the use of telecommunications and non-personal media to communicate product and organisational information to customers, who then can purchase products via mail, telephone or the Internet. Direct marketing can occur through catalogue marketing, direct response marketing, telemarketing, television home shopping and online retailing.

Catalogue marketing

In catalogue marketing, an organisation provides a catalogue from which customers make selections and place orders by mail, telephone or the Internet. Catalogue marketing began in 1872, when Montgomery Ward issued its first catalogue to rural families in the United States. The advantages of catalogue retailing include efficiency and convenience for customers. The retailer benefits by being able to locate in remote, low-cost areas, save on expensive store fixtures, and reduce both personal selling and store operating expenses. On the other hand, catalogue retailing is inflexible, provides limited service and is most effective for a selected set of products.

Direct response marketing

Direct response marketing occurs when a retailer advertises a product and makes it available through mail or telephone orders. Generally, a purchaser may use a credit card, but other forms of payment are acceptable. Examples of direct response marketing include a TV commercial offering a recording artist's musical collection available through a free-call number, and a newspaper or magazine ad for a series of children's books available by filling out the form in the ad or by calling a free-call number. Direct response marketing is also conducted by sending letters, samples, brochures or booklets to prospects on a mailing list and asking that they order the advertised products by mail or telephone. In general, products must be priced above $30 to justify the advertising and distribution costs associated with direct response marketing.

Telemarketing

A number of organisations use the telephone to strengthen the effectiveness of traditional marketing methods. Telemarketing is the performance of marketing-related activities by telephone. Some organisations use a prescreened list of prospective clients. Telemarketing can help to generate sales leads, improve customer service, speed up payments on past-due accounts, raise funds for non-profit organisations and gather marketing data.

Currently, the laws and regulations regarding telemarketing, while in a state of flux, are becoming more restrictive. Do-not-call lists of customers who do not want to receive telemarketing calls from companies have been created. In Australia, companies are subject to fines for each call made to a consumer listed on such registries. Certain exceptions apply

direct marketing
The use of telecommunications and non-personal media to introduce products to consumers, who then can purchase them via mail, telephone or the Internet

catalogue marketing
A type of marketing in which an organisation provides a catalogue from which customers make selections and place orders by mail, telephone or the Internet

direct response marketing
A type of marketing that occurs when a retailer advertises a product and makes it available through mail or telephone orders

telemarketing
The performance of marketing-related activities by telephone

to do-not-call lists. A company still can use telemarketing to communicate with existing customers. In addition, charitable, political and telephone-survey organisations are not restricted by registries.

Television home shopping

television home shopping
A form of selling in which products are presented to TV viewers, who can buy them by calling a free-call number and paying with a credit card

Television home shopping presents products to TV viewers, encouraging them to order through free-call numbers and pay with credit cards. The most popular products sold through TV home shopping are jewellery, clothing, housewares and electronics. The TV home shopping format offers several benefits. Products can be demonstrated easily, and an adequate amount of time can be spent showing the product so that viewers are well informed. The length of time a product is shown depends not only on the time required for doing demonstrations but also on whether the product is selling. Once the calls peak and begin to decline, a new product is shown. Other benefits are that customers can shop at their convenience and from the comfort of their homes.

Online retailing

online retailing
Retailing that makes products available to buyers through computer connections

Online retailing makes products available to buyers through computer connections. The phenomenal growth of Internet use has created new retailing opportunities. Many retailers have set up websites to disseminate information about their companies and products. Although

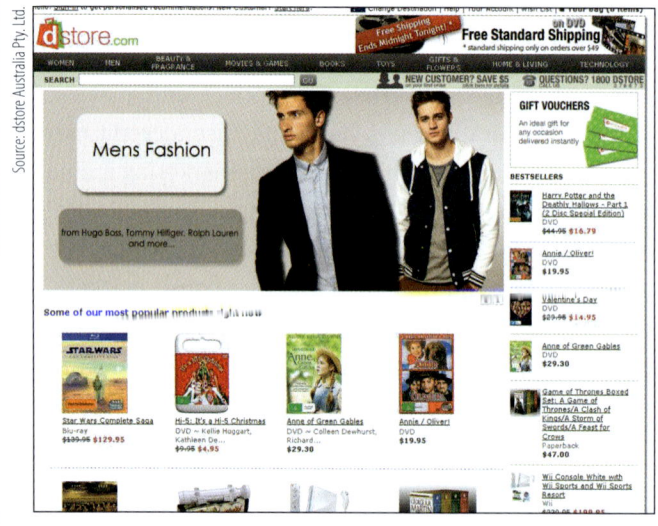

Source: dstore Australia Pty. Ltd.

most retailers with websites use them primarily to promote products, a number of companies, including OfficeMax, sell goods online. Consumers can purchase hard-to-find items on eBay. Banks and brokerage companies have established websites to give customers direct access to manage their accounts and enable them to trade online. With continuing advances in computer technology and consumers being ever more pressed for time, online retailing will escalate further.

Online retailers >>
Retailers such as dstore, Australia's biggest online shopping centre, are becoming increasingly popular among online consumers

Direct selling

direct selling
The marketing of products to ultimate consumers through face-to-face sales presentations at home or in the workplace

Direct selling is another form of retailing. **Direct selling** is the marketing of products to ultimate consumers through face-to-face sales presentations at home or in the workplace. Traditionally called door-to-door selling, direct selling began with peddlers and has since grown into a sizeable industry. Although direct sellers historically used a cold-canvass, door-to-door approach for finding prospects, many companies today, such as Amway, Mary Kay and Avon, use other approaches. They initially identify customers through the mail, telephone, Internet or shopping-centre intercepts and then set up appointments.

While the majority of direct selling takes place on an individual, or person-to-person, basis, it sometimes also includes the use of a group, or 'party', plan. With a party plan, a consumer acts as a host and invites friends and associates to view merchandise in a group setting, where a salesperson demonstrates products. The congenial party atmosphere helps to overcome customers' reluctance and encourages them to buy.

Direct selling has both benefits and limitations. It gives the marketer an opportunity to demonstrate the product in an environment – usually customers' homes – where it most likely would be used. The door-to-door seller can give the customer personal attention, and the product can be presented to the customer at a convenient time and location. Personal attention to the customer is the foundation on which some direct sellers, such as Mary Kay, have built their businesses. Because commissions for salespeople are so high, ranging from 30 to 50 per cent of the sales price, and great effort is required to isolate promising prospects, overall costs of direct selling make it the most expensive form of retailing. Furthermore, some customers view direct selling negatively, owing to unscrupulous and fraudulent practices used by some direct sellers in the past. Some communities even have local ordinances that control or, in some cases, prohibit direct selling. Despite these negative views held by some individuals, direct selling is still alive and well, bringing in annual revenues of $117 billion worldwide.[19]

Wholesaling

Wholesalers are also important channel members of channels designed to distribute consumer products. Wholesaling refers to all transactions in which products are bought for resale, for making other products or for general business operations. It does not include exchanges with ultimate consumers. A wholesaler buys products and resells them to resellers, governments and institutional users. Wholesaling activities are not limited to goods; service companies, such as financial institutions, also use active wholesale networks. For example, some banks buy loans in bulk from other financial institutions, as well as making loans to their own retail customers.

Wholesalers may engage in many supply-chain management activities, including warehousing, shipping and product handling, inventory control, information system management and data processing, risk taking, financing, budgeting and even marketing research and promotion. Regardless of whether there is a wholesaling company involved in the supply chain, all product distribution requires the performance of these activities. In addition to bearing the primary responsibility for the physical distribution of products from manufacturers to retailers, wholesalers may establish information systems that help producers and retailers better manage the supply chain from producer to customer. Many wholesalers are using digital and information technology and the Internet to allow their employees, customers and suppliers to share information between intermediaries and facilitating agencies such as trucking and warehouse companies. Other companies are making their databases and marketing information systems available to their supply-chain partners to facilitate order processing, shipping and product development and to share information about changing market conditions and customer desires. As a result, some wholesalers play a key role in supply-chain management decisions.

wholesaling
Transactions in which products are bought for resale, for making other products or for general business operations

wholesaler
An individual or organisation that sells products that are bought for resale, for making other products or for general business operations

Source: Shutterstock.com

Services provided by wholesalers

Wholesalers provide essential services to both producers and retailers. By initiating sales contacts with a producer and selling diverse products to retailers, wholesalers serve as an extension of the producer's sales force. Wholesalers also provide financial assistance. They often pay for transporting goods; they reduce a producer's warehousing expenses and inventory investment by holding goods in inventory; they extend credit and assume losses from buyers who turn out to be poor credit risks; and when they buy a producer's entire output and pay promptly or in cash, they are a source of working capital. Wholesalers also serve as conduits for information within the marketing channel, keeping producers up to date on market developments and passing along the manufacturers' promotional plans to other intermediaries. Using wholesalers therefore gives producers a distinct advantage because the specialised services wholesalers perform allow producers to concentrate on developing and manufacturing products that match customers' needs and wants.

Wholesalers support retailers by assisting with marketing strategy, especially the distribution component. Wholesalers also help retailers to select inventory. They are often specialists on market conditions and experts at negotiating final purchases. In industries in which obtaining supplies is important, skilled buying is indispensable. Effective wholesalers make an effort to understand the businesses of their customers. They can reduce a retailer's burden of looking for and coordinating supply sources. If the wholesaler purchases for several different buyers, expenses can be shared by all customers. Furthermore, whereas a manufacturer's salesperson offers retailers only a few products at a time, independent wholesalers always have a wide range of products available. Therefore, through partnerships, wholesalers and retailers can forge successful relationships for the benefit of customers.

The distinction between services performed by wholesalers and those provided by other businesses has blurred in recent years. Changes in the competitive nature of business, especially the growth of strong retail chains such as Bunnings, are changing supply-chain relationships. In many product categories, such as electronics, furniture and even food products, retailers have discovered that they can deal directly with producers, performing wholesaling activities themselves at a lower cost. An increasing number of retailers are relying on computer technology to expedite ordering, delivery and handling of goods. Technology, therefore, is allowing retailers to take over many wholesaling functions. However, when a wholesaler is eliminated from a marketing channel, wholesaling activities still have to be performed by a member of the supply chain, whether a producer, retailer or facilitating agency. These wholesaling activities are critical components of supply-chain management.

Types of wholesalers

Wholesalers are classified according to several criteria. Whether a wholesaler is independently owned or owned by a producer influences how it is classified. Wholesalers can also be grouped according to whether they take title to (own) the products they handle. The range of services provided is another criterion used for classification. Finally, wholesalers are classified according to the breadth and depth of their product lines. Using these criteria, we discuss three general types of wholesaling establishments: merchant wholesalers, agents and brokers, and manufacturers' sales branches and offices.

Merchant wholesalers

Merchant wholesalers are independently owned businesses that take title to goods, assume risks associated with ownership and generally buy and resell products to other wholesalers, business customers or retailers. A producer is likely to rely on merchant wholesalers when selling directly to customers would be economically unfeasible. Merchant wholesalers are also useful for providing market coverage, making sales contacts, storing inventory, handling orders, collecting market information and furnishing customer support. Some merchant wholesalers are even involved in packaging and developing private brands to help retail customers be competitive. Merchant wholesalers go by various names, including *wholesaler*, *jobber*, *distributor*, *assembler*, *exporter* and *importer*. They fall into one of two broad categories: full-service and limited-service (see Figure 11.3).

merchant wholesalers
Independently owned businesses that take title to goods, assume ownership risks and buy and resell products to other wholesalers, business customers or retailers

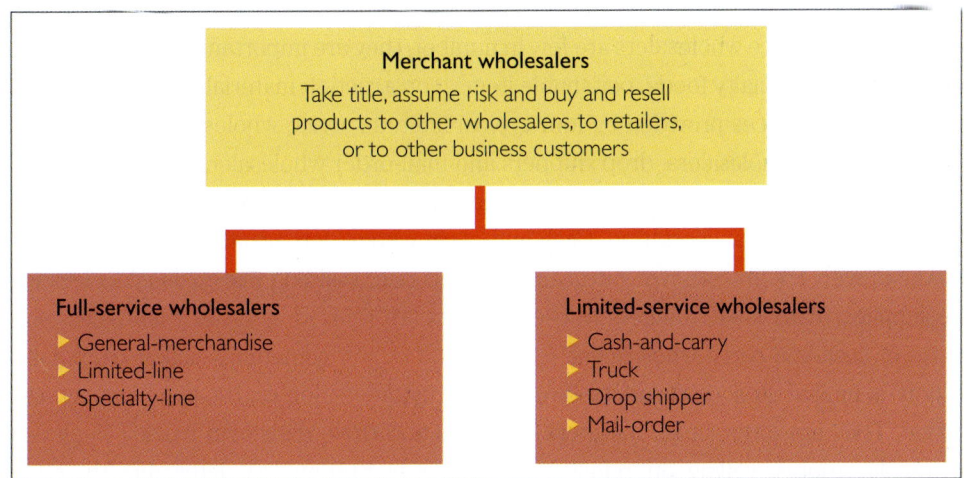

FIGURE 11.3 TYPES OF MERCHANT WHOLESALERS

full-service wholesalers
Merchant wholesalers that perform the widest range of wholesaling functions

Full-service wholesalers perform the widest possible range of wholesaling functions. Customers rely on them for product availability, suitable assortments, breaking large quantities into smaller ones, financial assistance and technical advice and service. Full-service wholesalers handle either consumer or business products and provide numerous marketing services to their customers. Many large grocery wholesalers help retailers with store design, site selection, personnel training, financing, merchandising, advertising, coupon redemption and scanning. Although full-service wholesalers often earn higher gross margins than other wholesalers, their operating expenses are also higher because they perform a wider range of functions

general merchandise wholesalers
Full-service wholesalers with a wide product mix but limited depth within product lines

general-line wholesalers
Full-service wholesalers that carry only a few product lines but many products within those lines

specialty-line wholesalers
Full-service wholesalers that carry only a single product line or a few items within a product line

rack jobbers
Full-service, specialty-line wholesalers that own and maintain display racks in stores

limited-service wholesalers
Merchant wholesalers that provide some services and specialise in a few functions

Full-service wholesalers are categorised as general merchandise, general-line and specialty-line wholesalers and as rack jobbers. General merchandise wholesalers carry a wide product mix but offer limited depth within product lines. They deal in products such as drugs, non-perishable foods, cosmetics, detergents and tobacco. General-line wholesalers carry only a few product lines, such as groceries, lighting fixtures or oil-well drilling equipment, but offer an extensive assortment of products within those lines. Bergen Brunswig Corporation, for example, is a general-line wholesaler of pharmaceuticals and health and beauty aids. General-line wholesalers provide a range of services similar to those of general merchandise wholesalers. Specialty-line wholesalers offer the narrowest range of products, usually a single product line or a few items within a product line. Rack jobbers are full-service, specialty-line wholesalers that own and maintain display racks in supermarkets, pharmacies and discount and variety stores. They set up displays, mark merchandise, stock shelves and keep billing and inventory records; retailers need furnish only space. Rack jobbers specialise in non-food items with high profit margins, such as health and beauty aids, books, magazines, hosiery and greeting cards.

Limited-service wholesalers provide fewer marketing services than do full-service wholesalers and specialise in just a few functions. Producers perform the remaining functions or pass them on to customers or to other intermediaries. Limited-service wholesalers take title to merchandise but often do not deliver merchandise, grant credit, provide marketing information, store inventory or plan ahead for customers' future needs. Because they offer restricted services, limited-service wholesalers are compensated with lower rates and have smaller profit margins than full-service wholesalers. The decision about whether to use a limited-service or a full-service wholesaler depends on the structure of the marketing channel and the need to manage the supply chain to provide competitive advantage. Although certain types of limited-service wholesalers are few in number, they are important in the distribution of products such as specialty foods, perishable items, construction materials and coal. Table 11.3 summarises the services provided by four typical limited-service wholesalers: cash-and-carry wholesalers, truck wholesalers, drop shippers and mail-order wholesalers.

cash-and-carry wholesalers
Limited-service wholesalers whose customers pay cash and furnish transportation

truck wholesalers
Limited-service wholesalers that transport products directly to customers for inspection and selection

Cash-and-carry wholesalers are intermediaries whose customers – usually small businesses – pay cash and furnish transportation. Cash-and-carry wholesalers usually handle a limited line of products with a high turnover rate, such as groceries, building materials and electrical or office supplies. Many small retailers whose accounts are refused by other wholesalers survive because of cash-and-carry wholesalers. Truck wholesalers, sometimes called truck jobbers, transport a limited line of products directly to customers for on-the-spot inspection and selection. They are often small operators who own and drive their own trucks. They usually have regular routes, calling on retailers and other institutions to determine their needs.

TABLE 11.3   SERVICES THAT LIMITED-SERVICE WHOLESALERS PROVIDE

Services	Cash-and-carry	Truck	Drop shipper	Mail-order
Physical possession of merchandise	Yes	Yes	No	Yes
Personal sales calls on customers	No	Yes	No	No
Information about market conditions	No	Some	Yes	Yes
Advice to customers	No	Some	Yes	No
Stocking and maintenance of merchandise in customers' stores	No	No	No	No
Credit to customers	No	No	Yes	Some
Delivery of merchandise to customers	No	Yes	No	No

Drop shippers, also known as desk jobbers, take title to products and negotiate sales but never take actual possession of products. They forward orders from retailers, business buyers or other wholesalers to manufacturers and arrange for carload shipments of items to be delivered directly from producers to these customers. They assume responsibility for products during the entire transaction, including the costs of any unsold goods. **Mail-order wholesalers** use catalogues instead of sales forces to sell products to retail and business buyers. Wholesale mail-order houses generally feature cosmetics, specialty foods, sporting goods, office supplies and automotive parts. Mail-order wholesaling enables buyers to choose and order particular catalogue items for delivery through Australia Post or other carriers. This is a convenient and effective method of selling small items to customers in remote areas that other wholesalers might find unprofitable to serve. The Internet has provided an opportunity for mail-order wholesalers to sell products over their own websites and have the products shipped by the manufacturers.

drop shippers Limited-service wholesalers that take title to products and negotiate sales but never take actual possession of products

mail-order wholesalers Limited-service wholesalers that sell products through catalogues

Agents and brokers

Agents and brokers negotiate purchases and expedite sales but do not take title to products (see Figure 11.4). Sometimes called *functional middlemen*, they perform a limited number

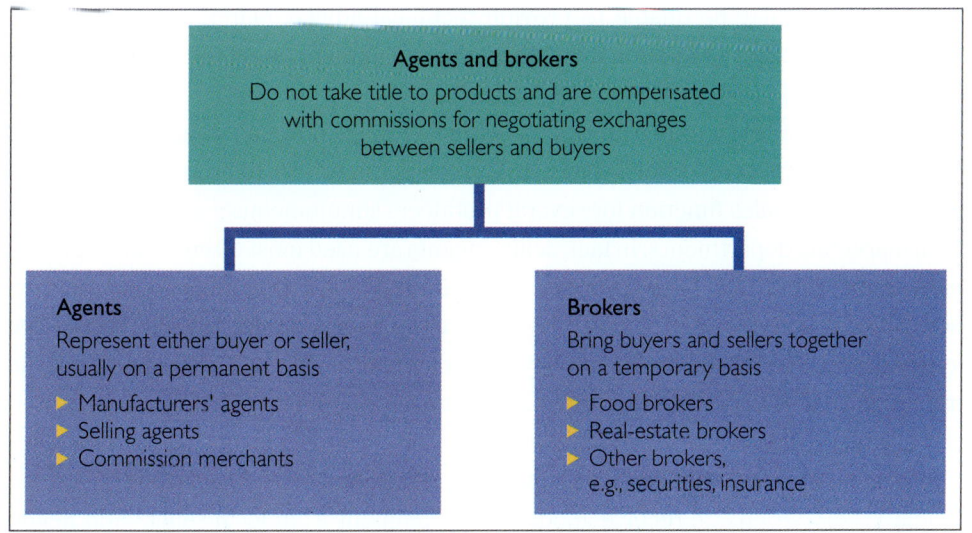

of services in exchange for a commission, which generally is based on the product's selling price. Agents represent either buyers or sellers on a permanent basis, whereas brokers are intermediaries that buyers or sellers employ temporarily.

Although agents and brokers perform even fewer functions than limited-service wholesalers, they are usually specialists in particular products or types of customers and can provide valuable sales expertise. They know their markets well and often form long-lasting associations with customers. Agents and brokers enable manufacturers to expand sales when resources are limited, to benefit from the services of a trained sales force and to hold down personal selling costs. Table 11.4 summarises the services provided by agents and brokers.

agents
Intermediaries that represent either buyers or sellers on a permanent basis

brokers
Intermediaries that bring buyers and sellers together temporarily

TABLE 11.4   SERVICES THAT AGENTS AND BROKERS PROVIDE

Services	Manufacturers' agents	Selling agents	Commission merchants	Brokers
Physical possession of merchandise	Some	Some	Yes	No
Long-term relationship with buyers or sellers	Yes	Yes	Yes	No
Representation of competing product lines	No	No	Yes	Yes
Limited geographic territory	Yes	No	No	No
Credit to customers	No	Yes	Some	No
Delivery of merchandise to customers	Some	Yes	Yes	No

manufacturers' agents
Independent intermediaries that represent two or more sellers and offer complete product lines

Manufacturers' agents, which account for more than half of all agent wholesalers, are independent intermediaries that represent two or more sellers and usually offer customers complete product lines. They sell and take orders year round, much as a manufacturer's sales force does. Restricted to a particular territory, a manufacturer's agent handles non-competing and complementary products. The relationship between the agent and the manufacturer is governed by written contracts that outline territories, selling price, order handling and terms of sale relating to delivery, service and warranties. Manufacturers' agents have little or no control over producers' pricing and marketing policies. They do not extend credit and may be unable to provide technical advice. Manufacturers' agents are commonly used in sales of apparel, machinery and equipment, steel, furniture, automotive products, electrical goods and certain food items.

selling agents
Intermediaries that market a whole product line or a manufacturer's entire output

Selling agents market either all of a specified product line or a manufacturer's entire output. They perform every wholesaling activity except taking title to products. Selling agents usually assume the sales function for several producers simultaneously and are used often in place of marketing departments. In fact, selling agents are used most often by small producers or by manufacturers that have difficulty maintaining a marketing department because of seasonal production or other factors. In contrast to manufacturers' agents, selling agents generally have no territorial limits and have complete authority over prices, promotion and distribution. To avoid conflicts of interest, selling agents represent non-competing product lines. They play a key role in advertising, marketing research and credit policies of the sellers they represent, at times even advising on product development and packaging.

commission merchants
Agents that receive goods on consignment and negotiate sales in large, central markets

Commission merchants receive goods on consignment from local sellers and negotiate sales in large, central markets. Sometimes called *factor merchants*, these agents have broad powers regarding prices and terms of sale. They specialise in obtaining the best price possible under market conditions. Most often found in agricultural marketing, commission merchants take possession of truckloads of commodities, arrange for necessary grading or storage, and transport the commodities to auction or markets where they are sold. When sales are completed, the agents deduct commission and the expense of making the sale and then turn over profits to the producer. Commission merchants also offer planning assistance and sometimes extend credit but usually do not provide promotional support.

A broker's primary purpose is to bring buyers and sellers together. Therefore, brokers perform fewer functions than other intermediaries. They are not involved in financing or physical possession, have no authority to set prices and assume almost no risks. Instead, they offer customers specialised knowledge of a particular commodity and a network of established contacts. Brokers are especially useful to sellers of certain types of products, such as supermarket products and real estate. Food brokers, for example, sell food and general merchandise to retailer-owned and merchant wholesalers, grocery chains, food processors and business buyers.

Manufacturers' sales branches and offices

Sometimes called *manufacturers' wholesalers*, manufacturers' sales branches and offices resemble merchant wholesalers' operations. Sales branches are manufacturer-owned intermediaries that sell products and provide support services to the manufacturer's sales force. Situated away from the manufacturing plant, they are usually located where large customers are concentrated and demand is high. They offer credit, deliver goods, give promotional assistance and furnish other services. Customers include retailers, business buyers and other wholesalers.

sales branches
Manufacturer-owned intermediaries that sell products and provide support services to the manufacturer's sales force

Sales offices are manufacturer-owned operations that provide services normally associated with agents. Like sales branches, they are located away from manufacturing plants, but unlike sales branches, they carry no inventory. A manufacturer's sales office (or branch) may sell products that enhance the manufacturer's own product line.

sales offices
Manufacturer-owned operations that provide services normally associated with agents

Manufacturers may set up these branches or offices to reach their customers more effectively by performing wholesaling functions themselves. A manufacturer may also set up such a facility when specialised wholesaling services are not available through existing intermediaries. A manufacturer's performance of wholesaling and physical distribution activities through its sales branch or office may strengthen supply-chain efficiency. In some situations, though, a manufacturer may bypass its sales office or branches entirely – for example, if the producer decides to serve large retailer customers directly.

Strategic issues in marketing channels

There is much evidence that supply chains can provide a competitive advantage for many marketers. If supply chains are not designed and managed properly, they can destroy company value. It is estimated that a significant supply-chain problem can reduce a company's market value by more than 10 per cent. Many well-known companies including Amazom.com, Dell, FedEx and Toyota owe much of their success to outmanoeuvring rivals with unique supply-chain capabilities.

To fulfill the potential of effective supply-chain management and ensure customer satisfaction, appropriate marketing channels have to be selected. Marketing channels also require the development of channel leadership, cooperation and the management of channel conflict. They may also require consolidation of marketing channels through channel integration.

Selecting marketing channels

Selecting appropriate marketing channels is important. While the process varies across organisations, channel selection decisions are usually significantly affected by one or more of the following factors: customer characteristics, product attributes, type of organisation, competition, marketing environmental forces and characteristics of intermediaries (see Figure 11.5).

FIGURE 11.5
SELECTING MARKETING
CHANNELS

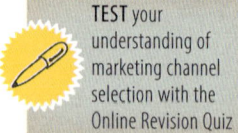

TEST your
understanding of
marketing channel
selection with the
Online Revision Quiz

Customer characteristics

Marketing managers must consider the characteristics of target-market members in channel selection. As we have discussed, the channels appropriate for consumers are different from those for business customers. A different marketing channel will be required for business customers purchasing carpet for commercial buildings compared with consumers purchasing carpet for their homes. As already mentioned, business customers often prefer to deal directly with producers (or very knowledgeable channel intermediaries such as industrial distributors), especially for highly technical or expensive products such as mainframe computers, planes and large mining machines. Moreover, business customers are more likely to buy complex products requiring strict specifications and technical assistance and/or to buy in considerable quantities.

Consumers, on the other hand, generally buy limited quantities of a product, purchase from retailers and often do not mind limited customer service. Additionally, when customers are concentrated in a small geographic area, a more direct channel may be ideal, but when many customers are spread across an entire state or nation, distribution through multiple intermediaries is likely to be more efficient.

Product attributes

The attributes of the product can have a strong influence on the choice of marketing channels. Marketers of complex and expensive products such as cars will likely employ short channels, as will marketers of perishable products such as dairy and food produce. Less expensive, more standardised products such as soft drinks and canned goods can employ longer channels with many intermediaries. In addition, channel decisions may be affected by a product's sturdiness: fragile products that require special handling are more likely to be distributed through shorter channels to minimise the risk of damage. Companies that desire to convey an exclusive image for their products may wish to limit the number of outlets available.

Type of organisation

Clearly, the characteristics of the organisation will have a great impact on the distribution channels chosen. Owing to their sheer size, larger companies may be better able to negotiate better deals with vendors or other channel members. Compared with small companies, they may be in better positions to have more distribution centres, which may reduce delivery times to customers. A smaller regional company using regional or local channel members may be in a position to better serve customers in that region compared with a larger, less flexible organisation. Compared with smaller organisations, large companies can use an extensive product mix as a competitive tool. Smaller companies may not have the resources to develop their own sales force, to ship their products long distances, to store or own products, or to extend credit. In such cases, they may have to include other channel members that have the resources to provide these services to customers efficiently and cost effectively.

Competition

Competition is another important factor for supply-chain managers to consider. The success or failure of a competitor's marketing channel may encourage or dissuade an organisation from considering a similar approach. A company may also be forced to adopt a similar strategy to remain competitive. In a highly competitive market, it is important for a company to keep its costs low so that it can underprice its competitors if necessary.

Environmental forces

Environmental forces can also play a role in channel selection. Adverse economic conditions might force an organisation to use a low-cost channel, even though customer satisfaction is reduced. In contrast, a booming economy might allow a company to choose a channel that previously had been too costly to consider. The introduction of new technology might cause an organisation to add or modify its channel strategy. For instance, as the Internet became a powerful marketing communication tool, many companies were forced to go online to remain competitive. Government regulations can also affect channel selection. As new labour and environmental regulations are passed, an organisation may be forced to modify its existing distribution channel structure. Companies may choose to make the changes before regulations are passed in order to appear compliant or to avoid legal issues. Governmental regulations can also include trade agreements with other countries that complicate the supply chain.

Characteristics of Intermediaries

When an organisation believes that a current intermediary is not promoting the organisation's products adequately, it may reconsider its channel choices. In these instances the company may choose another channel member to handle its products, or it may choose to eliminate intermediaries altogether and perform the eliminated intermediaries' functions itself. Alternatively, an existing intermediary may not offer an appropriate mix of services, forcing an organisation to change to another intermediary.

Channel leadership, cooperation and conflict

Each channel member performs a different role in the distribution system and agrees (implicitly or explicitly) to accept certain rights, responsibilities and rewards, and sanctions for nonconformity. Moreover, each channel member holds certain expectations of other channel members. Retailers, for instance, expect wholesalers to maintain adequate inventories and deliver goods on time. Wholesalers expect retailers to honour payment agreements and keep them informed of inventory needs.

Channel partnerships facilitate effective supply-chain management when partners agree on objectives, policies and procedures for physical distribution efforts associated with the supplier's products. Such partnerships eliminate redundancies and reassign tasks for maximum system-wide efficiency.

Channel leadership

channel captain
The dominant member of a marketing channel or supply chain

channel power
The ability of one channel member to influence another member's goal achievement

Many marketing channel decisions are determined by give and take among channel partners, with the idea that the overall channel will ultimately benefit. Some marketing channels, however, are organised and controlled by a single leader, or channel captain (also called *channel leader*). The channel captain may be a producer, wholesaler or retailer. Channel captains may establish channel policies and coordinate development of the marketing mix. To attain desired objectives, the captain must possess channel power, the ability to influence another channel member's goal achievement. The member that becomes the channel captain will accept the responsibilities and exercise the power associated with this role.

Source: Newspix/News Ltd/William West [Coles]; Getty Images [Woolworths]

<< Channel leadership
Coles and Woolworths dominate the supply chain for retail stores by virtue of the magnitude of their resources

Channel cooperation

Channel cooperation is vital if each member is to gain something from other members. Cooperation enables retailers, wholesalers, suppliers and logistics providers to speed up inventory replenishment, improve customer service and cut the costs of bringing products to the consumer.[20] Without cooperation, neither overall channel goals nor individual member goals can be realised. All channel members must recognise that the success of one company in the channel depends in part on other member companies. Therefore, marketing channel members should make a coordinated effort to satisfy market requirements. Channel cooperation leads to greater trust among channel members and improves the overall functioning of the channel. It also leads to more satisfying relationships among channel members.

There are several ways to improve channel cooperation. If a marketing channel is viewed as a unified supply chain competing with other systems, individual members will be less likely to take actions that create disadvantages for other members. Similarly, channel members should agree to direct efforts toward common objectives so channel roles can be structured for maximum marketing effectiveness, which in turn can help members achieve individual objectives. A critical component in cooperation is a precise definition of each channel member's tasks. This provides a basis for reviewing the intermediaries' performance and helps reduce conflicts because each channel member knows exactly what is expected of it.

Channel conflict

Although all channel members work toward the same general goal – distributing products profitably and efficiently – members may sometimes disagree about the best methods for attaining this goal. However, if self-interest creates misunderstanding about role expectations, the end result is frustration and conflict for the whole channel.

The increased use of multiple channels of distribution, driven partly by new technology, has increased the potential for conflict between manufacturers and intermediaries. For example, Hewlett-Packard makes products available directly to consumers through its website, thereby competing directly with existing distributors and retailers. Channel conflicts also arise when intermediaries over emphasise competing products or diversify into product lines traditionally handled by other intermediaries. Sometimes conflict develops because producers strive to increase efficiency by circumventing intermediaries. Such conflict is occurring in marketing channels for computer software. A number of software-only stores are establishing direct relationships with software producers, bypassing wholesale distributors altogether.

Although there is no single method for resolving conflict, partnerships can be re-established if two conditions are met. First, the role of each channel member must be specified. To minimise misunderstanding, all members must be able to expect unambiguous, agreed-on performance levels from one another. Second, members of channel partnerships must institute certain measures of channel coordination, which requires leadership and benevolent exercise of control. To prevent channel conflict from arising, producers or other channel members may provide competing resellers with different brands, allocate markets among resellers, define policies for direct sales to avoid potential conflict over large accounts, negotiate territorial issues among regional distributors and provide recognition to certain resellers for their importance in distributing to others.

Channel integration

Channel members can either combine and control most activities or pass them on to another channel member. Channel functions may be transferred between intermediaries and to producers and even to customers. However, a channel member cannot eliminate supply-chain functions; unless buyers themselves perform the functions, they must pay for the labour and resources needed to perform them.

Various channel stages may be combined under the management of a channel captain either horizontally or vertically. Such integration may stabilise supply, reduce costs and increase coordination of channel members.

VERTICAL CHANNEL INTEGRATION

vertical channel integration
Combining two or more stages of the marketing channel under one management

Vertical channel integration combines two or more stages of the channel under one management. This may occur when one member of a marketing channel purchases the operations of another member or simply performs the functions of another member, eliminating the need for that intermediary.

HORIZONTAL CHANNEL INTEGRATION

horizontal channel integration
Combining organisations at the same level of operation under one management

Combining organisations at the same level of operation under one management constitutes horizontal channel integration. An organisation may integrate horizontally by merging with other organisations at the same level in the marketing channel. The owner of a dry-cleaning company, for example, might buy and combine several other existing dry-cleaning establishments. Horizontal integration may enable a company to generate sufficient sales revenue to integrate vertically as well.

Although horizontal integration permits efficiencies and economies of scale in purchasing, marketing research, advertising and specialised personnel, it is not always the most effective method of improving distribution. Problems of size often follow, resulting in decreased flexibility, difficulties in coordination and the need for additional marketing research and large-scale planning. Unless distribution functions for the various units can be performed more efficiently under unified management than under the previously separate managements, horizontal integration will neither reduce costs nor improve the competitive position of the integrating company.

Chapter review

LO1   DESCRIBE THE ROLE OF MARKETING CHANNELS.

A marketing channel, or channel of distribution, is a group of individuals and organisations that direct the flow of products from producers to customers. The major role of marketing channels is to make products available at the right time, at the right place and in the right amounts. In most channels of distribution, producers and consumers are linked by marketing intermediaries. The two major types of intermediaries are retailers, who purchase products and resell them to ultimate consumers, and wholesalers, who buy and resell products to other wholesalers, retailers and business customers. Marketing channels serve many functions. They create time, place and possession utilities by making products available when and where customers want them and providing customers with access to product use through sale or rental. Marketing intermediaries facilitate exchange efficiencies, often reducing the costs of exchanges by performing certain services and functions. Although some critics suggest eliminating wholesalers, the functions of the intermediaries in the marketing channel must be performed. As such, eliminating one or more intermediaries results in other organisations in the channel having to do more. Because intermediaries serve both producers and buyers, they reduce the total number of transactions that otherwise would be needed to move products from the producer to the end customer.

LO2   RECOGNISE THE IMPORTANCE OF THE ROLE OF PHYSICAL DISTRIBUTION ACTIVITIES IN SUPPLY-CHAIN MANAGEMENT AND OVERALL MARKETING STRATEGIES.

Physical distribution, or logistics, refers to the activities used to move products from producers to customers and other end users. These activities include order processing, inventory management, materials handling, warehousing and transportation. An efficient physical distribution system is an important component of an overall marketing strategy because it can decrease costs and increase customer satisfaction. Within the marketing channel, physical distribution activities are often performed by a wholesaler, but they may also be performed by a producer or retailer or outsourced to a third party. Efficient physical distribution systems can decrease costs and transit time while increasing customer service.

Order processing is the receipt and transmission of sales order information. It consists of three main tasks – order entry, order handling and order delivery – which may be done manually but are more often handled through electronic data interchange systems. Inventory management involves developing and maintaining adequate assortments of products to meet customers' needs. Logistics managers must strive to find the optimal level of inventory to satisfy customer needs while keeping costs down. Materials handling, the physical handling of products, is a crucial element in warehousing and transporting products. Warehousing involves the design and operation of facilities for storing and moving goods; such facilities may be privately owned or public. Transportation, the movement of products from where they are made to where they are purchased and used, is the most expensive physical distribution function. The basic modes of transporting goods include railways, trucks, waterways, airways and pipelines.

 IDENTIFY THE MAJOR TYPES OF RETAILERS AND EXPLORE STRATEGIC ISSUES IN RETAILING.

Retail stores can be classified according to the breadth of products offered. Two broad categories are general merchandise retailers and specialty retailers. The primary types of general merchandise retailers include department stores, discount stores, convenience stores, supermarkets, superstores, hypermarkets, warehouse clubs and warehouse showrooms. Specialty retailers offer substantial assortments in a few product lines. They include traditional specialty retailers, category killers and off-price retailers, which sell brand-name manufacturers' seconds and product overruns at deep discounts.

To increase sales and store patronage, retailers must consider strategic issues. Location determines the trading area from which a store draws its customers and should be evaluated carefully. When evaluating potential sites, retailers take into account a variety of factors, including the location of the firm's target market within the trading area, kinds of products sold, availability of public transportation, customer characteristics and competitors' locations. Retailers can choose among several types of locations, including freestanding structures, traditional business districts, traditional planned shopping centres (local, community, regional and super-regional), or non-traditional shopping centres (lifestyle, power and outlet). Retail positioning involves identifying an unserved or underserved market segment and serving it through a strategy that distinguishes the retailer from others in those customers' minds. Store image, which various customers perceive differently, derives not only from atmospherics but also from location, products offered, customer services, prices, promotion and the store's overall reputation. Atmospherics refers to the physical elements of a store's design that can be adjusted to appeal to consumers' emotions and thus induce them to buy. Category management is a retail strategy of managing groups of similar, often substitutable products produced by different manufacturers.

 RECOGNISE THE VARIOUS FORMS OF DIRECT MARKETING AND SELLING.

Direct marketing is the use of the telephone, Internet and non-personal media to communicate product and organisational information to customers, who can then purchase products via mail, telephone or the Internet. Direct marketing is a type of non-store retailing, the selling of goods or services outside the confines of a retail facility. Direct marketing may occur through a catalogues (catalogue marketing), advertising (direct response marketing), telephone (telemarketing), TV (television home shopping) or online (online retailing). Two other types of non-store retailing are direct selling and automatic vending. Direct selling is the marketing of products to ultimate consumers through face-to-face sales presentations at home or in the workplace. Automatic vending is the use of machines to dispense products.

 LO5   UNDERSTAND THE NATURE AND FUNCTIONS OF WHOLESALERS.

Wholesaling consists of all transactions in which products are bought for resale, for making other products or for general business operations. Wholesalers are individuals or organisations that facilitate and expedite exchanges that are primarily wholesale transactions. For producers, wholesalers are a source of financial assistance and information; by performing specialised accumulation and allocation functions, they allow producers to concentrate on manufacturing products. Wholesalers provide retailers with buying expertise, wide product lines, efficient distribution and warehousing and storage.

 **LO6**   EXAMINE STRATEGIC ISSUES IN MARKETING CHANNELS, INCLUDING THE FACTORS THAT INFLUENCE MARKETING CHANNEL SELECTION, AND LEADERSHIP, COOPERATION AND CONFLICT.

Selecting an appropriate marketing channel is a crucial decision for supply-chain managers. To determine which channel is most appropriate, managers must think about customer characteristics, the type of organisation, product attributes, competition, environmental forces and the availability and characteristics of intermediaries. Careful consideration of these factors will assist a supply-chain manager in selecting the correct channel.

Each channel member performs a different role in the system and agrees to accept certain rights, responsibilities, rewards and sanctions for non-conformance. Although many marketing channels are determined by consensus, some are organised and controlled by a single leader, or channel captain. A channel captain may be a producer, wholesaler or retailer. A marketing channel functions most effectively when members cooperate; when they deviate from their roles, channel conflict can arise.

Integration of marketing channels brings various activities under one channel member's management. Vertical integration combines two or more stages of the channel under one management. Vertical marketing systems may be corporate, administered or contractual. Horizontal integration combines institutions at the same level of channel operation under a single management.

Key concepts

Use these key terms in **Search me! marketing** to find the latest relevant readings from a wide range of world-class journals, e-books and newspapers, including *The Australian*.

- agents
- atmospherics
- brokers
- cash-and-carry wholesalers
- catalogue marketing
- category killer
- category management
- channel captain
- channel management
- channel power
- commission merchants
- community shopping centres
- convenience store
- cycle time

- department stores
- direct marketing
- direct marketing channel
- direct response marketing
- direct selling
- discount stores
- distribution
- distribution centres
- drop shippers
- electronic data interchange (EDI)
- franchising
- freight forwarders
- full-service wholesalers
- general merchandise retailer
- general merchandise wholesalers
- general-line wholesalers
- horizontal channel integration
- hybrid marketing channel
- hypermarkets
- indirect marketing channel

- intermodal transportation
- inventory management
- just-in-time (JIT)
- lifestyle shopping centres
- limited-service wholesalers
- local shopping centres
- mail-order wholesalers
- manufacturers' agents
- marketing channel
- marketing intermediaries
- materials handling
- megacarriers
- merchant wholesalers
- multiple marketing channel
- off-price retailers
- online retailing
- operations management
- order processing
- outsourcing
- physical distribution
- rack jobbers
- regional shopping centres
- retailer

- retailing
- sales branches
- sales offices
- selling agents
- specialty-line wholesalers
- supermarkets
- super-regional shopping centres
- superstores
- supply chain
- television home shopping
- traditional specialty retailers
- transportation
- truck wholesalers
- vertical channel integration
- warehouse clubs
- warehouse showrooms
- warehousing
- wholesaler
- wholesaling

Issues for discussion and review

1 What is a marketing channel?

2 Compare and contrast the four major types of marketing channels for consumer products. Through which type of channel is each of the following products most likely to be distributed?

 a New Jeep Grand Cherokee vehicle
 b Tin of Heinz Baked Beans
 c Cut-your-own Christmas trees
 d This marketing textbook
 e New Adidas Basketball shoes.

3 Outline the four most common channels for business products. Describe the products or situations that lead marketers to choose each channel.

4 Under what conditions is a producer most likely to use more than one marketing channel?

5 Give an example of a consumer product that is likely to be distributed by each of the four typical channels for consumer products.

6 What is outsourcing?

7 What are the main tasks involved in order processing?

8 Explain the trade-offs inventory managers face when reordering products or supplies. How is the reorder point computed?

9 What combination of factors is considered when determining the appropriate transportation mode for products?

10 What major issues should be considered when determining a retail site location?

11 Give an example of the major grocery retail outlets that are operating within five kilometers of where you live. What type of general retailer are they? Is each category represented?

12 Identify and describe the factors that may influence marketing channel selection decisions.

13 What does the term 'atmospherics' refer to?

Marketing applications

1 Rob wants to open a small store that specialises in high-priced, high-quality, imported men's shoes. What types of competitors should he be concerned about in this retail environment? Why?

2 Supply-chain management involves long-term partnerships among channel members working together to reduce inefficiencies, costs and redundancies and to develop innovative approaches to satisfy customers. Select one of the following companies and explain how supply-chain management could increase marketing productivity.

   a Apple Computers
   b FedEx
   c Freedom Kitchens (http://www.freedomkitchens.com.au)

3 Think about the stores that you shop in. Identify your favourite and least favourite stores. Describe and contrast the atmospherics of both stores. Be specific about both exterior and interior elements, and indicate how the store is being positioned through its use of atmospherics. If necessary visit both stores.

4 Describe and compare the factors that might influence your choice of distribution channel for businesses selling the following:

   a guitar strings
   b women's shoes
   c telephone systems for small businesses
   d dolls for 5-year-olds.

ONLINE EXERCISE

5 Visit a website of an Internet-based computer retailer. Assume that you are responsible for the company's physical distribution of computers to customers. Which aspects of the website itself would you improve to ensure that the customers who have purchased a computer at the website have the best possible computer delivery experience to their home or workplace?

Developing your marketing plan

One of the key components in a successful marketing strategy is the plan for getting the products to your customer. In order to make the best decisions about where, when and how your products will be made available to the customer, you will need to know more about how these distribution decisions relate to other marketing-mix elements in your marketing plan. To assist you in relating the information in this chapter to your marketing plan, consider the following issues:

1   Marketing intermediaries perform many activities. Using Table 11.1 as a guide, discuss the types of activities where a channel member could provide needed assistance.

2   Considering your product's attributes and your target market(s)' buying behaviour, will your product likely be sold to the ultimate customer or to another member of the marketing channel?

3   Discuss the physical functions that will be required for distributing your product, focusing on materials handling, warehousing and transportation.

CengageNOW

Go to http:\\login.cengagebrain.com to link to CengageNOW, your online study tool. First take the Pre-Test for this chapter to get your Personalised Study Plan, and then:

❉ **Revise** your understanding of the key concepts of marketing with the online glossary

❉ **Watch** an interactive animation of strategic marketing to broaden your subject comprehension

❉ **Listen** to an audio summary of the learning objectives covered in this chapter.

After you have completed the activities in your Personalised Study Plan take the Post-Test to determine what concepts you have mastered and what you still need to work on.

Case study

WHY OWN WHEN YOU CAN SHARE? NEW MODELS OF OWNERSHIP AND DISTRIBUTION IN THE AUTOMOTIVE INDUSTRY.

In the wake of the recent global financial crisis, the automotive industry has experienced a drop in sales of new cars in many developed countries. In Australia, for example, 608 804 passenger cars were sold in 2005; this contrasts with 576 955 vehicles that were sold in 2012. This drop in sales poses serious challenges for both manufacturers and dealers.[21]

Source: Getty Images

The traditional way to sell cars has been through intermediaries; these car dealerships may sell just one brand or may sell cars from several manufacturers. These dealerships not only sell new cars but also provide additional services, such as servicing of cars under manufacturer's warranty (in which case the manufacturer carries the costs), general servicing of cars out of warranty and the sale of parts and accessories. This provides major sources of income for car dealerships. Dealerships are experiencing, however, new competition in the form of online websites such as **http://carpoint.com.au** and **http://carsales.com.au.** These websites provide an easy way for private car sellers to showcase their cars. These new online channels are now also being used by car dealerships to promote their cars and to reach customers not only in their immediate vicinity, but also in more distant locations.

While all these factors contribute to a very competitive industry, car manufactures have also noticed a lack of desire or ability to buy a new car by young people in cities with good public transport infrastructure and lack of parking facilities. The car has lost its place as a status symbol for many young people in developed countries.[22]

Why are people less interested in owning cars and are driving less than their parents did? This question is an important issue for the automotive industry. Technology has had an impact – why drive to meet friends when you can Skype or communicate via Facebook instead of driving through congested city streets and trying to find parking? Other factors that impact on the purchase decision to buy a new or used car are the high price of petrol, the trend of young people to live in inner-city areas with limited parking spaces and concerns about the environment.[23]

In cities such as Sydney, New York and Munich, car manufacturers are looking at new models of distribution and ownership. The leading luxury brands BMW and Mercedes have invested heavily in car sharing networks. In this new business model, people do not own a car outright but pay to use a car for short journeys, by kilometres driven and/or time spent in the car. It is predicted that by 2020 Mercedes and BMW will generate more than a billion euros each in revenues from their car sharing businesses in Germany.[24]

In this car sharing model, the cars are owned by a separate firm and are 'shared' among a number of people throughout the day. It is similar to traditional car rental, however the time span for each rental is usually shorter and may range from several hours to a few minutes. Important for the success of car sharing is effective fleet management which includes the servicing of the cars and the ability to locate suitable vehicles via smart phones. Access to parking facilities at reasonable rates will also be important for the success of the model. Car sharing also has environmental benefits, as each shared vehicle is replacing 15 personally owned vehicles.[25] In Sydney, 15 000 people have joined car sharing schemes and the City of Sydney has made 400 car parking spaces available for car sharing vehicles. According to a study conducted by SGS Economics, car sharing has contributed US$18.5 million in savings for residents through the deferral of car purchases.[26]

Petra Bouvain, University of Canberra

QUESTIONS FOR DISCUSSION

1 The distribution component of the marketing mix focuses on the decisions and activities involved in making products available to customers when and where they want to purchase them. How does car sharing fit in with this statement?

2 What type of channel is needed for car sharing to be successful?

3 How might strategic issues, such as issues in channel cooperation, conflict and leadership, apply to the car sharing model?

Chapter endnotes

1. 'Designers For Target: Roberto Cavalli,' Target Australia, accessed August 15, 2013, http://shop.target.com.au /designersfortarget/robertocavalli/stores.html; 'Target Australia,' Pinterest, accessed August 15, 2013, http:// pinterest.com/targetaus/quotes/; 'Gok Wan represents fashion brands for Target Australia,' Mumbrella, accessed August 15, 2013, http://mumbrella.com.au/gok-wan -represents-fashion-brands-for-target-australia-165434; 'Target Australia strips off its daggies,' Australian Creative, July 4, 2013, accessed August 15, 2013, http://www. australiancreative.com.au/news/target-australia-strips-off -its-daggies; P. Joye, 'Designer Cavalli hits his Target,' The Sydney Morning Herald, October 30, 2012, accessed August 15, 2013, http://www.smh.com.au/lifestyle/fashion /designer-cavalli-hits-his-target-20121030-28hhl.html.

2. Krista Mahr, 'Digging Deep for Smarter Heat,' Time, September 20, 2010, p. 74; 'IKEA Geothermal System Could Inform Others,' NREL.gov, August 19, 2010, accessed September 13, 2010, www.nrel.gov /features/20100819_geothermal.html; www.ikea.com, accessed October 27, 2010; http://www.ikea.com/us /en/about_ikea/newsitem/091713_kansas_merriam _geothermal.

3. Vicki O'Meara, 'Take a Deep Breath Before Diving into Global Outsourcing,' Inbound Logistics (September 2007): 36.

4. Eli Greenblat, 'TV show recipe for success: Woolies,' The Sydney Morning Herald, October 7, 2013, accessed January 18, 2014, http://www.smh.com.au/business/tv-show- recipe-for-success-woolies-20131006-2v29n.html.

5. Lee Pender, 'The Basic Links of SCM,' CIO, accessed February 25, 2009, http://www.itworld.com /CIO010205basic.

6. 'RedTail Solutions Announces Three New Modules for Its Managed EDI Service for Microsoft Dynamics GP,' Business Wire, March 9, 2009, http://www .supplychainmarket.com/article.mvc/RedTail -Solutions-Announces-Three -New-Modules- 0001?VNETCOOKIE=NO.

7. Anne T. Coughlan, Erin Anderson, Louis W. Stern, and Adel I. El-Ansary, Marketing Channels (Upper Saddle River, NJ: Prentice-Hall, 2006), 510.

8. Merrill Douglas, 'Taking an Eagle's-Eye View,' Inbound Logistics (July 2007): 20–22.

9. 'About Us,' Port Logistics, accessed March 20, 2012, www.portlogisticsgroup.com/about-us.

10. National Association of Convenience Stores (December 2007): http://www.naicsonline.com/NACS/News /FactSheet/Pages/IndustryStoreCount.aspx.

11. Katy Bachman, 'Suit Your Shelf,' Brandweek, January 19, 2009: 10.

12. Daniel Palmer, 'Hypermarkets in demand overseas, but will the concept ever take off in Australia?' Ausfoodnews, September 11, 2008, http://www.ausfoodnews.com .au/2008/09/11/hypermarkets-in-demand-overseas -butwill-the-concept-ever-take-off-in-australia.html.

13. Based on information in Willard Spiegelman, 'Etsy's Funky Brooklyn Headquarters,' Bloomberg Businessweek, February 9, 2012, www.businessweek.com; Ryan Kim, 'Etsy to Become an Indie Biz One-Stop Shop,' GigaOM,

February 2, 2012, www.gigaom.com; Nedra Rhone, 'Online Crafts Site to Co-Host Atlanta Event,' *Atlanta Journal-Constitution*, August 10, 2011, D1; Max Chafkin, 'Rob's World,' *Inc.*, April 2011, 56+.

14. Debra Hazel, 'Wide-Open Spaces,' *Chain Store Age*, November 2005: 120; 'ICSC Shopping Center Definitions,' *International Council of Shopping Centers*, http://icsc.org/srch/lib/USDefinitions.pdf.

15. Velitchka D. Kaltcheva and Barton A. Weitz, 'When Should a Retailer Create an Exciting Store Environment?' *Journal of Marketing* 70 (January 2006), http://www.marketingpower.com.

16. Mindy Fetterman and Jayne O'Donnell, 'Just Browsing at the Mall? That's What You Think,' *USA Today*, September 1, 2006, http://usatoday.com.

17. Anick Bosmans, 'Scents and Sensibility: When Do (In) Congruent Ambient Scents Influence Product Evaluations?' *Journal of Marketing* 70 (July 2006), http://www.marketingpower.com

18. Based on information in Adelaide Lancaster, 'Don't Buy This Jacket,' *Forbes*, December 1, 2011, www.forbes.com; Susan Carpenter, 'Online Shopping: Better for the Environment?' *Los Angeles Times*, December 16, 2011, www.latimes.com; Tim Nudd, 'Ad of the Day: Patagonia,' *AdWeek*, November 28, 2011, www.adweek.com.

19. 'What Is Direct Selling?' Direct Selling Association, accessed April 11, 2012, www.directselling411.com/about-direct-selling/.

20. Wroe Alderson, *Dynamic Marketing Behavior* (Homewood, IL: Irwin, 1965), 239.

21. 'PC [passenger car] Word sales,' OICA, accessed September 20, 2013, www.OICA.net.

22. Michael Borgman, 'Carsharing ein neues Geschaeftsmodel fuer Autobauer,' accessed September 12, 2013, http://www.frost.com/sublib/display-market-insight.do?id=190795176.

23. Richard Read, 'Young People are driving much less (but not for the Reasons you think),' carconnection, June 18, 2012, accessed September 12, 2013, http://www.thecarconnection.com/news/1077028_young-people-are-driving-much-less-but-not-for-the-reasons-you-think.

24. Nick Gibbs, 'Daimler, BMW bullish on car-sharing,' *Automotive News Europe*, August 13, 2013, accessed September 12, 2013, http://europe.autonews.com/article/20130813/ANE/308139999/daimler-bmw-bullish-on-car-sharing#axzz2eremVxR0.

25. David Zhao, 'Carsharing: A Sustainable and Innovative Personal Transport Solution with Great Potential and Huge Opportunities,' Frost & Sullivan, January 10, 2010, accessed September 12, 2013, http://www.frost.com/sublib/display-market-insight.do?id=190795176.; 'Car sharing,' City of Sydney, September 20, 2013, cityofsydney.nsw.gov.au.

26. 'Benefit-Cost Analysis of Car Share within the City of Sydney,' SGS Economics and Planning, 2012, accessed February 2, 2014, http://www.cityofsydney.nsw.gov.au/__data/assets/pdf_file/0012/122502/CarShareEconomicAppraisalFINALREPORT.pdf.

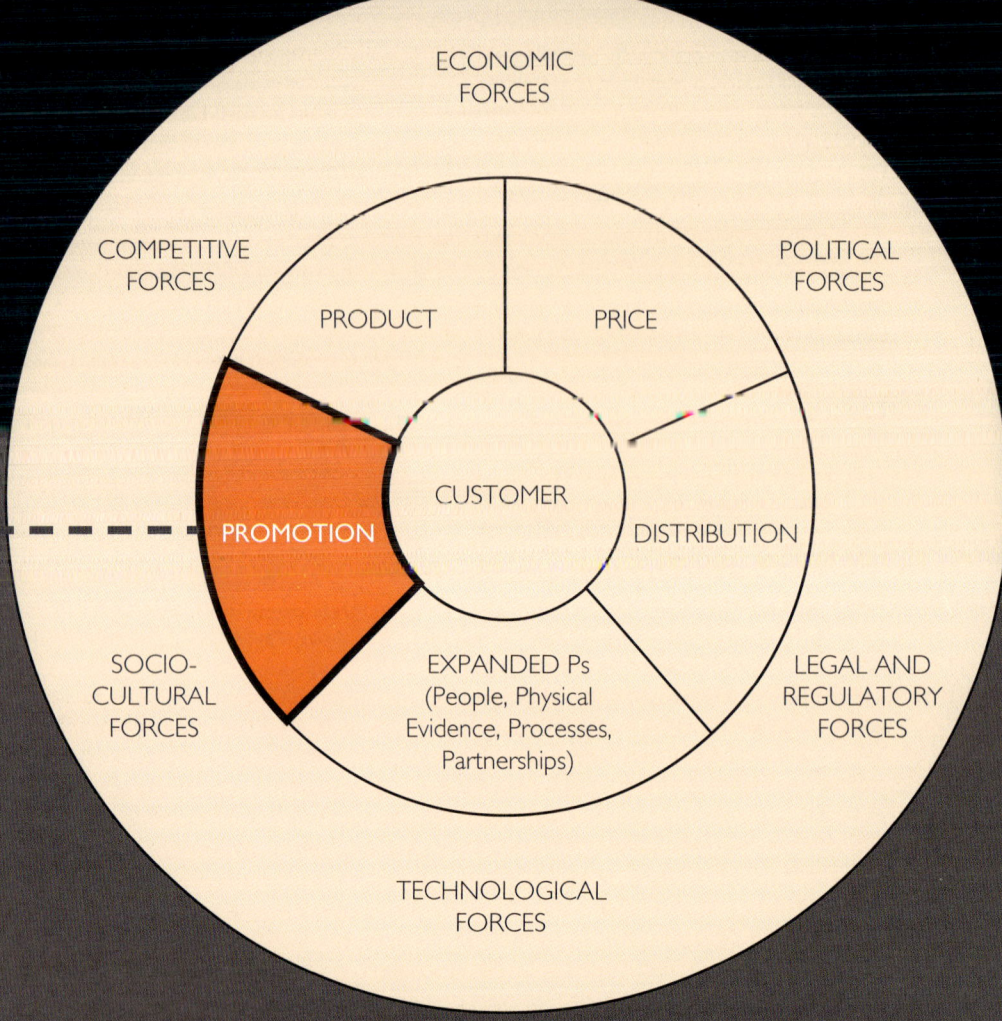

ECONOMIC FORCES

COMPETITIVE FORCES

POLITICAL FORCES

PRODUCT

PRICE

PROMOTION

CUSTOMER

DISTRIBUTION

SOCIO-CULTURAL FORCES

EXPANDED Ps (People, Physical Evidence, Processes, Partnerships)

LEGAL AND REGULATORY FORCES

TECHNOLOGICAL FORCES

INTEGRATING MARKETING COMMUNICATIONS: DESIGNING PROMOTIONAL CAMPAIGNS

What is integrated marketing communications?

The communication process

Message appeal styles
How target market characteristics and media channels guide message themes

The role and objectives of promotion
Create awareness
Stimulate demand
Encourage product trial
Identify prospects
Retain loyal customers
Facilitate reseller support
Reduce sales fluctuations/seasonality of demand
Combat competitive promotional efforts

Selecting elements for the marketing communications mix
Promotional resources, objectives and policies
Target market characteristics
Product characteristics
Costs and availability of promotional methods
Push and pull channel policies
The growing importance of word-of-mouth communications

Criticisms and defences of promotion
Offensive advertisements
Is promotion deceptive?
Does promotion increase prices?
Does promotion create needs?
Does promotion help customers without costing too much?
Should potentially harmful products be promoted?

   Throughout this chapter, Watch, Listen and Revise icons indicate an opportunity for online self-study through CengageNOW, linking you to animated chapter overviews, interactive diagrams, videos, quizzes and more.

INTEGRATING MARKETING COMMUNICATIONS: DESIGNING PROMOTIONAL CAMPAIGNS

Learning Objectives

LO1 Discuss the nature of integrated marketing communications

LO2 Understand how different stages in the communication process can guide the design of promotional campaigns

LO3 Appreciate how specific communication styles could be applied to the design of promotional campaigns

LO4 Explain the role and objectives of promotion

LO5 Describe the factors that affect the choice of marketing communications mix elements

LO6 Understand common criticisms and defences of promotion.

MARKETING CHALLENGE | 'NO ONE SEES IT LIKE YOU' BY CANON

In 2013 Canon launched its biggest ever promotional campaign targeting consumers, encouraging Australians to do more with their photographs. This campaign, estimated to cost $13m in media spend alone, is based on continuous feedback from Canon customers over a five year period. The campaign utilises in-store merchandising, TV, cinema, printed ads, outdoor ads as well as online versions of the same theme.

The promotions direct consumers to Canon's imageSpectrum online portal where they can find information about 'how to do more with my images'. The website includes suggestions and templates for making photos into canvas prints, photoboards and photobooks as well as links to Canon Academy courses and online tutorials.

The campaign aimed to 'reach as many digital imaging consumers as possible by the end of 2013', adding them to the existing database of 200 000 individuals. This expanded database will then be used by Canon and made available to Canon retailers.

Canon also recruited Guy Sebastian as their new Australian Ambassador to spearhead a 'Change Your Lens, Change Your Story' campaign to show how a new lens could make the picture-story even better.[1]

MARKETING CHALLENGE QUESTIONS

1   Where have you seen Canon's promotions?

2   Did the different platforms (e.g. TV ad, in-store merchandising) support the same campaign theme?

3   In your opinion, to what extent is the 'Change Your Lens, Change Your Story' campaign with Guy Sebastian an effective extension of the 'No One Sees It Like You' campaign?

Introduction

Organisations like Canon employ a range of promotional methods to communicate with their target markets. Providing information to customers and other stakeholders is vital to initiating and developing long term relationships with them.

In this chapter we look at promotion in general. First we discuss the nature of integrated marketing communications, a strategy for ensuring that promotional messages are consistent, unified and clearly inter-linked. Next, we analyse the meaning and process of communication and compare different styles of promotion. We then define and examine the role of promotion and explore some of the reasons for using promotion. We briefly consider major promotional methods and factors that influence marketers' decisions to use particular methods. Finally, we examine some common criticisms and defences of promotion. The elements of the marketing communications mix are detailed further in Chapter 13.

LO1

What is integrated marketing communications?

integrated marketing communications (IMC)
Coordination of promotional efforts for maximum informational and persuasive impact

Integrated marketing communications (IMC) refers to the coordination of promotional efforts to ensure maximum informational and persuasive impact on customers. Coordinating multiple marketing tools to produce this synergistic effect requires marketers to employ a broad perspective. A major goal of integrated marketing communications is to send a consistent message to customers and to avoid confusing them and other stakeholders who receive the message.

In the past, each department in an organisation planned and implemented their own promotional efforts. This way of operating, however, could easily lead to a lack of consistency in the messages being received by customers and other stakeholders. Confusing messages can erode the value of a brand and lower the perception of quality. Promotional messages that do not support the same theme is a wasteful use of company resources, as customers may not make the connection between promotional efforts. Why spend money on promotional campaigns that your customers fail to associate with your company? Integrated marketing communications allows a company to coordinate and manage its promotional efforts to transmit consistent messages. This approach fosters not only long term customer relationships but also efficient use of promotional resources. The Bundaberg Distilling Company uses different promotional methods with an integrated communication design for their Road to Recovery campaign. In

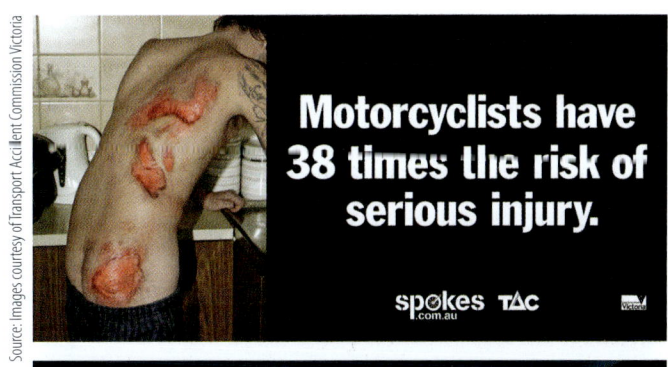

Source: Images courtesy of Transport Accident Commission Victoria

<< Integrated marketing communications
The Transport Accident Commission (TAC) employs integrated marketing communications across different media, from TV to billboards and magazine advertisements

addition, the company has strengthened its links with local stakeholders and loyal customers with generous donations to the recovery effort as well as the limited edition products (see the Marketing in Action box).

The concept of IMC is increasingly effective for several reasons. Advertising to a mass audience, a very popular promotional method in the past, is used less today because of

advertising
Paid non-personal communication about an organisation and its products transmitted to a target audience through mass media

MARKETING IN ACTION | RUM-ROAD TO RECOVERY AFTER FLOODS

Source: The Bundaberg Word, BDC Device and Associated Logos are Trademarks. © The Bundaberg Distilling Company Pty Limited 2013.

The Bundaberg Distilling Company's (BDC) Road to Recovery campaign aimed to collect funds for

Bundaberg's 2013 flood recovery work. Together with its parent company Diageo Australia, the BDC had already donated $200 000 to the Red Cross Queensland Flood Appeal and the aim of the second campaign was to make an additional $250 000 donation.

The Road to Recovery campaign included PR, advertising and social media communication aimed at attracting tourists back to the Bundaberg region. Loyal customers can also buy limited edition collectable Road to Recovery rum bottles. These bottles were only available at the Bundaberg distilleries for $60 each and they featured flood affected road names. Each flood affected house in Bundaberg was also offered a complimentary bottle to 'commemorate the spirit of Bundaberg and its strength of character in the face of adversity'.

its high cost and unpredictable audience size. Marketers can now take advantage of more precisely targeted promotional tools, such as pay TV, direct mail, the Internet, special-interest magazines, as well as a variety of apps running on smartphones or tablets. In other words, target markets of today are receiving promotional messages through a multitude of channels and therefore it is important that the messages communicated across all media platforms systematically communicate the same key message. Database marketing also allows marketers to target individual customers more precisely.

Until recently, suppliers of marketing communications were specialists. Advertising agencies developed advertising campaigns, sales promotion companies provided sales promotion activities and materials, and public relations companies engaged in publicity efforts. Today, several promotions-related companies provide one-stop shopping to clients seeking advertising, sales promotion and public relations, therefore reducing coordination problems for the sponsoring company. As the overall cost of marketing communications has risen significantly, there is a need for systematic evaluations of communication efforts and a reasonable return on investment. In a 2013 survey by World Federation of Advertisers some 80 per cent of advertising executives rated IMC as a 'top priority'.[3]

Unfortunately, simply having a united theme for promotional activities is not enough to ensure effective marketing communication. To maximise benefits from each promotional message, a company should create a detailed plan for the entire campaign, including message content, types of media to be used, as well as the timing of each communication. A GANTT chart is a good way to visualise planned activities over a longer period of time. Figure 12.1

Margin definitions

public relations
Communication efforts used to create and maintain favourable relations between an organisation and its stakeholders

publicity
A news story type of communication transmitted through a mass medium at no charge

GANTT chart
a graph that illustrates the different stages in a large project and the timing of all planned activities or tasks in the project

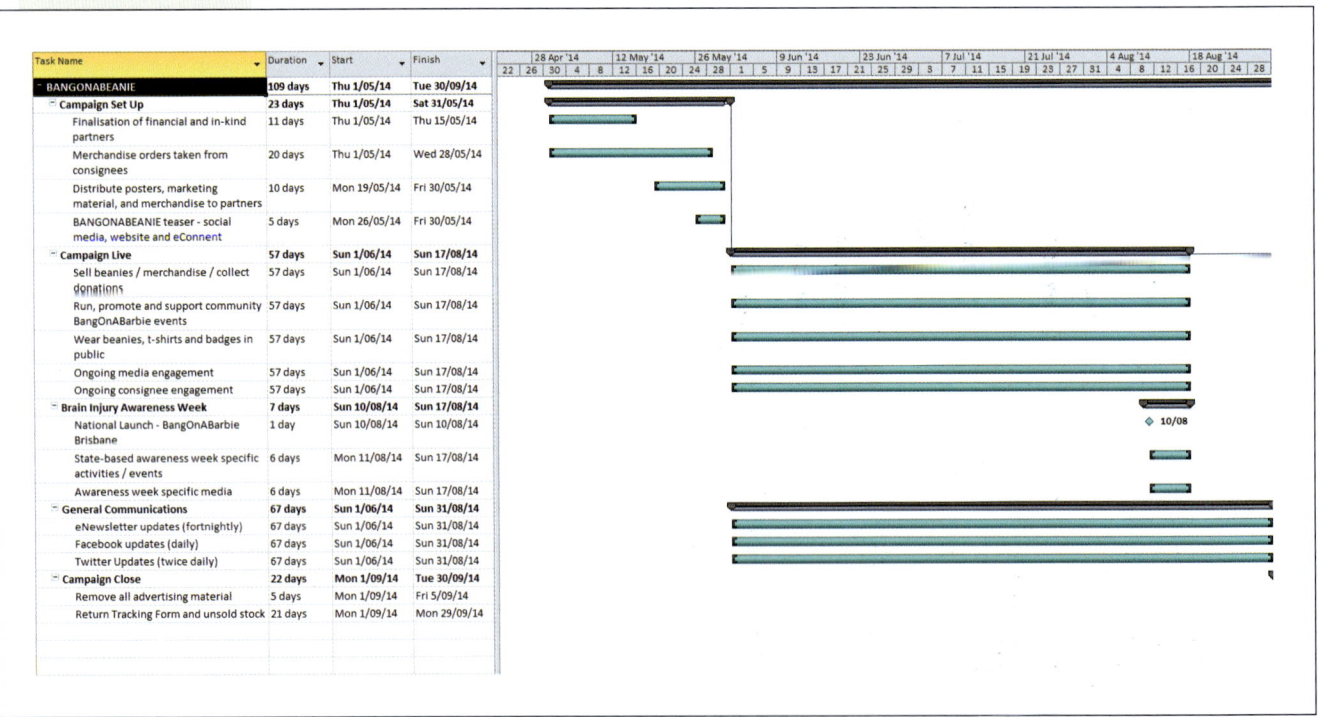

FIGURE 12.1
A GANTT CHART CAN BE USED TO OUTLINE THE TIMING OF EACH ACTIVITY IN A CAMPAIGN

Source: Image supplied courtesy of BANGONABEANIE - the national campaign for Brain Injury awareness facillitated by Synapse (http://synapse.org.au)

gives a week-by-week scheduling for all activities in the BangOnABeanie campaign which aims to increase Australians' awareness of Acquired Brain Injuries.[4]

Integration of all marketing communication is particularly important in today's world, with an ever-increasing number of electronic communication platforms and the speed of electronic communications reaching customers and other stakeholders. In other words, messages can be spread to wide audiences at unprecedented speeds.[5] The communication vehicles employed and the precision with which they are used are changing as both digital technology and customer interests become increasingly dynamic. For example, PLUS7 by Channel 7 allows viewers to catch up on programs they missed by making TV episodes freely available, but with embedded ads. All major Australian TV networks offer a similar service. By utilising streaming technology (and supported by advertising revenue), Channel 7 is able to offer this service to customers using broadband Internet. Such flexible TV viewing is attractive to a mobile and busy target audience, who want their entertainment when they have time, not on the network's schedule.

Today, marketers and customers can easily access online data about each other. Hence integrating and customising marketing communications while protecting customer privacy has become a major challenge. Through digital media, companies can provide product information and services that are coordinated with traditional promotional activities. In fact, gathering information about goods and services is one of the main reasons people go online. This has made online advertising a growing business. In Australia, an estimated $4.1 billion expenditure on Internet advertising exceeded TV advertising expenditure in 2013.[6] However, Internet advertising should only be used when the target audience for the promotion matches the profile of people regularly using online media, for example university students say they are influenced by Internet ads when buying online or researching product purchases.

The communication process

Communication is essentially the transmission of information. For communication to take place, both the sender and the receiver of information must share common ground. They must have a common understanding of the symbols, words and pictures used to transmit information. Thus we define communication as a sharing of meaning; for communication to have taken place both participants must understand the message content the same way.[7] Implicit in this definition is the notion of transmission of information because sharing necessitates transmission. The most basic example of lack of shared meaning takes place when individuals involved with the communication process simply do not speak the same language!

在工廠吾人製造化粧品,在商店吾人銷售希望。

Communication begins with a sender (as illustrated in Figure 12.2). A sender is a person, group or organisation with a meaning (message) it attempts to share with an audience. A sender could be a salesperson wishing to communicate a sales message or an organisation wanting to send a message to thousands of customers via an ad. Developing an integrated

communication
A sharing of meaning

<< Communication across language barriers is problematic
Communication has not taken place if you do not understand the language in which it was written

sender
A person, group, or organisation with a meaning it tries to share

marketing communications strategy can enhance the effectiveness of the sender's communication and will reduce the chances of confusing the receiver with conflicting messages. A receiver is the individual, group or organisation that receives and understands the encoded message, and an audience is two or more receivers.

WATCH an interactive animation on the communication process

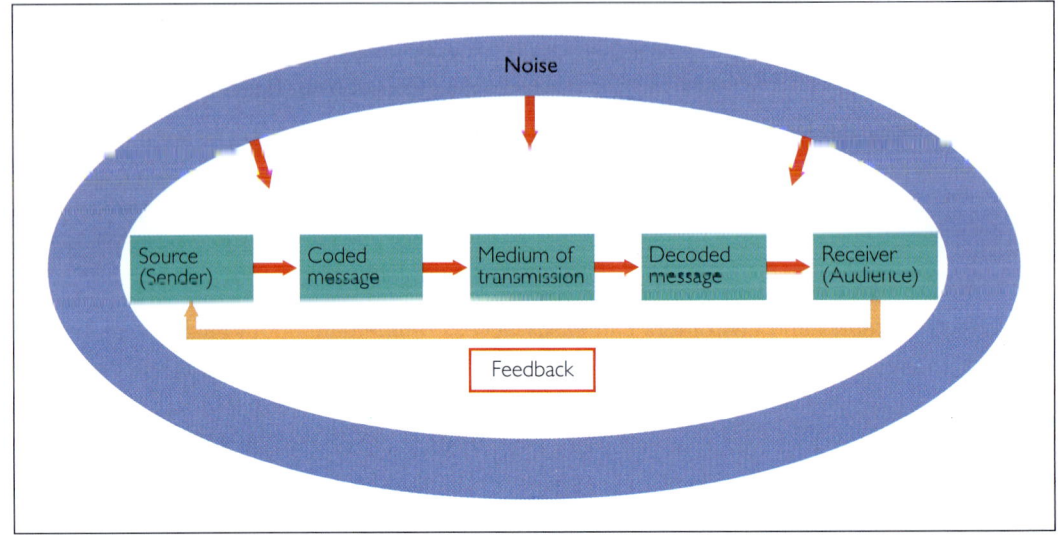

To share meaning, a sender must convert the meaning into a series of signs or symbols representing ideas or concepts. This is called the encoding process. When encoding meaning into a message, the sender must understand and appreciate the characteristics of the receiver or audience. To share meaning, the sender should use signs or symbols familiar to the receiver or audience. Market research can help a company reach a deep understanding of their target market; persuasive messages from a sender are more effective when the appeal matches an individual's personality.[8] Marketers who understand this realise the importance of knowing their target market and ensuring that an ad, for example, uses language the target market understands. For example, Gecko's Adventures promote their adventure holidays with the slogan 'May your heart be light, your step swift and your stories fucking epic' with a bold claim that 'they have found their language'. As the company targets 18–35-year-old travellers and sells thrilling holiday experiences in extreme destinations they feel that they have pitched the language used at a correct level that will help customers decide whether they might enjoy a Gecko holiday.[9]

When encoding a meaning, a sender needs to use signs or symbols that the receiver or audience uses for referring to the concepts the sender intends to convey. Instead of technical jargon, explanatory language that helps consumers to understand is more likely to result in positive attitudes and purchase intentions.[10] Conscientious marketers try to avoid signs or symbols that may have ambiguous meanings for an audience. For example, the Australian Association of National Advertisers (AANA) launched the 'Environmental Claims Advertising and Marketing Code' to ensure that claims regarding the environmentally green features of a product are substantiated. Such codes of conduct advise marketers in designing their communication to avoid unintentionally creating messages that could be misinterpreted by the receivers (see the Sustainable Marketing feature on green washing)

To share an encoded meaning with the receiver or audience, a sender selects and uses a medium of transmission. A communications channel, the medium of transmission, carries the encoded message from the sender to the receiver or audience. The media include print

communications channel
The medium of transmission that carries the encoded message from the sender to the receiver

SUSTAINABLE MARKETING | FIGHT AGAINST GREEN WASHING

As the communications process shows, consumers interact with the text, images and other stimuli used to interpret the meaning of an advertisement. A simple background picture of a clean lake could result in consumers concluding that the product advertised is environmentally friendly. To stop companies either accidentally or deliberately misleading consumers the Australian Consumer Law (in effect from 1 January 2011), states that companies 'must not mislead or deceive consumers in any way' and that environmental claims should be 'scientifically sound and appropriately substantiated'. Pictures of lush green meadows on packaging or in ads can also mislead consumers into thinking that the product is positively linked to sustainable practice. Penalties from misleading environmental claims can vary from refunds to customers to fines of up to $1.1 million.

Source: shutterstock.com

Green washing takes place when organisations give the impression that their products are environmentally friendly or sustainable. The Australian Competition and Consumer Commission (ACCC) spearheads the campaign against unsubstantiated claims of environmentally friendly attributes. According to the ACCC, complaints regarding suspicious green claims are a new phenomenon as in just over two years these have risen from zero to 500 per year. Whether this is an outcome of companies using environmentally friendly claims more liberally or consumers becoming more aware is not known.

For example, in July 2013 the ACCC announced an agreement with seven suppliers of bottled water to remove any 'organic' claims from the packaging as well as promotions. The ACCC is keen to remove any unsubstantiated credence claims as they are typically associated with higher prices. In other words, consumers pay more for 'organic' products whether the 'organic' is part of the brand name or acclaim made in advertisements.

Toyota advertisements in New Zealand feature Mother Nature driving a Toyota Prius. However, environment activists point out that since the launch of this campaign, 96 per cent of vehicles sold by Toyota are *not* hybrid and that the company is in fact only green washing. Whether this criticism will be adopted by the regulatory authorities is still not known.[11]

media (e.g. magazines), radio, TV and online and mobile applications. The final selection of media channels includes balancing the advantages and disadvantages of each media channel.

When a sender chooses an inappropriate communications channel, several problems may arise. The encoded message is likely to reach the wrong receivers or the encoded messages may not be received in the format they were designed for (e.g. software compatibility problems). For example, radio and broadcast TV signals are received effectively only over a limited range, which varies depending on climatic conditions. Members of the target audience living in rural areas area may receive a weak signal; others well within the broadcast area may also receive an incomplete message if, for example, they listen to the radio while driving or studying. Reports into consumer media preferences help marketers choose the communications channels used by specific target markets.

decoding process
Converting signs or symbols into concepts or ideas

In the decoding process, signs or symbols are converted into concepts and ideas. When a message contradicts a receiver's beliefs or attitudes, the characteristics of the sender will influence the decoding process (credibility, legitimacy, power). Seldom does a receiver decode exactly the same meaning that the sender encoded. When the result of decoding differs from what was encoded, noise exists. Noise is anything that reduces the clarity and accuracy of the communication; it has many sources and may affect any or all parts of the communication process. Noise sometimes arises within the communications channel itself. Radio static, poor or slow Internet connections, even the salesperson's sore throat are sources of noise. Noise also occurs when a sender uses signs or symbols that are unfamiliar to the receiver or have a different meaning from the one intended. Noise may also originate in the receiver; a receiver may be unaware of a coded message when perceptual processes block it out.

noise
Anything that reduces a communication's clarity and accuracy

feedback
The receiver's response to a message

The receiver's response to a message is feedback to the sender. The sender usually expects and normally receives feedback, although perhaps not immediately. This feedback is used to determine the success of the communication and how future communication can be further improved. Feedback is also encoded, sent through a communications channel and decoded by the receiver, the source of the original communication. Therefore, communication is a circular process, as indicated in Figure 12.2.

During face-to-face communication (e.g. personal selling and product sampling), verbal and nonverbal feedback can be immediate. Instant feedback lets communicators adjust messages quickly to improve the effectiveness of their communication. For example, when a salesperson realises through feedback that a customer does not understand a sales presentation, the salesperson adjusts the presentation to make it more meaningful to this customer. This may be why face-to-face sales presentations create higher behavioural intentions to purchase services than do telemarketing sales contacts.[12] In interpersonal communication, feedback occurs through talking, touching, smiling, nodding, eye movements and other body movements and postures. By contrast, when mass communication such as advertising is used, feedback is often slow and difficult to recognise.

channel capacity
limits the volume of information a communication channel can handle effectively

Each communication channel has a limit on the volume of information it can handle effectively. This limit, called channel capacity, is determined by the least efficient component of the communication process. For example, consider communications that depend on speech. An individual sender can speak only so fast, and there is a limit to how much an individual receiver can take in aurally. Beyond that point, additional messages cannot be decoded; therefore meaning cannot be shared. Although a radio announcer can read several hundred words a minute, a one-minute advertising message should not exceed about 150 words because most announcers cannot articulate words into understandable messages at a rate beyond 150 words per minute.

Message appeal styles

Have you noticed how you alter your communication style to fit the person or people you are talking to (e.g. making a formal presentation as part of a job interview process versus celebrating the end of exams with your friends). What you are discussing also affects your communication style (e.g. trying to explain how your computer is malfunctioning versus talking about your vacation plans). Similarly, the communication style used in promotions needs to consider the characteristics of the target audience, the communication channel, the objective of the promotion as well as what the communication is about (the product).

There are three major styles of promotional communication: rational, emotional and moral. A rational appeal features factual information perpetuating the merits of product features and attributes whereas an emotional appeal is designed to stir emotions like humour, fear, warmth, irritation or sexual arousal. Moral appeals rely on our sense of 'what is right or wrong' and as such should be reserved for promotional messages linked to a weighty cause such as helping the needy. Moral message appeals are most suited to promotional messages from authority figures, e.g. the government ('we must take action against global warming'), the police ('don't drink and drive') or health authorities ('smoking can harm your health').[13] Although many contemporary advertisements include both emotional and factual appeals, product attributes and benefits should guide the selection of the most appropriate message theme. For example, perfume commercials aim to create sensual moods by using figures of speech and emotion laden images.[14]

As consumers we use all our senses (vision, hearing, smell, feel/touch and taste) to interpret the situation we are in. Therefore the integrated marketing communication approach should be reflected in the whole marketing mix to ensure target customers receive complementary messages in a style designed to support the overall product branding. For example, the Optus 'Yes' stores feature 'clean, simple lines', environmentally friendly use of technology as well as interactive product demonstration areas. These changes are implemented in response to customers wanting experiences that are 'easier, simpler and better'.[15]

How target market characteristics and media channels guide message themes

The communication process shows how consumers need to interact with promotions to interpret message content. Therefore, a holistic approach is best when planning promotional campaigns. Consider the promotional content, the message theme, target market characteristics and product features as well as the limitations (or opportunities) dictated by the media channel.

As promotion aims to inform and persuade target audiences, careful attention needs to be paid to the content of promotional messages.[16] After all, consumers select brands that

rational appeal
a style of promotional communication that features factual information

emotional appeal
A style of promotional communication designed to stir emotions such as humour, fear, warmth, irritation or sexual arousal

moral appeal
a style of promotional communication that relies on our sense of 'what is right or wrong'

are most likely to satisfy both their emotional and rational needs. Successful promotion, therefore, creates distinctive and memorable messages that aim to engage both the heart (emotion laded messages) and the head (rational arguments for why the advertised brand will satisfy consumer needs).[17] Promotional messages are most effective when they match the style of product to target market characteristics.[18] Humour grabs attention and increases our engagement with advertisements. Humour is included in 10–30 per cent of all advertisements and is particularly powerful when launching new products or new brand names.[19] Advertising styles preferred by consumers include humour, animation and music. Preferred communication style divides consumers into three main categories: those who generally hold a positive attitude towards advertising, rational consumers who prefer advertisements with clear factual arguments and consumers who prefer metaphors or fantasy themes in advertisements.[20]

As discussed earlier, the medium (channel) used limits the quality and quantity of information that can be included in promotional messages, with personal communication offering the greatest quality/quantity. Careful consideration should also be given to target market characteristics as well as product type when deciding on the creative content[21] (e.g. Gecko's tagline of 'May your heart be light, your step swift and your stories fucking epic' is acceptable for the young target market of extreme adventure travellers).[22]

Generally speaking, TV ads aim to entertain audiences and grab viewers' attention as the pace of ads is relatively fast. Each commercial break is cluttered with competing messages and possibly overshadowed with viewer frustration at having their evening entertainment interrupted. In this environment, customers can successfully process only limited amounts of information. By contrast, customers can selectively browse printed advertisements and choose which advertisements they would like to focus on in line with their personal interests and information needs.[23]

The Internet succeeds in combining the desirable features of both print and TV commercials as consumers can control the pacing of information and choose what parts of the message (web page) to focus on. Moreover, the dynamic use of pictures, sound, video and live communication with company representatives makes the Internet a superior medium for promotion (provided that your target market uses the Internet to gather information). With the increased use of the Internet to support advertisements in traditional media (e.g. the '… for more information visit our web page' messages included in TV advertisements) the role of traditional media advertisements has become less informative and more concerned with enticing customers to visit company web pages for further information.[24]

The role and objectives of promotion

promotion
Communication to build and maintain relationships by informing and persuading one or more audiences

Promotion is communication that builds and maintains favourable relationships by informing and persuading one or more audiences to view an organisation more positively and to accept its products. Promotions can also be used by not-for-profit organisations with the aim of changing opinion or behaviour. For example, *CEO Sleep Out*, organised by the St Vincent de Paul Society, uses promotion to increase general awareness of the homelessness issue, and Worksafe uses promotion to reduce accidents or injuries at work.[25] While a company may pursue several promotional objectives (discussed later in this chapter), the overall role of promotion is to increase awareness of the product or the company or to stimulate product demand. To this end, many organisations spend considerable resources on promotion to build and enhance relationships with current or potential customers. For example, the Meat and Livestock Association has produced several good-humoured ads extolling the virtues of eating red meat.[26] Marketers also indirectly facilitate favourable relationships by focusing information about company activities and products on interest groups (such as environmental and consumer groups), current and potential investors, regulatory agencies and society in general. Table 12.1 offers a summary of common promotional objectives.

TABLE 12.1   POSSIBLE OBJECTIVES OF PROMOTION

Create awareness	Retain loyal customers
Stimulate demand	Facilitate reseller support
Encourage product trial	Combat competitive promotional efforts
Identify prospects	Reduce sales fluctuations

Marketing is not just about making profit as marketing techniques are also used by charities and not-for-profit organisations to enhance their cause. For example, Quitline aims to educate smokers about the health risks associated with cigarette smoking and about support programs available for smokers who wish to quit.[27] Companies also sometimes promote programs that help selected groups. For example, Mount Franklin water donates the use of its bottles (i.e. packaging design) to the McGrath Foundation to include messages encouraging consumers to get involved with this breast cancer charity or to make a donation.[28] Such cause-related marketing links the purchase of products to philanthropic efforts for one or more causes. By contributing to causes that its target markets support, cause-related marketing can help marketers to boost sales and generate goodwill. Marketers also sponsor or organise special events, often leading to news coverage and positive promotion of organisations and their brands. For example, the photographs of Australian celebrities serving customers in McDonald's restaurants during the 2012 McHappy Day helped raise over $3 million for the Ronald McDonald House Charity as well as promote McDonald's restaurants.[29] Celebrities like Delta Goodrem help raise consumers' awareness of this valuable cause.

cause-related marketing
Refers to companies linking up with charitable organisations with the aim of improving the company's image as well as 'giving something back' to the wider community. This practice is driven by customer demand

Source: © Ronald McDonald House Charities, used with permission

<< **Raising funds for Ronald McDonald House Charity**
Celebrities like Delta Goodrem help raise awareness of important issues

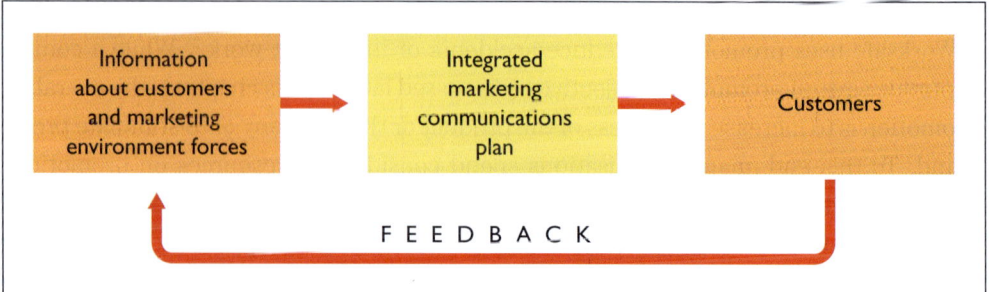

FIGURE 12.3
INFORMATION FLOWS
ARE IMPORTANT IN IMC

To obtain maximum benefit from promotional efforts, marketers strive for proper planning, implementation, coordination and control of communications. Effective management of integrated marketing communications is based on information about and feedback from customers or the marketing environment, often obtained from an organisation's marketing information system (see Figure 12.3). How successfully marketers use promotion to maintain positive relationships depends largely on the quantity and quality of information the organisation receives. Because customers derive information and opinions from many different sources, IMC planning also takes into account informal methods of communication such as word-of-mouth and independent information sources on the Internet. IMC strives for systematic communication of the brand positioning across all communication channels, therefore communicating an easily recognisable image utilising consistent visual and audible stimuli that strengthen brand values.[30]

Promotional objectives vary from one organisation to another and within organisations over time. Large companies with multiple promotional programs operating simultaneously may have a range of promotional objectives. For the purpose of analysis, we focus on commonly used promotional objectives as shown in Table 12.1. Although this set of possible promotional objectives is not exhaustive, one or more of the objectives discussed below underlie many promotional programs.

Create awareness

Creating awareness is a large part of promotion. For an organisation introducing a new product or product line extension, making customers aware of the product is crucial to initiating the product adoption process. A marketer who has invested heavily in product development strives to create product awareness quickly to generate revenues to offset the high costs of product development and introduction. For example, Cornetto Enigma won the 2013 Interactive Advertising Bureau award (Product Launch category) with a campaign using TV ads and social media activities. One measure for the success of this campaign was the 55 000 new Facebook fans it generated.[31] One way to capture attention is to create interactive outdoor advertisements, for example, Mini used electronic billboards in London to display complementary messages to Mini drivers (even including photos of drivers in their cars). As the Marketing in Transition box shows, printed advertisements can also be used to link consumers to interactive (and entertaining) content accessible on smartphones (e.g. using QR codes or **near field commnications (NFC)**).[32]

near field communication (NFC)
A wireless communication and data exchange technology that uses electromagnetic radio fields, works in a similar way to wi-fi, but only allows a very short distance between devices. This technology has been available since the 1980s but came to prominence recently when incorporated into mobile devices

MARKETING IN TRANSITION | NEAR FIELD COMMUNICATION (NFC) TURNS ADVERTISEMENTS INTO INTERACTIVE GAMES

Imagine the buzz you could create around a new movie or game launch by teasing your target audience with interactive online content? With smartphones it is possible to direct consumers from printed advertisements to video, audio, games and a countdown-to-release date online.

Tap your mobile phone to a movie poster and be immediately linked to interactive materials online. The Australian launch of the blockbuster movie 'Zero Dark Thirty' was promoted by 200 smart posters located in 91 shopping centres. By tapping the near field communication (NFC) tags consumers had quick access to movie trailers, image gallery and reviews. Movie enthusiasts could also elect to connect to the movie via Twitter or play the 'CIA' Facebook game.

NFC may also relegate Footy Cards to the Sports Museum. A tap-it campaign promoting the launch of the Halo 4 video game created a modern day treasure hunt: a competition to encourage consumers to tap the NFC tags of 376 posters located in Melbourne and Sydney. The first person to tap each poster won this poster as a prize. This campaign achieved 5664 taps. This is the future for poster advertising: consumers are enticed to tap NFC tags as they receive exciting online materials to enhance their consumption experience. Advertisers love NFC as the technology allows each mobile phone to be identified and they can collect real time statistical feedback to see how engaging the campaign is. Moreover, the content linked to the NFC tags can be programmed to vary according to the weather, time of the day or even the gender of the mobile phone owner. In other words, this could be the beginning of hyper-personalised promotional campaigns with a target market of just one — *you*. Additionally, the game/interactivity feature of posters can increase awareness of the promoted item in general as well as get the message to target segments that would not typically pay attention to poster campaigns.

Source: © Tapit, used with permission

NFC is not just for entertainment. Telstra's campaign allowing customers to tap and charge their pay-as-you-go mobile phone balance demonstrates a utilitarian use for NFC. Consumers on the move could also be delighted with NFC tags linked to maps and local information (provided they are placed in locations within mobile data coverage). Imagine being lost in a new city and only having to walk to the next street corner to access a map via NFC! Moreover, tourism businesses can involve visitors with interactive presentations of destination/location features at a relatively small cost.

The NFC chip is a short-range low-powered wireless connection between devices that requires no pairing codes (as with Bluetooth) and uses very little power (thus the two devices need to be just few centimetres away from each other). Both features make NFC ideal for promotional purposes. NFC chips are already incorporated in many Android handsets as well as in mobile phones by Samsung, HTC, Motorola, Nokia, LG and BlackBerry. Unfortunately, Apple elected NOT to include this technology in the iPhone 5. In 2013, some 285 million NFC-enabled devices were shipped and by 2017 this figure is expected to be 1.95 billion.[33]

Creating awareness is also important for existing products. Promotional efforts may aim to increase awareness of brands, product features and image-related issues (e.g. socially responsive behaviour by the company) or operational characteristics (e.g. store hours, locations and credit availability). Some promotional programs are unsuccessful because marketers fail to generate awareness of critical issues among a significant portion of target-market members or because programs do not target the right audience.

Pioneer demand >>
The Very Intelligent Pocket (VIP) has a desirable brand name as well as functionality. As the idea of a 'bag inside your bag' is new, the company needs to educate customers about the features and benefits of the product and give new customers instructions on how to use the product

Source: Pauline Ellis

Stimulate demand

When an organisation is the first to introduce an innovative product, it tries to stimulate primary demand – demand for a product category rather than for a specific brand of product – through pioneer promotion. Pioneer promotion informs potential customers about the product: what it is, what it does, how it can be used and where it can be purchased. In other words, when a company introduces a new product it must 'educate' customers about the benefits of the product. Because pioneer promotion is used at the beginning of the product life cycle, there are no competing brands, so it neither emphasises brand names nor compares brands. In their launch of The Very Intelligent Pocket (VIP), Tintamar introduced their novel concept of a pocket inside your handbag that organises the handbag and can easily be transferred from one handbag to another.

primary demand
Demand for a product category rather than for a specific brand

pioneer promotion
Promotion that informs consumers about a new product

selective demand
Demand for a specific brand

To build selective demand, demand for a specific brand, marketers employ promotional efforts that highlight the strengths and benefits of the brand. Building selective demand also requires singling out attributes important to potential buyers. Selective demand can be stimulated by differentiating the product from competing brands in the minds of potential buyers. It can also be stimulated by increasing the number of product uses and promoting them through advertising campaigns, as well as through price discounts, free samples, coupons, consumer contests and games, and sweepstakes. Promotions for large package sizes or multiple-product packages are directed at increasing consumption, which, in turn, can stimulate demand. In addition, selective demand can be stimulated by encouraging existing customers to use more of the product.

Encourage product trial

When attempting to move customers through the product adoption process (see also Chapter 8), marketers may successfully create awareness and interest, but customers may stall during the evaluation stage. In this case, certain types of promotion, such as free samples, coupons, test drives or limited free-use offers, contests and games, are employed to encourage product trial. For example, AVG offers potential customers the opportunity to download a free trial version of the company's antivirus or Internet security products.[34] Such free trial offers are especially convincing when the product in question is a complex service. Whether a marketer's product is the first of a new product category, a new brand in an existing category or simply an existing brand seeking customers, trial-inducing promotional efforts aim to make product trial convenient and low risk for potential customers. For example, the KFC ad shown here lists the ingredients of their new Black Edition Kentucky Burger. Once customers know the ingredients they know what flavours to expect. Steps like this to 'educate' customers are beneficial when the brand name offers few clues about ingredients and could therefore mislead customers.

Source: © 2014 Kentucky Fried Chicken Pty Limited. Image reproduced with permission by Kentucky Fried Chicken Pty Limited.

<< Encouraging product trial
Why is this ad by KFC a good example of trying to get customers to try something new?

Identify prospects

Some promotional efforts are directed at identifying customers who are interested in a company's product and are therefore more likely to buy it. For example, marketers may use a magazine ad with a direct-response information form, requesting readers to complete and mail the form to receive additional information. Some ads have free-call numbers to facilitate direct customer response.

Retain loyal customers

Clearly, maintaining long-term customer relationships is a major goal of most marketers. Such relationships are quite valuable. Promotional efforts directed at customer retention can help an organisation control its costs because the costs of retaining customers are usually considerably lower than those of acquiring new ones. Loyalty programs, such as those sponsored by airlines, car rental agencies and hotels, seek to reward loyal customers and encourage them to remain loyal. The Qantas Club allows members access to comfortable lounges at major airports worldwide where they can use complimentary business facilities and hot showers or enjoy light snacks and beverages.[35] To retain loyal customers, marketers not only advertise loyalty programs but also use reinforcement advertising, which assures current users that they have made the right brand choice and tells them how to get the most satisfaction from the product.

Another way to retain loyal clients is to reward their continuous custom. For example, Waze (a free app sharing traffic updates from other drivers in the same area) rewards frequent use with points that rank drivers in the Waze scoreboard.[36]

Facilitate reseller support

Reseller support is a two-way street. Producers generally want to provide support to resellers to maintain sound working relationships, and in turn, they expect resellers to support their products. When a manufacturer advertises a product to consumers, resellers should view this promotion as a form of strong manufacturer support. In some instances, a producer agrees to pay a certain proportion of retailers' advertising expenses for promoting its products. When a manufacturer is introducing a new consumer brand in a highly competitive product category, it may be difficult to persuade supermarket managers to carry this brand. However, if the manufacturer promotes the new brand with free samples and coupon distribution in the retailer's area, a supermarket manager views these actions as strong support and is much more likely to handle the product. To encourage wholesalers and retailers to market its products more aggressively, a manufacturer may provide them with special offers, buying allowances, contests or service. In the Fast Moving Consumer Goods (FMCG) industries, a producer's salesperson may provide support to a retailer by setting up special offer displays, maintaining the regular product displays or supporting the retailer at special events or exhibitions. Strong relationships with resellers are important in terms of a company's ability to maintain a sustainable competitive advantage. Using a range of promotional methods can help an organisation achieve this goal.

Reduce sales fluctuations/seasonality of demand

Demand for many products varies from one month to another because of factors such as climate, holidays and seasons. Promotional techniques are often designed to stimulate sales during sales slumps. For example, ads promoting price reduction of lawn-care equipment can increase sales during autumn and winter months. During peak periods, marketers may refrain from advertising to prevent stimulating sales to the point where the company cannot handle demand. Occasionally, organisations advertise that customers can be served better by coming in on particular days. A pizza outlet, for example, might distribute coupons that are valid only Monday through Thursday because on Friday through Sunday the restaurant is extremely busy.

Combat competitive promotional efforts

At times, a marketer's objective in using promotion is to offset or lessen the effect of a competitor's promotional or marketing programs. This type of promotional activity does not necessarily increase the organisation's sales or market share, but it may prevent a sales or market share loss. A combative promotional objective is used most often by firms in extremely competitive consumer markets, such as the fast-food, convenience store and cable/Internet/phone markets. It is not unusual for competitors to respond with a counter-pricing strategy or even match a competitor's pricing.

To achieve the major objectives of promotion discussed here, companies must develop appropriate promotional programs. In the next section we consider the basic components of such programs, referred to as the marketing communications mix elements.

Selecting elements for the marketing communications mix

Organisations can use several promotional methods to communicate with their customers and other stakeholders. A combination of promotional methods is called the marketing communications mix. An effective marketing communications mix (also known as the promotions mix or promotional mix) requires the right combination of components – the 'right' combination is determined by variables such as advertising objectives, target market characteristics and preferences, product features and the desired positioning for the product and available budget. The traditional elements of a promotion mix are advertising, personal selling, public relations and sales promotion. However, many new digital communication channels could also be utilised for promotions. Word-of-mouth is included in this mix as social networks can be used for promotions (these are covered in greater detail in the next chapter) (see Table 12.2). To see how such a mix is created we now examine the factors and conditions affecting the selection of elements that an organisation uses for a specific marketing communications mix.

marketing communications mix
A combination of marketing communications methods used to promote a specific product

TABLE 12.2   MARKETING COMMUNICATIONS MIX VARIABLES EXPLAINED

Marketing communications mix variables	Short definition
Advertising	Paid non-personal communication about an organisation and its products transmitted to a target audience through mass media
Personal selling	Paid for personal presentations aiming to inform and/or persuade the customers
Public relations (PR)	Communication efforts used to create and maintain favourable relations between an organisation and its stakeholders
Sales promotion (SP)	An activity and/or material meant to induce resellers or salespeople to sell a product or consumers to buy it
Product placement	The strategic location of products or product promotions within entertainment content (such as movies) to reach the product's target market
Digital marketing	Marketing communications mix elements that rely on digital technology, e.g. mobile coupons or banner advertisements.
Word-of-mouth communication (WOM)	Personal, informal exchanges of information that customers share with one another about products, brands and companies

So what is the relationship between the marketing mix, marketing communications mix and integrated marketing communications? The first two describe a 'mix', or a bundle, of tools marketing managers can use to make sure they are responding to customers' needs. The *marketing mix* refers to the types of decisions made in marketing including the promotion component. The variety of possible promotional tools is known as the *marketing communications mix*, a sub-component of the marketing mix. As organisations can use a variety of promotional tools, ranging from advertising to product placements, they need to select the most suitable promotional methods in a strategic manner. This selective use of promotional alternatives is *integrated marketing communications* at work. Figure 12.4 shows the relationship between the marketing mix, the marketing communications mix and integrated marketing communications.

Marketers vary the composition of the marketing communications mix for many reasons. Although a marketing communications mix can include all six elements, frequently marketers select fewer than four. In Table 12.2, a seventh variable of 'word of mouth' is included. This isn't considered an official part of the marketing communications mix, but is included here as many companies are now trying to use it to their benefit. Companies that market multiple product lines use several marketing communications mixes simultaneously (GANTT charts can help the coordination of these promotional activities, see Figure 12.1). The marketing communications mix is something a company can control to be more effective in serving the needs of their customers and as a way of responding to changes in the competitive business environment.

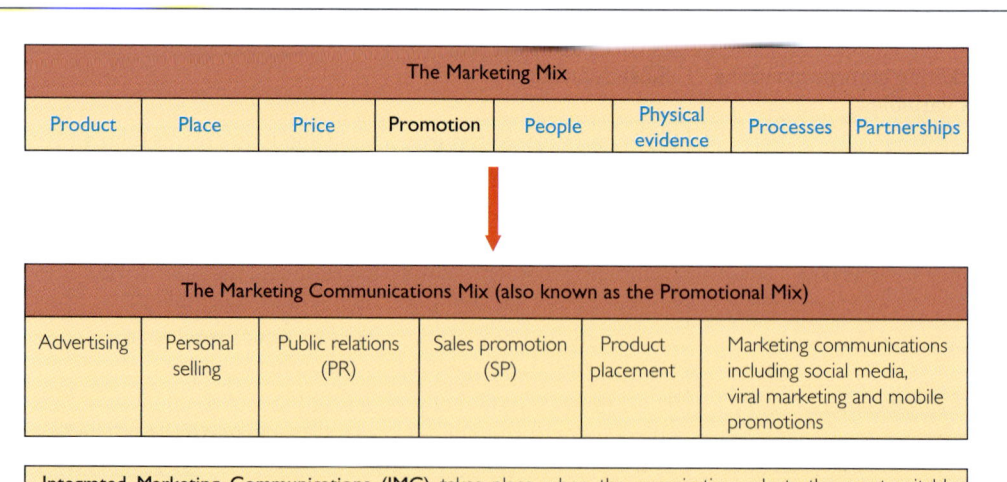

FIGURE 12.4
THE RELATIONSHIP BETWEEN INTEGRATED MARKETING COMMUNICATIONS AND THE EXPANDED MARKETING MIX

Promotional resources, objectives and policies

The size of an organisation's promotional budget affects the number and relative intensity of promotional methods included in a marketing communications mix. An organisation's promotional objectives and policies also influence the types of promotion selected. If a company's objective is to create mass awareness of a new convenience good, such as a breakfast cereal, its marketing communications mix probably leans heavily toward advertising, sales promotion and possibly public relations. For example, Mother (the energy drink) utilised media partnerships, TV and cinema ads, printed promotions on Mother packaging as well as interactive point-of-sale displays for their Call of Duty campaign. Fans could also participate in a 'secret rescue op'.[37]

Another factor to consider when creating an effective marketing communication mix is the stage of the product life cycle and stage of buyer readiness, as shown in Figure 12.5 which lists the type of promotions that could be used at different stages of buyer readiness. At the initial stages (introduction and growth stages), when the objective is to increase general awareness of the product, mass media communications, such as advertising or publicity, are most effective. These mass media communication channels lose their effectiveness soon after the initial buyer awareness stages, with the exception, perhaps, of reminder advertising. Once potential customers are aware of a product but need to understand its benefits, communication like personal selling is appropriate. At the ordering stage, customers are aware of the features and benefits of the product but their order could be prompted by a targeted sales promotion campaign.

Target market characteristics

Size, geographic distribution and demographic characteristics of its target market help a company to decide what to include in the marketing communications mix for their products. To some degree, market size determines composition of the mix. Companies selling to business markets and companies marketing products through only a few wholesalers frequently make personal selling the major element in their marketing communications mix. When a product's market consists of millions of customers, businesses rely on advertising and sales promotion because these methods reach large numbers of people at a low per-person cost. Table 12.3 demonstrates how consumers in New Zealand use media according to their age. For example, if your product is typically used by the elderly, it would be wise not to invest in a heavy Internet presence. Age of your target customers is an important variable when deciding which media to use. The differences in media use in Table 12.3 could be explained by existing media habits as well as the type of information, news or entertainment sought by different age groups.

Geographic distribution of a company's customers also affects the choice of promotional methods, especially in a country like Australia where population densities vary greatly between major cities and rural areas. The cost of sending a sales representative from Melbourne to meet a customer in Swan Hill includes travel,

REVISE each chapter with myriad of resources including flashcards

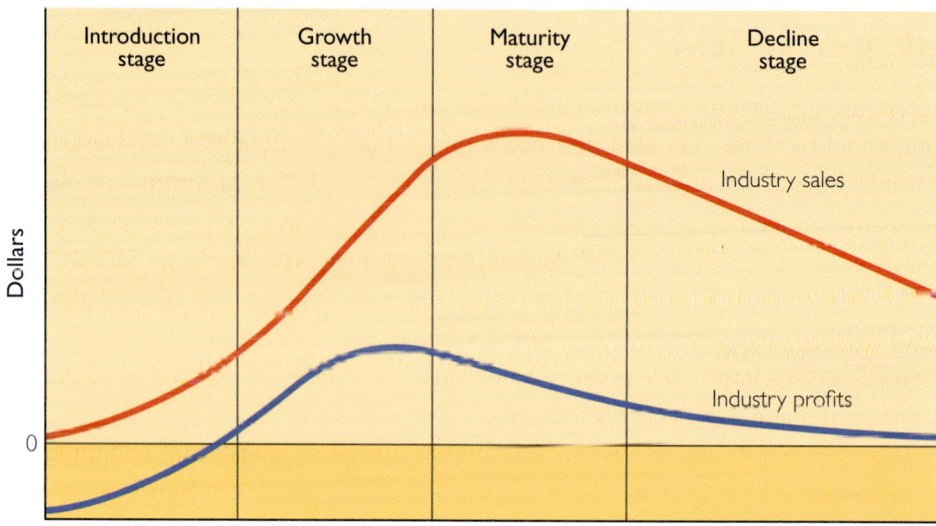

Key challenges	Customers are unaware of the new product type. You have to bear the cost of 'educating' them as no substitute products available yet	Competitors/ substitute product emerging. Aim for loyal clientele	Many competitors results in cuts in profit margins	Number of competitors reducing but as volume of sales reduces the related costs increase
Promotional strategy	Aim at the needs of early adopters	Make the mass market aware of the brand benefits	Use promotion as a vehicle for differentiation among otherwise similar brands	Emphasise low price to reduce stock
Promotional emphasis	High, to generate awareness and interest among early adopters and persuade dealers to stock the brand	Moderate, to let sales rise on the sheer momentum of word-of-mouth recommendations	Moderate, since most buyers are aware of brand characteristics	Minimum expenditures required to phase out the product
Consumer sales and promotion expenditures	Heavy, to entice target groups with samples, coupons, and other inducements to try the brand	Moderate, to create brand preference (advertising is better suited to do this job)	Heavy, to encourage brand switching, hoping to convert some buyers into loyal users	Minimal, to let the brand coast by itself

Source: Pride, W and Ferrell, OC, *Foundations of Marketing*, 4th Edition, 2010, Cengage Learning; Dhalla, NK and Yuspeh, S, 1976, 'Forget the product life cycle concept', *Harvard Business Review*, January–February, p. 104.

FIGURE 12.5 COST EFFECTIVENESS OF DIFFERENT TYPES OF PROMOTION

TABLE 12.3   TIME SPENT WITH MEDIA VARIES ACCORDING TO AGE (HOURS PER WEEK)

	<40 years	40+ years
Television	19h 50m	21h 52m
Radio	16h 53m	20h 43m
Newspapers	2h 14m	4h 22m
Magazines	1h 38m	2h 17m
Internet	10h 30m	7h 8m
Total	51h 05m	56h 22m

Source: Roy Morgan Research

accommodation and insurance charges incurred by such a visit. Geographical variables are also important in urban areas, for example when considering the use of billboards or targeting specific neighbourhoods through bus ads (either inside the bus where patrons will see the ad or by wrap-around ad on the outside) that focus on consumers somewhere on that bus route.[38]

Distribution of a target market's demographic characteristics, such as age, income or education, may affect the type of communications marketing mix-variables marketers select, as well as the messages and images employed. The characteristics of the target audience should also be noted when deciding on the encoding of promotional messages and the channels of communication to be used (see also Figure 12.2). Using digital billboards allows marketers to tempt audiences to greater interaction with the communication, as can be seen in the Marketing in Transition box below.

MARKETING IN TRANSITION | TECHNOLOGY IS CHANGING BILLBOARDS

Latest technological trends are making out-of-home (OOH) (i.e. billboards) into interactive communication that engages and, at times, delights technology savvy consumers. The willingness of consumers to adopt new technology is a key segmentation variable for many new ICT products.

→ Bluetooth enabled billboards let consumers download music or entertainment content to their mobile phones (e.g. movie trailers)

→ Touch screen technology enables consumers to interact with pre-programmed features

→ QR codes or near field communication (NFC) link outdoor advertisements seamlessly to online content

→ Through gesture-tracking technology consumers can direct interaction with the billboard with their hands (as you would conduct a symphony orchestra).

→ Advancements in facial recognition technology allowed Streets' Magnum Infinity Promotions to have a smile activate an interaction where users could virtually eat a whole Magnum ice cream.

Fluent interaction between out-of-home advertisements and smart phones allow consumers to redeem special offers/vouchers online or use

their mobile phones to make payments/complete purchases on the go. Unfortunately, widespread use of this new digital-out-of-home (DOOH) channel is hampered by the lack of NFC technology being routinely incorporated into mobile phones. In 2011 only five per cent of mobile phones included NFC but by 2016 approximately 50 per cent of mobile phones are expected to incorporate this technology. In Australia, the adoption of moving billboards by road sides is further limited by government concern that enticing DOOH advertisements will distract drivers.[39]

Product characteristics

Generally, a marketing communications mix for business products concentrates on personal selling, whereas advertising plays a major role in promoting consumer goods. This generalisation should be treated cautiously, though. Marketers of business products use some advertising to promote products. Personal selling is used extensively for consumer durables, such as home appliances, automobiles and houses, whereas consumer convenience items are promoted mainly through advertising and sales promotion. Public relations appears in marketing communications mixes for both business and consumer products.

Marketers of highly seasonal products often employ advertising, and sometimes sales promotion as well, because off-season sales generally do not support an extensive year-round sales force. Although most toy producers have sales forces to sell to resellers, many of these companies depend heavily on advertising to promote their products.

A product's price also influences the composition of the marketing communications mix. High-priced products call for personal selling because consumers associate greater risk with the purchase of such products and usually want information from a salesperson. Few people, for example, are willing to purchase a refrigerator from a self-service establishment. For low-priced convenience items (low involvement buying decisions), marketers use advertising rather than personal selling. When products are marketed through intensive distribution, companies depend heavily on advertising and sales promotion. Many convenience products, such as lotions, cereals and coffee, are promoted through samples, coupons and money refunds. Furthermore, when marketers choose selective distribution, marketing communication mixes vary considerably. Items handled through exclusive distribution, such as expensive watches, jewellery and high-quality furniture, typically require a significant amount of personal selling. Manufacturers of highly personal products, such as laxatives, non-prescription contraceptives and feminine hygiene products, depend on advertising because many customers do not want to talk with salespeople about these products. Finally, customers considering the purchase of a complex item, such as a new computer, appreciate marketing communication messages they can revisit easily to check the exact product features or to enable a comparison between different brands. Printed or online advertisements enable this.

Costs and availability of promotional methods

Costs associated with marketing communication methods are major factors to analyse when developing a marketing communications mix. National advertising and sales promotion require large expenditures. If these efforts succeed in reaching extremely large audiences, however, the cost per individual reached may be quite small, possibly a few cents. Some forms of advertising are relatively inexpensive. Many small, local businesses advertise goods and services through local newspapers, radio and TV stations, outdoor displays, search engine result ads and signs on vehicles. Figure 12.6 shows how young people routinely use the Internet for communication and information searches, making the future of Internet-based promotions appear rosy. Unfortunately, it is not possible to say at this stage if heavy website traffic always results in increased sales.

Another factor marketers consider when formulating a marketing communications mix is the availability of marketing communications techniques. The problem of media availability becomes more pronounced when marketers advertise in foreign countries. Some media, such as TV, simply may not be available, or it may be illegal to advertise on TV.

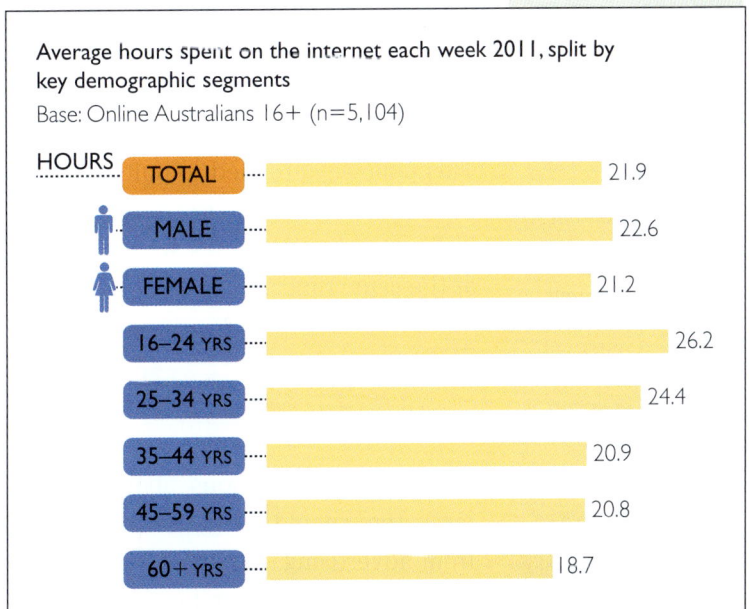

Source: Nielsen: The Australian Online Consumer Landscape, March 2012, p. 7.

FIGURE 12.6
IS THE FUTURE OF PROMOTIONS ONLINE? THE AVERAGE HOURS SPENT ONLINE EACH WEEK IN 2011 SPLIT BY KEY DEMOGRAPHIC SEGMENTS.

push policy
Promoting a product only to the next institution down the marketing channel

Push and pull channel policies

Another element marketers consider when planning a marketing communications mix is whether to use a push policy or a pull policy. With a push policy, producers promote products only to the next institution down the marketing channel. In a marketing channel with wholesalers and retailers, producers promote to wholesalers, the channel member just below producers (see Figure 12.7). Each channel member, in turn, promotes to the next channel member. A push policy normally stresses personal selling. Sometimes sales promotion and advertising are used in conjunction with personal selling to push products down through the channel.

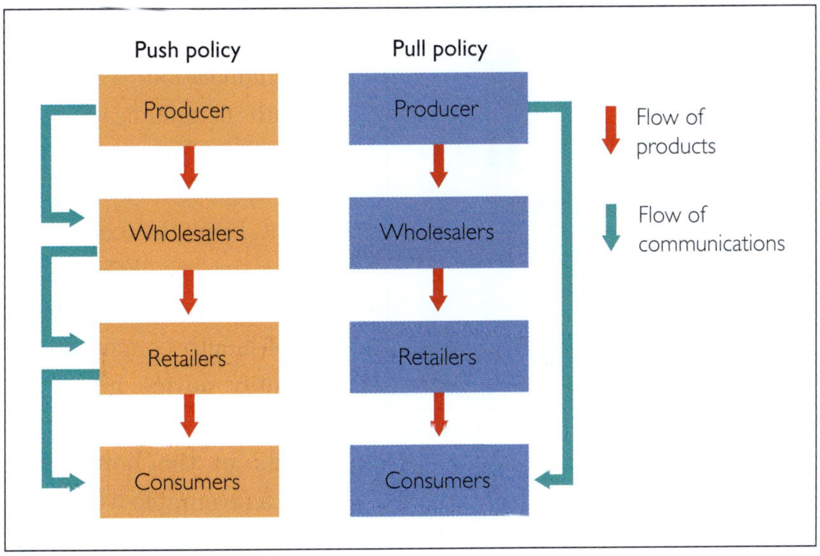

FIGURE 12.7
COMPARISON OF PUSH AND PULL PROMOTIONAL STRATEGIES

pull policy
Promoting a product directly to consumers to develop strong consumer demand that pulls products through the marketing channel

word-of-mouth communication (WOM)
Personal, informal exchanges of information that customers share with one another about products, brands and companies

As Figure 12.7 shows, a company using a pull policy promotes directly to consumers to develop strong consumer demand for its products. It does so primarily through advertising and sales promotion. Because consumers are persuaded to look for products in retail stores, retailers, in turn, go to wholesalers or producers to buy the products. This policy is intended to pull the goods down through the channel by creating demand at the consumer level. Consumers are told that if the stores don't have it, ask them to get it. Push and pull policies are not mutually exclusive. At times, an organisation uses both at the same time.

The growing importance of word-of-mouth communications

When making decisions about the composition of marketing communication mixes, marketers should recognise the limited extent to which commercial messages, whether from advertising, personal selling, sales promotion or public relations, can inform and persuade customers and move them closer to making purchases. Depending on the type of customers and products, buyers to some extent rely on word-of-mouth communication from personal sources such as family members and friends. Word-of-mouth communication (WOM) refers to personal, informal exchanges in which customers share information about products, brands and companies.[41] Most consumers are likely to seek information from knowledgeable friends, family members and experts when buying medical, legal and car repair services. Word-of-mouth communication is also important when people are selecting restaurants and entertainment, as well as banking and personal services such as haircare.

Strictly speaking, word-of-mouth communication is not part of an organisation's marketing communications mix since the message content and its delivery are not 100 per cent controlled by the organisation. So why are marketers so attracted to this type of communication? The allure of word-of-mouth communication is based on the impartial nature of the message as it originates from an individual and not from the company aiming to increase sales. Effective marketers who understand the importance of word-of-mouth communication attempt to identify advice givers and opinion leaders and encourage them to try their products in the hope that they will spread a favourable word about them.

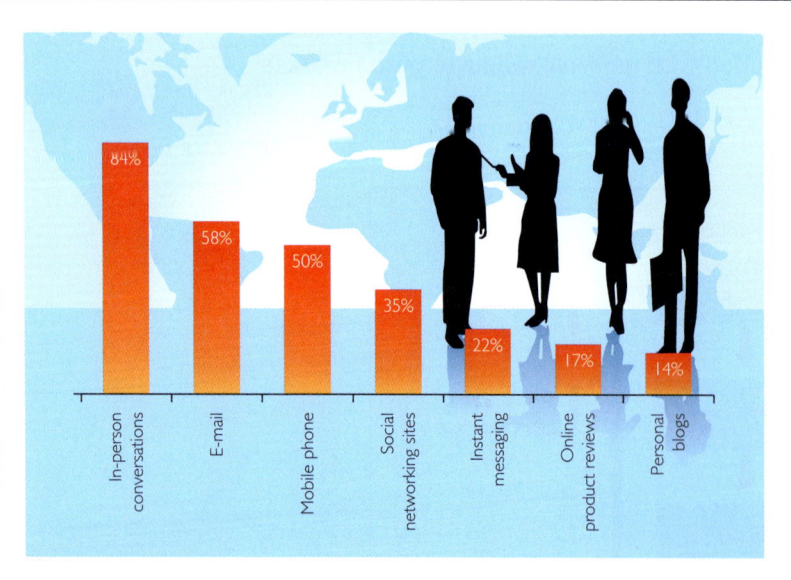

FIGURE 12.8
HOW CONSUMERS DISCUSS PRODUCTS AND SERVICES

Source: *E-Marketer*; Word of Mouth Marketing Association. Reprinted in "Crunching the Numbers," Inc., March 2012, p. 26.

Increasingly, customers are going online to share their opinions about goods and services as well as about the companies that market them (see Figure 12.8). Digital-word-of-mouth is communicating about products through websites, blogs, email, social networks or online forums. A number of consumer-oriented forums, such as

<< Dangers of negative word of mouth
Dave Carroll's 'United Breaks Guitars' songs transformed him from 'just a musician' to an author, sought after speaker, consumer advocate and business consultant

http://productreview.com.au and http://whirlpool.net.au allow consumers to learn about other consumers' experiences of specific products. Users can also search within product categories and compare consumers' viewpoints on different brands and models. Buyers can peruse Internet-based newsgroups, forums and blogs to find word-of-mouth information. A consumer looking for a new mobile phone service, for example, might inquire in forums about other participants' experiences and level of satisfaction to gain more information before making a purchase decision. A Nielsen Global Online Consumer Survey found that 90 per cent of consumers trust recommendations they get from their friends, while 70 per cent trust consumer comments posted online.[42]

Irrespective of how it is transmitted, word of mouth is not effective in all product categories. It seems to be most effective for new-to-market and more expensive products. Despite the obvious benefits of positive word of mouth, marketers must also recognise the potential dangers of negative word of mouth. For example, United Airlines has reportedly lost over US$180 million from its market value after musician Dave Carroll chronicled his experiences with the airline in his YouTube music video. By June 2013 his complaint song had been viewed more than 13 million times. Moreover, Dave has since posted two additional songs 'United Breaks Guitars Song 2' and 'United Breaks Guitars Song 3', published a book called 'United breaks guitars – The power of one voice in the age of social media' and launched a company called Gripevine (a website where consumers can complain about poor service).[43]

Criticisms and defences of promotion

LO6

Even though promotional activities can help customers make informed purchasing decisions, social scientists, consumer groups, government agencies and members of society in general have at times criticised promotion. The two main reasons for such criticism are: promotion does have flaws, and it is a highly visible business activity that pervades our daily lives. Although complaints about too much promotional activity are almost universal, a number of more specific criticisms have been lodged. In this section, we discuss some of the criticisms and defences of promotion.

Offensive advertisements

In the quest to catch consumers' attention, advertisers occasionally offend their audiences. A study by the UK Advertising Standards Authority found that 16 per cent of adult respondents had been offended by advertisement in the past 12 months. In the same time period 30 per cent of children complained about advertisements that featured sex, violence or other frightening materials. Moreover, advertisements created for charities often upset audiences as consumers are not comfortable with highly charged emotional scenes addressing animal cruelty or child abuse.[44]

In Australia the advertising industry administers a national self-regulatory system to maintain high standards in advertising, to protect consumers against offensive advertising content and maintain consumer trust. The Advertising Standards Bureau (ASB), the Advertising Standards Board and Advertising Claims Board are funded by a 0.035 per cent levy based on advertising spend (i.e. $3.50 for every $10 000 of gross media expenditure). This self-regulating system is based on various codes of conduct and other industry initiatives with the aim that 'advertisements should be legal, decent, honest and truthful, prepared with a sense of social responsibility to the consumer and society as a whole and with due respect to the rules of fair competition'. This system of maintaining acceptable advertising standards is built on voluntary compliance by the industry and it is not underpinned by Government legislation.[45]

Table 12.4 summarises the top 10 most complained about ads in Australia in 2012. Two thirds of all complaints lodged with the Advertising Standards Bureau (ASB) in 2012 were about advertisements containing material considered discriminatory or vilifying most likely to prompt a complaint. Overall, almost 500 complaints were lodged with the ASB in 2012 but only about 60 ads were found to breach the code.[46]

offensive advertising
Advertisements considered offensive by the consumers due to insulting, unfair or morally wrong content

Advertising Standards Bureau (ASB)
The Advertising Standards Bureau administers a national, self-regulating system aimed at maintaining responsible advertising practice. For detailed information on codes and initiatives guiding the Australian advertising industry see http://www.adstandards.com.au

TABLE 12.4 SUMMARY OF ADVERTISING COMPLAINTS IN AUSTRALIA IN 2012

	Advertiser	Media	Short description of advertisement	Number of complaints	Outcome
1	Johnson & Johnson Pacific Pty Ltd	TV	A younger woman in her mid-20s talks about how amazing our bodies are and about the body's way of keeping the vagina healthy and why Carefree has designed acti-fresh liners	149	Dismissed
2	Red Bull Aust Pty Ltd	TV	Three cartoon characters fishing on a lake. One of the characters, named Jesus, says he is bored and decides to leave the boat and appears to walk on water as he departs.	96	Dismissed
3	Unilever Australasia	TV	An infomercial style scenario with a presenter and guest appearance by tennis player, Sophie Monk. She shows how the Lynx product can clean a variety of dirty balls.	92	Dismissed

	Advertiser	Media	Short description of advertisement	Number of complaints	Outcome
4	Pacific Magazines	TV	As a cart and horse driven by an Amish elder couple stops to pick up a mother and son, the boy notices a discarded magazine lying in the grass nearby. In a series of vignettes the elderly couple become increasingly concerned by changes occurring in their community and toss the magazine away	85	Dismissed
5	SCA Hygiene Australasia	Internet	A drag queen and a woman in the bathroom of a nightclub or bar taking part in a friendly duel which ends with the woman pulling out her Libra tampon and giving the drag queen a cheeky smile.	78	Dismissed
6	Unilever Australasia	TV	Set in a TV studio with a mixed female and male audience and featuring a female presenter and another woman, 'Amber Jones', introduced as former champion of a fictitious tennis tournament who talks about dirty sports balls and the difficulties of cleaning them properly.	58	Upheld – Modified or Discontinued
7	Pilot Pen Australia Pty Ltd	TV	A man is following a hand written recipe for soup. The word 'leek' is misspelled 'leak'. The man unzips his trousers and through sound effects we are led to understand that he is urinating in the soup.	54	Dismissed
8	Kimberly-Clark Aust Pty Ltd	TV	A Labrador puppy sniffs his way through the day, approaching various people from behind, including the backside of a plumber with his head under the kitchen sink.	40	Dismissed
=9	Transport Accident Commission	TV	Shows in reverse the reconstructed actions of a motorbike crashing into a car.	19	Dismissed
=9	ACP Publishing Pty Ltd	Social	People are invited to comment on images on the Facebook page. Examples include a woman on the beach, separated into top and bottom halves and Facebook users were asked which half they would prefer.	19	Upheld – Modified or Discontinued
10	Energy Australia	TV	Features a man sitting inside a fridge	19	Upheld – Modified or Discontinued

Source: Advertising Standards Bureau, 17 December, 2012.

Is promotion deceptive?

A common criticism of promotion is that it is deceptive and unethical. During the 19th and early 20th centuries, much promotion was blatantly deceptive. Although no longer widespread, some deceptive promotion still occurs. For example, an Australian Competition and Consumer Commission (ACCC) investigation in June 2013 highlighted the practice of partially baked goods that arrive to the supermarket frozen and the in-store bakery simply completes the cooking process. The ACCC is taking Coles to court for 'false, misleading and deceptive conduct' due to claims like 'Baked Today, Sold Today' as well 'Freshly Baked In-Store' attached to packaging or displayed near items that are only partially baked in-store. A blatant example of such practice is the 'baked in-store' Danish pastry that is actually made in Belgium.[47]

The diet products and exercise equipment industry is subject to a high number of truthfulness-related claims, with advertisers being criticised for using pictures that are 'too perfect'. By creating pictures of models or celebrities that are digitally improved to physical perfection, the advertising industry is contributing towards unhealthy trends like eating disorders and stress associated with not being able to achieve the 'perfect' body image (see the Ethical Marketing box below).

Some promotions deceive unintentionally. For example, ads aimed at children can easily be misleading because children are more naïve than adults and less able to separate fantasy from reality. A promotion may also mislead receivers, because words and images can mean different things to different people. However, not all promotion should be condemned because a small portion is flawed. Laws, government regulation and industry self-regulation have helped decrease the number of deceptive promotions.

ETHICAL MARKETING | IMAGES IN ADVERTISING ARE ROUTINELY PHOTOSHOPPED

Should Photoshopped images be banned from advertisements?

As discussed elsewhere in this chapter, the receiver of a coded message interprets the combination of text, sound and images into a meaningful communication. Understanding of the message is not limited to the product features being promoted but includes any message from the communication perceived as important. Unfortunately, pictures of beautiful, ultra-thin models not only sell products but also communicate an unrealistic expectation of what we should look like (distorting the perception of a healthy body image and contributing towards eating disorders).

The Dove Campaign for Real Beauty has been running for decades (it won a Grand Prix in Cannes in 2007) and this campaign is making headlines again! The latest attention grabbing promotion included a fake Photoshop plug-in called 'Beautify' that claimed to make models' skin appear radiant but in reality reverted any photoshopped images back to their original appearance complete with a superimposed screen message of 'Don't manipulate our perceptions of real beauty'. Although this Photoshop plug-in was not used to any great extent, the video outlining the case study brought the debate about airbrushing images of already skinny models and research on eating disorders back into the news headlines.

Here are the historical highlights of the Dove campaign:

→ 2004 – Dove Real Beauty campaign was launched featuring real women who were beautiful outside stereotypical expectations.

→ 2005 – Advertisements featured real women, real bodies and real curves.

→ 2006 – Dove Self-Esteem Fund was launched to inspire and educate girls and women.

→ 2007 – Dove global study: Beauty Comes of Age 'celebrated the essence of women 50+ – wrinkles, age spots, grey hair and all'.

→ 2010 – Dove: Movement for Self-Esteem created educational program aimed at building self-esteem.

→ 2011 – Dove launched The Real Truth About Real Beauty: Revisited campaign.

Dove is not the only campaigner against unrealistic, airbrushed advertising photographs. For example, in the UK the high street department store Debenhams has

banned all images of airbrushed lingerie models and vows a 'moral obligation to ban the airbrush'. In Australia, the government has launched a voluntary industry code of conduct for the fashion industry as well as the Positive Body Image Awards.[48]

Challenge questions

1. In your opinion, will a voluntary code of conduct make a difference to the practice of airbrushing images of models for advertisements?
2. Can a campaign like this help reduce eating disorders?

Does promotion increase prices?

Promotion is also criticised for raising prices, but in fact it often tends to lower them. The ultimate purpose of promotion is to stimulate demand. If it does, a business should be able to produce and market products in larger quantities and thus reduce per-unit production and marketing costs, which can result in lower prices. For example, as demand for flat-screen TVs and MP3 players increases, their prices drop. When promotion fails to stimulate demand, the price of the promoted product increases because promotion costs must be added to other costs. Promotion also helps keep prices lower by facilitating price competition. When firms advertise prices, they tend to remain lower than when they are not promoting prices.

Does promotion create needs?

Some critics of promotion claim that it manipulates consumers by persuading them to buy products they do not need, hence creating 'artificial' needs. In his theory of motivation,

Abraham Maslow indicates that an individual tries to satisfy five levels of needs: physiological needs, such as hunger, thirst and sex; safety needs; needs for love and affection; needs for self-esteem and respect from others; and self-actualisation needs, or the need to realise one's potential. When needs are viewed in this context, it is difficult to demonstrate that promotion creates them. If there were no promotional activities, people would still have needs for food, water, sex, safety, love, affection, self-esteem, respect from others and self-actualisation.

Although promotion may not create needs, it does capitalise on them (which may be why some critics believe promotion creates needs). Many marketers base their appeals on these needs. For instance, several mouthwash, toothpaste and perfume ads associate these products with needs for love, affection and respect. These advertisers rely on human needs in their messages, but they do not create the needs.

Does promotion help customers without costing too much?

Every year, firms spend billions of dollars on promotion. The question is whether promotion helps customers enough to be worth the cost. Consumers do benefit because promotion informs them about product uses, features, advantages, prices and store locations. Thus, consumers gain more knowledge about available products and can make more intelligent buying decisions. Promotion also informs consumers about services such as health care, educational programs and day care, and about important social, political and health-related issues. For example, The 'Dumb Ways to Die' advertisement by Melbourne's Metro Trains highlights safe consumer behaviour near trains. This advertisement was named the best ad in the world after winning five top prizes at the Cannes International Festival of Creativity in 2013.[49]

Should potentially harmful products be promoted?

Finally, some critics of promotion, including consumer groups and government officials, suggest that certain products should not be promoted at all. Primary targets are products associated with violence and other unhealthy activities, such as handguns, alcohol and tobacco. Cigarette advertisements, for example, promote smoking, a behaviour proven to be harmful and even deadly. Tobacco companies, who spend billions on promotion, have countered criticism of their advertising by pointing out that advertisements for red meat and coffee are not censored, even though these products may also cause health problems. Those who defend such promotion assert that, as long as it is legal to sell a product, promoting that product should be allowed.

Study Tools

Chapter review

 **DISCUSS THE NATURE OF INTEGRATED MARKETING COMMUNICATIONS.**

Integrated marketing communications is the coordination of promotion and other marketing efforts to ensure maximum informational and persuasive impact on customers. Sending consistent messages to customers is a major goal of integrated marketing communications. As both digital technology and customer interests become increasingly dynamic, the specific communication vehicles employed and the precision with which they are used are changing.

 **UNDERSTAND HOW DIFFERENT STAGES IN THE COMMUNICATION PROCESS CAN GUIDE THE DESIGN OF PROMOTIONAL CAMPAIGNS.**

Communication is a sharing of meaning. The communication process involves several steps. First, the sender translates meaning into code, a process known as coding or encoding. The sender employs signs or symbols familiar to the receiver or audience. The coded message is sent through a communications channel to the receiver or audience. The receiver or audience then decodes the message and usually supplies feedback to the source. When the decoded message differs from the encoded one, a condition called noise exists.

 **APPRECIATE HOW SPECIFIC COMMUNICATION STYLES COULD BE APPLIED TO THE DESIGN OF PROMOTIONAL CAMPAIGNS**

Elements such as language, images, video and music contribute to communication styles. Most advertisements fall into the categories of emotional, rational or moral appeals. Communication style should match the type of product being promoted, e.g. rational appeals work best with products that are promoted with facts and figures (e.g. computers and mobile phones), emotional appeals are most effective when the product being promoted has emotional value (e.g. medicines for your baby when he/she has a high temperature), and moral appeals are most suited to communications that 'aim to improve the world we live in', that is, the message has some greater meaning emphasising local moral codes and norms.

 EXPLAIN THE ROLE AND OBJECTIVES OF PROMOTION.

Eight primary objectives underlie most promotional programs. Promotion aims to create awareness of a new product, new brand or existing product, to stimulate primary and selective demand, to encourage product trial through the use of free samples, coupons, limited free-use offers, contests and games, to identify prospects, to retain loyal customers, to facilitate reseller support, to combat competitive promotional efforts, and to reduce sales fluctuations.

 **DESCRIBE THE FACTORS THAT AFFECT THE CHOICE OF MARKETING COMMUNICATIONS MIX ELEMENTS.**

The promotional methods to include in an organisation's marketing communications mix are determined by the organisation's promotional resources, objectives and policies, target market characteristics, product characteristics, and cost and availability of promotional methods. Marketers also consider whether to use a push or a pull policy. With a push policy, producers promote the product only to the next institution down the marketing channel. Normally, a push policy stresses personal selling. Companies that use a pull policy promote directly to consumers, with the intention of developing strong consumer demand for products. Once consumers are persuaded to look for the products in retail stores, retailers go to wholesalers or the producer to buy the products.

 LO6 UNDERSTAND COMMON CRITICISMS AND DEFENCES OF PROMOTION.

Promotional activities can help consumers make informed purchasing decisions, but they have also been the subject of much criticism, including accusations of deception. Although some deceiving or misleading promotions do exist, laws, government regulation and industry self-regulation minimise deceptive promotion. Promotion has been blamed for increasing prices, but it actually tends to lower them. When demand is high, production and marketing costs decrease, which can result in lower prices. Promotion also helps to bring prices down by facilitating price competition. Other criticisms of promotional activity are that it manipulates consumers into buying products they do not need, that it leads to a more materialistic society and that consumers do not benefit sufficiently from promotional activity to justify its high cost. Finally, some critics of promotion suggest that potentially harmful products, especially those associated with violence, sex and unhealthy activities, should not be promoted at all.

Key concepts

Use these key terms in **Search me! marketing** to find the latest relevant readings from a wide range of world-class journals, e-books and newspapers, including *The Australian*.

- cause-related marketing
- channel capacity
- coding process
- communication
- communications channel
- decoding process
- feedback

- integrated marketing communications
- noise
- pioneer promotion
- primary demand
- promotion
- promotional mix

- pull policy
- push policy
- receiver
- selective demand
- source (in communication process)

Issues for discussion and review

1 What is the major task of promotion? Do companies ever use promotion to accomplish this task and fail? If so, give several examples.

2 What does the term 'integrated marketing communications' mean? Why should communication be integrated?

3 What is communication? What possible difficulties could marketers face during the communication process when consumers encode and decode messages being conveyed to them? How can this be avoided?

4 Identify several causes of noise. How can a sender reduce noise?

5 How do companies retain customer loyalty, create awareness and stimulate demand through their promotional activities?

6 How do target-market characteristics determine which marketing communications-mix variables to include in a marketing mix? Assume that a company is planning to promote a breakfast cereal to both adults and children. How would these two promotional efforts have to differ from each other?

7 How can a product's characteristics affect the composition of its promotion mix?

8 Why is it important to match communication style with product features?

9 Why should communication style be matched with target market characteristics?

10 How do promotional methods vary at different stages in product life cycles? Explain with examples.

11 Explain the difference between a pull policy and a push policy. Under what conditions should each policy be used?

12 Which criticisms of promotion do you believe are the most valid? Why? Suggest actions marketers could use to counteract such criticism.

13 Should organisations be allowed to promote offensive, violent, sexual or unhealthy products that can be sold and purchased legally? Support your answer with recent examples.

Marketing applications

1 Identify three TV commercials, one appealing to consumers' rational needs, another to their emotional needs and the third to their sense of morality. Describe each commercial, and discuss how each attempts to achieve its objective.

2 Suppose that marketers at Microsoft Surface tablet have come to you for recommendations on how they should promote their products. They want to develop a comprehensive promotional campaign and they have a generous budget with which to implement their plans. What questions will you ask them, and what will you suggest they consider before developing a promotional program?

3 Identify a product for which marketers should use a push policy, another for which a pull policy would be appropriate and a third product that might best be promoted using a mix of the two policies. Explain your answers.

4 Many factors need to be considered when developing a promotion mix, including the type of product and the product's attributes. Which of the four promotional methods – advertising, personal selling, public relations or sales promotion – would you emphasise if you were developing the promotion mix for the following products? Explain your answers.

  a Washing machine
  b Cereal
  c Mobile data service/SIM card
  d Students carpooling to university (i.e. students from the same area travelling together and taking turns to drive).

ONLINE EXERCISE

5 Familiarise yourself with the Advertising Standards Bureau website (http://www.adstandards.com.au)

   a Identify key areas that are likely to cause an advertisement to be determined inappropriate (look for 'determination summaries'). Provide a brief explanation for each key heading.

   b Explain why a self-regulating system is more beneficial to the advertising industry than government legislation.

   c Provide a summary of recent advertisements that attracted complaints. Why do you think these advertisements were viewed as offensive by Australian consumers? Can you think of an advertisement that offended receivers simply because the media (channel) used was inappropriate?

Developing your marketing plan

A vital component of a successful marketing strategy is a company's plan for communicating with its stakeholders. A segment of the communications plan is included in the marketing mix as the marketing communications-mix element. Developing a promotional plan requires a clear understanding of the role that promotion plays and the different ways to promote products. The following questions should assist you in relating the information in this chapter to several decisions in your marketing plan.

1 Review the communication process in Figure 12.2. Identify the different players in the communication process for promoting your product.

2 What are your objectives for promotion?

3 What are the characteristics of your product (or service)? What type of marketing communication is most suited to your product type?

4 Who is in your target market?

5 What media is best suited to communicating with your target market? What alternative or support promotions could you use?

6 What is the likely 'noise' reducing the impact of your communication with your target market? Suggest ways to overcome this 'noise'.

 # CengageNOW

Go to http:\\login.cengagebrain.com to link to CengageNOW, your online study tool. First take the Pre-Test for this chapter to get your Personalised Study Plan, and then:

 * **Revise** your knowledge of target market characteristics with online flashcards.

 * **Watch** an interactive animation of the communication process.

 * **Listen** to an audio summary to refresh your knowledge of social media-based marketing.

After you have completed the activities in your Personalised Study Plan take the Post-Test to determine what concepts you have mastered and what you still need to work on.

Case study

PROMOTING AN ALTERNATIVE TO THE SMARTPHONE

The Australian mobile phone market is one of the strongest in the world, showing substantial growth and continuing to expand steadily as late adopters purchase phones. Any global trends are likely to be mirrored in this market.

It is the next stage in the development of the mobile phone market that has the industry buzzing. A Nielsen Research report shows that, while statistics on mobile phone ownership are difficult to accurately predict because at least 20 per cent of Australians own more than one phone, it is known that at least 86 per cent of Australians own a mobile phone.[50] Phones with an advanced operating system are referred to as smartphones while those without a touch screen and advanced operating system are called feature phones. Telstra's Research Director, Foad Fadaghi reported that 'More than 50 per cent of Australians have a smartphone, so we are now looking to the second half of the population, that don't have the economic means, and are relying on "hand me downs" and things like that. That market has really gravitated towards lower end products'.[51] Fadaghi indicated that there is a market for lower price-point phones and plans. Market leader Apple iPhone has shown little interest in pursuing this market, while Samsung with the Android operating system has some lower-priced products.

It came as no great surprise to junior account manager Daniel Knights, a keen marketer who constantly updates his knowledge of mobile communication devices, that a new competitor would eventually enter the mobile phone market. He was delighted when Geoffrey Bowll, Managing Director of Starship Advertising, offered him the opportunity to prepare a fully integrated promotion campaign to launch a new mobile phone developed by a Chinese manufacturer that would retail at about half the price of the smartphone devices currently being

Source: Getty Images

sold by Apple and Samsung. The new phone would have a touch screen but limited capabilities for video and data downloads. He knew the main users of the lower priced 'feature' phones were likely to be the very young who had been given 'hand me downs' and were connected on pay-as-you-go plans, males in the 45–65 age group and those who had owned their mobile phone for a considerable period. More research was needed to provide insights into this campaign.

He started to plan the task in hand. He knew that a fully integrated promotional plan was essential for this market and the target audience was most likely different to the target market. Younger consumers relied on their parents to make the purchase and they needed to be informed and convinced about the product. This would mean communicating with at least two distinctly different audiences. Likewise, to reach the non-phone users and the more senior groups such as the 45–65-age cohorts, would mean that besides reaching these distinct groups, the campaign would need to involve those who provide advice and influence their decision making.

He pondered on the list of media that might be required for this diverse audience and realised that besides traditional TV, print ads, brochures, radio, in-store retail, ambient (taxi, train and billboard) and shopping-centre promotions, the campaign would need to reach those already online with mobile devices who currently use the web to search for information. This cohort currently use their phones, tablets and computers and source information from social media such as Facebook, Youtube clips and online banner

advertising. The task offered Daniel the opportunity to demonstrate the breadth of his promotional management expertise and he welcomed the challenge.

Wayne Binney
Deakin University, Melbourne

QUESTIONS FOR DISCUSSION

1 Help Daniel define and estimate the market by setting out an analysis of the possible target markets and target audiences. Both of these need to be prioritised for the phone manufacturer.

2. What key messages would be conveyed and how would you ensure that it is fully integrated across the audiences so

that there is a consistent story being conveyed to each audience?

3 Try to estimate the reaction from the current phone manufacturers. Are retailers required for this product introduction? If retailers were to be used as information providers, how could this message be coordinated?

Chapter endnotes

1. 'Canon drops $13m in biggest ever consumer push,' *Marketing*, April 15, 2013, accessed November 13, 2013, http://www.marketingmag.com.au/tags/integrated -campaign/#.UoLIXJ24bcs; 'Canon Australia launches biggest-ever integrated marketing campaign "No One Sees It Like You"', agencyne.ws, April 15, 2013, accessed November 13, 2013, http://agencyne.ws/canon-australia -launches-biggest-ever-integrated-marketing-campaign -no-one-sees-it-like-you-2/; 'Canon campaign says "No One Sees It Like You"' *Mumbrella*, April 18, 2013, accessed November 13, 2013, http://mumbrella.com.au/canons -13-million-campaign-says-no-one-sees-it-like-you-151111; Keith Shipton, 'Canon sinks $13 mil into new campaign and consumer website,' photocounter, April 18, 2013, accessed November 13, 2013, http://www.photocounter. com.au/2013/canon-sinks-13-mil-into-new-campaign -and-consumer-website/; Nadia Cameron, 'Canon invests in digital platforms to drive $13m consumer campaign,' *CMO*, April 17, 2013, accessed November 13, 2013, http://www.cmo.com.au/article/459301/canon_invests _digital_platforms_drive_13m_consumer_campaign/; 'Canon launches it biggest promotion,' *Connected Media*, October 23, 2008, http://www.connectedaustralia.com /News/BreakingNews/tabid/119/selectmoduleid/579 /ArticleID/769/reftab/91/Default.aspx; 'Guy Sebastian named the new face of Canon,' *Marketing*, November 7, 2013, accessed November 13, 2013, http://www .marketingmag.com.au/news/guy-sebastian-names-the -new-face-of-canon-46047/#.UoLN8524bcs.

2. 'Bundy cracks open its Road to Recovery flood relief campaign,' *B&T*, March 8, 2013, http://www.bandt.com.au /news/creative/bundy-cracks-open-its-road-to-recovery -flood-relief.

3. 'Advertisers face IMC challenges,' WARC, April 30, 2013, accessed August 23, 2013, http://www.warc.com /LatestNews/News/EmailNews.news?ID=31331&Origin =WARCNewsEmail#wgsSBb8jHZHFTjY7.99.

4. 'About Us,' Bangonabeanie Campaign website, accessed January 28, 2014, https://bangonabeanie.com.au/#about -us; 'With millions of people banging on and on about 'bangonabeanie', perhaps it's time you joined us?' *Synapse*, April 2013, accessed November 25, 2013, http://synapse .org.au/newsletters.aspx?contentId=2303.

5. S. Madhavaram, V. Badrinarayanan, and R. E. McDonald, 'Integrated marketing communication (IMC) and brand identity as critical components of brand equity strategy: A conceptual framework and research propositions,' *Journal of Advertising* 34:4 (2005): 69–80.

6. Darren Davidson, 'Spending on internet ads to overtake TV ads in 2013 for first time,' *B&T*, June 19, 2013, accessed August 23, 2013, http://www.bandt.com.au /news/advertising/gecko-s-reveals-fucking-brave-rebrand.

7. Terence A. Shimp, *Advertising, Promotion, and Supplemented Aspects of Integrated Marketing Communications* (Fort Worth: Dryden Press, 2000), 117.

8. Salvador Ruiz and María Sicilia, 'The Impact of Cognitive and/or Affective Processing Styles on Consumer Response to Advertising Appeals,' *Journal of Business Research* 57 (2004): 657–664.

9. Anne Majumdar, 'Gecko's fucking brave rebrand,' *Bandt*, 17 January, 2013, accessed August 23, 2013Http://www .bandt.com.au/news/advertising/gecko-s-reveals-fucking -brave-rebrand.

10. Samuel D. Bradley III and Robert Meeds, 'The Effects of Sentence-Level Context, Prior Word Knowledge, and Need for Cognition on Information Processing of

Technical Language in Print Ads,' *Journal of Consumer Psychology* 14, no. 3 (2004): 291–302.

11. 'Green marketing and the Australian Consumer Law,' ACCC, March 11, 2011, accessed January 28, 2014, http://www.accc.gov.au/system/files/Green%20marketing%20and%20the%20ACL.pdf, http://www.accc.gov.au/publications/green-marketing-and-the-australian-consumer-law; Bryan Walker, 'Greenwash: Big Brands and Carbon Scams,' *Hot Topic*, October 18, 2012, accessed January 28, 2014, http://hot-topic.co.nz/greenwash-big-brands-and-carbon-scams/.

12. David M. Szymanski, 'Modality and Offering Effects in Sales Presentations for a Good Versus a Service,' *Journal of the Academy of Marketing Science* 29, no. 2 (2001): 179–189.

13. Zeinab Rostami, Mohammad Reza Abedi, and W. B. Schaufeli, 'Does interest predict burnout?' *Interdisciplinary Journal of Contemporary Research in Business* (2012); Alessandro Iannuzzi, 'Understanding advertising appeals,' MBA&Company, April 4, 2013, accessed June 4, 2013, http://blog.mbaco.com/understanding-advertising-appeals/.

14. Mark Toncar, and Marc Fetscherin, 'A study of visual puffery in fragrance advertising: Is the message sent stronger than the actual scent?' *European Journal of Marketing* 46.1/2 (2012): 52–72.

15. 'Optus new concept 'Yes' Store,' Greatergroup, 2013, accessed January 28, 2013, http://www.greatergroup.com.au/optus-new-concept-yes-store/; Claire Reilly, 'Optus goes solo in retail with new format,' Retailbiz, March 12, 2013, accessed January 28, 2013, http://www.retailbiz.com.au/2013/03/12/article/Optus-goes-solo-in-retail-with-new-format/QULTHQMZCN.html.

16. S. M. Choi, N. J. Rifon, C. S. Trimble, and B. B. Reece, 'Information content in magazine, television and web advertising: a comparison and update,' *The Marketing Management Journal* 16, 1 (2006): 188–203.

17. S. Verma, 'Do all advertising appeals influence consumer purchasing decision: An exploratory study,' *Global Business Review* 10, 1 (2009): 33–43.

18. Ibid.

19. J. Hansen, M. Strick, R. B. van Baaren, M. Hooghuis, and D. H. J. Wigboldus, 'Exploring memory for product names advertised with humour,' *Journal of Consumer Behaviour* 8 (2009): 135–148.

20. Freitas, Elsa-Simões-Lucas, and Paulo Ribeiro-Cardoso, 'What makes an ad enjoyable? Analysing advertising appeals as viewed by Portuguese consumers.' (2012).

21. S. M. Choi, N. J. Rifon, C. S. Trimble, and B. B. Reece, 'Information content in magazine, television and web advertising: a comparison and update.'

22. Anne Majumdar, 'Gecko's fucking brave rebrand.'

23. S. M. Choi, N. J. Rifon, C. S. Trimble, and B. B. Reece, 'Information content in magazine, television and web advertising: a comparison and update.'

24. Ibid.

25. B. Glanville, 'CEOs rough it for homeless fundraiser,' abc.net.au (19 June, 5 August, 2010) http://www.abc.net.au/news/stories/2009/06/19/2602704.htm; '2010 Vinnies CEO Sleepout – Rise to the Challenge,' The Vinnies CEO Sleepout Team (2010): http://www.vinnies.org.au

/ceo-sleepout-2010-act; 'TAC News,' Transport Accident Commission, accessed 5 August, 2010, http://www.tac.vic.gov.au/jsp/corporate/homepage/home.jsp?s_kwcid=TC|9327|t.a.c||S|b|4289835771&gclid=CPPP0anfoaMCFQPMbwod0W7g3Q.

26. M. Ligerakis, 'Re-thinking red meat,' 5 September, 2003: http://www.bandt.com.au/features/re-thinking-red-meat.

27. 'Welcome to Quitnow Website,' Australian Government Department of Health and Ageing, 26 February, 2010: http://www.quitnow.info.au/.

28. 'Mount Franklin extends its iconic pink lids campaign,' Mount Franklin, 2012, Media Release, http://ccamatil.com/InvestorRelations/md/2012/'MountFranklin'_Pink.pdf (accessed June 7, 2013).

29. 'Celebrities like Delta Goodrem help rise consumers' awareness of this valuable cause,' McHappy Day, http://www.mchappyday.com.au/ (accessed June 7, 2013).

30. 'Adshel Mobile – Sherlock Holmes,' adshel.com.au, (2010): http://www.adshel.com.au/how/insights/casestudies/detail/index_html?content_id=27354; 'Commonwealth Bank gets into music in interactive outdoor ads,' Mumbrella, 24 March, 2010, http://mumbrella.com.au/commbank-gets-into-music-in-interactive-outdoor-ads-21396; A. Saenz, 'Interactive Billboards That Talk To Your Phone – Welcome to Marketing 2.0 (video),' February 8, 2011, http://singularityhub.com/2011/02/08/interactive-billboards-that-talk-to-your-phone-welcome-to-marketing-2-0-video/.

31. 'Product Launch Winner: Cornetto Enigma,' IAB Australia, 2013, http://www.iabaustralia.com.au/-/media/IAB/Resources/IAB%20Awards%20Case%20Study/2012/Product%20Launch%20Winner.ashx (accessed August 24, 2013); 'Media Release: The Monkeys raise the bar to win Creative Showcase 6.5,' IAB Australia, April 11, 2012, accessed August 24, 2013, http://iabaustralia.com.au/en/About%20IAB/Media%20Releases/2012%20-%20The%20Monkeys%20raise%20the%20bar%20to%20win%20Creative%20Showcase%206-5.aspx?&p=1.

32. T. Wasserman, 'Electronic Billboards in London Deliver Special Messages to Mini Drivers,' *Mashable.com*, September 6, 2013, accessed November 25, 2013, http://mashable.com/2013/09/06/london-mini-billboards/?utm_campaign=Mash-BD-Synd-Pulse-Bus-Full&utm_cid=Mash-BD-Synd-Pulse-Bus-Full&utm_medium=feed&utm_source=rss&utm_medium=referral&utm_source=pulsenews.

33. N. Bakos, 'From apping to tapping,' *U Talk Marketing*, March 5, 2013, accessed April 3, 2013, http://www.utalkmarketing.com/Pages/Article.aspx?ArticleID=23575&title=From%20apping%20to%20tapping; N. Bakos, 'How to turn branded content into powerful high-tech marketing with NFC,' The Marketer, March 27, 2013, accessed April 3, 2013, http://blog.themarketer.co.uk/2013/03/how-to-turn-branded-content-into-powerful-high-tech-marketing-with-nfc/; J. Carter, 'What is NFC and why is it in your phone? NFC is coming to the UK - but what can you do with it?' *Techradar*, January 16, 2013, accessed April 3, 2013, http://www.techradar.com/au/news/phone-and

-communications/what-is-nfc-and-why-is-it-in-your
-phone-948410; S. Clark, 'South Downs Way gets NFC
sign posts,' NFC World, January 11, 2013, accessed April 4,
2013, http://www.nfcworld.com/2013/01/11/321877
/south-downs-way-gets-nfc-sign-posts/; M. Clinch, 'After
Apple Snub, Can This Mobile Payment Method Take
Off?' CNBC.com, 28 February, 2013, accessed April 3,
2013, http://www.cnbc.com/id/100504466; M. Keferl,
'Near-Field Communication Is Shifting Marketing in
Japan: Brands From Revlon to Gap and Sony Are Using
Technology for Payments, Identity Verification,' Ad Age, June
12, 2012, accessed April 3, 2013, http://adage
.com/article/global-news/field-communication-shifting
-marketing-japan/235246(); K. Smith-Strickland, 'Outdoor
NFC Campaign Promotes Australian Launch of Zero
Dark Thirty,' NFC Times, January 16, 2013, accessed April 3,
2013, http://nfctimes.com/news/outdoor-nfc
-campaign-promotes-australian-launch-zero-dark-thirty;
F. Smith-Strickland, 'Australian Mobile Operator Telstra
Expands NFC Tag Campaign, Mobile News,' February 20,
2013, accessed April 4, 2013 http://nfctimes.com
/news/australian-mobile-operator-telstra-expands-nfc-tag
-campaign, accessed April 4, 2013.

34. 'Returns & Refunds,' AVG (AU/NZ), 2010, http://www
    .avg.com.au/terms/refunds/.

35. 'Qantas Club Membership,' Qantas, http://www.qantas
    .com.au/fflyer/dyn/program/usingPoints/qantas-club
    -membership?alt_cam=au:ff:WelcomeMicrosite:200906:A
    ustralia:UsingPointsFlying:WOWlaunch:QantasClubMem
    bership:TextLink.

36. 'FAQs,' Waze, 2013, http://www.waze.com/faq/#1
    (accessed August 24, 2013); Waze, http://www.waze.com/
    (accessed August 24, 2013).

37. 'Mother's energetic campaign with Call of Duty,' B&T,
    August 22, 2013, http://www.bandt.com.au/breaking-
    campaigns/mother-s-energetic-campaign-with-call-of-duty
    (accessed August 24, 2013).

38. 'Bus Advertising,' Bus Advertising, http://busadvertising
    .com.au/bus-advertising.html.

39. Adshel Mobile – Sherlock Holmes,' adshel.com
    .au, (2010): http://www.adshel.com.au/how/insights
    /casestudies/detail/index_html?content_id=27354;
    'Commonwealth Bank gets into music in interactive
    outdoor ads,' Mumbrella, 24 March, 2010,
    http://mumbrella.com.au/commbank-gets-into-music
    -in-interactive-outdoor-ads-21396; A. Saenz, 'Interactive
    Billboards That Talk To Your Phone – Welcome to
    Marketing 2.0 (video),' February 8, 2011,
    http://singularityhub.com/2011/02/08/interactive-
    billboards-that-talk-to-your-phone-welcome-to
    -marketing-2-0-video/; 'Global Trends,' Adshels, 2013,
    http://adshel.com.au/blog/global-trends-march13/
    (accessed June 11, 2013); 'Out-of-Home is moving on up,'
    B&T, 2013, http://www.bandt.com.au/news/media
    /out-of-home-is-moving-on-up (accessed June 11, 2013);
    C. Scharf, 'The Importance of Innovation in Outdoor
    Advertising,' Trend Reports, 2013, www.trendreports.com/
    article/outdoor-advertising (accessed June 11, 2013);
    'Digital Outdoor: Opportunities of going digital,' Stroer,
    www.stroer.pl/innovations/digital-outdoor?language=en

(accessed June 11, 2013); 'Outdoor Advertising Facial
& Gesture Recognition Technology,' JCDecaux – One
World, 2012, www.jcdecaux-oneworld.com/2012/05
/facial-gesture-recognition-outdoor-adverts/ (accessed
June 11, 2013); M. Ross, 'New technology promises
interactive outdoor advertising,' B&T, 2011,
http://www.bandt.com.au/news/latest-news/new-
technology-promises-interactive-outdoor-advert
(accessed June 11, 2013); R. Hicks, 'The future of outdoor
advertising?' mUmBRELLA, 2012, http://mumbrella.com
.au/the-future-of-outdoor-advertising-96141 (accessed
June 11, 2013).

40. Don Reisinger, 'The Internet is becoming more mobile by
    the day,' CNET, 2013, http://news.cnet.com/8301-1023_3
    -57586644-93/the-internet-is-becoming-more-mobile-by
    -the-day/?part=pulse&subj=latest-news&tag=title&utm
    _medium=referral&utm_source=pulsenews (accessed
    June 7, 2013).

41. John Eaton, 'e-Word-of-Mouth Marketing,' Teaching
    Module (Boston: Houghton Mifflin Company, 2006).

42. 'Global Advertising: Consumers Trust Real Friends and
    Virtual Strangers the Most,' NielsenWire, July 7, 2009,
    http://blog.nielsen.com/nielsenwire/consumer
    /global-advertising-consumers-trust-real-friends-and
    -virtualstrangers-the-most/ (accessed April 19, 2011).

43. 'Singer gets his revenge on United Airlines and soars to
    fame,' The Guardian, http://www.theguardian.com/news
    /blog/2009/jul/23/youtube-united-breaks-guitars-video
    (accessed June 11, 2013); K. Gibbons, 'United Airlines lose
    millions following YouTube complaint song,' SeOptimise,
    2009, http://www.seoptimise.com/blog/2009/07/united
    -airlines-lose-millions-youtube.html (accessed June 11,
    2013); K. Parker, 'Carroll's broken guitar has clear story to
    tell,' Herald Business, 2012, http://thechronicleherald
    .ca/business/131860-carroll-s-broken-guitar-has-clear
    -story-to-tell (accessed June 11, 2013); A. Broverman, 'The
    'United Breaks Guitars' Guy Resolves Your Consumer
    Complaints,' Walletpop, http://www.walletpop
    .ca/blog/2012/09/17/the-united-breaks-guitars-guy
    -resolves-your-consumer-complaint/ (accessed
    June 11, 2013).

44. Tom de Castella, 'What makes ads controversial?' BBC
    News, May 12, 2011, http://www.bbc.co.uk/news
    /magazine-13372751 (accessed June 4, 2013); Tom de
    Castella, 'What is it that really offends people about
    adverts?' BBC News, July 31, 2012, http://www.bbc.co.uk
    /news/magazine-19048807 (accessed June 4, 2013).

45. The Advertising Standards Bureau, http://www
    .adstandards.com.au/ (accessed June 4, 2013).

46. 'A year of language and lifestyle choices - 10 most
    complained about ads for 2012,' Advertising Standards
    Bureau, 2012, Media Release, http://post.cre8ive.com
    .au/t/ViewEmail/r/B7B067F3912C9953 (accessed June 4,
    2013).

47. Amy Kellow, 'Coles guilty of deceptive bread slogans:
    ACC,' Ad News, June 12, 2013, http://www.adnews.com
    .au/adnews/coles-guilty-of-deceptive-bread-slogans-accc
    (accessed August 26, 2013).

48. 'Positive Body Image Awards,' youth.gov.au, August 9,
    2013, http://www.youth.gov.au/sites/youth/bodyimage

/awards/pages/default (accessed December 4, 2013); 'Body Image,' youth.gov.au, August 9, 2013, http://www.youth.gov.au/sites/Youth/bodyImage (accessed December 4, 2013); Bonnie Malkin, 'Australia to force magazines to carry airbrush warning,' Telegraph UK, June 29, 2010, http://www.telegraph.co.uk/news/worldnews /australiaandthepacific/australia/7860766/Australia-to -force-magazines-to-carry-airbrush-warning.html (accessed December 4, 2013); Deni Kirkova, 'We have a moral obligation to ban the airbrush: Debenhams vows not to retouch model shots... and calls on others to follow suit,' Dailymail UK, June 13, 2013, http://www.dailymail.co.uk/femail/article-2340800 /Retailers-moral-obligation-ban-airbrush-Debenhams -spearheads-ban-retouched-model-shots-calls-follow-suit .html#ixzz2cs1A74gp (accessed December 4, 2013); Joe Berkowitz, 'Dove Canada uses photoshop Trojan horse to shame potential body-shamers,' Fast Company, March 6, 2013, http://www.fastcocreate.com/1682534 /dove-canada-uses-photoshop-trojan-horse-to-shame

-potential-body-shamers (accessed December 4, 2013); Tim Nudd, 'Ad of the Day: Dove Ogilvy's Photoshop hacktivism is clever but questionable for a brand built on honesty,' Ad Week, March 11, 2013, http://www.adweek .com/news/advertising-branding/ad-day-dove-147846 (accessed December 4, 2013); 'The Dove Campaign for Real Beauty,' Dove, http://www.dove.us/social-mission /campaign-for-real-beauty.aspx (accessed December 4, 2013).

49. Jenna Clarke, 'Not so dumb: Ad catches on in big way at Cannes,' Canberra Times, June 24, 2013, http://www .canberratimes.com.au/business/media-and-marketing /not-so-dumb-ad-catches-on-in-big-way-at-cannes -20130623-2or15.html (accessed August 26, 2013).
50. Nielson Research (2013), 'The Mobile Consumer-A Global Snapshot', http://www.slideshare.net/duckofdoom /mobile-consumerreport2013-17748641.
51. Paul Smith, '2013 mobile battleground takes shape', Financial Review, 24 December 2012.

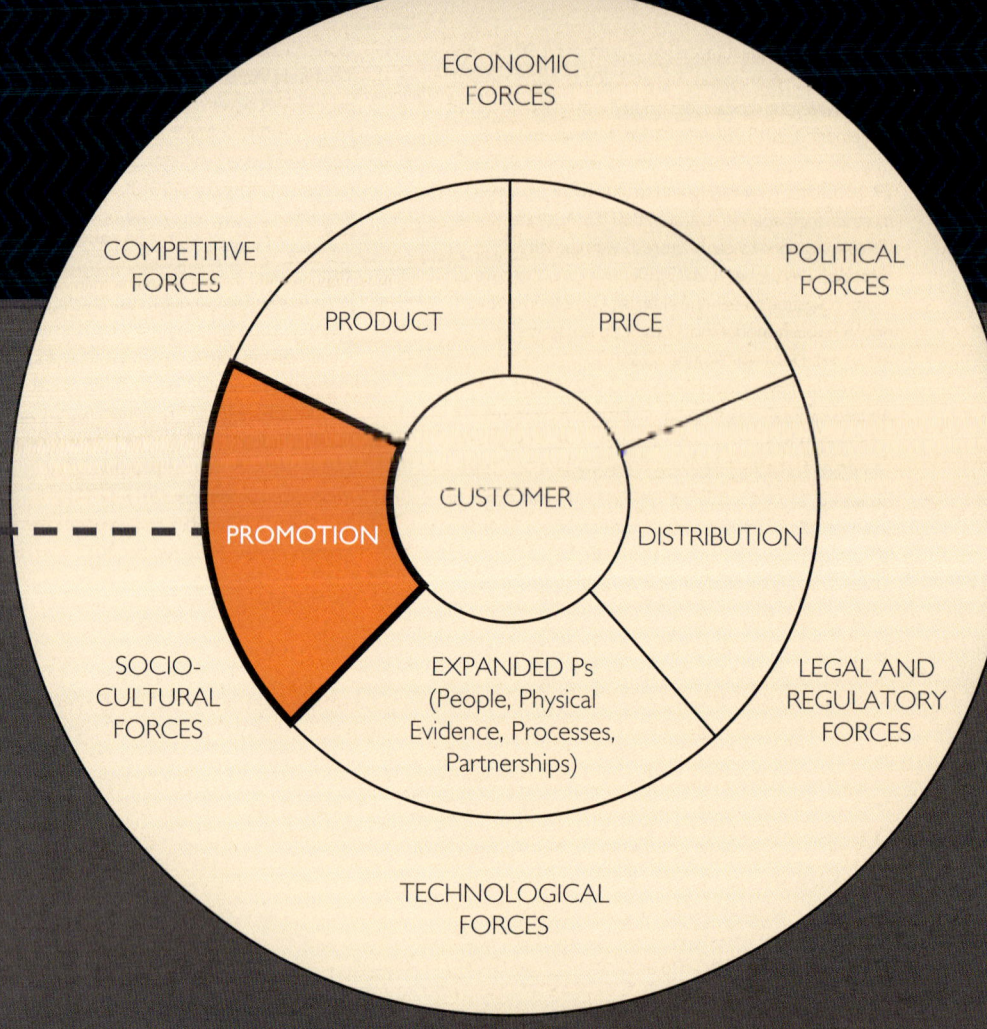

MARKETING COMMUNICATIONS MIX VARIABLES: APPLICATION

Advertising
- Developing an advertising campaign
- Executing the campaign and evaluating advertising effectiveness
- Advertising you should be aware of

Product placement

Public relations
- Public relations tools

Sponsorship
- Common types of sponsorship
- Evaluating the effectiveness of sponsorship
- Dealing with unfavourable sponsorship contracts

Personal selling
- The personal selling process
- Managing the sales force

Sales promotion
- Consumer sales promotion methods
- Trade sales promotion methods

   Throughout this chapter, Watch, Listen and Revise icons indicate an opportunity for online self-study through CengageNOW, linking you to animated chapter overviews, interactive diagrams, videos, quizzes and more.

MARKETING COMMUNICATIONS MIX VARIABLES: APPLICATION

Learning Objectives

LO1 Understand how to use advertising as a marketing communications tool

LO2 Appreciate the power of product placement as a promotional method

LO3 Understand how public relations practices can be used to influence company/brand reputation

LO4 Appreciate the power of successful sponsorship arrangements whilst being aware of potential mishaps linked to sponsorship deals

LO5 Comprehend the personal selling practices for both consumer and trade sales situations

LO6 Describe sales promotion methods used for consumer markets as well as trade sales.

MARKETING CHALLENGE | L'ORÉAL SLOGAN CELEBRATES 40 YEARS OF EMPOWERING WOMEN

A successful company slogan may only be a few words in length, but it is a key factor in telling the story behind the brand. As brands and consumer tastes evolve, many companies change their advertising slogans over time. French cosmetics brand L'Oréal Paris is an exception. Changes to the company slogan 'Because I'm Worth It' have been limited to pronouns (it recently changed its slogan to say 'Because We're Worth It'). The slogan has been translated into 40 languages and continues to be a part of most L'Oréal advertising.

L'Oréal's trademark slogan was created in 1971 during a time when women were seeking to become more empowered. Created by advertising agency McCann Erickson, the slogan first appeared in a

Source: © L'Oréal Paris, used with permission

commercial with actress Joanne Dusseau speaking the words while attempting to rationalise her L'Oréal purchases. Four decades later, L'Oréal celebrated 40 years of the slogan by throwing a large party attended by the company's brand ambassadors.

Although L'Oréal is the largest cosmetics company worldwide, selling an estimated 50 products per second, sales have slipped in recent years. Experts feel that the onset of the digital age and shorter attention spans may be making the slogan less effective and more outdated. Despite these concerns, L'Oréal Paris' CEO has announced that he intends to keep the advertising slogan. Although the slogan's sense of female empowerment may not be as relevant in Europe or America, he sees opportunity in Africa and Asia where women's rights are taking hold. Combine this with L'Oréal Paris' 30 brand ambassadors, who spend a significant amount of time promoting the slogan, and L'Oréal's brand might gain the same level of prominence as it had four decades ago[1].

MARKETING CHALLENGE QUESTIONS	**1** In your opinion, does this 40-year-old slogan still connect with women of today?	**2** Would this slogan be suitable for L'Oreal Men's skin care products as well?

Introduction

In today's complex world it is very difficult to achieve 100 per cent control over any of the marketing communications tools and therefore the need for an integrated marketing communications approach is even greater. The six most common elements of a marketing communications mix are advertising, personal selling, public relations, product placement, digital marketing communication and sales promotion (see Figure 13.1). For some products, companies use all six elements; for others, they use only two or three. For example, The IKEA 'Time for Living' campaign includes TV commercials, online content, print advertisements and a brochure (IKEA Manifesto 2013) and the Priceline Pharmacy's '30 days of fashion and beauty' campaign includes special events, in-store promotions/beauty workshops, TV, magazine advertisements and editorials, how-to videos online, catalogues and social media activity.[2]

In Chapter 12 the broader concepts of promotion and integrated marketing communications were introduced. In this chapter we explore in more detail the marketing communications-mix elements of advertising, product placement, public relations, sponsorship, personal selling and sales promotion. We start with a detailed exploration of the eight steps involved in developing an advertising campaign, followed by a discussion on the growing trend of product placement in modern entertainment mediums and how sponsorship can be used for promotion. We then look into the powerful tools used in public relations. Next, the chapter outlines the seven steps in the personal selling process and the finishes with a discussion of the methods used in consumer sales and trade sales promotion methods. By the end of the chapter you will be familiar with the commonly used marketing communications-mix variables available to today's marketers.

Advertising

Advertising permeates our daily lives. At times, we may view it positively as a source of information or entertainment; at other times, we avoid it. Some advertisements inform, persuade, or entertain us; some bore or even offend us.

As mentioned in Chapter 12, advertising is a paid non-personal communication about an organisation and its products transmitted to a target audience through mass media, including TV, radio, the Internet, newspapers, magazines, direct mail, outdoor displays and signs on vehicles. Individuals and organisations use advertising to promote goods, services, ideas, issues and people. Advertising is the highly visible 'tip of the iceberg' of 'marketing' and many non-marketers assume (wrongly) that advertising is the only task performed by the

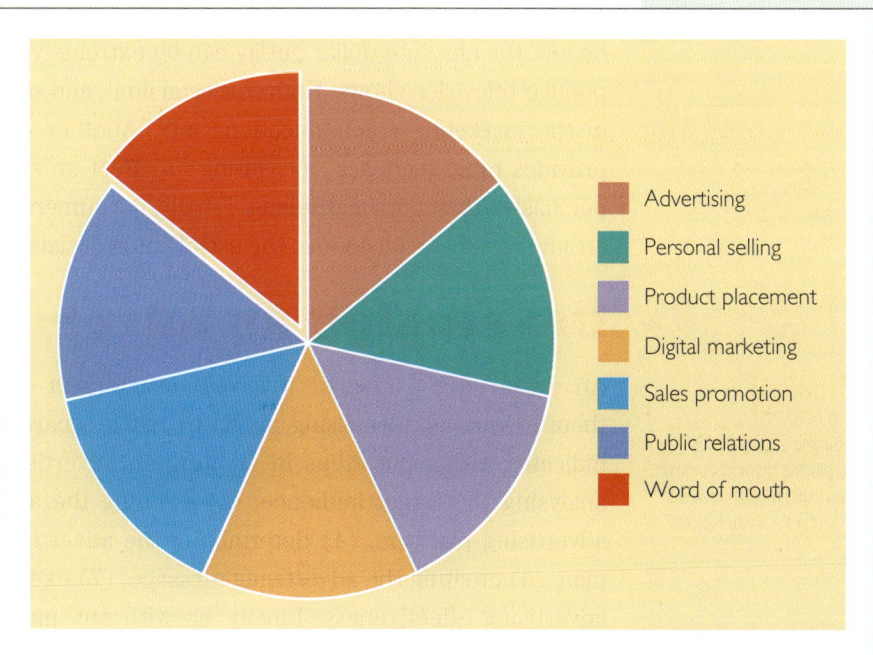

marketing department. Being highly flexible, advertising can reach an extremely large target audience or focus on a small, precisely defined segment. For instance, Pizza Hut's advertising focuses on a large audience of potential fast-food customers, ranging from children to adults, whereas an advertisement for Gulfstream jets is aimed at a much smaller and more specialised target market.

When asked to name major advertisers, most people immediately mention business organisations. However, many non-business companies, including governments, churches, universities and charitable organisations, employ advertising to communicate with stakeholders. Although we analyse advertising in the context of business organisations here, much

of the material in this chapter applies to all types of companies, including not-for-profit organisations and charities.

Advertising is also used in long-term campaigns to change our opinions of important community-based issues, such as the Transport Accident

FIGURE 13.1 THE SIX COMMON ELEMENTS OF A MARKETING COMMUNICATIONS MIX; WORD-OF-MOUTH COMMUNICATIONS IS INCLUDED EVEN THOUGH IT IS NOT 100 PER CENT CONTROLLED BY THE ORGANISATION

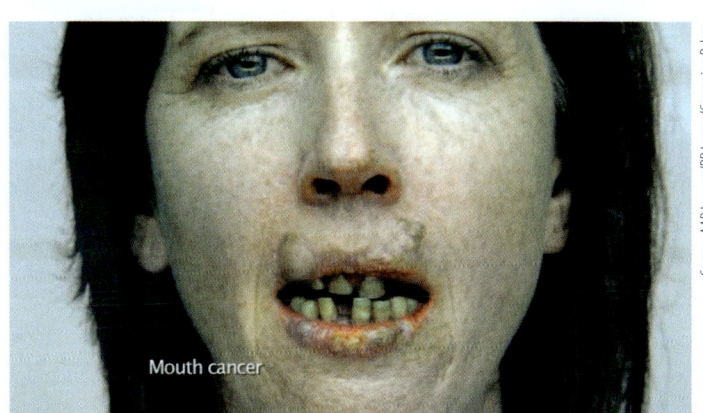

Source: AAP Images/PR Image/Campaign Palace

Mouth cancer

<< Advertising community-based issues
This anti-smoking campaign uses graphic images to show what smoking can do to your health

Commission campaign to reduce the Victorian road toll, discussed in Chapter 12, and the long-term anti-smoking campaign by Quit.

Advertising offers several benefits. It is cost-efficient, reaches a large number of people at a low cost per person and advertisements can be repeated several times. Today, clever ads can also incorporate touchable elements, interactivity, scents and sounds to generate a positive sensory feedback as well as a stronger positive persuasive communication.[3]

Advertising has disadvantages as well. Even though the cost per person reached may be low, the absolute dollar outlay can be extremely high, especially for commercials during popular television shows. High costs can limit, and sometimes prevent, the use of advertising in the marketing communications mix. Another disadvantage is that advertising rarely provides rapid feedback, measuring its effect on sales is difficult, and it is ordinarily less persuasive than personal selling. Finally, consumers give only a few seconds of attention to an advertisement. Of course, the use of 'infomercials' can increase exposure time for viewers.

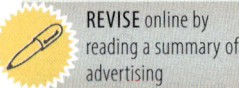

REVISE online by reading a summary of advertising

Developing an advertising campaign

advertising campaign
Designing a series of ads and placing them in various advertising media to reach a particular target audience

An advertising campaign involves designing a series of advertisements and placing them in various advertising media to reach a particular target audience. As Figure 13.2 indicates, the major steps in creating an advertising campaign are: (1) identifying and analysing the target audience, (2) defining the advertising objectives, (3) creating the advertising platform, (4) determining the advertising budget, (5) developing the media plan, (6) creating the advertising message, (7) executing the campaign and (8) evaluating advertising effectiveness. Finally, as with any management process we learn from our experiences and incorporate these lessons into future advertising processes (9). The number of steps and the exact order in which they are carried out may vary according to an organisation's resources, the nature of its product and the type of target audience to be reached. Nevertheless, these general guidelines for developing an advertising campaign are relevant for all types of organisations. The feedback from all steps is often ignored in marketing textbooks. As intelligent marketing professionals we learn from our mistakes

FIGURE 13.2 GENERAL STEPS IN DEVELOPING AND IMPLEMENTING AN ADVERTISING CAMPAIGN

and successes all the time; for example, if an advertising objective we thought was clearly communicated was misunderstood by our media planners we would insist on additional checks being built into the process of developing future advertising campaigns.

Identifying and analysing the target audience

The target audience is the group of people at whom ads are aimed. Advertisements for Barbie cereal are targeted towards young girls who play with Barbie dolls, whereas those for Special K cereal are directed at health-conscious adults. Identifying and analysing the target audience are critical actions as the information yielded helps to determine other steps in developing the campaign; for example, ads at petrol stations would benefit from a link to car driving or vehicle maintenance. The target audience for a campaign may include everyone in the company's target market or only a portion of the target market.

Advertisers research and analyse target audience to establish an information base for a campaign. Information commonly needed includes location and geographic distribution of the target group, the distribution of demographic factors such as age, income, ethnic origin, sex and education, lifestyle information, and consumer attitudes regarding purchase and use of both the advertiser's products and competing products. The exact kind of information an organisation finds useful depends on the type of product being advertised, the characteristics of the target audience as well as the type and amount of competition. Generally, the more an advertiser knows about the target audience, the more likely the company is to develop an effective advertising campaign. When the target audience is not precisely identified and properly analysed, the campaign may fail.

target audience
The group of people at whom advertisements are aimed

<< Target audience
Digital advertising at petrol stations aims to capture our attention during those few minutes it takes to fill up our car

Defining the advertising objectives

An advertiser's next step is to determine what the company hopes to accomplish with the campaign. Because advertising objectives guide campaign development, advertisers should define objectives carefully. Advertising objectives should be stated clearly, precisely and in measurable terms. Precision and measurability allow advertisers to evaluate advertising success at the end of a campaign in terms of whether or not objectives were met. To provide precision and measurability, advertising objectives should contain benchmarks and indicate how far the advertiser wishes to move from these standards. If the goal is to increase sales, the advertiser should state the current sales level (the benchmark) and the amount of sales increase sought through advertising. An advertising objective should also specify a timeframe so that advertisers know exactly how long they have to accomplish the objective. An advertiser with average monthly sales of $450 000 (the benchmark) might set the following objective: 'Our primary advertising objective is to increase average monthly sales from $450 000 to $540 000 within 12 months'.

If an advertiser defines objectives on the basis of sales, the objectives focus on increasing absolute dollar sales or unit sales, increasing sales by a certain percentage or increasing the company's market share. Even if an advertiser's long-run goal is to increase sales, not all campaigns are designed to produce immediate sales. Some campaigns are designed to increase product or brand awareness, make consumers' attitudes more favourable or increase consumers' knowledge of product features. The type of objectives determines the execution of the advertising campaign.

Creating the advertising platform

Before launching a political campaign, party leaders develop a political platform stating the major issues on which the campaign is based. Like a political platform, an advertising platform consists of the basic issues or selling points that an advertiser wishes to include in an advertising campaign. For example, tablet computers are positioned as a convenient-on-the-go way to access the internet, e-mail and some basic functions of a computer. The low price, small size and light weight make these computers of interest to travellers, students and, increasingly, traditional laptop computer consumers as the performance of these ultra-portable computers improves.[4]

A single ad in an advertising campaign may contain one or several issues from the platform. Although the platform sets forth the basic issues, it does not indicate how to present them. An

advertising platform should consist of issues important to customers. One of the best ways to determine those issues is to survey customers about what they consider most important in the selection and use of the product involved.

Determining the advertising budget

The advertising budget is the total amount of money allocated for advertising for a specific time period. It is hard to decide how much to spend on advertising for a specific period because the potential effects of advertising are so difficult to measure precisely. We will now discuss the common steps in setting advertising budgets. First is a list of seven initial issues that must be considered when planning an advertising budget.

* Geographic size of the market and the distribution of buyers within the market.
* Type of product (frequency of purchase, cost of each transaction, e.g. B2B transactions require less advertising compared to fast moving consumer goods).

✳ Industry 'norms' regarding advertising frequency, chosen media and so on, e.g. highly competitive products like confectionaries require more frequent (and often more elaborate) campaigns.

✳ Company's position on a perceptual map and their desired position.

✳ The company's sales volumes versus competitors' sales volumes.

✳ How often will the advertising campaigns be reviewed? Many companies (or advertising agencies) review competitive spending on a quarterly basis, comparing competitors' dollar expenditures on print, radio and television with their own spending levels.

✳ Budgets should include contingency funds for unexpected events.

Table 13.1 summarises the common methods of deciding an advertising budget.

TABLE 13.1   COMMON METHODS OF SETTING ADVERTISING BUDGETS

Method	Description	Comments	Issues
Per cent-of-sales approach	Adjust past sales according to expected increase/decrease. Budget will be determined by a proportion of this adjustment. Exact percentage figures applied based on industry average or company tradition.	Very common method. Easy to implement.	Based on a flawed assumption that sales create advertising (and not vice versa). Could lead to vicious circle when reduction in expected sales (e.g. recession) leads to a reduced budget. Thus further diminishing sales.
Objective-and-task approach	Determine campaign objectives and list tasks that will achieve these objectives. Total budget determined by the total cost of these tasks.	The most logical approach. Useful especially if setting the budget for a new product type (i.e. when there are no past budgets to consult).	Difficult to estimate which tasks will achieve the campaign objectives.
Competition-matching approach	Aim to match the major competitors' budgets in absolute dollars or to allocate the same percentage of sales for advertising that competitors do.	Yes it is good to be aware of competitors' actions, but this method is not enough as the only determinant for an advertising budget, since competitors might have different promotional objectives and resources.	Simply following the trend is not a route to success. Misses the opportunity to 'stand out', to develop a unique selling proposition (USP) (a feature of a product or service that differentiates it from substitute products).
Arbitrary approach	A high-level executive in the company states how much to spend on advertising for a certain period.	Although hardly a scientific budgeting technique, it is expedient. Past experience and recent marketing research should be allowed to influence actual budget figures.	Often leads to underspending or overspending.

Developing the media plan

media plan
Specifies media vehicles and schedule for running ads

Getting your ads included in popular TV shows or magazines is very expensive. To derive maximum results from media expenditure, marketers must develop effective media plans. A media plan sets forth the exact media vehicles to be used (specific magazines, TV stations, newspapers and so forth) as well as the dates and times advertisements will appear. The plan focuses on how many people in the target audience will be exposed to a message and the frequency of exposure.

To formulate a media plan, planners select the media for campaigns and prepare a time schedule for each medium. A media planner's primary goal is to reach the largest number of people in the target audience that the budget will allow. A secondary goal is to achieve the appropriate message reach and frequency for the target audience while staying within budget. Reach refers to the percentage of consumers in the target audience actually exposed to a particular advertisement in a stated period. Frequency is the number of times these targeted consumers are exposed to the advertisement.

Media planners take many factors into account when devising a media plan. They analyse location and the demographic characteristics of people in the target audience, because people's tastes in media differ according to demographic groups and locations. With a fragmented media landscape the success of an advertising campaign relies heavily on understanding the media habits of the intended target market. Media planners also consider the size and type of audiences that specific media reach. The content of the message sometimes affects media choice. Print media can be used more effectively than broadcast media to present complex issues or numerous details in single ads.

Media are selected by weighing the various advantages and disadvantages of each as shown in Table 13.2.

TABLE 13.2   ADVANTAGES AND DISADVANTAGES OF MAJOR ADVERTISING MEDIA

Medium	Advantages	Disadvantages
Newspapers	Reaches large audience; purchased to be read; geographic flexibility; short lead time; frequent publication; favourable for cooperative advertising, merchandising services.	Not selective for socioeconomic groups or target market; short life; limited reproduction capabilities; large advertising volume limits exposure to any single advertisement.
Magazines	Demographic selectivity; good reproduction; long life; prestige; geographic selectivity when regional issues are available; read in leisurely manner.	High costs; 30- to 90-day average lead time; high level of competition; limited reach; communicates less frequently.
Direct mail	Little wasted circulation; highly selective; circulation controlled by advertiser; few distractions; personal; stimulates actions; use of novelty; relatively easy to measure performance; hidden from competitors.	Very expensive; lacks editorial content to attract readers; often thrown away unread as junk mail; criticised as invasion of privacy; consumers must choose to read the ad.
Radio	Reaches 95 per cent of consumers; highly mobile and flexible; very low relative costs; ad can be changed quickly; high level of geographic and demographic selectivity; encourages use of imagination.	Lacks visual imagery; short life of message; listeners' attention limited because of other activities; market fragmentation; difficult buying procedures; limited media and audience research.

Medium	Advantages	Disadvantages
Television	Reaches large audiences; high frequency available; dual impact of audio and video; highly visible; high prestige; geographic and demographic selectivity; difficult to ignore. Digital TV offers greater flexibility and allows for better targeting.	Very expensive; highly perishable message; size of audience not guaranteed; amount of prime time limited; lack of selectivity in target market.
Internet	Immediate response; potential to reach a precisely targeted audience; ability to track customers and build databases; highly interactive medium.	Costs of precise targeting are high; inappropriate ad placement; effects difficult to measure; concerns about security and privacy.
Yellow Pages	Wide availability; action and product category oriented; low relative costs; ad frequency and longevity; non-intrusive.	Market fragmentation; extremely localised; slow updating; lack of creativity; long lead times; requires large space to be noticed.
Outdoor	Allows for frequent repetition; low cost; message can be placed close to point of sale; geographic selectivity; operable 24 hours a day; high creativity and effectiveness.	Message must be short and simple; no demographic selectivity; seldom attracts readers' full attention; criticised as traffic hazard and blight on countryside; much wasted coverage; limited capabilities.

Sources: William F. Arens, Contemporary Advertising (Burr Ridge, IL: Irwin/McGraw-Hill, 2011); George E. Belch and Michael Belch, *Advertising and Promotion* (Burr Ridge, IL: Irwin/McGraw-Hill, 2011).

Like media selection decisions, media scheduling decisions are affected by numerous factors, such as target-audience characteristics, product attributes, product seasonality, customer media behaviour and size of the advertising budget. There are three general types of media schedules: continuous, flighting and pulsing. When a continuous schedule is used, advertising runs at a constant level with little variation throughout the campaign period. With a flighting schedule, advertisements run for set periods of time, alternating with periods in which no ads run. For example, an advertising campaign might have an ad run for two weeks, then suspend it for two weeks, and then run it again for two weeks. A pulsing schedule combines continuous and flighting schedules. During the entire campaign, a certain portion of advertising runs continuously, and during specific time periods of the campaign, additional advertising is used to intensify the level of communication with the target audience.

The changing media landscape

Declining broadcast television ratings and newspaper/magazine readership have led many companies to explore alternative media, including not only cable television and digital advertising but also ads on mobile phones and product placements in video games. New media such as social networking websites are also attracting advertisers due to their large reach. Research has found that, when advertising is a part of a social networking website, consumers need to see the advertising as beneficial, or it may lead them to abandon the website.[5]

Furthermore, the line between brand management and media activities is blurring with the emergence of owned media. The key goals for owned media are to entertain and inform target audiences as well as create exclusive environments where the brand (owner of the

owned media
Owned media describes media owned by organisations traditionally involved with branded goods and services. The original business focus of these companies was not media [6]

media) can be demonstrated. User generated content is often incorporated to increase customer involvement with the brand [7] For example, the Red Bull Media House operates TV stations and magazines, and develops cross-linked product deals for events, soap operas, music, games, films and documentaries. By contrast, Procter & Gamble has linked up with NBC Universal to target the baby boomer market with their Life Goes Strong bundle of websites.[8]

Digital marketing in particular is growing, with spending on online advertising expected to exceed $49 billion by 2015.[9] For example, the revenue predictions for mobile advertisements have to be frequently revised (Google is now expected to earn US$8.9 billion from mobile advertising in 2013, that is 56 per cent of the total mobile advertising market).[10] Digital technology is also introducing new ways for TV ads to reach specific target audiences, as the Marketing in Transition box below shows.

MARKETING IN TRANSITION | WILL TV ADVERTISING BE REVITALISED THROUGH TARGETED ADVERTISEMENTS?

Gracenote is a new ad replacement system from Sony that tracks what shows people watch on TV and combines this with geo demographic data based on household address (age, gender, income etc) to select the type of TV ads most appreciated by the residents. When there is a commercial break in a TV show viewers receive TV commercials most suited to their lifestyle. For example, whilst watching a popular TV show Mr Smith (a middle aged father of two with interest in fishing and camping) sees advertisements for 4x4 vehicles or fishing and camping gear during commercial breaks. By contrast, in a neighbour's house this commercial break is taken up by advertisements for spa breaks and designer jeans since the owner occupant is 35-year-old career-minded lawyer, Ms Jones.

Such 'precision targeting for TV ads' is made possible by monitoring resident's TV viewing preferences through a set-top box or smartTV functions. This Gracenote ad replacement technology is being trialled at the moment, and hopes to get incorporated into TV manufacturing from late 2013[11]

Printed magazines are also feeling the pinch from the emerging digital versions of established magazines, consumer created digital content (e.g. newsletters) as well as from competing (printed) magazines in an over fragmented market (i.e. too many specialist/niche magazines now compete for small target audiences). The increase in digital magazine subscriptions can be partly attributed to an increase in the number of Australians owning smartphones or tablets (Figure 13.3). According to the Audit Bureau of Circulation (ABC) figures from December 2012, the circulation for 'traditional women's monthly magazines' dropped by an average of 6 per cent (e.g. *Cleo* -24% and *Cosmopolitan* -16%) whereas health magazines reported a slight increase (e.g. *Women's Health* +0.3% and *Men's Fitness* +8.3%). The real boom areas for magazine circulation included home and lifestyle magazines (e.g. *Real Living* +15.3%). The increase in digital magazine subscriptions appears healthy, but it is too early to see a trend since digital magazine sales have only been reported since 1st July 2013.[12]

Digital media poses a threat to traditional print magazines but the new revenue opportunities digital magazines offer have prompted some publishers to maximise their use of digital channels, for example, Condé Nast (publisher for *Vogue, Vanity Fair* and *New Yorker*) are selling subscriptions to both print and digital magazines through Amazon.com.[13]

Smartphones can also be used for ad campaigns as consumers already use the multimedia functions on their mobile phones for entertainment. Future opportunities for targeted, permission-based promotions are endless (how does your smartphone use vary from the average? See Figure 13.4). Mobile phones are the perfect media for targeted promotions as consumers usually carry their phones at all times. Moreover, each phone can be identified and targeted to allow personalised promotions. GPS can make promotions location-based and multimedia enables interactive communications.

The challenge for mobile advertising is to capture the attention of their multitasking target audience in just a few seconds. Moreover, for a campaign to be successful, these consumers need instant gratification.[14] Worldwide mobile ad spending doubled from $4 billion in 2011 to $8.41 billion in 2012. By 2016 mobile advertising expenditure globally is expected to reach $37 billion.[15]

Despite the increase in adopting digital media, advertisers are constantly challenged by the unique characteristics of this medium as well as the fast pace of changing consumer preferences. Table 13.3 summarises common shortcomings associated with digital advertising.

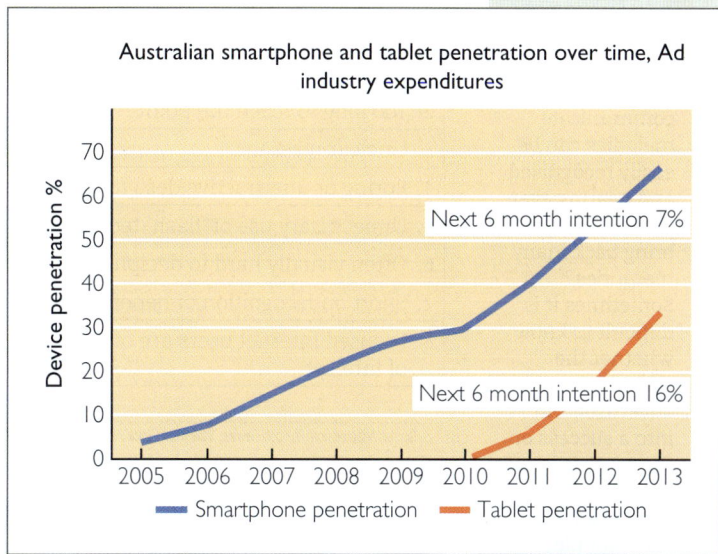

Source: IAB Australia, Australian Mobile Advertising Landscape, 2013, p.5, http://www .iabaustralia.com.au/uploads/uploads/2013-10/1382047200 _38df9ff3739286e374d73252834e624a.pdf.

FIGURE 13.3 TABLET AND SMARTPHONE OWNERSHIP IN AUSTRALIA

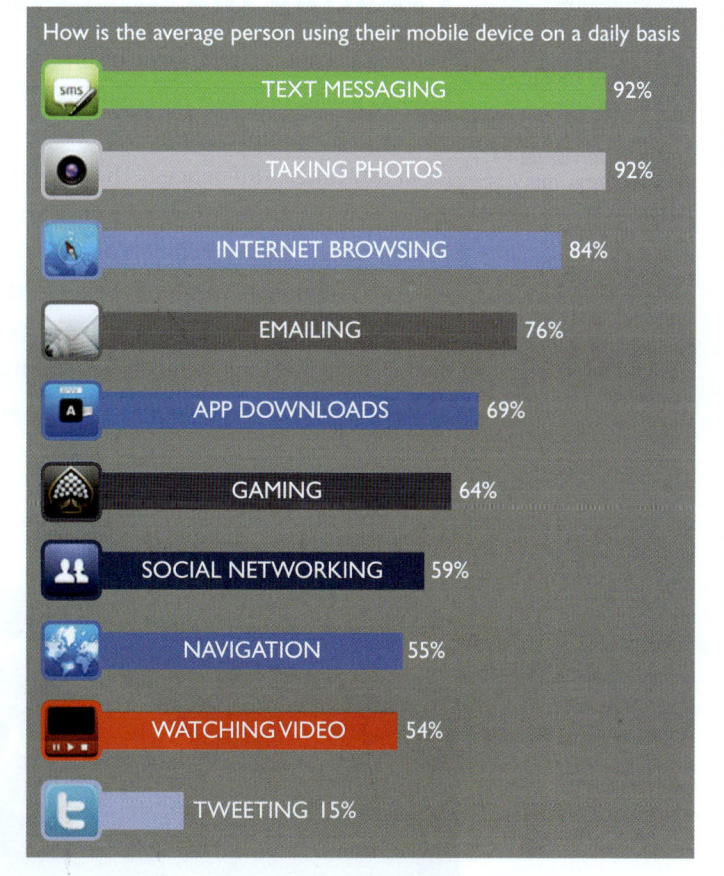

Source: http://www.anchormobile.net/

FIGURE 13.4 WHAT ARE SMARTPHONES REALLY USED FOR?

copy
The verbal portion of advertisements

Components of a print ad >>
This Jaguar ad contains most of the components of a print ad, including a headline, body copy, signature and illustration. It does not have a sub-headline

TABLE 13.3 SHORTCOMINGS OF DIGITAL ADVERTISING

1. Overly detail-focused
2. Too long to reach the point
3. Unclear message
4. Boring or unattractive design that fails to catch audience's attention
5. Unnecessary use of 'flash' technology that is not effective in reaching the target audience
6. Often visually hard to decipher or read
7. Short on recognition of benefits
8. Focused Internet users are often angered by promotions that do not deliver immediate messages of interest.

Source: Adapted from Phillip W. Sawyer, 'Why Most Digital Ads Still Fail to Work', *Advertising Age*, 27 January 2010, http://adage.com/digitalnext/post/article_id=141751 (accessed April 9, 2010).

Irrespective of the media channel, integrated marketing communications should use a communication style appropriate to the target audience and feature a coherent message that emphasises product benefits as well as brand themes. The next section outlines key issues in creating message content.

Creating the advertising message

The basic content and form of an advertising message are functions of several factors. A product's features, uses and benefits affect the content of the message. Characteristics of the people in the target audience – gender, age, education, race, income, occupation, lifestyle and other attributes – influence both content and form. When GlaxoSmithKline promotes Macleans Junior Jaws toothpaste for children, the company emphasises daily brushing and cavity control. For the adults, the company promotes the teeth whitening varieties of Macleans toothpaste.

To communicate effectively, advertisers use words, symbols and illustrations that are meaningful, familiar and attractive to people in the target audience. Sounds and music are also used in ads to grab attention and make the ads memorable. At times, the popularity of a song could be based on its use in an ad.

Source: © AP Images/PRNewsFoto/Jaguar North America

COPY

Copy is the verbal portion of an ad and may include headlines, sub-headlines, body copy and a signature. Not all advertising contains all these copy elements. Even handwritten notes on direct-mail advertising that say, 'Try this. It works!' seem to increase requests for free samples.[18] The headline is critical because it is often the only part of the copy that people read. It should attract readers' attention and create enough interest to make them want to read the body copy.

ARTWORK

Artwork consists of an ad's illustrations and layout. Although illustrations are often photographs, they can also be drawings, graphs, charts and tables. Illustrations can be more important in capturing attention than text or brand elements, independent of size.[19] Colours (or simple black and white) can make an advertisement stand out from competing messages. They are used to attract attention, encourage audiences to read or listen to the copy, communicate an idea quickly, or communicate ideas that are difficult to put into words.[20] Advertisers use various illustration techniques. They may show the product alone, in a setting, or in use, or they may show the results of its use. Illustrations also can be in the form of comparisons, contrasts and diagrams.

artwork
An ad's illustrations and layout

illustrations
Photos, drawings, graphs, charts and tables used to spark audience interest

layout
The physical arrangement of an ad's illustration and copy

Source: courtesy Beaurepaires

<< Colour versus black-and-white
This ad highlights the importance of using colour when advertising certain products

Executing the campaign and evaluating advertising effectiveness

Execution of an advertising campaign requires extensive planning and coordination because many tasks must be completed on time, as well as due to the high number of people and companies involved. This is achieved by creating and adhering to detailed schedules.

Advertising can be evaluated before, during and after the campaign. An evaluation performed before the campaign begins is called a pre-test. A pre-test usually attempts to evaluate the effectiveness of one or more elements of the message. To pre-test ads, marketers sometimes use a consumer panel, a group of actual or potential buyers of the advertised product.

pre-test
Evaluation of ads performed before a campaign begins

consumer panel
A group of a product's actual or potential buyers who pre-test ads

To measure advertising effectiveness during a campaign, marketers can use 'inquiries'. In a campaign's initial stages, an advertiser may use several ads simultaneously, each containing a coupon, form or a unique phone number linked to a specific ad through which potential customers can request information. In short, the number, as well as the type, of inquiries help in assessing the effectiveness of each ad as well as the type of media used. Advertisers record the number of inquiries returned from each type of ad. If an advertiser receives 78 528 inquiries from ad A, 37 072 from ad B and 47 932 from ad C, then ad A is judged superior to ads B and C.

post-test
Evaluation of advertising
effectiveness after the
campaign

Evaluation of advertising effectiveness after the campaign is called a post-test. Advertising objectives often determine what kind of post-test is appropriate. If the objectives focus on communication – to increase awareness of product features or brands or to create more favourable customer attitudes – the post-test should measure changes in these dimensions. For campaign objectives stated in terms of sales, advertisers should determine the change in sales or market share attributable to the campaign. However, changes in sales or market share brought about by advertising cannot be measured precisely. Many factors independent of ads affect a company's sales and market share. Competitors' actions, government actions and changes in economic conditions, consumer preferences and weather are only a few factors that might enhance or diminish a company's sales or market share. By using data about past sales, current sales and advertising expenditures, advertisers can make gross estimates of the effects of a campaign on sales or market share.

recognition test
A post-test in which
individuals are shown the
actual ad and asked if they
recognise it

Because it is difficult to determine the direct effects of advertising on sales, some advertisers evaluate ads according to how well consumers can remember them. Post-test methods based on memory include recognition and recall tests. Such tests are usually performed by research organisations through surveys. In a recognition test, respondents are shown the actual ad and asked whether they recognise it. If they do, the interviewer asks additional questions to determine how much of the ad each respondent observed. When recall is evaluated, the respondents are not shown the actual ad but instead are asked about what they have seen or heard recently. Recall can be measured through either unaided or aided recall methods. In an unaided recall test, respondents identify ads they have seen recently but are not shown any clues to help them remember.

unaided recall test
A post-test in which
respondents identify ads they
have recently seen but are
given no recall clues

For digital advertising, e.g. in social media, the most common measures for effectiveness are: the number of times the brand name gets mentioned, what consumers feel about the brand (brand sentiment) as well as measures of what influencers are thinking about the brand.[21] Basic web analytics can be achieved through Google Alerts and more sophisticated web analysis tools can be purchased, e.g. BlitzMetrics can monitor communication about your brand across most social media platforms.[22] Google is also developing a new type of online ad tracker to replace the privacy-challenged cookie. This is a significant move since Google is the world leader in digital advertising and claims their Chrome browser has top position. The new AdID identifier will track web browsing anonymously.[23] To maintain competitiveness, most social media platforms are also developing their own ad tracking to demonstrate how advertisements are received by the initial target audience as well as the extent to which advertisements are forwarded to secondary audiences (e.g. Pinterest Web Analytics was introduced in March 2013).[24]

Advertising you should be aware of

Comparative advertising is a subcategory of advertising you should be aware of. It compares a sponsored brand with one or more identified brands on the basis of one or more product characteristics, i.e. direct product comparisons. This is a bold strategy, aimed at drawing customers' attention to the superior features of a product. Comparative advertising strategies attract additional scrutiny from competitors and government agencies, such as the Australian Competition and Consumer Commission (ACCC). In January 2011, the *Trade Practices Act 1974* was replaced by the *Competition and Consumer Act 2010*. Under the provisions of this legislation, marketers using comparative advertisements must not misrepresent the qualities or characteristics of competing products.[25]

Often the brands promoted through comparative advertisements have low market shares and are compared with competitors that have the highest market shares in the product category. Product categories that commonly use comparative advertising include soft drinks, toothpaste, pain relievers, foods, tyres, cars and detergents. Another specific form of advertising you should be aware of is reminder advertising which tells customers that an established brand is still around and still offers certain characteristics, uses and benefits.

comparative advertising
Compares a sponsored brand with one or more identified brands on the basis of one or more product characteristics

reminder advertising
Reminds consumers about an established brand's uses, characteristics and benefits

Product placement

Today's average city dweller could see up to 5000 marketing messages each day. As the public move away from traditional printed magazines and newspapers, marketing managers have to be smarter with their promotional expenditure. A growing technique for reaching consumers is the strategic placement of products or product promotions within TV programs, movies, video games or other entertainment venues to reach the product's target market. New technology allows post-production product placement where branded items can be added to popular TV shows like *Packed to the Rafters* even when those brands were not part of the original scene. Such flexibility is likely to attract more organisations into using product placement in the future.[26]

Product placement is a popular marketing choice for a number of reasons. Audiences are already pre-segmented according to the media content, making targeting easier. It can also provide access to market segments difficult to reach through traditional media channels, such as young males. Traditional TV advertising is also losing out as new technologies allow consumers to fast-forward commercial breaks. Viewers do not try to avoid product placement if it combines branded goods with actual storylines. Brands used by key characters of a successful movie can enhance brand familiarity and greatly increase demand for that item.

Branded products add realism to storylines and engage the consumer on a more emotional level (e.g. the latest mobile application helped an action hero to save the world from terrorists). Product placement can be an essential part of the storyline (e.g. detectives finding an empty Pepsi Max can at the crime scene could narrow down their list of suspects). Furthermore, movies set in the contemporary world would not appear realistic if the characters did not consume commonly known branded goods.

product placement
The strategic location of products or product promotions within TV program (or other entertainment media) content to reach the product's target market

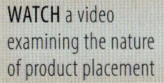**WATCH** a video examining the nature of product placement

Product placement is a very subtle and powerful communication but falls largely outside the traditional consumer protection laws and professional codes of conduct, as a product placement rarely makes claims regarding the value of the item or its specific attributes. Moreover, if a product is featured in a fictional setting, surely the audience will understand their personal experience with the same product might be different (e.g. the additional features in James Bond's cars are not available for cars bought in the real world)? There are some obvious legal limitations to the use of product placement; for example, products like cigarettes or alcohol are already banned from most media. Moreover, the UK government has regulated product placement even further by forbidding alcohol as well as junk food placements in BBC licensed fee-funded TV programs. If future research finds a positive impact on viewers' health these regulations could be copied in Australia.[27]

Product placement is big business: the global growth for brand placement expenditure in 2012 was 11.7 per cent, with the greatest growth taking place in China (27.7% but due to limited market size this was valued at 'only $103 million'). In the USA the 2012 growth was only 11.4 per cent but this was valued at $4.75 billion. Worldwide product placement is estimated to be almost $10 billion per annum.[28] The winner of the 2012 Brandcameo Product Placement award for most frequently appearing brand in top performing feature films was Mercedes-Benz with their vehicles featured in a third of the qualifying movies.[29] The nomination for the most blatant product placement award must go to Avril Lavigne for starting her 'Rock n Roll' video with 'Oh, my new Sony phone is ringing'…[30]

Public relations

LO3

public relations
Communication efforts used to create and maintain favourable relations between an organisation and its stakeholders

Public relations (often referred to as PR) is a broad set of communication efforts used to create and maintain favourable relationships between an organisation and its stakeholders. An organisation communicates with both internal and external stakeholders and public relations efforts can be directed toward any and all of these. A company's stakeholders can include customers, suppliers, employees, stockholders, the media, educators, potential investors, government officials and society in general. Public relations can be used to promote people, places, ideas, activities and even countries. It focuses on enhancing the image of the total organisation. Assessing public attitudes and creating a favourable image are no less important than direct promotion of the organisation's products. Because the public's attitudes toward a company are likely to affect the sales of its products, it is very important for companies to maintain positive public perceptions. In addition, employee morale is strengthened if the public perceives the company positively.[31] By getting the media to report on a company's accomplishments, public relations helps the company maintain positive public visibility.

Public relations tools

Companies use a range of public relations tools to convey messages and create images. Public relations professionals prepare written materials, such as brochures, newsletters, company magazines, news releases, websites, blogs and annual reports that reach and influence company stakeholders. Public relations personnel also create corporate identity materials, such as logos, business cards, stationery and signs, that make companies immediately recognisable. Speeches are another public relations tool. What a company executive says publicly at meetings or to the media can affect the organisation's image, so his or her speech must convey the desired message clearly. The best PR results are achieved by organisations that participate in positive and exciting activities that can touch the hearts of average citizens. The 'best jobs in the world' campaigns are good examples of this.

viral marketing
A strategy to get consumers to share a marketer's message, often through email or online video, in a way that spreads dramatically and quickly

MARKETING IN ACTION | THE SIX BEST JOBS IN THE WORLD?

Tourism Queensland's 'The Best Job In the World' PR campaign in 2009 was a **viral marketing** phenomenon. It attracted worldwide attention as well as an estimated 647 million media impressions and a total media coverage valued at AU$430 million worldwide. Some estimates suggest that in the US and Canada alone, the campaign achieved free publicity to the advertising value of AU$106 million. The huge number of media impressions was also impressive; for example, in just two days the campaign received 1100 TV placements in the US and Canada.

In 2013 Tourism Australia ran a 'six best jobs in the world' promotion as part of its $4 million campaign targeting 18–30 year old travellers and promoting the Australian Working Holiday Maker program. The working holiday segment accounts for a quarter of international visitors to Australia and contributes $2.5 billion to the Australian economy. On average, working holiday makers spend $13000 each during their stay. These travellers stay longer, are scattered across the whole country and take on seasonal employment in the tourism industry and other sectors of the economy.

The six best jobs in the world were designed to showcase Australia to the youth target market. Jobs ranged from wildlife caretaker in South Australia to lifestyle photographer in Victoria and attracted over 500000 applications. The applications were used to create a database of individuals interested in an Australian working holiday and the six successful applicants started their six-month $100000 positions towards the end of 2013.[32]

Publicity is part of public relations. Publicity is communication in a news story form about the organisation, its products, or both, and transmitted through a mass medium at no charge. Examples of publicity-based public relations tools include **news releases** (sometimes called press or media releases), **press conferences** and **feature articles**. Media channels select stories with the best fit to their audience preferences. Stories need to add value to normal programming in the form of entertainment or by featuring

news release
A short piece of copy publicising an event or a product

press conference
A meeting used to announce major news events to the media

feature article
A manuscript of up to 3000 words prepared for a specific publication

interesting people. The Red Bull Stratos story outlined in the Did you know? box is a good example of a story that captured the world. Ordinarily, public relations efforts are planned and implemented to be consistent with and support other elements of the marketing communication mix. Public relations efforts may be the responsibility of an individual or of a department within the organisation, or the organisation may hire an independent public relations agency. Although public relations has a larger, more comprehensive communication function than publicity, publicity is a very important aspect of public relations. Publicity can be used to provide information about goods or services, to announce expansions, acquisitions, research, or new-product launches, or to enhance a company's image.

The most common publicity-based public relations tool is the news release, which is usually a single page of typewritten copy containing fewer than 300 words and describing a company event or product (see the Virgin Australia and AFL partnership announcement). A news release gives the company's or agency's name, address, phone number and contact person. News releases can tackle a multitude of specific issues, as suggested in Table 13.4. A feature article is a manuscript of up to 3000 words prepared for a specific publication. A **captioned photograph** is a photograph with a brief description explaining the picture's content. Captioned photographs are effective for illustrating new or improved products with highly visible features.

captioned photograph
A photo with a brief description of its contents

News release >>
Virgin extends partnership with AFL

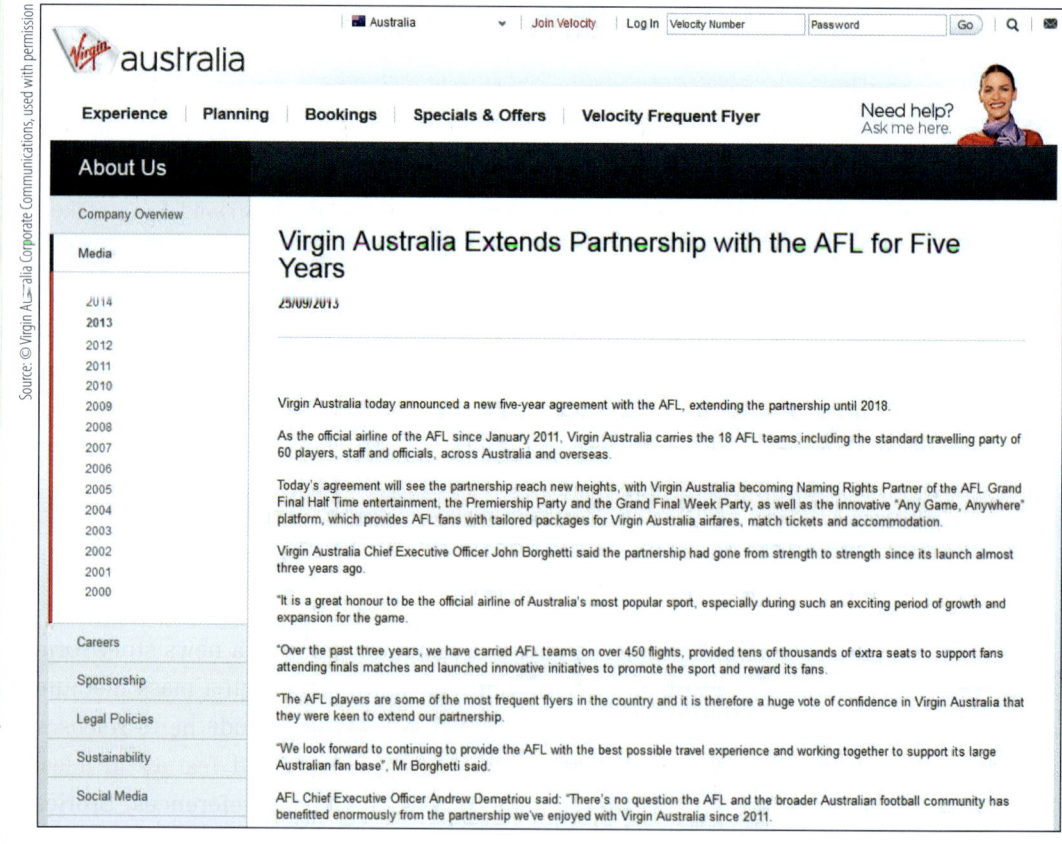

Source: © Virgin Australia Corporate Communications, used with permission

TABLE 13.4 POSSIBLE ISSUES FOR NEWS RELEASES

Support of a social cause	New products
Improved warranties	New slogan
Reports on industry conditions	Research developments
New uses for established products	Company's history and development
Product endorsements	Employment, production and sales records
Quality awards	Award of contracts
Company name changes	Opening of new markets
Interviews with company officials	Improvements in financial position
Improved distribution policies	Opening of an exhibit
International business efforts	History of a brand
Athletic event sponsorship	Winners of company contests
Visits by celebrities	Logo changes
Reports on new discoveries	Speeches of top management
Innovative business practices	Merit awards
Economic forecasts	Anniversary of inventions

There are several other kinds of publicity-based public relations tools. A press conference is a meeting called to announce major news events. Media personnel are invited to press conferences and are usually supplied with written materials and photographs. Letters to the editor and editorials are sometimes prepared and sent to newspapers and magazines. Videos and audiotapes may be distributed to broadcast stations in the hope that they will be aired.

Publicity-based public relations tools offer several advantages, including credibility, news value, significant word-of-mouth communications and a perception of being endorsed by the media. The public may consider news coverage more truthful and credible than an advertisement because the media are not paid to provide the information. In addition, stories regarding a new product or a new environmentally responsible company policy, for example, which are handled as news items are likely to receive notice. Finally, the cost of publicity is low compared with the cost of advertising.[34]

Publicity-based public relations tools also have some limitations. Media personnel must judge company messages to be newsworthy if the messages are to be published or broadcast at all. Consequently, messages must be timely, interesting, accurate and in the public interest. Many communications do not qualify. It may take a great deal of time and effort to convince media personnel of the news value of publicity releases. Although public relations personnel usually encourage the media to air publicity releases at certain times, they control neither the content nor the timing of the communication. Media personnel alter length and content of publicity releases to fit publishers' or broadcasters' requirements and may even delete the parts of messages that company personnel view as most important. Furthermore, media personnel use publicity releases in time slots or positions most convenient for them. Therefore messages sometimes appear in locations or at times that may not reach the company's target audiences. Although these limitations can be frustrating, properly managed publicity-based public relations tools offer an organisation substantial benefits.

Evaluating public relations effectiveness

Because of the potential benefits of good public relations, it is essential that organisations evaluate the effectiveness of their public relations campaigns. Research can be conducted to determine how well a company is communicating its messages or image to its target audiences. Environmental monitoring identifies changes in public opinion affecting an organisation. A public relations audit is used to assess an organisation's image among the public or to evaluate the effect of a specific public relations program. A communications audit may include a content analysis of messages, a readability study or a readership survey. If an organisation wants to measure the extent to which stakeholders view it as being socially responsible, it can conduct a social audit.

One approach to measuring the effectiveness of publicity-based public relations is to count the number of exposures in the media (as in 'The Six Best Jobs In the World' example). To determine which news releases are published in print media and how often, an organisation can hire a clipping service, a company that clips and sends news releases to client companies. To measure the effectiveness of TV coverage, a company can enclose a card with its publicity releases asking TV stations to record their name and the dates when the news item was broadcast (although station personnel do not always comply). Although some TV and radio tracking services exist, they are extremely costly.

Counting the number of media exposures does not reveal how many people have actually read or heard the company's message or what they thought about the message afterwards. However, measuring changes in product awareness, knowledge and attitudes resulting from the publicity campaign does. To assess these changes, companies must measure these levels before and after public relations campaigns. Although precise measures are difficult to obtain, company marketers should attempt to assess the impact of public relations efforts on the organisation's sales figures.

Dealing with unfavourable public relations

So far, we have discussed public relations as a planned element of the marketing communications mix. Unpleasant situations and negative events, such as product tampering or an environmental disaster, may provoke unfavourable public relations for an organisation. To minimise the damaging effects of unfavourable coverage, effective marketers have policies and procedures in place to help manage public relations problems. Public relations should not be viewed as a set of tools to be used only during crises. To get the most from public relations, an organisation should have someone responsible for public relations either internally or externally and should have an ongoing public relations program.

However, companies may have to deal with unexpected and unfavourable publicity resulting from an unsafe product, an accident, controversial actions by employees or some other negative event or situation. For example, a December 2012 prank call to the London hospital treating the Duchess of Cambridge by the DJs of the Australian 2Day FM radio station led to the suicide of a British nurse. The poor handling of this critical event by the station owner, Southern Cross Austereo, inflamed the situation and turned the whole event into 'PR 101 in what not to do'.

One of the poor judgement calls made by the station owner was to aggressively deny any wrong-doing when the appropriate communication style should have been apologetic or remorseful. Furthermore, the decision to place the two DJs behind the prank call in a current affairs TV interview only enraged the British media further and made the story bigger. At the height of this PR disaster the two DJs and the station manager had to be placed under 24-hour security after receiving death threats. In July 2013 the story was resuscitated when one of the prank call DJs lodged a complaint against her employer for 'failing to provide a safe workplace'. In August 2013 the Royal prank call made the news again as contributing to the poor financial performance for Southern Cross Austereo.[35]

LISTEN to the Audio Summary for a recap of the key concepts of public relations

Today's mass media, including online services and the Internet, disseminate information faster than ever before and, unfortunately, bad news generally receives considerable media attention.

Sponsorship

Sponsorship should be viewed 'holistically and strategically' as part of the integrated marketing communications.[36] The most successful sponsorship deals are built around the needs of the target audience, not those of the sponsoring organisation or receivers of the sponsorship income. The best sponsorship deals add value to the customers' experience of the sponsored event.[37] For example, Nike views sponsorship deals as a partnership with the sponsored athletes that results in advanced product designs. These innovative products can then help amateur athletes to achieve their own goals.[38]

In 2013, the global sponsorship expenditure reached US$53.3 billion with sport as the biggest category to receive sponsorship income.[39] The London Olympics alone attracted over AU$1.7 billion in sponsorship revenue.[40] Surprisingly, the 116 top brands in the world spend 25% more on sponsorship in the post Global Financial Crisis (GFC) environment than they did before the GFC era of 2008.[41]

The most important trends influencing sponsorship in recent times are the emergence of a range of digital media, an explosion in the number of potential channels of communication including social media and a greater need for accountability of sponsorship expenditure. Furthermore, the Internet has facilitated an expansion of online gaming/gambling as well as the spread of international brands across the world. Since advertising for gambling, tobacco, alcohol, unhealthy food or promotions targeting children in general are heavily regulated in most developed countries, these brands are using sponsorship as a primary tool for increasing awareness.[42]

Sponsorship is a versatile form of communication that works at multiple levels. For example, it has been linked to improved corporate culture within the sponsor's own organisation as well as achieving promotional objectives for external target markets. Furthermore, sponsorship can be used to communicate with business customers as well as with consumers.[43]

Table 13.5 demonstrates the long reaching and multilevel benefits the animal feed company, Alltech, gained by sponsoring the 2010 Equestrian Games. From the original investment of $30 million, the company calculated a $131 million return (a 409% return on their investment), a significant drop in staff turnover and a tenfold increase in their sales to the consumers.[44]

TABLE 13.5   BENEFITS OF EVENT SPONSORSHIP

Stakeholder	Who	Sample of results
Internal	Employers and others directly involved with Alltech	33% drop in employee turnover; 400 participated in games; 128 articles published by staff
Customers	Organisations who purchase Alltech's products – feed, pet food, food, beverages and crop solutions	Equine sales doubled with the games sponsorship; doubling of overall 'partner' sales; pet food sector sales up fourfold; tenfold increase in B2C sales
Suppliers	Of products or services to Alltech – banks, equipment and ingredients	Better terms: including by key bank in top-30 client list
Co-suppliers	Companies offering products and services that complement what Alltech offers	Industry board participation increases; requests to do business increase; supplier visits during the games
Competitors	Companies that offer substitute services or products to Alltech's technologies	Job applications double; tenfold increase in visits to the website
Influencers	People or organisations who influence Alltech's business environment, nutritional consultants, universities, politicians, NGOs, media, children (future audience)	Access to key people; local support for growth initiatives; massive coverage in mass media (CNN, NBC, etc.). Coverage valued at $31 million
Estimated total value resulting from sponsorship: $131 million		

Source: Alltech, in Meenaghan, Tony, Damien McLoughlin, and Alan McCormack. 'New Challenges in Sponsorship Evaluation Actors, New Media, and the Context of Praxis', *Psychology & Marketing*, 30.5 (2013): 444–60.

Common types of sponsorship

Common types of sponsorship include:

* social sponsorship (organisations sponsor social causes, charitable organisations or events)
* arts sponsorship (e.g. Ernst & Young Global Limited sponsoring various galleries, ballet and classical music in Australia)
* sponsorship of professional athletes, sports teams or sports events (e.g. Nike sponsors Tiger Woods; All Blacks (New Zealand Rugby Union) are sponsored by Coca-Cola New Zealand, Unilever, Sanitarium, Barkers and Bvlgari).[46]

It is estimated that 60–80 per cent of all sponsorship money is spent on sport as many clubs have strong loyal followings and sponsoring a professional sports team creates great brand exposure.[47]

The strength of sport sponsorship lies in linking the attributes of the sponsoring brand/company, the desired brand personality and the emotions the sport evokes for the target segment. Look, for example, at the obvious functional connection between the sponsoring product and the event when Kumho Tyres sponsored the Australian V8 Touring Car Series in 2013.[48] Prestige and status associated with attending events are also key criteria for all sponsorships, e.g. attending a

social sponsorship
Social sponsorship is used when organisations want to influence customer perceptions of their socially responsible/ethical merits or to improve their image[45]

ballet performance, visiting an art gallery or viewing the Olympic Games.[49]

Another public relations tool is event sponsorship which involves a company paying for part or all of a special event, such as a benefit concert or a tennis tournament. Sponsoring special

Source: Shutterstock.com

event sponsorship
When an organisation contributes financially to a special event with a view to gaining positive publicity

<< Event sponsorship
Pirtek and V8 Supercars signed a four-year deal for the Enduro Cup naming-rights

events can be an effective way to increase company or brand recognition with relatively minimal expenditures. Event sponsorship can gain companies considerable amounts of free media coverage. McDonald's is one of the largest corporate sponsors in the sports world. From the Olympics to grassroots youth programs, McDonald's has donated large sums of money to help promote sporting events.[50]

An even more extreme form of event sponsorship is practised by Red Bull energy drink: the company prefers to create and organise their own extreme events rather than be one of many organisations sponsoring a mega event. To date, Red Bull has created over 90 Red Bull branded events worldwide – as the inventor of these new extreme challenges and through creating branded events like Red Bull Air Race World Championships the company 'owns' the events. The Red Bull strategy is a good example of how it is becoming more and more difficult to separate sponsorship, product placement and branded entertainment. The company spends an estimated billion pounds on marketing per year (one third of their profits) and the Red Bull events match the energy drink brand image with extreme challenges that are also exciting viewing. The Red Bull sponsorship strategy also involves long term partnerships with athletes; for example, the Red Bull Stratos flight took seven years of planning and preparation.

The extreme challenges theme of Red Bull events has also brought the company under scrutiny after a seventh person died participating in an extreme sports event sponsored by Red Bull. However, the company ethos has always been to assist 'extraordinary people to reach extraordinary goals'. The brand personality is humorous, even whimsical, so it is no surprise that one Red Bull event features teams of everyday people trying to pilot their 'home-made' human-powered flying machines from a 10-metre-high starting platform to land in water. Competitors in this Red Bull Flugtag event are judged on flight distance achieved, the creative design of their craft as well as the showmanship exhibited by the flight crew.[51]

Evaluating the effectiveness of sponsorship

Sponsorship is most effective when there is a logical fit between the event and the sponsor.[52] For example, Red Bull's involvement in extreme sports events is a good match with the energy drink product category in general as well as with their slogan 'Red Bull gives you wings'.

The effectiveness of any sponsorship is best measured against the set sponsorship objectives. Typical objectives for sponsorship include enhancing the brand image and customers' perception of the brand/company and creating good will towards the sponsor.[53]

Table 13.6 offers a list of commonly used sponsorship objectives.

TABLE 13.6 COMMON SPONSORSHIP OBJECTIVES

Increase brand awareness in general
Improve perceived company image
Gain media exposure
Increase social media engagement with the brand/company
Build brand preference and loyalty
Increase customers' engagement with the brand
Increase traffic to company website
Increase sales and market share for B2C and B2B customers as well as for dealership network
Entertain clients or prospective clients at sponsored events
Network with co-sponsors during sponsored events
Market internally, e.g. excite employees, motivate sales force by inviting them to sponsored events as an incentive or bonus

Source: Meenaghan, Tony, Damien McLoughlin, and Alan McCormack. 'New Challenges in Sponsorship Evaluation Actors, New Media, and the Context of Praxis', *Psychology & Marketing*, 30.5 (2013): 444–60.

Companies can achieve greater results from sponsorship if they engage in sponsorship activation by organising sweepstakes and competitions or offering discounted entry fees to sponsored events.[54] Social media platforms are well placed to activate sponsorship audiences and the following measures are used to gauge the impact sponsored events can have on a brand or company.

* Buzz refers to the volume of references gained in the social media.

* Sentiment analysis explores the positive and negative references to a brand in the social media environment.

* Engagement with a brand refers to a more deliberate involvement with the brand within a social media environment. For example, 'Likes', 'Twitter followers' or 'Facebook fans'.[55]

Dealing with unfavourable sponsorship contracts

Not all sponsorship agreements result in positive outcomes and sponsorship deals can be terminated if one party is not keeping to the letter of the contract. One would have thought, for example, that the Australian Crime Commission (ACC) report into drugs and sport might have led to an avalanche of sponsorship agreement terminations, but it did not. The report contained allegations of doping (recreational and performance enhancing drug use) and match fixing, as well as identifying links between professional sporting bodies and organised crime. It appears that sponsors are willing to 'wait and see' in a country where there are few major sponsorship opportunities and the support for sports teams is fanatical. In other words, the withdrawal of a major sponsor could be blamed for the downfall of a club! Key sponsors, however, are not shy to penalise individual players if their behaviour breaks 'disrepute' clauses embedded in sponsorship agreements. For example, The Transport Accident Commission fined Melbourne Stars after the club's captain was caught speeding.[56]

Nike is 'the big spender' of the sponsorship world with a commitment to endorsement contracts worth $3.8 billion.[57] Nike athletes have also featured in negative news stories, resulting in Nike cancelling sponsorship deals with high profile athletes involved in scandals. For example, a $2 million deal with Oscar Pistorious (double amputee Olympic athlete) was cancelled after he was accused of murder. Nike also ended a long term arrangement with Lance Armstrong who admitted to using performance enhancing drugs after denying such allegations for years. Nike paid Lance $40 million annually and helped the Livestrong Foundation to raise a further $80 million. By contrast, Nike was one of the few companies to continue their sponsorship deal with Tiger Woods after he admitted to multiple extra-marital affairs. It has been suggested that sponsorship deals based on 'winning only assumption' are unlikely to endure in the long term.[58] This explains, to some extent, why Nike initially stood by Armstrong who is also a cancer survivor and because of his work to support other cancer sufferers. Similarly, Tiger Woods is valuable to Nike since he opened golf to a new demographic segment and had been raising money to assist underprivileged kids from early in his golf career.[59]

There are times when sponsored athletes refuse to be associated with their sponsors' brand or logo, as the Ethical Marketing box below shows.

ETHICAL MARKETING | PROFESSIONAL ATHLETE REFUSES TO DON SPONSOR'S LOGO FOR RELIGIOUS REASONS

issue

Can a professional athlete refuse to wear a team uniform emblazed with a sponsor's logo and still claim the benefits from lucrative sponsorship deals?

Fawad Ahmed, an Australian cricketer of Muslim faith made news headlines when he said he was not comfortable wearing the Cricket Australia (CA) uniform emblazed with the VB logo of their sponsor Carlton & United Breweries (CUB). He was also photographed wearing the CA shirt without the VB logo. By contrast, another Australian cricketer Usman Khawaja (also Muslim) did not object to wearing the uniform as he sees himself as an Australian player, not a Muslim cricketer.

The following arguments are relevant.

We must respect personal beliefs. Ahmed is not the only professional athlete who has objected to wearing their club sponsor's logos. Hashim Amla (South African cricketer) refused to wear a Castle Lager branded uniform and Papiss Cisse (English Premier League player) refused to don a shirt promoting a loan company. Religion was given as the reason for the players not wanting to wear the logo emblazed uniforms.

If you don't want to wear the team gear you should not be part of the team. But if you are happy to play without pay then that's OK. A former rugby union international player and two former Australian test cricketers feel that sponsorship is far too important for teams and the grassroot development of sport for an individual athlete to ignore the contract negotiated between sponsors and teams. In this instance, CA and CUB negotiated a wide-ranging sponsorship agreement with CUB paying in excess of $10 million. Through this sponsorship deal CUB is looking to reposition and placing the mighty VB on Australian players' shirts is an important part of this communication strategy. 'Major sponsorship deals like this enable players to claim their substantial salaries' and 'players should abide by the terms of their employment contract' is the message coming from a former Australian test player. To put it bluntly, if you do not like the terms of your employment contract, you can choose to work somewhere else. Finally, as long as alcohol, tobacco, gaming and fatty foods remain legal, athletes should abide by their contractual agreements.

The outcome. By allowing Ahmed to play in a VB-less uniform, Cricket Australia demonstrated great respect for an individual's religious beliefs. Since CA promotes diversity as one of its cultural values, perhaps this is just the first of many culturally respectful exclusions to sponsorship deals? In a twist of fate, Ahmed's VB-less shirt brought CUB incredible media exposure and by not forcing a Muslim player to wear a beer logo, the company found itself basking in a glow of positive PR.[60]

What is your opinion? Should professional players simply 'shut up and put up' with sponsorship demands since the income from these sponsorship deals enables better training for junior players at the grassroot level? If a professional player refuses to abide by any part of their contract (e.g. wearing a uniform with a sponsor's logo) should their wages be forfeited? Or are we allowing commercial gains to cloud our moral judgement? And finally, if professional athletes stop wearing team uniforms emblazed with sponsors' logos, what effect will that have on the willingness of sponsors to commit to supporting teams in the future?

Source: Newspix

^ **Australia's Fawad Ahmed, centre, with teammates Shaun Marsh, left, and Shane Watson, right**
The VB logo is missing from Ahmed's uniform

Personal selling

Personal selling is a paid personal communication that seeks to inform customers and persuade them to purchase products in an exchange situation. The phrase 'purchase product' is interpreted broadly to encompass acceptance of ideas and issues. Telemarketing (direct marketing over the telephone) relies heavily on personal selling.

When a salesperson and customer meet face to face, they use several types of interpersonal communication. The predominant communication form is language, both spoken and written.

Personal selling gives marketers the freedom to adjust a message according to the feedback received during this communication process so that it will satisfy customers' information needs. For example, a skilled car salesperson is happy to explain the meaning of the latest technological developments to all potential buyers in a language that is meaningful to that customer. Compared to other promotional methods, personal selling is very focused, as it enables marketers to focus on the most promising sales prospects. Other marketing communications-mix elements are aimed at groups of people, some of whom may not be prospective customers. However, personal selling is generally the most expensive element in the marketing communications mix. The average cost of a business sales call is more than $400.[61]

Source: © pcruciatti/Shutterstock.com

<< **The importance of personal selling** When Microsoft released the Windows Phone, representatives engaged in personal selling to inform consumers about the benefits of the new smartphone

Recruiting and training salespeople can also be very expensive as salespeople must be experts in their field of business, skilled in using their own products as well as aware of their competitors. They must also monitor the development of new products and know about competitors' sales efforts in their sales territories, how often and when the competition calls on their accounts, and what the competition is saying about their product in relation to its own. Salespeople must emphasise the benefits that their products provide, especially when competitors' products do not offer those specific benefits.

Identifying potential buyers interested in the organisation's products is also critical. Because most potential buyers seek information before making purchases, salespeople can ascertain prospects' informational needs and then provide relevant information. To do so, sales personnel must be well trained regarding both their products and the selling process in general.

Feedback from salespeople is also an opportunity to develop and maintain a marketing mix that better satisfies both the company and its customers.[62]

The personal selling process

Specific activities involved in selling vary among salespeople, selling situations and cultures. No two salespeople use exactly the same selling methods. Nonetheless, many salespeople move through the same general process as they sell products. This process consists of seven steps, outlined in Figure 13.5: prospecting, pre-approach, approach, making the presentation, overcoming objections, closing the sale and following up.

Prospecting for customers

Developing a list of potential customers is called prospecting. Salespeople seek names of prospects from company sales records, trade shows, commercial databases, newspaper announcements (of marriages, births, deaths and so on), public records, telephone directories, trade association directories and many other sources. Sales personnel also use responses to traditional and online ads that encourage

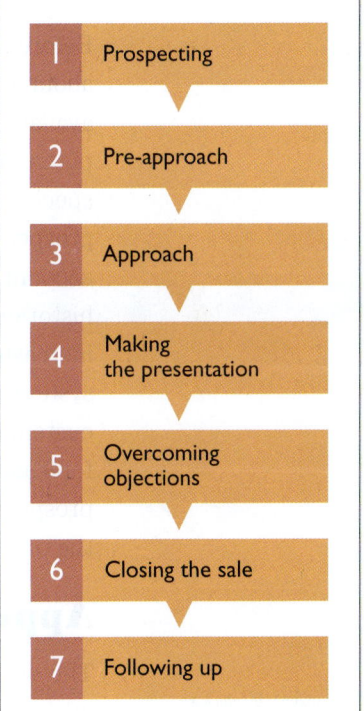

1 Prospecting

2 Pre-approach

3 Approach

4 Making the presentation

5 Overcoming objections

6 Closing the sale

7 Following up

FIGURE 13.5 GENERAL STEPS IN THE PERSONAL SELLING PROCESS

prospecting
Developing a list of potential customers

interested persons to send in information request forms. Seminars and meetings attended by particular types of clients, such as attorneys or accountants, may also produce leads.

Most salespeople prefer to use referrals – recommendations from current customers – to find prospects. Obtaining referrals relies on salespeople having a good relationship with current customers since they must have performed well to be asking customers for this kind of help. Research shows that one referral is as valuable as 12 cold calls. Interestingly, 80 per cent of clients are willing to give referrals, but only 20 per cent are ever asked! The advantages of using referrals, according to sales experts, are that the resulting sales leads are highly qualified, sales rates are higher, initial transactions are larger and the sales cycle is shorter.[63]

Consistent activity is critical to successful prospecting. Salespeople must actively search the customer base for qualified prospects who fit the target-market profile. After developing the prospect list, a salesperson evaluates whether each prospect is able, willing and authorised to buy the product. Based on this evaluation, prospects are ranked according to desirability or potential.

Pre-approaching prospects

Before contacting acceptable prospects, a salesperson finds and analyses information about each prospect's specific product needs, current use of brands, feelings about available brands and personal characteristics. In short, salespeople need to know what potential buyers and decision makers consider most important and why they need a specific product.[64] The most successful salespeople are thorough in their evaluations of prospects. This pre-approach step involves identifying key decision makers, reviewing account histories and problems, contacting other clients for information, assessing credit histories, preparing sales presentations and identifying product needs. Marketers are increasingly using digital technologies and customer relationship management (CRM) systems to comb through their databases and identify their most profitable products and customers. CRM systems can also help sales departments manage leads, track customers, forecast sales and assess performance. A salesperson with a lot of information about a prospect is better equipped to develop a presentation that communicates precisely with the prospect.

Approaching the customer

approach
The manner in which a salesperson contacts a potential customer

The approach, the manner in which a salesperson contacts a potential customer, is a critical step in the sales process. In more than 80 per cent of initial sales calls, the purpose is to gather information about the buyer's needs and objectives. Creating a favourable impression and building rapport with prospective clients are important tasks in the approach. During the initial contact, the salesperson strives to develop a relationship rather than just push a product. The salesperson may have to call on a prospect several times before the product is considered. The approach must be designed to deliver value to targeted customers. If the sales approach is inappropriate, the salesperson's efforts are likely to have poor results.

As mentioned earlier, one type of approach is based on referrals. The salesperson approaches the prospect and explains that an acquaintance, associate or relative suggested the call. Another type of approach is the 'cold canvass/cold call', in which a salesperson calls on potential customers without prior consent. The exact type of approach depends on the salesperson's preferences, the product being sold, the company's resources and the prospect's characteristics.

Making the presentation

During the sales presentation, the salesperson must attract and hold the prospect's attention, stimulate interest and spark a desire for the product. Research indicates that salespeople who carefully monitor the selling situation and adapt their presentations to meet the needs of prospects are associated with effective sales performance.[65] Salespeople should match their influencing tactics – such as information exchange, recommendations, threats, promises, ingratiation and inspirational appeals – to their prospects. Different types of buyers respond to different tactics, but most prospects respond well to information exchange and recommendations, and virtually no prospects respond to threats.[66] Salespeople should have the prospect touch, hold or use the product. If possible, the salesperson should demonstrate the product. Audio visual equipment and software also may enhance the presentation.

During the presentation, the salesperson must listen as well as talk. Non-verbal modes of communication are especially beneficial in building trust during the presentation.[67] The sales presentation gives the salesperson the greatest opportunity to determine the prospect's specific needs by listening to questions and comments and observing responses. Even though the salesperson plans the presentation in advance, he or she must be able to adjust the message to meet the prospect's informational needs.

Virtual sales presentations have been touted as a better alternative to face-to-face sales presentations due to their convenience. Yet in reality, they come with their own set of challenges. Virtual sales presentations require an adequate bandwidth, and users must be familiar with the technology to create an effective sales presentation virtually. This requires additional training for a company's sales force. The salesperson cannot always see the customer, and the customer cannot touch the product. On the other hand, virtual sales presentations can eliminate long travel times, can be sent to a large number of prospects simultaneously, and can be viewed from a location of the prospect's choosing.[68]

Overcoming objections

An effective salesperson usually seeks out a prospect's objections so that he or she can address them. If they are not apparent, the salesperson cannot deal with them, and the prospect may not buy. One of the best ways to overcome objections is to anticipate and counter them before the prospect raises them. However, this approach can be risky because the salesperson may mention objections that the prospect would not have raised. If possible, the salesperson should handle objections as they arise. They can also be addressed at the end of the presentation. Research demonstrates that adapting the message in response to the customer's needs generally enhances performance, particularly in new-task or modified rebuy purchase situations.[69]

Closing the sale

closing
The stage in the selling process when the salesperson asks the prospect to buy the product

Closing is the stage of the selling process when the salesperson asks the prospect to buy the product. During the presentation, the salesperson may use a 'trial close' by asking questions that assume the prospect will buy the product. The salesperson might ask the potential customer about financial terms, desired colours or sizes, or delivery arrangements. One questioning approach uses broad questions (what, how and why) to probe or gather information and focused questions (who, when and where) to clarify and close the sale. Reactions to such questions usually indicate how close the prospect is to buying. A trial close allows prospects to indicate indirectly that they will buy the product without having to say those sometimes difficult words, 'I'll take it'.

A salesperson should try to close at several points during the presentation because the prospect may be ready to buy. One closing strategy involves asking the potential customer to place a low-risk tryout order. An attempt to close the sale may result in objections. Thus, closing can uncover hidden objections, which the salesperson can then address.

Following up

After a successful closing, the salesperson must follow up the sale. In the follow-up stage, the salesperson determines whether the order was delivered on time and installed properly, if installation was required. He or she should contact the customer to learn if any problems or questions regarding the product have arisen. The follow-up stage is also used to determine customers' future product needs.

Managing the sales force

The sales force is directly responsible for generating one of an organisation's primary inputs – sales revenue. Without adequate sales revenue, businesses cannot survive. In addition, a company's reputation is often determined by the ethical conduct of its sales force. A positive ethical climate, which is one component of corporate culture, has been linked with decreased stress and turnover and improved job attitudes and performance in sales.[70] The morale and ultimately the success of a company's sales force depend in large part on adequate compensation, room for advancement, adequate training and management support – all key areas of sales management. Salespeople who are not satisfied with these elements may leave. Evaluating the input of salespeople is an important part of sales force management because of its strong bearing on a company's success.

Sales promotion

sales promotion
An activity and/or material meant to induce resellers or salespeople to sell a product or consumers to buy it

Sales promotion (often abbreviated to SP) is an activity or material that acts as a direct inducement, offering added value or another type of incentive (e.g. discounted price) for a specified product/brand during a set period of time. These incentives can be aimed at resellers, salespeople or consumers.[71] Examples include free samples, games, rebates, displays, sweepstakes, contests, premiums and coupons. Some websites also help consumers manage their access to coupons. One popular website (http://www.ozbargain.com.au) is an Australian-based community of online shoppers who share their tips for best bargains with each other.

Sales promotion should not be confused with promotion; sales promotion is just one aspect of promotion. Marketers spend more on sales promotion than on advertising, and sales promotion also appears to be a faster-growing area than advertising. This shift in how promotional dollars are used has occurred for several reasons. Heightened concerns about value have made customers more responsive to promotional offers, especially price discounts and point-of-purchase displays. Thanks to their size and access to checkout scanner data, retailers have gained considerable power in the supply chain and are demanding greater promotional efforts from manufacturers to boost retail profits. General decline in brand loyalty has produced an environment in which sales promotions aimed at persuading customers to switch brands are more effective. Finally, the stronger emphasis placed on improving short-term performance results calls for greater use of sales promotion methods that yield quick (albeit perhaps short-lived) sales increases.[72]

Generally, when companies employ advertising or personal selling, they depend on them either continuously or cyclically. However, a marketer's use of sales promotion tends to be irregular. Many products are seasonal. Marketers frequently rely on sales promotion to improve the effectiveness of other marketing communication-mix elements, especially advertising and personal selling. Company sponsorship of popular TV programs can allow a close connection between brand and target market. For example, the producers of MasterChef have teamed up with several companies, such as Qantas, Coles, Handee Ultra (a kitchen towel) and many more. These key partners get integrated into the TV show; for example, the contestants are flown by Qantas to cook on location, spills on the floor are cleared with the Handee Ultra towels and the contestants get their ingredients from Coles.[73]

Marketers often use sales promotion to facilitate personal selling, advertising or both. Companies also employ advertising and personal selling to support sales promotion activities. For example, marketers frequently use advertising to promote contests, free samples and premiums. The most effective sales promotion efforts are highly interrelated with other promotional activities. Decisions regarding sales promotion often affect advertising and personal selling decisions, and vice versa.

Sales promotion can increase sales by providing extra purchasing incentives. Many opportunities exist to motivate consumers, resellers and salespeople to take desired actions. Some kinds of sales promotion are designed specifically to stimulate resellers' demand and effectiveness, some are directed at increasing consumer demand and some focus on both consumers and resellers. Regardless of the purpose, marketers must ensure that sales promotion objectives are consistent with the organisation's overall objectives, as well as with its marketing and promotion objectives.

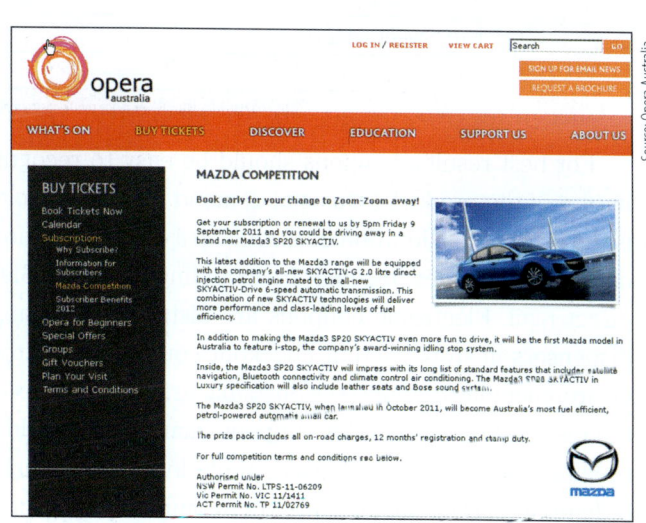

Source: Opera Australia

<< **Sales promotion**
Competitions are another form of sales promotion

Consumer sales promotion methods

Consumer sales promotion methods encourage or stimulate consumers to patronise specific retail stores or try particular products. These methods initiated by retailers often aim to attract customers to specific locations, whereas those used by manufacturers generally introduce new products or promote established brands. In this section we discuss coupons and cents-off offers, money refunds and rebates, frequent-user incentives, point-of-purchase materials and demonstrations free samples and premiums, and consumer contests, games and sweepstakes.

Coupons and cents-off offers

Coupons reduce a product's price and are used to prompt customers to try new or established products, increase sales volume quickly, attract repeat purchasers or introduce new package sizes or features. Savings may be deducted from the purchase price or offered as cash. Research indicates that coupons are most effective when a small-face-value coupon is used in conjunction with a lower product price available for all consumers.[74] Coupons are the most widely used consumer sales promotion. Consumer packaged-goods manufacturers distribute about 253 billion coupons, of which about 1 per cent are redeemed, saving consumers an estimated $3 billion. Nearly 90 per cent of all consumers use coupons.[75] While consumers can find coupons for a wide variety of products and services, Table 13.7 shows the product categories with the greatest coupon distributions.

TABLE 13.7 TOP 10 COUPON CATEGORIES IN 2013

1. Boxed cereal
2. Household cleaning supplies
3. Yogurt
4. Butter/margarine
5. Adult vitamins
6. Nappies
7. Dinner meats
8. Cheese
9. Lotion
10. Sweet snacks

Source: Recipe.com, http://www.recipe.com/blogs/cooking/how-to-coupon-top-coupon-categories-year.

For best results, coupons should be easy to recognise and state the offer clearly. The nature of the product (seasonal demand for it, life cycle stage and frequency of purchase) is the prime consideration in setting up a coupon promotion. Paper coupons are distributed on and in packages, through freestanding inserts (FSIs), in print advertising and through direct mail. Electronic coupons are distributed online, via in-store kiosks, through shelf dispensers in stores and at checkout counters. Electronic coupons also claim to be more environmentally friendly (see Sustainable Marketing box on the next page). When deciding on the distribution method for coupons, marketers should consider strategies and objectives, redemption rates, availability, circulation and exclusivity. The coupon distribution and redemption arena has become very competitive. To draw customers to their stores, some supermarkets double and sometimes even triple the value of customers' coupons.

SUSTAINABLE MARKETING | E-COUPONS BENEFIT A VARIETY OF STAKEHOLDERS, INCLUDING THE ENVIRONMENT

While coupon redemption rates fell in the last decade, recent years have seen an uptake in coupon usage. In fact, electronic coupon (e-coupon) redemption rates are growing rapidly. The increasing use of e-coupons benefits consumers, manufacturers and the environment. E-coupons seem less intrusive than paper ones. With the growth of websites like http://www.groupon.com.au, consumers can search for digital coupons they want at their leisure. A growing trend in electronic couponing is the use of mobile devices. One study revealed that 46 per cent of those owning mobile devices are willing to try mobile coupons. Manufacturers like mobile coupons as well, because they are 10 times more likely to be redeemed than paper coupons.

E-coupons also benefit the environment. They save paper because consumers can print only those coupons they want. Some stores even allow consumers to download e-coupons directly onto their rewards cards, which eliminates paper use entirely. From the manufacturer's standpoint, e-coupons reduce the cost

Source: iStockphoto/© trekandshoot

(in paper and energy) of having to deliver coupons through direct mail.

Indeed, 45 per cent of people say they prefer receiving mobile coupons through text messages. As more businesses and consumers realise the advantages of e-coupons, this sales promotion is likely to take off in a big way.[76] ✕

Source: RedPlum Survey of 23,000 adults

Where Shoppers Get Coupons and Discounts

Newspapers	76%
E-mails and coupon alerts	59%
Internet searches	33%
Retail circulars	30%
Postal mail	28%

<< Discount offers
Newspapers are still the most common source for coupons and discount vouchers

Coupons offer several advantages. Print ads with coupons are often more effective at generating brand awareness than are print ads without coupons. Generally, the larger the coupon's cash offer, the better the recognition generated. Coupons reward current product users, win back former users and encourage purchases in larger quantities. Because they are returned, coupons also help a manufacturer determine whether it reached the intended target market. The advantages of using electronic coupons over paper coupons include lower cost per redemption, greater targeting ability, improved data-gathering capabilities and improved experimentation capabilities to determine optimal face values and expiration cycles.[77] However, newspapers are still the most common source for coupons and discount vouchers and motivated consumers are likely to consider information in a print coupon more carefully than in an online coupon.[78]

Drawbacks of coupon use include fraud and mis-redemption, which can be expensive for manufacturers. Another disadvantage, according to some experts, is that coupons are losing their value; because so many manufacturers offer them, consumers have learned not to buy without some incentive, whether it is a coupon, rebate or refund. Furthermore, brand loyalty influences coupon use as many consumers redeem coupons only for products they normally buy. It is believed that about 75 per cent of coupons are redeemed by people already using the brand on the coupon. Thus coupons have questionable success as an incentive for consumers to try a new brand or product. An additional problem with coupons is that stores often do not have enough of the coupon item in stock. This situation generates ill will toward both the store and the product.

cents-off offer
A promotion that lets buyers pay less than the regular price to encourage purchase

With a **cents-off offer**, buyers pay a certain amount less than the regular price shown on the label or package. Similar to coupons, this method can serve as a strong incentive for trying new or unfamiliar products. Commonly used in product introductions, cents-off offers can stimulate product sales, yield short-lived sales increases and promote products in off-seasons. It is an easy method to control and is often used for specific purposes. If used on an ongoing basis, however, cents-off offers reduce the price for customers who would buy at the regular price and may also cheapen a product's image. In addition, the method often requires special handling by retailers who are responsible for giving the discount at the point of sale.

Refunds and rebates

money refunds
A sales promotion technique offering consumers money when they mail in a proof of purchase, usually for multiple product purchases

rebates
A sales promotion technique whereby customers are sent a specific amount of money for purchasing a single product

With **money refunds**, consumers submit proof of purchase and are refunded a specific amount of money. Usually manufacturers demand multiple product purchases before consumers qualify for refunds. Money refunds, used primarily to promote trial use of a product, are relatively low in cost, but because they sometimes generate a low response rate, they have limited impact on sales. With **rebates**, the customer is sent a specified amount of money for making a single purchase. Rebates generally are given on more expensive products than money refunds and are used to encourage customers. Marketers also use rebates to reinforce brand loyalty, provide promotion buzz for salespeople and as advertisements for the product. On larger items, such as cars, rebates are often given at the point of sale. Most rebates, however, especially on smaller items, offer a delayed discount because it takes time for the customer to receive the rebate.

Money refunds and rebates also attract criticism. One problem with money refunds and rebates is that many people perceive the redemption process as too complicated hence only about 40 per cent of individuals who purchase rebated products actually apply for the rebates.[79] To reduce administrative costs associated with these offers, marketers are increasingly encouraging customers to apply for rebates online. Consumers may also have negative perceptions of manufacturers' reasons for offering rebates. They may believe the products are new, untested or not selling well. If these perceptions are not changed, rebate offers may actually degrade the image and desirability of the products.

Frequent-user incentives

Many companies develop incentive programs to reward customers who engage in repeat (frequent) purchases. Most major airlines offer frequent-flyer programs that reward customers who have flown a specified number of kilometres with free tickets for additional travel. Frequent-user incentives foster customer loyalty to a specific company or group of cooperating companies. They are favoured by service businesses, such as airlines, car rental agencies, hotels and restaurants.

Point-of-purchase materials and demonstrations

Point-of-purchase (P-O-P) materials include outdoor signs, window displays, counter pieces, display racks and self-service cartons. Innovations in P-O-P displays include sniff-teasers, which give off a product's aroma in the store as consumers walk within a radius of a metre, and computerised interactive displays. These items, often supplied by producers, attract attention, inform customers and encourage retailers to carry particular products. A retailer is likely to make use of P-O-P materials if they are attractive, informative, well constructed and in harmony with the store's image.

Demonstrations are excellent attention getters. Manufacturers offer them temporarily to encourage trial use and purchase of a product or to show how a product works. Because labour costs can be extremely high, demonstrations are not widely used. They can be highly effective for promoting certain types of products, such as appliances, cosmetics and cleaning supplies. For example, many health and wholefood stores provide cooking classes and demonstrations to teach consumers how to prepare different cuisines and to give them ideas on how to use products sold in the stores.

Free samples and premiums

Marketers use free samples to stimulate trial of a product, increase sales volume in the early stages of a product's life cycle and obtain desirable distribution. Sampling is the most expensive sales promotion method because production and distribution – at local events, by mail or door-to-door delivery, online, in stores and on packages – incur high costs. Big cosmetics brands regularly offer free samples to shoppers, for example. Many consumers prefer to get their samples by mail. Other consumers like to sample new food products at supermarkets or to try samples of new recipes featuring foods they already like. In designing a free sample, marketers should consider factors such as seasonal demand for the product,

point-of-purchase (P-O-P) materials
Signs, window displays, display racks and similar means used to attract customers

demonstrations
A sales promotion method manufacturers use temporarily to encourage trial use and purchase of a product or to show how a product works

free samples
Samples of a product given out to encourage trial and purchase

market characteristics and prior advertising. Free samples are usually not appropriate for slow-turnover products.

Premiums are items offered free or at minimal cost as a bonus for purchasing a product. Like the prize in a cereal box, premiums are used to attract competitors' customers, introduce different sizes of established products, add variety to other promotional efforts and stimulate consumer loyalty. Creativity is essential when using premiums; to stand out and achieve a significant number of redemptions, the premium must match both the target audience and the brand's image. Premiums must also be easily recognisable and desirable. Premiums are placed on or in packages and can also be distributed by retailers or through the mail. Examples include a service station giving a free carwash with a fuel purchase, a free toothbrush available with a tube of toothpaste and a free plastic storage box given with the purchase of cheese.

Consumer games, contests and sweepstakes

In consumer contests, individuals compete for prizes based on analytical or creative skills. This method can be used to generate retail traffic and frequency of exposure to promotional messages. Contestants are usually more highly involved in consumer contests than in games or sweepstakes, even though total participation may be lower. Contests may also be used in conjunction with other sales promotional methods, such as coupons. For example, the Cartoon Network Australia regularly hosts contests.[80]

Source: iStockphoto

In consumer games, individuals compete for prizes based primarily on chance – often by collecting game pieces such as bottle caps or a sticker on the side of a packet. Because collecting multiple pieces may be necessary to win or increase an individual's chances of winning, the game stimulates repeat business. Games are typically conducted over a long period of time and are commonly used by fast-food chains, soft-drink companies and hotels to stimulate traffic and repeat business. Development and management of consumer games are often outsourced to an independent public relations company, which can help marketers navigate federal and state laws applying to games. Although games may stimulate sales temporarily, there is no evidence to suggest that they affect a company's long-term sales. Marketers should exercise care in developing and administering games: problems or errors may anger customers and could result in lawsuits. Some games are also open to fraud.

Entrants in consumer sweepstakes (or competitions) submit their names for inclusion in a draw for prizes. For example, just 25 words could win you the Big Brother house experience compliments of the Ambi Pur 'Breathe Happy' campaign.[81] Sweepstakes are employed more often than consumer contests and tend to attract a greater number of participants. Contests, games and sweepstakes may be used in conjunction with other sales promotion methods, such as coupons. It is important to know regulations and laws for contests and sweepstakes because some state laws may consider certain types of events to be forms of gambling or lotteries.[82]

Trade sales promotion methods

To encourage resellers, especially retailers, to carry their products and to promote them effectively, producers use sales promotion methods. Trade sales promotion methods stimulate wholesalers and retailers to carry a producer's products and market those products more aggressively. These methods include buying allowances, buy-back allowances, scan-back allowances, merchandise allowances, cooperative advertising, dealer listings, free merchandise, dealer loaders, premium or push money and sales contests.

Trade allowances

Many manufacturers offer trade allowances to encourage resellers to carry a product or stock more of it. One such trade allowance is a buying allowance, which is a temporary price reduction offered to resellers for purchasing specified quantities of a product. A soap producer, for example, might give retailers $1 for each case of soap purchased. Such offers provide an incentive for resellers to handle new products, achieve temporary price reductions or stimulate purchase of items in larger than normal quantities. The buying allowance, which takes the form of money, yields profits to resellers and is simple and straightforward. There are no restrictions on how resellers use the money, which increases the method's effectiveness. One drawback of buying allowances is that customers may buy 'forward', meaning they buy large amounts that keep them supplied for many months. Another problem is that competitors may match (or beat) the reduced price, which can lower profits for all sellers.

A buy-back allowance is a sum of money that a producer gives to a reseller for each unit the reseller buys after an initial promotional deal is over. This method is a secondary incentive in which the total amount of money that resellers receive is proportional to their purchases during an initial consumer promotion, such as a coupon offer. Buy-back allowances foster cooperation during an initial sales promotion effort and stimulate repurchase afterward. The main disadvantage of this method is expense.

A scan-back allowance is a manufacturer's reward to retailers based on the number of pieces moved through the retailers' scanners during a specific time period. To participate in scan-back programs, retailers are usually expected to pass along savings to consumers through special pricing. Scan-backs are becoming widely used by manufacturers because they link trade spending directly to product movement at the retail level.

A merchandise allowance is a manufacturer's agreement to pay resellers certain amounts of money for providing promotional efforts such as advertising or P-O-P displays. This method is best suited to high-volume, high-profit easily handled products. A drawback is that some retailers perform activities at a minimally acceptable level simply to obtain allowances. Before paying retailers, manufacturers usually verify their performance. Manufacturers hope that retailers' additional promotional efforts will increase sales substantially.

Cooperative advertising and dealer listings

Cooperative advertising is an arrangement whereby a manufacturer agrees to pay a certain amount of a retailer's media costs for advertising the manufacturer's products. The amount allowed is usually based on the quantities purchased. As with merchandise allowances, a

trade sales promotion methods Ways of persuading wholesalers and retailers to carry a producer's products and market them aggressively

buying allowance A temporary price reduction to resellers for purchasing specified quantities of a product

buy-back allowance A sum of money given to a reseller for each unit bought after an initial promotion deal is over

scan-back allowance A manufacturer's reward to retailers based on the number of pieces scanned

merchandise allowance A manufacturer's agreement to pay resellers certain amounts of money for providing special promotional efforts

cooperative advertising An arrangement in which a manufacturer agrees to pay a certain amount of a retailer's media costs for advertising the manufacturer's products

retailer must show proof that ads did appear before the manufacturer pays the agreed-on portion of the advertising costs. These payments give retailers additional funds for advertising. Some retailers exploit cooperative advertising agreements by crowding too many products into one advertisement. Not all available cooperative advertising dollars are used. Some retailers cannot afford to advertise, whereas others can but do not want to advertise. A large proportion of all cooperative advertising dollars are spent on newspaper advertisements.

dealer listings
Advertisements that promote a product and identify the names of participating retailers that sell the product

Dealer listings are ads promoting a product and identifying participating retailers that sell the product. Dealer listings can influence retailers to carry the product, build traffic at the retail level and encourage consumers to buy the product at participating dealers.

Free merchandise and gifts

free merchandise
A manufacturer's reward given to resellers for purchasing a stated quantity of products

Manufacturers sometimes offer free merchandise to resellers that purchase a stated quantity of products. Occasionally, free merchandise is used as payment for allowances provided through other sales promotion methods. To avoid handling and bookkeeping problems, the free merchandise usually takes the form of a reduced invoice.

dealer loader
A gift, often part of a display, given to a retailer purchasing a specified quantity of merchandise

A dealer loader is a gift to a retailer who purchases a specified quantity of merchandise. Dealer loaders are often used to obtain special display efforts from retailers by offering essential display parts as premiums. For example, a manufacturer might design a display that includes a sterling silver tray as a major component and give the tray to the retailer. Marketers use dealer loaders to obtain new distributors and to push larger quantities of goods.

Premium (push) money

premium money (or push money)
Extra compensation to salespeople for pushing a line of goods

Premium money (or push money) is additional compensation to salespeople offered by the manufacturer as an incentive to push a line of goods. This method is appropriate when personal selling is an important part of the marketing effort; it is not effective for promoting products sold through self-service. The method often helps manufacturers obtain a commitment from the sales force, but it can be very expensive.

Sales contests

sales contest
A promotion method used to motivate distributors, retailers and sales personnel through recognition of outstanding achievements

A sales contest is designed to motivate distributors, retailers and sales personnel by recognising outstanding achievements. To be effective, this method must be equitable for all persons involved. One advantage is that it can achieve participation at all distribution levels. Positive effects may be temporary, however, and prizes are usually expensive.

Study Tools

Chapter review

 **UNDERSTAND HOW TO USE ADVERTISING AS A MARKETING COMMUNICATIONS TOOL**

Advertising is a paid form of non-personal communication transmitted to consumers through mass media such as TV, radio, the Internet, newspapers, magazines, direct mail, outdoor displays and signs on vehicles. Both non-business and business organisations use advertising. Institutional advertising promotes organisational images, ideas and political issues. To make direct product comparisons, marketers use comparative advertising, in which two or more brands are compared. Another form of competitive advertising is reminder advertising, which tells customers that an established brand is still around.

 **APPRECIATE THE POWER OF PRODUCT PLACEMENT AS A PROMOTIONAL METHOD**

A growing technique for reaching consumers is the strategic placement of products or product promotions within TV programs, movies, video games or other entertainment venues to reach the product's target market. Product placement is a popular marketing choice for a number of reasons. Audiences are already pre-segmented according to the media content, making targeting easier. Branded products add realism, as any form of entertainment set in the contemporary world would not appear realistic if the characters did not consume commonly known branded goods. Product placement is a subtle and powerful communication but falls largely outside the traditional consumer protection laws and professional codes of conduct, as a product placement rarely makes claims regarding the value of the item or its specific attributes.

 **UNDERSTAND HOW PUBLIC RELATIONS PRACTICES CAN BE USED TO INFLUENCE COMPANY/BRAND REPUTATION**

Public relations is a broad set of communication efforts used to create and maintain favourable relationships between an organisation and its stakeholders. Public relations can be used to promote people, places, ideas, activities and countries and to create and maintain a positive company image. Public relations tools include: written materials, such as brochures, newsletters and annual reports; corporate identity materials, such as business cards and signs; speeches; event sponsorships; and special events. Publicity is communication in news-story form about an organisation, its products, or both, transmitted through a mass medium at no charge. Publicity-based public relations tools include news releases, feature articles, captioned photographs and press conferences. Problems that organisations confront in using publicity-based public relations include reluctance of media personnel to print or air releases and lack of control over timing and content of messages.

APPRECIATE THE POWER OF SUCCESSFUL SPONSORSHIP ARRANGEMENT WHILST BEING AWARE OF POTENTIAL MISHAPS LINKED TO SPONSORSHIP DEALS

Sponsorship is a versatile form of promotion that influences multiple audiences from target markets to company employees. Digital media and increased controls for advertising products like tobacco, alcohol and gambling are increasing the popularity of sponsorship deals.

Sponsorship deals are commonly used in sport, social causes, art or special events. The most successful sponsorship agreements are based on partnerships where together the sponsor and sponsored individuals enhance the public's enjoyment or experience of an event.

Sponsorship agreements can be questioned or terminated when the sponsored individuals fail to behave in line with the sponsorship contract.

COMPREHEND THE PERSONAL SELLING PRACTICES FOR BOTH CONSUMER AND TRADE SALES SITUATIONS

Many salespeople move through a generally accepted set of steps when they sell products. In prospecting, a salesperson develops a list of potential customers. Before contacting prospects, the salesperson conducts a pre-approach that involves finding and analysing information about prospects and their needs. The approach is the way in which a salesperson contacts potential customers. During a sales presentation, the salesperson must attract and hold the prospect's attention to stimulate interest in and desire for the product. If possible, the salesperson should handle objections as they arise. During the closing, the salesperson asks the prospect to buy the product or products. After a successful closing, the salesperson must follow up the sale.

DESCRIBE SALES PROMOTION METHODS USED FOR CONSUMER MARKETS AS WELL AS TRADE SALES

Sales promotion (SP) is an activity or material that acts as a direct inducement, offering added value or another type of incentive (e.g. discounted price) for a specified product/brand during a set period of time. These incentives can be aimed at resellers, salespeople or consumers. Sales promotion should not be confused with promotion; sales promotion is just one aspect of promotion. Marketers frequently rely on sales promotion to improve the effectiveness of other marketing communication-mix elements, especially advertising and personal selling.

Consumer sales promotion methods encourage or stimulate consumers to patronise specific retail stores or try particular products. These include coupons and cents-off offers, refunds and rebates, frequent-user incentives, point-of-purchase (P-O-P) materials and demonstrations, free samples and premiums, and consumer games, contests and sweepstakes.

Trade sales promotion methods stimulate wholesalers and retailers to carry a producer's products and market those products more aggressively. These methods include buying allowances, buy-back allowances, scan-back allowances, merchandise allowances, cooperative advertising, dealer listings, free merchandise, dealer loaders, premium or push money and sales contests.

Key concepts

Use these key terms in **Search me! marketing** to find the latest relevant readings from a wide range of world-class journals, e-books and newspapers, including *The Australian*.

- advertising budget
- advertising campaign
- advertising platform
- artwork
- captioned photograph
- closing
- comparative advertising
- consumer panel
- consumer sales promotion methods

- copy
- event sponsorship
- feature article
- illustrations
- layout
- media plan
- news release
- personal selling
- post-test
- press conference

- pre-test
- product placement
- prospecting
- recognition test
- reminder advertising
- sales promotion
- target audience
- trade sales promotion methods
- unaided recall test

Issues for discussion and review

1 What is a target audience? How does a marketer analyse the target audience after identifying it?

2 Why is it necessary to define advertising objectives?

3 What factors affect the size of an advertising budget? What techniques are used to determine an advertising budget?

4 What are two key features of product placement?

5 What is public relations? Whom can an organisation reach through public relations?

6 In what ways is the effectiveness of public relations evaluated?

7 What are some sources of negative public relations? How should an organisation deal with unfavourable public relations?

8 Why is sport sponsorship such a powerful form of promotional communication? Give examples of successful and unsuccessful sponsorship arrangements.

9 What is personal selling? How does personal selling relate to other types of promotional activities?

10 Identify steps in the personal selling process. Must a salesperson include all these steps when selling a product to a customer? Why or why not?

11 What is sales promotion? Why is it used?

12 For each of the following, identify and describe three techniques and give several examples:

   a consumer sales promotion methods

   b trade sales promotion methods.

Marketing applications

1   Select a print ad and identify how it:

    a   identifies a specific problem
    b   recommends the product as the best solution to the problem
    c   states the product's advantages and benefits
    d   substantiates the ad's claims
    e   asks the reader to take action.

2   Look through several recent newspapers and magazines, or search the Internet, and identify a news release, a feature article or a captioned photograph used to publicise a product. Describe the type of product.

3   Identify a company that has recently been the target of negative public relations. Describe the situation, and discuss the company's response. What did marketers at this company do well? What, if anything would you recommend that they change about their response?

4   Briefly describe an experience you have had with a salesperson at a clothing store or a car dealership. Describe the steps used by the salesperson. Did the salesperson skip any steps? What did the salesperson do well? Not so well?

5   Identify which sales promotion method or methods a producer might use in the following situations, and explain why the method would be appropriate.

    a   A golf ball manufacturer wants to encourage retailers to add a new type of golf ball to current product offerings.
    b   A life insurance company wants to increase sales of its universal life products, which have been lagging recently (the company has little control over sales activities).
    c   A notebook manufacturer is concerned that the competitor's new 'tablet' notebook due to be launched in three months will make his stock redundant. How can he encourage his distributors/IT store salespeople to 'sell his product'?

ONLINE EXERCISE

6   The LEGO company has been making toys since 1932 and is one of the most recognised brand names in the toy industry. With the company motto 'Only the best is good enough', it is no surprise that the LEGO company has developed such an exciting and interactive website. Visit http://www.lego.com and see how the company promotes the LEGO products and encourages consumer involvement with the brand.

    a   Which type of advertising is LEGO using on its website?
    b   What target audience is the LEGO company wanting to reach?
    c   Identify the advertising objectives the LEGO company is attempting to achieve through this website.

Developing your marketing plan

A vital component of a successful marketing strategy is the company's plan for communicating with its stakeholders. One segment of the communications plan is the marketing communications mix. A clear understanding of the role that promotion plays, as well as the various methods of promotion, is important when developing a promotional plan. The following questions should help you relate to the information in this chapter and to decisions in your marketing plan.

1   Remind yourself of the target markets for your product: what segmentation variables did you use to identify these people (for example, 'environmental awareness' could be a key consideration in your promotional plan)

2   What product features/attributes are appreciated by each target market? How does each target market use the product?

3   What resources (financial, human capital/skills/alliances) do you have available for the duration of this marketing communications plan? Are there any short-term objectives like improving cash flow or reducing stock that you should take into account?

4   What are your objectives for promotion?

5   Which elements of the marketing communications mix are most appropriate for achieving your objectives? Discuss the advantages and disadvantages of each.

6   What role should word-of-mouth communications, buzz marketing or product placement play in your promotional plan?

7   Discuss the different methods for determining the advertising budget.

8   What methods would you use to evaluate the effectiveness of your advertising campaign?

9   Evaluate each type of consumer sales promotion as it relates to accomplishing your promotional objectives.

CengageNOW

Go to http:\\login.cengagebrain.com to link to CengageNOW, your online study tool. First take the Pre-Test for this chapter to get your Personalised Study Plan, and then:

 ✳ **Revise** the learning objectives related to integrated marketing communications by reviewing the chapter summary.

 ✳ **Watch** a video exploring the impact of product placement in greater detail.

 ✳ **Listen** to an overview of the public relations sphere in the audio summary.

After you have completed the activities in your Personalised Study Plan take the Post-Test to determine what concepts you have mastered and what you still need to work on.

Case study

BLOGGERS AND SOCIAL MEDIA INFLUENCE: NEW OPPORTUNITIES FOR BRAND MARKETERS

Word of mouth is recognised as one of the most, if not the most, powerful forms of brand communications.[83] When a consumer hears favourable (or unfavourable) information about a brand from a friend, family member, colleague or referential other they are likely to trust that information and believe it to be true. Marketers have long tried to identify ways to encourage positive word of mouth communications about their brands, and research indicates that brand information communicated through word of mouth is highly credible, highly likely to be passed along to other consumers, and has a positive effect on purchase intent.[84] Similarly, e-wom (word of mouth through electronic means) may have the same power.

The rise of social media, including consumer generated blogs, has created both opportunities and challenges for brand marketers. Social media has given individual consumers the ability to reach large audiences very inexpensively, with both brand advocates and dissatisfied consumers using a range of different social media outlets to share their opinions. In Australia at the end of 2013, there were 11.5 million user accounts on Facebook, over 2.5 million Tumblr accounts and over 2 million Twitter accounts. Between them, Blogspot and Wordpress (the top two blogging platforms) had approximately 6 million Australian user accounts in March 2013.[85] There is clearly potential for large amounts of brand communications to occur in an online C2C (consumer to consumer) environment.

Bloggers in particular present an interesting phenomenon. Blogs such as http://kottke .org (popular culture/liberal arts), http://perezhilton.com (celebrity gossip) http://whatwouldkarldo.com (fashion), http://dooce .com/ and http://retromummy.com/ ('mommy bloggers') attract large numbers of dedicated followers, and present an income source for the bloggers behind them. With daily postings (often more) on the most successful blogs,

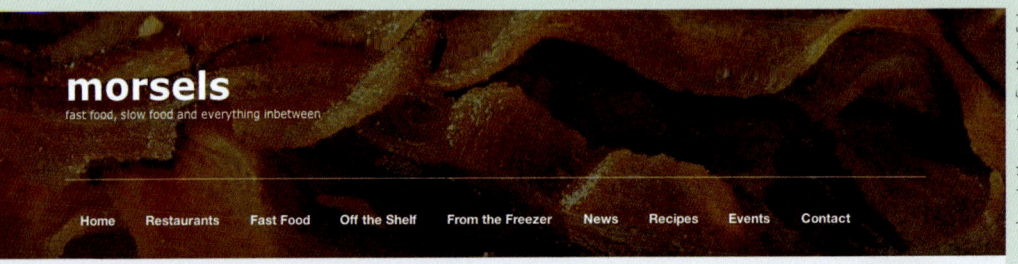

Latest Blog Posts

Visit Blog

12 January 2014 / Leave a comment

Breakfast review: The Brook Bar & Bistro, Ellenbrook

The Brook Bar & Bistro in Ellenbrook is our "local", the place you go to by default to catch up with friends who live nearby or grab a chicken parmy when you've had a rough day and can't be bothered cooking. We've been there a few times since moving to Ellenbrook nearly six months ago – [...]

05 January 2014 / 1 Comment

Lunch at Madhatters on Milston, Swan Valley

Renay and I have decided to explore more places in the Swan Valley this year, particularly since we're so close by in Ellenbrook. The first place on our list was Madhatters on Milston (formerly Milston Gardens) on West Swan Road in Henley Brook, only 15 minutes from home. We tried to get in for lunch once [...]

03 January 2014 / Leave a comment

Quick breakfast (with a surprise) at Coffee Break, Malaga Markets

Some days I just fancy a decent sized breakfast with no frills: an unglamorous plate of bacon, eggs, sausages, hash browns, baked beans and toast is perfect – nothing difficult, complex or fancy. Well today was one of those days and since half of Perth was still closed after Christmas / New Year I decided [...]

31 December 2013 / 1 Comment

Fast Food Review: KFC Aussie vs English Burgers

It's been a while since KFC had anything interesting to review so I was excited to see these new "Aussie vs English" burgers as part of its current "green and gold" promotion in support of the Aussie Ashes team (not that they need it, but there you go). The Aussie burger includes an original recipe [...]

blog readers comment on and engage with the bloggers, and may become attached to them, seeing them as aspirational or referential others.

Acknowledging the power of these bloggers as opinion leaders, marketers are seeking different ways to associate with them, either through placing ads on the blogs, through blog sponsorships, affiliate link programs or publicity. The financial benefit to bloggers is obvious, with some bloggers making a lucrative income from advertising, sponsored posts and brand integration from brands as diverse as Xbox, Woolworths, Asos, Westfield and Toyota. The benefit to marketers comes from positive e-wom associations with the blog. Kristen Young, Group Manager, Retail Communications at Woolworths cites the 'the ability to engage directly and authentically with a highly engaged readership that trusts their blogger to bring them news and information about things that they care about and are interested in' as one of the most exciting things about brand partnerships with bloggers.[86]

Bloggers' links with brand marketers, and the professionalisation of the blogging industry raise a potentially controversial issue. Conferences such as BlogHer in the US and Problogger in Australia educate bloggers about how they can link to brand marketers, and make money from blogging activities. As a result many bloggers include brand mentions within the editorial content of their sites, some as an attempt to attract the favour of potential future advertisers, others as paid brand communications, and others as genuine posts without commercial intent. But it can be difficult for readers to discern the difference. Many bloggers disclose sponsored posts, and offer sales promotions (such as competitions) to their readers to encourage them to read, comment on and have more favourable attitudes towards sponsored content. However many readers express their dismay at the intrusion of brand marketers in the blogs which raises issues for the future in terms of the legal disclosure of paid content (as is the case in the print publishing industry). Some firms even pay individuals with large Facebook followings to post positive brand mentions in status updates! It's a brave new world of e-wom and brand associations with online opinion leaders out there.

Anita Love, Griffith University

QUESTIONS FOR DISCUSSION

1 What promotional objective(s) might underlie a brand's association with a blogger? What types of brand communications could be used to reinforce these objectives?

2 Why are bloggers appealing to marketers as a message source? Consider factors such as characteristics of the source, reach and feedback.

3 Could some forms of sponsored content within blogs (and other forms of media) be considered deceptive? Should all relationships between bloggers and brand marketers be disclosed to readers? What about cases where a blogger is promoting a favoured brand to their readers in the hope of attracting future benefits (free product/future sponsorship)?

Chapter endnotes

1. Christina Passariello and Max Colchester, 'L'Oreal's Slogan Proves Timeless', *The Wall Street Journal*, November 15, 2011, B14; Amy Verner, 'L'Oreal's 'Because I'm worth it' Slogan Marks a Milestone', *The Globe and Mail*, December 2, 2011, www.theglobeandmail.com/life/fashion-and -beauty/beauty/beauty-features/lorals-because-im-worth -itslogan-marks-a-milestone/article2256825/ (accessed December 7, 2011); Kate Shapland, 'It Was Worth It: L'Oreal Celebrates 40th Anniversary of Landmark Slogan', *Telegraph.co.uk*, November 16, 2011, http://fashion .telegraph.co.uk/beauty/news-features/TMG8894450 /It-was-worth-it-LOreal-celebrates-40th-anniversary -of-landmark-slogan.html (accessed December 7, 2011); Rebecca Leffler, 'L'Oreal Fetes 40th Anniversary of 'Because You're Worth It' in Paris', *The Hollywood Reporter*, November 14, 2011, www.hollywoodreporter.com/fash -track/l-orealjane-fonda-freida-pinto-261216 (accessed December 7, 2011).

2. Bob Liodice, 'Essentials for Integrated Marketing', *Advertising Age*, June 9, 2008, http://adage.com/ print?article_id=127599.

3 Joann Peck and Jennifer Wiggins, 'It Just Feels Good: Customers' Affective Response to Touch and Its Influence in Persuasion', *Journal of Marketing* 70 (October 2006): http://www.marketingpower.com.

4. Stewart Cockburn, 'Netbooks—The New Breed of Ultra Portable Laptops', *Ezine @rticles*, March 28, 2009, http://ezinearticles.com/?Netbooks—The-New-Breed-of -Ultra-Portable-Laptops&id=2155901.

5. David G. Taylor, Jeffrey E. Lewin, and David Strutton, 'Friends, Fans, and Followers: Do Ads Work on Social Networks? How Gender and Age Shape Receptivity', *Journal of Advertising Research* 51, no. 1 (2011): 258–275.

6. Baetzgen, Andreas, and Jörg Tropp, 'Owned Media': Developing a Theory from the Buzzword', *Studies in Media and Communication* 1:2 (2013): 1–10.

7. Baetzgen, Andreas, and Jörg Tropp, 'Owned Media': Developing a Theory from the Buzzword.'

8. Ibid.; Mike Taylor, 'NBC Digital launches 'Life Goes Strong' site for boomers', Fishbowl NY, May 11, 2010, accessed October 4, 2013, http://www.mediabistro.com/fishbowlny /nbc-digital-launches-life-goes-strong-site-for-boomers _b14863.

9. Salvador Ruiz and María Sicilia, 'The Impact of Cognitive and/or Affective Processing Styles on Consumer Response to Advertising Appeals', *Journal of Business Research* 57 (2004): 657–664.

10. Sheila Shayon, 'Google is the Mobile Ad King, but Facebook, Twitter are Taking Notes', Brand Channel, June 14, 2013, accessed October 4, 2013, http://www .brandchannel.com/home/post/2013/06/14/Google -Mobile-Ads-061413.aspx.

11. Alex Halperin, 'Targeted ads coming to TV', salon.com, December 27, 2012, accessed October 4, 2013, http://www.salon.com/2012/12/26/predictive_ads _coming_to_tv/; Josh Constine, 'Gracenote's Ad Replacement System That Personalizes TV Commercials Will Start Trials In 2013', *TechCrunch*, December 26, 2012, accessed October 4, 2013, http://techcrunch .com/2012/12/26/gracenote-tv-targeted-ads/.

12. Madeleine Ross, 'ABCs: Beauty and lifestyle dives, health and home hikes in monthlies', Bandt, February 15, 2013, accesses September 2, 2013, http://www.bandt.com .au/news/media/abcs-beauty-and-lifestyle-dives-health -and-home-hi?utm_source=SilverpopMailing&utm _medium=email&utm_campaign=BandT%20 Newsletter%20-%20send%20-%3E%2015/02/2013%20 8:29:43%20AM&utm_content=&spMailingID=5610359& spUserID=Njg0NzU4NDE3MQS2&spJobID=66155510 &spReportId=NjYxNTU1MTAS1.

13 Christina Chaey, 'Condé Nast cuts deal with Amazon to turn magazine subscriptions into an all-access business', Fast Company, http://m.fastcompany.com/3016076 /fast-feed/conde-nast-cuts-deal-with-amazon-to-turn -magazine-subscriptions-into-an-all-access?partner=rss ?partner=rss&utm_medium=referral&utm_source =pulsenews.

14. Christopher Heine, 'Talking Mobile Ads Are No Joke', Ad Week, April 1, 2013, accessed September 2, 2013.

15. 'Nuance Unveils Voice Ads: A Game Changer in Interactive Advertising', April 1, 2013, accessed September 2, 2013, http://www.nuance.com/company/news-room /press-releases/voiceads.docx

16. Lucy Clark, 'Music man', *B&T*, February 1, 2013, accessed September 20, 2013, http://www.bandt.com.au/features /music-man?utm_source=SilverpopMailing&utm _medium=email&utm_campaign=BandT%20 Newsletter%20-%20send%20-; Vanessa Apaolaza-Ibáñez, Mark Zander, Patrick Hartmann. Memory, 'Emotions and rock 'n' roll: The influence of music in advertising, on brand and endorser perception', *African Journal of Business Management*, 2010; 4:17 (2010): 3805–3816, http://www .sciencedaily.com/releases/2011/06/110622045135.htm.

17. U. Reese, 'The power of sound: audio drives award winning work at the 2013 Cannes lions', *iV interactive*, accessed September 20, 2013, http://blog.ivgroup .cc/2013/06/18/the-power-of-sound-audio-drives-award -winning-work-at-the-2013-cannes-lions/.

18. Daniel J. Howard and Roger A. Kerin, 'The Effects of Personalized Product Recommendations on Advertisement Response Rates: The "Try This. It Works!" Technique', *Journal of Consumer Psychology* 14: 3 (2004): 271–279.

19. Rik Pieters and Michel Wedel, 'Attention Capture and Transfer in Advertising: Brand, Pictorial, and Text-Size Effects', *Journal of Marketing* (April 2004): 36–50.

20. William F. Arens, *Contemporary Advertising* (Burr Ridge, IL: Irwin/McGraw-Hill, 2007).

21. Anil Batra, 'Social Media Analytics Part I', Web Analytics, Behavioral Targeting and Optimization by Anil Batra, June 29, 2009, accessed October 7, 2013, http://webanalysis .blogspot.com/2009/06/social-media-analytics-part-i .html#ixzz2h0N2k6os.

22. Pam Dyer, '50 Top Tools for Social Media Monitoring, Analytics, and Management', *Social Media Today*, May 13, 2013, accessed October 7, 2013, http://socialmediatoday

.com/pamdyer/1458746/50-top-tools-social-media
-monitoring-analytics-and management-2013.

23. Alistair Barr, 'Google may ditch 'cookies' as online ad
tracker', *USA Today*, September 17, 2013, accessed
October 7, 2013, http://www.usatoday.com/story
/tech/2013/09/17/google-cookies-advertising/2023183/.

24. Tim Peterson, 'Pinterest, Twitter Step Up Their Analytics
Games', Ad Week, March 13, 2013, accessed October 4,
2013, http://www.adweek.com/news/technology
/pinterest-twitter-step-their-analytics-games-147910.

25. 'Legislation', ACCC, http://www.accc.gov.au/about-us
/australian-competition-consumer-commission/legislation,
accessed January 28, 2014; 'False or misleading claims',
ACCC, http://www.accc.gov.au/business/advertising
-promoting-your-business/false-or-misleading-claims,
accessed January 28, 2014.

26. D. Knox, 'Digital product placement coming to Seven', *TV
Tonight*, December 28, 2010, http://www.tvtonight.com
.au/2010/12/digital-product-placement-coming-to
-seven.html

27. '"Junk" food product placement banned in UK', *Australian
Food News*, 10 February, 2010, http://www.ausfoodnews
.com.au/2010/02/10/junk-food-product-placement-
banned-in-uk.html; C. Gascoyne, 'Australia: Product
Placement, it's powerful, but is it legal?', http://www
.mondaq.com/australia/article.asp?articleid=52338.

28. 'Announcing the 2013 Brandcameo Product Placement
Award Winners', *Brand Channel*, accessed September 2,
2013, http://www.brandchannel.com/features_effect
.asp?pf_id=538; Abe Sauer, 'Product Placement Sees
Global Rise as Fans Face Saturated Entertainment', *Brand
Channel*, April 24, 2013, accessed October 7, 2013,
http://www.brandchannel.com/home/post/2013/04/24
/Product-Placement-On-The-Rise-042413.aspx#continue.

29. 'Announcing the 2013 Brandcameo Product Placement
Award Winners', *Brand Channel*, accessed September 2,
2013, http://www.brandchannel.com/features_effect
.asp?pf_id=538

30. Abe Sauer, 'Avril Lavigne May Have Just Pulled Off the
Greatest (and Worst) Product Placement of All Time',
Brand Channel, August 20, 2013, accessed October 7,
2013, http://www.brandchannel.com/home
/post/2013/08/20/Avril-Lavigne-Product-Placement-Rock
-N-Roll-082013.aspx; Avril Lavigne, 'Rock N Roll',
http://www.youtube.com/watch?v=uuNTO31FIY8.

31. George E. Belch and Michael A. Belch, *Advertising and
Promotion* (Burr Ridge, IL: Irwin/McGraw-Hill, 2001),
576–577.

32. Robert Upe, 'Winners for "best jobs in the world"
announced', *The Sydney Morning Herald*, June 21, 2013,
http://www.smh.com.au/travel/travel-news/winners-for
-best-jobs-in-the-world-announced-20130621-2omxf
.html#ixzz2fQBLiZpu; Brendan Coyne, 'Best job in the
world is back. And this time, there are six', *Ad News*,
March 4, 2013, http://www.adnews.com.au/adnews
/best-job-in-the-world-is-back-and-this-time-there-are-six;
Angela Saurine, 'Tourism Australia to launch Six Best Jobs
in the World campaign', News Limited Network, March
5, 2013; http://www.news.com.au/travel/news/tourism
-australia-to-launch-six-best-jobs-in-the-world-campaign/

story-e6frfq80-1226590095882#ixzz2fQCz7OT4; Kevin
May, 'Best Jobs in the World stunt works wonders for PR
again, but technology needed to relieve strain', *tnooz*, April
4, 2013, http://www.tnooz.com/article/best-jobs-in-the
-world-stunt-works-wonders-for-pr-again-but-technology
-needed-to-relieve-strain/#sthash.Z4w5W95S.dpuf (all
accessed September 20, 2013).

33. 'Publicity Felix Baumgartner speaking in a press
conference', http://www.youtube.com/user/redbull/about;
'Confirmed: Felix Baumgartner's free fall from space sets
five new world records', *Guinness World Records News*,
October 15, 2012, http://www.guinnessworldrecords
.com/news/2012/10/confirmed-felix-baumgartners-free
-fall-from-space-sets-five-new-world-records-45463/;
Janet Fouts, 'What Online Marketers Can Learn From
the Red Bull Jump', *Social Media Today*, October 16, 2012,
http://socialmediatoday.com/jfouts/910631/what-online
-marketers-can-learn-red-bull-jump; Jenny Shaw, 'Red Bull
Stratos', *Mindshare*, http://www.wpp.com/wpp/marketing
/digital/red-bull-stratos/ (all accessed October 4, 2013).

34. George E. Belch and Michael A. Belch, *Advertising
and Promotion* (Burr Ridge, IL: Irwin/McGraw-
Hill, 2001), 598.

35. Stephen McMahon, '2Day FM's PR strategy after royal
prank call a "major cock-up"', News Limited Network,
December 12, 2012, http://www.theaustralian.com
.au/news/hoax-pair-pr-strategy-a-major-cock-up/story
-e6frg6n6-1226534836565; Alison Rourke, 'Prank call DJs
receive death threats', *theguardian.com*, December, 14
2012, http://www.theguardian.com/world/2012/
dec/14/prank-call-djs-death-threats; 'Royal prank weighs
on Southern Cross', *The Sydney Morning Herald*, August
14, 2013, accessed September 9, 2013, http://www.smh
.com.au/business/earnings-season/royal-prank-weighs-on
-southern-cross-20130814-2rw7h.html#ixzz2dh1TA2Y1;
'Royal prank call DJ Mel Greig sues employer', *BBC News*,
accessed September 9, 2013, http://www.bbc.co.uk/news
/world-asia-23243308.

36. Tony Meenaghan, Damien McLoughlin, and Alan
McCormack, 'New Challenges in Sponsorship Evaluation
Actors, New Media, and the Context of Praxis',
Psychology & Marketing 30.5 (2013): 444–460.

37. Alicia Beachley, 'Maximising sponsorship investment is not
rocket science (but it is a science)', Marketing Mag, March
4, 2013, accessed September 9, 2013,
http://www.marketingmag.com.au/blogs/maximising-your
-sponsorship-investment-is-not-rocket-science-but-there
-is-a-science-to-it-37151/#.Ui1OUcZmjTo.

38. Denise Lee Yohn, 'Lance Armstrong's Biggest Offense',
Brand Channel, January 14, 2013, accessed September 6,
2013, http://www.brandchannel.com/brand_speak
.asp?bs_id=322.

39. Tony Meenaghan, 'Measuring Sponsorship Performance:
Challenge and Direction', *Psychology & Marketing* 30.5
(2013): 385–393.

40. Simon Rogers, 'London 2012 Olympic sponsors list: who
are they and what have they paid?', *The Guardian*, July 19,
2012, accessed September 9, 2013, http://www
.theguardian.com/sport/datablog/2012/jul/19/london
-2012-olympic-sponsors-list.

41. 'Post recession sponsorship spend 25% higher than pre', *Marketing Mag*, accessed September 6, 2013, http://www .marketingmag.com.au/tags/sponsorship/#.UiIJosZmjTo.

42. Tony Meenaghan, 'Measuring Sponsorship Performance: Challenge and Direction', *Psychology & Marketing* 30.5 (2013): 385–393; Tony Meenaghan, Damien McLoughlin, and Alan McCormack, 'New Challenges in Sponsorship Evaluation Actors, New Media, and the Context of Praxis', *Psychology & Marketing* 30.5 (2013): 444–460.

43. Tony Meenaghan, 'Measuring Sponsorship Performance: Challenge and Direction', *Psychology & Marketing* 30.5 (2013): 385–393.

44. Tony Meenaghan, Damien McLoughlin, and Alan McCormack, 'New Challenges in Sponsorship Evaluation Actors, New Media, and the Context of Praxis', *Psychology & Marketing* 30.5 (2013): 444–460.

45. Reinhard Grohs, Heribert Reisinger, 'Sponsorship effects on brand image: The role of exposure and activity involvement', *Journal of Business Research*, In Press, Corrected Proof, Available online August 22, 2013.

46. Ibid.

47. Anna Harrington, 'Why sponsors take scandals in their stride', *Business Spectator*, February 22, 2013, accessed September 9, 2013, http://www.businessspectator.com.au /article/2013/2/22/commodities/why-sponsors-take -scandals-their-stride.

48. 'Kumho V8 Touring Car Series confirms 2013 technical regulations', Kumho, December 14, 2012, accessed September 9, 2013, http://www.kumho.com.au/ blog/2012/12/14/kumho-v8-touring-car-series-confirms -2013-technical-regulations/.

49. Reinhard Grohs, Heribert Reisinger, 'Sponsorship effects on brand image: The role of exposure and activity involvement.'

50 Ben Klayman, 'McDonald's Not Cutting 09 Sponsorship Budget', *Reuters*, March 9, 2009), http://www.reuters.com /article/sportsNews/idUSTRE52864Q20090309.

51. Tom Porter, 'Red Bull Under Fire Over Seventh Death at Tyrol Stunt Event', *International Business Times*, May 5, 2013, accessed October 4, 2013, http://www .ibtimes.co.uk/articles/464619/20130505/red-bull -stunt-marketing-extreme-sports-death.htm; Calum McGuigan, 'Red Bull: Masterminds of New Age Marketing', creativeguerrillamarketing, October 16, 2012, accessed October 4, 2013, http://www.creativeguerrillamarketing .com/viral-marketing/red-bull-masterminds-of-new-age -marketing/#sthash.mbarmlsa.dpuf; Russell Scibetti, 'HBO Real Sports – Red Bull Extreme Marketing', *Marketing*, August 20, 2013, accessed October 4, 2013, http://www .thebusinessofsports.com/2013/08/20/hbo-real-sports -red-bull-extreme-marketing/#sthash.zuqio92v.dpuf; Jenny Shaw, 'Red Bull Stratos', *Mindshare*, http://www.wpp.com /wpp/marketing/digital/red-bull-stratos/, accessed October 4, 2013; David Aaker, 'Red Bull: The Ultimate Brand Builder', May 15, 2013, accessed October 4, 2013, http://www.prophet.com/blog/aakeronbrands/140 -red-bull.

52 Reinhard Grohs, Heribert Reisinger, 'Sponsorship effects on brand image: The role of exposure and activity involvement.'

53. Ibid.

54. Alicia Beachley, 'Maximising sponsorship investment is not rocket science (but it is a science).'

55. Tony Meenaghan, Damien McLoughlin, and Alan McCormack, 'New Challenges in Sponsorship Evaluation Actors, New Media, and the Context of Praxis.'

56. 'Drug allegations could cost Aussie sport millions in sponsorship dollars' Marketing, February 8, 2013, accessed September 6, 2013, http://www.marketingmag .com.au/tags/sponsorship/#.UiIJosZmjTo; Anna Harrington, 'Why sponsors take scandals in their stride.'

57. Chris Isidore, 'Nike suspends contract with Pistorius', CNN Money, February 21, 2013, accessed September 6, 2013, http://money.cnn.com/2013/02/21/news/ companies/nike-pistorius/index.html.

58. Denise Lee Yohn, 'Lance Armstrong's Biggest Offense.'

59. 'Celine Dion, Tiger Woods Help Underprivileged Youths', *Chicago Tribune*, August 9, 1999, accessed September 19, 2013, http://articles.chicagotribune.com/1999-08-09 /news/9908100089_1_tiger-woods-foundation-rene -angelil-celine-dion.

60. 'Cricket Australia agree to Fawad Ahmed's request not to wear Victoria Bitter logo in England', *Herald Sun*, September 3, 2013, accessed September 9, 2013, http://www.heraldsun.com.au/sport/cricket /cricket-australia-agree-to-fawad-ahmeds-request -not-to-wear-victoria-bitter-logo-in-england/story -fni2usfi-1226709612838; Martin Hardy, 'Papiss Cisse will refuse to wear Wonga sponsored Newcastle shirt – but seeks a pay rise to stay at St James' Park', *The Independent*, June 11, 2013, accessed September 9, 2013, http://www.independent.co.uk/sport/football/premier- league/papiss-cisse-will-refuse-to-wear-wonga-sponsored -newcastle-shirt--but-seeks-a-pay-rise-to-stay-at-st-james -park-8652995.html; John Lehmann, and Jamie Pandram, 'Doug Walters tells Pakistan-born Fawad Ahmed: if you don't like the VB uniform, don't play for Australia', *The Daily Telegraph*, September 6, 2013, accessed September 9, 2013, http://www.dailytelegraph.com.au/news/nsw/ doug-walters-tells-pakistanborn-fawad-ahmed-if-you -don8217t-like-the-vb-uniform-don8217t-play-for -australia/story-fni0cx12-1226712644439; Jamie Pandaram, 'Fawad Ahmed has inadvertently handed VB "priceless" marketing coup no amount of money could buy', *news.com.au*, September 7, 2013, accessed September 9, 2013, http://www.news.com.au/breaking -news/fawad-ahmed-has-inadvertently-handed-vb -priceless-marketing-coup-no-amount-of-money-could -buy/story-e6frfkp9-1226713581591#ixzz2eM0SoOQd; Chloe Saltau, 'CA slams "bigotry" against Ahmed', *The Sydney Morning Herald*, September 7, 2013, accessed September 9, 2013, http://www.smh.com.au/sport /cricket/ca-slams-bigotry-against-ahmed-20130906-2t9yz .html#ixzz2eLxgPguc; Glenn Valencich, 'Calls for Ahmed to play for free', *Sports Fan*, September 6, 2013, accessed September 9, 2013, http://www.sportsfan.com.au/calls-for -ahmed-to-play-for-free/tabid/91/newsid/111227/default .aspx.

61. 'Research and Markets: The Cost of the Average Sales Call Today Is More Than 400 Dollars', *M2 Presswire*, February 28, 2006.

62. Eli Jones, Paul Busch, and Pater Dacin, 'Firm Market Orientation and Salesperson Customer Orientation: Interpersonal and Intrapersonal Influence on Customer Service and Retention in Business-to-Business Buyer-Seller Relationships', *Journal of Business Research* 56 (2003): 323–340.

63. Sarah Lorge, 'The Best Way to Prospect', *Sales & Marketing Management* (January 1998): 80.

64. Bob Donath, 'Tap Sales "Hot Buttons" to Stay Competitive', *Marketing News*, March 1, 2005: 8.

65. Ralph W. Giacobbe, Donald W. Jackson, Jr., Lawrence A. Crosby, and Claudia M. Bridges, 'A Contingency Approach to Adaptive Selling Behavior and Sales Performance: Selling Situations and Salesperson Characteristics', *Journal of Personal Selling & Sales Management* 26 (Spring 2006): 115–142

66. Richard G. McFarland, Goutam N. Challagalla, and Tasadduq A. Shervani, 'Influence Tactics for Effective Adaptive Selling', *Journal of Marketing* 70 (October 2006), http://www.marketingpower.com.

67. John Andy Wood, 'NLP Revisted: Nonverbal Communications and Signals of Trustworthiness', *Journal of Personal Selling & Sales Management* 26 (Spring 2006): 198–204.

68. Harvey Chipkin, 'Insufficient Bandwidth Can Ruin a Meeting, Expert Says', *Travel Market Report*, December 5, 2011, http://travelmarketreport.com/meetings?articleID=6663&LP=1 (accessed December 9, 2011); 'How to Design and Deliver Effective Sales Presentations', *Slideshare*, www.slideshare.net/gotomeeting/how-to-design-and-deliver-effective-virtualsales-presentations (accessed December 9, 2011).

69. Stephen S. Porter, Joshua L. Wiener, and Gary L. Frankwick, 'The Moderating Effect of Selling Situation on the Adaptive Selling Strategy—Selling Effectiveness Relationship', *Journal of Business Research* 56 (2003): 275–281.

70. Fernando Jaramillo, Jay Prakash Mulki, and Paul Solomon, 'The Role of Ethical Climate on Salesperson's Role Stress, Job Attitudes, Turnover Intention, and Job Performance', *Journal of Personal Selling & Sales Management* 26 (Summer 2006): 272–282.

71. K. S. Fam, L. Yang, and G. Tanakinjal, 'Innovative sales promotion techniques among Hong Kong advertisers–a content analysis', *Innovative Marketing* 4 (2008): 1, 8–15, businessperspectives.org; M. Leppäniemi, and H. Karjaluoto, 'Mobile Marketing: From Marketing Strategy to Mobile Marketing Campaign Implementation', Mobiphonica (2008).

72. George E. Belch and Michael A. Belch, *Advertising and Promotion* (Burr Ridge, IL: Irwin/McGraw-Hill, 2001): 526–532.

73. K. Quinn, 'Supermarket slip as Coles confirms MasterChef deal', *The Age* (27 July, 2010): theage.com.au, http://www.theage.com.au/entertainment/tv-and-radio/supermarket-slip-as-coles-confirms-masterchef-deal-20100727-10tel.html; K. Quinn, 'MasterChef mops up in a whole new

way', *Brisbane Times* (31 May, 2010): brisbanetimes.com.au, http://www.brisbanetimes.com.au/opinion/blogs/the-vulture/masterchef-mops-up-in-a-whole-new-way/20100531-wobc.html.

74. Eric T. Anderson and Inseong Song, 'Coordinating Price Reductions and Coupon Events', *Journal of Marketing Research* (November 2004): 411–422.

75. D. Anderson, 'National Coupon Month: Fun facts and actual statistics', accessed September 9, 2013, http://c2cwriter.com/blog/, http://www.examiner.com/article/national-coupon-month-fun-facts-and-actual-statistics, accessed January 28, 2014; Betsy Spethmann, 'FSI Coupon Worth Reaches $300 Billion in 2006: MARX', *Promo*, January 4, 2007, http://promomagazine.com/othertactics/news/fsi_coupon_worth_300_billion_010407/.

76. Timothy W. Martin, 'Coupons Are Hot. Clipping Is Not.' *The Wall Street Journal*, February 25, 2009, http://online.wsj.com/article/SB123551425475363603.html (accessed November 30, 2011); Brandon Munson, 'The Mobile Coupon: What's the Bang for the Buck?' *FoodService.com*, November 7, 2010, www.foodservice.com/articles/show.cfm?contentid=19550 (accessed November 30, 2011); 'Go Green with Electronic Grocery Coupons', WOWPONS, June 27, 2011, www.wowponsmobilegrocerycoupons.com/Green-Shopping/go-green-withelectronic-grocery-coupons.html (accessed November 30, 2011).

77. Arthur L. Porter, 'Direct Mail's Lessons for Electronic Couponers', *Marketing Management Journal* (Spring/Summer 2000): 107–115.

78. Rajneesh Suri, Srinivasan Swaminathan, and Kent B. Monroe, 'Price Communications in Online and Print Coupons: An Empirical Investigation', *Journal of Interactive Marketing* (Autumn 2004): 74–86.

79. Brian Grow, 'The Great Rebate Runaround', *BusinessWeek* (December 5, 2005): 34–7.

80. 'Home Page', Cartoon Network Australia, 2011, http://www.cartoonnetwork.com.au/.

81. 'Breathe happy competition', 2013, http://www.bigbrother.com.au/win/ambipur/, accessed January 28, 2014.

82. Burt A. Lazar, 'Agencies Held Liable for Client Ads, Promos', *Marketing News* (February 15, 2005).

83. E. Keller, 2007, 'Unleashing the Power of Word of Mouth: Creating Brand Advocacy to Drive Growth', *Journal of Advertising Research*, 47 (4), 448-52.

84. E. Keller, 2007, 'Unleashing the Power of Word of Mouth: Creating Brand Advocacy to Drive Growth'.

85. D. Cowling, 'Social Media Statistics Australia – March 2013', Retrieved on September 9, 2013 from http://www.socialmedianews.com.au/social-media-statistics-australia-march-2013/.

86. L. Murphy, (Interviewer) and K. Young, (Interviewee), 31 July 2013, *Café Remarkables Catch Up with Kristen from Woolworths* [Interview transcript], Retrieved on September 6, 2013 from: http://theremarkablesgroup.com.au/news/cafe-remarkable-catch-up-kristen-woolworths/.

Marketing mix diagram

ECONOMIC FORCES

COMPETITIVE FORCES

POLITICAL FORCES

PRODUCT

PRICE

CUSTOMER

PROMOTION

DISTRIBUTION

SOCIO-CULTURAL FORCES

EXPANDED Ps (People, Physical Evidence, Processes, Partnerships)

LEGAL AND REGULATORY FORCES

TECHNOLOGICAL FORCES

EXPANDING THE MARKETING MIX

Strategic use of the expanded marketing mix variables

A marketing mix for the 'experience economy'
Mapping the customer experience

The people variable

Personnel
Aesthetic labour
Emotional labour
'Me as the customer' and other customers as participants
Passers-by (or accidental participants)
Can marketing help solve these problems?

The physical evidence/physical assets variable

Buildings, grounds and other physical assets
Atmospherics

Processes

Flow and progress of customers
Sensitivity, privacy and confidentiality of customer–company interactions
Digital technology and the service process
Curated convenience

The partnerships variable

Throughout this chapter, Watch, Listen and Revise icons indicate an opportunity for online self-study through CengageNOW, linking you to animated chapter overviews, interactive diagrams, videos, quizzes and more.

14 EXPANDING THE MARKETING MIX

Learning Objectives

 LO1 Understand how competitive advantage can be achieved through strategic use of the expanded marketing mix variables

 LO2 Appreciate how the people variable of the expanded marketing mix can be used to create exceptional experiences for the customers

 LO3 Understand how the design of physical assets (physical evidence) can make operations run more smoothly as well as enhance customer satisfaction

 LO4 Appreciate how a step-by-step analysis of customers' interaction with the organisation can improve profitability

 LO5 Learn how companies can use partnerships with external organisations to improve their competitiveness.

MARKETING CHALLENGE | 5-STAR AFTER SALES SERVICE FROM KUBOTA AUSTRALIA

Jeremy works for Kubota Tractor Australia (KTA) at the company headquarters in Melbourne. Today he is visiting a rural Kubota dealer to conduct a '5-Star Service Program' inspection. Kubota is a Japanese manufacturer of heavy machinery, which has a proud history of making quality products since 1890. The company has won prestigious awards for manufacturing excellence and claims International brand leadership with their products sold in over 130 countries. As a manufacturer, Kubota recognises the importance of partnerships through a network of independent dealers to ensure distribution of Kubota's agricultural machinery across Australia. KTA and these independent agricultural machinery dealerships have a partnership agreement that allows the end-users for Kubota products to buy Kubota machines from a conveniently located dealership. Accredited Kubota dealers also offer after-sales service to

Source: Kubota

501

their customers (the end-users) as many of these machines are used in commercial agricultural settings where speed of repairs is essential.

Kubota has only a handful of its own employees in Australia and uses its 5-star service program to ensure consistent high standards for all their agricultural customers. The 5-star quality drive is linked to significant financial incentives aimed at motivating the independent partners across Australia to gain, and maintain, 5-star status.

To achieve (and maintain) their 5-star status, key team members have to attend training courses provided by KTA. For example, mechanics need to learn how to diagnose the reasons for engine failure to make sure that customers don't return with the same problem. By correctly diagnosing engine failure, customers can be advised of changes they need to make (e.g. to use the correct oil) or of another Kubota model that would better suit their needs. Workshop managers also need to make sure that all mechanics are up to date with the latest technological innovations or changes in service procedures.

The 5-star service program recognises the value of customer satisfaction and brand loyalty while aiming to improve dealers' business on several levels; for example, by maintaining service and workshop facilities that promote fast, as well as professional, service work. Qualified mechanics use specialist diagnostic equipment and maintain their expert knowledge through regular training. Even tidy premises and the way signage is used attract positive feedback. By participating in the 5-star service program the independent agricultural dealers learn how to make the most of their marketing mix variables to improve overall profitability.

The program is based on results from a self-assessment conducted by dealers every two years, followed by a KTA inspection. The 5-star dealership status is highly desirable, not just for the financial rewards it brings, but also because dealers can use their 5-star status in promotions.[1]

| MARKETING CHALLENGE QUESTIONS | 1 What minimum standards has Kubota set for their 5-star dealers? | 2 How do these required minimum standards impact the service experienced by customers? |

Introduction

Although the Kubota brand is linked to tractors, industrial engines, generators and construction equipment, their 5-star dealership certification specifies minimum requirements for the appearance of premises as well as expectations and standards related to customer service. Through their 5-star dealership program Kubota Tractors Australia (KTA) controls marketing activities beyond the four traditional marketing mix elements of product, price, place and promotion. Through this approach, KTA can better respond to the challenges presented by a dynamic business environment.

In this chapter we review the development of the traditional marketing mix and examine reasons for adding more elements. We consider why attention to additional marketing mix elements is essential for competitive advantage in today's ever changing world. In the second half of the chapter we explore in detail the additional marketing mix variables of people, physical evidence, processes and partnerships.

Strategic use of the expanded marketing mix variables

The marketing mix, often referred to as the 'controllable factors' or 'the tools of the marketing trade' (first introduced in Chapter 1), includes key factors that marketing managers can vary in response to changes in their business environment. These variables are key decisions a company can take to ensure they satisfy their customers and remain profitable.

The idea of business managers using a mix of key decisions to maximise business gains from limited resources emerged in the late 1940s, but the marketing mix concept as we know it (product, place, price and promotion) was introduced by McCarthy in 1964 as the 'combination of factors at the marketing manager's command to satisfy the target market'.[2] These four key marketing mix variables emerged during an era of intense manufacturing as a set of key controllable variables (key decisions) that could be used to respond to changes in the external business environment. The focus of the original four marketing mix variables was, therefore, on tangible goods. Figure 14.1 summarises decisions that need to be made within the traditional 4Ps marketing mix framework.

The key marketing mix ingredients of product, place, price and promotions reigned without great challenge until the late 1970s when greater focus was given to the marketing of services coinciding with the growing financial importance of the service economy. In this new environment, the marketing mix model needed to be rethought.[3]

Product
Service
Quality
Range
Brand name
Alternatives
Benefits
Guarantees
Packaging: either as the tangible wrapping for products or the bundling of goods and services into a package purchased by customers. This term is typically used in the tourism industry, e.g. EU Package Travel Directive.

Place
Distribution (including downloading digital products)
Physical location, e.g. for a hotel, accessibility, e.g. local bank, transport to the location
Convenience

Price
List price
Discounts (coupons, bulk/group purchases, early/late bookings)
Payment period, credit terms
Special situations, such as skimming or penetration pricing
Price elasticity

Promotion
Marketing communications mix (promotional channels)
- Advertising
- Personal selling
- Product placement
- Public relations (PR)
- Digital marketing communications
- Sales promotion (SP)
Production channels
- Frontline staff
- Service outlets
- Franchises
External communications (not in our control)
- Word of mouth (WOM +/−)
- Media editorials

FIGURE 14.1
SUMMARY OF THE FOUR MARKETING MIX VARIABLES

The boundaries between marketing tangible goods and intangible services are obscured when companies focus on building long-lasting relationships with their customers. The trend towards personalisation (also referred to as customisation, tailoring or individualisation) of goods and services encourages even business-to-business (B2B) manufacturers to engage in the customer service process.

The expanded marketing mix (also known as the extended marketing mix or 8Ps) evolved from the traditional four variables in response to the expanding services sector, and aimed to accommodate the intangible nature of service- and experience-based products.[4] Labels for the variables differ from one publication to another, but the seven elements shown in Table 14.1 are the most commonly agreed upon: product, place, price, promotion, people, physical evidence and processes.[5] The eighth 'P' in the marketing mix has a number of different names; for example, *personalisation* referring to a customers' desire for individualised products, *publications* as a consistent and systematic use of a company's visual identity. *Procedures* and *programming* have also been used, but these are too similar to *processes*. Partnerships is used in this book since partnerships may be essential to achieving customer satisfaction and new product development processes, as well as making a company's products available at locations far away from their traditional stronghold.

Figure 14.2 outlines the four expanded marketing-mix variables and typical decisions marketing managers make in relation to them. Which marketing mix variables are used most depends on the type of organisation, as well as opportunities presented to marketing managers. For example, an organisation operating from rented premises with a limited budget could use the people and processes variables together with product, place and price.

Using the additional variables allows marketers to create functional as well as psychologically pleasing environments for interaction between a company and its customers. Companies can eliminate all possible causes of frustration (e.g. telephone queues) and create a well-functioning workplace (e.g. office layout or stock-keeping system) enabling qualified and trained staff members to successfully deliver goods and services

People/participants	Physical evidence
Staff (frontline to support roles)	Tangible components, e.g. furnishing, décor, staff uniforms/grooming
'Moments of truth'	The 'atmospherics' or 'servicescape': the ambience, background music, comfort of waiting areas
Influences quality perceptions	
Guests and other participants	Design of physical assets
Customer-oriented culture	Typical of service companies
Internal marketing	Promotion must support the style adopted
Degree of empowerment	
Interpersonal behaviour	
Appearance	
Training	
Discretion	
Commitment	
Incentives	
Attitudes	
Aesthetic labour	
Emotional labour	
Processes	**Partnerships**
True to the marketing philosophy, i.e. what more can we offer to our customers, what would they really appreciate?	Partnership, e.g. FlyBuys
	Joint venture between small-scale local partnerships, for example a restaurant serving local produce
Customer oriented	
Timing	
Interactions with customers, e.g. 'touch points'	
Degree of automation	
Degree of personalisation	
Payment systems (e.g. online)	
'Educating' customers, e.g. recycling in hotels	

FIGURE 14.2 THE EXPANDED MARKETING-MIX ELEMENTS

to customers. Satisfied customers will patronise the company again and even recommend it to their friends (see Chapter 1 for reasons why companies want to have loyal clients).

Adding these additional variables to the traditional marketing mix helps companies achieve competitive advantage, positive word-of-mouth communication, brand loyalty (or brand differentiation) as well as a positive attitude towards the company and its products. This usually translates into an improved financial performance by the organisation.[6]

A marketing mix for the 'experience economy'

In the current competitive and fast changing consumer environment, the line between goods and services has been blurred to the extent that the 'quality' of goods and services is now gauged from the overall 'experience' of buying and consuming. In this new environment, marketers must consider the 'experience' of a good or service and how they can manage it to ensure customer satisfaction and repeat business. This **experience** economy emerged from two key trends. First, affluent

Source: Shutterstock.com

consumers can now expect most products and services to meet advertised functional quality standards and brand image. Second, companies find it increasingly difficult to sell goods and services based solely on their functional qualities. Moreover, over time the 'share of consumers' wallet' spent on commodities and goods has declined with an increasing proportion of expenditure being directed to experiencing leisure activities and entertainment. In this highly competitive environment, companies look for ways to differentiate their product from those of competitors – they want to turn the consumption of goods and services into a memorable and emotional experience.[7] This development process is illustrated in Figure 14.3 which shows the relationship between premium pricing and competitive position.

The trend of moving from 'services' to 'experiences' has implications for marketing managers as well as society as a whole. Many customers now expect more than just a pure 'service', they want service plus experience options, so experiences are becoming the key requirement for anything with a premium price tag. Consequently the competitive marketplace is changing as organisations that can supply experiences strive to do so; other businesses need to revisit their strategic positioning (see Chapter 2) as well as seek ways to better utilise their expanded marketing mix variables.

In today's competitive environment, even manufacturing companies are using the expanded marketing-mix variables for greater competitiveness as well as differentiation

partnerships
Alliances between independent organisations that have complimentary skills or assets. Partnership agreements aim to utilise complimentary skills and resources to satisfy company objectives

<< Expanded marketing mix
What makes luxury hotels so luxurious? A combination of factors including the bedding, sumptuous bathrooms, the concierge, dining opportunities, extra services, recreational facilities, décor, size of property and the room types, club and or/loyalty program memberships and safety and security

experience
An event staged by an organisation, aimed at evoking an emotional response from customers by trying to engage the five senses in order to make the experience more memorable

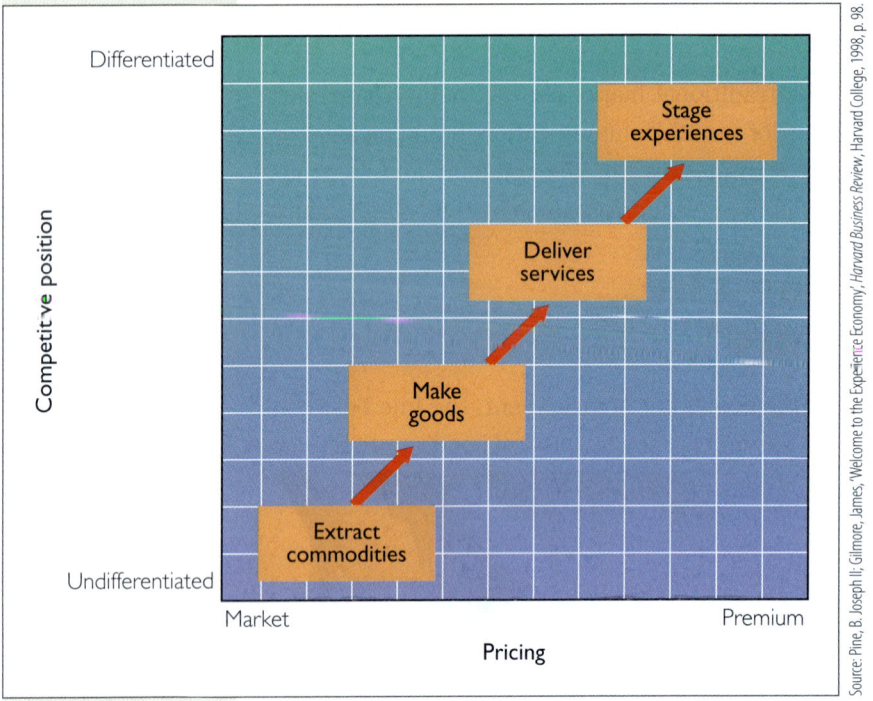

Source: Pine, B. Joseph II; Gilmore, James, 'Welcome to the Experience Economy,' *Harvard Business Review*, Harvard College, 1998, p. 98.

FIGURE 14.3 THE PROGRESSION OF ECONOMIC VALUE – COMPANIES AIMING FOR PREMIUM PRICING SHOULD FOCUS ON STAGING EXPERIENCES THAT ARE HIGHLY DIFFERENTIATED, I.E. EACH CUSTOMER EXPERIENCES SIMILAR EVENTS IN A UNIQUE WAY

from substitute products. Examples of this trend outside traditional service industries include maintaining tidy gardens outside factories, ensuring staff uniforms are clean (physical evidence), providing customer service training for warehouse staff, and using partnerships to facilitate product development. The Eddie Stobart haulage company featured in the Marketing in Action box on page 508 is a good example of this.

Table 14.1 offers examples of how expanded marketing-mix variables are used in service and manufacturing industries. More emphasis is placed on the additional marketing- mix variables of people, physical evidence, processes and partnerships.

TABLE 14.1   EXAMPLES OF HOW THE EXPANDED MARKETING MIX CAN BE UTILISED BY BOTH SERVICE AND MANUFACTURING COMPANIES

Expanded marketing-mix variable	Services examples	Manufacturing examples
Product	Many intangible services have been developed into experiences to make them unique and therefore more desirable, e.g. themed restaurants.	Key trends to consider are: -just in time, i.e. raw materials arrive as they are needed -individualised or tailor-made products, e.g. made-to-measure Levi jeans -partnership arrangements for new product developments. -collaborating with customers (finding out what the customer wants and tailor making goods -a 24/7 customer support service.
Place	Digital distribution for some experiences, e.g. entertainment.	Digital distribution for some products, e.g. software.
Promotion	Digital media and interactivity used to engage customers.	Personal sales still play a key role.
Price	Internet offers greater transparency of pricing and substitute products available.	Problem solving and continuous after-sales support can be more important for customers.
People	Matching the type of service employees with the type of customers is important to achieve an easy communication style.	Expert knowledge of contact personnel is essential. Some organisations use uniforms to enhance brand message.

Expanded marketing-mix variable	Services examples	Manufacturing examples
Physical evidence	Essential for giving correct clues to customers about what to expect from their service experience. For example, what makes a 5-star hotel?	Not as important if customers never visit manufacturing premises (but how is the company 'presented' online?). Very important for smooth running of the manufacturing process and employee wellbeing.
Processes	Poor processes create queues and many consumers will not tolerate queuing unless products are unique (e.g. new product launch) or the price is exceptional (e.g. big sales).	Speedy expert service is essential to solve customer's problems quickly. Diagnostic processes like 'why did the product fail' are essential to save money in warranty claims as well as educating customers to avoid future product malfunctioning.
Partnerships	Used for expert skills to enhance customer experience, e.g. actors used to bring a historic castle alive.	Distinction between manufacturer and customer more fluid as both work together to improve a product or service.

Companies offering experiences recognise that these are unique for each customer and technology can be used to great effect to create memorable experiences. For example, museums use flooring texture and scents to create a medieval streetscape. Companies can charge premium prices for experiences that engage all five senses and successful businesses work on continuously refreshing experiences to ensure a healthy repeat visitor rate. For example, Warner Brothers Movie World, on the Gold Coast of Australia, offers a wide range of themed rides, shows, restaurants and shops and employs people who dress up as well-known movie characters.

Source: Shutterstock/Li Chaoshu

Creating 5-star experiences
When visiting a 5-star hotel, we experience a friendly welcome from the Concierge, smell the fresh flowers, hear the soothing music in the lobby and check-in at a Reception desk that offers a functional work environment for well-qualified staff.

We use our five senses all the time to collect clues from and understand our environment. Similarly, customers use their five senses to collect clues about a company; for example, neatly presented and polite staff members observed in a clean and functional work environment are indicators of a well-managed organisation. In other words, customers use all this information to form an opinion about products, companies and even other individuals. When we split the whole customer experience into smaller steps it is easy to see how many opportunities customers have to absorb clues about an organisation and the most appropriate stages for companies to engage with customers.

Mapping the customer experience

As companies aspire towards a positive brand image, it is important for marketing managers to understand the clues customers use to form opinions and attitudes about a company's products or services. To do this, managers can plan the total customer experience with their company by mapping 'customer journeys' or 'touch points', that is, when and how customers interact with the company or staff members (see Figure 14.4). So how can a

MARKETING IN ACTION | EXPANDED MARKETING MIX USED TO TRANSFORM A UK HAULAGE COMPANY INTO A SUPERBRAND

Source: © Stobart Group, used with permission

Eddie Stobart started with just 12 employees and eight trucks in 1976 and today the company operates 2500 trucks, owns two airports and employs 6000 people in 50 sites across Europe. Although the company is now involved with environmental initiatives like Stobart Biomass and Stobart Rail low-carbon service, it is the Eddie Stobart truck fleet that has captured the imagination of the general public. Can you name another B2B brand that has a 25000 strong fan club (Eddie Stobart Members Club)?

The primary target market for a haulage company may be businesses requiring transport services, but Edward Stobart courts the travelling public as well. Trucks are immaculately presented and clean, drivers wear collars and ties and acknowledge waves from other road users by sounding their horn.

Some call Edward Stobart a genius because he captured the imagination of families travelling on UK motorways before social media was even invented and without the help of marketing consultants! He used the core function of his business, trucks on roads, to communicate the company values of reliability, professionalism and brand differentiation. Eddie Stobart drivers stood out from the crowd because of their professional behaviour, formal uniform and friendly interaction with other road users. In other words social and emotional features were employed to make the brand almost human.

People started talking about the Eddie Stobart trucks and drivers they encountered on their travels, families played 'I spy' games, scoring points for each Eddie Stobart truck spotted. Trucks were given female names to make it easy for people to identify them and enabling Stobart Spotters to keep a record of the trucks they had

seen. The Stobart Fan Club encourages truck spotting by supplying bi-annual spotters handbooks, offering truck depot tours and allowing members to name future trucks. Today Stobart Club members can use an interactive website to upload photos and spotting data or order Stobart merchandise at a discounted price.

Other notable Stobart activities include the Steady Eddie Kids Club that helps families to plan long journeys in a child-friendly manner. Members can also download activities to keep kids entertained during trips. In 2012 the company hosted their first-ever Stobart Fest over two days. This free festival combined Stobart's interest in Rugby League games, Fan Club activities and filming for the Stobart TV series. Visitors to this festival were also able to meet some of the (now famous) Stobart drivers, collect autographs, explore the diverse display of 15 Stobart trucks and buy Stobart merchandise. Can you guess what the top prize for the draw was? A chance to go on a delivery trip with their favourite Stobart driver or jump the three-year waiting list to name a brand new Stobart truck![8] Can you name the Expanded marketing mix variables Eddie Stobart used to transform his company?

company ensure that each interaction (or touch point) enhances a customer's perception of the company's products and services?[9]

There may not be a rule book about touch points, but there are guidelines to rank customer touch points, according to their impact on the overall quality perception of a product. Customers combine clues from their total product/service experience (customer journey) to form an overall quality impression of a company.[10] Customer expectations can also vary greatly from one generation to another (e.g. the service expected by your grandparents is likely to be different from what you expect) as well as between differing cultural backgrounds (e.g. what an American sees as friendly service may be seen as 'fake' by a Finnish person in an identical situation). This is another reason why so many organisations are looking for ways to customise their product or service offerings by using the expanded marketing-mix variables.[11]

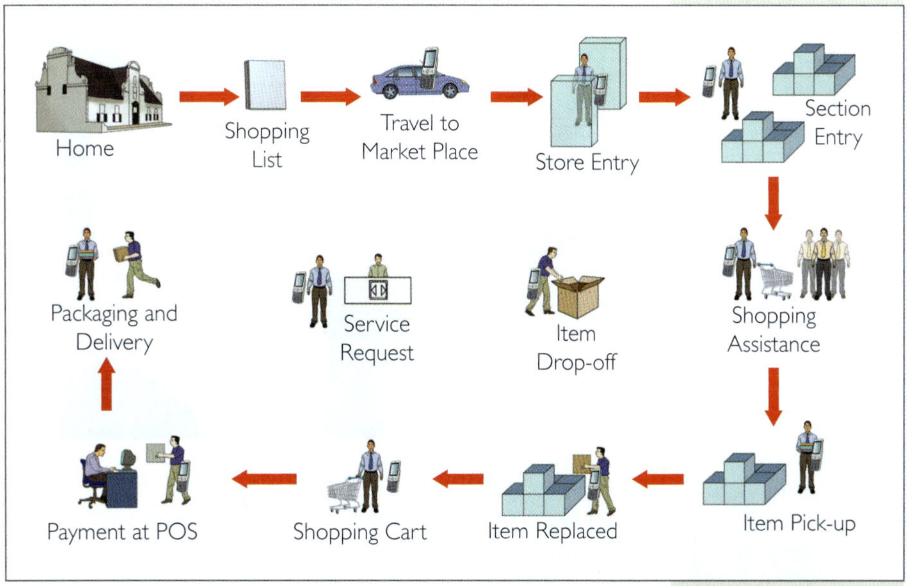

FIGURE 14.4 THE 12 TOUCH POINTS OF RETAIL

The remainder of this chapter focuses on the four extra marketing mix variables that have not been covered elsewhere in this book. The *product* variable is discussed in Chapters 7–9, *price* in Chapter 10, *place* in Chapter 11 and *promotion* in Chapters 12 and 13. Let's turn now to the additional variables of *people*, *physical evidence*, *processes* and *partnerships*. Keep in mind that the expanded marketing-mix variables can be used by all organisations, from farming to futuristic theme parks, to achieve organisational goals.

The expanded marketing mix variables outlined in Table 14.1 (see also Figures 14.1 and 14.2) allow organisations to communicate with customers at different levels. Now that you appreciate the changes in the business environment, we introduce the four variables of the expanded marketing mix.

The people variable

The 'people' variable of the expanded marketing mix refers to the 'human' aspect of products, services or experiences. This includes those people involved with producing the product, offering the service or experience, as well as customers who share the experience with fellow customers and personnel. In other words, 'people' includes company employees, customers present at the time of consumption (e.g. other guests in a restaurant) and all those individuals (or groups of people) who happen to be present at the time (e.g. passersby).

In this section, we first discuss the role of employees and the impact they have on a customer's experience. We then discuss the impact fellow customers might have on an individual's experience (both positive and negative) and the impact unexpected participants might have.

Personnel

Employees are the 'face of the company'. Recruiting the right type of staff and offering them suitable training and a functional work environment can enhance a customer's

Source: Shutterstock.com

overall impression of a company. Interaction between staff members and customers is often called the 'moment of truth' because each interaction can test an employer's skills and training around customer service processes. Service employees also need to have excellent social skills and be highly organised so that they can reply to customer requests promptly and keep within set company policies.[12]

From a customer's perspective, interaction with a company representative is central to their degree of satisfaction with the goods and services they purchase. Customer satisfaction is 'highly dependent upon individual interactions between the guests and associates … It is very difficult for the [customer] to psychologically distinguish between company actions and employee actions'.[13]

Customer-employee interaction can be seen as the greatest contributor to overall quality perception, that is, if a customer has a positive experience.[14] At times, a disastrous service experience can be 'rescued' by a sympathetic staff member who tries to recover the situation. What incentives are there for staff to offer exceptional service? The *Cornell Hospitality Quarterly* lists the following as prerequisites for excellent service:

* a belief that everyone is 'on the same team, working toward the same goals'
* a perception that management goes out of its way to ensure that everyone feels equally included
* effective training to support excellent customer service
* policies and procedures that make it easy to satisfy customers
* decisions by management and leaders that reflect a commitment to customers.[15]

Internal marketing is a cross between human resources management and marketing, and it is the way an organisation interacts with its employees. An organisation should view their personnel as internal customers not just staff members. Managerial support contributes to employees' organisational commitment which, in turn, fosters high-quality service performance. Satisfied and committed employees lead to satisfied customers (see Chapter 2).[16]

Aesthetic labour

The intangible nature of services and experiences means that customers use staff appearance, numbers and behaviour to make a judgement on service quality.[17] Small details in the appearance of staff members can lead to unflattering conclusions about the organisation as a whole. For these reasons, employers may insist on uniforms (always clean and neatly pressed), limit the amount or type of jewellery staff can wear at work (nose rings are a 'no-no' for some companies) or insist that staff have no visible tattoos (or cover their body art while at work). Other regulations seem more logical, for example chefs have to cover their hair at work to make sure none of it ends up in the food!

Management expectations about the appearance of staff members is not new, but the label aesthetic labour is a relatively new concept in the services industry. Managers know how important staff members are in creating a desirable company image, but maybe the need for 'political correctness' delayed the introduction of this name tag. Aesthetic labour can be defined as body language, dress sense, grooming, posture, voice/accent, body shape, demeanour and general stylishness and the way a staff member interacts with customers while representing his or her employer.[18] Service industry staff training has long reflected the concept of aesthetic labour, where staff members are 'on stage' every time they interact with members of the public.[19]

In the hospitality and airline industries aesthetic labour has been acknowledged more widely as an opportunity to maintain a perception of high quality, enhance brand image as well as a way of creating competitive advantage. Typical dress codes include guidelines regarding personal grooming, hairstyle (e.g. length of hair, changing the natural colour of hair, how long hair should be secured), acceptable jewellery and accessories as well as detailed instructions regarding make-up.[20] Organisations like Disney are known for protecting their wholesome, family-friendly image with detailed requirements for 'the Disney Look'. But even these guidelines are reviewed periodically to ensure that employees match the appearance expected of them by theme park patrons. The latest Disney look even allows neatly trimmed facial hair![21] This is quite a contrast to news reports of Australian police officers having to shave off facial hair, as detailed below in the Ethical Marketing box.

ETHICAL MARKETING | 'THE COMMUNITY HAS A RIGHT TO EXPECT A PROFESSIONAL IMAGE FROM ITS POLICE OFFICERS'

issue

Uniformed police officers are a common sight in cities, but have you actually looked at the person inside the uniform? Did you know that in some Australian police forces, male officers could face disciplinary action if their hair reaches below their shirt collar? Or that female police officers are not allowed to wear nail varnish or make-up that is not in natural/neutral tones? Sixteen male Victorian police officers are challenging the new grooming standards at the Victorian Civil and Administrative Tribunal (VCAT) as being discriminatory

Are visible tattoos and beards offensive on a police officer? Should police officers be given the freedom to choose whether they have facial hair?

on the grounds that female officers can have long hair tied in a bun. One officer even gave evidence that his children did not recognise him, their dad, with a clean shaven look.

Police forces in Australia are debating the extent to which a police force job should restrict an individual's rights to have visible tattoos (under consideration in South Australia, New South Wales and Victoria). Those arguing against visible tattoos say '[members of the] community [do not] want someone knocking on their door with a Mike Tyson tattoo on their face or neck….'[22]

Source: Newspix

^ Aesthetic labour and mordern policing
South Australian Police employment application form: 'Visible tattoos or body art must not be excessive or offensive to recognised standards of decency or reflect adversely on the professional image the community would reasonably expect from its police officers'

Aesthetic labour can also play a small part in the recruitment of new staff members. Allegedly, some companies interpret 'attractive appearance' as a pleasant smile, good teeth, neat hair style and pleasing bodily proportions.[23] A company is allowed to guard its overall image, and given situations where applicants for a job have equal résumés, preference could be given to individuals who fit the company's desired aesthetic. For example, airlines are keen to recruit staff members capable of creating confidence, whereas security companies and the armed forces are keen to promote strength.[24] Discrimination on the basis of aesthetic labour is not acceptable and Australian employers are warned against 'Fattism' (discrimination of obese individuals in the work place).[25]

Emotional labour

The interaction between customers and staff members can have an impact on customers' emotions and this interaction is a key contributor to overall customer satisfaction and perceived quality. For some experience-based products, employees are required to engage with customers, i.e. to make a personal or emotional connection with customers. The levels of this engagement vary; for example, a bank teller processing a quick deposit transaction is not as engaged in the process as a loan officer is when trying to sell a mortgage to clients in an hour-long meeting. But in all such situations, a staff member is engaged in emotional labour.[26]

Emotional labour refers to the requirement (or expectation) of staff members to communicate appropriate emotional messages when interacting with customers. For example, apologies after a product failure should be delivered in a sympathetic style to maintain good customer relations; enthusiastic demonstrations of the latest technological advances can create higher sales than a simple statement of facts.

The concept of emotional labour arose in the 1980s and has been traditionally linked to employee wellbeing, fatigue, burnout and staff turnover. However, recent focus on the quality of service encounters as a competitive tool has led to including the emotional labour concept in mainstream service design.

Expressions of emotional labour could be contradictory to the current emotional state of an employee (e.g. even during bereavement we are expected to 'put on a brave face' at work). Companies are keen to ensure a specific style of interaction with customers; staff training can be used to educate employees about the emotional nuances of communications.[27]

emotional labour
When staff members are expected to display emotion and feel empathy/sympathy, with the aim of enhancing customer satisfaction

Source: Getty Images

<< **Emotional labour**
Cathay Pacific flight attendants threatened to stop smiling if their pay demands were not met

'Me as the customer' and other customers as participants

If customers do not participate in planned processes there is no service or experience: imagine a personal trainer whose client refuses to exercise! At the moment you are engaging in a learning experience where your lecturers aim to help you by splitting difficult concepts into smaller, meaningful pieces and making these theoretical constructs meaningful through examples. You can also enhance your learning experience by asking questions, participating in exercises and reading around key topics. However, the key component of your learning experience is your desire to learn and participate. As you have probably observed, it is possible to participate in all lectures and tutorials without learning anything (e.g. after a sleepless night it is virtually impossible to learn anything). Co-creation occurs when customers play a key part in the service experience. Co-creation explains situations where customers take an active role in their experience and drive the experience according to their preferences or values. For example, physically fit tourists might choose the longer and more strenuous track to the sightseeing lookout. Co-creation is a term commonly used in, for example, a tourism context.[28]

In other situations, services and experiences are consumed in the presence of other customers. These other participants need to be considered when assessing if these individuals can have a direct or indirect impact on the service or experience. Direct impact arises in situations where customer experiences depend on all participants interacting with each other or even working as a team, for example, while white-water rafting. Indirect impact takes place when the other customers are consuming their service at the same time in a shared space but they are not expected to work as a team towards a common goal, for example, diners in a restaurant. Other customers present at the service or product experience can have an indirect impact on the overall quality of the product consumption, as well as repeat purchase intentions; for example, a night out dancing could be enjoyable simply due to the positive atmosphere created by other patrons.[29] This is referred to as customer-to-customer (C2C) interaction. As with the rest of life, extreme positive or negative experiences are rare. Much of our pleasure or displeasure at sharing experiences with other individuals does not change our lives and the impact of these interactions is moderate (see the three middle stages of Figure 14.5).[30]

co-creation
When the customer takes an active role in their experience and drives the experience according to their own preferences or values

customer-to-customer (C2C) interaction
This takes place when two or more customers share the consumption experience

Very negative	Negative	Neutral	Positive	Very Positive
'he [the other customer] was rude, dishonest, abusive, violent, aggressive, disruptive'	'I wish she [the other customer] was not here'	'the other customers did not have any impact on my experience'	'excellent, these people are very nice'	'interaction with other customers was the best part of this experience'
'they had to call in the police, paramedics.'				'we shared something very special'
				'we became a real team'
				'we became real friends'

FIGURE 14.5 SCALE OF CUSTOMER-TO-CUSTOMER INTERACTION

How much does it take for other customers to spoil our experience? Not very much, as you can see from the following list of behaviours that can make us feel uncomfortable about fellow customers:

* standing too close/invading personal space
* exceeding the capacity for specific places, such as a beach – this creates an unwelcome perception of overcrowding

* not enough participants to make the experience enjoyable for everyone, for example would you stay in a nightclub that only had a handful of other customers?

* physical appearance of other customers may appear threatening

* physical appearance of other customers may result in stereotypical assumptions

* too little or too much eye contact

* body odour

* smoking or mobile telephone use that impacts on other customers

* breaking the line/pushing at the front of the queue

* refusing to cooperate with the service process, for example the compulsory security screening before a flight or refusing to wait for their turn in the bank

* dysfunctional customer behaviour, for example thieves, drunks or vandals

* loud or hysterical behaviour aimed at getting faster service or a discounted rate

* any behaviour that is not congruent with the service situation, for example allowing children to run around a fine dining restaurant.[31]

Passersby (or accidental participants)

The third type of individuals involved in some service experiences are the accidental participants, people who are not supposed be part of your service experience. The key criteria for classifying these people as passersby is that neither the customer nor the service provider anticipated their presence. In some situations, the customer, as well as the service provider, do not know what to do when these passersby become involved with the experience. These unplanned interactions could either enhance or reduce the quality of your experience. The best interactions with accidental participants will delight the customer and give the service providers ideas on how to enhance their future services/experience offerings. Remember your first day at university? It was exciting but you felt a bit nervous as well. In the past, students were left to their own devices to cope with their first few weeks of university life, and it was pure luck if they

Source: Shutterstock.com

<< **Accidental participants**
To establish minimum standards, signs can be used to direct behaviour

bumped into a friendly older student who could show them around. Today, universities go to great lengths to make your transition to university life more pleasurable; for example, orientation weeks and older students acting as guides and mentors who sometimes also arrange social gatherings.

The worst case scenario is when accidental participants are seen as undesirable and neither the customer nor the company providing the service benefit. Imagine attending a luxury day spa and outside loud people are protesting against animal testing in the cosmetics industry. You have to walk past the angry crowd and, once inside, the loud noise and chanting ruin any chance of relaxation.

Can marketing help solve these problems?

Can marketing managers take action to maximise positive C2C encounters, facilitate co-creation and eliminate negative encounters? Marketing managers should consider the following actions to reduce potentially negative C2C interactions.

* *Create a homogenous customer group.* Clearly positioning the service in the market place through targeted promotional methods and with message content that encourages customers to 'self-select' suitable service experiences. For example, the Contiki brand name and promotions clearly indicate that the holidays they provide are for young, single adults.

* *Group compatible customers.* Use space layout and staff training to place compatible customers near each other. For example:
  - a garden can reduce noise and dust pollution from a busy road
  - fences, garden beds, water features and so on tend to make us walk on footpaths or other tracks designed for foot traffic, e.g. zoos need to keep people at a safe distance from the animals
  - a fence or a hedge can be used to protect the privacy of paying customers.

* *Establish minimum standards.* An organisation should clearly communicate the acceptable minimum standards (e.g. dress code) or codes of conduct (e.g. respectful behaviour when visiting a historic monastery). How many signs have you seen today that aim to set your behaviour at the minimum acceptable standard?

* *Promote desirable behaviour.* The design of physical assets should be conducive towards behaviour the organisation deems most appropriate. For example, plush carpets absorb sounds in libraries and restaurants, and long tables set up for a medieval banquet encourage C2C interaction.

* *Empower staff members to monitor C2C interaction.* Staff members should be empowered to 'police' potentially negative C2C interaction and resolve the situation before customers' experiences are negatively impacted, for example moving on a drunken passerby. If the disturbance cannot be moved then the staff are empowered to move customers, for example, upgrading them to a better hotel room.[32]

The physical evidence/ physical assets variable

Physical evidence includes tangible and intangible clues customers may observe during their customer journey. Managing physical evidence is especially important for service organisations as the intangible nature of services (and experiences) often prompts customers to look for tangible quality clues from the service environment.[33] Psychological responses to a physical environment can stimulate customers' emotions and moods, which may enhance their pleasure or satisfaction when interacting with a company. More importantly, the emotional responses initiated by the company's physical assets can be transferred to other people (staff and guests) within that same space. For example, a poorly ventilated waiting room without adequate seats may irritate customers who then transfer these negative feelings to a customer-service representative.[34]

In this section we explore the range of buildings, grounds and other physical assets that marketing managers should consider.

Buildings, grounds and other physical assets

'We shape our building, and afterwards, they shape us.'

Winston Churchill looking at the bombed House of Commons, 1943[35]

This quote from Winston Churchill highlights the symbiotic relationship between people and buildings. Marketing managers focus on building facilities and design as a core contributor to customer satisfaction. The design of buildings and other physical characteristics can also become part of the company identity (e.g. the Sydney Opera House is used overseas as a symbol of Australia). A building may offer particular character or appeal to visitors (e.g. the Tahbilk vineyard in Victoria allows visitors to explore the historical artefacts of winemaking and simultaneously learn about the vineyard).[36] The traditional wine cellars with wooden barrels, surrounded by tranquil countryside, help create the image of quality wines.

There has been research in the tourism and hospitality industries into the positive and negative impact of architecture and design on customers' overall impressions, but it is best to apply these findings to other situations with a 'pinch of salt'. However, examples from the tourism and hospitality industry provide an insight into the role of buildings as a tangible asset. For example, a key argument is that the physical design of a hotel impacts on customer perceptions of quality. Tangible attributes of the hotel design and the aesthetic impressions created by the building can also enrich our experience of a vacation destination. The design of a hotel's lobby is viewed as critical to its impact on first impressions of the hotel.[37]

Source: Shutterstock.com

Source: Flickr/Fred Garrecht/Getty Images

<< Physical assets
Both these buildings have character and appeal to visitors

The age or condition of a hotel building also affects a customer's overall perceptions of quality: older facilities may lower the quality appraisal.[38] In the restaurant industry, décor is seen as a core factor attracting customers, with evidence of a 20 per cent sales increase attributed to updated décor.[39]

In today's world, it is also important for buildings and facilities to match customer expectations regarding sustainable use of limited resources (e.g. electricity and water) as well as environmental protection.[40] In summary, the tangible elements (building architecture, furniture and décor) and intangible elements (atmosphere, music or even smells) contribute to customer satisfaction while on company premises.[41] In services literature, these physical assets are commonly known as the servicescape.[42]

servicescape
A collective term for the physical evidence (or assets) used to create desirable brand or service quality perception

Today's retail design blends online shopping with retail spaces, playing games (read: interacting with products) with social media and smartphone apps with shopping trolleys. Engaging customers through retail design innovations is also highly competitive: for example, Shoes of Prey (online retailer of custom made shoes for women) employed a theatre set designer, interior designer, an architect as well as a musician to create a space enticing customers to engage with the lengthy process of customising their own shoes. This theatrical retail space can be experienced at David Jones' Sydney store.

By contrast, Nike used interactive technology for their Nike Fuel Station concept store. This store focuses on the Nike+ Fuel Band product (a high-tech wrist band designed to record our activity levels and encourage us to move more). The stores invite customers to run or jump at special activity stations that record movement with displays changing colour from red to green the more activity a shopper shows. By providing the store with their email address customers can share the resulting 30-second video through social media. When did you last post a video of yourself shopping on Facebook?

Many retail stores provide interactive stations for customers to acquire more information about products or check for availability as well as the price of products. In some stores employees also carry iPads to demonstrate product features or to answer customer enquiries. The USA retail giant Walmart even encourages customers to use their location-aware smartphone app in the store to scan purchases as they go for a speedy self-service checkout.

Atmospherics

Research from environmental psychology has been used in the design of physical environments to evoke desirable emotions and responses from customers. In a marketing context, these variables are collectively known as atmospherics – the management of atmospheric variables with the aim of creating a compelling and engaging atmosphere.[43] Atmospherics are included here since they can be used to communicate a company's image, ideals and attributes to stakeholders.[44] Atmospheric elements can impact a customer's mood, behaviour within commercial spaces, length of time spent in the establishment, as well as customer satisfaction with products.[45] Figure 14.6 outlines common atmospheric variables and the possible impacts they are perceived to have by staff members and customers. A good a match between physical evidence, personnel and customer profiles results in higher satisfaction ratings.

environmental psychology
Psychological study of how people react to changes in the environment

Much of the research into atmospherics is based in the retail environment, concentrating initially on learning about whether shelf space allocations per brand had an impact on sales volumes. However, the concept of atmospherics is more widely defined (and investigated) today when atmospheric variables include the use of space and any specialty displays.[46]

How to use atmospherics for retail space design

Customers interpret the atmosphere of a shop (retail space) from the sensory clues retailers use (e.g. colours, designs, textures, smells, sounds, temperatures and distribution of space). Clever retailers use these sensory clues systematically to manipulate shopping behaviour, but how is this possible?

As customers, our impression of a shop starts outside the building; at times we are lured into the shop by loud promises of discounted goods, appealing music or attractive window displays. The smell of freshly baked bread draws customers to bakeries at lunch times as well! By contrast, sewage works outside a shop, a dirty shop front or crackling sound system playing 'elevator music' tend to keep customers away.

In the first 2–3 metres inside the shop entrance, we tend to 'get organised': put away sunglasses/umbrella and gain our first impression of the shop (e.g. not a hot spot for sales). Most Western customers tend to start walking to the right (cultural tendency to pass obstacles at right!) and retailers can invite us further into the shop by creating walkways/ aisles. Large department stores emphasise these walkways by using smooth flooring materials (e.g. wood) to contrast with the thick carpet of the 'strike zones' designed to slow customer traffic to browse the merchandise. Naturally, high demand items and attractive bargains are located at the back of the store to ensure customers are exposed to maximum buying opportunities. Walkways encourage customer traffic around the shop without frustrating 'bottlenecks' or 'dead ends' while maximising our exposure to merchandise. High displays are against walls so that they do not block customers' view of the rest of the merchandise and spotlights draw attention to items on display.[47]

1.

2.

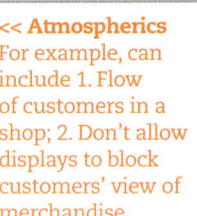

<< Atmospherics
For example, can include 1. Flow of customers in a shop; 2. Don't allow displays to block customers' view of merchandise

Use of music to control customers' perceptions

Background music is commonly used to create (or enhance) the atmosphere in a retail or service environment. Past research suggests that slow tempo music in the background makes shoppers spend more time (and money) at the supermarket and the impact on restaurant customers is similar. Background music may make customers spend more time at a restaurant and order more drinks. The type of music needs to support the overall theme or design of each service or retail establishment. A tavern may experience a surge of sales when drinking songs are played and a wine store may sell more French wines when French music is played. By contrast, classical music in the background tends to create an atmosphere of sophistication, class and even intelligence.[48]

Background music plays a vital role in blocking other (possibly undesirable) sounds in the background from, for example, the restaurant kitchen or passing traffic. At the same time, background music can stop an establishment feeling empty. Music also influences how we interact with each other – soothing music can be used to trigger conversation and increase eye contact.

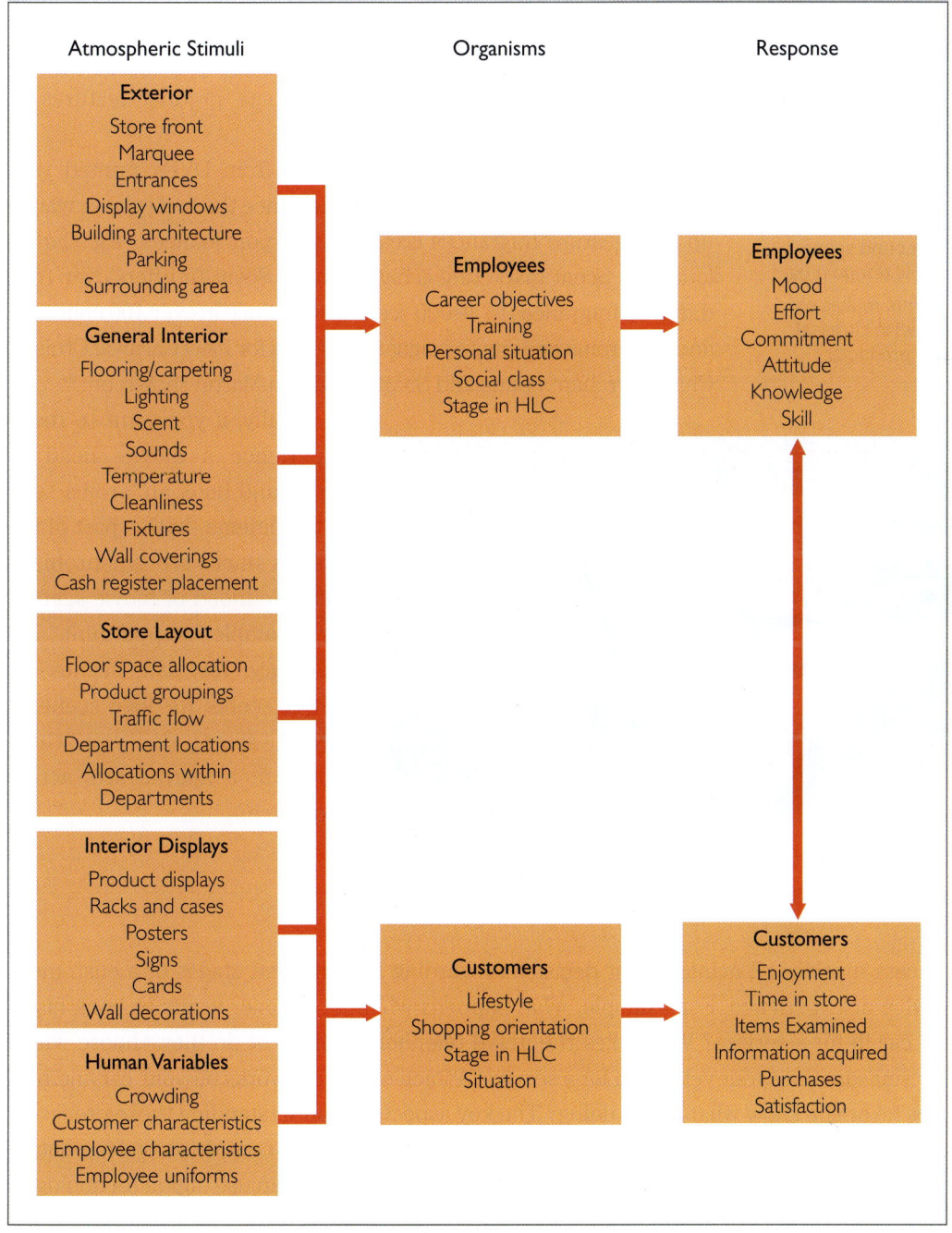

Source: L. W. Turley, Ronald E. Milliman, Atmospheric Effects on Shopping Behavior: A Review of the Experimental Evidence,' Vol 49, Issue 2, *Journal of Business Research*, Elsevier, 2000, p. 196.

FIGURE 14.6
COMMON ATMOSPHERIC VARIABLES

olfaction effect
Refers to sensing and interpreting smells and taste flavours; may result in an emotional reaction

Scents and smells influencing customers' perceptions

A relatively new area for research is the impact scents have in retail and service environments (the olfaction effect). Traditionally, marketers have relied on audiovisual materials, but today there are just too many of these, so how else can subliminal messages be sent? The sense of smell is unique because it engages a direct emotional response without the rational analysis applied to other forms of communication. Scents linked to products enhance our memory of products and increase their distinctiveness.[50] Interestingly, the actual 'flavour' of a scent is not as important as the presence of a pleasant smell when consumers evaluate product features or engage with a service.

Scent marketing includes everything from DVDs printed with pizza scented inks releasing a pizza smell once the DVD player warms up, to signature fragrances created for airport lounges (e.g. Qantas lounges). Scent marketing is big business: ScentAir offers over 1600 different fragrances to 40 000 scent installations in over 100 countries and Air Aroma has created signature scents for P&O Carnival Cruises, China Merchants Bank and Shanghai Aston Martin showroom.[51]

Source: Shutterstock.com

Finally, if you want to really experience a movie, head to Japan and book an 'aroma seat' in the cinema. In this part of the cinema smells are synchronised with the mood of movie scenes; for example, peppermint and rosemary for sad scenes or flower scents for love scenes.[52] Which scent do you think would fit a martial arts action sequence?

<< Olfaction effect
Some cinemas in Japan offer 'aroma seats'

Processes

Process involves all management decisions regarding the different stages of a customer's service or experience. For example, what happens when a customer wants to book his or her car in for a service? Who takes the initial telephone call? How do they choose which day you can bring your vehicle in for a service? Which mechanic works on your car and how does he or she know what needs doing? The key aspects for understanding these processes can be grouped into: the flow and progress of customers; special considerations in relation to the type of information customers share with us; and how we can use digital technologies for a more positive customer experience.

Flow and progress of customers

A key consideration for managing processes is queue management. Waiting for services impacts negatively on customer satisfaction, product quality perception and customer loyalty.

Queues are part of everyday living, they form when customer demand exceeds service capacity, and managing short-term peaks of demand can at times be difficult. Companies can reduce customers' displeasure at waiting in a number of ways as listed below.

* Customers observe fair waiting procedures such as 'first come, first served'.

* When priorities are clearly explained or justifiable (e.g. triage in an emergency room).

* A well-designed, attractive and sociable waiting environment is provided (e.g. comfortable seats, magazines to read, air-conditioning, tea/coffee/cold drinks available).

* Relaxing music plays in the background.

* There are activities for customers to fill in time (e.g. interesting TV programs or relevant DVDs).

* Wait-time guarantees are offered (e.g. 'if your pizza takes more than 15 minutes from when you ordered, the next pizza is free').[53]

Simple processes like managing waiting times can have a significant impact on customers' overall satisfaction. Waiting during a telephone conversation can cause greater irritation than actually standing in a queue. Irritability at being 'on hold' on the telephone is fuelled by not being able to see the number of people ahead of us in the queue or that employees are working hard to reduce waiting times. The Marketing in Action box shows how Carnival Cruises have made queuing into an enjoyable experience with clear signals that the Caribbean vacation has already started!

MARKETING IN ACTION | WAS IT REALLY A QUEUE?

Queues are probably the most common reason for customer complaints. Some of us just cannot tolerate queues and get frustrated after only a few minutes of waiting for service.

What if there was a very long queue between you and your dream holiday? Imagine a beautiful white cruise liner waiting for you at the dock, ready to take you and 2000 other impatient passengers on a beautiful Caribbean holiday. This scenario has all the ingredients for an irritating queue: 2000 or more people with heavy luggage needing to board a vessel in just a few hours. The first bottleneck is the narrow entry ramp which is no more than the size of normal double doors. How can Carnival Cruise Lines stop each check-in day from becoming a long queue of frustrated customers? The following scenario outlines tactics used at each potential bottleneck.

Customers can speed up the check-in process by completing a registration form online before departure. The completed online form also satisfies immigration requirements, thereby speeding up the process even more.

The first step at port is to relieve customers of their heavy luggage, check tickets, passports and allocate cabins. All this is done in an airport-like check-in terminal building. From the check-in counter, customers are directed to a lounge where the ship's entertainers are performing.

Source: Shutterstock.com

The second potential bottleneck is the walkway from the terminal building to the vessel. Depending on the departure port, the gangway could be just one metre wide, suspended 10 metres above the concrete dock, which is a potential hazard in itself. The ship's photographer is now responsible for policing traffic; when there is no queue at the walk way he will whisk passengers through the memorabilia photograph opportunity, or take his time to arrange the perfect pose (to allow more time for previous passengers to clear the gangway). Incidentally, the cruise liner also earns revenue from this transaction as many customers later purchase these photos!

The third potential bottleneck is the entry lobby with its magnificent design features. The risk here is that passengers will stop to admire the construction and décor, thus blocking the entry for customers crossing the gangway after them. This is where several crew members entice customers to head towards the (more spacious) outdoor decks with calls to 'free drinks on the Sun Deck'.

While passengers step through all the above stages, their luggage is being delivered directly to their cabin.

This is a good example of customers queuing for a service without realising they are actually waiting in turn to be served. Can you think of other good examples where queuing was not a stressful experience?[54] ✉

Organisations can reduce irritation at telephone waiting times by:

* playing relaxing music, which can help reduce frustration and result in better overall customer satisfaction levels
* informing customers when service is in great demand and advising them to call back at a later time
* periodically updating information on the number of customers in the queue and
* offering customers alternative service options, for example accessing bank accounts via the Internet (a form of self-service).[55]

Sensitivity, privacy and confidentiality of customer–company interactions

Managers need to design processes or systems that ensure the anonymity of customers and provide safe storage of confidential information. Specific attention should be paid to customer service situations (or touch points) to ensure that the necessary information exchange is not witnessed by other members of the public.[56] Below are good examples of protecting confidentiality, implementing safeguards to protect privacy and demonstrating sensitivity at key touch points in service situations:

* signs saying 'please wait behind this line to be served' at banks and ATMs; separate meeting rooms for discussions regarding personal loans or mobile bankers visiting customers at home to discuss a mortgage

* professional service area at pharmacies for private discussions of symptoms and medications

* confidentiality in relation to customer lists, contact details and services purchased

* ATM and EFTPOS terminals designed so that people waiting in a queue cannot see (or guess) the PIN a customer is using

* privacy filters for computer screens

* ensuring telephone conversations involving confidential or sensitive information cannot be overheard by members of the public (e.g. the clerk repeating the credit card number to confirm a purchase/payment over the phone).

Digital technology and the service process

Digital technologies can be used in two key ways to improve the service process: by offering customers the opportunity for self-service, or by making the steps taken by staff members in the service interaction faster, cheaper and more efficient. Self-service technology is changing the way we interact with companies and purchase goods or services. For example, major retailers, such as Big W and Woolworths, use self-service checkouts where customers scan their purchases and pay with a credit or debit card.

By using technology many routine steps in the customer interaction chain can be automated; for example, the use of online banking to pay bills, rather than queuing at a local branch with the bills and cash. With your mobile phone you can access a pre-arranged loan should the need to borrow cash arise when banks are closed or you don't have time to see the bank manager (see 'Did you know?'). The use of online banking by customers gives bank employees more time to help us with complex processes like applying for a mortgage or a new credit card. Customers also like the privacy offered by online banking. The greater flexibility (e.g. 24/7 availability) and potential savings associated with automated processes make them attractive to both companies and customers. However, it is important to note that employees dealing with complex transactions still need to be highly trained and more empowered to solve potential problems.[58]

The use of technology has been integrated into customer service, manufacturing and organisational processes to improve product or service quality, speed up processes and reduce overall costs. For example, as the Marketing in Transition story shows, a quick 3D

LISTEN to the Audio Summary for a recap of the physical evidence/physical assets principle

curated convenience
Curated convenience merges the trends of curated consumption and convenient delivery of customer orders to their home/work address

body scan can provide you with a list of clothes that are going to fit perfectly so that you don't even need to try the clothes on! Unfortunately, slow and inflexible technological systems can become major barriers to quality interaction with customers. Ineffective technology can frustrate staff members and become a major source of dissatisfaction and reduce productivity.

MARKETING IN TRANSITION | BODY SCANNING HELPS YOU FIND PERFECTLY FITTING CLOTHES

New body scanning technology can eliminate the pain of finding well-fitting clothes. Using infra-red technology 3D scanners measure shoppers' body type and recommend clothes that will fit. The scanners collect 200 000 data points to describe body types (size and shape) and some retailers let consumers create their own on-screen body avatars to try on clothes. These scanners are bulky and expensive, costing in excess of $100 000, so currently only the largest clothes retailers offer this service, e.g. Target in Australia, Levi's in the USA and Marks & Spencer in the UK.

Contributing to the ill-fitting clothes problem are factors such as a person's body shape changing, consumers preferring certain types of clothes (e.g. loose fitting versus skinny leg jeans), out of date national body type standards and clothes made to fit unrealistic body shapes.

Solutions for body scanning at home are being developed using webcam and image processing software or infrared sensors (as used in Microsoft Kinect). Naturally, body scanning at home is more convenient and cheaper – but home scanning may also be less accurate. Perhaps in the future we can send our body scan results directly to clothes manufacturers and receive tailor made outfits by return post?[59]

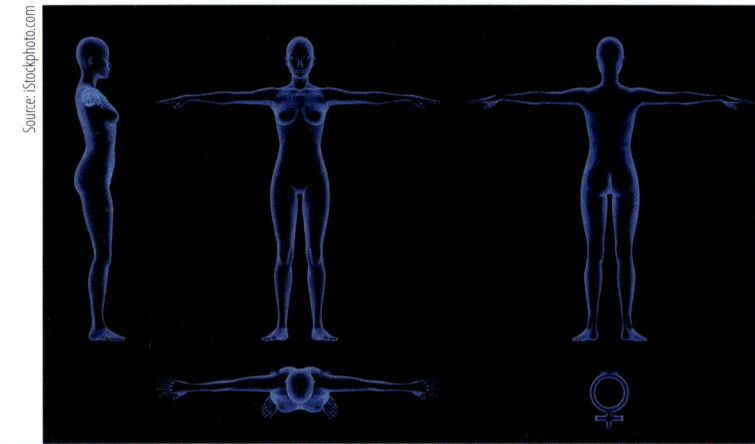

Source: iStockphoto.com

curated consumption
Curated consumption refers to a trend of consumers electing to follow the style advice or expertise of a curator through communication made available, e.g. via magazines, TV shows and blogs

curator
Traditionally a curator is a person working for a museum or a place of exhibition. They hold the position due to their expertise in the field being exhibited, e.g. a curator for the National Sports Museum of Australia is an expert in significant sport related trends in Australia. In a marketing context, a curator is a person viewed as an authority in their field of expertise whose recommendations for brands to buy are received well by many consumers

Curated convenience

Amazon.com changed the way we expect to obtain goods and services: the variety of products on offer is phenomenal, prices are competitive and the whole process from ordering to delivery is easy. The environment of a wide range of products offered to time-poor consumers who are information savvy with easy access to the internet has led to the concepts of curated consumption and curated convenience. This relates to large numbers of consumers following the advice of perceived experts. For example, Jennifer Hawkins could influence our fashion choices and Michelle Bridges could direct our health and fitness activities; in other words, Jennifer Hawkins can be seen as a fashion curator and Michelle Bridges as a fitness curator.[60]

Typically, a curated convenience service starts with a customer answering online questions about style preferences and how they like to use products. For example, a service for monthly delivery of workout gear will ask about workout preferences (gym versus running), favourite sports clothes styles, colours and cuts before customers receive personalised recommendations. Some services allow customers to choose between 'economy' and 'luxury' deliveries. Curators source trendy product combinations (e.g. a complete gym outfit) that are sent at regular intervals to customers in smartly put together product bundles at competitive prices, with customer convenience being the key feature.

Another trend emerging from a time-poor lifestyle and a willingness to buy products online is subscription services made possible through developments in e-commerce. Manufacturers are also keen to use this opportunity for direct sales to consumers with deliveries made to a home or work address. It's now possible to subscribe to regular deliveries of a wide range of products – from razors to designer clothes.[61] Local 'corner shops' with extended opening hours also benefit from this trend by renting out safe delivery lockers.

The partnerships variable

In the context of an expanded marketing-mix, partnerships refer to alliances between independent organisations with the twin goals of improving service to customers and enhancing the business performance of each organisation. Typically, partnerships are formed between organisations that have complementary skills or assets.[62] Other reasons for partnerships include lack of resources or expertise to meet company objectives and customer needs in a changing market place, or a desire to develop new products (when the cost of product development is beyond the resources of an organisation on its own).[63] For example, John West partnered with WWF for their responsible fishing and marine environment conservation initiatives.

subscription service
Subscription service (also known as subscription commerce) refers to an arrangement of regular deliveries of products to customers against a regular (often automated) payment or fee for this service (e.g. direct debit arrangement). Developments in e-commerce have facilitated these kind of direct sales to customers

LO5

e-commerce
The online purchasing of goods, services and experiences, mainly through the Internet, email or mobile phones

---

ETHICAL MARKETING | DOES YOUR TUNA HAVE THE WWF STAMP OF APPROVAL?

issue

In December 2012, Greenpeace launched a six week intensive 'Reject John West' campaign after three years of unsuccessful conversation with the company about stopping unsustainable fishing practices. Greenpeace claimed that 20000 Australians supported their campaign to end John West's 'destructive fishing'. John West refers to 'recent proactive engagement with Greenpeace' in a statement confirming that the company will end sourcing tuna from unsustainable fisheries by 2015.

In November 2013, John West announced a partnership with the WWF for two new marine conservation programs as well as a three year, $600000 commitment under the John West Conservation Program. One of these new programs aims to promote sustainable fishing methods and to make responsibly sourced tuna easier to source.[64]

After a Greenpeace campaign against destructive fishing methods, John West partners with the World Wildlife Fund (WWF) on a conservation program.

Source: iStockphoto.com

Successful partnerships are built on trust and mutual commitment to honest, open communication. Discussions with potential partners should cover possible barriers to collaboration in the future as well as common ground for the partnership. The leadership group of the new alliance needs to agree on accountability, governance and the degree of transparency before assets are committed to new ventures.[65] Trust is viewed as a 'very effective lubricant … to help spread risk and pool resources' thus enabling successful partnerships.[66] Naturally, links between alliance members can be 'cemented' by organisations investing in their partner companies.[67]

Tourism Australia as an organisation has alliances with some 200 partners from key sectors of the Australian travel industry. For example, Tourism Australia and Virgin Australia announced a three year partnership valued at $12 million in total until the end of 2015. The aim of this partnership is to attract tourists to Australia from the USA, New Zealand, the UK, continental Europe and Asia.

An example of using complementary products can be seen in an alliance between Google and the Hyundai Motors Group. This involves the Google Maps API being incorporated into the hands-free vehicle technology platforms of Hyundai and Kia cars. In other words, Google Maps with Voice Search will enable hands-free navigation. Moreover, the Google Send-to-Car allows users to send directions to their car remotely from their smartphones.

FlyBuys, the largest loyalty program in Australia, is another good example of partnerships in action. FlyBuys understands key trends in consumer buying behaviour and responds to these trends with one major innovation after another. For example, a recent alliance with Yahoo!7 introduces the Toolbar application (free to registered FlyBuys members) rewarding members with up to 100 points per month for valid search terms. Through this partnership Yahoo!7 gains access to a new target audience in Australia with increased advertising opportunities.

The American Express and Twitter alliance introduced Amex Synch on Twitter to enable tweet purchases of selected goods, i.e. purchases made by tweeting! The system is still in its infancy with a complicated procedure: (1) Connect your Amex card to your Twitter account, (2) find a hashtag from the American Express Twitter account, (3) tweet this hashtag for your purchase and (4) reply to the Amex confirmation tweet within 15 minutes.

The Australian Farm Business Management Network (AFBMN) offers further insight into successful partnerships. The AFBMN is a not-for-profit organisation that has individuals and organisations as its members. The common characteristic across all members is the desire to promote education and research services for Australian primary producers. This network was formed when members did not have the capacity to achieve AFBMN goals individually. However, as a partnership they have managed to enhance communication, innovation and involvement across the primary production industries.[68] Table 14.2 lists the types of members in the network.

A specialist project initiated by AFBMN demonstrates best practice in communication. By outlining, from the beginning of the project, a communications schedule and the target audience for each message, each partner is able to share information about achieving goals

application (or app)
a small self-contained program that can run on computers, tablets and smartphones to achieve a specific purpose, e.g. accessing the latest weather forecast

more efficiently.[69] Table 14.3 contains a guide to the ground rules that need to be in place from the beginning of any partnership.

TABLE 14.2   EXAMPLES OF PARTNERSHIPS FROM THE AGRICULTURAL INDUSTRY

Partner type	Examples
Small/medium businesses	Beef producers, beef enterprises
Large businesses	Pastoral companies, feedlots, processors, retailers
Government departments	State DPIs, regional bodies
Industry agencies	MLA, MWNZ, AgForce, breed societies
Commercial organisations	Consultants, Elders, Landmark, banks
Education/training institutions	Schools, colleges, universities

Source: Clark R.A. 2008, The Partnership and Network Strategy, *AFBM Journal*, vol. 5 nos. 1 & 2 – Special Edition 2008, 57–62, © Charles Sturt University.

TABLE 14.3   ESTABLISHING PARTNERSHIP PROTOCOLS FROM THE BEGINNING – PLANNED COMMUNICATION IN AN AGRICULTURAL PARTNERSHIP

Activity	Date due
Regional newsletter	When appropriate
State newsletter	When appropriate
Internal newsletter	Every 90 days, after the 90-day BPP Management meetings
Calendar	For distribution each year in December
Reporting templates	These will be revised/updated when appropriate
Feedback form	These will be revised/updated when appropriate
PowerPoint presentations	These will be developed as required
Conference proceedings	These will be produced in conjunction with the BPP Forum
Annual report	April each year
Flyers	When appropriate

Source: Mulholland C and G.R. Griffith (2008), Paper 7. The Communication, Information and Marketing Strategy, *AFBM Journal*, vol. 5 nos. 1 & 2 – Special Edition 2008, 43–47,
© Charles Sturt University.

REVIEW your knowledge of this chapter's key concepts by taking the online Post-test

Study Tools

Chapter review

LO1

UNDERSTAND HOW COMPETITIVE ADVANTAGE CAN BE ACHIEVED THROUGH STRATEGIC USE OF THE EXPANDED MARKETING MIX VARIABLES.

The expanded marketing mix consists of eight variables: product, place, promotion, price, people, physical evidence, processes and partnerships. This mix offers companies more ways to create satisfying customer experiences. By analysing each customer touch point, companies can identify specific stages of interaction with customers. The next step is to evaluate how the expanded marketing-mix variables are used at each of these touch points.

Through market research, an organisation can learn what their customers like, e.g. using self-service technology. Armed with the results of market research, marketing managers can decide how to use limited funds and other resources, for example, if recruiting qualified staff is problematic, perhaps the best alternative would be to develop self-service technologies for customers to use.

We live in an 'experience economy' and many organisations are already using the expanded marketing-mix variables to create memorable experiences. At the same time, consumers are more aware of possible substitute products and how to switch to competitive product offerings (the Internet has created more transparency by allowing individuals access to information previously only available to businesses). The final key trend is the empowerment of consumers where they are aware of their rights and can easily contact other individuals about their experiences with products.

LO2

APPRECIATE HOW THE PEOPLE VARIABLE OF THE EXPANDED MARKETING MIX CAN BE USED TO CREATE EXCEPTIONAL EXPERIENCES FOR THE CUSTOMERS.

The 'people' variable of the expanded marketing mix refers to the 'human' aspect of products, services or experiences. This includes those people involved with producing the product, those offering the service or experience, as well as customers who share the experience with fellow customers and personnel. Customer–employee interaction can be seen as the greatest contributor to overall quality perception – that is, if a customer has a positive experience. Organisations know that staff appearance/presentation contributes to the overall quality judgements of the company and its products, therefore managers might enforce rules regarding suitable hair styles for staff or insist on neatly pressed uniforms. Furthermore, staff training can be used to help employees better communicate with customers.

LO3

UNDERSTAND HOW THE DESIGN OF PHYSICAL ASSETS (PHYSICAL EVIDENCE) CAN MAKE OPERATIONS RUN MORE SMOOTHLY AS WELL AS ENHANCE CUSTOMER SATISFACTION.

Physical evidence includes tangible and intangible clues customers observe during their customer journey. Managing physical evidence is especially important for service organisations, as the intangible nature of services (and experiences) often prompts customers to look for tangible quality clues from the service environment. Psychological responses to a physical environment can stimulate customers' emotions and moods, which may enhance their pleasure or satisfaction when interacting with a company. More importantly, the emotional responses initiated by the company's physical assets can be transferred to other people (staff and guests) within that same space. Using the physical assets of an organisation includes managing the appearance of buildings, grounds and online presence to strengthen the company/brand positioning.

 **LO4 APPRECIATE HOW A STEP-BY-STEP ANALYSIS OF CUSTOMERS' INTERACTION WITH THE ORGANISATION CAN IMPROVE PROFITABILITY.**

This process involves all management decisions regarding the different stages of a customer's service or experience. The key aspects for understanding these processes can be grouped into: the flow and progress of customers; special considerations in relation to the type of information customers share with us; and how we can use digital technologies for a more positive customer experience.

To achieve positive brand image, an organisation aims to understand the clues customers use to form opinions and attitudes about their company's products or services. To do this, managers can plan the total customer experience with their company by mapping 'customer journeys' or 'touch points', that is, when and how customers interact with the company or staff members.

 **LO5 LEARN HOW COMPANIES CAN USE PARTNERSHIPS WITH EXTERNAL ORGANISATIONS TO IMPROVE THEIR COMPETITIVENESS.**

Partnerships refer to alliances between independent organisations with the twin goals of improving service to customers and enhancing the business performance of each organisation. Typically, partnerships are formed between organisations that have complementary skills or assets. Other reasons for partnerships include lack of resources or expertise to meet company objectives and customer needs in a changing market place, or a desire to develop new products (when the cost of product development is beyond the resources of an organisation on its own).

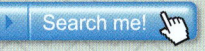

Key concepts

Use these key terms in **Search me! marketing** to find the latest relevant readings from a wide range of world-class journals, e-books and newspapers, including *The Australian*.

- aesthetic labour
- application (app)
- atmospherics
- co-creation
- curator
- curated convenience
- curated consumption
- customer-to-customer (C2C) interaction
- e-commerce
- emotional labour
- environmental psychology
- experience
- internal marketing
- olfaction effect

- partnerships
- people
- physical evidence
- processes
- servicescape
- subscription service

Issues for discussion and review

1 Why are there different versions of the marketing mix models?

2 'The expanded marketing mix is an opportunity to enhance your company's competitiveness.' Discuss.

3 What is meant by the 'people' variable of the marketing mix?

4 Why are partnerships an opportunity for organisations?

5 Why is it important to ensure that customer service processes work well?

6 Why does the physical evidence variable of the marketing mix need to match the other marketing mix variables?

7 To what extent can manufacturing companies benefit from utilising expanded marketing mix variables?

8 How would you determine whether the marketing mix variables of your company match the expectations of your customers?

ONLINE EXERCISE

9 Visit the live webcam for Cairns & Great Barrier Reef Live Webcams at **http://www.cairns-greatbarrierreef.org.au/quick-facts/see-live-webcams.aspx**.

  a Why would Tropical North Queensland Tourism be keen to include a live feed on their website?

  b Would the live feed make customers prefer this destination over competing destinations?

  c Does the live webcam feed add to the online promotion of this vacation destination?

  d What improvements would you suggest for this webcam feed?

Marketing applications

1 You are taking your car in for a service. What clues from the immediate vicinity of the vehicle service centre, combined with the design and décor of the premises, would help you gauge the cost of this service? Would you expect a link between the cost of servicing your vehicle and the quality of the customer service you receive?

2 When travelling, have you caught yourself thinking that 'this is not a safe neighbourhood' or 'that company is in financial trouble'? By using the expanded marketing mix framework, identify stimuli/clues from the environment that caused you to reach your conclusions of a company in financial trouble or a neighbourhood that is not very safe.

3 Identify two manufacturing organisations that are using some of the expanded marketing-mix variables and give details of the variables used.

Developing your marketing plan

A company's strategic plan should be revisited when significant changes are observed in the organisation's external business environment.

Analyse your product/service offering as it is experienced by your customers.

1 What is the core product (see Chapter 8)? Has this changed from your last review? Are your customers still using the products for the same purpose?

2 Create a list of recent key changes under these headings: economic forces, political forces, legal and regulatory forces, sociocultural forces and competitive forces. How will these impact on your customers?

3 Map out the customer touch points or the customer journey for your company. What observations or clues can customers make about the quality of your product or your company at any of these touch points?

4 Collect feedback from your current customers (e.g. through interviews) as well as your customer service personnel. How pleasurable or smooth is the customers' progression through the different touch points?

5 Identify mismatches between current customer touch points and customer expectations (based on your answers to questions 1–3 in this section). Initiate changes required.

6 Analyse to what extent your company has used all feasible marketing mix variables for each of the touch points. Is it possible to strengthen your brand/company/quality image by using a wider range of marketing mix variables at each of the customer touch points?

CengageNOW

Go to http:\\login.cengagebrain.com to link to CengageNOW, your online study tool. First take the Pre-Test for this chapter to get your Personalised Study Plan, and then:

❋ **Revise** your understanding of the expanded marketing mix by completing the interactive quizzes.

❋ **Watch** an online video activity on the service industry.

❋ **Listen** to an audio summary of digital technology and the service process.

After you have completed the activities in your Personalised Study Plan take the Post-Test to determine what concepts you have mastered and what you still need to work on.

Case study

THE EXPERIENCE OF LEARNING IN A MUSEUM

In the past, a museum visit involved observing fossils and other artefacts. These days, however, museums have interactive tools to engage visitors and make them active participants in the learning process. The Natural History Museum (NHM) in London is an example of how to turn science into a fun experience. With five million visitors in 2012, this free-entry museum is home to 70 million natural history specimens and a recognised research centre.[70] Relatively easy to access by public transport, the museum is known for constantly adapting their exhibitions to suit a varied audience. Permanent galleries are complemented by new exhibitions and events. Once in the precinct, children, adults, families, school groups, teachers and communities can choose from a wide range of activities in line with their interests.

Source: Alamy

The museums' comprehensive website allows visitors to create their itinerary before they reach the museum. Learning resources, activities for children and adults, and short videos are some of the sources available online. The provision of information online is an incentive to visit the website by providing information about the activities available. Once at the museum, visitors can choose to wander around or go straight to their chosen exhibition or event. Additionally, printed versions of maps, brochures and timetables are available at certain points. The layout of the museum is colour coded – orange, blue, green and red zones distributed across two floors. Each colour represents a theme, for example the green zone displays birds and minerals while the earth's evolution is in the red zone. Facilities include restaurants, cloakroom, toilets, picnic area, faith room, Centre for UK Biodiversity and two learning rooms.

Every exhibit has been made with the purpose of involving visitors as the main participants. All elements combine to appeal to visual, auditory and tactile senses. Therefore, it is possible to observe strange specimens, hear a dinosaur roar and touch colourful screens that explain aspects of the planet. In the Central Hall is one of the highlights of the museum, a diplodocus skeleton frequently referred as Dippy. Another popular gallery is the dinosaur room that displays skeletons and a T-Rex animatronics that create an environment for discovering more about those prehistoric giants. Opened in 2009, the Darwin Centre is considered the most significant expansion at the museum. Here, museum visitors can explore the science world via displays and observe scientists at work. Located in the ground floor of the Darwin Centre is the Attenborough Studio, a multimedia facility where visitors learn about human evolution in a 45-minute interactive video.

The NHM has 1400 employees that include scientists, internships and 450 volunteers. Some scientists and curators are also part of the whole experience of visiting the museum. They interact with the audience at certain times and also appear in videos. In addition there are volunteers who are responsible for providing information and assistance. They also walk around the museum engaging audiences via the use of skeletons, so that visitors, especially children, can touch and experience the feel of these exhibits. The museum also uses high end technology to create a user friendly environment that appeals to children and adults. As an example, the Climate Change Wall is a 12-metre-wide interactive wall with screens that respond to a visitor's presence by changing in colour, light and sound.

Due to the great number of visitors, certain galleries or exhibitions may experience long queues, especially in school holidays. Signals along the way indicate the waiting period; however this may act as deterrent for tourists on holidays with limited time. On the other hand, the considerable collection in the museum seems to provide a variety of options for those with specific interests.

The NHM was established as a charity so it requires funding from patrons or other sources. Considering its incredible infrastructure and artefacts, some galleries can be hired out for private functions or events, which provides the museum with another source of income. Memberships are also available for visitors with benefits that include free fast-track for exhibitions, discounts and exclusive members-only events. Additionally, the museum hosts special events, namely Wildlife Photographer of the Year and the Annual Science Lecture. Attendance at these events has an additional cost. An event called 'Dino Snores' was created to invite children from 7–11 years old to spend a night at the museum. It is a monthly sleepover that includes activities such as chasing dinosaurs with a torch and a live show. There is also an adult version, 'Dino Snores for Grownups' that consists of a three-course dinner, live music and a horror movie marathon.

The NHM shows how innovative ways can be used to encourage visitors to learn while enjoying the experience. The museum certainly possesses a great collection but it also combines technology, targeted strategies and social media to engage potential visitors and keep current patrons coming back.

Sandra Osorio, La Trobe University

QUESTIONS FOR DISCUSSION

1 Identify and describe the 8Ps for the NHM in London.

2 How do you think that 'Place' is being used to give the NHM a competitive advantage?

3 Suggest ways to improve the customer service 'processes' in this museum.

Chapter endnotes

1. 'Kubota Tractor Australia celebrates its 120th anniversary', Kubota Tractor Australia, 16 April, 2010, http://kubota .com.au/news/default.asp?ne_id=125; '5 star service rating for Kubota Tractor Australia dealers', Kubota Tractor Australia, 15 April, 2009, http://www.ferret.com.au/c /Kubota-Tractor-Australia/5-star-service-rating-for-Kubota -Tractor-Australia-dealers-n832523; 'Five-star Status for Tractor Outlet', Newcastle Herald, 28 July, 2005, http://www.machineryspareparts.com.au/machinery -spare-parts-articles/2005/7/28/fivestar-status-for -tractor-outlet/.

2. Chai Lee Goi, 'Marketing Mix: A Review of P', Array Development (2005), accessed Febraury 2, 2014, www.arraydev.com/commerce/JIBC/2005-08/goi.HTM.

3. OECD, 'The Service Economy', Science, Technology and Industry; Business and Industry Policy Forum Series report (2000), http://www.oecd.org/dataoecd/10/33/2090561 .pdf; Pine, B. Joseph II; Gilmore, James, 'Welcome to the Experience Economy', Harvard Business Review, Jul–Aug 1998; Gilmore, J.H. and Pine, B.J. II, 'The Experience Is the Marketing – A Special Report', 2002, http://www.soloseo .com/blog/files/experience-is-the-marketing.pdf; Dominici,

G, 'From Marketing Mix to e-Marketing Mix: a literature overview and classification', *International Journal of Business and Management*, 4 (9) (2009) (September), 17–24.

4. V. P. Magnini and E. E. Parker, 'The psychological effects of music: Implications for hotel firms', *Journal of Vacation Marketing* 15 (1) (2009), http://jvm.sagepub.com /content/15/1/53.abstract.

5. Mary Jo Bitner and Bernard H. Booms, 'Marketing Strategies and Organization Structures for service firms.' In *Marketing of Services*, James H. Donnelly and William R. George (eds), Chicago: American Marketing Association (1992: 47–52).

6. V. P. Magnini and E. E. Parker, 'The psychological effects of music: Implications for hotel firms.'

7. Hsien-Tang Ko, Hsi-Peng Lu & Hueiju Yu, 'Comparative analysis of experience-oriented customer needs based on the Kano model: an empirical study', *The Service Industries Journal*, 32:12 (2012): 1973–1990; Johan Swinnen, Kristine Van Herck, and Thijs Vandemoortele, 'The Experience Economy as the Future for European Agriculture and Food?' *LICOS Discussion Paper, No. 313*. (2012), accessed November 10, 2013, http://www.econstor.eu/ bitstream/10419/74959/1/dp313.pdf.

8. 'Eddie Stobart', Superbrands, accessed March 15, 2013, http://www.superbrands.uk.com/eddie-stobart; Alex Aspinall, 'News analysis: The secret to Eddie Stobart's success', *B2B Marketing*, accessed March 15, 2013, http://www.b2bmarketing.net/knowledgebank/branding /features/news-analysis-secret-eddie-stobart%E2%80%99s -success; Vanessa Barford, 'How did Eddie Stobart become so famous?' *BBC News*, April 1, 2011, accessed March 15, 2013, http://www.bbc.co.uk/news/ magazine-12925163; 'How did Eddie Stobart become a superbrand without any help from marketers?' *The Drum*, April 1, 2011, accessed March 15, 2013, http://www .thedrum.com/news/2011/04/01/how-did-eddie-stobart -become-superbrand-without-any-help-marketers; 'Stobart Fest Delivers Family Fun to Manchester', Stobart Group, accessed March 15, 2013, http://www .stobartgroup.co.uk/news/general/stobart-fest-delivers -family-fun-to-manchester/; 'Thousands pack out first ever Stobart fest', Stobart Group, accessed March 15, 2013, http://www.stobartgroup.co.uk/news/general/ thousands-pack-out-first-ever-stobart-fest/; 'TV series helps Eddie Stobart top business superbrand category', Stobart Group, accessed March 15, 2013, http://www .stobartgroup.co.uk/news/general/tv-series-helps-eddie -stobart-top-business-superbrand-category/; 'About', Stobart Group, http://www.stobartgroup.co.uk/about -us/; 'Stobart sport and benefits of being a Stobart club member', Stobart Group, accessed March 15, 2013, http://www.stobartclubandshop.co.uk/; Steady Eddie, http://www.steadyeddieworld.com/ (accessed March 15, 2013).

9. L. G. Zomerdijk and C. A. Voss, 'Service Design for Experience-Centric Services', *Journal of Service Research* 13, no. 1 (2010): http://jsr.sagepub.com/content/ early/2009/12/03/1094670509351960.abstract.

10. Ibid.

11. R. E. Goldsmith, 'The personalized marketplace: beyond the 4P's', *Marketing Intelligence and Planning*

(17 April, 1999): www.emeraldinsight.com/journals. htm?articleid=854461&show=pdf.

12. M. Fernandez-Barcala, M. Gonzales-Diaz and J. Pierto -Rodriguez, 'Factors Influencing Guests, Hotel Quality Appraisals', *European Journal of Tourism Research* 2 (1) (2009); A. Sergeant and S. Frenkel, 'When do Customer Contact Employees Satisfy Customers', *Journal of Service Research* 3 (18) (2000): http://jsr.sagepub.com/ content/3/1/18.abstract.

13. V. P. Magnini and E. E. Parker, 'The psychological effects of music: Implications for hotel firms': 53–62.

14. L. G. Zomerdijk and C. A. Voss, 'Service Design for Experience-Centric Services.'

15. Rick Garlick, 'Do Happy Employees Really Mean Happy Customers? Or Is There More to the Equation?', *Cornell Hospitality Quarterly*, August 2010; 51 (3): 305–06.

16. A. Sergeant and S. Frenkel, 'When do Customer Contact Employees Satisfy Customers', *Journal of Service Research* 3:18 (2000): http://jsr.sagepub.com/content/3/1/18.abstract.

17. C. Ezeh and L. Harris, 'Servicescape research: a review and a research agenda', *The Marketing Review* 7, no. 1 (2007): 59–78.

18. B. Quinn, 'Aesthetic labor, rocky horrors, and the 007 Dynamic', *International Journal of Culture, Tourism and Hospitality Research* 2, no. 1 (2008): 78.

19. C. Ezeh and L. Harris, 'Servicescape research: a review and a research agenda.'

20. Sheng-Hshiung Tsaur & Wei-Hsin Tang, 'The burden of esthetic labour on front-line employees in hospitality industry', *International Journal of Hospitality Management* 35 (2013): 19–27, http://www.sciencedirect.com/ science/article/pii/S0278431913000571 (accessed November 12, 2013).

21. 'The Disney Look', Disney Careers, http://cp .disneycareers.com/en/about-disney-college-program/ disney-look/ (accessed November 12, 2013); 'Disneyland allows employees to grow beards', *The Australian*, http://www.theaustralian.com.au/news/ latest-news/disneyland-allows-employees-to-grow- beards/story-fn3dxity-1226252289707 (accessed November 12, 2013).

22. Emily Portelli, 'Bearded police battle Chief Commissioner Ken Lay's ban at tribunal', *Herald Sun*, September 25, 2013, http://www.heraldsun.com.au/news/law-order/ bearded-police-battle-chief-commisioner-ken-lay8217s -ban-at-tribunal/story-fni0fee2-1226726421949 (accessed November 10, 2013); Anthony Dowsley, 'Rebel Victorian police officers fight bans on ponytails, beards', *Herald Sun*, January 17, 2012, http://www.news.com.au/national/rebel -victorian-police-officers-fights-bans-on-ponytails-beards /story-e6frfkvr-1226246066037 (accessed November 10, 2013); Amy Noonan, 'SA Police plans new policy to ban visible tattoos on officers', *Adelaide Now*, November 4, 2012, http://www.adelaidenow.com .au/news/south-australia/police-edict-to-cover-up-and -ban-offensive-body-art/story-e6frea83-1226510202723 (accessed November 10, 2013); Yoni Bashan, 'Tattoos could rule out a career in police', *The Sunday Telegraph*, January 29, 2012, http://www.news.com.au/national/fresh -ink-rules-out-a-career-in-police/story-e6frfkp9 -1226256410737 (accessed November 10, 2013).

23. Sheng-Hshiung Tsaur & Wei-Hsin Tang, 'The burden of esthetic labour on front-line employees in hospitality industry'.

24. C. Ezeh and L. Harris, 'Servicescape research: a review and a research agenda'; B. Quinn, 'Aesthetic labor, rocky horrors, and the 007 Dynamic.'

25. Mary-Jane Ierodiaconou & Laura Douglas, 'Fattism – a new legal risk at work', *The Australian Financial Review*, January 30, 2013, accessed November 10, 2013, http://www.afr.com/p/national/work_space/fattism _new_legal_risk_at_work_11OKwV7Lm7IkRltrR63ckO.

26. L. G. Zomerdijk and C. A. Voss, 'Service Design for Experience-Centric Services.'

27. Cho, Yoon-Na, Brian N. Rutherford, and JungKun Park, 'The impact of emotional labor in a retail environment', *Journal of Business Research* 66.5 (2013): 670–677; Chu, Kay H., Melissa A. Baker, and Suzanne K. Murrmann, 'When we are onstage, we smile: The effects of emotional labor on employee work outcomes', *International Journal of Hospitality Management* 31.3 (2012): 906–915; Skaalvik, Einar M., and Sidsel Skaalvik, 'Teacher job satisfaction and motivation to leave the teaching profession: Relations with school context, feeling of belonging, and emotional exhaustion.' *Teaching and Teacher Education* 27.6 (2011): 1029–1038.

28. Prebensen, N. K. & Foss, L, 'Coping and co-creating in tourist experiences', *International Journal of Tourism Research*, 13 (2011): 54–67. doi: 10.1002 /jtr.799.

29. L. G. Zomerdijk and C. A. Voss, 'Service Design for Experience-Centric Services'; Wu, C, H-J, 'The impact of customer-to-customer interaction and customer homogeneity on customer satisfaction in tourism service—The service encounter prospective', *Tourism Management*, 28:6 (December 2007): 1518–1528.

30. L. C. Harris and K. L. Reynolds, 'The consequences of dysfunctional customer behaviour', *Journal of Service Research* 6:2 (2003): 144–161; E. J Arnold and L. L. Price, 'River Magic: Extraordinary Experience and the Extended Service Encounter', *Journal of Consumer Research* 20:1 (1993): 24–45.

31. Wu, C, H-J, 'The impact of customer-to-customer interaction and customer homogeneity on customer satisfaction in tourism service—The service encounter prospective': 1520.

32. Ibid.; W-H Huang and C.H.C. Hsu, 'The Impact of Customer-to-Customer Interaction on Cruise Experience and Vacation Satisfaction', *Journal of Travel Research* 49:1 (February 2010): 79–92; W-H Huang, 'The impact of other-customer failure on service satisfaction', *International Journal of Service Industry Management* 19:4 (2008): 521–536; A.G.Tombs, and J.R. McColl-Kennedy, 'The Impact of Social Density, Purchase Occasion and Displayed Emotions of Others on Customer Affect and Behavioural Intensions', Paper presented at 34th EMAC Conference. Milan, Italy, (2005, May).

33. M. Fernandez-Barcala, M. Gonzales-Diaz and J. Pierto -Rodriguez, 'Factors Influencing Guests, Hotel Quality Appraisals'; C. Ezeh and L. Harris, 'Servicescape research: a review and a research agenda.'

34. V. P. Magnini and E. E. Parker, 'The psychological effects of music: Implications for hotel firms.'

35. Winston Churchill looking at the bombed House of Commons, 1943 (as cited in Ezeh and Harris 2007, p. 59)

36. A. D. Alonso and A. Ogle, 'Exploring design among small hospitality and tourism operations', *Journal of Retail and Leisure Property* 7 (2008): http://ro.ecu.edu.au/ ecuworks/892/.

37. Ibid.

38. M. Fernandez-Barcala, M. Gonzales-Diaz and J. Pierto -Rodriguez, 'Factors Influencing Guests, Hotel Quality Appraisals.'

39. N. Rahman, 'Toward a Theory of Restaurant Décor: An Empirical Examination of Italian Restaurants in Manhattan', *Journal of Hospitality and Tourism Research* 34 (2010).

40. A. D. Alonso and A. Ogle, 'Exploring design among small hospitality and tourism operations.'

41. Ibid.

42. I. Y. Lin, 'Evaluating a servicescape: the effect of cognition and emotion', *Hospitality Management* 23 (2004): 163–178; C. Ezeh and L. Harris, 'Servicescape research: a review and a research agenda.'

43. L. G. Zomerdijk and C. A. Voss, 'Service Design for Experience-Centric Services.'

44. L. W. Turley and R. E. Milliman, 'Atmospheric Effects on Shopping Behavior: A Review of the Experimental Evidence', *Journal of Business Research* 49:2.

45. K. Quartier, H. Christiaans, and K. Van Cleempoel, 'Retail design: lighting as an atmospheric tool, creating experiences which influence consumers' mood and behaviour in commercial spaces', Sheffield Hallam University Research Archive (SHURA) (2009): http://shura.shu.ac.uk/496/.

46. L. W. Turley and R. E. Milliman, 'Retail atmospherics', *Journal of Business of Research* 49:2 (2000): 196.

47. Ibid.

48. Gus Lubin, '8 Amazing Effects That Background Music Has On Sales', *Business Insider*, July 21, 2011, http://www .businessinsider.com/effects-of-music-on-sales-2011 -7?op=1#ixzz2Nrlix86f .

49. Ibid.

50. K. Aradhna, M. Lwin, and M. Morrin, 'Does scent enhance consumer product memories?' *ScienceDaily. University of Chicago Press Journals* (December 15, 2009): http://www .sciencedaily.com/releases/2009/12/091214143732.htm.

51. 'Car Showrooms', Air Aroma, http://www.air-aroma.com .au/who-scenting/car-showrooms'; 'Scent Marketing: The Smell That Sells', *Gigabiting*, September 6, 2013, accessed November 10, 2013, http://gigabiting.com/scent -marketing-the-smell-that-sells/.

52. 'MAANZ Home', The Marketing Assaociation of Australia and New Zealand, http://www.marketing.org.au/sample _mextra.aspx#_Toc139891680.

53. C. M. Voorhees, J. Baker, B. L. Bordeau, E. D. Brocato and J. Croin Jr., 'It Depends: Moderating the Relationships Among Perceived Waiting Time, Anger and Regret', *Journal of Service Research* 12:2(2009), http://jsr.sagepub.com /content/early/2009/05/18/1094670509336744; A. Rafaeli, G. Barron and K. Haber, 'The Effects of Queue Structure on Attitudes', *Journal of Service Research* 5:2 (2002),

http://jsr.sagepub.com/content/5/2/125.abstract; P. Kumar and P. Krishnamurthy, 'The Impact of Service-Time and Anticipated Congestion on Customers' Waiting-Time', *Journal of Service Research* 10 (2008): http://jsr.sagepub.com/content/10/3/282.abstract; V. P. Magnini and E. E. Parker, 'The psychological effects of music: Implications for hotel firms.'

54. O. Niininen, personal observation 1994; Carnival.com 2010, Fund Pass, https://funpass.carnival.com/signIn.aspx, accessed January 24, 2011.

55. V. P. Magnini and E. E. Parker, 'The psychological effects of music: Implications for hotel firms.'

56. A. I. Canhoto, 'Safeguarding customer information: the role of staff', *Journal of Consumer Marketing* 26:7 (2009): 487–495; A. C. Beetles, and L. C. Harris, 'The role of intimacy in service relationships: an exploration', *Journal of Services Marketing*, 24:5 (2010): 347–358.

57. A. Sergeant and S. Frenkel, 'When do Customer Contact Employees Satisfy Customers.'

58. Pikavippi tekstiviestillä, https://www.viestilaina.fi/pikavippi/pikavippi-tekstiviestilla, accessed March 28, 2013; Pikavippi, http://www.lainafakta.fi/lainat/pikavippi/; N. Broström, (2012), Turun Sanomat: Pikavippien suosio kasvoi, Kauppalehti, 24.03, http://www.kauppalehti.fi/etusivu/turun+sanomat+pikavippien+suosio+kasvoi/201203141573, accessed March 28, 2013.

59. 'Sizing up Australia – is Target's 3D body scanner the shape of things to come?' *The Conversation*, May, 2012, accessed March28, 2013, http://theconversation.edu.au/sizing-up-australia-is-targets-3d-body-scanner-the-shape-of-things-to-come-6690; B. Jopson, 'Clothes shops prepare for body scanning', *The Financial Times*, September 14, 2012, accessed March 28, 2013, http://www.ft.com/intl/cms/s/0/fb0ef6e2-fa0c-11e1-9f6a-00144feabdc0.html#axzz2NrDrDQuN.

60. Mikko Villi, 'Social curation in audience communities: UDC (user-distributed-content) in the networked media ecosystem', *Participations. Journal of Audience & Reception Studies* 9:2 (2012): 614–632; Chen, Bingxin, et al., 'Comic circuit: an online community for the creation and consumption of news comics.' CHI'13 Extended Abstracts on Human Factors in Computing Systems, ACM, 2013.

61. M. Carney, 'Duck, Duck, Acquisition: Wittlebee Taps Kids Clothing Company Cottonseed', *Pando Daily*, August 28, 2012, accessed March 28, 2013, http://pandodaily.com/2012/08/28/duck-duck-acquisition-wittlebee-taps-childrens-clothing-company-cottonseed/; K. Freeman, 'Buying Baby Clothes Is Easier With Mail Subscription Service', *Mashable*, August 13, 2012, accessed March 28, 2013, http://mashable.com/2012/08/13/buying-baby-clothes-subscription-services/; K. A. Fetters, 'Deal Alert: Subscription Service for Workout Gear: A new monthly apparel service will make over your fitness wardrobe with just a few clicks', *Women's Health Magazine Blog*, February 11, 2013, accessed March 28, 2013, http://blog.womenshealthmag.com/beauty-style-buzz/workout-clothes/.

62. T. T. Huang and A. L. Yaroch, 'A Public-Private Partnership Model for Obesity Prevention', *Preventing Chronic Disease Public Health Research, Practise, and Policy* 6:3 (2009), http://www.cdc.gov/pcd/issues/2009/jul/09_0034.htm.

63. J. H. Cheng, C. H. Tang and H. P. Chen, 'Interorganizational Partnership, Switching Cost, and Strategic Flexibility in Supply Chain', *WSEAS Transactions on Information Science and Applications* 12:5 (2008); H. Kriel, 'Partnership Marketing: A New Approach to Ensure Sustainability in a Digital Library', (2003), http://www.iatul.org/doclibrary/public/Conf_Proceedings/2003/KRIEL_fulltext.pdf

64. 'Consumer pressure changes John West's ways', *B & T*, December 4, 2012, accessed November 12, 2013, http://www.bandt.com.au/news/media/consumer-pressure-changes-john-west-s-ways; Aoife Boothroyd, 'John West launches conservation projects with WWF', *Food Mag*, November 1, 2013, accessed November 12, 2013, http://www.foodmag.com.au/news/john-west-launches-conservation-projects-with-wwf.

65. T. T. Huang and A. L. Yaroch, 'A Public-Private Partnership Model for Obesity Prevention.'

66. J. H. Cheng, C. H. Tang and H. P. Chen, 'Interorganizational Partnership, Switching Cost, and Strategic Flexibility in Supply Chain.'

67. Ibid.

68. C. Mulholland and G. R. Griffith, 'Paper 7. The Communication, Information and Marketing Strategy', *AFBM Journal Special Edition* 5: 1–2 (2008), http://www.csu.edu.au/faculty/science/saws/afbmnetwork/.

69. Ibid.

70. National History Museum, 2013, http://www.nhm.ac.uk/.

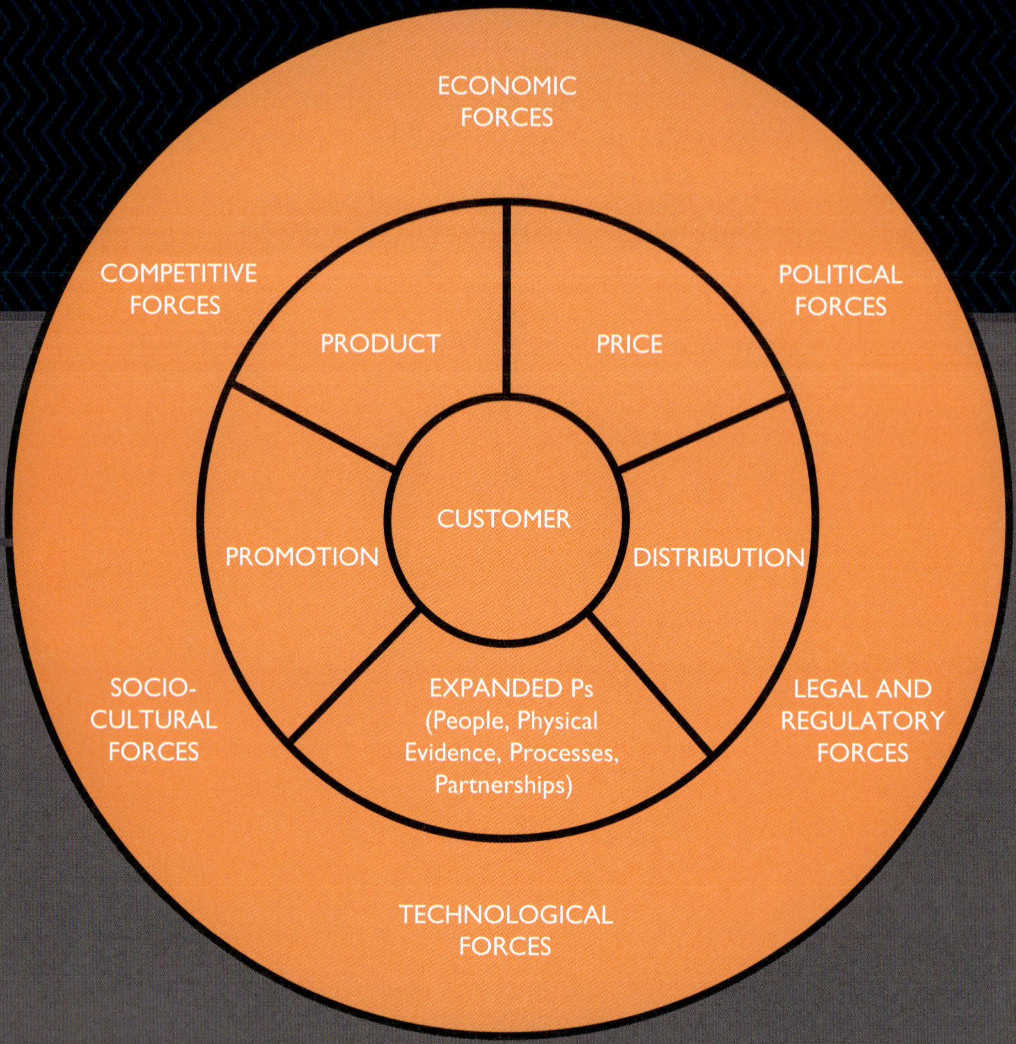

ECONOMIC
FORCES

COMPETITIVE
FORCES

POLITICAL
FORCES

PRODUCT

PRICE

CUSTOMER

PROMOTION

DISTRIBUTION

SOCIO-
CULTURAL
FORCES

EXPANDED Ps
(People, Physical
Evidence, Processes,
Partnerships)

LEGAL AND
REGULATORY
FORCES

TECHNOLOGICAL
FORCES

DIGITAL MARKETING AND SOCIAL NETWORKING

Growth and benefits of digital marketing
The interactivity of social media

Consumer-generated marketing and digital media
Social networks
Media-sharing websites
Virtual websites
Mobile devices
Applications and widgets
Wearable technology

Trends in digital marketing consumer behaviour
Online consumer behaviour
E-marketing strategy
Product considerations

Distribution considerations
Promotion considerations
Pricing considerations

Digital media and the expanded marketing mix
People considerations
Physical evidence considerations
Process considerations
Partnership considerations

Ethical and legal issues
Privacy
Online fraud
Intellectual property

 Throughout this chapter, Watch, Listen and Revise icons indicate an opportunity for online self-study through CengageNOW, linking you to animated chapter overviews, interactive diagrams, videos, quizzes and more.

15 DIGITAL MARKETING AND SOCIAL NETWORKING

Learning Objectives

LO1 Appreciate how digital media and electronic marketing are changing strategic planning

LO2 Understand how consumer-generated content can impact marketing strategy

LO3 Understand digital marketing consumer behaviour

LO4 Appreciate how digital media affects the expanded marketing mix

LO5 Identify legal and ethical issues related to digital media and electronic marketing.

MARKETING CHALLENGE | FACEBOOK BEFRIENDS SMALL BUSINESSES

Although more than 9 million small businesses promote their organisations through 'free' pages on Facebook, not as many choose to pay for advertising. Chief operating officer of Facebook, Sheryl Sandberg wants to change this. In 2012, Sandberg, formerly vice president of global online sales and operations at Google, began offering incentives to small businesses to advertise on Facebook. This took the form of advertising credits worth $50 to as many as 200 000 small businesses.

Normally, Facebook charges a set rate for each time a user clicks on an ad, but in this campaign, no charges were made until the number of clicks exceeded $50 worth. With rates at 25 cents or less per click, businesses had an opportunity to target a wide range of consumers with their $50 credit.

The aim of the campaign was to make businesses aware of the valuable word-of-mouth marketing opportunities that Facebook offers. The ability to target specific markets has led to success stories. For example, a wedding photographer used Facebook advertising to target women who had just changed their Facebook status from 'single' to 'engaged'. Another advantage of Facebook is the ease of creating a marketing platform and interacting directly with consumers through free pages. Sandberg believes Facebook is the key to helping small companies achieve growth and says she will not 'stop until all of them are using it to grow their business'.[1]

MARKETING CHALLENGE QUESTION

1 From the perspective of a small company, what are the advantages and disadvantages of paying for advertising space on social media when promotion can be done freely on these platforms?

Introduction

Since the 1990s, the Internet and information technology have dramatically changed the marketing environment and the way in which marketing success is achieved. Digital media have created exciting opportunities for companies to target specific markets more effectively, develop new marketing strategies and gather information about customers. Using digital media channels, marketers are better able to analyse and address consumer needs.

A defining characteristic of information technology in the twenty-first century is accelerating change. New systems and applications advance so rapidly that it is virtually impossible for a chapter on this topic to project into the future. For example, when Google first arrived on the scene in 1998, a number of search engines were fighting for dominance. Google, with its fast, easy-to-use format, soon became the number-one search engine. Today, Google provides additional competition to many industries, including advertising, newspaper, mobile phone services, book publishing and social networking. However, even Google must constantly innovate to keep its competitive advantage. For instance, the Chinese search engine Baidu is gaining ground with 75 per cent of the Chinese search engine market. Baidu has also announced it will create its own mobile technology to challenge Google's more than 40 per cent market share in mobile operating systems in China.[2] These examples show how rapidly the marketing environment is changing and it is likely to change even more and in unexpected directions as advances in information technology continue.

In this chapter, we focus on digital marketing strategies, particularly new communication channels such as social networks, and discuss how consumers are changing their information searches and consumption behaviours to fit with these emerging technologies and trends. Most importantly, we analyse how marketers can use new media to their advantage to better connect with consumers, gather more information about their target markets and convert this information into successful marketing strategies.

LO1

Growth and benefits of digital marketing

digital media
Electronic media that function using digital codes available via computers, mobile phones, smart phones and other digital devices

Digital media are electronic media that function using digital codes and are available on computers, mobile phones, smart phones and other digital devices. A number of terms have been coined to describe marketing activities on the Internet.

Digital marketing uses all digital media, including the Internet and mobile and interactive channels, to develop communication and exchanges with customers. In this chapter, we focus on how the Internet relates to all aspects of marketing, including strategic planning. The term **electronic marketing (e-marketing)** refers to the strategic use of the expanded marketing mix variables, as well as identifying customer preferences through digital marketing. Our definition of e-marketing goes beyond the Internet to include mobile phones, banner ads, digital outdoor marketing and social networks.

The phenomenal growth of the Internet has provided unprecedented opportunities for marketers to forge interactive relationships with consumers. Advances in Internet and digital communication technologies have made it possible to target markets more precisely and reach previously inaccessible markets. The Internet has become an important component of firms' marketing strategies because it opens up new ways of exchanging information between marketers and customers. Internet marketing is now integrated into strategies for all digital media, including television advertising and mobile as well as interactive media that do not use the Internet (advertising media are discussed in Chapters 12 and 13). In fact, marketers are using the term *digital marketing* as a catch-all for all the digital channels they use to reach customers. This area is evolving quickly, and the integration of the digital world into overall marketing strategies is still at an early stage.[3]

The speed of growth for Internet traffic is best illustrated historically:

* 1992 – 100 gigabytes per day
* 2002 – 100 gigabytes per second
* 2012 – 12 000 gigabytes per second
* 2017 forecast – 35 000 gigabytes per second[4]

One of the most important benefits of e-marketing is the capacity for marketers and customers to share information. Through websites, social networks and other digital media, consumers can learn about everything they consume and use in life. Since one third of the world's population now has Internet access, the Internet is changing the way marketers communicate and develop relationships with customers, employees and suppliers.[5] Many companies use not just email and mobile phones, but also social networking, wikis, media sharing sites, podcasts, blogs, videoconferencing and other technologies to coordinate activities and communicate with employees. Modes of communication are changing as well. For instance, many consumers prefer to text rather than call on their mobile phones. Among those who text on their mobiles, men send an average of 555 text messages monthly, while women send 716 text

Source: © NetPhotos/Alamy

digital marketing
Uses all digital media, including the Internet and mobile interactive channels, to develop communication and exchanges with customers

electronic marketing (e-marketing)
The strategic process of distributing, promoting and pricing products and identifying customer preferences through digital marketing

<< Digital marketing
Companies like Adidas build their brand equity and gain market share with their digital marketing strategies

messages.[6] Women also lead the way in social networking, with 53 per cent of women using blogs or social networks compared with 47 per cent of men.[7]

Figure 15.1 shows the rapidly growing contribution made by non-PC devices (mobile phones, tablets, TVs, machine-to-machine) to total global IP traffic (Internet Protocol Traffic). By 2017, wired devices (e.g. a PC connecting via cable to the Internet) are expected to account for only 45 per cent of total global IP traffic.[8]

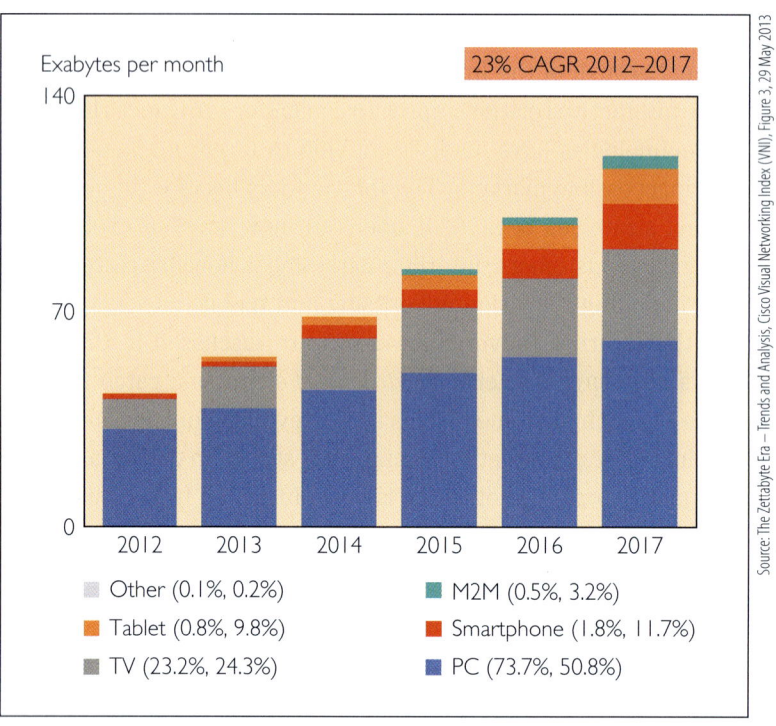

Source: The Zettabyte Era – Trends and Analysis, Cisco Visual Networking Index (VNI), Figure 3, 29 May 2013

FIGURE 15.1 GLOBAL IP TRAFFIC BY DEVICE TYPE 2012–2017

Some digital forms of communication merge two or more technologies. Twitter, considered both a social network and micro blog, illustrates how these digital technologies combine to create new communication opportunities. Social networking in particular is changing the dynamics of marketing and business communication. Because they facilitate communications in an extremely cost effective way, these new information technologies represent a tremendous opportunity for industries or activities that depend on the flow of information.

For many businesses, engaging in digital and online marketing activities is essential to maintaining a competitive advantage. Increasingly, small businesses can use digital media to develop strategies to reach new markets and access inexpensive communication channels. In addition, large companies like Target use online catalogues and company websites to supplement their brick-and-mortar stores. At the other end of the spectrum, companies like Amazon.com, which have no physical stores and sell products solely online, are challenging traditional brick-and-mortar businesses. Social networking sites are advancing e-marketing by providing special features, e.g. Facebook developed its own currency for consumers to purchase products, send gifts and engage in the entire shopping experience.[9] Finally, some corporate websites and social media sites provide feedback mechanisms through which customers can ask questions, voice complaints, indicate preferences, and otherwise communicate about their needs and desires.

One of the biggest mistakes marketers can make when engaging in digital marketing is to treat it like a traditional marketing channel. Digital media offer a whole new dimension that marketers must consider when developing their companies' marketing strategies. Table 15.1 outlines some of the characteristics that distinguish online media from traditional marketing channels.

TABLE 15.1   CHARACTERISTICS OF ONLINE MEDIA

Characteristic	Definition	Example
Addressability	The ability of the marketer to identify customers before they make a purchase	Amazon.com installs cookies on a user's computer that allow the company to identify the user when he or she returns to the website
Interactivity	The ability of customers to express their needs and wants directly to the firm in response to its marketing communications	Dell interacts with its customers on its Facebook page by answering concerns and posting updates
Connectivity	The ability for consumers to be connected with marketers along with other consumers	The Avon Voices website encourages singers to upload their singing videos, which can then be voted on by other users for the chance to be 'discovered'
Control	The customer's ability to regulate the information they view as well as the rate and exposure to that information	Consumers use Travelzoo to discover the best travel deals

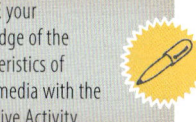

REVISE your knowledge of the characteristics of online media with the Interactive Activity

The interactivity of social media

Interactivity, the main distinguishing feature of digital media, enables an easy two-way flow of information between companies and stakeholders, unlike traditional marketing which usually involves one-way forms of communication. In the traditional model, marketers contact customers through an advertising message. If customers have questions or concerns, they contact company representatives by phone or other feedback mechanisms. This sometimes lengthy process requires companies to employ service representatives and/ or call centres to interact with customers who often have to wait an unreasonably long time to receive answers, leading to customer dissatisfaction.

Interactivity helps to solve this problem by focusing on the kinds of digital media that can make interpersonal connections possible. By using appropriate digital media, companies can facilitate interactivity and

interactivity
Allows customers to express their needs and wants directly to the firm in response to its marketing communications

Source: © Hartswood Films, used with permission of Hartswood Films and Sherlockology

<< Connectivity
Companies can bring networks of individuals together to share their love of a product as illustrated by the Sherlockology fan website

initiate conversations with customers. Features like interactive links on websites allow Internet users to view marketing messages at their own pace – a much less intrusive form of promotion than television commercials or sales calls. Digital media like blogs and some social networks allow marketers to interact with prospective customers in real or close to real time. The one-sided communication style of traditional marketing channels is being replaced with interactive conversations between customers and marketers. Thus, through greater interaction, digital communication can move marketing away from being an intrusion into the realm of relationship building.

Interactivity helps marketers maintain high-quality relationships with existing customers by shaping their expectations and perceptions. Additionally, digital media has created a myriad of relationships. Where traditionally a relationship existed between a company and a consumer, the Internet allows consumers to form relationships with one another as well – through online chats, blogs and electronic word of mouth.[10] By providing information, ideas and a context for interacting with other customers, interactive marketers can enhance customers' interest in and involvement with their products.

Consumer-generated marketing and digital media

Digital and e-marketing may have generated exciting opportunities for producers of products to interact with consumers, but businesses need to recognise that social media channels are more consumer-driven than traditional media. Consumer-generated material is having a profound effect on marketing. As the Internet becomes more accessible worldwide, consumers are creating and reading consumer-generated content like never before. Social networks and advances in software technology provide an environment for marketers to use consumer-generated content.

Consumer-generated information has gained prominence for two main reasons:

✳ Consumers enjoy publishing their own thoughts, opinions, reviews and product discussions through blogs or digital media.

✳ Consumers trust other consumers over corporations. Consumers often rely on the recommendations of friends, family and fellow consumers when making purchasing decisions.

By understanding where online users are likely to express their thoughts and opinions, marketers can use these forums to interact with consumers, address problems and promote their companies. Types of digital media in which Internet users are likely to participate include social networking sites, blogs, wikis, media-sharing sites, virtual reality sites, mobile devices, applications and widgets.

Social networks

social network
Web-based meeting place for friends, family, co-workers and peers that allow users to create a profile and connect with other users for purposes that include getting acquainted, keeping in touch and building a work-related network

Social networks have evolved quickly in a short period of time. A social network is defined as 'a web-based meeting place for friends, family, co-workers and peers that allows users to create a profile and connect with other users for purposes that range from getting acquainted, to keeping in touch, to building a work related network'.[11] Many large companies are experts in using social media to their advantage, but in Australia only 30 per cent of small businesses have a social media presence.[12] Each wave of social networking is more sophisticated than its predecessor and mishaps are possible when adopting any new technology, but rarely are these mistakes as public as what took place at HMV (see the Ethical Marketing box below). Today's social networks offer a multitude of consumer benefits, including music downloads, apps, forums and games. Marketers are therefore using the popularity of these sites as a way of promoting products, handling questions and complaints, and providing information to assist customers with buying decisions.

ETHICAL MARKETING DON'T LEAVE SACKED EMPLOYEE IN CHARGE OF YOUR SOCIAL MEDIA ACCOUNT!

HMV, the British entertainment retailer, is undergoing a restructure and looking for savings through layoffs. The company provided a chilling example of 'How not to manage'. Here are key points to consider:

→ 60 employees were called into a group meeting and told the bad news.

→ One of these 60 employees was the HMV Community Manager who was still in charge of HMV Twitter. She started tweeting the news during the meeting.

→ Lessons we should *not* forget from this incident:

■ A company should control its own social media account.

■ If considering layoffs, change passwords and restrict access to social media accounts *before* you dismiss employees managing those accounts.

■ *Regularly* update administrator status for social

Source: Shutterstock.com

media accounts (remove ex-employees and those who no longer need access to company social media accounts).[13]

As the number of social network users increases, interactive marketers are finding opportunities to reach out to consumers in new target markets. LonelyPlanet.com offers information and advice about everything travel related. The site currently boasts 10.3 million unique visitors and 45.9 million views. The site incorporates over 8000 destination pages and the ThornTree online community discussions feature a variety of travel activities with 100 000 new posts each month. For advertisers, this online community offers a well educated target market with above average household income and the desire to travel.[14]

Many countries have their own much smaller social networking websites. Orkut is a Google-owned service that is popular in India and Brazil. In China, QQ is a major social networking website; others are VKONTAKTE in Russia and CyWorld in South Korea. Social networking websites also offer ways for marketers to promote their companies. More information on how marketers use social networks is provided later in this chapter.

Internet users join social networks for many reasons, from chatting with friends to professional networking. In Australia, the majority of social media users are under 40 years of age and females are slightly more active users of social networks as shown in Figure 15.2.

FIGURE 15.2
FREQUENCY OF
SOCIAL MEDIA USE
BY AUSTRALIANS (BY
GENDER AND AGE)

Frequency of using social media	Total	Male	Female	14–19	20–29	30–39	40–49	50–64	65+
At least once a day	45%	44%	47%	72%	76%	66%	42%	28%	10%
Most days	5%	4%	5%	8%	3%	5%	5%	6%	2%
A few times a week	6%	6%	6%	8%	5%	6%	9%	5%	2%
About once a week	4%	3%	4%	4%	4%	3%	7%	2%	3%
Less often than weekly	5%	5%	6%	0%	0%	6%	3%	11%	7%
Never	35%	38%	32%	8%	13%	15%	34%	48%	76%

Source: YellowTM Social Media Report, p.10, Yellow Social Media Report 2013, "What Australian people and businesses are doing with social media," Sensis, May 2013, http://about.sensis.com.au/IgnitionSuite/uploads/docs/Yellow per cent20Pages per cent20Social per cent20Media per cent20Report_F.PDF (accessed, October 31, 2013).

An important question relates to how social media websites are adding value to the economy. Marketers at companies like Amazon.com and PayPal, for instance, are using social media to promote products and build consumer relationships. Many corporations are supporting Facebook pages and Yammer accounts for employees to communicate across departments and divisions. Professionals like doctors, professors and engineers also share ideas on a regular basis. Even staffing organisations use social media, bypassing traditional email and telephone channels. Billions of dollars in investments are being funnelled into social media, but it may be too early to assess the exact economic contribution of social media to the entire economy.[15]

Facebook

When Facebook overtook Myspace in membership numbers, it became the most popular social networking website in the world.[16] Internet users create Facebook profiles and then search the network for people to connect with. Facebook markets to parents and grandparents as well as to teenagers. At the time of writing, consumers aged 55 and over are the fastest-growing group on Facebook.[17]

Because social media can also be used for business, many marketers are turning to Facebook to promote products, interact with consumers and take advantage of free publicity. For example, Oreo celebrated its 100th birthday on Facebook by creating 100 new Facebook posts for 100 consecutive days. These posts were celebrating world events like the Gay Pride Month with an image of the Oreo biscuit featuring rainbow coloured filling. This 'Daily Twist' campaign was designed to tempt the 'child inside us' and resulted in 110 per cent increase in fan interaction per social media post.[18]

Source: © Kit Kat and Logo are registered trademarks of Société des Produits Nestlé S A, Vevey, Switzerland, used with permission

<< **Social networks**
Kit Kat engages consumers through Facebook. The Kit Kat page shows how a brand can sell a global product by using local market expertise

Additionally, social networking websites are useful for relationship marketing – the creation of relationships that benefit both businesses and customers. Companies are using relationship marketing through Facebook to help consumers feel more connected to their products. For instance, Kit Kat uses localised pages to target customers with localised promotions.[19] Thanks to Facebook, companies like Kit Kat are able to understand who their customers are and how they can better meet their needs.

Myspace

Myspace is a social networking website that offers users the chance to create profiles and connect with other Myspace members across the world. Like Facebook, Myspace allows users to watch videos, listen to and promote music, instant message friends, write on various topics (called forums), network with friends/colleagues, play games and more. Due to what some analysts say was a failure to innovate, Myspace now trails behind Facebook in popularity. Myspace hopes that recent redesign and content changes will help to reinvigorate the website. In 2011, News Corporation sold Myspace to Specific Media for $35 million. Pop star Justin Timberlake is also a co-owner of the website.[20]

Despite its decrease in popularity, Myspace retains a loyal following who prefer its layout and interface to other online social networking websites. Myspace also offers aspiring artists a chance to demonstrate their talent, becoming the largest artist community on the Web. Emerging musicians are using Myspace to record and share their music, and users can create social playlists of music from famous artists.[21] Justin Timberlake is determined to use Myspace's library of songs and music videos to turn the website around.

He announced the company would launch Myspace TV, a way to integrate television with instant communication among Myspace members.[22] For businesses, Myspace can be a creative means of marketing through the use of profiles, advertising, music, videos and other forms of online media.

Twitter

Twitter is a website that combines social networking with micro-blogging. It asks viewers one simple question, 'What's happening?' Users can post answers of up to 140 characters, which are then available for their 'followers' to read. A limit of 140 characters may seem too little for companies to send an effective message, but some have become experts at using Twitter in their marketing strategies. For instance, Xbox Support claims to be the world's most responsive brand on Twitter with a staggering 1.3 million tweets. Communication is also very informal: customers are called 'mates' and the support team goes to extreme lengths to solve their mates' problems.[23] Like other social networking websites, Twitter is also being used to enhance customer service and create publicity about company products. Some companies are paying influencers to use Twitter to create 'buzz' around their products, while others use it to gain a competitive advantage. Marketers can pay Twitter to highlight advertisements or company brands to a wider range of users when they search for specific terms or topics.[24] The race is on for companies who want to use Twitter to get an edge over the competition.

Blogs and wikis

Marketers should not ignore the impact of consumer-generated material like blogs and wikis, as their significance to online consumers has increased significantly. Blogs (short for 'weblogs') are web-based journals in which writers editorialise and interact with other Internet users. More than 75 per cent of Internet users read blogs.[25]

Sometimes blogs give consumers more control than companies would like. Blogs don't have to be factually accurate, so bloggers can post whatever opinions they like about a company or its products. Although companies have filed lawsuits against bloggers for defamation, they usually cannot prevent the blog from going viral. Responding to a negative review is a delicate matter. When a Korean Dunkin' Donuts worker created a blog alleging that a company factory had unsanitary conditions, the company forced him to remove the blog. However, readers had already created copies of the blog, and they spread it across the Internet after the removal of the original.[26] Similarly, an author made the mistake of angrily responding to a negative blog post about her book. The comments quickly went viral and were used as an example of how *not* to treat criticism on the Internet.[27] In other cases, a positive review of a product or service posted on a popular blog can result in large increases in sales. Thus, blogs can be both opportunities for and potent threats to corporations.

Blogs have major advantages as well. Rather than trying to eliminate blogs that cast their companies in a negative light, some businesses are using such blogs to answer consumer concerns or defend their corporate reputations. Many major corporations have created their own blogs or encourage employees to blog about the company.

A wiki is a type of software that creates an interface that enables users to add or edit the content of websites. One of the best known is Wikipedia, an online encyclopedia with more than 17 million entries in more than 250 languages on almost every subject imaginable (*Encyclopedia Britannica* has only

Source: Shutterstock.com

<< **Wikis**
Wikipedia is an online encyclopedia that allows users to add or edit information in more than 250 languages

120 000 entries).[28] Wikipedia is consistently one of the top 10 most popular websites on the web. Because Wikipedia can be edited and read by anyone, it is easy for online consumers to correct inaccuracies in content.[29] This website is expanded, updated and edited by a large team of volunteer contributors. For the most part, only information that is verifiable through another source is considered appropriate. Access to some entries, however, is restricted because of the risk of vandalism. Because of its open format, Wikipedia has suffered from some high-profile instances of vandalism in which incorrect information was disseminated. Such problems have usually been detected and corrected quickly. Like all social media, wikis have advantages and disadvantages for companies. Wikis on controversial companies like Nike often contain negative publicity, such as alleged violations of workers' rights. However, some companies have begun to use wikis as internal tools for teams working on a project requiring lots of documentation.[30]Additionally, monitoring wikis provides companies with a better idea of how consumers feel about a company brand.

There is too much at stake financially for marketers to ignore blogs and wikis. Despite this fact, statistics show that less than 25 per cent of *Fortune* 500 companies have a corporate blog.[31] Marketers who want to form better customer relationships and promote their company's products should not underestimate the power of these two tools as media outlets.

Media-sharing websites

Businesses can promote corporate messages in visual ways through media sharing websites which allow marketers to share photos, videos and podcasts. These websites tend to be promotional rather than reactive which means there is limited or no interaction with consumers through personal messages or responses. Nevertheless, the popularity of these websites offers the potential to reach a global audience of consumers.

Well-known photo sharing websites include Flickr, SmugMug, Picasa Web Albums and Photobucket. Flickr is owned by Yahoo! and is the most popular photo-sharing website on the Internet. A Flickr user can upload images, edit them, classify the images, create photo albums and share photos or videos with friends without having to email bulky image files or send photos through the mail. Photo sharing represents an opportunity for companies to market themselves visually by displaying snapshots of company events, company staff and/or company products. Companies can direct viewers to their photostreams (sets of photographs) by marking their pictures with the appropriate keywords or tags.[32] Many businesses with pictures on Flickr link their Flickr photostreams to their corporate websites.[33] Even Austrade (The Australian Trade Commission) uses Flickr photostream to help Australian companies grow their overseas business, attract international companies to Australia and promote Australian education internationally.[34]

Video-sharing websites allow virtually anybody to upload videos, from professional marketers at Fortune 500 corporations to the average Internet user. Some of the most popular video-sharing websites include YouTube, Metacafe.com and Hulu. Video-sharing websites give companies the opportunity to upload ads and informational videos about their products. A few videos become viral at any given time, and although many of these gain popularity because they embarrass the subject in some way, others reach viral status because people find them entertaining. Marketers are capitalising on the viral nature of these websites to promote awareness of their companies. McDonald's, for instance, has partnered with YouTube to have advertisements posted during videos by YouTube's partners. With YouTube's biggest partner generating more than five million subscribers, such exposure guarantees that McDonald's reaches a large audience.[35]

A new trend in video marketing is the use of amateur filmmakers. Businesses have begun to realise that they can use consumer-generated content, which saves them a great deal of money by not having to hire advertising firms to develop professional advertising campaigns. GoPro was transformed from a small camera firm into a $250 million company due to the videos consumers took of themselves using GoPro cameras. The company is partnering with YouTube to create its own network for consumer-generated GoPro videos.[36] Marketers believe consumer videos look more authentic and create enthusiasm for products among potential customers.

Podcasting, traditionally used for music and radio broadcasts, is also an important digital marketing tool. Podcasts are audio or video files that can be downloaded from the Internet with a subscription that automatically delivers new content to listening devices or personal computers. Podcasts offer the benefit of convenience, giving users the option to listen to or view content when and where they choose. The fact that the majority of current podcast users are between 18 and 29 years of age makes podcasts a key tool for businesses marketing to this demographic.[37] For instance, the podcast *Mad Money*, hosted by Jim Cramer, provides investment advice and teaches listeners how to analyse stocks and other financial instruments.[38]

Companies can use podcasts to demonstrate features of their products, create brand awareness and encourage customer loyalty.

podcast
Audio or video files that can be downloaded from the Internet with a subscription that automatically delivers new content to listening devices or personal computers, giving consumers the option to listen to or view content when and where they choose

Source: © iStockphoto.com/William Perugini

Photo-sharing >>
Flickr is a popular website that allows photo and video sharing

Virtual websites

Virtual websites offer significant opportunities for marketers to connect with consumers in unique ways. Virtual websites include Second Life, Everquest, Sim City and the role-playing game World of Warcraft. Such virtual worlds can be classified as social networks with a twist. Virtual realities are user-created, three-dimensional worlds that have their own economies and currencies, lands and residents who come in every shape and size. Internet users who participate in virtual realities like Second Life choose a fictional persona called an avatar. Residents of Second Life connect with other users, communicate with one another, purchase goods with virtual Linden dollars (which are convertible to real dollars on a floating exchange rate of around 250 Linden dollars per $1), and even own virtual businesses. For entertainment purposes, residents can shop, attend concerts or travel to virtual environments – all while spending real money.

Source: © iStockphoto.com/Micah Young

<< Virtual realities
World of Warcraft is a virtual reality game that allows consumers to completely immerse themselves in a fictional environment

Real-world marketers and organisations have been eager to capitalise on the popularity of virtual realities. Second Life allows businesses to reach consumers in a way that is creative and fun. For instance, in an effort to connect with consumers and build brand loyalty, Domino's Pizza created a shop in Second Life where users can order pizzas online.[39] Other businesses are looking to virtual worlds as a way of informing consumers about their products and services. For instance, McDonald's has partnered with the virtual gaming website Zynga to bring its virtual store and brand to Zynga's popular virtual gaming website Cityville.[40]

Firms are also using virtual technology for recruiting purposes. Major companies like Boeing, Procter & Gamble, Citigroup, and Progressive Corp. hold virtual career fairs to recruit candidates from across the world. The companies promote the fairs on Facebook and Twitter. By interacting with the public virtually, businesses hope to connect with younger generations of consumers.[41]

Mobile devices

Mobile devices, such as smart phones, mobile computing devices and tablet computers, allow customers to leave their desktops and access digital networks from anywhere. More than 80 per cent of Americans have a mobile device and 52 per cent of Australians now own a smart phone.[42] Because users can access the Internet, download apps, listen to music and take photographs, smart phones offer many opportunities for marketing businesses. In addition, these phones incorporate location based apps and due to the near field communication (NFC) feature they can also be used as a mobile wallet. Apps are a key driver for smart phone usage. By the end of 2014 it is likely that mobiles will be the main way of accessing the Internet in Australia.[43]

near field communication (NFC)
A wireless communication and data exchange technology that uses electromagnetic radio fields, works in a similar way to wi-fi, but only allows a very short distance between devices. This technology has been available since the 1980s but came to prominence recently when incorporated into mobile devices.

Mobile marketing has proved effective in grabbing consumers' attention. In one study, 88 per cent of smart phone users said they had noticed mobile ads. This rate is unusually high in a world where consumers are often inundated with ads. Ironically, mobile advertisement revenues are now growing faster than predicted. For example, the US mobile advertising industry was expected to be worth US$7.29 billion in 2013. Part of the success can be attributed to Facebook and Twitter joining Google in the mobile advertising business.[44]

According to the Interactive Advertising Bureau (IAB) online advertising across smart phones and tablets recorded 183 per cent growth in Australia from January to March 2013 and the total online ad expenditure for the same period was AU$ 910.8 million. Ads designed for tablets exceeded mobile ads for the first time in the same time period.[45] Although, the mobile ad expenditure is the fastest growing ad category in Australia (1.8 per cent of the total media expenditure), it is still low compared to the global figure of 2.8 per cent of total revenue.[46] Moreover, mobile advertisements in the future are likely to have a meaningful two way conversation with consumers once voice recognition applications for mobiles are refined.[47] Already today, some companies are sending location-based promotions (e.g. 'come and visit our store just 200m away from your current location') as well as location-based coupons to select mobile phones.[48]

Shopping by phones is another increasing trend. Some 50 per cent of Australians research products online which often leads to buying items either in stores or online. There are no significant age differences between Australians who explore products online (Gen Y 74 per cent, Gen X 62 per cent and Baby Boomers 49 per cent[49]. Table 15.2 provides insight into m-Commerce in Australia which is valued at $5.6 billion.[50]

TABLE 15.2　MOBILE BUYING BEHAVIOUR BY AUSTRALIANS

Where Australians make mobile purchases	37 per cent when travelling; 42 per cent at work; 42 per cent at school, park, restaurant or out-of-home location
Mobiles are also used in stores	73 per cent check prices, take photos, find product details compare deals between stores 53 per cent did not buy in store after finding a better deal by using their mobile
Product searchers	From smart phones and tablets spike in evenings
Convenience and impulse	71 per cent of Australian mobile shoppers are attracted by the convenience: 29 per cent like transactions on the go; 26 per cent buy with mobile when they think of the product (e.g. reminder or prompt from TV); 38 per cent buy by mobile 'because device is where they are'.

Source: PayPal: Mobilising sales / Making money in the mobile commerce revolution, pp. 5–6

Despite these promising trends, many brands have yet to take advantage of mobile marketing opportunities. Although most major businesses have websites, these are not always easily viewed on mobile devices.[51] Similarly email marketing messages are often not mobile friendly.[52]

To avoid being left behind, brands need to recognise the importance of mobile marketing. Some of the more common mobile marketing tools include:

✳ SMS messages: text messages of 160 words or less. SMS messages are an effective way of sending coupons to prospective customers.[53]

✳ Multimedia messages: multimedia messaging takes SMS messaging a step further by allowing companies to send video, audio, photos and other types of media over mobile devices. For instance, Anytime Fitness clubs successfully used MMS to promote their 12 hour sale.[54]

✳ Mobile advertisements: visual advertisements that appear on mobile devices. Companies might choose to advertise through search engines, websites or even games accessed on mobile devices.

✳ Mobile websites: websites designed for mobile devices. By 2014 the volume of mobile Internet traffic is expected to exceed Internet traffic from landlines.[55] In Australia the most visited news-type website is the Bureau of Meteorology (across both mobile and fixed line).[56]

✳ Location-based networks: These are built for mobile devices. One of the most popular networks is Foursquare, which lets users check in and share their location with others.[57]

✳ Mobile applications: software programs that run on mobile devices and give users access to particular content.[58] Businesses release apps to help consumers access more information about their company or to provide incentives or sales. These are discussed further in the next section.

Applications and widgets

Applications, or apps, are adding an entirely new layer to the marketing environment in Australia which has the second highest smart phone usage in the world. According to *Choice*, in 2013, the average smart phone contains 27 apps. The most important feature of apps is the convenience and cost savings they offer to consumers. Some apps allow consumers to scan a product's barcode and then compare it with the price of identical products in other stores. Other uses include downloading in-store discounts and finding homes for abandoned pets. Figure 15.3 shows the top 10 free apps per operating system. The differences between operating systems could be due to availability of free apps as well as the typical target markets for iPhones, Android phones and Windows phones.[59] Although many apps are associated with entertainment, business or social networking, some aim to make ethical buying behaviour a little easier (see Marketing in Transition box on the next page).

To remain competitive, companies are beginning to use mobile marketing to offer additional incentives to consumers. International Hotel Group, for instance, has both a mobile website and a Priority Club Reward app. As a result of its mobile marketing strategy, the company experienced a 20 per cent boost in mobile website jumps per month.[61] The QR scanning app is also becoming popular with marketers as a way of promoting their companies and offering consumer discounts.[62] QR codes are black and white squares that appear in magazines, posters and storefront displays. Smart phone users with the QR scanning application can scan the code and be directed to a web page, video or image on the phone's screen.

QR code
A QR (quick response) code is a two dimensional barcode that links to a website

	Top Android free apps		Top iPhone free apps		Top Windows free apps	
	App Name	**Category**	**App Name**	**Category**	**App Name**	**Category**
1	Facebook	Social	Deer Hunter 2014	Games	Facebook	Social
2	Candy Crush Saga	Game	Guide for iOS 7 – Tips and Tricks	Reference	Adobe Reader	Tools + Productivity
3	Skype	Social	Grand Theft Auto: iFruit	Games	YouTube	Music + Video
4	Snapchat	Social	The Human Body by Tinybop	Education	Skype	Social
5	eBay	Shopping	Wallpapers iOS 7 Edition	Catalogues	WhatsApp	Social
6	Pet Rescue Saga	Game	Where's My Water? 2	Games	Flashlight XT	Tools + Productivity
7	Viber	Social	ScreenMotion Wallpapers iOS 7	Entertainment	Viber	Social
8	Instagram	Social	Hanger	Games	Carsales	Lifestyle
9	Gumtree Australia	Shopping	Turbo Racing League	Games	Kik Messenger	Social
10	Facebook Messenger	Social	Pet Rescue Saga	Games	6tag	Social

FIGURE 15.3 TOP 10 FREE APPS PER OPERATING SYSTEM

Source: Based on http://www.gizmodo.com.au/2013/10/the-20-most-popular-android-iphone-and-windows-phones-apps-right-now-and-our-favourite-alternatives/

MARKETING IN TRANSITION | ETHICAL APPS

Mobile phone and social media apps make ethical consumer behaviour and shopping so much easier. For example, Shop Ethical!, Australia's most popular ethical shopping app for both iPhone and Android phones, gives consumers access to some 4000 products which are rated based on recommendations from Greenpeace, Choose Cruelty Free, WWF, Friends of the Earth and Free2Work. At the time of writing, there were 20 000 downloads for this app and over 110 000 printed copies of the product/company guide in use.

The Free2Work app helps consumers judge companies, products and brands according to their efforts in helping to reduce the exploitation of child labour around the world. By scanning the product's bar code, customers can see the company's grade for ethical practices.

Pet food manufacturer, Pedigree offers a Dog-A-Like app which aims to find homes for dogs in shelters by matching you to the look of rescue dogs in need of a home. This app plays on the notion that dogs and owners tend to look alike and by simply uploading a picture of your face this helps to match you with your new 'K9' family member. This app is available for iPhone, Android phones or on Facebook and has already led to thousands of dogs being rescued from euthanasia.[60]

Mobile payments are also gaining traction, and companies like Google are working to capitalise on this opportunity.[63] Google Wallet is a mobile app that stores credit card information on a smart phone. When shoppers are ready to check out, they can tap the phone at the point of sale to register the transaction.[64] Another example is PayPal: over 20 per cent of Australian PayPal transactions are now mobile.[65]

Software widgets on websites, desktop or mobile devices enable users 'to interface with the application and operating system'. Marketers use widgets to display news headlines, clocks or games on their web pages.[66] Widgets downloaded to desktops can update users on the latest company or product information, enhancing relationship marketing between companies and their fans. For example, the Australian Tourism booking widget can be used to make bookings for events, accommodation, attractions or tours.[67] Widgets are an innovative digital marketing tool to personalise web pages, alert users to the latest company information and spread awareness of a company's products.

Wearable technology

Over the next 3–5 years the wearable technology business is set to increase dramatically in value to somewhere between AU$30 and AU$50 billion. Wearable technology clothing and accessories require a connection to a smart phone app for functionality and interconnectivity. It is estimated that approximately 250 million smart phones could support wearable technology devices and some 15 per cent of current smart phone users are likely to purchase wearable technology once it becomes more easily available.[68]

Currently wearable technology development is driven by Apple, Google, Samsung and Nike but new players are entering the market, for example the Pebble smartwatch was funded by Kickstarter, a crowdfunding website.[69]

Wearable technology takes the form of, for example, smartwatches, which are computerised wrist watches with data processing functionality similar to tablets and smart phones. Health conscious consumers might be interested in wearable technology solutions that monitor vital signs/health or physical activity. Modern day pedometers count steps taken each day (e.g. Gymboss) or there are activity trackers which record moods, sleep patterns and activity levels (e.g. UP by Jawbone). The UP by Jawbone wristband also lets you know if you have been inactive too long and it can be programmed to wake you up at the optimal point of your sleep cycle so that you feel refreshed.[70]

More advanced examples of wearable technology with a health focus include:

* *Handyscope* smart phone body scanner designed to detect early signs of skin cancer[71]
* *Conscious Clothing* – wearable air quality monitors measuring the amount of air pollution[72]
* gloves designed to change colour if they come into contact with toxins (a welcome development for anyone who regularly handles potentially harmful chemicals)[73]
* ultraviolet monitoring bracelets that change colour after too long spent in the sun[74]
* smart bras that can detect breast cancer with greater accuracy than mammograms.[75]

Wearable technology app development is in its infancy but already some clothes are infused with technology for more novel purposes. For example, the TshirtOS is a 100 per cent cotton T-shirt with added Bluetooth connectivity, an LED display, microphone, accelerometer and speakers that allow wearers to record daily activities as well as display their creativity on this 'wearable billboard'.[77]

wearable technology
Technology that can be worn like any piece of clothing or accessory with seamless connectivity to smart phone apps

DID YOU KNOW?

Social media addicts might appreciate the Social Denim jeans by Replay with built in Twitter and Facebook connectivity, as well as the 'Like-A-Hug' vest that gives wearers a hug-like squeeze for every 'Like' they receive on Facebook. Go online to find out more about these products and what they can do.[76]

Trends in digital marketing consumer behaviour

Since e-marketing started, businesses have seen a range of changes in consumer behaviour. Today, with the click of a button, consumers expect to be able to access detailed information on companies, products and issues that can help them make purchasing decisions. 'Deal' websites, for example, allow online shoppers to find the best deals, giving retailers a run for their money. E-marketers like Amazon.com and eBay, have taken market share away from brick and mortar bookstores and movie rental stores. Companies are finding ways to provide creative incentives to consumers and market to them in new ways.

Through social networking websites and blogs, consumers are able to connect with one another in ways unheard of a decade ago. They can share information and experiences without company interference, allowing them to get more of the 'real story' on a product or company. In many ways, some of the power of professional marketers to control and dispense information has been placed in the hands of consumers who are now able to regulate the information they view as well as the rate and sequence of their exposure to that information. The Internet is sometimes referred to as a pull medium because users determine which websites they want to view, leaving marketers with limited ability to control the content to which users are exposed, and in what sequence. Today, blogs, wikis, podcasts and ratings are used to publicise, praise or challenge companies. Digital media forces marketers to approach their jobs differently compared with traditional marketing.[78] However, many companies miss the opportunity to gather information by not routinely monitoring consumer postings to social networking websites.

The changing social behaviour of consumers need not be all 'doom and gloom' for marketers. Some companies are using the power of consumers to their advantage While negative ratings and reviews damage a company, positive customer feedback is free publicity that can be more effective than corporate messages. Because consumer-generated content appears more authentic than corporate messages, it can significantly increase a company's credibility. Additionally, while consumers can use digital media to access more information about companies, marketers can use the same websites to get information about consumers – often more information than could be gathered through traditional marketing avenues. They can examine how consumers use the Internet to improve target marketing messages to their audiences. Marketers increasingly use consumer-generated content to supplement their own marketing efforts, even going so far as to incorporate Internet bloggers in their publicity campaigns. Finally, marketers are also using the Internet to track the success of online marketing campaigns, creating an entirely new approach to market research.

Online consumer behaviour

Digital media marketers need to continually adapt to new technologies and changing consumer behaviour. With the emergence of so many new technologies, the attrition rate for digital media channels is high, with some dying off each year as new ones emerge. The trend with social networks is similar: early social networks like Six Degrees disappeared when they failed to capture the interest of the general public. With the passing of time, digital media are becoming more sophisticated and effective in the way they reach consumers.

Mastering digital media is a daunting task for marketers, particularly those used to more traditional means of marketing. For this reason, it is essential that marketers focus on the changing social behaviour of consumers and how they interact with digital media. Social networking and other digital technologies are changing how consumers gather and use information. They have access to more information than ever before, and the Internet makes it possible for consumers to become involved in the marketing process.

Marketers who want to capitalise on social and digital media need to consider how the media channels are being used – are online consumers creating content, conversing, rating, collecting, joining or simply reading information? In markets where the online population are 'spectators', companies should post corporate messages promoting their organisations. In a population of 'joiners', companies could try to connect with their target audience by creating profile pages and inviting consumers to post their thoughts. In areas where a significant portion of the online community are 'creators', marketers should continually monitor what consumers are saying and incorporate bloggers into their public relations strategies.

Companies need to exercise care, however. Firms that try to use their influence to stifle online criticism run the risk of consumer backlash. The power of consumers in the online world should not be underestimated by marketers. By knowing how to segment the online population, marketers can tailor messages to their target markets.

E-marketing strategy

Although the Internet has yet to take off in many countries due to a lack of infrastructure, basic Internet literacy is becoming commonplace. More than 25 per cent of the world's population uses the Internet, and this number is growing at a fast pace. In June 2013, there were 12.4 million Internet subscribers in Australia.[79] These trends highlight a growing need for businesses to use the Internet to reach an increasingly web-savvy population. As more and more shoppers go online for purchases, the power of traditional brick and mortar businesses is decreasing. Online retailers like Amazon.com are challenging traditional retailers like Collins bookstores, and even small businesses are finding ways to reach customers and take share away from established competitors.

Most businesses now use digital marketing to gain or maintain market share. This 'brick and clicks' model is now standard for businesses from neighbourhood family-owned restaurants to national chain retailers. In the process, companies that use digital marketing well receive the added benefit of streamlining their organisations and offering entirely new benefits and convenience to consumers. The following sections examine how businesses are effectively using social media forums to create effective online marketing strategies.

Product considerations

In traditional marketing models, marketers anticipate consumer needs and preferences and tailor their products to meet those needs. The same is true for digital media but it has something extra – the opportunity to add a service dimension to traditional products and to create new products that can only be accessed through the Internet. The Internet can also blur the line between organisations and consumers, for example, crowdsourcing showcases the knowledge or expertise of 'everyday people'. Crowdsourcing refers to companies using the expertise of crowds of people outside their company to complete tasks that have been traditionally performed by staff members. Internet platforms are typically used to collect information from consumers or other experts. The following examples illustrate the varied nature of crowdsourcing activities:

* Open Street Map (http://www.openstreetmap.org) is best described as the Wikipedia of maps, a free-to-use map of the world.
* Weather Underground (http://www.wunderground.com) incorporates local weather observations into weather forecasts
* Instragram (http://instagram.com) transforms ordinary photos into filter-driven art you want to share.
* Kickstarter (http://www.kickstarter.com) claims to be 'world's largest funding platform for creative works'.
* Utest (http://www.utest.com/soft) promotes itself as 'the world's largest marketplace for software testing.

Some companies, for example Nissan, Citroen and Levi, also use online advertising campaigns and contests to help develop better products.[80]

geocaching
A modern day treasure hunt where participants use smart phone apps or handheld GPS units to locate caches (small treasure chests).

Affordable, handheld GPS technology has been used to create a whole new product/ experience called Geocaching – a modern day treasure hunt where participants use smart phone apps or handheld GPS units to locate caches (small treasure chests). These caches have a logbook for participants to sign and some of them also include low cost trinkets that treasure hunters can take away with them by replacing it with an item of similar value. Geocaching is increasing in popularity. In March 2013 there were over 2 million active caches around the world for over 5 million treasure hunters to locate. Geocaching can be an inexpensive hobby for the whole family, e.g. the Scouts promote geocaching as a family oriented opportunity for bushwalking. By contrast, tourism destinations can use well designed geocache trails to attract visitors and encourage them to extend their stay. Online companies sell specialist smart phone apps that allow gamers to log their treasure hunt activities, e.g. Geocaching Australia lists Top Hiders and Top Finders on its website (http://geocaching.com.au).[81]

Applications available on the iPad, for instance, provide examples of products that are only available in the digital world. The ability to access product information for any product can have a major impact on buyer decision making. However, with larger companies now launching their own extensive marketing campaigns, and with the constant sophistication of digital technology, many businesses are finding it necessary to continually upgrade their product offerings to meet consumer needs.

Distribution considerations

The role of distribution is to make products available at the right time, at the right place and in the right quantities. Digital marketing can be seen as a new distribution channel that helps businesses increase efficiency. Digital products are usually distributed digitally: downloading software, a smart phone app or music now comes naturally to many consumers. It can be argued that digital distribution is environmentally friendly since physical shipping of goods is not required and the electronic distribution of e-books eliminates the printing process (see the Sustainable Marketing box overleaf). Figure 15.4 shows how Australian game sales

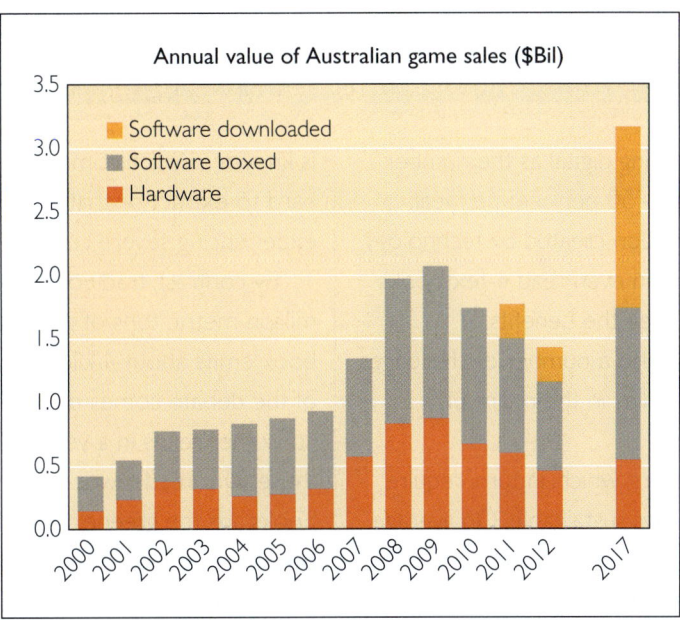

Source: The NPD Group Australia, PwC Australia

are shifting online. Other developments in the pipeline include the delivery of entertainment and news content for consumers on the go, for example Network Ten and GoConnect are trialling free to use wi-fi TV at central Melbourne locations funded by advertisements.[82]

The ability to process orders electronically and the speed of Internet communication reduce inefficiencies, costs and redundancies while increasing speed throughout the marketing channel. Shipping times and costs have become an important consideration in attracting consumers, prompting many companies to offer consumers low shipping costs or next-day delivery. The delivery of online purchases can be a problem for some customers, for example, who can receive parcels for you if your job keeps you on the road? Amazon.com has addressed this issue by giving customers the option of receiving parcels at Amazon.com lockers placed in convenient locations like train stations. At the time of writing, this service was unique to Amazon.com, giving them a real competitive advantage.

Finland Post offers parcel lockers that let consumers send and receive packages: senders enter relevant address information into Smartpost lockers and pay for postage with a debit card. Parcels are transported through regular postal services and when they arrive at their destinations, recipients receive a text message with an 'unlock code' for their nearest Smartpost locker.[83] Finland Post is also trialling a grocery delivery service where consumers order their groceries online and nominate a convenient Smartpost locker for collecting them – the perishable nature of food items forces consumers to commit to a two-hour window for collecting their shopping.[84]

Source: Getty Images

<< **Distribution**
24/7 retailing online sounds great, but not everyone can collect their purchases from the post office between 9 a.m. and 5 p.m. Amazon has taken a proactive role in addressing this issue by placing automated delivery lockers in convenient locations

SUSTAINABLE MARKETING | ARE ELECTRONIC TEXTBOOKS REALLY BETTER FOR THE ENVIRONMENT?

University textbooks are going digital as the number of e-textbooks is growing by 50 per cent per year. With the help of an application created by technology company Inkling, students can even read e-textbooks on their iPads. It is easy to see the benefits of e-textbooks, but there are also a number of challenges to overcome. One of these lies in the realm of sustainability.

E-books require e-readers, which, in turn, require resources that are not always sustainable. On average, manufacturing an e-reader requires 15 kilos of minerals, 300 litres of water, and emits about 30 kilos of carbon dioxide. The iPad also requires what is known as 'conflict minerals' – minerals that are either hard to extract or that come from parts of the world experiencing severe conflict.

By contrast, traditional books use approximately 1.5 million metric tons of paper annually, and the average book emits about 4 kilos of carbon dioxide. Thus, much of the debate comes down to how many books a consumer reads in a year. One study indicates that, for those who read fewer than 10 books a year, traditional books are the greener option. Those who read many books a year would be better off using digital books. Of course, there is one option that trumps both of these in sustainability: the library![85]

Distribution involves a push–pull dynamic: firms that provide products push to get them in front of consumers. At the same time, connectivity aids those channel members who want to find each other – the pull side of the dynamic. For example, an iPhone app can help consumers find the closest McDonald's or KFC. Furthermore, a blog or Twitter feed can help a marketer communicate the availability of products and how and when they can be purchased. This process helps companies push products through the marketing channel and enables customers to pull products through the marketing channel.

These changing distribution patterns are not limited to the Western world. Businesses in countries all around the world are choosing to sell products over the Internet. This represents a revolutionary shift in countries like China, where online shopping had not been widely adopted by consumers. One of the first Chinese companies to adopt Internet selling was Taobao, an auction website for consumers that also features sections for Chinese brands and retailers. Taobao has been successful, with the majority of online sales in China going through its website.[86] The changing consumer trends in China indicate that the shift to digital media is well underway.

Promotion considerations

So far, this chapter has focused on how marketers can use digital media and social networking websites to promote products to consumers. However, almost any traditional promotional event can be enhanced or replaced by digital media. Banks are using blogs, podcasts and Twitter to post rates and financial products or to answer financial questions. Even direct selling representatives from firms like Avon and Amway are gathering their consumers on

Facebook to discuss products, much like socialising around the kitchen table or engaging in a focus group. Social media profiles also offer companies great intelligence about buying preferences and general consumer behaviour habits (see the Marketing in Transition box on page 567).

Social media websites need to balance the preferences of users, moderators and potential advertisers. Advertising via social media websites is a hot debate: the industry is making the news with projections of advertising revenue. In the US, for example, social media ad revenue is expected to be US$11 billion by 2017 (almost 19 per cent growth over five years).[87] However, social media advertisers are concerned about the impact negative publicity attached to Facebook advertising could have on their brand image. In fact, several high-profile companies have withdrawn advertisements from Facebook after a campaign urging consumers to target advertisers whose promotions appear next to content promoting domestic violence or violence against women in general. In other words, Facebook appears to be struggling to balance freedom of expression, 'crude attempts at humour' and the diversity of moral norms entwined in the Facebook community of over a billion members. Facebook's own terms of use ban posts that 'attack others based on their race, ethnicity, national origin, religion, sex, gender, sexual orientation, disability or medical condition'.[88] Yet initially the company refused to remove a photograph of a woman with her mouth covered with tape next to a caption 'Don't tap her and rap her. Tape her and rape her' as this image 'did not violate [Facebook] community standards'.[89] Facebook has since bowed to pressure from campaigners by admitting that its 'systems for identifying and removing hate speech failed to work effectively' and that the company needs to step up the policing of hate speech.[90]

Pricing considerations

Pricing relates to perceptions of value and is the most flexible element of the marketing mix. Digital online media marketing facilitates both price and non-price competition, because Internet marketing gives consumers access to more information about costs and prices. As consumers become more informed about their options, the demand for low-priced products has grown, leading to the creation of daily deal websites like Groupon. Figure 15.5 shows that, in Australia, 80 per cent of group buying revenue can be attributed to Groupon, Scoop, LivingSocial, Cudo and OurDeal.[91] These companies partner with local businesses to offer major discounts to subscribers in order to generate new business. Several marketers are also offering buying incentives like online coupons or free samples to generate consumer demand for their products.

Digital connections can help customers find competitive prices for products in an instant. Websites provide price information, and mobile applications help customers find the lowest price. Consumers can even bargain with retailers in the store by using a smart phone to show the lowest price available during a transaction. Showrooming refers to consumers using bricks and mortar retailers to 'get a feel for a product' but actually buying the item from often cheaper online stores.[92] This new access to price information benefits consumers, but it places new pressures on sellers to be competitive and to differentiate products so

showrooming
Buying behaviour whereby consumers use bricks and mortar retailers to get a feel for products but actually buy them more cheaply through online stores.

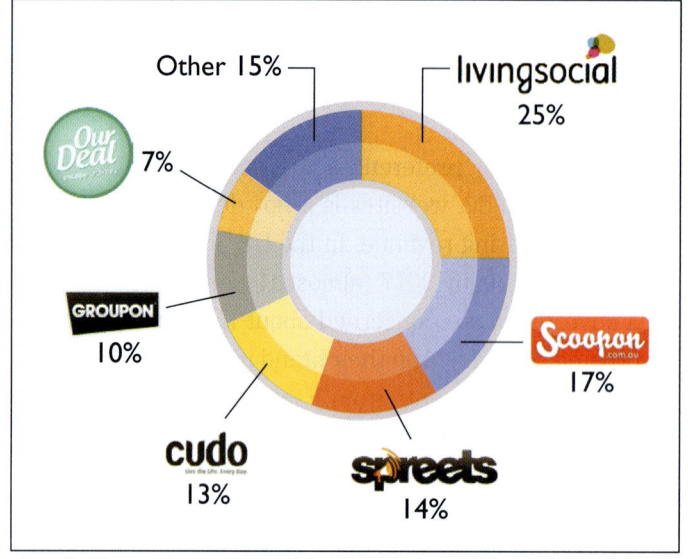

FIGURE 15.5 MARKET SHARE OF LEADING DAILY DEALS COMPANIES IN AUSTRALIA

that customers focus on attributes and benefits other than price. Traditional retailers can also use price matching promises as well as well-trained sales staff to discourage showrooming behaviour.[93]

Until recently, social networks like Facebook and Twitter were mainly used for promotional purposes and customer service. Those who wanted to purchase items were often redirected to a company's website. However, retailers and other organisations are developing e-commerce stores on Facebook so that consumers do not have to leave the website to purchase items. The top Facebook stores are Amazon.com, Best Buy (technology and entertainment products), Gap (clothes retailer), Lady Gaga (music and Lady Gaga branded goods) and Arsenal, the UK Premier league soccer team selling Arsenal branded products.[94] The Facebook store offers smaller businesses an excellent opportunity to have their products viewed around the world, e.g. Sydney-based Show Pony Fashion sells clothes worldwide. For businesses wanting to compete on price, digital marketing provides unlimited opportunities.

Digital media and the expanded marketing mix

L04

REVISE your knowledge of digital media and the expanded marketing mix with the Online Revision Quiz

Developments in digital media also impact on the expanded marketing mix variables. Consider the following: social media helps companies to connect with their customers (people variable); the design features of company websites (e.g. type of media incorporated) is part of the physical evidence portrayed by the organisation; the 24/7 availability of automated services online contributes to customers' convenience (process); and finally, digital communication has introduced new opportunities for global partnerships. In this section we look at each one in turn.

People considerations

In the era of social media, companies should have clear policies and procedures in relation to who within the organisation contributes content to company branded social media websites. Views on this range from using external agencies that specialise in social media to encouraging all employees to make contributions. Those advocating wider participation recognise the importance of educating employees about the power of social media through in-house social media training courses.[95] Table 15.3 shows the relationship between the style of social media communication and the impression it makes on consumers

TABLE 15.3 WHO SHOULD REPRESENT YOUR COMPANY IN SOCIAL MEDIA?

Account structure	Impression this gives the brand
Company account with anonymous person tweeting	Impersonal, mysterious, corporate. Does not 'humanise' the brand. This approach works well for 'mysterious' brands that people do not expect to be personal or accessible.
Company account with employees tweeting from company account	Personal and gives the brand a 'humanised' element, but lacks insight into the lives of the people behind the company. Often results in an inconsistent mixture of corporate and personal tone or message.
Company account with fictional character tweeting	Personal, fun and interactive. Lacks the human element, but if a brand is associated with a mascot, this can be effective. Wonga, SEOmoz and Compare the Market are great examples of brands using this approach.
Employees tweeting from personal accounts	Highly personal and human, gives insight into the lives of the people behind the company, reducing friction between brand and customers.
Company account with employees tweeting + employees tweeting from personal accounts	Good balance of being personal, human, allowing people to develop relationships with the people behind the brand if they want to, but company account also maintains corporate feel.

Source: http://www.stateofdigital.com/who-should-represent-your-brand-on-the-social-web/

Physical evidence considerations

In a digital context, the physical evidence element of the expanded marketing mix consists of getting customers involved with the brand irrespective of the digital media platform they use. This is done by designing engaging, brand-focused web pages or m-sites (mobile-optimised pages).

Today a compelling website is likely to include seamless functionality between multimedia objects and video. In the not too distant future we can expect to be able to buy products through YouTube channels.[96] So far, technology has not advanced to the point where seamless use of rich media is available through mobile devices. As the popularity of smart phones and tablets grows, the demand for creating websites across these different platforms increases. Today, m-site is no longer 'an afterthought' or the 'poor cousin' of the website, since, for some online retailers, the mobile website is actually more profitable than their main website! Naturally this depends very much on the characteristics of your target market. For digital marketing managers, m-sites can be challenging since mobile browsing can easily be interrupted by SMS, an incoming call or poor 3G/4G coverage. A slow loading mobile website is likely to irritate customers too.[97]

In 2014 the expectation is that Australians are more likely to browse the Internet on a mobile phone than on a computer,[98] so the demand for mobile-optimised websites is great. For m-sites to function well, the total content (weight) needs to be small. Alternatively,

m-sites
Websites optimised for on the go use via mobile devices.

companies can invest in creating responsive websites that are designed to be accessed via desktop computers, smart phones and tablets alike. Unfortunately these responsive websites can be expensive to create (and still slower downloading than m-sites) but if your business relies on constantly updating web pages then these responsive websites are worth considering. Mobile phone apps could also be the answer to creating 'rich' customer experiences with opportunities for personalisation as well.[99]

Process considerations

Internet and mobile technologies have already made customer service processes smoother, faster and convenient for all parties. From the multitude of examples available we have selected ones that demonstrate how mobile and digital communication can be used beyond browsing the Internet or updating your Facebook status.

Smart phones have given rise to a new lifestyle that features on-the-go convenience and mini-experiences that are (liberally) shared with other consumers through different social media platforms. A recent *TIME* magazine study identified that 84 per cent of people worldwide could not live a day without their mobile phones, and 20 per cent of consumers are even checking their phones every 10 minutes.[100] As the study from *TIME* magazine indicates, mobile phones have already made evolutionary changes to our everyday lives.

Convenience

Convenience is a major feature of the Internet, mobile phones and other hand held devices. The following examples illustrate how processes have been streamlined for our use.

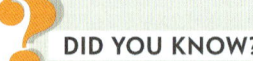

DID YOU KNOW?

Smartphones are changing our daily routines, to the extent that physical and mental changes are already evident. This is a revealing quote from the TIME magazine editor:

'It's hard to think of any tool, any instrument, any object in history with which so many developed so close a relationship so quickly as we have with our phones' …. 'Only money comes close – always at hand, don't leave home without it. But most of us don't take a wallet to bed with us,' BUT a smart phone 'can replace your wallet now anyway.'

Our dependence on mobile devices is even having physical and mental effects. 'There's a smart phone gait: the slow sidewalk weave that comes from being lost in conversation rather than looking where you're going,' ….. [Furthermore] 'Thumbs are stronger, attention shorter, temptation everywhere. We can always be mentally, digitally, someplace other than where we are.' We're also never far from our mobile devices, even in sleep – 75 per cent of 25-to-29-year-olds say they take their phones to bed.[101]

- Mobile phones with a QR code reader allow us to connect to websites simply by scanning the QR code. For example, Mercedes-Benz uses QR codes to speed up road accident rescue (see the Marketing in Action box on the next page), in Korea consumers can complete their grocery shopping by scanning QR codes in a virtual supermarket at metro stations, and in Klagenfurt (Austria) residents can access the town's virtual library by scanning QR codes conveniently located at bus stops.[102] QR codes are easy to generate, so with a QR code you could link your professional blog to your business cards or promote your personal web page via a T-shirt!

- Image conscious clubbers can leave their wallets at home after opting for an RFID implant to pay for drinks and gain access to VIP lounges (see Ethical Marketing box on page 566).

- *GateGuru* is a free app that helps you negotiate busy international airports by helping you find food that you like and the type of souvenirs you need to buy before the next leg of your journey.[103]

- *Waze* (another free app) is a GPS navigator that incorporates real-time traffic updates from other people on the road.[104]

When emergency or rescue personnel respond to a serious car crash they cannot 'just cut into the crashed vehicle to release trapped drivers or passengers'. The first step in using rescue shears is to identify the make and model of the vehicle to ensure they proceed with the rescue in a safe manner. After a bad accident, rescue workers need to call in the vehicle licence plates to obtain safe rescue information.

Mercedes has developed QR code based vehicle specific rescue information sheets to speed up this process. One QR code is placed in the fuel tank flap and one in a pillar (as both of these locations rarely get damaged simultaneously) so the emergency response personnel only need to use their smart phone to scan this QR code for the complete rescue information sheet.

Source: Getty Images

Mercedes is considering retrofitting these QR codes to older vehicles and waiving the patent right for this innovation so that other car manufacturers can take advantage of it.[105] ☒

The 'virtual wallet' is a clever way of reducing queues by making the payment process faster. Unfortunately, not all online/mobile buying experiences are positive and improvements in the process are still required. Retailers are going to extremes to attract customers to their online stores without realising that 66 per cent of mobile transactions are being abandoned at check-out. Customers get frustrated at having to type and re-type personal information in the tiny boxes offered by mobile devices or they are not happy about disclosing credit card information on mobiles.[106]

Enhanced experience

Museum exhibitions come to life when visitors can be directed to a website or an entertaining in-depth audio tour relevant to the exhibits. QR codes can be used to guide visitors to such additional information. A more 'high tech' way to enhance customer experience is to use augmented reality (AR), that is, to combine virtual reality features with real life experience. Today augmented reality experiences can be achieved by giving customers specialist goggles or glasses (e.g. Google's Project Glass),

Source: Getty Images

<< **Online consumer behaviour**
Imagine completing your grocery shop while waiting for your train

or by using smart phones or computers (e.g. AR games like Droid Shooting, Zombie, Run and Speck Treck).[107] Smart phone apps like Layar Reality Browser use GPS to determine locations so that consumers can access further details about businesses simply by pointing their smart phone camera to a building or landmark. For example, by pointing their smart phones at a restaurant, consumers can see the menu displayed on screen.[108] Check out the latest AR solutions from Total Immersion, one of the industry leaders (http://www .t-immersion.com)

ETHICAL MARKETING | IS IT OK TO OFFER MINOR MEDICAL PROCEDURES TO CUSTOMERS AS A CONVENIENCE?

The Baja Beach Club in Barcelona (Spain) achieved notoriety by offering VIP club members radio frequency identification (RFID) microchip implants. The benefits of VIP membership includes jumping entrance queues and using the club's VIP lounge. Each VIP member can choose between a 'normal' VIP card and one implanted with an RFID microchip. The RFID implant removes the need to carry membership cards, ID cards and cash to the beach themed club. Patrons can also pay for their drinks simply by waving their RFID chipped arm under special scanners installed at bars as the microchips can be linked to debit cards.

Each microchip is approximately the size of a long grain rice granule and they are implanted by medical professionals under local anaesthetic.

And before you even ask: yes – the same microchip technology is used to ensure lost pets can be returned home; and no – patrons cannot get their implants during a night of partying![109]

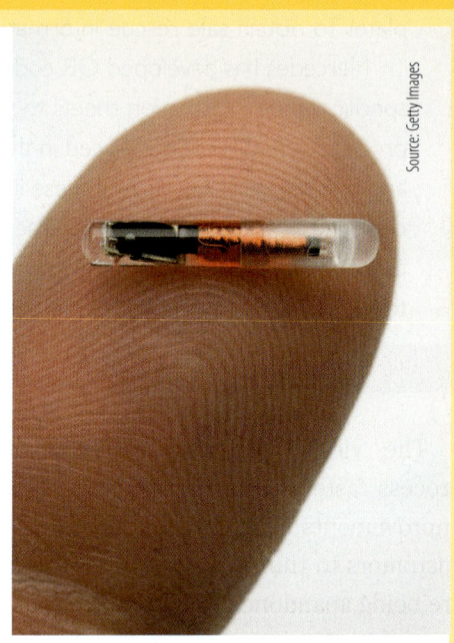

Source: Getty Images

---

radio frequency identification (RFID)
Contactless, wireless data exchange using radio frequency electromagnetic fields for automated/quick communication between a very small chip and the reading device. Examples include the ID chips that veterinarians insert into pets for pet registration schemes.

Partnership considerations

The partnership variable of the expanded marketing mix is ideal for implementation in the online or mobile environment where technology providers need to secure meaningful content to increase sales of their hardware products. On one hand, these collaborations often involve an existing entertainment content provider (e.g. a TV channel) who wants to secure a position in the area of media/entertainment consumption on-the-go. On the other hand, ICT/mobile hardware companies are keen to ensure continuous demand for new models with innovative product features (e.g. how to make tablet computers into 'a must have' when consumers already have smart phones). Finally, organisations specialising in customer data analysis can offer services to improve segmentation and targeting of products. The following are examples of effective partnership arrangements involving digital communication.

* The Yahoo!7 and Samsung partnership brings entertainment from the Seven TV network directly to Samsung smart phones and Samsung tablets.[110]

* Unilever is consulting an online community of 250 000 creative thinkers via eYeka to fine tune promotional campaigns for Unilever brands like Cornetto and Lipton.[111]

* Ikea, Yahoo!7 and Acxiom are collaborating to create a database of Australians interested in home decorating. This customer database also recognises any overlap with the Yahoo!7 audience, thus opening a creative channel for promotions in the future.[112]

Ethical and legal issues

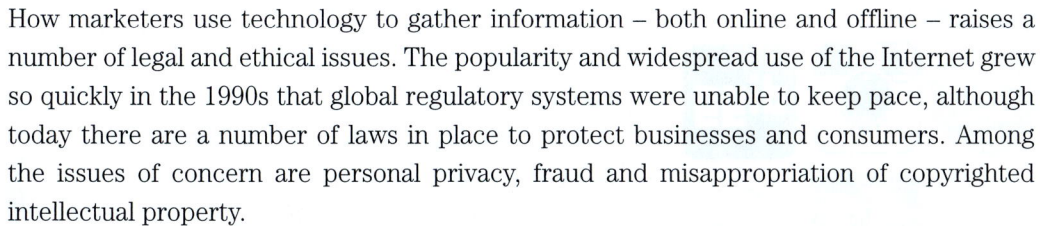

How marketers use technology to gather information – both online and offline – raises a number of legal and ethical issues. The popularity and widespread use of the Internet grew so quickly in the 1990s that global regulatory systems were unable to keep pace, although today there are a number of laws in place to protect businesses and consumers. Among the issues of concern are personal privacy, fraud and misappropriation of copyrighted intellectual property.

Privacy

One of the most significant privacy issues involves the use of personal information that companies collect from website visitors in their efforts to foster long-term relationships with customers. Some people fear that the collection of personal information from website users may violate users' privacy, especially when it is done without their knowledge. Hackers may break into websites and steal users' personal information, enabling them to commit identity theft. Mobile phone payments are another source of concern. Consumers worry that their information could be hacked, or their phones could be targeted with malware.[113] Consumers should also be aware that their social media profiles can be linked to their High Street buying behaviour (see Marketing in Transition box below). Many of these breaches occur at banks, universities and other businesses that handle sensitive consumer information.[114] All this leads to the need for organisations to implement security measures to prevent database theft.

MARKETING IN TRANSITION | YOU AS THE TARGET AUDIENCE: SOCIAL MEDIA PROFILES ARE CATCHING UP WITH OUR REAL LIFE PURCHASES

The use of data included in our social media profiles (e.g. age, gender, location, interests) for targeted advertisements via our social media accounts is to be expected. The 'Lookalike audiences' feature on Facebook even allows advertisers to target our 'friends', thereby improving the effectiveness of targeted ads. The advertising feature is based on the assumption that 'birds of a feather, flock together'.

But did you know that the information you provide to high street retailers can now be linked to your Facebook profile? Facebook has launched 'Custom Audiences', a feature where advertisers can overlay their customer database information (e.g. your phone number, email address, mobile app user ID, Facebook user ID) to target select customers via Facebook advertisements. Through independent consumer

Source: iStockphoto.com

profiling companies, advertisers can link our social media profiles to store loyalty cards and mailing lists.

If consumers feel overwhelmed by advertisements targeting them through social media, there are several ways to separate your real life buying behaviour from your social media profiles.

→ AdChoices is a self-regulatory program by the advertising industry where consumers can now 'opt out' from advertisements via social media (AdChoices works in a similar manner to 'Do Not Call' registries.)

→ Facebook Disconnect allows consumers to stop Facebook receiving data from web pages using Facebook Connect

→ Adblock Plus blocks your browsing history from being linked to your Facebook account

→ DoNotTrackMe works in a similar way to Adblock Plus

→ Finally, you can disable 'Social Ads' from your Facebook settings ('Social Ads' uses your 'Likes' and 'Share' to promote brands to your friends.)[115] ✖

Facebook and other social networking websites have also come under fire about privacy issues. Facebook and Google both agreed to undergo independent privacy audits for 20 years due to alleged privacy transgressions. Another Internet privacy issue occurring more frequently is 'scraping', an activity where companies offer to collect personal information from social networking websites and other forums.

The amended Australian *Privacy Act* which came into force in March 2014, contains strict privacy principles. Companies that use direct marketing or share data across national borders with partner organisations should take particular note. In preparation for this new law, companies should update their privacy policies and statements, credit check procedures and implement processes for handling complaints as well as ensuring compliance with the Act. Penalties can be as high as $1.1 million.[116]

Marketers must also comply with the *Spam*

Ethical and legal issues in digital media >>
Twitter freely shares its online security measures with consumers

Source: Courtesy of Twitter Inc.

About   English ▾   Have an account?   Sign in

Products   Company   Press   Investor relations   Blogs   Careers

We value your online security as much as you do. Our team works continuously to protect the security of your account, and we take steps every day to provide a secure Twitter experience for our users.

Reporting possible vulnerabilities

If you've found an issue that affects only **your own account**, please fill out this form.

If you think you've discovered a security issue that affects many users, please fill out this form with detailed instructions about how to reproduce the issue.

If you're researching security issues, please use a private Twitter account to test possible security vulnerabilities; that will give us time to fix any issues.

Security is a community effort

Maintaining top-notch security online is always a community effort, and we're lucky to have a vibrant group of independent security researchers who volunteer their time to help us spot potential issues. We applaud their efforts and the important role they play in keeping Twitter safe for everyone.

Act 2003 that bans any unsolicited commercial electronic messages with an Australian link. This refers to messages originating from or commissioned by an Australian company and to messages sent from overseas to an Australian address. In other words, all electronic messages sent for commercial purposes can be addressed to a person only if they have given their consent. Furthermore, all such messages must include a functioning 'unsubscribe' option.[117] In October 2013, GraysOnline, the Australian online retailer, was fined $165 000 and in May 2013 Cellarmasters Wines paid $110 000 for failure to comply with the *Spam Act 2003*.[118]

Online fraud

Online fraud refers to any attempt to conduct dishonest activities online, including attempts to deceive consumers into releasing personal information. Online fraud is becoming a major source of frustration for social networking websites because cybercriminals are forever discovering ways to use websites like Facebook and Twitter to carry out fraudulent activities. For instance, it has become common for cybercriminals to create profiles under a company's name. These fraudulent profiles are often created either to damage the company's reputation (particularly common with larger, more controversial companies) or as a way of luring that company's customers into releasing personal information that the cybercriminal can then use for monetary gain. Another tactic used by fraudsters is to create typo squatting websites based on common misspellings of search engines or social networks (e.g. Faecbook versus Facebook). Fraudsters then trick visitors into releasing their information.[119] Perhaps most disturbing is the practice of using social networking websites to pose as charitable institutions. For instance, fake charities were established on Facebook after the 2011 earthquake and tsunami disaster in Japan.

Organisations and social networking websites alike are developing ways to combat fraudulent activity. For instance, organisations known as brand-protection firms monitor social networks for fraudulent accounts. Whenever these websites are found, the company notifies their clients and helps them to remove the fraudulent account.[120] However, the best protection for consumers is to be careful when divulging information online. Privacy advocates say the best way to stay out of trouble is to avoid giving out personal information, such as social security numbers or credit card information, unless the website is definitely legitimate.

Intellectual property

The Internet has also created issues associated with intellectual property, the copyrighted or trademarked ideas and creative materials developed to solve problems, carry out applications, and educate or entertain others. YouTube has often faced lawsuits on intellectual property infringement. With millions of users uploading content to YouTube, it is hard for the company to monitor and remove all videos that may contain copyrighted materials.

The software industry is particularly hard-hit when it comes to the pirating of materials and illegal file sharing. The Business Software Alliance estimates that the global computer software industry loses more than US$50 billion a year to illegal theft.[121] Consumers view illegal downloading in different ways, depending on why they are doing it. If the motivation is primarily utilitarian, or for personal gain, then the act is viewed as less ethically acceptable

online fraud
Any attempt to conduct fraudulent activities online, including deceiving consumers into releasing personal information

% illegal downloaders by annual household income

FIGURE 15.6 PIRACY INCREASES WITH INCOME

Source: APRA

than if it is for a hedonistic reasons, or just for fun.[122] Australia ranks in the top 10 countries of peer-to-peer infringement (P2P infringement) in the world. Figure 15.6 shows that the typical Australian downloading pirated materials is well educated and earning over $100 000 per year.[123]

Consumers rationalise pirating software, video games and music for a number of reasons. First, many consumers feel they do not have the money to pay for what they want. Second, they do it because their friends engage in piracy and swap digital content. Third, for some, the attraction is the thrill of getting away with it and the slim risk of consequences. Finally, there are people who think they are smarter than others and engaging in piracy allows them to show how tech savvy they are.[124]

As digital media continues to evolve, more legal and ethical issues will certainly arise. As a result, marketers and all other users of digital media should make an effort to learn and abide by ethical practices to ensure they get the most out of the resources available in this growing medium. Doing so will allow marketers to maximise the tremendous opportunities digital media has to offer.

Study Tools

Chapter review

L01 APPRECIATE HOW DIGITAL MEDIA AND ELECTRONIC MARKETING ARE CHANGING STRATEGIC PLANNING.

Digital media are electronic media that function using digital codes. They include media available via computers, mobile phones, smart phones and other digital devices released in recent years. Digital marketing uses all digital media, including the Internet and mobile and interactive channels, to develop communication and exchanges with customers. Electronic marketing refers to the strategic process of distributing, promoting and pricing products, and discovering the desires of customers using digital media. Our definition of e-marketing goes beyond the Internet to include mobile phones, banner ads, digital outdoor marketing and social networks.

L02 UNDERSTAND HOW CONSUMER-GENERATED CONTENT CAN IMPACT MARKETING STRATEGY.

Digital media in marketing is advancing at a rapid rate. The self-sustaining nature of digital technology means that current advances act as catalysts for even more development. As faster digital transmissions evolve, marketing applications emerge that offer an opportunity for companies to reach consumers in entirely new ways.

As a result, digital marketing is moving from being a niche strategy to being a core consideration in the marketing mix. At the same time, digital technologies are changing the dynamic between marketer and consumer. Consumers use social networking websites and mobile applications to do everything from playing games to booking airline and hotel reservations. The menu of digital media alternatives continues to grow, requiring marketers to make informed decisions about strategic approaches.

 LO3 UNDERSTAND DIGITAL MARKETING CONSUMER BEHAVIOUR.

It is essential that marketers focus on the changing social behaviours of consumers and how they interact with digital media. Consumers now have a greater ability to regulate the information they view as well as the rate and sequence of their exposure to that information. This is why the Internet is sometimes referred to as a *pull* medium because users determine which websites they are going to view; marketers have only limited ability to control the content to which users are exposed, and in what sequence. Marketers must modify their marketing strategies to adapt to the changing behaviour of online consumers.

 LO4 APPRECIATE HOW DIGITAL MEDIA AFFECTS THE EXPANDED MARKETING MIX.

The reasons for a digital marketing strategy are many. The low costs of many digital media channels can provide major savings in promotional budgets. Laptops, smart phones, mobile broadband, webcams and other digital technologies can provide low-cost internal communication as well as external connections with customers. Digital marketing allows companies to connect with market segments that are difficult to reach with traditional media. Despite the challenges, digital marketing is opening up new avenues in the relationship between businesses and consumers, for example, social media helps companies connect with their customers (people variable). Moreover, the design features of company websites (e.g. type of media incorporated) is part of the physical evidence portrayed by the organisation, the 24/7 availability of automated services online contributes to customers' convenience (process), and, finally, digital communication has introduced new opportunities for global partnerships.

Because digital tools, strategies, tactics and channels are not static, marketers must prepare to learn new ways of reaching customers. There is still a need to balance traditional and digital media. Developing skills to manage the appropriate mix of traditional and digital media is important for success. Assuming that everything is now digital can be a mistake when targeting some market segments. Collaboration across organisations is necessary to ensure that digital marketing decisions break down the walls between products and customers. Customers should be engaged to help this bond evolve.

L05 IDENTIFY LEGAL AND ETHICAL ISSUES IN RELATION TO DIGITAL MEDIA AND ELECTRONIC MARKETING.

How marketers use technology to gather information – both online and offline – raises a number of legal and ethical issues.

Privacy, one of the most significant issues, involves the use of personal information that companies collect from website visitors in their efforts to foster long-term relationships with customers. Some people fear that the collection of personal information from website users may violate users' privacy, especially when it is done without their knowledge.

Online fraud refers to any attempt to conduct dishonest activities online, including attempts to deceive consumers into releasing personal information. It is becoming a major source of frustration for social networking websites because cybercriminals are forever discovering entirely new ways to use websites like Facebook and Twitter to carry out fraudulent activities.

The Internet has also created issues associated with intellectual property, the copyrighted or trademarked ideas and creative materials developed to solve problems, carry out applications, and educate and entertain others. Each year, intellectual property losses are estimated to be billions of dollars stemming from the illegal copying of computer programs, movies, compact discs and books.

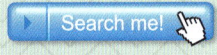

Key concepts

Use these key terms in **Search me! marketing** to find the latest relevant readings from a wide range of world-class journals, e-books and newspapers, including *The Australian*.

- digital marketing
- digital media
- electronic marketing (e-marketing)
- geocaching
- interactivity
- m-sites
- near field communication (NFC)
- online fraud
- podcast
- QR code
- radio frequency identification (RFID)
- showrooming
- social network
- wearable technology

Discussion and review

1 How does e-marketing differ from traditional marketing?

2 Define interactivity and explain its significance. How can marketers exploit this characteristic to improve relations with customers?

3 Explain the distinction between push and pull media. What is the significance of control in terms of using websites to market products?

4 Why are social networks becoming an increasingly important marketing tool? Find an example online in which a company has improved the effectiveness of its marketing strategy by using social networks.

5 How has new media changed consumer behaviour? What opportunities and challenges do marketers face with regard to this?

6 How can marketers exploit the characteristics of the Internet to improve the product element of their marketing mixes?

7 How do the characteristics of e-marketing affect the promotion element of the marketing mix?

8 How has digital media affected the pricing of products? Give examples of the opportunities and challenges presented to marketers in light of these changes.

9 Name and describe the major ethical and legal issues that have developed in response to the Internet. How should policymakers address these issues?

Marketing applications

1 Amazon.com is one of the Internet's most recognisable marketers. Visit their website at http://www.amazon.com and describe how the company adds value to its customers' buying experiences.

2 Social networking has become a popular method of communication not only for individuals but also for businesses. Visit social networking websites, such as Facebook and Twitter, and identify how companies are using these websites in their marketing strategies.

3 Marketers have a keen interest in social media because of the notion of influence. The assumption is that you have certain friends on Facebook, or specific authors whom you follow on Twitter, who affect the kinds of products that you buy. A recent start-up called Klout attempts to quantify this online influence by assigning people a Klout score, which ranges from 0 to 100 and which, according to the company, reflects a person's influence across the social network. Marketers can then try to use people with high Klout scores as influencers of consumption behaviours. Critics of Klout suggest that the algorithm that it uses to calculate the Klout score is too reliant on Facebook and Twitter, does not account for the quality of the online interactions and neglects other important social media. But its rise (and the growth of other similar services like Kred and PeerIndex) suggests that it has some influence over social media marketing.

   Identify and map your habits on social networking websites over the past week. Did you create content through blogs? Did you rate or recommend products or companies? Did you post photos of yourself at particular events or places on Facebook? Rate each of your online social activities according to how much influence you think they may have had on your friends or followers. Use 0 if you believe a particular activity had zero influence, 1 for slight influence, 2 for moderate influence and 3 for significant influence. After you finish ranking the impact of your online activities, decide whether you are an influencer of consumer behaviours. Do you think your friends would agree with you?

ONLINE EXERCISE

When was the last time you Googled your own name? Did you get any surprise hits or were you amazed about the number of web pages that mention your name? Imagine you are currently job hunting, or already working as the PR manager for a sports team.

Wouldn't it be great to receive alerts whenever your name or your customer gets a mention online? By setting up an alert you can have time to prepare your response to an online posting before you are asked to prepare a press release addressing the latest online rumours. The very basic online monitoring app is a Google Alert.

Create a Google Alert for your name:

✳ Sign in to your Google account (if you do not have a Google account, you can create one easily by following the prompts at https://accounts.google.com; please remember to read the Google User Agreement before you accept it)

✳ Go to http://www.google.com.au/alerts or http://www.google.com/alerts

✳ In the 'Search query' box enter your search terms in the same way as you would for a Google search

✳ You can refine your alerts by result type (e.g. news versus blogs); choose the frequency of alerts (from 'As it happens' to 'Once a week'); select the volume of alerts you wish to receive (i.e. would you like Google to filter alerts to include 'only the best results'?)

✳ Create alert. You can 'Manage your alerts' from this same page

✳ Your Alert will be activated once you have replied to the email requesting confirmation. Please note:

  ▪ Google Alert 'behaves' like a normal web search, so if you are not receiving any alerts your search/alert terms are set too narrow or if you are overwhelmed by alerts you could tighten your alert criteria

  ▪ You might need to add Google Alerts to your email Contacts to stop these alerts being sent to Junk/Spam box

  ▪ Google Alerts is a free service but http://www.googlealerts.com is a separate fee-charging service.

Next time you are given an assignment focusing on a specific industry or company, consider setting up a Google Alert for it at the beginning of the semester. Simply file your alerts away until you are ready to start compiling your assignment.

Alternatives to Google Alert

✳ http://socialmention.com/alerts helps you keep track of what is said about you/your company/brand, etc. in social media such as Twitter, Facebook, YouTube and so on.

✳ https://en.mention.net is more powerful monitoring app than Google Alert offering both free and paid accounts.

✳ http://www.meltwater.com/products/meltwater-news/online-media-monitoring is ideal for PR companies wanting fast alerts if their customers are mentioned online. Alerts vary from industry-level monitoring of online material to tracking of specific brand names.

✳ https://ifttt.com (IFTTT stand for 'If This, Then That'). For companies that have very specific trends they wish to be alerted about.[125]

Developing your marketing plan

When developing a digital media marketing strategy, marketers must be aware of the strengths and weaknesses of these media which are relatively new in the marketing field and have pros and cons that differ from those in traditional media.

1 Review the key concepts of addressability, interactivity, accessibility, connectivity and control in Table 15.1, and explain how they relate to social media. Think about how a marketing strategy focused on social media would differ from a marketing campaign reliant on traditional media sources.

2 Irrespective of marketing media used, determining the correct marketing mix for your company is always important. Think about how social media might affect your company's marketing mix.

3 Discuss different digital media and the pros and cons of using each as part of your marketing plan.

The information obtained from these questions should assist you in developing aspects of your marketing plan found in the *Interactive Marketing Plan* exercise at http://www .cengagebrain.com.

CengageNOW

Go to http:\\login.cengagebrain.com to link to CengageNOW, your online study tool. First take the Pre-Test for this chapter to get your Personalised Study Plan, and then:

* **Revise** your understanding of business markets throughout the semester by completing the interactive quiz.

* **Watch** an online video examining the different types of business purchases and complete the activity.

* **Listen** to a comprehensive summary of business markets, transactions and products to further clarify your knowledge.

After you have completed the activities in your Personalised Study Plan take the Post-Test to determine what concepts you have mastered and what you still need to work on.

Case study

HOW A PLUSH TOY MANUFACTURER PLANS ITS MARKETING THROUGH CROWDSOURCING

With an increasingly connected and digitally involved population, marketers are discovering innovative ways of engaging consumers through each stage of the marketing planning process. One new trend, known as crowdsourcing, has become particularly popular among technology companies and new start-ups. At the heart of crowdsourcing is the idea that rather than keep product design and strategy within the organisation's marketing planning team, outside stakeholders are invited to have a say in how things should be done. In other words, it is a form of distributed problem solving, where customers and users outside the organisation contribute ideas, services and content.

Although technology companies have engaged in crowdsourcing for quite some time, the rapid spread of social media is leading other industries to try this customer-oriented way of planning their marketing activities. One example is the plush toy manufacturer Squishable. Founded in 2007, the New York based company specialises in plush toys resembling everything from cartoon-like animals such as pandas, hedgehogs and owls through to fantasy creatures like unicorns, 'ice dragons' and the suspicious looking drooling 'worrible', one of its best-selling models. The toys are distinguished by a round, almost balloon-like shape, and range in sizes from bean bags to nimble little minis that could fit into a handbag.

What sets Squishable apart from the competition is the way it goes about planning new toy designs. The typical design process at most companies is concentrated on the work of an in-house design team, whereas Squishable turns to its customers to seek advice on what the next species in the Squishable family should be. Through its project Open Squish on the Squishable website, customers are invited to submit their own designs in a simple three-step process. A template for how the drawing should be presented, along with concise instructions on file and copyright requirements are listed on the website. Once a design has been submitted, it is evaluated by the Squish design team, which ensures that the design does not infringe on another character's copyright, is appropriate for children and that the design is 'plush-manufacturer-friendly', meaning its details are not excessively intricate. Once successful, a candidate design is entered into a public voting round, where friends of the designer, fans and other customers are able to vote on their favourite design. Designs must meet a certain average score threshold before they are manufactured. A winning designer can be paid up to $500, with the designer's name printed on the hangtag.

Squishable's approach to customer engagement is more than simply another form of mass-customisation. By involving customers and fans in the production process, Squishable generates significant buzz on different social media platforms. A candidate designer encourages friends and followers on websites like Facebook and Twitter to vote for her/his design on the Open Squish page, thereby driving and spreading awareness of other Squishable products. On its Facebook page, Squishable takes customer and fan interaction seriously, by responding to every single question and comment posted on its wall. Engaging customers in this kind of genuine two-way conversation shifts the traditional customer relationship, turning customers into 'partners' and 'advocates' for sustainable competitive advantage.

By outsourcing key aspects of the design process to a dedicated crowd of fans and customers, Squishable is able to create products that customers want, while at the same time building loyalty and establishing a customer-oriented culture. This type of marketing planning is in part enabled by social media culture, where customers expect to be able to interact more genuinely with brands, and have a say in the production process.[126]

Sandra Osorio, La Trobe University

QUESTIONS FOR DISCUSSION

1 How does the way consumers behave on social media make the promotion of Squishable products so appealing to marketers?

2 How does Squishable's approach to strategic marketing planning differ from conventional marketing planning?

3 How does the Squishable approach to product design and marketing address elements of the expanded marketing mix?

Chapter endnotes

1. Sarah E. Needleman, 'Facebook "Likes" Small Business,' *The Wall Street Journal*, September 26, 2011, B11; Jefferson Graham, 'Facebook wants to be big among small businesses,' *USA Today*, September 16, 2011, 3B; Edward Lovett and Melinda Arons, 'Facebook Is Friend to Jobless and Small Business, Says Company COO,' *ABC News*, September 15, 2011, accessed November 8, 2011, http://abcnews.go.com/Business/facebook-friend-jobless-small-business-creates- jobs-coo/story?id=14521237.

2. Trefis Team, 'Baidu Girds For Google Battle In China,' *Forbes*, December 7, 2011, accessed February 10, 2012, www.forbes.com/sites/greatspeculations/2011/12/07/baidu-girds-for-google- battle-in-china/.

3   Piet Levy, 'The State of Digital Marketing,' *Marketing News*, March 15, 2010: 20–21.

4. 'The Zettabyte Era – Trends and Analysis,' Cisco, May 29, 2013, accessed October 31, 2013, http://www.cisco.com/en/US/solutions/collateral/ns341/ns525/ns537/ns705/ns827/VNI_Hyperconnectivity_WP.html.

5. Maya Shwayder, 'One Third of World's Population Using Internet, Developing Nations Showing Biggest Gains.'

International Business Times, September 24, 2012, accessed July 12, 2013, http://www.ibtimes.com/one-third-worlds-population-using-internet-developing-nations-showing-biggest-gains-795299.

6. Mike Snider, 'Study Details Digital Lives by Age, Sex and Race,' *USA Today*, February 24, 2012, 4A.

7. 'Crunching the Numbers,' *Inc.*, April 2011, 24.

8. 'The Zettabyte Era – Trends and Analysis,' Cisco, May 29, 2013, accessed October 31, 2013, http://www.cisco.com/en/US/solutions/collateral/ns341/ns525/ns537/ns705/ns827/VNI_Hyperconnectivity_WP.html.

9. Don Fletcher, 'Gift Giving on Facebook Gets Real,' *TIME*, February 15, 2010, accessed April 12, 2011, www.time.com/time/magazine/article/0,9171,1960260,00.html.

10. '17 Key Differences Between Social Media and Traditional Marketing,' Microgeist, April 20, 2009, accessed February 18, 2010, http://microgeist.com.

11. '2009 Digital Handbook,' *Marketing News*, April 30, 2009, 13.

12. 'Yellow Social Media Report 2013: 'What Australian people and businesses are doing with social media,' Sensis, May 2013, accessed, October 31, 2013, http://about.sensis.

com.au/IgnitionSuite/uploads/docs/Yellow%20Pages%20
Social%20Media%20Report_F.PDF.

13. Susan Adams, 'Don't Fire An Employee And Leave Them
In Charge Of The Corporate Twitter Account,' *Forbes*,
January 2, 2013, accessed June 27, 2013, http://www
.forbes.com/sites/susanadams/2013/02/01/dont-fire-an
-employee-and-leave-them-in-charge-of-the-corporate
-twitter-account/; Veronica Pullen, 'Sacked HMV Employee
- A Lesson In Social Media Security!' The Experts' Social
Media Expert, January 2, 2013, accessed June 27, 2013,
http://veronicapullen.co.uk/2013/02/sacked-hmv
-employee-a-lesson-in-social-media-security/.

14. 'Lonely Planet: Reach and Audience,' *BBC Worldwide*,
accessed July 12, 2013, http://advertising.bbcworldwide.
com/home/mediakit/reachaudience
/brandedentertainment/lonelyplanet; 'About
lonelyplanet.com,' Lonely Planet, accessed July 12, 2013,
http://www.lonelyplanet.com/about/lonely-planet-
digital/#ixzz2Yo1gbhLb.

15. Zachary Karabell, 'To Tweet or Not to Tweet,' *TIME*, April
12, 2011: 24.

16. 'Facebook: Largest, Fastest Growing Social Network,' Tech
Tree, August 13, 2008, accessed April 12, 2011, http://
archive.techtree.com/techtree/jsp/article.jsp?article
_id=92134&cat_id=643.

17 Courtney Rubin, 'Internet Users Over Age 50 Flocking to
Social Media,' *Inc.*, August 30, 2010, accessed February 13,
2012, www.inc.com/news/articles/2010/08/users-over-50
-are-fastest-growing-social-media-demographic.html.

18. Ann-Christine Diaz, 'Oreo's 100-Day 'Daily Twist'
Campaign Puts Cookie in Conversation,' *Ad Age*,
September 10, 2012, accessed October 31, 2013, http://
adage.com/article/digital/oreo-s-daily-twist-campaign-
puts-cookie-conversation/237104/; Laura Stampler,
'Facebook Says These Are The 20 Best Brands On The
Social Network,' *Business Insider*, April 30, 2013, accessed
October 31, 2013, http://www.businessinsider.com.au/
facebook-says-these-are-the-20-best-brands-on-the-
social-network-2013-4#2-blue-award-360i-was-also-
awarded-for-working-on-the-daily-twist-campaign-3.

19 Brittany Darwell, 'Facebook launches 'global pages' for
brands to offer localized experiences,' *Inside Facebook*,
October 17, 2012, accessed July 12, 2013, http://www
.insidefacebook.com/2012/10/17/facebook-launches-
global-pages-for-brands-to-offer-localized-experiences/.

20. Jon Swartz, 'Timberlake Could Revive Popularity of
Myspace,' *USA Today*, July 5, 2011, 5B.

21. 'Myspace Homepage', www.myspace.com/, accessed April
11, 2011.

22. 'Justin Timberlake Debuts Myspace TV,' *Rolling Stone*,
January 10, 2012, accessed February 10, 2012, www
.rollingstone.com/music/news/justin-timberlake-debuts
-myspace-tv-20120110.

23. David Moth, 'Five good and four bad examples of brands
using Twitter,' *eConsultancy*, May 1, 2013, accessed October
31, 2013, http://econsultancy.com/au/blog/62639-five-
good-and-four-bad-examples-of-brands-using-twitter.

24. 'As Twitter Grows and Evolves, More Manpower Is
Needed,' *Marketing News*, March 15, 2011, 13.

25. 'Social Media Summit,' Harrisburg University, 2012,
accessed February 16, 2012, www.harrisburgu.edu/
academics/professional/socialmedia/index-2012.php.

26. 'Couldn't Stop the Spread of the Conversation in
Reactions from Other Bloggers,' from Hyejin Kim's May 4,
2007, blog post, 'Korea: Bloggers and Donuts' on the blog
Global Voices, http://globalvoicesonline.org/2007/05/04
/korea-bloggers-and-donuts/ (accessed April 12, 2011).

27. 'How Not to Handle Bad Reviews,' *The Guardian*,
accessed February 16, 2012, www.guardian.co.uk/ books
/booksblog/2011/mar/30/jacqueline-howett-bad-review.

28. Drake Bennett, 'Ten Years of Inaccuracy and Remarkable
Detail: Wikipedia,' *Bloomberg Businessweek*, January 10,
2011: 57–61.

29. Charlene Li and Josh Bernoff, *Groundswell* (Boston:
Harvard Business Press, 2008): 24.

30. Ibid.: 25–26.

31. Nora Ganim Barnes and Justina Andonian, 'The 2011
Fortune 500 and Social Media Adoption: Have America's
Largest Companies Reached a Social Media Plateau?'
University of Massachusetts, 2011, accessed February 16,
2012, www.umassd.edu/cmr/studiesandresearch/2011fort
une500/.

32. Bianca Male, 'How to Promote Your Business on Flickr,'
The Business Insider, accessed April 12, 2011, http://www
.businessinsider.com.au/how-to-promote-your-business
-on-flickr-2009-12.

33. 'How to Market on Flickr,' *Small Business Search Marketing*,
accessed August 5, 2013, http://www
.smallbusinesssem.com/how-to-market-on-flickr/6031/.

34. Austrade, http://www.austrade.gov.au/ (accessed
November 20, 2013).

35. Emily Glazer, 'Who Is Ray WJ? YouTube's Top Star,' *The Wall
Street Journal*, February 2, 2012, B1.

36. Tom Foster, 'The GoPro Army,' *Inc.*, February 2012,
52–59.

37. '2009 Digital Handbook,' *Marketing News*, April 30, 2009, 14.

38. 'About Mad Money,' *CNBC*, accessed February 28, 2012,
www.cnbc.com/id/17283246/.

39. 'Dominos Pizza,' Second Places, accessed February
16, 2012, www.secondplaces.net/opencms/ opencms/
portfolio/caseStudies/caseStudy_dominospizza.html.

40. Brandy Shaul, 'CityVille Celebrates the Golden Arches
with Branded McDonald's Restaurant,' Games.com,
October 19, 2011, http://blog.games.com/2011/10/19/
cityville-mcdonalds-restaurant.

41. Emily Glazer, 'Virtual Fairs Offer Real Jobs,' *The Wall Street
Journal*, October 31, 2011, B9.

42. 'Mobilising sales - Making money in the mobile commerce
revolution, a whitepaper from PayPal,'
Paypal, July 3, 2013, accessed November 1, 2013,
https://www.drivingbusinessonline.com.au/media/30746
/mobilewhitepaper.pdf.

43. Ibid.

44. John McDermott, 'Mobile Advertising Grows So Fast
That Analysts Revise Forecasts Marketers to Spend $100
Million More on Mobile Than Previously Projected,' Ad
Age, April 3, 2013, accessed June 16, 2013, http://adage.
com/article/digital/mobile-advertising-grows-fast-analysts-
revise-forecasts/240673/?utm_source=Digital&utm_
medium=feed&utm_campaign=Feed:+AdvertisingAge/
Digital&utm_medium=referral&utm_source=pulsenews;
Madeleine Ross, 'Marketing Trends in 2012,' *B&T*, January
25, 2012, accessed June 17, 2013, http://www.bandt.com.
au/features/marketing-trends-in-2012.

45. Madeleine Ross, 'Mobile ad spend fuels growth in online expenditure,' *B&T*, 20 May, 2013, accessed November 1, 2013, http://www.bandt.com.au/news/digital/mobile-ad-spend-fuels-growth-in-online-expenditure.

46. 'Australia yet to tap mobile advertising potential,' *Ad News*, October 1, 2013, accessed November 1, 2013, http://www.adnews.com.au/adnews/australia-yet-to-tap-mobile-advertising-potential; Ben Hurley, 'Ad group InMobi targets Australian rise of mobile commerce,' *Business Review Weekly*, July 2, 2013, accessed November 1, 2013, http://www.brw.com.au/p/business/ad_group_inmobi_targets_australian_5ljo8ysTQL9Es8yNJfMwvK.

47. Christopher Heine, 'Talking Mobile Ads Are No Joke - Leo Burnett, OMD and Digitas will pitch the promos to brands,' *AdWeek*, April 1, 2013, accessed June 17, 2013, http://www.adweek.com/news/technology/talking-mobile-ads-are-no-joke-148303.

48 Abigail Phillips, 'Geofencing rises as the latest advertising phenomenon,' *Business Review Europe*, April 20, 2012, accessed June 17, 2013, http://www.businessrevieweurope.eu/marketing/mobile-marketing/geofencing-rises-as-the-latest-advertising-phenomenon.

49. 'Making Money with mobile commerce, 2013 PayPal White Paper: Mobilising sales/Making money in the mobile commerce revolution,' Pay Pal, https://www.drivingbusinessonline.com.au/articles/making-money-with-mobile-commere/.

50. 'Infographic: M-commerce and mobile shopping in Australia,' *Marketing*, May 17, 2013, http://www.marketingmag.com.au/news/infographic-m-commerce-and-mobile-shopping-in-australia-40000/#.UnNXFPlmjTp.

51. Thomas Claburn, 'Google Tells Businesses 'Fall In Love With Mobile,' *Information Week*, February 28, 2012, accessed February 28, 2012, www.informationweek.com/news/ mobility/business/232601587.

52. 'Brands Continue Limited Mobile Site Offerings,' *eMarketer*, January 30, 2012, accessed February 28, 2012, www.emarketer.com/Article.aspx?id=1008803&R=1008803.

53. Mark Milian, 'Why Text Messages Are Limited to 160 Characters,' *Los Angeles Times*, May 3, 2009, accessed February 28, 2012, http://latimesblogs.latimes.com/technology/2009/05/invented-text-messaging.html; 'Eight Reasons Why Your Business Should Use SMS Marketing,' Mobile Marketing Ratings, accessed February 28, 2012, www.mobilemarketingratings.com/eight-reasons-sms- marketing.html.

54. 'MMS helps boost Anytime Fitness 12 Hour Sale (Case Study),' *Mobipost*, March 7, 2013, accessed November 1, 2013, http://blog.mobipost.com.au/index.php/2013/03/07/mms-helps-boost-anytime-fitness-12-hour-sale-case-study-2/.

55. Danyl Bosomworth, 'Mobile Marketing Statistics 2013,' *Smart Insights*, June 10, 2013, accessed June 17, 2013m http://www.smartinsights.com/mobile-marketing/mobile-marketing-analytics/mobile-marketing-statistics/.

56. 'Hitwise: Australians' news and media consumption is 51 per cent higher on mobile devices,' *mUmBRELLA*, http://mumbrella.com.au/hitwise-australians-news-and-media-consumption-is-51-per-cent-higher-on-mobile-devices-150007, (accessed June 22, 2013).

57. Foursquare website, https://foursquare.com/ (accessed February 16, 2012).

58. Anita Campbell, 'What the Heck Is an App?' *Small Business Trends*, March 7, 2011, http://smallbiztrends.com/2011/03/what-is-an-app.html (accessed February 28, 2012).

59. 'App purchases by Australian consumers on mobile and handheld devices', *Choice*, February 2013 , http://ccaac.gov.au/files/2013/02/Choice.pdf ACCESSED 03112013; Campbell Simpson, 'The 20 Most Popular Android, iPhone and Windows Phones Apps Right Now (And Our Favourite Alternatives),' *Gizmodo*, October 16, 2013, accessed November 3, 2013, http://www.gizmodo.com.au/2013/10/the-20-most-popular-android-iphone-and-windows-phones-apps-right-now-and-our-favourite-alternatives/.

60. A. J. Dellinger, '8 Apps for Fair Trade and Ethical Shopping,' *MacLife*, April 10, 2012, http://www.maclife.com/article/gallery/8_apps_fair_trade_and_ethical_shopping (accessed June 17, 2013); Michelle Starr, 'Buycott app lets you boycott dodgy companies,' *CNet*, May 15, 2013, http://www.cnet.com.au/buycott-app-lets-you-boycott-dodgy-companies-339344284.htm (accessed June 17, 2013); 'Dog-A-Likeapplication,' The PEDIGREE Adoption Drive, http://www.pedigreeadoptiondrive.com.au/iphonefeedback.aspx (accessed June 17, 2013); 'Shop Ethical! App – Shop with a clear conscience!' Shop Ethical, http://www.ethical.org.au/get-involved/resources/shop-ethical-app/ (accessed June 17, 2013).

61. Todd Wasserman, '5 Innovative Mobile Marketing Campaigns,' Mashable, March 8, 2011, http://mashable.com/2011/03/08/mobile-marketing-campaigns/ (accessed February 13, 2012).

62. Umika Pidaparthy, 'Marketers Embracing QR Codes, for Better or Worse,' *CNN Tech*, March 28, 2011, accessed April 11, 2011, http://articles.cnn.com/2011-03-28/ tech/qr.codes.marketing_1_qr-smartphone-users-symbian?_s=PM:TECH.

63. Brad Stone and Olga Kharif, 'Pay As You Go,' *Bloomberg Businessweek*, July 18–July 24, 2011: 66–71.

64. 'Google Wallet,' www.google.com/wallet/what-is-google-wallet.html (accessed February 16, 2012).

65. 'Mobilising sales – Making money in the mobile commerce revolution, a whitepaper from PayPal,' Paypal, July 3, 2013, accessed November 1, 2013, https://www.drivingbusinessonline.com.au/media/30746/mobilewhitepaper.pdf.

66. Vangie Beal, 'All About Widgets,' *Webopedia*, August 31, 2010, accessed February 28, 2012www.webopedia.com/DidYouKnow/Internet/2007/widgets.asp.

67. 'Australian Booking Widget,' Australian Tourism Data Warehouse, 2013, http://www.bookingwidget.com.au/ (accessed November 3, 2013).

68 Vikram Alexei Kansara, 'Wearable Technology Market Set to Explode, Could Reach $50 Billion, Says Credit Suisse,' *Business of Fashion*, May 19, 2013, accessed July 12, 2013, http://www.businessoffashion.com/2013/05/wearable-technology-market-set-to-explode-could-reach-50-billion-says-credit-suisse.html.

69. Zach Honig, 'Pebble smartwatch review,' *Engadget*, January 25, 2013, http://www.engadget.com/2013/01/25/pebble-smartwatch-review/, (accessed July 12, 2013); Vikram Alexei Kansara, 'Wearable Technology Market Set

to Explode, Could Reach $50 Billion, Says Credit Suisse';
Daniel Ionescu, 'Samsung confirms new smartwatch is
in the works,' *Marketing Mag*, March 21, 2013, accessed
June 22, 2013, http://www.marketingmag.com.au/
news/samsung-confirms-new-smartwatch-is-in-the-
works-37891/#.UgDjfY3I2Sq.

70. 'About UP by Jawbone,' *Pedometer*, April 30, 2013,
accessed June 22, 2013, http://www.pedometersaustralia
-blog.com/about-up-by-jawbone/; 'GYMBOSS Interval
timers have a new look,' *Pedometer*, May 8, 2013, accessed
June 22, 2013, http://www.pedometersaustralia
-blog.com/gymboss-interval-timers-have-a-new-look/.

71. Bridgette Meinhold, 'Handyscope is a Smartphone Body
Scanner That Checks for Skin Cancer,' *Ecouterre*, January 7,
2013, accessed July 12, 2013, http://www.ecouterre
.com/handyscope-is-a-smartphone-body-scanner-that-
checks-for-skin-cancer/.

72. Bridgette Meinhold, 'EPA, NIH Award $100K to
Conscious Clothing's Wearable Pollution Monitor,'
Ecouterre, July 6, 2013, accessed July 12, 2013, http://www
.ecouterre.com/epa-nih-award-100000-to-conscious
-clothings-wearable-air-pollution-monitor/.

73. Bridgette Meinhold, 'Color-Changing Glove Alerts Wearer
to Presence of Invisible Toxins,' *Ecouterre*, May 20, 2013,
accessed July 12, 2013, http://www.ecouterre.com
/color-changing-glove-alerts-wearer-to-presence-of
-invisible-toxins/.

74. Jasmin Malik Chua, 'UV-Monitoring Bracelet Warns You
When You've Had Enough Sun,' *Ecouterre*, August 14,
2012, accessed July 12, 2013, http://www.ecouterre.com
/uv-monitoring-bracelet-warns-you-when-youve-had
-enough-sun/.

75. Bridgette Meinhold, 'Cancer-Detecting Smart Bra Could
Soon Surpass Mammograms in Accuracy,' *Ecouterre*,
October 15, 2012, accessed July 12, 2013, http://www
.ecouterre.com/this-cancer-detecting-smart-bra-could
-one-day-surpass-mammograms-in-accuracy/.

76. Bridgette Meinhold, "Like-A-Hug 'Vest Gives You a
Squeeze for Every Facebook 'Like' You Get,' *Ecouterre*,
October 8, 2012, accessed July 12, 2013, http://www
.ecouterre.com/like-a-hug-vest-gives-you-a-squeeze
-for-every-facebook-like-you-get/; Bridgette Meinhold,
'Replay's 'Social Denim' Lets You Update Your Facebook
Status on the Fly,' *Ecouterre*, November 7, 2012, accessed
July 12, 2013, http://www.ecouterre.com/replays-social
-denim-lets-you-update-your-facebook-status-on-the-fly/.

77. Bridgette Meinhold, 'Meet TshirtOS, a Programmable Tee
That Displays Anything You Want,' Ecouterre, August 13,
2012, accessed July 12, 2013, http://www.ecouterre.com
/meet-tshirtos-a-programmable-t-shirt-that-displays-your
-tweets/.

78. '17 Key Differences Between Social Media and Traditional
Marketing.'

79. '8153.0 - Internet Activity, Australia, June 2013,' ABS,
October 8, 2013, accessed November 3, 2013, http://
www.abs.gov.au/ausstats/abs@.nsf/Products/D6B00147BF
1749E1CA257BFA00127708?opendocument.

80. David Moth, 'Eight brands that crowdsourced marketing
and product ideas,' *econsultancy*, April 11, 2013, accessed
June 27, 2013, http://econsultancy.com/au/blog/62504-
eight-brands-that-crowdsourced-marketing-and-product-
ideas; 'P&G Drives New Product Innovation to the
Next Level with Increased Crowdsourcing Program,'
Daily Crowdsourcing, accessed June 27, 2013, http://
dailycrowdsource.com/20-resources/projects/203-pg-
drives-new-product-innovation-to-the-next-level-with-
increased-crowdsourcing-program.

81. Joanne Steele, 'Geocaching, a Perfect Rural Tourism
Attraction,' *Rural Tourism Marketing*, April 15, 2010,
accessed June 28, 2013, http://ruraltourismmarketing.
com/2010/04/geocaching-a-perfect-rural-tourism-
attraction/; Keir Clarke, 'The World's Geocaching on
Google Maps,' Google Maps Mania, April 12, 2011,
accessed June 28, 2013, http://www.mapsmaniac.
com/2011/04/worlds-geocaching-on-google-maps.html;
'Geocaching Australia,' Geochaching, http://geocaching.
com.au/; 'Geocaching 101,' Geochaching, http://www
.geocaching.com/ (accessed June 28, 2013); 'Are you good
at finding things that are hidden?' Scouts Australia, http://
www.vicscouts.com.au/geocaching.html (accessed June
28, 2013).

82. 'Network Ten partners GoConnect to offer free WiFi
TV,' *Marketing Mag*, June 11, 2013, accessed June 27, 2013,
http://www.marketingmag.com.au/news/network
-ten-partners-goconnect-to-offer-free-wifi-tv-41358/#.
UgDyvl3I2Sp.

83. 'Näin toimii Postin pakettiautomaatti,' *Posti*, http://www
.posti.fi/smartpost/ (accessed June 28, 2013).

84. 'Näin käytät Kauppakassi-pakettiautomaattia,' *Foodie, FM*,
January 22, 2013, accessed June 28, 2013, https://fi.foodie.
fm/#!/blog/post/smartpost.

85. 'Hitting the e-books,' *Inc.*, September 2011: 36; Leon Kaye,
'Will iPads Kindle a Massive Carbon Footprint,' April 13,
2011, accessed December 8, 2011, *The Guardian*, www.
guardian.co.uk/sustainable-business/carbon
-footprint-ipad-kindle; Nancy Davis Kho, 'E-readers or
Print Books—which Is Greener?' *San Francisco Chronicle*,
December 4, 2011, accessed December 8, 2011, www
.sfgate.com/ cgi-bin/article.cgi?f=/c/a/2011/12/01/
HOCR1MUJ6B.DTL; Nick Bilton, 'Replacing a Pile of
Textbooks With an iPad,' *The New York Times*, August
23, 2010, accessed December 8, 2011, http://bits.blogs.
nytimes.com/2010/08/23/replacing-a-pile-of-textbook
-with-an-ipad/.

86. Aaron Back, 'China's Big Brands Tackle Web Sales,' *The
Wall Street Journal*, December 1, 2009, B2; 'The Taobao
Affair from China Largest Auction Website,' PR Log,
February 7, 2010, accessed February 16, 2012, www.
prlog.org/10552554- the-taobao-affair-from-china-largest-
auction-website.html.

87. Ryan Northover, 'Social Media Advertising to Hit $11
Billion,' *Washington Business Journal*, April 17, 2013 http://
socialmediatoday.com/ryannorthover/1389076/social-
media-advertising-spent-hit-11-billion; 'Social media ad
revenue expected to grow by $6.3B over next five years,'
Washington Business Journal, April 11, 2013, http://www
.bizjournals.com/washington/blog/techflash/2013/04/social
-media-ad-revenue-expected-to.html.

88. Soraya Chemaly, 'Facebook rejects rape culture. Can you?'
CNN, May 31, 2013, accessed June 18, 2013, http://edition.
cnn.com/2013/05/30/opinion/chemaly-facebook.

89. Ibid.

90. Kristin Shorten, '#FBrape: Facebook relents to anti-women Facebook groups,' news.com.au, May 29, 2013, accessed June 18, 2013, http://www.news.com.au/technology/fbrape-campaign-against-anti-women-facebook-groups/story-e6frfro0-1226651223664#ixzz2WXeCx5qL.

91. Jon Beros ,'Are daily deals dead?' The Sydney Morning Herald, May 28, 2013, accessed June 27, 2013, http://www.smh.com.au/small-business/managing/are-daily-deals-dead-20130528-2n8za.html#ixzz2XNrXiXjm.

92. Helen Leggatt, '57% of showroomers head to Amazon,' Biz Report, June 5, 2013, accessed June 22, 2013, http://www.bizreport.com/2013/06/57-of-showroomers-head-to-amazon.html.

93. Ibid.

94. Kris Kash, 'Checkout these 5 Best Facebook Ecommerce Store of 2012,' DJ Designer Lab, October 4, 2012, accessed June 22, 2013, http://djdesignerlab.com/2012/10/04/checkout-these-5-best-facebook-ecommerce-store-of-2012/.

95. Jeanne Meister, 'To Do: Update Company's Social Media Policy ASAP,' Forbes, July 2, 2013, http://www.forbes.com/sites/jeannemeister/2013/02/07/to-do-update-companys-social-media-policy-asap/ (accessed July 8, 2013); Amy Gesenhues, 'Study: 76% Of Executives Believe CEOs Should Be Utilizing Social Media Channels,' Marketing Land, May 30, 2013, http://marketingland.com/study-ceos-active-on-social-media-channels-rate-higher-as-leaders-compared-to-ceos-not-using-social-media-46040 (accessed July 8, 2013).

96. 'YouTube enables viewers to shop products on videos,' Marketing Mag, May 17, 2013, accessed June 22, 2013, http://www.marketingmag.com.au/news/youtube-enables-viewers-to-shop-products-on-videos-40456/#.UgEWhI3I2Sq.

97. Joe Barber, 'Brand in hand: the strengths and weaknesses of responsive web design,' Marketing Mag, May 21, 2013, accessed June 22, 2013, http://www.marketingmag.com.au/blogs/brand-in-hand-the-strengths-and-weaknesses-of-responsive-web-design-40558/#.UgEXd43I2Sq.

98. 'Mobilising sales – Making money in the mobile commerce revolution a whitepaper from PayPal,' Paypal, July 3, 2013, accessed November 1, 2013, https://www.drivingbusinessonline.com.au/media/30746/mobilewhitepaper.pdf.

99. Shaun Dobbin, 'Mobile sites vs native apps: which one suits your brand?' Marketing Mag, March 12, 2013, accessed June 22, 2013, http://www.marketingmag.com.au/blogs/mobile-sites-vs-native-apps-which-one-suits-your-brand 37511/#.UgEYVI3I2Sq.

100. '10 Crucial Consumer Trends For 2013: How will YOU deliver on consumer expectations in the next 12 months?' Trendwatch, http://www.trendwatching.com/trends/10trends2013/ (accessed March 28, 2013).

101. Meena Hart Duerson, 'We're addicted to our phones: 84% worldwide say they couldn't go a single day without their mobile device in their hand,' NY Daily News, http://www.nydailynews.com/life-style/addicted-phones-84-worldwide-couldn-single-day-mobile-device-hand-article-1.1137811#ixzz2IALHgH1c (accessed November 20, 2013); Nancy Gibbs, 'Your Life is Fully Mobile,' TIME Tech, http://techland.time.com/2012/08/16/your-life-is-fully-mobile/#ixzz2Y9P5CbI7 (accessed November 20, 2013).

102. '10 Crucial Consumer Trends For 2013: How will YOU deliver on consumer expectations in the next 12 months?' Trendwatch, http://www.trendwatching.com/trends/10trends2013/ (accessed March 28, 2013); Hunter Phillips, 'MobileDay Favorites: 10 Mobile Apps Designed to Save you Time, Money, and Stress,' Mobile Day, April 22, 2013, http://mobileday.com/productivity/9-other-mobile-apps-to-save-you-time/ (accessed July 5, 2013); Ekaterina Walter, '10 Creative Ways to Use QR Codes for Marketing,' Mashable, January 14, 2012, http://mashable.com/2012/01/13/qr-code-marketing/ (accessed July 5, 2013).

103. Hunter Phillips, 'MobileDay Favorites: 10 Mobile Apps Designed to Save you Time, Money, and Stress,' Mobile Day, April 22, 2013, http://mobileday.com/productivity/9-other-mobile-apps-to-save-you-time/ (accessed July 5, 2013).

104. Ibid.

105. Helen Leggatt, 'Mercedes introduces QR Code rescue sheets for emergency responders,' BizReport, May 28, 2013, http://www.bizreport.com/2013/05/mercedes-introduces-qr-code-rescue-sheets-for-emergency-resp.html (accessed June 22, 2013).

106. Kristina Knight, 'Skava: Mobile shoppers having negative experiences, not returning,' BizReport, June 20, 2013, http://www.bizreport.com/2013/06/skava-mobile-shoppers-having-negative-experiences-not-return.html.

107. Robin Sandhu, '5 Applications of Augmented Reality Technology, How Augmented Reality is Changing the Market Today,' About.com New Tech, http://newtech.about.com/od/augmentedreality/tp/5-Applications-Of-Augmented-Reality-Technology.htm (accessed July 8, 2013); Tim Perdue, 'Applications of Augmented Reality, Augmented Reality is Evolving as Computing Power Increases,' About.com New Tech, http://newtech.about.com/od/softwaredevelopment/a/Applications-Of-Augmented-Reality_2.htm (accessed July 8, 2013); Ekaterina Walter, '10 Creative Ways to Use QR Codes for Marketing,' Mashable, January 14, 2012, http://mashable.com/2012/01/13/qr-code-marketing/ (accessed July 5, 2013).

108. 'What is Layar Reality Browser?' Layar, April 23, 2010, https://layar.zendesk.com/entries/161304-What-is-Layar-Reality-Browser (accessed July 8, 2013); Jennifer L Schenker, 'Layar: Augmenting Reality via Smartphone,' Bloomberg Businessweek, September 2, 2010, http://www.businessweek.com/stories/2010-09-02/layar-augmenting-reality-via-smartphonebusinessweek-business-news-stock-market-and-financial-advice (accessed July 8, 2013).

109. Duncan Graham-Rowe, 'Clubbers choose chip implants to jump queues,' New Scientist, May 21, 2004, http://www.newscientist.com/article/dn5022-clubbers-choose-chip-implants-to-jump-queues.html#.UgUPe5LI2So (accessed March 25, 2013).

110. 'Yahoo!7 and Samsung partnership means catch-up TV for mobiles and tablets,' mUmBRELLA, http://mumbrella.com.au/yahoo7-and-samsung-partnership-means-catch-up-tv-for-mobiles-and-tablets-143191 (accessed June 22, 2013).

111. 'Unilever partners co-creation firm to boost crowdsourcing capabilities,' Marketing Mag, June 13, 2013,

http://www.marketingmag.com.au/news/unilever-partners-co-creation-firm-to-boost-crowdsourcing-41453/#. UgEsiY3I2Sp (accessed June 22, 2013).

112. 'Ikea and Yahoo!7 team up to match customer data with audience data,' *Marketing Mag*, May 2, 2013, http://www.marketingmag.com.au/news/ikea-and-yahoo7-team-up-to-match-customer-data-with-audience-data-39665/#. UgEsiI3I2Sp (accessed June 22, 2013).

113. Stone and Kharif, 69.

114. Larry Barrett, 'Data Breach Costs Surge in 2009: Study,' *eSecurity Planet*, January 26, 2010, www.esecurityplanet.com/features/article.php/3860811/article.htm (accessed April 12, 2011).

115. Kashmir Hill, 'Facebook Lays Out All Of Its New Targeting Techniques In One Easy-To-Read Blog Post,' *Forbes*, January 10, 2012, http://www.forbes.com/sites/kashmirhill/2012/10/01/facebook-lays-out-all-of-its-new-targeting-techniques-in-one-easy-to-read-blog-post/ (accessed June 19, 2013); Thorin Klosowski, 'How Facebook Uses Your Data to Target Ads, Even Offline,' *Lifehacker*, April 11, 2013, http://lifehacker.com/5994380/how-facebook-uses-your-data-to-target-ads-even-offline (accessed June 19, 2013); 'Facebook ads guide,' Social ads tool, http://www.socialadstool.com/facebook-ads-guide/how-facebook-ads-work/ (accessed June 19, 2013); Maura McGowan, 'Facebook Rolling Out Video Ads to News Feeds,' *Adweek*, May 7, 2013, http://www.adweek.com/news/technology/facebook-rolling-out-video-ads-news-feeds-149239 (accessed June 19, 2013); Maura McGowan, 'Facebook Gives Developers and Brands Ability to Target Consumers,' *Adweek*, May 3, 2013, http://www.adweek.com/news/technology/facebook-gives-developers-and-brands-ability-target-consumers-149128 (accessed June 19, 2013); Katy Bachman, 'Facebook Ads Will Soon Display AdChoices Icon,' *Adweek*, February 4, 2013, http://www.adweek.com/news/technology/facebook-ads-will-soon-display-adchoices-icon-147039 (accessed June 19, 2013); Christopher Heine, 'Facebook Debuts Hashtags, Urges Advertisers to Use Them,' *Adweek*, June 12, 2013, http://www.adweek.com/news/technology/facebook-debuts-hashtags-urges-advertisers-use-them-150254 (accessed June 19, 2013); Tim Peterson, 'Facebook Adopts Direct Marketing Tactics for Display Ads,' *Adweek*, August 31, 2012, http://www.adweek.com/news/technology/facebook-adopts-direct-marketing-tactics-display-ads-143295 (accessed June 19, 2013); Tim Peterson, 'What Twitter's Ad API Really Means for Social Advertising,' *Adweek*, February 20, 2013, http://www.adweek.com/news/technology/what-twitters-ad-api-really-means-social-advertising-147421 (accessed June 19, 2013).

116. Brian Karlovsky, 'Privacy laws: Act now or else,' *ARN*, http://www.arnnet.com.au/article/530962/privacy_laws_act_now_else/ (accessed November 8, 2013); Kaman Tsoi, 'A primer to Australia's new privacy laws,' *Business Spectator*, December 3, 2012, http://www.businessspectator.com.au/article/2012/12/3/technology/primer-australias-new-privacy-laws (accessed November 8, 2013).

117. 'Key Elements of the Spam Act,' *ACMA*, July 19, 2013, http://www.acma.gov.au/Industry/Marketers/Anti-Spam/Ensuring-you-dont-spam/key-elements-of-the-spam-act-ensuring-you-dont-spam-i-acma (accessed November 8, 2013).

118. Harrison Polites, 'ACMA fines GraysOnline for breaching Spam Act,' *Business Spectator*, October 9, 2013, http://www.businessspectator.com.au/news/2013/10/9/technology/acma-fines-graysonline-breaching-spam-act (accessed November 8, 2013); Yolanda Redrup, 'Cellarmaster Wines slammed with $110,000 fine for spam,' *Smart Company*, May 29, 2013, http://www.smartcompany.com.au/marketing/advertising-and-marketing/31928-cellarmaster-wines-slammed-with--110-000-fine-for-violating-spam-act.html (accessed November 8, 2013).

119. 'Friend Me On Faecbook,' *Bloomberg Businessweek*, November 7– November 13, 2011, 36–37.

120. Sarah Needleman, 'Social-Media Con Game,' *The Wall Street Journal*, October 12, 2009, http://online.wsj.com/article/SB10001424052748704471504574445502831219412.html (accessed April 12, 2011).

121. '2010 Global PC Software Theft Reaches Record 59 Billion,' *BSA*, http://portal.bsa.org/globalpiracy2010/ (accessed February 16, 2012).

122. Aubry R. Fowler III, Barry J. Babin, and May K. Este, 'Burning for Fun or Money: Illicit Consumer Behavior in a Contemporary Context,' presented at the Academy of Marketing Science Annual Conference, May 27, 2005, Tampa, FL.

123. Michael Bodey, 'Online piracy appeals most to those who are better educated,' *The Australian*, June 10, 2013, http://www.theaustralian.com.au/media/digital/online-piracy-appeals-most-to-those-who-are-better-educated/story-fna03wxu-1226660999120# (accessed November 8, 2013).

124. Kevin Shanahan and Mike Hyman, 'Motivators and Enablers of SCOUR-ing: A Study of Online Piracy in the US and UK,' *Journal of Business Research*, 63 (2010): 1095–1102.

125. Sara Angeles, 'Hate the New Google Alerts? Here Are 6 Alternatives,' *BusinessNewsDaily*, January 24, 2014, http://www.businessnewsdaily.com/5822-google-alerts-alternatives.html; 'Homepage,' Google Alerts, http://www.google.com.au/alerts, accessed February 2, 2014; 'Homepage,' Mention, https://en.mention.net/, accessed February 2, 2014; 'Homepage,' Meltwater, http://www.meltwater.com/products/meltwater-news/online-media-monitoring/, accessed February 2, 2014; 'Homepage,' IFTTT, https://ifttt.com/, accessed February 2, 2014.

126. C. Leahey, 'Why Your Teen Loves Wanelo,' *CNN Money*, accessed September 20, 2013, http://money.cnn.com/2013/05/23/technology/wanelo-deena-varshavskaya.pr.fortune/index.html; A. Popescu, 'An Online Toy Company Turns to Facebook for Design Ideas,' *Mashable*, accessed September 20, 2013, http://mashable.com/2013/06/27/squishable-crowdsource-toys/; 'About Us,' Squishable, accessed September 20, 2013, http://www.squishable.com/s/.

Glossary

A

accessory equipment Equipment that does not become part of the final physical product but is used in production or office activities

advertising Paid non-personal communication about an organisation and its products transmitted to a target audience through mass media

advertising budget Advertising budget for a specified period, also known as advertising appropriation

advertising campaign Designing a series of ads and placing them in various advertising media to reach a particular target audience

advertising platform Basic issues or selling points to be included in the advertising campaign

aesthetic labour The tendency for companies to manage the appearance and personal characteristics of their employees, through requiring them to tailor their grooming, clothing and behaviour to fit the company image

aesthetic modifications Changes to the sensory appeal of a product

agents Intermediaries that represent either buyers or sellers on a permanent basis

allowance A concession in price to achieve a desired goal

application or app A small self-contained program that can run on computers, tablets and smartphones to achieve a specific purpose, e.g. accessing the latest weather forecast

approach The manner in which a salesperson contacts a potential customer

artwork An ad's illustrations and layout

atmospherics The physical elements in a store's design that appeal to consumers' emotions and encourage buying

attitude An individual's enduring evaluation of, feelings about and behavioural tendencies towards an object or idea

Australian Association of National Advertisers (AANA) Represents the rights and responsibilities of the major advertisers (and their industry partners). These companies are responsible for 85 per cent of Australia's mainstream advertising spend (in 2008 this was $11 billion). Further information from http://www.aana.com.au

Australian Competition and Consumer Commission (ACCC) The ACCC promotes competition and fair trade in the market place to benefit consumers, businesses and the community. Its primary responsibility is to ensure that individuals and businesses comply with the Commonwealth competition, fair trading and consumer protection laws

B

bait pricing Pricing an item in the product line low with the intention of selling a higher priced item in the line

benefit segmentation The division of a market according to benefits that customers want from the product

blogs Internet-based journals which can be edited as well as accommodate interactions with other Internet users

brand A name, term, design, symbol or any other feature that identifies one marketer's product as distinct from those of other marketers

brand association The set of associations linked to a brand which connect a particular lifestyle or, in some instances, a certain personality type with a specific brand

brand awareness The extent to which a brand is recognised by potential customers, and correctly associated with a particular product or service

brand competitors Firms that market branded products with similar brand features and brand benefits to the same customers at similar prices

brand equity The marketing and financial value associated with a brand's strength in a market

brand extension Using an existing brand to brand a new product in a different product category

brand insistence The degree of brand loyalty in which a customer strongly prefers a specific brand and will accept no substitute

brand licensing An agreement whereby a company permits another organisation to use its brand on other products for a licensing fee

brand loyalty A customer's favourable attitude toward a specific brand

brand mark The part of a brand not made up of words, but symbols

brand name The part of a brand that can be spoken

brand preference The degree of brand loyalty in which a customer prefers one brand over competitive offerings

brand recognition A customer's awareness that the brand exists and is an alternative purchase

breakdown approach Measuring company sales potential based on a general economic forecast for a specific period and the market potential derived from it

brokers Intermediaries that bring buyers and sellers together temporarily

buildup approach Measuring company sales potential by estimating how much of a product a potential buyer in a specific geographic area will purchase in a given period, multiplying the estimate by the number of potential buyers, and adding the totals of all the geographic areas considered

bundle pricing Packaging together two or more complementary products and selling them for a single price

business analysis Evaluating the potential contribution of a product idea to the company's sales, costs and profits

business (organisational) buying behaviour The purchase behaviour of producers, government units, institutions and resellers

business cycle A pattern of economic fluctuations that usually has four stages: prosperity, recession, depression and recovery

business market Individuals or groups that purchase a specific kind of product for resale, direct use in producing other products or for use in general daily operations

business products Products bought to use in an organisation's operations, to resell, or to make other products

business services The intangible products that many organisations use in their operations

buy-back allowance A sum of money given to a reseller for each unit bought after an initial promotion deal is over

buying allowance A temporary price reduction to resellers for purchasing specified quantities of a product

buying centre The people within an organisation, including users, influencers, buyers, deciders and gatekeepers, who make business purchase decisions

buying power Resources, such as money, goods and services, that can be traded in an exchange

C

captioned photograph A photo with a brief description of its contents

captive pricing Pricing the basic product in a product line low while pricing related items at a higher level

cash-and-carry wholesalers Limited-service wholesalers whose customers pay cash and furnish transportation

cash discount Price reduction given to buyers for prompt payment or cash payment

catalogue marketing A type of marketing in which an organisation provides a catalogue from which customers make selections and place orders by mail, telephone or the Internet

category killer A very large specialty store concentrating on a major product category and competing on the basis of low prices and product availability

category management A retail strategy of managing groups of similar, often substitutable, products produced by different manufacturers

cause-related marketing Refers to companies linking up with charitable

organisations with the aim of improving the company image as well as 'giving something back' to the wider community. This practice is driven by customer demand

centralised organisation A structure in which top management delegates little authority to levels below it

cents-off offer A promotion that lets buyers pay less than the regular price to encourage purchase

channel capacity The limit on the volume of information a communication channel can handle effectively

channel captain The dominant member of a marketing channel or supply chain

channel management The total set of managerial activities used by an organisation to distribute products in the right quantities to the right locations at the right time

channel power The ability of one channel member to influence another member's goal achievement

client-based relationships Interactions that result in satisfied customers who use a service repeatedly over time

closing The stage in the selling process when the salesperson asks the prospect to buy the product

co-branding Using two or more brands on one product

co-creation When the customer takes an active role in their experience and drives the experience according to their own preferences or values

codes of conduct Formalised rules and standards that describe what the company expects of its employees

cognitive dissonance A buyer's doubts shortly after a purchase about whether the decision was the right one

commercialisation Deciding on full-scale manufacturing and marketing plans and preparing budgets

commission merchants Agents that receive goods on consignment and negotiate sales in large, central markets

communication A sharing of meaning

communications channel The medium of transmission that carries the encoded message from the sender to the receiver or audience

community shopping centres Shopping centres with one or two

department stores, some specialty stores and convenience stores

company sales potential The maximum percentage of market potential that an individual company can expect to obtain for a specific product

comparative advertising Compares the sponsored brand with one or more identified brands on the basis of one or more product characteristics

comparison pricing Setting a price at a specific level and comparing it with a higher price

competition Other firms that market products that are similar to or can be substituted for a firm's products in the same target market segment

competition-based pricing Pricing influenced primarily by competitors' prices

competitive advantage The result of a company's matching a core competency to opportunities in the marketplace

component parts Items that become part of the physical product and are either finished items ready for assembly or products that need little processing before assembly

concentrated targeting strategy A strategy in which an organisation targets a single market segment using one marketing mix for each

concept testing Seeking potential buyers' responses to a product idea

consistency of quality The degree to which a product has the same level of quality over time

consumer behaviour Behaviour of people who purchase products for personal or household use and not for business purposes

consumer buying decision process A five-stage purchase decision process that includes problem recognition, information search, evaluation of alternatives, purchase and post-purchase evaluation

consumer contests Sales promotion methods in which individuals compete for prizes based on analytical or creative skills

consumer games Sales promotion method in which individuals compete for prizes based primarily on chance

consumer market Purchasers and household members who intend to consume or benefit from the purchased products and do not buy products to make profits

consumer panel A group of a product's actual or potential buyers who pre-test ads

consumer products Products purchased to satisfy personal and family needs

consumer sales promotion methods Ways of encouraging consumers to patronise specific stores or try particular products

consumer socialisation The process of acquiring knowledge and skills in order to function as a consumer

consumer sweepstakes Sales promotion in which entrants submit their names for inclusion in a draw for prizes

convenience products Relatively inexpensive, frequently purchased items for which buyers exert minimal purchasing effort

convenience store A small self-service store that is open long hours and carries a narrow assortment of products, usually convenience items

cooperative advertising An arrangement in which a manufacturer agrees to pay a certain amount of a retailer's media costs for advertising the manufacturer's products

copy The verbal portion of advertisements

core competency Something a company does extremely well, which sometimes gives it an advantage over its competition

corporate strategy A strategy that determines the means for using resources in the various functional areas to reach the organisation's goals

cost-plus pricing Adding a specified dollar amount or percentage to the seller's cost. Also known as markup pricing

coupons Written price reductions used to encourage consumers to buy a specific product

crowdsourcing A research method that combines the words crowd and outsourcing. Crowdsourcing is usually performed by a marketer or researcher who outsources a research question to a crowd, or potential market, through an open call, usually online

curated consumption Refers to a trend of consumers electing to follow the style advice or expertise of a curator through communication made available via magazines, TV shows and blogs

curated convenience Merges the trends of curated consumption and convenient delivery of customer orders to their home/work address

curator Traditionally a person working for a museum or a place of exhibition. They hold the position due to their expertise in the field being exhibited, e.g. a curator for the National Sports Museum of Australia is an expert in significant sport-related trends in Australia. In a marketing context, a curator is a person viewed as an authority in their field of expertise whose recommendations for brands to buy are received well by many consumers

customary pricing Pricing on the basis of tradition

customer advisory boards Small groups of actual customers who serve as sounding boards for new product ideas and offer insights into their feelings and attitudes toward a company's products and other elements of marketing strategy

customer contact The level of interaction between provider and customer needed to deliver the service

customer relationship management (CRM) Using information about customers to create marketing strategies that develop and sustain desirable customer relationships

customer services Human or mechanical efforts or activities that add value to a product

customer-to-customer (C2C) interaction This takes place when two or more customers share the consumption experience

customers Customers are the purchasers of products, such as goods, services, ideas and experiences. Customers are the focal point of all marketing activities

cycle time The time needed to complete a process

D

dealer listings Advertisements that promote a product and identify the names of participating retailers that sell the product

dealer loader A gift, often part of a display, given to a retailer purchasing a specified quantity of merchandise

decentralised organisation A structure in which decision-making authority is delegated as far down the chain of command as possible

decline stage The stage of a product's life cycle when sales fall rapidly

decoding process Converting signs or symbols into concepts and ideas

demand curve A graph of the quantity of a product taken by buyers in the market at various prices, given that all other factors are held constant

demographic segmentation Market segmentation based on factors such as age, gender, income, education and ethnicity

demonstrations A sales promotion method manufacturers use temporarily to encourage trial use and purchase of a product or to show how a product works

department stores Large retail organisations characterised by wide product mixes and organised into separate departments to facilitate marketing and internal management

depth of product mix The average number of different product items offered in each product line

derived demand Demand for industrial products that stems from demand for consumer products

descriptive research Research conducted to clarify the characteristics of certain phenomena and thus solve a particular problem

differential pricing Charging different prices to different buyers for the same quality and quantity of product

differentiated targeting strategy A strategy in which an organisation targets two or more segments by developing a marketing mix for each

digital marketing Uses all digital media, including the Internet and mobile interactive channels, to develop communication and exchanges with customers

digital media Electronic media that function using digital codes available via computers, mobile phones, smartphones and other digital devices

direct marketing The use of telecommunications and non-personal media to introduce products to consumers, who then can purchase them via mail, telephone or the Internet

direct marketing channel A marketing channel owned and managed by a single channel member to supply a target market segment

direct response marketing A type of marketing that occurs when a retailer advertises a product and makes it available through mail or telephone orders

direct selling The marketing of products to ultimate consumers through face-to-face sales presentations at home or in the workplace

discount stores Self-service, general merchandise stores offering brand name and private brand products at low prices

discretionary income Disposable income available for spending and saving after an individual has purchased the basic necessities of food, clothing and shelter

disposable income After-tax income

distribution The decisions and activities that make products (goods and services) available to customers when and where they want to purchase or access them

distribution centres Large, centralised warehouses that focus on moving rather than storing goods

drop shippers Limited-service wholesalers that take title to products and negotiate sales but never take actual possession of products

early adopters Careful choosers of new products

early majority Those adopting new products just before the average person

e-commerce The online purchasing of goods, services and experiences, mainly through the Internet, email or mobile phones

electronic data interchange (EDI) A computerised means of integrating order processing with production, inventory, accounting and transportation

electronic marketing (e-marketing) The strategic process of distributing, promoting and pricing products and identifying customer preferences through digital marketing

emotional appeal A style of promotional communication designed to stir emotions such as humour, fear, warmth, irritation or sexual arousal

emotional labour When staff members are expected to display emotion and feel empathy/sympathy, with the view of enhancing customer satisfaction

encoding process Converting meaning into a series of signs or symbols that are meaningful to the intended receiver

environmental analysis The process of assessing and interpreting the information gathered through environmental scanning

environmental psychology Psychological study of how people react to changes in the environment

environmental scanning The process of collecting information about forces in the marketing environment

evaluative criteria Objective and subjective characteristics important to a consumer

everyday low prices (EDLP) Setting a low price for products on a consistent basis

event sponsorship When an organisation contributes financially to a special event with a view to gaining positive publicity

evoked set A group of brands that a buyer views as alternatives for possible purchase

exchanges The provision or transfer of goods, services and ideas in return for something of value

expanded marketing mix Also known as the extended marketing mix, the concept includes the eight key variables a company can use to manage its markets under changing market conditions: product, place, promotion, price, people, physical evidence, process and partnership

experience An event staged by an organisation, it usually evokes an emotional response from the customer and it will try to engage the five senses in order to make the experience more memorable

experimental research Research that allows marketers to make causal inferences about relationships

exploratory research Research conducted to gather more data about a problem or to make a tentative hypothesis more specific

extended problem solving A type of consumer problem-solving process employed when purchasing unfamiliar, expensive or infrequently bought products

external customers Individuals who patronise a business

external reference price A comparison price provided by others

external search An information search in which buyers seek information from outside sources

family branding Branding all of a company's products with the same name

family packaging Using similar packaging for all of a company's products, or packaging that has one common design element

feature article A manuscript of up to 3000 words prepared for a specific publication

feedback The receiver's response to a message

focus-group interview A research method involving observation of group interaction when members are exposed to an idea or a concept

franchising An arrangement in which a supplier (franchiser) grants a dealer (franchisee) the right to sell the franchiser's products in exchange for some type of consideration such as a percentage of the franchisee's sales or an annual fee. Some of the benefits that the franchisee receives from the franchiser, apart from the right to sell the franchiser's products (goods or services), include furnishing equipment, management know-how and marketing assistance

free merchandise A manufacturer's reward given to resellers for purchasing a stated quantity of products

free samples Samples of a product given out to encourage trial and purchase

freight forwarders Organisations that consolidate shipments from several firms into efficient lot sizes

full-service wholesalers Merchant wholesalers that perform the widest range of wholesaling functions

functional modifications Changes affecting a product's versatility, effectiveness, convenience or safety

G

GANTT chart A graph that illustrates different stages of a large project and the timing of all planned activities or tasks the large project is split into

general-line wholesalers Full-service wholesalers that carry only a few product lines but many products within those lines

general merchandise retailer A retail establishment that offers a variety of product lines that are stocked in considerable depth

general merchandise wholesalers Full-service wholesalers with a wide product mix but limited depth within product lines

geocaching A modern day treasure hunt where participants use smartphone apps or handheld GPS units to locate caches (small treasure chests)

generic competitors Firms that provide very different products that solve the same problem or satisfy the same basic customer need

geodemographic segmentation Market segmentation that clusters people in postcode areas and smaller neighbourhood units based on lifestyle and demographic information

geographic and demographic subcultures Groups of individuals whose characteristic values and behaviour patterns are similar to each other and differ from those of the surrounding culture

geographic segmentation Market segmenting by national boundaries, regional districts or even suburban postcode

good A tangible physical entity

government markets Federal, state and local governments that buy goods and services to support their internal operations and provide products to their constituencies

green marketing A strategic process involving stakeholder assessment to create meaningful long-term relationships with customers while maintaining, supporting and enhancing the natural environment

growth stage The stage of a product's life cycle when sales rise rapidly and profits reach a peak and then start to decline

H

heterogeneity Variation in quality

heterogeneous markets Markets made up of individuals or organisations with diverse needs for products in a specific product class

homogeneous market A market in which a large proportion of customers have similar needs for a product

horizontal channel integration Combining organisations at the same level of operation under one management

house brands Brands initiated and owned by resellers

hybrid marketing channel A marketing channel that is a combination of direct and indirect channels whereby different channels are used to reach the same target market segment

hypermarkets Stores that combine supermarket and discount store shopping in one location

hypothesis An informed guess or assumption about a certain problem or set of circumstances

I

idea A concept, philosophy, image or issue

idea generation Seeking product ideas to achieve objectives

illustrations Photos, drawings, graphs, charts and tables used to spark audience interest

impulse buying An unplanned buying behaviour resulting from a powerful urge to buy something immediately

in-home (door-to-door) interview A personal interview that takes place in the respondent's home

indirect marketing channel A marketing channel comprised of several independently owned channel members who work together to serve a target market segment

individual branding A policy of naming each product differently

inelastic demand Demand that is not significantly altered by a price increase or decrease

information inputs Sensations received through the sense organs

innovators First adopters of new products

inseparability An aspect that is produced and consumed at the same time

installations Facilities and immobile major equipment

institutional markets Organisations with charitable, educational, community or other non-business goals

intangibility An aspect that is not physical and cannot be touched

integrated marketing communications (IMC) Coordination of promotional efforts for maximum informational and persuasive impact

interactivity Allows customers to express their needs and wants directly to the firm in response to its marketing communications

intermodal transportation Two or more transportation modes used in combination

internal customers A company's employees

internal marketing Coordinating internal exchanges between the company and its employees to achieve successful external exchanges between the company and its customers

internal reference price A price developed in the buyer's mind through experience with the product

internal search An information search in which buyers search their memories for information about products that might solve their problem

introduction stage The initial stage of a product's life cycle – its first appearance in the marketplace – when sales start at zero and profits are negative

inventory management Developing and maintaining adequate assortments of products to meet customers' needs

J

joint demand Demand involving the use of two or more items in combination to produce a product

just-in-time (JIT) An inventory-management approach in which supplies arrive just when needed for production or resale

L

labelling Providing identifying, promotional or other information on package labels

laggards The last adopters, who distrust new products

late majority Sceptics who adopt new products when they feel it is necessary

layout The physical arrangement of an ad's illustration and copy

learning Changes in an individual's thought processes and behaviour caused by information and experience

level of involvement An individual's degree of interest in a product and the importance of the product for that person

level of quality The amount of quality a product possesses

lifestyle An individual's pattern of living expressed through activities, interests and opinions

lifestyle shopping centres A type of shopping centre that is typically open air and features upscale specialty, dining and entertainment stores

limited problem solving A type of consumer problem-solving process that buyers use when purchasing products occasionally or when they need information about an unfamiliar brand in a familiar product category

limited-service wholesalers Merchant wholesalers that provide some services and specialise in a few functions

line extension Development of a product that is closely related to existing products in the line but meets different customer needs

local shopping centres Shopping centres usually consisting of several small convenience and specialty stores

M

m-sites Websites optimised for on-the-go use via mobile devices

mail-order wholesalers Limited-service wholesalers that sell products through catalogues

mail survey A research method in which respondents answer a questionnaire sent through the mail

manufacturer brands Brands initiated by producers

manufacturers' agents Independent intermediaries that represent two or more sellers and offer complete product lines

market A group of individuals and/or organisations that have needs for products in a product class and have the ability, willingness and authority to purchase those products

market density The number of potential customers within a unit of land area

market opportunity A combination of circumstances and timing that permits an organisation to take action to reach a target market

market-growth/market-share matrix A strategic planning tool based on the philosophy that a product's market growth rate and market share are important in determining marketing strategy

market orientation An organisational culture expressed through the organisation-wide (1) generation of market intelligence in relation to current and future customer needs, to the competition and to collaborators, (2) dissemination and inter-functional coordination of the market intelligence across business functions, and (3) responsiveness to the market intelligence

market potential The total amount of a product that customers will purchase within a specified period at a specific level of industry-wide marketing activity

market segment Individuals, groups or organisations with one or more similar characteristics that cause them to have similar product needs

market segmentation The process of dividing a total market into meaningful groups with relatively similar product needs and wants

market share The percentage of a market that actually buys a specific product from a particular company

marketing The process of maximising returns to stakeholders by developing exchanges with valued customers and creating an advantage for them

marketing channel The aggregate of all individuals and organisations that direct the flow of products from producers to customers; marketing channels are referred to as 'place' in the marketing mix

marketing communications mix A combination of marketing communications methods used to promote a specific product

marketing concept A managerial philosophy that an organisation should try to satisfy customers' needs through a coordinated set of activities that also allows the organisation to achieve its goals

marketing control process Establishing performance standards and trying to match actual performance to those standards

marketing decision support system (MDSS) Customised computer software that aids marketing managers in decision-making

marketing environment The competitive, economic, political, legal and regulatory, technological, and sociocultural forces that surround the customer and affect the marketing mix

marketing goal A statement of what is to be accomplished through marketing activities

marketing implementation The process of putting marketing strategies into action

marketing information system (MIS) A framework for the management and structuring of data gathered regularly from data sources inside and outside an organisation

marketing intermediaries The middlemen between producers and customers in a marketing channel linking producers to consumers

marketing management The process of planning, organising, implementing and controlling marketing activities to facilitate exchanges effectively and efficiently

marketing mix Four marketing activities (or variables) – product, pricing, distribution and promotion – that an organisation controls to meet the needs of customers within its target market

marketing objective A statement of what is to be accomplished through marketing activities

marketing plan A written document that specifies the activities to be performed to implement and control an organisation's marketing activities

marketing planning The process of assessing opportunities and resources, determining objectives, defining strategies and establishing guidelines for implementation and control of the marketing program

marketing research The systematic design, collection and interpretation of data, as well as the reporting of the information gained to help marketers solve specific marketing problems or take advantage of marketing opportunities

marketing strategy A plan of action for identifying and analysing a target market segment and developing a marketing mix to meet the needs of that market segment

markup pricing Adding to the cost of the product a predetermined percentage of that cost

materials handling Physical handling of tangible goods, supplies and resources

maturity stage The stage of a product's life cycle when the sales curve peaks and starts to decline as profits continue to fall

media plan Specifies media vehicles and schedule for running the ads

megacarriers Freight transportation firms that provide several modes of shipment

merchandise allowance A manufacturer's agreement to pay resellers certain amounts of money for providing special promotional efforts

merchant wholesalers Independently owned businesses that take title to goods, assume ownership risks, and buy and resell products to other wholesalers, business customers or retailers

micromarketing An approach to market segmentation in which organisations focus precise marketing efforts on very small geodemographic markets

mission statement A long-term view of what the organisation wants to become

modified-rebuy purchase A new-task purchase that is changed on subsequent orders or when the requirements of a straight-rebuy purchase are modified

money refunds A sales promotion technique offering consumers money when they mail in a proof of purchase, usually for multiple product purchases

monopolistic competition A competitive structure in which a firm

has many potential competitors and tries to develop a marketing strategy to differentiate its product

monopoly A competitive structure in which an organisation offers a product that has no close substitutes, making that organisation the sole source of supply

moral appeal A style of promotional communication that relies on our sense of 'what is right or wrong'

motive An internal energising force that directs a person's behaviour towards satisfying needs or achieving goals

MRO supplies Maintenance, repair and operating items that facilitate production and operations but do not become part of the finished product

multiple marketing channel A marketing channel that is a combination of direct and indirect channels whereby each channel is used to reach a different target market segment

multiple sourcing An organisation's decision to use several suppliers

multiple-unit pricing Packaging together two or more identical products and selling them for a single price

N

Near Field Communication (NFC) A wireless communication and data exchange technology that uses electromagnetic radio fields, works in a similar way to wi-fi, but only allows a very short distance between devices. This technology has been available since the 1980s but came to prominence recently when incorporated into mobile devices

negotiated pricing Establishing a final price through bargaining

new-product development process A seven-phase process for introducing products

new-task purchase An initial purchase by an organisation of an item to be used to perform a new job or solve a new problem

news release A short piece of copy publicising an event or a product

noise Anything that reduces a communication's clarity and accuracy

non-price competition Emphasising factors other than price to distinguish a product from competing brands

non-probability sampling A sampling technique in which there is no way to calculate the likelihood that a specific element of the population being studied will be chosen

odd-even pricing Ending the price with certain numbers to influence buyers' perceptions of the price or product

offensive advertising Advertisements considered offensive by the consumers due to insulting, unfair or morally wrong content

off-price retailers Stores that buy manufacturers' seconds, overruns, returns and off-season merchandise for resale to consumers at deep discounts

olfaction effect Refers to sensing and interpreting smells and tasting flavours; may result in an emotional reaction

oligopoly A competitive structure in which a few sellers control the supply of a large proportion of a product

online fraud Any attempt to conduct fraudulent activities online, including deceiving consumers into releasing personal information

online retailing Retailing that makes products available to buyers through computer connections

online survey A research method in which respondents answer a questionnaire via email or on a website

operations management The total set of managerial activities used by an organisation to transform resource inputs into products; primarily concerned with production

opinion leader A member of a reference group who provides specific information that interests reference-group participants

order processing The receipt and transmission of sales order information

outsourcing The contracting of physical distribution tasks to third parties who do not have managerial authority within the marketing channel

owned media Media owned by organisations traditionally involved with branded goods and services. The original business focus of these companies was not media

P

partnerships Alliances between independent organisations that have complimentary skills or assets. Partnership agreements aim to utilise complimentary skills and resources to satisfy company objectives

penetration pricing Setting prices below those of competing brands to penetrate a market and gain a significant market share quickly

people The actors involved with the process/experience, including personnel as well as other customers (and even passersby) present when the product/service/experience took place, also referred to as participants

perceived brand quality An intangible, overall brand evaluation

perception The process of selecting, organising and interpreting information inputs to produce meaning

performance standard An expected level of performance

periodic discounts Temporary reduction of prices on a patterned or systematic basis

perishability The inability of unused service capacity to be stored for future use

personal interview survey A research method in which participants respond to survey questions face to face

personal selling Paid personal presentations aiming to inform and/or persuade customers

physical evidence The facilities visible to a customer, e.g. building design and decor, gardens, overall ambience, staff uniforms and appearance, background music, etc

pioneer promotion Promotion that informs consumers about a new product

podcast Audio or video files that can be downloaded from the Internet with a subscription that automatically delivers new content to listening devices or personal computers, giving consumers the option to listen to or view content when and where they choose

point-of-purchase (P-O-P) materials Signs, window displays, display racks and similar means used to attract customers

population All the elements, units or individuals of interest to researchers for a specific study

post-test Evaluation of advertising effectiveness after the campaign

premium pricing Pricing the highest quality or most versatile products higher than other models in the product line

premium money (or push money) Extra compensation to salespeople for pushing a line of goods

premiums Items offered free or at a minimal cost as a bonus for purchasing a product

press conference A meeting used to announce major news events to the media

prestige pricing Setting prices at an artificially high level to convey prestige or a quality image

prestige-sensitive Drawn to products that signify prominence and status

pre-test Evaluation of ads performed before a campaign begins

price Value exchanged for products in a marketing transaction

price competition Emphasising price and matching or beating competitors' prices

price-conscious Striving to pay low prices

price leader Product priced below the usual markup, near cost or below cost

price lining Setting a limited number of prices for selected groups or lines of merchandise

price skimming Charging the highest possible price that buyers who most desire the product will pay

pricing objectives Goals that describe what a company wants to achieve through pricing

primary data Data observed and recorded or collected directly from respondents

primary demand Demand for a product category rather than for a specific brand

probability sampling A sampling technique in which every element in the population being studied has a known chance of being selected for study

process materials Materials that are used directly in the production of other products but are not readily identifiable

processes The flow and progress of the customers when they engage with the product or the company, also referred to as programming

producer markets Individuals and business organisations that purchase products to make profits by using them to produce other products or using them in their operations

product A good, a service, an idea or a combination thereof

product adoption process The stages buyers go through in accepting a product

product competitors Firms that compete in the same target market segment but market products with different features, benefits and prices

product deletion Eliminating a product from the product mix

product design How a product is conceived, planned and produced

product development Determining if producing a product is technically feasible and cost effective

product differentiation Creating and designing products so that customers perceive them as different from competing products

product features Specific design characteristics that allow a product to perform certain tasks

product item A specific version of a product that can be designated as a distinct offering among a company's products

product life cycle The progression of a product through four stages: introduction, growth, maturity and decline

product line A group of closely related product items viewed as a unit because of marketing, technical or end-use considerations

product-line pricing Establishing and adjusting prices of multiple products within a product line

product mix The total group of products that an organisation makes available to customers

product modification Change in one or more characteristics of a product

product placement The strategic location of products or product promotions within a TV program (or other entertainment media) to reach the product's target market

product positioning Creating and maintaining a certain concept of a product in customers' minds

professional pricing Fees set by people with great skill or experience in a particular field

promotion Communication to build and maintain relationships by informing and persuading one or more audiences

prospecting Developing a list of potential customers

psychographic segmentation Market segmentation based on factors such as personality and lifestyle

psychological influences Factors that partly determine people's general behaviour, thus influencing their behaviour as consumers

psychological pricing Pricing that attempts to influence a customer's perception of price to make a product's price more attractive

public relations Communication efforts used to create and maintain favourable relations between an organisation and its stakeholders

publicity A news story type of communication transmitted through a mass medium at no charge

pull policy Promoting a product directly to consumers to develop strong consumer demand that pulls products through the marketing channel

pure competition A market structure characterised by an extremely large number of sellers, none strong enough to significantly influence price or supply

push policy Promoting a product only to the next institution down the marketing channel

Q

QR (quick response) code A two dimensional barcode that links to a website

quality Characteristics of a product that allow it to perform as expected in satisfying customer needs

quality modifications Changes relating to a product's dependability and durability

quantity discounts Deductions from list price for purchasing large quantities

quota sampling A non-probability sampling technique in which researchers divide the population into groups and then arbitrarily choose participants from each group

R

rack jobbers Full-service, specialty-line wholesalers that own and maintain display racks in stores

radio frequency identification (RFID) Contactless, wireless data exchange using radio frequency electromagnetic fields for automated/quick communication between a very small chip and the reading device. Examples include the ID chips that veterinarians insert into pets for pet registration schemes

random discounts Temporary reduction of prices on an unsystematic basis

random sampling A type of probability sampling in which all units in a population have an equal chance of appearing in a sample

rational appeal A style of promotional communication that features factual information

raw materials Basic natural materials that become part of a physical product

rebates A sales promotion technique whereby a customer is sent a specific amount of money for purchasing a single product

receiver A specific term relating to the communications process. A receiver is the individual, group or organisation that decodes a coded message

reciprocity An arrangement unique to business marketing in which two organisations agree to buy from each other

recognition test A post-test in which individuals are shown the actual ad and asked if they recognise it

reference group A group that positively or negatively affects a person's values, attitudes or behaviour

reference pricing Pricing a product at a moderate level and displaying it next to a more expensive model or brand

regional shopping centres A type of shopping centre with the largest department stores, the widest product mix and the deepest product lines of all shopping centres

relationship marketing Establishing long-term, mutually satisfying buyer–seller relationships

reliability A condition existing when a research technique produces almost identical results in repeated trials

reminder advertising Reminds consumers about an established brand's uses, characteristics and benefits

research design An overall plan for obtaining the data needed to address a research problem or issue

reseller markets Intermediaries who buy finished goods and resell them for profit

retailer An organisation that purchases products for the purpose of reselling them to ultimate consumers

retailing All transactions in which the buyer intends to consume the product through personal, family or household use

role A set of actions and activities associated with an individual's position

routinised response behaviour A type of consumer problem-solving process used when buying frequently purchased, low-cost items that require very little search and decision effort

S

sales branches Manufacturer-owned intermediaries that sell products and provide support services to the manufacturer's sales force

sales contest A promotion method used to motivate distributors, retailers and sales personnel through recognition of outstanding achievements

sales offices Manufacturer-owned operations that provide services normally associated with agents

sales promotion An activity and/or material meant to induce resellers or salespeople to sell a product or consumers to buy it

sample A limited number of units chosen to represent the characteristics of the population

sampling The process of selecting representative units from a total population

scan-back allowance A manufacturer's reward to retailers based on the number of pieces scanned

screening Choosing the most promising ideas for further review

seasonal discount A price reduction given to buyers for purchasing goods or services out of season

secondary data Data compiled both inside and outside the organisation for some purpose other than the current investigation

secondary-market pricing Setting one price for the primary target market and a different price for another market

segmentation variables Characteristics of individuals, groups or organisations used to divide a market into segments

selective demand Demand for a specific brand

selective distortion An individual's changing or twisting of information when it is inconsistent with personal feelings or beliefs

selective exposure The process of selecting inputs to be exposed to our awareness while ignoring others

selective retention Remembering information inputs that support personal feelings and beliefs and forgetting inputs that do not

self-concept A person's view or perception of himself or herself

selling agents Intermediaries that market a whole product line or a manufacturer's entire output

sender A person, group or organisation with a meaning it tries to share

service A mostly intangible result of the application of human and mechanical efforts to people or objects

servicescape A collective term for the physical evidence (or assets) used to create desirable brand or service quality perception

shopping-centre intercept interviews A research method that involves interviewing a percentage of persons passing by 'intercept' points in a centre

shopping products Items for which buyers are willing to expend considerable effort in planning and making purchases

showrooming Buying behaviour whereby consumers use bricks and mortar retailers to get a feel for products but actually buy them more cheaply through online stores

single-source data Data provided by a single marketing research firm

situational influences Influences from physical and social surroundings, time and reason considerations as well as the buyer's mood, affect the consumer buying decision process

social influences External social forces on an individual's buying behaviour

social media Involves digital technologies that link people to networks and allow the exchange of personal and professional information as well as common interests such as product and brand preferences

social network Web-based meeting place for friends, family, co-workers and peers that allow users to create a profile and connect with other users for purposes that include getting acquainted, keeping in touch and building a work-related network

social networking websites Used to gather useful data in understanding consumer decisions

social sponsorship Social sponsorship is used when organisations want to influence customer perceptions of their socially responsible/ethical merits or to improve their image

sociocultural forces The influences in a society and its culture(s) that change people's attitudes, beliefs, norms, customs and lifestyles

sole sourcing An organisation's decision to use only one supplier

special-event pricing Advertised sales or price cutting linked to a special event

specialty products Items with unique characteristics that buyers are willing to expend considerable effort to obtain

specialty-line wholesalers Full-service wholesalers that carry only a single product line or a few items within a product line

stakeholders Constituents who have a 'stake', or claim, in some aspect of a company's products, operations, markets, industry and outcomes

statistical interpretation Analysis of what is typical or what deviates from the average

straight-rebuy purchase A routine purchase of the same products under approximately the same terms of sale by a business buyer

strategic business unit (SBU) A division, product line or other profit centre within a parent company

strategic planning The process of establishing an organisational mission and formulating goals, corporate strategy, marketing objectives, marketing strategy and a marketing plan

strategic windows Temporary periods of optimal fit between the key requirements of a market and a company's capabilities

stratified sampling A type of probability sampling in which the population is divided into groups according to a common attribute, and a random sample is then chosen within each group

styling The physical appearance of a product

subcultures Groups of individuals whose characteristic values and behavioural patterns are similar to each other and different from those of the surrounding culture

subcultures of consumption A subculture defined and unified through shared consumption practices

subscription service (also known as subscription commerce) refers to an arrangement of regular deliveries of products to customers against a regular (often automated) payment or fee for this service (e.g. direct debit arrangement). Developments in e-commerce have facilitated these kind of direct sales to customers

super-regional shopping centres A type of shopping centre with the widest and deepest product mixes that attracts customers from many kilometres away

supermarkets Large, self-service stores that carry a complete line of food products, along with some non-food products

superstores Giant retail outlets that carry food and non-food products found in supermarkets, as well as most routinely purchased consumer products

supply chain All the activities associated with the flow and transformation of products from raw materials through delivery to the end customer

sustainable competitive advantage An advantage that the competition cannot copy

SWOT analysis A tool that marketers use to assess an organisation's strengths, weaknesses, opportunities and threats

 T

target audience The group of people at whom advertisements are aimed

target market Customers on whom an organisation focuses its marketing efforts

technology The application of knowledge and tools to solve problems and perform tasks more efficiently

telemarketing The performance of marketing-related activities by telephone

telephone depth interview An interview that combines the traditional focus group's ability to probe with the confidentiality provided by telephone surveys

telephone survey A research method in which respondents' answers to a questionnaire are recorded by interviewers on the phone

television home shopping A form of selling in which products are presented to TV viewers, who can buy them by calling a free-call number and paying with a credit card

tensile pricing Refers to a broad statement about price reductions as opposed to detailing specific price discounts

test marketing Introducing a product on a limited basis to measure the extent to which potential customers will actually buy it

total budget competitors Firms that compete for the financial resources of the same customers

trade (functional) discount A reduction off the list price given by a producer to an intermediary for performing certain functions

trade name Full legal name of an organisation

trade sales promotion methods Ways of persuading wholesalers and retailers to carry a producer's products and market them aggressively

trademark A legal designation of exclusive use of a brand

traditional specialty retailers Stores that carry a narrow product mix with deep product lines

transportation The movement of products from where they are made to intermediaries and end users

truck wholesalers Limited-service wholesalers that transport products directly to customers for inspection and selection

U

unaided recall test A post-test in which respondents identify ads they have recently seen but are given no recall clues

undifferentiated targeting strategy A strategy in which an organisation designs a single marketing mix and directs it at the entire market for a particular product

unsought products Products purchased to solve a sudden problem, products of which customers are unaware and products that people do not necessarily think about buying

V

validity A condition existing when a research method measures what it is supposed to measure

value A customer's subjective assessment of benefits relative to costs in determining the worth of a product

value analysis An evaluation of each component of a potential purchase

value-based pricing Pricing based on the level of benefits the product offers

value-conscious Concerned about price and quality of a product

vendor analysis A formal, systematic evaluation of current and potential vendors

vertical channel integration Combining two or more stages of the marketing channel under one management

viral marketing A strategy to get consumers to share a marketer's message, often through email or online video, in a way that spreads dramatically and quickly

W

warehouse clubs Large-scale members-only establishments that combine features of cash-and-carry wholesaling with discount retailing

warehouse showrooms Retail facilities in large, low-cost buildings with large on-premises inventories and minimal services

warehousing The design and operation of facilities for storing and moving goods

wearable technology Technology that can be worn like any piece of clothing or accessory with seamless connectivity to smartphone apps

wholesaler An individual or organisation that sells products that are bought for resale, for making other products or for general business operations

wholesaling Transactions in which products are bought for resale, for making other products or for general business operations

width of product mix The number of product lines a company offers

wikis Websites that enable users to add or edit content collaboratively

willingness to spend An inclination to buy because of expected satisfaction from a product, influenced by the ability to buy and numerous psychological and social forces

word-of-mouth communication (WOM) Personal, informal exchanges of information that customers share with one another about products, brands and companies

Index

A

AC Nielsen, 297, 300
accessory equipment, 260–1
accidental participants, 514
advertising, 453–65
  to be aware of, 465
  budget, 456–7
  campaign execution, 463–4
  colour vs black-and-white, 463
  community-based issues, 453
  comparative, 465
  cooperative, 487
  effectiveness, evaluating, 463–4
  objectives, 455–6
  offensive, 436–7
  platform, 456
  print, components of, 462
  product placement, 465–6
  recognition test, 464
  reminder, 465
  TV, 465–6
  see also promotion
advertising campaign development, 454–63
  artwork, 463
  budget, 456–7
  changing media landscape, 459–2
  consumer panel, 463
  copy, 462–3
  creating advertising message, 462–3
  media plan, 458–9
  objectives, 455–6
  platform, 456
  post-test, 464
  pre-test, 463
  target audience, 455
  unaided recall test, 464
Advertising Standards Bureau (ASB), 48, 436
aesthetic labour, 510–12
aesthetic modifications, 303
age-based segmentation, 160
agents and brokers, 393–5
Air Asia, 119–20, 121
Alcohol Beverages Advertising Code (ABAC), 48
Aldi, 39–40, 64
allowances, 354
Amazon.com, 63, 92, 106, 331–2
American Express, 526
American Marketing Association (AMA), 5
Apple, 9, 11, 18, 54, 56, 180–1, 221, 223, 230, 234, 445
applications (apps), 526, 553–5
artwork, advertising, 463

atmospherics (store design), 385, 517–20
attitudes (buying decision process), 133–4
Australia Post, 376
Australian Association of National Advertisers (AANA), 416
Australian Competition and Consumer Commission (ACCC), 48, 167–8, 231, 417, 438, 465
Australian Consumer Law, 47, 417
Australian Crime Commission (ACC), 474
Australian Farm Business Management Network (AFBMN), 526
Australian Market & Social Research Society, 105
automotive industry (case study), 407–8

B

bait pricing, 348
BangOnABeannie campaign, 415
basic trading (evolution of marketing), 19
Ben & Jerry's ice cream, 57
behavioural change in social marketing (case study), 150–1
behaviouristic variables (consumer markets), 159, 166–9
benefit segmentation, 168
billboards, 431
BlitzMetrics, 44
blogger (case study), 494–5
blogs, 141, 548–9
BMW, 92
body scanning and clothing fit, 524
Bonds, 173–4, 230
Boost Juice, 297
Boston Consulting Group (BCG), 60
brainstorming, 292
brand(s)
  association, 225
  awareness, 223
  building and sustaining, 235–9
  competitors, 43
  definition, 221
  equity, 223–9
  essence, 238–9
  evaluation, 239
  experience, 242
  extensions, 232–3
  global, 227
  house, 228
  insistence, 224
  licensing, 234–5
  loyalty, 224, 225
  manufacturer, 227
  mark, 222

  names, 221, 229–1
  negotiation, 224
  objectives, 238
  preference, 224
  and pricing, 240
  protection, 230–1
  resourcing, 239
  values, 237
  vision, 237
brand marketers (case study), 494–5
branding, 221–43
  auditing the brand sphere, 238
  co-branding, 233–4
  and corporate social responsibility, 241
  family, 232
  individual, 131
  internal implementation, 239
  and marketing mix, 239–3
  and physical distribution, 240–1
  policies, 231–2
  and products, 242–3
  and promotion, 241–2
  strategic power of, 221–2
  strategy within an unbranded market (case study), 247–8
  value of, 222–3, 237
breakdown approach, 177
Bridges, Michelle, 524
Bright, Torah, 9
Build-A-Bear Workshop, 94
buildup approach, 177
Bundaberg Distilling Company, 413
bundle pricing, 349
bundling services, 311–14
Bunnings, 71, 175
business and marketing, 28
business analysis (new product development), 295
business banking (case study), 212–13
business buying
  decision process stages, 205–8
  decisions, 203–5
  methods of, 196, 199–200
  PEST factors, 207
business customers
  customer attributes, 196, 197
  demand, 196, 201–3
  marketing to, 196–201
  methods of business buying, 196, 199–200
  primary concerns, 196, 197–9
  transaction characteristics, 196, 197
  types of business purchases, 196, 200–1
business cycle, 46

business market(s), 156, 157, 192–6
business markets, variables for segmenting, 169–70
  customer size, 169
  geographic location, 169
  product use, 170
  type of organisation, 169
business product demand, 196, 201–3
business products, 255, 258–2
business purchases, types of, 196, 200–1
business services, 262
Business Software Alliance, 569
business-to-business (B2B), 157, 192
business-to-consumer (B2C), 192
business-unit strategy, 59–61
buy-back allowances, 487
buyer's momentary moods (buying decision process), 129
buying allowances, 487
buying centre, 203–5
buying decision process
  decision process stages, 205–8
  influences, 207–8
  psychological influences, 130–7
  situational influences, 128–9
  social influences, 137–45
buying power, 45–6

C

Cadbury, 259, 296, 299
Caltex, 234
Campbell's, 15–16
Cannon, 411–12
Capital One Financial, 106
captioned photograph, 468
captive pricing, 348
career prospects, 30
Carlton & United Breweries (CUB), 475–6
Carrefour, 380
Carsales.com, 29
cash discounts, 353
cash-and-carry wholesalers, 392
catalogue marketing, 387
category killer, 382
category management, 385–6
cause-related marketing, 421
centralised organisation, 69
cents-off offers, 482–4
Channel 7, 415
channel capacity, 418
channel conflict, 399–400
channel cooperation, 399
channel integration, 400
channel leadership, 398
channel management, 365
channel policies, push and pull, 433–4
Christian Dior, 28
Christian Louboutin, 231, 255
Chrysler, 319

Cisco, 89, 230
Clark, Maxine, 94
client-based relationships, 309
co-branding, 233–4
Coca-Cola, 43, 70, 90, 101–2, 177, 181, 227, 232, 276, 283–5, 291, 300
co-creation, 513
codes of conduct, 73
Coffee Club, 257
cognitive dissonance, 126
Coles, 22, 39–40, 54, 94–5, 254, 380, 438
Colgate-Palmolive, 181
combo deals, 350
commercialisation (new product development), 298–300
commission merchants, 394
  communication, 415–9
  across language barriers, 415
  channel capacity, 418
  decoding process, 418
  definition, 415
  encoding process, 416
  face-to-face, 418
  feedback, 418
  noise, 418
  out-of-home (OOH), 431
  receiver, 416
  sender, 415
  word-of-mouth, 428, 434–5
  see also marketing communications mix
communications channel, 417
community shopping centres, 384
company sales potential, 177
comparison pricing, 352
comparative advertising, 465
competition, 43
  and marketing channels, 397
  non-price, 333–4
  price, 333
Competition and Consumer Act 2010, 465
competition-based pricing, 345–6
competitive advantage, 55
  sustainable, 63–4
competitive assessment (market segments), 178
competitive forces (marketing environment), 43–5
component parts, 261
concentrated targeting strategy, 172–3
concept testing (new product development), 294–5
connectivity, 543
consumer adoption categories, 270–1
consumer awareness, 28
consumer behaviour, 121–2
  digital marketing, 556–62
  distribution considerations, 558–60
  e-marketing strategy, 557
  online, 556–7
  pricing considerations, 561–2
  product considerations, 557–8

  promotion considerations, 560–1
consumer buying decision process, 122–6
  definition, 122
  evaluation of alternatives, 124–5
  information search, 124
  post-purchase evaluation, 126
  problem recognition, 123–4
  purchase, 125
consumer contests, 486
consumer games, 486
consumer market, 156
consumer markets, variables for segmenting, 159–69
  behaviouristic variables, 159, 166–9
  demographic variables, 159–4
  geographic variables, 159, 164–6
  psychographic variables, 159, 166
consumer privacy, 106
consumer problem-solving processes, 126–8
consumer products, 255, 256–8
consumer sales promotion methods, 482–6
  consumers games, contests and sweepstakes, 486
  coupons and cents-off offers, 482–4
  free samples and premiums, 485–6
  frequent-user incentives, 485
  point-of-purchase materials and demonstrations, 485
  refunds and rebates, 484–5
consumer socialisation, 138
consumer sweepstakes, 486
consumer-generated marketing and digital media, 544–55
  applications (apps), 553–5
  blogs, 548–9
  Facebook, 546–7
  media-sharing websites, 549–50
  mobile devices, 551–3
  Myspace, 547–8
  social networks, 544–9
  Twitter, 548
  virtual websites, 551
  wearable technology, 555
  widgets, 553–5
  Wikis, 548–9
consumption
  habits and technology, 125
  subcultures, 144–5
control process (marketing management), 27
convenience, 564–5
convenience products, 256–7
convenience stores, 378, 379
cooperative advertising, 487
copy, advertising, 462–3
core competency, 54
corporate identity, 57
corporate social responsibility, 74
  and branding, 241

corporate strategy, 59
cost and pricing objective, 335
cost estimates (market segments), 178
cost-plus pricing, 343–4
Costco, 39–40, 204, 378, 380, 381
coupons, 482–4
Cricket Australia (CA), 475–6
crowdsourcing, 97, 576–7
culture (buying decision process), 141–5
curated consumption, 524
curated convenience, 524–5
customary pricing, 351
customer advisory boards, 94
customer and stakeholder relationship, 14–15
customer characteristics, 396–7
customer–company interactions, 522–3
customer contact, 309–10
customer experience, mapping, 507–9
customer interpretation of price, 336
customer lifetime value (CLV), 66
customer loyalty, 425–6
customer perception of product, 338–9
customer relationship management (CRM), 22, 66, 104, 478
customer relationships, managing, 22–5
customer services, 320
customer size (business markets), 169
customer-to-customer (C2C) interactions, 513, 514
customers, 7
  external, 67
  flow and progress of, 521–2
  internal, 67
  as participants, 512–14
  prospecting for, 477–8
  see also business customers
cycle time, 371

D

data
  analysis, 101–2
  analysis, technology to improve, 102–5
  collection and preparation, 91–101
  primary, 91, 92–101
  secondary, 91–2
  types of, 91
databases, 104–5
David Jones, 377, 378, 379
DB Export breweries, 181
dealer listings, 488
dealer load, 488
decentralised organisation, 69
deceptive promotion, 438
decoding process (communication), 418
Dell, 366
demand
  curve, 339
  and pricing decisions, 339–40
  primary, 424

seasonality of demand, 426
  selective, 424
demographic segmentation, 159
demographic variables (consumer markets), 159–4
demonstrations, 485
department stores, 378, 379
depth of product mix, 262–4
derived demand, 201
descriptive research, 90
differential pricing, 346
differentiated targeting strategy, 173–4
digital marketing, 540–70
  definition, 451
  ethical and legal issues 567–70
  growth and benefits of, 540–4
digital marketing consumer behaviour
  distribution considerations, 558–60
  e-marketing strategy, 557
  online, 556–7
  pricing considerations, 561–2
  product considerations, 557–8
  promotion considerations, 560–1
  trends, 556–62
digital media, 461
  applications (apps), 553–5
  blogs, 548–9
  and consumer-generated marketing, 544–55
  definition, 540
  ethical and legal issues, 567–70
  and the expanded marketing mix, 562–7
  Facebook, 546–7
  media-sharing websites, 549–50
  mobile devices, 551–3
  Myspace, 547–8
  social networks, 544–5
  Twitter, 548
  virtual websites, 551
  wearable technology, 555
  widgets, 553–5
  Wikis, 548–9
digital networks (buying decision process), 141
digital technology and the service process, 523–4
Dinnigan, Collette, 28
direct marketing, 387–9
direct marketing channels, 367–8
direct response marketing, 387
direct selling, 388–9
discount stores, 378, 379
discretionary income, 45
Disneyland, 242
disposable income, 45
distribution
  considerations, 557–8
  definition, 364
  of services, 315–16
  see also physical distribution

distribution centres, 374
distribution (place) variable (marketing mix), 11, 503, 509
Domain, 315
Domino's Pizza, 121–2
Dove, 231, 438–9
drop shippers, 393
'Dumb Ways to Die' 440, 462

E

Eagle Boys Pizza, 177
Earth Choice, 260
eBay, 106
e-books, 560
e-commerce, 525
economic conditions (marketing environment), 46–7
economic forces (marketing environment), 45–7
  buying power and willingness to spend, 45–6
  economic conditions, 46–7
Eddie Stobart haulage, 506, 508
electronic coupons (e-coupons), 482–3
electronic data interchange (EDI), 372
Ella Baché salons, 56
e-marketing, 23, 541, 556
  strategy, 557
emotional appeal, 419
emotional labour, 512
encoding process (communication), 416
enhanced experience, 565–6
environmental analysis, 41
environmental forces, 398
environmental scanning, 41
ethical and legal issues, 567–70
ethical marketing, 16, 17, 68, 73–4, 122, 161, 193, 228, 293–4, 337, 386, 438–9, 475–6, 511, 525, 566
ethics, 73–4
  marketing research, 105–6, 107
evaluation of alternatives, 124–5
evaluative criteria, 124
everyday low prices (EDLP), 351
evoked set, 124
exchanges, 14
expanded marketing mix (8Ps), 7–8, 505
and digital media, 562–7
  experience economy, 505–7
  partnership variable, 13–14, 504, 509, 525–7
  people variable, 12–13, 504, 509–15
  physical evidence variable, 13, 504, 509, 515–21
  process variable, 13, 504, 509, 521–5
  strategic use of variables, 503–9
  experience economy, 505–7
experimental research, 90
exploratory methods (primary data collection), 94–5
exploratory research, 89

extended problem solving, 127
external customers, 67
external reference price, 338
external search, 124

F

Facebook, 62, 98, 141, 142, 173, 539, 546–7
face-to-face communication, 418
family branding, 232
family packaging, 273
fast moving consumer goods (FMCGs), 267
feature articles, 467
FedEx, 103, 376
feedback (communication), 418
Flickr, 549–50
fluctuating demand, 203
FlyBuys, 526
focus group interviews, 94
food labelling, 278
Food Standards of Australia and New Zealand (FSANZ), 278
Ford, 8, 172, 227
Foster's Australia, 320
franchising, 383
free merchandise, 488
free samples, 485
freight forwarders, 376
frequent-user incentives, 485
full-service wholesalers, 392
functional modifications, 302

G

GANNT chart, 414, 428
Gecko's Adventures, 416
gender-based segmentation, 161–2
general-line wholesalers, 392
general merchandise wholesalers, 392
Generation Y, 155
generic competitors, 43
geocaching, 558
geodemographic segmentation, 165
geographic location (business markets), 169
geographic segmentation, 164–5
geographic variables (consumer markets), 159, 164–6
Gillette, 72
GlaxoSmithKline, 462
global economy, marketing in a, 26–30
good (definition), 252
Google, 42, 58, 68, 106, 223, 526
government markets, 195
green marketing, 30, 167–8, 276–7
Greenpeace, 525
greenwashing, 167, 260, 417
Grey Goose Vodka, 9
growth stage (product life cycle), 265–6
Gucci, 271
Grylls, Bear, 21

H

Hamel, Gary, 292
Harley-Davidson, 144–5, 223
Hawkins, Jennifer, 524
headphones, 253–4
Hello Kitty, 224
heterogeneity, 309
heterogeneous market, 158
Hilton, 23, 224
Holden, 28, 62, 227, 291, 301
homogenous market, 158
Honda, 227, 232
horizontal channel integration, 400
house brands, 228
Hudson's Coffee, 22
hybrid marketing channels, 369
hypermarkets, 378, 380
Hyundai Motors Group, 526

I

IBM, 70, 191–2, 222
idea generation, 291–4
IKEA, 368, 378, 381, 452
implementation (marketing management), 27
impulse buying, 128
indirect marketing channels, 368
inelastic demand, 201–2
information inputs, 130
information search, 124
information systems
    social media role in, 85–6
in-home (door-to-door) interview, 98
innovators, 270
inseparability, 307
installations (business products), 259
institutional markets, 195–6
intangibility, 306–7
integrated marketing communications (IMC), 412–15, 428
communication mix, 427–35
    communication process, 415–9
    message appeal styles, 419–20
    planning, 422
    promotion, criticisms and defences, 435–40
    promotion, role and objectives of, 420–7
Intel, 42
intellectual property, 569–70
Interactive Advertising Bureau (IAB), 552
interactivity of social media, 543–4
intermodal transportation, 376
internal customers, 67
internal implementation, 239
internal marketing, 67–8
internal reference price, 337
internal search, 124
international issues in marketing research, 106–7

Internet and marketing, 29, 50
Internet-based marketing strategies (e-marketing), 23
interviews
    focus group, 94
    in-home (door-to-door), 98
    personal interview survey, 98
    shopping-centre intercept, 99
    telephone depth, 95
introduction stage (product life cycle), 264–5
inventory management, 372–3

J

JetStar, 7, 182, 233
Johnson & Johnson, 11
joint demand, 202
just-in-time (JIT), 373

K

Kellogg, 24, 232, 234
Kickstarter, 292
Kimberly-Clark, 63
Kindle, 5
Kmart (case study), 112–14
Kraft, 20, 48, 293
    case study, 35–6
Kubota Tractor Australia (KTA), 501–2

L

labelling
    definition, 276
    food, 278
    legal issues, 276–89
laggards, 270
learning (buying decision process), 132–3
legal forces (marketing environment), 47–9
legal issues and labelling, 276–89
Lego, 292, 293
level of involvement, 126–7
Levi's, 132
lifestyle segmentation, 166, 167, 175
lifestyle shopping centre, 384
lifestyles (buying decision process), 135–7
limited problem solving, 127
limited-service wholesalers, 392
line extensions, 300
LinkedIn, 98
local shopping centres, 384
location (retailing), 383–5
L'Oréal, 451–2
Louis Vuitton, 10, 231

M

McDonald's, 11, 97, 100, 166, 230, 319, 421, 550
McGrath Foundation, 421
mail survey, 96
mail-order wholesalers, 393

maintenance, repair and operating (MRO) supplies, 261–2
manufacturer brands, 227
manufacturers' agents, 394
manufacturers' sales branches/offices, 395
market
  business, 156, 157, 192–6
  consumer, 156
  definition, 60, 156–7
  density, 165
  heterogeneous, 158
  homogenous, 158
  opportunity, 54
  orientation, 18–2
  potential, 177
  share, 60
market-growth/market-share matrix, 60
Market Research Society of New Zealand, 105
market segment, 158
  evaluating relevant segments, 177
  profiles, 176
market segmentation, 157–70
  business market variables, 169–70
  consumer market variables, 159–69
  definition, 14, 158
marketing
  activities, organising, 68–9
  career prospects, 30
  catalogue, 387
  cause-related, 421
  concept, 18–2
  control process, 71
  and consumer awareness, 28
  costs and buyers' dollars, 27
  customer and stakeholder relationship, 14–15
  definition, 5–6
  direct, 387–9
  direct response, 387
  ethical, 16, 17, 68, 73–4, 122, 161, 193, 228, 293–4, 337, 386, 438–9, 475–6, 511, 525, 566
  evolution, 19–20
  existing products, 299–4
  in a global economy, 26–30
  goals, 57
  green, 30, 167–8, 276–7
  importance to business, 28
  and Internet, 29, 50
  key concepts, 2
  modern, 20–2
  new products, 67
  non-profit organisations, 27
  objectives, 52
  and the people variation, 515
  people are the focus, 6–7
  social network, 51
  socially responsible, 30, 73–4
  strategic variables, 7–14

sustainable, 28, 29, 140, 167, 200, 241, 271, 320, 342, 368, 483, 560
  and technology, 29–30
  value-driven, 23–5
  virtual, 191–2, 467
  see also integrated marketing communications (IMC)
marketing activities, controlling, 71–2
marketing activities, organising, 68–71
  by functions, 70
  by products, 70
  by regions, 70
  by target market segments, 71
marketing channel(s)
  channel integration, 400
  create utility, 366
  definition, 365
  direct, 367–8
  facilitate exchange efficiencies, 366–7
  hybrid, 369
  indirect, 368
  multiple, 368
  role of, 365–9
  selecting, 396–8
  significance of, 366–7
  strategic issues in, 395–400
  types of, 367–9
marketing communications mix, 427–35
  advertising, 453–65
  definition, 427
  personal selling, 476–80
  product characteristics, 432
  product placement, 465–6
  promotional methods, costs and availability, 432–3
  promotional resources, objectives and policies, 429
  public relations, 466–71
  push and pull channel policies, 433–4
  sales promotion, 480–8
  sponsorship, 471–6
  target market characteristics, 429–31
  variables, 427
  word-of-mouth communication, 428, 434–5
marketing decision support systems (MDSS), 105
marketing environment, 15–17, 41–52
  competitive forces, 43–5
  economic forces, 45–7
  legal and regulatory forces, 47–9
  political forces, 47
  shaping and responding to, 42
  sociocultural forces, 51–2
  technological forces, 49–51
marketing implementation, 66
marketing information systems (MIS), 103
marketing intermediaries, 365
marketing managers and C2C encounters, 515
marketing management process, 25–6

marketing mix (4Ps), 7, 9–12, 428
and brands, 239–3
  creating for services, 311–17
  creating the, 63–4
  distribution (place) variable, 11, 503, 509
  price variable, 10, 503
  product variable, 9–10, 503
  promotion variable, 11–12, 503
  variables other than price, 336
  see also expanded marketing mix
marketing plan
  components, 65
  creating a, 64–5
  definition, 54
marketing planning, 64
marketing research
  data analysis, 101–5
  data collection, 91–101
  definition, 86
  determining the scope, 88–9
  ethics, 105–6, 107
  importance of, 86–8
  international issues, 106–7
  issues in, 105–7
  process, 88–102
  reliability and validity, 90–1
  selecting the method, 89–91
  types of research, 89–90
Marketing Research Association, 105
marketing strategies, implementing, 65–72
  controlling market activities, 71–2
  customer relationship management (CRM), 66
  organising marketing activities, 68–1
  through internal marketing, 67–8
  marketing strategy, 53, 61–4
  creating the marketing mix, 63–4
  and packaging, 273–5
  and physical distribution, 369–7
  and product life cycles, 263–9
  target market segment selection, 62–3
markup pricing, 343
Maslow, Abraham, 440
materials handling, 373
media
  changing landscape, 459–2
  plan (advertising campaign), 458–9
media-sharing websites, 549–50
megacarriers, 377
Mercedes-Benz, 565
merchandise allowance, 487
merchant wholesalers, 391–3
message appeal styles, 419–21
Metacafe, 550
micromarketing, 165
Microsoft, 42
Mini-Coopers, 11, 12
mission statement, 57
mobile devices, 551
mobile optimism pages (m-sights), 563

modified-rebuy purchase, 201
money refunds, 484
monopolies, 44
monopolistic competition, 44
Mont Blanc, 10, 172
moral appeal, 419
Mossman Gorge, 219–20
Mother, 429
Mothers Against Drunk Driving
  (MADD), 253
motives (buying decision process), 132
m-sights (mobile optimism pages), 563
multiple marketing channels, 368
multiple sourcing, 206
multiple-unit pricing, 349–51
music, 518–9, 520
Myer, 22, 257, 377, 378, 379
Myspace, 547–8

N

Nando's, 25
NapoleanPerdis, 255
National Australia Bank (NAB), 259
Natural History Museum (NHM) London
  (case study), 532–3
NBC Universal, 460
near field communications (NFC),
  422, 551
negotiated pricing, 346
Nespresso, 255
Nestlé, 291, 296
new-product development system, 291
new-product pricing, 347
news releases, 487, 469
new-task purchase, 200
Nielsen, 98–9
Nike, 243, 234, 243, 319, 475
Nissan, 227
noise (communication), 418
non-price competition, 333–4
non-probability sampling, 93
non-profit organisations, 27

O

observation methods (primary data
  collection), 100–1
odd-even pricing, 351
offensive advertisements, 436–7
OfficeMax, 366
off-price retailers, 382
olfaction effect, 520
oligopoly, 44
Olympic Games, 301
Omega, 301
online consumer behaviour, 556–7
online fraud, 569
online retailing, 388
online shopping, 254
online survey, 97
operations management, 365

opinion leaders (buying decision process),
  139–40
order processing, 371–2
organisation type (business markets), 169
organisational buying decisions, 203–5
organisational culture, 237–8
organisational mission, 57–8
organisational resources and
  opportunities, 54–7
  SWOT analysis, 56–7
organising (marketing management
  process), 27
out-of-home (OOH) communication, 431
outsourcing, 193, 369
owned media, 459

P

Pacific Coast Eco Bananas, 276
Pacific Micromarketing, 165
packaging, 271–5
  altering the, 274
  category-consistent, 275
  family, 273
  functions, 272
  handling-improved, 275
  innovative, 275
  major considerations, 272–3
  and marketing strategy, 273–5
  multiple, 275
  secondary-use, 275
  sustainable, 271
Panasonic, 61
Pancake Parlour, 24
partnership considerations, 566–7
partnership variable (expanded marketing
  mix), 13–14, 504, 525–7
passerby (accidental participants), 514
penetration pricing, 347
people and marketing, 6–7
people considerations, 562–3
people variable (expanded marketing
  mix), 12–13, 504, 509–15
  aesthetic labour, 510–12
  customer as participants, 512–14
  emotional labour, 512
  and marketing, 515
  'me as the customer' 512–14
  passerby (accidental customer), 514
  personnel, 509–10
PepsiCola, 43, 101–2, 232
perceived brand quality, 225
perception (buying decision process),
  130–2
perceptual mapping (product
  positioning), 180
performance standard, 72
periodic discounts, 354
perishability, 308
personal interview survey, 98
personal selling, 476–80
  approaching the customer, 478–9

closing the sale, 480
  definition, 476
  following up, 480
  making the presentation, 479
  managing the sales force, 480
  overcoming objections, 479
  pre-approaching prospects, 478
  process, 477–80
  prospecting for customers, 477–8
  personnel, 509–10
Photobucket, 549
photo-sharing, 550
physical distribution
  and branding, 240–1
  inventory management, 372–3
  and marketing strategies, 369–77
  materials handling, 373–4
  order processing, 371–2
  physical distribution, 369–7
  in supply-chain management, 369–7
  transportation, 374–7
  warehousing, 374
physical evidence considerations, 563–4
physical evidence variable (expanded
  marketing mix), 13, 504, 509, 515–20
  atmospherics, 517–20
physical surrounding (buying decision
  process), 128–9
Picasa, 549
Pilates Studio (case study), 325–7
pioneer promotion, 424
Pirate Bay, 41
Pizza Capers, 5
Pizza Hut, 177, 453
place (distribution) variable (marketing
  mix), 11, 503, 509
planning (marketing management
  process), 26–7
podcasts, 550
point-of-purchase (P-O-P) materials, 485
political forces (marketing environment),
  47
Ponds, 231
population, 92
Porsche, 72
portable compact disc (CD) players, 60–1
post-purchase evaluation, 126
Prada, 10
premium pricing, 348
premium (push) money, 488
premiums, 486
press conferences, 467
prestige pricing, 352
prestige-sensitive, 339
price
  competition, 333
  customer interpretations, 336–8
  definition, 332
  determination of a specific, 352–4
  evaluation of competitors' 343
  external reference price, 338

price (Continued)
    internal reference, 337
    leader, 352
    lining, 348–9
    and marketing mix variables, 336,
        503, 509
    new-product, 347
    non-price competition, 333–4
    penetration, 347
    product-line, 347–9
    role of, 332–3
    setting, 340–6
    skimming, 347
    target market's evaluation of, 342–3
    variable (marketing mix), 10
price-conscious, 339
Priceline, 22, 452
Prices Surveillance Act 1983 48
pricing, basis for, 343–6
    competition, 345–6
    cost, 343–5
    value, 345
pricing and brands, 240
pricing considerations, 561–2
pricing decisions, factors affecting, 334–40
    consumer perceptions of product,
        338–9
    costs, 335
    customer interpretations, 336–8
    demand, 339–40
    marketing mix variables, 336
    organisational and marketing
        objectives, 335
pricing objectives
    development of, 341–2
    types of, 335
pricing of services, 314–15
pricing strategy, 346–54
    determination of a specific price, 352–4
    differential pricing, 346
    new-product pricing, 347
    product-line pricing, 347–9
    professional pricing, 352
    psychological pricing, 349–2
primary data, 92–101
    collection methods, 92–101
    definition, 91
    exploratory methods, 94–5
    observation methods, 100–1
    questionnaire construction, 99–100
    sampling procedures, 92–3
    survey methods, 95–9
    primary demand, 424
privacy, 567–9
probability sampling, 93
problem recognition, 123–4, 206
Procter & Gamble, 460
process considerations, 564–6
process materials, 261
process variable (expanded marketing
    mix), 13, 504, 520–5

curated convenience, 524–5
customer–company interactions, 522–3
digital technology and the service
    process, 523–4
flow and progress of customers, 521–2
producer markets, 194
product adoption process, 269–71, 425
product attributes, 397
product competitors, 43
product components, managing intangible
    (service), 310–17
    bundling services, 311–14
    distribution of services, 315–16
    pricing of services, 314–15
    promotion of services, 316–17
product considerations, 557–8
product deletions, 303–4
product demand, 426
product design, 319
product development, 296
product differentiation
    definition, 317
    quality, design and services, 317–21
product features, 319
product item, 262
product life cycle, 263–9
    decline stage, 267–9
    growth stage, 265–6
        introduction stage, 264–5
        maturity stage, 266–9
        product line, 262–4
        pricing, 347–9
        product mix, 262–4
product modifications, 300–3
product placement, 465–6
product positioning, 179–81
    bases for, 180–1
    definition, 179
    perceptual mapping, 180
product quality, 318–9
product repositioning, 181–3
product trials, 425
product variable (marketing mix), 9–10,
    503, 509
products
    and branding, 242–3
    business, 255, 258–62
    characteristics (marketing
        communication mix), 432
    classifying, 255
    customer perception of, 338–9
    consumer, 255, 256–8
    definition, 252–5
    marketing existing, 299–304
    orientation (evolution of marketing), 19
    support services, 320–1
    use (business markets), 170
products, developing new, 291–9
business analysis, 295
    commercialisation, 298–300
    concept testing, 294–5

idea generation, 291–4
product development, 296
screening, 294
test marketing, 296–8
professional pricing, 343
promotion (marketing communication mix)
    competitive promotional efforts, 426–7
    creating awareness, 422–4
    customer loyalty, 425–6
    definition, 420
    methods, cost and availability, 432–3
    product trial, 425
    reseller support, 426
    resources, 429
    role and objectives, 420–7
    sales fluctuation/seasonality of demand,
        426
    stimulate demand, 424
promotion, criticisms and defences,
    435–40
    and creation of needs, 439–40
    and customers, 440
    does it increase prices, 439
    is it deceptive? 438
    harmful products, 440
    offensive advertising, 436–7
promotion and branding, 241–2
promotion considerations, 560–1
promotion of services, 316–17
promotion variable (marketing mix),
    11–12, 503
prospecting for customers, 477–8
psychographic segmentation, 166
psychographic variables (consumer
    markets), 159, 166
psychological influences (buying decision
    process), 130–7
psychological pricing, 349–2
public relations, 414, 466–71
    definition, 466
    effectiveness evaluation, 470
    publicity-based, 468–9
    tools, 466–71
    unfavourable, 470–1
publicity, 414
publicity-based public relations, 468–9
pull policy, 434
purchase, 125
purchase reason (buying decision
    process), 129
pure competition, 44
push policy, 433

Q

Qantas, 174, 182, 224, 233, 481
QR codes, 131, 553, 564, 565
quality, 318
quality modifications, 301–2
quantity discounts, 353
Queensland tourism industry (case study),
    79–81

questionnaire construction (primary data collection), 99–100
queues, 521–2
quota sampling, 93

R

R. M. Williams, 142–3, 235
rack jabbers, 392
radio frequency identification (RFID), 566
random discounts, 354
random sampling, 93
rational appeal, 419
raw materials, 260–1
Ray-Ban, 9
rebates, 484–5
receiver (communication), 416
reciprocity, 197
recognition test (advertising campaign), 464
Red Bull, 11, 252–3, 460, 468
Red Cross, 27
Red Rooster, 23
reference group (buying decision process), 139
reference pricing, 349
regional shopping centres, 384
regulatory agencies, 48–9
regulatory forces (marketing environment), 47–9
relationship marketing, 22
reliability of research, 90–1
reminder advertising, 465
research design, 89
reseller markets, 194–5
reseller support, 426
retailers, 377–86
    general merchandise, 378–81
    off-price retailers, 382
    specialty, 381–2
retailing
    and atmospherics (store design), 385, 517–20
    category management, 385
    definition, 377
    location, 383–5
    online, 388
    store image, 385
    strategic issues, 382–6
Rexona, 231
Ribena, 42
Ritz-Carlton, 57
roles (buying decision process), 138–9
Rolex, 221, 318
routinised response behaviour, 127
Roy Morgan Research, 136

S

sales contests, 488
sales estimates (market segments), 177–8
sales orientation (evolution of marketing), 20

sales promotion, 480–8
    consumer methods, 482–6
    definition, 480
    trade methods, 487–8
    sampling
    non-probability, 93
    probability, 93
    procedures (primary data collection), 92–3
    quota, 93
    random, 93
    stratified, 93
Samsung, 302, 303, 445
scan-back allowances, 487
screening (new product development), 294
scents and smells (customer perception), 620
seasonal discounts, 353
secondary data, 91–2
secondary-market pricing, 346
segment profile, 176
    understanding you, 178
segmentation variables, 159
segmenting markets see market segmentation
selective demand, 424
selective distortion, 132
selective exposure, 131
selective retention, 132
self-concept (buying decision process), 134–5
selling agents, 394
sender (communication), 415
service(s)
    bundling of, 311–14
    creating marketing mixes for, 311–17
    definition, 252
    digital technology and the service, 523–4
    distribution of, 315–16
    nature and importance of, 305–10
    pricing of, 314–15
    product components, 310–17
    promotion of, 316–17
    traditional characteristics of, 306–10
shopping-centre intercept interviews, 99
shopping centres, 383–5
shopping products, 257
showrooming, 561
single-source data, 104
situational influences (buying decision process), 128–9
Sizzler, 166
small and medium enterprises (SMEs), 195
smartphones, 445–6, 461, 564
SmugMug, 549
social influences (buying decision process), 137–45
social marketing, behavioural change in (case study), 150–1

social media, 14
    case study, 494–5
    interactivity, 543–4
    role in information systems, 85–6
social network marketing, 51
social networking websites, 98, 141
social networks, 544–9
social surrounding (buying decision process), 129
socially responsible marketing, 30, 73–4
sociocultural forces (marketing environment), 51–2
sole sourcing, 206
Sony, 9, 28, 61, 303–4
Spa Ceylon (case study), 359–60
Spanx, 295
special event pricing, 354
specialty products, 258
specialty-line wholesalers, 392
specialty retailers, 381–2
sponsorship, 471–6
    common types of, 472–3
    effectiveness evaluation, 473–4
    event, 473
    social, 472
    unfavourable contracts, 474–5
St Vincent de Paul Society, 10, 420–1
stakeholders
    and customer relationship, 14–15
    definition, 15
statistical interpretation, 101
Steelcase, 202–3
store image, 385
straight-rebut purchase, 200
strategic business unit (SBU), 60
strategic planning
    business-unit strategy, 59–61
    components, 53
    and corporate social responsibility, 73–4
    corporate strategies, 59
    definition, 52
    and ethics, 73–4
    marketing goals, 57–8
    marketing strategy, 61–4
    organisational mission, 57–8
    organisational resources and opportunities, 54–7
    process, 52–64
strategic window, 54
stratified sampling, 93
Streets, 232
styling, 319
subcultures
    buying decision process, 141–5
    of consumption, 144–5
sub-regional shopping centres, 384
subscription services, 525
Subway, 166
Suncorp Bank, 316, 317
Suntory, 241
supermarket wars, 39–40, 254

supermarkets, 378, 380
superstores, 378, 380
supply chain, 365
supply-chain management, 369–7
   inventory management, 372–3
   materials handling, 373–4
   order processing, 371–2
   physical distribution, 369–7
   transportation, 374–7
   warehousing, 374
Surfer Girl, 256, 257
survey methods (primary data collection), 95–9
Susilo Bambang Yudhoyono, 313
sustainable competitive advantage, 63–4
sustainable marketing, 28, 29, 140, 167, 200, 241, 271, 320, 342, 368, 483, 560
SWOT analysis, 56–7

T

2Day FM radio station, 470–1
1M, 9, 292
Target, 364–5
target audience, 455
target market, 7
   characteristics, 419–20, 429–31
   segment selection, 62–3, 179
   segments, organising by, 71
   selecting specific, 179
target market selection process, 170–9
appropriate targeting strategy, 170–4
   market segment profiles, 176
   relevant market segments, 177–8
   segmentation variables, 174–6
   specific target markets, 179
TATA Group, 265–6
technological forces (marketing environment), 49–51
technology
   and billboards, 431
   and consumption habits, 125
   to improve data analysis, 102–5
   and marketing, 29–30
   wearable, 555
telemarketing, 387–8
telephone depth interview, 95
telephone survey, 96
television home shopping, 388–9
Telstra, 55
tensile pricing, 353
Tesco, 254

test marketing, 296–8
The Good Guys, 28
Therapeutic Goods Administration (TGA), 278
time dimension (buying decision process), 129
Time Warner, 100
tobacco industry (case study), 247–8, 268
Toshiba, 28
total budget competitors, 44
Tourism Australia, 526
Toyota, 28, 62, 121, 140, 227, 232, 291
trade allowances, 487
trade discounts, 353
trade name, 222
Trade Practices Act 1974 (TPA), 47, 48, 465
trade sales promotion methods, 487–8
   cooperative advertising and dealer listings, 487–8
   definition, 487
   free merchandise and gifts, 488
   premium (push) money, 488
   sales contests, 488
   trade allowances, 487
trademark, 222
traditional specialty retailers, 381–2
transportation, 374–7
   coordinated, 376–7
   intermodal, 376
   modes, 375–6
Trek Bicycle (case study), 186–7
triple j radio station, 241–2
truck wholesalers, 392
TV advertising, 465–6
Twitter, 98, 140, 526, 548

U

unaided recall test (advertising campaign), 464
undifferentiated targeting strategy, 170–2
Unilever Australasia, 231–2
UNIQLO, 226–7
United Airlines, 435
unsought products, 258
UPS, 376

V

validity of research, 90–1
value analysis, 206
value of branding, 222–3

value-based pricing, 345
value-conscious, 338
value-driven marketing, 23–5
vendor analysis, 206
vertical channel integration, 400
video game market, 158–9
video-sharing websites, 550
Village Roadshow, 289–90
Virgin, 182, 233
Virgin Australia, 526
Virgin Blue, 233
virtual marketing, 191–2, 467
virtual websites, 551
Visa, 9
Volkswagen, 10

W

Walmart, 380
warehouse clubs, 378, 380–1
warehouse showrooms, 378, 381
warehousing, 374
Warner Brothers Movie World, 507
WaterFurnace, 198
wearable technology, 555
WeDoGeo.com, 198
Weet-Bix, 225–5
Wet 'n' Wild, 289–90, 312
wholesalers
   agents and brokers, 393–5
   manufacturers', 395
   merchant, 391–3
   services provided, 390–1
   types of, 391
wholesaling, 389–95
width of product mix, 262–4
wikis, 141, 548–9
willingness to spend, 45–6
Woolworths, 13, 22, 39–40, 54, 226, 234, 251, 370
word-of-mouth communication (WOM), 428, 434–5
Wrigleys, 9

Y

YHA Backpacker Hostels, 23
youth subculture, 143–4
YouTube, 141, 550, 563

Z

ZANA Network, 195